1970

University of St. Francis
GEN 808.82 D568

W9-DBH-302

3 0301 00026458 6

THE ART OF

MODERN

DRAMA

book may be kent

THE ART OF
MODERN
DRAMA

R. F. DIETRICH
University of South Florida

WILLIAM E. CARPENTER
University of Delaware

KEVIN KERRANE
University of Delaware

HOLT, RINEHART AND WINSTON, INC.
NEW YORK CHICAGO SAN FRANCISCO ATLANTA DALLAS

Copyright © 1969 by Holt, Rinehart and Winston, Inc.
All rights reserved
Library of Congress Catalog Card Number 69–14252
SBN: 03–074660–4
Printed in the United States of America
90123 19 987654321

808.82
D568

For Linn, Melinda, and Sheila

J.

Publisher 3

6-29-70

54267

PREFACE

This anthology contains plays that are excellent in themselves, but of course we had additional reasons for choosing them and for doing this anthology.

Perhaps the most important consideration was our belief, apparently shared by many, that an anthology should provide stimulation for the instructor without usurping his function as a teacher. Nearly every modern anthology has such an abundance of critical apparatus that the instructor finds himself either fighting the text or being replaced by it. Our text avoids both problems by reserving almost all the critical material for an instructor's manual, which the instructor may use as he pleases. The manual contains material that we hope will stimulate fresh thinking about the plays, but, at the same time, will allow the instructor to approach his students without a barrier of preconceived opinion.

Our selection of plays, was made on the following bases: we sought, overall, to pick plays that are representative of important types and periods so that the instructor would be able to give a balanced view of drama; we tried as well to mix in some of the less anthologized plays for the sake of freshness and variety; where translations were involved, we selected the very best available; and, finally, many of our plays were chosen because they have been made into films that are readily available to colleges.

In short, we hope you will find this anthology both useful and enjoyable.

Newark, Delaware   *R. F. D.*
JANUARY, 1969   *W. E. C.*
                                                          K. K.

CONTENTS

THE ART OF
MODERN
DRAMA

TO THE STUDENT

Fiction and Drama. Suppose that you are a budding writer with a "story to tell," and that you wish to render it through the medium of prose fiction. The story will deal primarily with how a young man has been deeply changed by his experience of war, how this change coincides with his passage from adolescence to mature manhood, and how he is no longer capable of living a "simple" civilian life.

Assume you decide, in order to lend immediacy to your story, to make the Vietnam war your main character's experience. But, in order to focus on his conflicts in civilian life, you put the war itself in the background, beginning your narrative with the day after his return home. To emphasize the universal applicability of your theme, you decide to make your main character an "average" young man, relatively unsophisticated. You make his home a small town, and you decide to intensify his conflicts by setting this town in the South, as part of a "traditional" society. Once you have arrived at this decision, you see an extra advantage in it—hot, steamy weather, which can mirror a mood of depression, and which can also provoke people to fits of temper. Your story takes place in midsummer.

Finally, after arriving at other strategic decisions about the pattern of events which will take place in the story, you write a draft of its opening paragraphs:

> Men go to war, and they return. But they are different men.
>
> It was a hot southern day in late June, the morning after Bobby Joe's return. He stepped out of the house warily, feeling slightly improper without his uniform. The smothering Louisiana heat depressed him. He could see that it was starting to drizzle; but the rain would be a light one, and would only add to the burden of the heat.
>
> He walked down the front steps. Suddenly a baseball kicked up dust at his feet and rolled past him, hitting the steps. Bobby Joe retrieved it, then looked up to see a gangly boy loping toward the yard, wearing a catcher's mitt. It was Little Davy Chapman—but not so little now. "God, that kid sure has grown in two years!" Bobby Joe thought. "He's almost big enough for a uniform." After shouting hello, Bobby Joe signaled to Davy that he wanted to pitch the ball to him, and he pegged back a curve, the way he used to in high school. The ball broke neatly and popped into the mitt, but Bobby Joe felt vaguely that something was wrong. He turned toward the street, thinking uneasily of the day before him. Familiar faces asking silly questions: "How were things in Vietnam?" "Hey, how are them Oriental chicks, Bobby Joe?"
>
> He dreaded the thought of conversation with his friends, but still he needed to see them. He started walking up the street, toward Jamie's house. When he came to the middle of the block he began to run.

These opening paragraphs, written especially for this purpose, illustrate explicitly the options open to you as a writer of fiction. You are free to make a thematic statement: "Men go to war, and they return. But they are not the same men." You can inform the reader directly of the story's setting and describe the weather objectively. You are free to add exposition, so that the reader quickly learns that Bobby Joe has just come home from the military, and that he has not seen Davy Chapman for two years. Most important, you have the option of providing *subjective* information: what the central character is thinking, feeling, and experiencing. You can *tell* the reader that Bobby Joe feels "improper" without his uniform; that the heat "depresses" him; that as he looks at Davy Chapman, he "thinks" about how quickly things can change; that he feels strangely uneasy after throwing the ball; and, finally, that he experiences mixed emotions as he thinks about seeing his friends once again.

Now suppose that you had the job of rendering your story in the medium of *drama*—through actors, on a stage, before a live audience. How much of the opening "scene" of your fictional version could be acted out? Very little—for what you could *tell* to the reader of fiction, you must now *show* to the audience of drama. The dramatist makes plays, not for a reader, but for spectators. Or perhaps a better way of stating this obvious fact is that a playwright writes speeches for actors and instructions about sets, costumes, or movements for directors, who, in turn, render the material for the spectators. (This is not to say that plays should not be read, a point that will be dealt with later.)

Your freedom to dramatize your story is inhibited most obviously by the physical limitations of the stage. The sets might suggest a "house" and a "yard," but Bobby Joe's movements will be confined. It would be impossible, for example, to show him walking "to the middle of the block." And what about that baseball? How could it "kick up dust"? Would it not be impractical for the actor to throw the ball within the confines of a normal stage? And who in the audience will be able to see that it is a "curve"? Furthermore, how can the audience be made so specifically aware of the weather? Bobby Joe can react to the heat, of course; he might be wearing light clothes (shorts, perhaps), and he might fan himself. But there will not be much room here for nuance, and it will be difficult to call the audience's attention to such details as the impending rain, unless a character on stage *mentions* it aloud or extensive use is made of special effects such as thunder and lightning.

More serious difficulties await you. How will exposition be provided? The theatre program might tell the audience that the setting of the action is in Rayville, Louisiana, and that the time is "the present." But how can the audience be made aware, seeing Bobby Joe in civilian clothes, that he had been wearing a uniform until the day before? Or that he has not seen Davy Chapman for two years? Or that he pitched baseball in high school? Again, these details will become known only when a character *talks* about them (and has reason or motivation to do so).

Even more important, how can you give the audience a clear impression of Bobby Joe's thoughts and emotions? Stage directions might call for the actor to *step warily out of the house*, and they might provide him with pantomimic gestures for expressing his indecision near the end of the scene. But enlightening as the actor's gestures may be, they represent a less analytical "language" than that which is available to the writer of fiction. (And they will almost certainly depend more on the actor's use of his body rather than his face—which cannot be caught in "closeup," and which the people in the back rows might not even be able to see clearly.) Once again, your "dramatic" solution would have to involve dialogue, and you would have to take special pains to make this dialogue believable. Only rarely in real life do people reveal their innermost thoughts and feelings aloud. This happens far more often in drama (and it has every right to), but when it does there should be some dramatic "occasion" for it. You cannot write the scene so that Bobby Joe, after throwing the ball to Davy Chapman, then says, "I feel vaguely that something is wrong," and then begins to describe to Davy the mixed emotions he feels about seeing his friends.

At this point, it should be clear just how much the dramatic medium *limits* the freedom of the writer, creating barriers between him and his audience, and pushing him towards "objective" presentation. But it would be a mistake to think that this objectivity is ever total. The dramatic audience, even more than the audience at a movie, is aware that what it is seeing is *"artificial"*: that the performers are acting out episodes conceived, selected, and arranged by a drama-tist—episodes which have their own internal coherence, but which are never-theless "unreal." Usually, theatrical "props" are far more suggestive than real-istic; they, like other details in a drama, are meant to convey an impression. The audience of a drama undergoes a "willing suspension of disbelief"; but they do not undergo an illusion that commands total "belief."

Moreover, the great tradition of drama has been nonrealistic. Dramatists have always taken liberties with the supposed "objectivity" of the action onstage, using accepted conventions of performance in order to "tell" as well as "show" things to the audience. Greek drama used a "chorus," a group of actors who might represent characters (for example, the Theban citizens in *Oedipus Rex*), but who also interrupted the action with chanted odes—filling in the story, com-menting directly on events and motives, and guiding the audience's emotions (sometimes by expressing the emotions the dramatist wanted the audience to experience). Elizabethan drama used the "soliloquy" and the "aside"—conven-tions whereby an actor on stage speaks his thoughts aloud to himself when alone, or speaks them to the audience in the presence of other actors who are not supposed to be able to hear him. These conventions are occasionally revived in modern dramas, and some contemporary plays use "narrators"—as in *The Glass Menagerie* or *A View from the Bridge*—who speak directly to the audience, and who are also characters in the dramatic action. And these—the chorus, solil-oquy, aside, and narrator—are not the final limitations. Imaginative dramatists, feeling cramped by the traditional conventions of the stage, continually expand the medium of drama.

It does seem safe to suggest, however, that even the most inventive of dramatists will always be faced with the task of rendering scenes "objectively." And even with the freedom that *all* the conventions can give, you would still have a difficult time writing your fictional opening as a dramatic scene. It is likely, in fact, that you would have to rethink the *whole* story in dramatic terms to make that first scene work. (You might use the time-tested device of delaying the appearance of your main character, allowing other people who have reason to do so—for example, Bobby Joe's mother and father—to talk about him.) "But why bother?" you might ask. Is drama merely a secondary form of art, doing crudely and with-out credibility what prose fiction (and even the movies) can do better? The answer is that the dramatist, like every other artist, renounces in order to gain. The medium of drama presents the writer with inherent difficulties, but it offers "compensations" not available in any other form of art.

Above all, the drama offers a sense of immediacy. The opening paragraphs of your story about Bobby Joe are (except for the thematic statement) in the past tense—the tense most natural to fiction. By contrast, a drama exists, even in written form, in the present tense; the action is always happening "now." No matter how well we know a play, no matter how many times we have seen or read it before, its action always pulls us forward, commanding our active atten-tion.

This leads to the second "compensation" of drama: the demands that it makes upon its audience. The more trivial forms of storytelling (for example, the fiction in love-story magazines) are those which force their readers into a passive role by "telling" them everything, making no requirements on the imagination or intellect. In fact, one of the drawbacks to the opening paragraphs of the story about Bobby Joe is that they lack subtlety; the reader can afford to be passive, since he is being hit over the head with the main point from the very beginning. The difference between enjoying fiction of this kind and enjoying a more subtle work like Hemingway's "The Big Two-Hearted River" (also a story about a young man's return from war) is, in one sense, the difference between enjoying checkers and enjoying chess.

Similarly, the medium of drama—with its apparent "objectivity"—forces our imagination and intellect to probe below the surface, to fill in gaps. When we hear two characters conversing at the beginning of a play, a part of our mind should be interpolating the motives of each for saying what he does; another should be deducing the situation as it existed before the play began; another part should grasp certain repeated ideas, phrases, or foreshadowing (for example, the "wild duck" in Ibsen's play of that name), and think, "Something may come of this." In addition, the "point" of a drama is almost always something we arrive at by seeing a number of characters react to a problem in different ways, each illuminating one aspect of the problem—rather than having the author *tell* us "the whole truth."

Aristotle, in his seminal work of dramatic criticism, the *Poetics* (about 340 B.C.), claimed that other forms of storytelling (for example, the epic) aspire to the condition of drama. The same point has been made in modern times—by Henry James, in speaking about prose fiction, and by T. S. Eliot, in speaking of poetry. These three critics all seem to have had in mind a concept of the superior subtlety of objective presentation. They may also have been thinking of the immense possibilities for irony within the dramatic mode. In a "dramatic monologue" (like Eliot's "The Love Song of J. Alfred Prufrock") the poet himself remains in the background. The speaker addresses another character, or perhaps talks to himself; he is unaware of being "overheard" by an audience. Invariably, there is a discrepancy between what we think of him and what he thinks of himself. The result is that a character unwittingly stands revealed. And if we judge him negatively, the effect is all the stronger because he has damned himself with his own words; the author has "told" us nothing. Ballads are another kind of poetry (significantly, a storytelling form) that exploit the resources of dramatic irony. In "Sir Patrick Spence," for example, the anonymous medieval balladeer has arranged his narrative so that things are suggested rather than stated directly. In the first three stanzas we see the king deciding to send Sir Patrick Spence, an expert sailor, on a dangerous mission; he notifies him in a letter. Here are stanzas four through seven:

> The first line that Sir Patrick red,
>   A loud lauch lauced he;
> The next line that Sir Patrick red,
>   The teir blinded his ee.

> "O wha is this has don this deid,
>   This ill deid don to me,
> To send me out this time o' the yeir,
>   To sail upon the se!

> "Mak haste, mak haste, my mirry men all,
>   Our guid schip sails the morne."
> "O say na sae, my master deir,
>   For I feir a deadlie storme.

"Late late yestreen I saw the new moone,
   Wi' the auld moone in hir arme,
And I feir, I feir my deir master,
   That we will cum to harme."

The poet does not probe Sir Patrick Spence's motives and emotions, but we are intensely aware of them. In stanza five, Sir Patrick stands alone, bewailing his fate; in stanza six he addresses his men with a confident tone, as though nothing were wrong. Our imagination fills in the "gap" between these two stanzas; we can attribute a complex personality to Sir Patrick, even though the poet has not "described" him from the inside. In addition, when a sailor (unidentified) voices a fearful warning, we know, although he does not, that Sir Patrick is aware of the danger but has chosen to go anyway. This ballad, like many other ballads, jumps without transition from one situation to another, usually concentrating on what is most "dramatic," and, like many ballads, it tends toward a direct transcription of dialogue.

Needless to say, the possibilities for irony inherent in the dramatic monologue and the ballad are multiplied many times in the medium of drama itself. It is worth remarking, however, that irony in a dramatic production can also be more intense, because we are aware *as a group* of something which a character on stage does not know. The appeal of a play to a "group mind" is probably the most difficult to discuss of all the qualities of drama. Many scholars are agreed that drama had its origins in primitive rituals, in which a community or tribe, intensely aware of itself as a group, "imitated" events that they wished to take place (for example, the coming of spring, or a successful hunt). Later, at the Theatre of Dionysus in Athens, the ancient Greeks produced (and attended) plays as part of a collective religious festival. There may be less sense of a religious rite in Elizabethan drama, and even less in modern drama—but the fact remains that plays continue to address themselves to the group spirit. Consider for a moment the experience of watching a play (say, Molière's *The Misanthrope*) as the only person in the audience. Not only would you tend to laugh less at the humor, but you would also be more immediately aware of the props *as props*, the costumes *as costumes,* and the dialogue *as dialogue.* It would become more difficult, in short, to suspend your disbelief. A willing suspension of disbelief seems somehow to thrive upon a *group* will; collectively we sustain the conventions which make dramas "playable."

Reading Plays: The Stage in The Mind. The previous discussion raises the whole question of the difference between *seeing* a play and *reading* it. This textbook is a collection of plays meant to be "taught" in a classroom. But is it possible to do this? Are you, the student, being forced to consider second-rate realities? In a sense, yes. Certainly you will understand any play in this book better if you see a production of it—even a poor production—for the exigencies of stage presentation are such that you are bound to "experience" the play more fully, becoming aware of options in the text that you had not seen before. We should remember, however, that both the actors and the director began as "readers." In fact, the play exists in the form of words before the performance and after, and we can experience what is most essential in it as we read. But in order for any play to "come alive" when we read it, we must willingly allow our imaginations to work, to participate actively in the play, to visualize, and by so doing, to discover a way for the language on the printed page to "play" on the physical stage. Reading dramas requires great concentration, but it yields worthwhile rewards and distinct pleasures. The mind delights in building its own stage, making its own costumes and sets, choosing the perfect actors for every part, and directing the play exactly as it wants. (If, for example, Paul Newman is your perfect Hamlet, so be it.) But the mind does not have to imagine the events in the play as "staged" events with actors, costumes, and props; it may instead visualize the scenes as reality, things happening to real people in real environments. Either way, the good reader experiences the play by visualizing it. Obviously there is no "one right way" a play should be performed or imagined; quite the contrary, one great appeal of drama is that it lends itself to almost endless possibilities of presentation—with different actors, different sets, different direction. So, as you read a work, experiment with the possibilities, always keeping your imaginative eye on the words of the author.

Plays can be read quickly, so we suggest that each be read at least twice. The first reading should reveal, in broad terms, "what happens" in the play. *Drama* comes from a Greek verb *dran* meaning *to act* or *to do;* this action answers the question, What happens? Action arises from all the elements of the drama, but particularly from characters in conflict; therefore, try to comprehend the central conflict of the work, for all drama depends on conflict to show us the true nature of the central character (protagonist) and his opponent (the antagonist). From conflicts spring the excitement that we expect from great plays, as well as the resolutions which make us feel, This should be. So, as you read, look for dramatic moments, confrontation scenes between protagonist and antagonist or between other characters, any scenes in which a character makes important revelations about himself, and scenes in which expectations—a character's or the audience's—are reversed. (When a character's expectations are reversed, the result is often ironic; when the audience's expectations are reversed, the dramatic result can be a shock of recognition, a clarification of the play's major themes.)

If the first reading answers the question *what* happens, the second explores the questions of *why* and *how* it happens. A second reading will show *why* the situations in the plot are arranged as they are; *why* the characters behave as they do (motivation); *how* the characters speak and *why* the author wishes them to speak that way; *how* minor characters and incidents relate to the major themes of the play; and a host of other similar *how-why* questions. In answering these questions it is useful to examine the first scene very closely, almost line for line, because this scene usually provides very important exposition, suggests the play's mood and atmosphere, establishes the nature of the central conflict, and introduces through its language, imagery fundamental to the play's themes. Also, examine the stage directions—something the spectator at a play cannot do —because directions are often significantly revelatory of the author's ideas and his conception of the play. (An excellent example is Tennessee Williams' *The Glass Menagerie,* in which the stage directions support and help explain the patterns of imagery in the work, and through them the mood and theme it presents.) The second reading, then, should reveal nuances of the play's architecture and theme.

In *As You Like It* Shakespeare wrote about the stage and the nature of man:

> All the world's a stage
> And all the men and women merely players;
> They have their exits and their entrances;
> And one man in his time plays many parts.

Consider this idea in another way: the drama is a "world" in itself, an imaginary one that may or may not be a mirror image of the world we live in. (Interestingly enough, Shakespeare's theater was called the Globe.) The audience's acceptance of this world on the stage, which is governed by a set of rules or conventions, constitutes the dramatic illusion, and, although we know that this world is not literally real, we also know that it has a special imaginative reality. Each dramatist creates his make-believe "play" world, arranges his material so that from the work emerges meaning, significance, and pleasure. By way of explanation, consider for a moment the ghost in *Hamlet:* Shakespeare does not examine the question of whether ghosts exist; he merely states that, for his dramatic purpose, in the world of Elsinore, where Hamlet lives, one ghost does indeed exist. This ghost makes the point that Elsinore and Hamlet are haunted by the past—Elsinore by the horrors of regicide, and Hamlet by the demands of vengeance. In Molière's *The Misanthrope* the characters speak in couplets; thus, in his excellent translation, Richard Wilbur has retained this convention of dialogue. Obviously seventeenth-century Parisians did not speak in rhyme, but rhymed dialogue was a convention of classical French drama, and this dialogue aids Molière in creating a world preoccupied with polished manners, elegant conversation, and sparkling wit—a stage world that simultaneously mirrors and criticizes the fashionable society of his day. In *The Glass Menagerie*, Tennessee Williams uses the convention of a narrator who talks directly to the audience and then steps back into the action of the play as a central character. This device gives Williams both the immediacy of drama and the interpretive quality of fiction, an excellent combination for his "memory play," a work that achieves its emotional impact by showing both the narrator's memory and its effects on him.

Quite clearly, then, the ghost in *Hamlet,* the rhymed dialogue in *The Misanthrope,* and the narrator in *The Glass Menagerie* contribute meaningfully to the total dramatic worlds presented in these plays. Why emphasize this obvious point? Because, as students of the drama, we must understand *how* an author creates his dramatic world and then *why* he does so; only then can we experience the full force and meaning of the play as it relates to the world we inhabit.

In this volume we have presented eight modern plays. Each contains a brilliantly conceived world inhabited by endlessly fascinating people. As you read these plays, we hope you will begin to explore and understand more about the nature of drama and about human nature.

HENRIK IBSEN
[1828–1906]

There were two Henrik Ibsens, the one who inspired a social and political revolution under the banner of "Ibsenism," and the one who protested his complete innocence of any revolutionary intentions. That the two Ibsens were the same man is testimony to both the complexity of the man and the misunderstanding that plagued him all his life. The truth seems to be that Ibsen underwent a great change of character. He did indeed begin as the social reformer his disciples took him for, but when disillusionment with his fellow Norwegians forced him inward and away from political and social reform to an examination of man's inner being, his disciples did not notice either the change in Ibsen or the change in his art. But then, neither did Ibsen when he insisted upon the unchanging tenor of his life's work. In 1890 he wrote ingenuously, "I was surprised that I, who had made it my chief life-task to depict human characters and human destinies, should, without conscious or direct intention, have arrived in several matters at the same conclusions as the social democratic moral philosophers had arrived at by scientific processes." This was Ibsen reacting against the simplified view of himself as the great fighting liberal emancipator invented by his disciples. He wished to make it clear that his art was greater than mere political melodrama.

Henrik Ibsen was the product of a frustrated and embittered childhood. When he was eight, his wealthy merchant family lost its fortune, bringing down upon him the full force of all the provincial narrowness and social ostracism of which the small Norwegian town of Skien was capable. He received an inferior education at a poor people's school, and was further disappointed by his parents' lack of sympathy for his artistic ambitions. He was so alienated by his father's indifference and his mother's religious dogmatism that, after leaving home at the age of fifteen, he scarcely bothered to keep up family connections. But the family and its middle class sensibility left its mark on Ibsen. He spent a great deal of his time either flouting middle-class conventions or trying to live up to them. He was considered a revolutionary, but he dressed with unusual care, often revealing the temperament of a conservative banker. He also liked to display the orders of merit that governments and royalty bestowed on him in the days of his international fame, before the scandalous publication of *A Doll's House* and *Ghosts* made his name an anathema to the conventionally pious. The unfavorable public reaction he received in his later years added to the already well-known dourness of his temperament, and pushed him further into himself. It might be said that he emerged only in the great symbolic dramas of his later years.

In his launching of modern drama, Ibsen progressed along the entire range of dramatic production. After an immature excursion into the field of folk and nationalistic drama, he experimented successfully with romantic drama, came into his own with realistic drama, and ended with symbolic drama. His major plays were *Brand* (1866), *Peer Gynt* (1867), *The League of Youth* (1869), *Emperor and Galilean* (1873), *Pillars of Society* (1877), *A Doll's House* (1879), *Ghosts* (1881), *An Enemy of the People* (1882), *The Wild Duck* (1884), *Rosmersholm* (1886), *The Lady from the Sea* (1888), *Hedda Gabler* (1890), *The Master Builder* (1892), *Little Eyolf* (1894), *John Gabriel Borkman* (1896), and *When We Dead Awaken* (1899).

THE WILD DUCK

HENRIK IBSEN
A New Translation by Otto Reinert

CHARACTERS

WERLE, *a manufacturer and merchant*
GREGERS WERLE, *his son*
OLD EKDAL
HJALMAR EKDAL, *his son, a photog-rapher*
GINA EKDAL, HJALMAR'S *wife*
HEDVIG, *their daughter, fourteen years old*
MRS. SØRBY, WERLE'S *housekeeper*
RELLING, *a physician*
MOLVIK, *a former student of theology*

GRÅBERG, *a bookkeeper in* WERLE'S *office*
PETTERSEN, WERLE'S *servant*
JENSEN, *a hired waiter*
A FLABBY GENTLEMAN
A THIN-HAIRED GENTLEMAN
A NEARSIGHTED GENTLEMAN
SIX OTHER GENTLEMEN, WERLE'S *dinner guests*
OTHER HIRED WAITERS

SCENE   *The first act takes place at* WERLE'S; *the other four, in* HJALMAR EKDAL'S *studio.*

"The Wild Duck" by Henrik Ibsen, English translation by Otto Reinert, is re-printed by permission of the publishers from *Drama: An Introductory Anthology*, edited by Otto Reinert, and *Modern Drama: Alternate Edition*, edited by Otto Reinert. Copyright © 1961, and Copyright 1961, 1962, 1964, © 1966 (respectively), by Little, Brown and Company (Inc.)

ACT I

> An expensive-looking and comfortable study in WERLE'S house;
> bookcases and upholstered furniture; in the middle of the room a
> desk with papers and ledgers; lamps with green shades give the
> room a soft, subdued light. In the rear, open double doors with
> portieres pulled apart reveal a large, elegant drawing room,
> brightly illuminated by lamps and candles. Front right, a small
> door to the office wing. Front left, a fireplace with glowing coals
> in it. Farther back on the left wall, double doors to the dining
> room.
>
> PETTERSEN, WERLE'S servant, in livery, and the hired waiter JENSEN,
> in black, are setting the study in order for the guests. In the
> drawing room, two or three other hired waiters are lighting can-
> dles, moving chairs, etc. Sounds of conversation and laughter of
> many people come from the dining room. Someone signals he
> wishes to make a speech by touching his glass with his knife. Si-
> lence follows, a short speech is made, there are noises of approval,
> then again conversation.

PETTERSEN [lights a lamp by the fireplace and puts a shade on it] Just listen
to that, Jensen. There's the old man now, proposing a long toast to Mrs.
Sørby.

JENSEN [moving an armchair] Do you think it's true what people say, that
the two of 'em—y'know—?

PETTERSEN Couldn't say.

JENSEN I bet he used to be quite a goat in the old days.

PETTERSEN Maybe so.

JENSEN They say this dinner is for his son.

PETTERSEN That's right. He came home yesterday.

JENSEN It's the first I've heard Werle has a son.

PETTERSEN He has a son, all right. But he's up at the works at Høydal all the
time. He hasn't been home as long as I've been here.

A HIRED WAITER [in the drawing room doorway] Pst, Pettersen, there's an old
fellow here, says he—

PETTERSEN [under his breath] Dammit! Can't have anybody in here now!
[OLD EKDAL appears from the right in the drawing room. He is dressed in a
shabby old coat with a high collar. Wool mittens. He carries a walking stick
and a fur cap in his hand. Under his arm a parcel in thick paper. Dirty,
reddish brown wig. Small, gray mustache.]

PETTERSEN [going towards him] Good Lord! What are you doing here?

EKDAL [in the doorway] Got to get into the office, Pettersen.

PETTERSEN The office closed an hour ago, and—

EKDAL They told me that downstairs. But Gråberg is still in there. Be a good
boy, Pettersen; let me in this way. [Points to the small office door.] Been
through here before.

PETTERSEN Oh well, all right. [Opens the door.] But see you go out the other
way. We're having guests tonight.

EKDAL I know, I know—h'm! Thanks a lot, Pettersen, old boy. Good old friend.
Thanks. [Mutters.] Ass!
[He enters the office. PETTERSEN closes the door behind him.]

JENSEN Is he one of them office people, too?

PETTERSEN Oh no. He just does some extra copying for them, when they need
it. But he's been a fine enough fellow in his day, old Ekdal has.

JENSEN   You know, he sort of looked like that.

PETTERSEN   Oh yes. He used to be a lieutenant.

JENSEN   I'll be damned! A lieutenant!

PETTERSEN   Yessir: Then he got mixed up in some forest deal or something. They say he pretty near ruined Werle once. The two of 'em were partners—owned the Høydal works together. Oh yes, Ekdal and I are good friends. We've had many a drink together at Madam Eriksen's place, we have.

JENSEN   Didn't look to me like he'd have much to buy people drinks with.

PETERSEN   Good Lord, Jensen. It's my treat, of course. I always say one should be nice to people who've seen better days.

JENSEN   So he went bankrupt?

PETTERSEN   Worse than that. He went to prison.

JENSEN   Prison!

PETTERSEN   Or something.—[*Listens.*] Shhh. They are getting up from the table. [*Servants open the doors to the dining room.* MRS. SØRBY *appears, in conversation with a couple of the dinner guests. The rest of the company follows in small groups.* WERLE *is among them. The last to appear are* HJALMAR EKDAL *and* GREGERS WERLE.]

MRS. SØRBY   [*to the servant, in passing*]   Pettersen, tell them to serve the coffee in the music room, will you?

PETTERSEN   Very well, Mrs. Sørby.
[*She and the two guests go into the drawing room and disappear, right.* PETTERSEN *and* JENSEN *follow them out.*]

A FLABBY GENTLEMAN   [*to* A THIN-HAIRED *one*]   Phew! That dinner—It was almost too much for me.

THE THIN-HAIRED GENTLEMAN   Oh, I don't know. With a little bit of good will, it's amazing what one can accomplish in three hours.

THE FLABBY GENTLEMAN   Yes, but afterwards, afterwards, my dear chamberlain!

A THIRD GENTLEMAN   I am told the coffee and liqueurs will be served in the music room.

THE FLABBY GENTLEMAN   Wonderful! Then maybe Mrs. Sørby will play something for us.

THE THIN-HAIRED GENTLEMAN   [*in a low voice*]   If only she doesn't play us a different tune one of these days.

THE FLABBY GENTLEMAN   Don't worry. Bertha isn't one to let old friends down.
[*They laugh and enter the drawing room.*]

WERLE   [*in a low and troubled voice*]   I don't think anybody noticed, Gregers.

GREGERS   [*looks at him*]   Noticed what?

WERLE   You didn't either?

GREGERS   What?

WERLE   We were thirteen at the table.

GREGERS   Really? Were we thirteen?

WERLE   [*with a glance at* HJALMAR EKDAL]   Usually we are only twelve. [*To the other guests*] Gentlemen!
[*He and the remaining guests, except* HJALMAR *and* GREGERS, *leave through the drawing room, rear right.*]

HJALMAR   [*who has overheard the conversation*]   You shouldn't have invited me, Gregers.

GREGERS   Nonsense! This is supposed to be a party for *me*. Shouldn't I invite my one and only friend?

HJALMAR   But I don't think your father approves. I never come to this house.

GREGERS   So I hear. But I wanted to see you and talk to you.—Well, well,

we two old school fellows have certainly drifted apart. It must be sixteen—
seventeen years since we saw each other.

HJALMAR   Is it really that long?

GREGERS   It is indeed. And how are you? You look fine. You're almost stout.

HJALMAR   Stout is hardly the word, but I suppose I look a little more manly
than I used to.

GREGERS   Yes, you do. Your appearance hasn't suffered any all these years.

HJALMAR   [*gloomily*] But the inner man—! Believe me, that's a different
story. You know, of course, how utterly everything has collapsed for me
and mine since we last met.

GREGERS   [*in a lower voice*]   How is your father these days?

HJALMAR   I'd just as soon not talk about him. My poor, unfortunate father
lives with me, of course. He has no one else in the whole world to turn to.
But it is so terribly difficult for me to talk about these things. Tell me
rather how you have been—up there at the works.

GREGERS   Lonely—blissfully lonely. I've had all the time in the world to think
over all sort of things.—Here. Let's make ourselves comfortable.
[*He sits down in an armchair near the fireplace and gets* HJALMAR
to take another chair beside him.]

HJALMAR   [*softly*]   All the same, I do want to thank you, Gregers, for inviting
me to your father's table. It proves to me you no longer bear me a grudge.

GREGERS   [*surprised*]   Grudge? What makes you think I ever did?

HJALMAR   You did at first, you know.

GREGERS   When?

HJALMAR   Right after the tragedy. Of course, that was only natural. After all,
your own father only escaped by the skin of his teeth. Oh, that terrible
old business!

GREGERS   And so I bore you a grudge? Who told you that?

HJALMAR   I know you did, Gregers. Your father said so himself.

GREGERS   [*startled*]   Father! Really? H'm. So that's why you've never written—
not a single word.

HJALMAR   Yes.

GREGERS   Not even when you decided to become a photographer?

HJALMAR   Your father thought it would be better if I didn't write about anything at all.

GREGERS   [*looking straight ahead*]   Oh well, maybe he was right, at that.—But
tell me, Hjalmar—do you feel you have adjusted pretty well to your situation?

HJALMAR   [*with a small sigh*]   Oh yes, I think I have. Can't say I haven't, anyway. At first, of course, things seemed very strange. My circumstances were
so completely different. But then, everything had changed. Father's great,
ruinous tragedy—The shame—The disgrace—

GREGERS   [*feelingly*]   Yes, yes. I see.

HJALMAR   Of course there was no way in which I could pursue my studies.
There wasn't a penny left. Rather the opposite; there was debt. Mainly to
your father, I think.

GREGERS   H'm—

HJALMAR   Well—then I thought it best to take the bull by the horns and
make a clean break with the past—you know, all at once. Your father
thought so, too, and since he had been so helpful, and—

GREGERS   Father helped you?

HJALMAR   Yes, surely you know that? Where do you think I got the money
to learn photography and to set up my own studio? Things like that are
expensive, I can tell you.

GREGERS And father paid for all that?

HJALMAR Yes, didn't you know? I understood him to say he had written to you about it.

GREGERS Not a word that it was *he*. He must have forgotten. We only write business letters. So it was father—!

HJALMAR It certainly was. But he has never wanted people to know that. It was he who made it possible for me to get married, too. Or maybe—maybe you didn't know that, either?

GREGERS No! How could I? [*Shakes* HJALMAR's *arm.*] My dear Hjalmar, I can't tell you how happy all this makes me—and pains me, too. Perhaps I have been unfair to father. In some respects, anyway. For this shows he has a heart, you know. A kind of conscience—

HJALMAR Conscience?

GREGERS Or whatever you want to call it. No, really, I can't tell you how glad I am to hear this about father.—So you are married, Hjalmar. That's more than I ever will be. I trust you find yourself happy as a married man?

HJALMAR Yes, I certainly do. She is as good and competent a wife as any man could ask for. And she is by no means without culture.

GREGERS [*a little taken aback*] No, of course not.

HJALMAR Life itself is an education, you see. Being with me every day—And then there are a couple of remarkable men we see quite a lot of. I assure you, you'd hardly recognize Gina.

GREGERS Gina?

HJALMAR Yes. Surely you remember her name was Gina?

GREGERS Whose name? I haven't the slightest idea—

HJALMAR But don't you remember she was here in the house for a while?

GREGERS [*looks at him*] Is it Gina Hansen—?

HJALMAR Of course it is Gina Hansen.

GREGERS —who kept house for us the last year of mother's illness?

HJALMAR That's it. But my dear friend, I know for a fact that your father wrote you about my marriage.

GREGERS [*who has risen*] Yes, so he did, that's true, but not that—[*paces the floor*]. Wait a minute—Yes, he did—now when I think back. But father always writes such short letters. [*Sits down on the arm of the chair.*] Listen, Hjalmar—this interests me—how did you make Gina's acquaintance—your wife, I mean?

HJALMAR Quite simply. You remember she didn't stay here very long. Everything was so unsettled during your mother's illness. Gina couldn't take that, so she gave notice and moved out. That was the year before your mother died. Or maybe it was the same year.

GREGERS It was the same year. I was up at Høydal at the time. Then what happened?

HJALMAR Well, Gina moved in with her mother, Madam Hansen, an excellent, hardworking woman, who ran a small eating place. And she had a room for rent, too. A nice, comfortable room.

GREGERS Which you were lucky enough to get?

HJALMAR Yes. Through your father, in fact. And it was there I really learned to know Gina.

GREGERS And then you got engaged?

HJALMAR Yes. It's easy for young people to fall in love, you know. H'm—

GREGERS [*gets up, walks up and down*] Tell me—after you'd become engaged, was that when father—I mean, was that when you took up photography?

HJALMAR That's right. Naturally, I wanted to get married and have a place of my own, the sooner the better. And both your father and I agreed that photography was the best thing I could get into. Gina thought so, too. Oh yes, that was another reason. It so happened that Gina had learned how to retouch.

GREGERS What a wonderful coincidence.

HJALMAR [*smiling contentedly*] Yes, wasn't it? Don't you think it worked out very well?

GREGERS Remarkably well, I should say. So father has really been a kind of Providence for you, Hjalmar; hasn't he?

HJALMAR [*moved*] He did not abandon his old friend's son in his days of need. That's one thing about your father: he does have a heart.

MRS. SØRBY [*enters on* WERLE'S *arm*] I don't want to hear another word, my dear sir. You are not to stay in there staring at all those bright lights. It isn't good for you.

WERLE [*letting go of her arm and moving his hand across his eyes*] I almost think you are right.

[PETTERSEN *and* JENSEN *enter carrying trays with glasses of punch.*]

MRS. SØRBY [*to the guests in the drawing room*] Gentlemen, if you want a glass of punch, you'll have to take the trouble to come in here.

THE FLABBY GENTLEMAN [*to* MRS. SORBY] Dear Mrs. Sørby, please tell me it isn't so. You have not withdrawn your cherished permission to smoke?

MRS. SØRBY Yes, Chamberlain. No smoking here in Mr. Werle's own sanctum.

THE THIN-HAIRED GENTLEMAN And when did you append these harsh paragraphs to the tobacco regulations, Mrs. Sørby?

MRS. SØRBY After the last dinner, Chamberlain, when certain persons abused their liberties.

THE THIN-HAIRED GENTLEMAN And will not even the smallest infraction be tolerated, Mrs. Sørby? Really none at all?

MRS. SØRBY None whatsoever, Chamberlain.

[*Most of the guests are gathered in the study. The servants are serving punch.*]

WERLE [*to* HJALMAR, *over by a table*] Well, Ekdal, what is that you are looking at?

HJALMAR Oh, just an album, sir.

THE THIN-HAIRED GENTLEMAN [*moving about*] Ah yes! Photographs! That's your line, of course.

THE FLABBY GENTLEMAN [*seated*] Haven't you brought some of your own along?

HJALMAR No, I haven't.

THE FLABBY GENTLEMAN Too bad. Looking at pictures is good for the digestion, you know.

THE THIN-HAIRED GENTLEMAN And then it would have contributed a mite to the general entertainment.

THE NEARSIGHTED GENTLEMAN And all contributions are gratefully received.

MRS. SØRBY The chamberlains think that when one has been invited to dinner, one ought to work for one's food, Mr. Ekdal.

THE FLABBY GENTLEMAN With a cuisine like this that's only a pleasure.

THE THIN-HAIRED GENTLEMAN Oh well, if it's a question of the struggle for existence—

MRS. SØRBY You are so right!

[*They continue their conversation, laughing and joking.*]

GREGERS [*in a low voice*] You must join in, Hjalmar.

HJALMAR [*with a twist of his body*] What am I to say?

THE FLABBY GENTLEMAN Don't you believe, sir, that Tokay may be considered relatively beneficial to the stomach?

WERLE [*by the fireplace*] I'll guarantee the Tokay you were served tonight, at any rate. It is one of the very best years. I am sure you noticed that yourself.

THE FLABBY GENTLEMAN Yes, it really was unusually delicate-tasting.

HJALMAR [*hesitantly*] Do the years differ?

THE FLABBY GENTLEMAN [*laughs*] Ah, Mr. Ekdal! Splendid!

WERLE [*with a smile*] I see it is hardly worth while to serve you fine wine.

THE THIN-HAIRED GENTLEMAN Tokay is like photographs, Mr. Ekdal. Both need sunshine. Or isn't that so?

HJALMAR Yes, sunshine has something to do with it.

MRS. SØRBY Just the same with chamberlains. They need sunshine, too—royal sunshine, as the saying goes.

THE THIN-HAIRED GENTLEMAN Ouch! That's a tired old joke, Mrs. Sørby.

THE NEARSIGHTED GENTLEMAN The lady will have her fun—

THE FLABBY GENTLEMAN —and at our expense. [*Wagging his finger.*] Madam Bertha! Madam Bertha!

MRS. SØRBY But it is true that vintages differ widely sometimes. The older the better.

THE NEARSIGHTED GENTLEMAN Do you count me among the older vintages?

MRS. SØRBY Far from it.

THE THIN-HAIRED GENTLEMAN Well, well! But what about me, Mrs. Sørby?

THE FLABBY GENTLEMAN And me? What vintages do we belong to?

MRS. SØRBY I reckon you among the sweet vintages, gentlemen.
[*She sips a glass of punch. The chamberlains laugh and flirt with her.*]

WERLE Mrs. Sørby always finds a way out—when she wants to. But gentlemen, you aren't drinking! Pettersen, please see to it that—! Gregers, let's have a glass together.
[GREGERS *does not move.*]
Won't you join us, Ekdal? I had no opportunity at the table—
[GRÅBERG *comes in through the office door.*]

GRÅBERG Beg your pardon, Mr. Werle, but I can't get out.

WERLE They've locked you in again, eh?

GRÅBERG Yes, they have, sir. And Flakstad has left with the keys.

WERLE That's all right. You just come through here.

GRÅBERG But there is somebody else—

WERLE Doesn't matter. Come on, both of you.
[GRÅBERG *and* OLD EKDAL *enter from the office.*]

WERLE [*involuntarily*] Damn!
[*Laughter and talk among the guests cease.* HJALMAR *gives a start when he sees his father, puts down his glass, and turns away toward the fireplace.*]

EKDAL [*does not look up but makes quick little bows to both sides, as he mutters*] Beg pardon. Came the wrong way. Gate's locked. Gate's locked. Beg pardon. [*He and* GRÅBERG *go out, rear right.*]

WERLE [*between his teeth*] That idiot Gråberg!

GREGERS [*staring, his mouth hanging open, to* HJALMAR] Don't tell me that was—!

THE FLABBY GENTLEMAN What is it? Who was that?

GREGERS Nothing. Just the bookkeeper and somebody else.

THE NEARSIGHTED GENTLEMAN [*to* HJALMAR] Did *you* know that man?

HJALMAR I don't know—I didn't notice—

THE FLABBY GENTLEMAN [*getting up*] What the devil has gotten into everybody? [*He walks over to some other guests, who are talking in low voices.*]

MRS. SØRBY [*Whispers to the servant*] Give him something from the kitchen to take home. Something good.

PETTERSEN   [*nods his head*]   I'll do that, ma'am. [*Goes out.*]

GREGERS   [*shocked, in a low voice to* HJALMAR]   Then it really was he?

HJALMAR   Yes.

GREGERS   And you stood there and denied him!

HJALMAR   [*in a fierce whisper*]   But how *could* I—?

GREGERS   —acknowledge your own father?

HJALMAR   [*pained*]   Oh, if you had been in my place, maybe—
[*The low conversation among the guests changes to forced gaiety.*]

THE THIN-HAIRED GENTLEMAN   [*approaching* HJALMAR *and* GREGERS, *in a friendly mood*]   Aha! Reminiscing about university days, gentlemen?—Don't you smoke, Mr. Ekdal? Can I give you a light? Oh that's right. We are not allowed—

HJALMAR   Thanks, I don't smoke.

THE FLABBY GENTLEMAN   Don't you have a nice little poem you could recite for us, Mr. Ekdal? You used to do that so beautifully.

HJALMAR   I am sorry. I don't remember any.

THE FLABBY GENTLEMAN   That's a shame. Well, in that case, Balle, what do we do?
[*They both walk into the drawing room.*]

HJALMAR   [*gloomily*]   Gregers—I am leaving! You see, when a man has felt Fate's crushing blow—Say goodbye to your father for me.

GREGERS   Yes, of course. Are you going straight home?

HJALMAR   Yes. Why?

GREGERS   I thought I might come up and see you a little later.

HJALMAR   No, don't do that. Not to my home. My home is a gloomy one, Gregers, particularly after a brilliant banquet such as this. We can meet somewhere in town.

MRS. SØRBY   [*has come up to them; in a low voice*]   Are you leaving, Ekdal?

HJALMAR   Yes.

MRS. SØRBY   Say hello to Gina.

HJALMAR   Thank you. I'll do that.

MRS. SØRBY   Tell her I'll be up to see her one of these days.

HJALMAR   Fine. [*To* GREGERS]   You stay here. I'll slip out without anybody noticing. [*Drifts off. A little later he goes into the drawing room and out right.*]

MRS. SØRBY   [*in a low voice to the servant who has returned*]   Well, did you give the old man something?

PETTERSEN   Oh yes. A bottle of brandy.

MRS. SØRBY   Oh dear. Couldn't you have found something better?

PETTERSEN   But Mrs. Sørby, there's nothing he likes better than brandy.

THE FLABBY GENTLEMAN   [*in the doorway to the drawing room, with a sheet of music in his hand*]   Will you play a duet, Mrs. Sørby?

MRS. SØRBY   Yes, gladly.

THE GUESTS   Good! Good!
[*She and all the guests go out rear right.* GREGERS *remains standing by the fireplace.* WERLE *is looking for something on the desk and appears to wish to be left alone. Since* GREGERS *does not leave,* WERLE *walks towards the drawing room door.*]

GREGERS   Father, do you have a moment?

WERLE   [*stops*]   What is it?

GREGERS   I'd like a word with you.

WERLE   Couldn't it wait till we're alone?

GREGERS   No, it can't, for maybe we'll never be alone again.

WERLE   [*coming closer*]   What does that mean?

[*During the following scene, the sound of a piano is faintly heard from the music room.*]

GREGERS   How is it that that family has been allowed to go to ruin so miserably?

WERLE   I suppose you refer to the Ekdals?

GREGERS   Yes, I do mean the Ekdals. Lieutenant Ekdal was once your close friend.

WERLE   Yes, unfortunately. Too close. I have felt that keenly enough for many years. It was his fault that my good name and reputation, too, were—somewhat tarnished.

GREGERS   [*in a low voice*]   Was he the only one who was guilty?

WERLE   Who else, do you mean?

GREGERS   The two of you were together on that big purchase of forest land, weren't you?

WERLE   But it was Ekdal who surveyed the area—surveyed it fraudulently. It was he who felled all that timber on state property. He was responsible for everything that went on up there. I didn't know what he was doing.

GREGERS   I doubt that Lieutenant Ekdal himself knew what he was doing.

WERLE   That may well be. The fact remains that he was convicted and I was not.

GREGERS   Yes, I know there were no proofs.

WERLE   Acquittal is acquittal. Why do you want to bring back that miserable old business that gave me gray hairs before my time? Is that what has been on your mind all these years up there? I can assure you, Gregers, here in town that whole story has been forgotten long ago, as far as *I* am concerned.

GREGERS   But what about that unfortunate family?

WERLE   Well, now, exactly what do you want me to do for those people? When Ekdal got out, he was a broken man, beyond help altogether. Some people go to the bottom as soon as they've got some buckshot in them and never come up again. Believe me, Gregers, I've done all I possibly could do, if I didn't want to put myself in a false light and give people occasion for all sorts of talk and suspicion—

GREGERS   Suspicion? I see.

WERLE   I have given Ekdal copying work to do for the office, and I pay him far, far more than he is worth.

GREGERS   [*without looking at him*]   H'm. I don't doubt that.

WERLE   You are laughing? Don't you think I am telling you the truth? Oh, to be sure, you won't find it in my books. I never enter expenses like that.

GREGERS   [*with a cold smile*]   No, I suppose there are certain expenses that are better not entered.

WERLE   [*puzzled*]   What do you mean?

GREGERS   [*being brave*]   Have you entered what it cost you to let Hjalmar Ekdal learn photography?

WERLE   I? What do you mean—entered?

GREGERS   I know now it was you who paid for it. And I also know it was you who set him up in business—quite comfortably, too.

WERLE   All right! And you still say I have done nothing for the Ekdals! I assure you, Gregers, those people have cost me a pretty penny!

GREGERS   Have you entered those expenses?

WERLE   Why do you ask?

GREGERS   I have my reasons. Listen—at the time you were providing so kindly for your old friend's son, wasn't that just when he was getting married?

WERLE   Damn it, Gregers! How can I remember—! After so many years—!

GREGERS   You wrote me a letter at the time. A business letter, of course. And in a postscript you mentioned very briefly that Hjalmar Ekdal had married one Miss Hansen.

WERLE   That's right. That was her name.

GREGERS   But you did not say anything about Miss Hansen being Gina Hansen, our ex-housekeeper.

WERLE   [*with scornful but forced laughter*] No, to tell the truth, it didn't occur to me that you were particularly interested in our ex-housekeeper.

GREGERS   I wasn't. But—[*Lowers his voice.*] somebody else in this house was.

WERLE   What do you mean? [*Flaring up.*] Don't tell me you're referring to me!

GREGERS   [*in a low but firm voice*] Yes, I am referring to you.

WERLE   And you dare—! You have the audacity—! How can that ingrate, that—photographer fellow—how dare he make accusations like that!

GREGERS   Hjalmar hasn't said a word. I don't think he has the faintest suspicion of anything like this.

WERLE   Then where do you get it from? Who could have said a thing like that?

GREGERS   My poor, unfortunate mother. The last time I saw her.

WERLE   Your mother! I might have thought so! You and she—you always stood together. It was she who first turned you against me.

GREGERS   No, it was all she had to go through, till things became too much for her and she died in sheer misery.

WERLE   Oh, nonsense! She didn't have to go through anything! No more than what others have had to, anyway. There's just no way of getting on with morbid, hysterical people—that's something *I* have had to learn! And here you are, with a suspicion like that—dabbling in old rumors and gossip against your own father. Listen here, Gregers. It really seems to me that at your age you might find something more useful to do.

GREGERS   Yes, it is about time.

WERLE   Then maybe your mind would be more at ease than it seems to be now. What is the point of working away, year in and year out, as just an ordinary clerk up there at Høydal, with not so much as a penny beyond regular wages? It's plain silly!

GREGERS   I wish I could believe that.

WERLE   Not that I don't understand, mind you. You want to be independent, don't want to be obliged to me for anything. But right now there is a chance for you to become independent, to be on your own in everything.

GREGERS   Oh? How so?

WERLE   When I wrote you that I needed you here in town right away—h'm—

GREGERS   Yes, what is it you want of me? I've been waiting to hear all day.

WERLE   I am offering you a partnership in the firm.

GREGERS   I! In your firm? As a partner?

WERLE   Yes. That doesn't mean we have to be together all the time. You could take over the business here in town and I could go up to Høydal.

GREGERS   You would want to do that?

WERLE   Well, you see, Gregers. I can't work as well as I used to. I'll have to save my eyes. They are getting weaker.

GREGERS   You have always had weak eyes.

WERLE   Not as bad as now. Besides—there are other things, too, that may make it advisable for me to live up there—for a while, anyway.

GREGERS   Nothing like this has ever even occurred to me.

WERLE   Look here, Gregers. I know there are many things that stand between us. But after all, we are father and son. It seems to me we ought to be able to come to some sort of understanding.

GREGERS   For appearance's sake, I suppose you mean.

WERLE   Well, that would be something, anyway. Think it over, Gregers.

HEDVIG [*closing her book*]   Well, father doesn't care much for reading, anyway.

GINA [*puts her sewing aside and picks up a pencil and a small notebook from the table*]   Do you remember how much we spent for the butter today?

HEDVIG One crown and sixty-five øre.

GINA That's right. [*Writes it down.*] We're using an awful lot of butter in this family. Then there was the sausage and the cheese—let me see— [*writing*] —and the ham— [*mumbles figures while adding up*]. Goodness! it does add up—

HEDVIG And the beer.

GINA Right. [*Writes.*] It gets terrible expensive, but it can't be helped.

HEDVIG And you and I didn't need anything hot for supper since father was out.

GINA No, that's right. That helps some. And I did get eight crowns and fifty øre for the pictures.

HEDVIG Was it that much?

GINA Eight-fifty, exactly.

[*Silence.* GINA *picks up her sewing.* HEDVIG *takes paper and pencil and starts drawing, her left hand shading her eyes.*]

HEDVIG Isn't it nice to think that father is at that big dinner party at Mr. Werle's?

GINA Can't rightly say he's *his* guest. It was the son who invited him. [*After a pause.*] We have nothing to do with the old man.

HEDVIG I can't wait till father comes home. He promised to ask Mrs. Sørby if he could take home something good for me.

GINA Why yes, you can be sure there are plenty of good things in *that* house.

HEDVIG [*still drawing*]   Besides, I think I am a little bit hungry, too.

[OLD EKDAL *enters right rear, the brown paper parcel under his arm, another parcel in his coat pocket.*]

GINA So late you are today, Grandpa.

EKDAL They'd locked the office. Had to wait for Gråberg. And then I had to go through—h'm—

HEDVIG Did they give you any more copying to do, Grandpa?

EKDAL This whole parcel. Look.

GINA That's nice.

HEDVIG And you've got another one in your pocket.

EKDAL What? Oh never mind. That's nothing. [*Puts his walking stick away in the corner.*] This will keep me busy a long time, Gina. [*Slides one of the double doors half open.*] Shhh! [*Peeks into the attic for a while, then he cautiously slides the door shut. Chuckling.*] They're sound asleep the whole lot of 'em. And she herself's in the basket.

HEDVIG Are you sure she won't be cold in that basket, Grandpa?

EKDAL Cold? With all that straw? Don't you worry about that. [*Goes towards the door left rear.*] There are matches, aren't there?

GINA On the dresser.

[EKDAL *goes into his room.*]

HEDVIG It's nice that he got all that new work to do.

GINA Yes, poor old thing. It will give him a little spending money.

HEDVIG And he won't be able to stay down at the awful Madam Eriksen's all morning.

GINA No; there's that, too.

HEDVIG Do you think they're still at the table?

GINA Lord knows. Could be.

HEDVIG Just think of all that delicious food. I'm sure he'll be in a good mood when he comes home. Don't you think so, mother?

GINA   Yes, but what if we could tell him we'd rented the room. Wouldn't that be nice?

HEDVIG   But we don't need that tonight.

GINA   Oh yes we do. We could always use the money. The room is no good to us as it is.

HEDVIG   No, I mean that father will be in a good mood tonight, anyway. It's better to have the room for some other time.

GINA   [*looking at her*]   You like it when you have something nice to tell father when he comes home nights, don't you?

HEDVIG   It makes things more pleasant.

GINA   [*reflectively*]   Yes, I guess you're right about that.
   [OLD EKDAL *enters from his room, heads for the kitchen door, left front.*]

GINA   [*turning half around in her chair*]   Do you need anything in the kitchen, Grandpa?

EKDAL   Yes. But don't you get up. [*Goes out.*]

GINA   I hope he isn't fooling around with the fire out there. [*After a while.*] Hedvig, go out and see what he's doing.
   [OLD EKDAL *enters with a pitcher of hot water.*]

HEDVIG   Getting hot water, Grandpa?

EKDAL   That's right. Got some writing to do, but the ink's as thick as gruel. H'm—

GINA   But hadn't you better have supper first? It's all ready for you in your room.

EKDAL   Never mind supper, Gina. I tell you I'm busy. I don't want anybody coming in to me. Not anybody. H'm.
   [*He goes into his room.* GINA *and* HEDVIG *look at each other.*]

GINA   [*in a low voice*]   I can't think where he got the money from. Can you?

HEDVIG   From Gråberg, maybe.

GINA   No, it wouldn't be that. Gråberg always gives me the money.

HEDVIG   Maybe he got a bottle on credit.

GINA   Him! Who'd give him credit?
   [HJALMAR EKDAL, *in overcoat and gray hat, enters right.*]

GINA   [*throws down her sewing, gets up*]   Heavens, Ekdal! Home already?

HEDVIG   [*getting up at the same time*]   Father? So soon!

HJALMAR   [*lays down his hat*]   Most of them seemed to be leaving now.

HEDVIG   Already?

HJALMAR   Well, it was a dinner party, you know. [*Takes his coat off.*]

GINA   Let me help you.

HEDVIG   Me too. [*They help him off with his coat.* GINA *hangs it up in the rear.*] Were there many there, father?

HJALMAR   Not too many. About twelve or fourteen at the table.

GINA   Did you get to talk to all of them?

HJALMAR   Oh yes, a little. Though Gregers kept me engaged most of the evening.

GINA   Is he as ugly as he used to be?

HJALMAR   Well—I suppose nobody would call him handsome. Is father back?

HEDVIG   Yes, he is in there writing.

HJALMAR   Did he say anything?

GINA   No. About what?

HJALMAR   He didn't mention—? I thought I heard he'd been with Gråberg. I think I'll go in to him for a moment.

GINA   No, you'd better not.

HJALMAR   Why not? Did he say he didn't want to see me?

GINA   He doesn't want to see anybody.

HEDVIG   [*making signs to her*]   Ahem!

GINA   [*doesn't notice*]   He's gotten himself some hot water.

HJALMAR   Ah! So he is—

GINA   Looks that way.

HJALMAR   Ah yes—my poor old white-haired father. Let him enjoy his little pleasures as best he can.

[OLD EKDAL, *a lighted pipe in his mouth, enters in an old smoking jacket.*]

EKDAL   Home again? Thought it was you I heard talking.

HJALMAR   Yes. I just came back.

EKDAL   Guess you didn't see me, did you?

HJALMAR   No, but they told me you'd gone through, so I thought I'd catch up with you.

EKDAL   H'm. That's good of you, Hjalmar. Who were they—all those people?

HJALMAR   Oh—all sorts. Chamberlain Flor and Chamberlain Balle and Chamberlain Kaspersen and chamberlain this and that. I don't know—

EKDAL   [*nodding his head*]   Hear that, Gina? He's been with nothing but chamberlains all evening.

GINA   Yes, I hear as they've become quite fancy in that house now.

HEDVIG   Did the chamberlains sing, father? Or recite poetry?

HJALMAR   No. They just talked nonsense. They wanted *me* to recite, though, but I didn't want to.

EKDAL   They couldn't get you to, eh?

GINA   Seems to me you might have done that.

HJALMAR   No. I don't see any reason why one has to oblige every Tom, Dick, and Harry all the time. [*Walks up and down.*] At any rate, I won't.

EKDAL   No point in being too obliging, you know. That's Hjalmar for you.

HJALMAR   I don't see why *I* always have to be the one who provides entertainment on the rare occasions when I am out for dinner. Let the others exert themselves for a change. Those fellows go from one big meal to the next, stuffing themselves day in and day out. Let *them* do something for all the food they are getting!

GINA   You didn't tell them that though, did you?

HJALMAR   [*humming a little*]   Well, I don't know about that. They were told a thing or two.

EKDAL   The chamberlains?

HJALMAR   Mmm—[*Casually.*]   Then we had a little controversy over Tokay wine.

EKDAL   Tokay, no less! Say, that's a fine wine!

HJALMAR   [*stops his walking*]   It *may* be a fine wine. But let me tell you: not all the vintages are equally fine. It depends on how much sunshine the grapes get.

GINA   If you don't know everything—!

EKDAL   And they quarreled with that?

HJALMAR   They tried to, but then it was pointed out to them that it was the same way with chamberlains. Not all vintages are equally fine among chamberlains, either—so they were told.

GINA   Goodness! What you don't think of!

EKDAL   Heh-heh! So they got that to put in their pipe.

HJALMAR   Right to their face. That's how they got it.

EKDAL   Gina, d'ye hear that? He gave it to them right to their face!

GINA   Right to their face! Imagine!

HJALMAR   Yes, but I don't want you to talk about it. One doesn't talk about such things. Of course, the whole thing was done in the friendliest possible way. They are all of them pleasant, easy-going people. Why should I hurt them? No!

EKDAL   Right to their face, though—

HEDVIG   [*ingratiatingly*]   It's so nice to see you all dressed up, father. You look very well in tails.

HJALMAR   Yes, don't you think so? And it really fits me perfectly. As if it were tailor-made. Possibly a trifle tight in the armpits, that's all. Help me, Hedvig. [*Takes his dinner jacket off.*] I'd rather wear my own coat. Where is it, Gina?

GINA   Here it is. [*Helps him on with it.*]

HJALMAR   There now! Be sure to have Molvik get his suit back first thing in the morning.

GINA   [*putting the clothes away*]   I'll take care of it.

HJALMAR   [*stretching*]   Aaahh. This feels cozier after all. And this kind of loose-fitting, casual wear is really more in keeping with my whole appearance; don't you think so, Hedvig?

HEDVIG   Oh yes, father!

HJALMAR   Especially when I tie my neckcloth with loose, flying ends—like this? What do you think?

HEDVIG   Yes, it goes extremely well with your mustache. And with your curls, too.

HJALMAR   I'd hardly call my hair curly. Wavy, rather.

HEDVIG   Yes, for the curls are so large.

HJALMAR   Waves, really.

HEDVIG   [*after a moment, pulling his sleeve*]   Father?

HJALMAR   What is it?

HEDVIG   Oh, you know very well what it is!

HJALMAR   I certainly don't.

HEDVIG   [*laughing and pleading*]   Oh come on, father! Don't tease me!

HJALMAR   But what is it?

HEDVIG   [*shaking him*]   Father! Give it to me! You know, you promised me. Something good to eat.

HJALMAR   Oh, dear! I completely forgot!

HEDVIG   You are only teasing, father. Shame on you! Where is it?

HJALMAR   No, honest, I really did forget. But wait a moment. I have something else for you, Hedvig. [*Goes and searches his coat pockets.*]

HEDVIG   [*jumps up and down, clapping her hands*]   Oh mother, mother!

GINA   See what I mean? If you just give him time—

HJALMAR   [*with a piece of paper*]   Here it is.

HEDVIG   That? But that's just a piece of paper.

HJALMAR   It's the menu, Hedvig, the entire menu. Look here. It says "Menu." That means what you get to eat.

HEDVIG   Haven't you anything else for me?

HJALMAR   I tell you, I forgot all about it. But take my word for it: it's not such a great treat, all that rich food. You just sit down and read the menu, now, and I'll tell you later what the things taste like. Here you are, Hedvig.

HEDVIG   [*swallowing her tears*]   Thank you.
    [*She sits down but doesn't read.* GINA *signals to her.* HJALMAR *notices.*]

HJALMAR   [*pacing the floor*]   It is really unbelievable all the things a father is supposed to keep in mind. And if he forgets the smallest item—! Long faces right away. Oh well. One gets used to that, too. [*Stops by the stove where* OLD EKDAL *is sitting.*] Have you looked at them tonight, father?

EKDAL   I certainly have! She's in the basket!

HJALMAR   No! Really? In the basket? She is getting used to it then, I guess.

EKDAL   Didn't I tell you she would? But look, Hjalmar, there are still a few things—

HJALMAR   —improvements, yes, I know.

54267

LIBRARY
College of St. Francis
JOLIET, ILL.

EKDAL   They've got to be done.

HJALMAR   Right. Let's talk about it now, father. Come over here to the sofa.

EKDAL   All right. H'm. Guess I want to fill my pipe first, though. Need to clean it, too—h'm—[*Goes into his room.*]

GINA   [*with a smile, to* HJALMAR]   Cleaning his pipe—

HJALMAR   Oh well, Gina—let him. The poor shipwrecked old man.—About those improvements—We'd better get to them tomorrow.

GINA   You won't have time tomorrow, Ekdal.

HEDVIG   [*interrupting*]   Oh, yes, mother.

GINA   For remember those prints you were going to retouch? They came for 'em again today.

HJALMAR   I see. It's those prints again, is it? Well, they'll get done. You can be sure of that. Perhaps there are some new orders come in, too?

GINA   Not a thing, worse luck. Tomorrow I've got only those two portraits I told you about.

HJALMAR   Is that all? Well, if one doesn't exert oneself, what can you expect?

GINA   But what can I do? I advertise in the papers all I can, seems to me.

HJALMAR   The papers, the papers—you see yourself how far that gets us. I suppose there hasn't been anyone to look at the room, either?

GINA   No, not yet.

HJALMAR   Just as I thought. Well, no—if one doesn't *do* anything—One has to make a real effort, Gina!

HEDVIG   [*going to him*]   Shall I get your flute, father?

HJALMAR   No, not the flute. *I* need no pleasures. [*Paces up and down.*] You'll see if I don't work tomorrow! You don't need to worry about *that!* You can be sure I shall work as long as my strength holds out—

GINA   But Ekdal, dear—I didn't mean it that way.

HEDVIG   How about a bottle of beer, father?

HJALMAR   Not at all. I don't need anything—[*Stops.*] Beer? Did you say beer?

HEDVIG   [*brightly*]   Yes, father; lovely, cool beer.

HJALMAR   Oh well—all right—since you insist, I suppose you may bring me a bottle.

GINA   Yes, do that. That'll be nice and cozy.

[HEDVIG *runs towards the kitchen door.*]

HJALMAR   [*by the stove, stops her, looks at her, takes her by the head and presses her to him*]   Hedvig! Hedvig!

HEDVIG   [*happy in tears*]   Oh father! You are so sweet and good!

HJALMAR   No, no, don't say that. There I was—seated at the rich man's table—gorging myself on his ample fare—and I couldn't even remember—

GINA   [*seated by the table*]   Nonsense, Ekdal.

HJALMAR   It is not nonsense. But you must not reckon too strictly. You know I love you, regardless.

HEDVIG   [*throwing her arms around him*]   And we love you, father, so much, so much!

HJALMAR   And if I am unreasonable at times, remember—God forgive me—remember I am a man beset by a host of sorrows. Well, well! [*Drying his eyes.*] No beer at such a moment. Give me my flute.

[HEDVIG *runs to the shelf and fetches it.*]

HJALMAR   Thank you. There now. With my flute in my hand and you two around me—ah!

[HEDVIG *sits down by the table next to* GINA. HJALMAR *walks back and forth, playing a Bohemian folk dance. He plays loudly but in slow tempo and with pronounced sentiment.*]

HJALMAR   [*interrupts his playing, gives his left hand to* GINA, *and says with strong emotion*]   Our home may be mean and humble, Gina. But it is our home. And I say to you both: here dwells contentment!

[*He resumes his playing. Presently there is a knock on the door.*]

GINA   [*getting up*]   Shh, Ekdal. I think somebody's coming.

HJALMAR   [*putting the flute back on the shelf*]   Yes, yes of course. Somebody would—

[GINA *goes to open the door.*]

GREGERS WERLE   [*out in the hall*]   I beg your pardon—

GINA   [*taking a step back*]   Oh!

GREGERS   —isn't this where Mr. Ekdal lives, the photographer?

GINA   Yes, it is.

HJALMAR   [*going to the door*]   Gregers! So you did come, after all. Come in.

GREGERS   [*entering*]   I told you I wanted to see you.

HJALMAR   But tonight—? Have you left the party?

GREGERS   Both party and home. Good evening, Mrs. Ekdal. I don't know if you recognize me.

GINA   Oh yes. Young Mr. Werle isn't hard to recognize.

GREGERS   No, for I look like my mother, and you remember her, I am sure.

HJALMAR   You have left your home?

GREGERS   Yes. I have taken a room at a hotel.

HJALMAR   Really?—Well, since you're here, take off your coat and sit down.

GREGERS   Thanks. [*Removes his overcoat. He has changed clothes and is now dressed in a plain, gray suit, of somewhat unfashionable cut.*]

HJALMAR   Here on the sofa. Make yourself comfortable.

[GREGERS *sits down on the sofa,* HJALMAR *on a chair by the table.*]

GREGERS   [*looking around*]   So this is your residence, Hjalmar. This is where you live.

HJALMAR   This is the studio, as you can see.

GINA   It's roomier in here, so this is where we mostly keep ourselves.

HJALMAR   The apartment we had before was really nicer than this, but there is one big advantage here: we have plenty of space.

GINA   And we have a room across the hallway that we're renting out.

GREGERS   [*to* HJALMAR]   You have lodgers, too?

HJALMAR   No, not yet. These things take time, you see. One has to be on the lookout. [*To* HEDVIG.] What about that beer?

[HEDVIG *nods her head and goes out into the kitchen.*]

GREGERS   So that's your daughter.

HJALMAR   Yes, that's Hedvig.

GREGERS   Your only child, isn't she?

HJALMAR   Our only one. Our greatest joy in the world, and [*lowers his voice*] our greatest sorrow, as well.

GREGERS   What are you saying!

HJALMAR   Yes, Gregers, for there is every probability that she'll lose her sight.

GREGERS   Becoming blind!

HJALMAR   Yes. So far, there are only early symptoms, and things may be well with her for some time yet. But the doctor has warned us. It is coming, irresistibly.

GREGERS   But this is nothing less than a tragedy! How do you account for it?

HJALMAR   [*with a sigh*]   Heredity, most likely.

GREGERS   [*struck*]   Heredity?

GINA   Ekdal's mother had weak eyes.

HJALMAR   That's what father says. I of course don't remember her.

GREGERS   Poor child. How does she take it?

HJALMAR   Oh, we can't bring ourselves to tell her—I'm sure you can understand that. She suspects nothing. Joyous and carefree, chirping like a little bird, she'll flutter into life's endless night. [*Overcome by emotion.*] Oh Gregers, this is such a terrible burden for me.

[HEDVIG *enters with a tray with beer and glasses. She puts it down on the table.*]

HJALMAR [*stroking her hair*]   Thanks. Thank you, Hedvig.

HEDVIG [*puts her arms around his neck and whispers something in his ear.*]

HJALMAR   No. No sandwiches now. [*Looks off.*] That is—unless Gregers wants some?

GREGERS [*with a gesture of refusal*]   No. No thanks.

HJALMAR [*still in a melancholic mood*]   Oh well, you might as well bring in some, all the same. A crust, if you have one. And plenty of butter, please.

GREGERS [*who has followed her with his eyes*]   Otherwise she seems healthy enough.

HJALMAR   Yes, thank God, there is nothing else wrong with her.

GREGERS   I think she is going to look like you, Mrs. Ekdal. How old is she?

GINA   Hedvig is just about fourteen. Her birthday is day after tomorrow.

GREGERS   Quite big for her age, isn't she?

GINA   Yes, she has grown a lot lately.

GREGERS   It's by the children we tell we're growing older ourselves. How long have you two been married now?

GINA   We've been married for—let's see—fifteen years, pretty near.

GREGERS   Just imagine! Has it really been that long?

GINA [*taking notice, looks at him*]   It certainly has.

HJALMAR   That's right. Fifteen years, less a few months. [*Changing topic.*] Those must have been long years for you up there at the works, Gregers.

GREGERS   They were long while they lasted. Now afterwards I hardly know where they went.

[OLD EKDAL *enters from his room, without his pipe, but with his old-fashioned lieutenant's cap on his head. His walk is a trifle unsteady.*]

EKDAL   I'm ready for you now, Hjalmar. Let's talk about this—h'm—What was it again?

HJALMAR [*going towards him*]   Father, there's someone here. Gregers Werle. I don't know if you remember him?

EKDAL [*looks at* GREGERS, *who has stood up*]   Werle? That's the son, isn't it? What does he want from me?

HJALMAR   Nothing. He has come to see me.

EKDAL   Then there's nothing wrong?

HJALMAR   Of course not.

EKDAL [*swinging one arm back and forth*]   Not that I am scared, mind you, but—

GREGERS [*goes up to him*]   I just wanted to bring you greetings from your old hunting grounds, Lieutenant Ekdal.

EKDAL   Hunting grounds?

GREGERS   Yes, the woods up around the Høydal works.

EKDAL   Oh yes, up there. Yes, I used to know that country quite well in the old days.

GREGERS   You were quite a hunter then, weren't you?

EKDAL   Could be. Maybe I was. You're looking at my get-up. I don't ask anybody's permission to wear it in the house. Just as long as I don't go outside—

[HEDVIG *brings a plate with open-faced sandwiches, which she puts down on the table.*]

HJALMAR   You sit down, father, and have a glass of beer. Help yourself, Gregers.

[EKDAL *mutters something and shuffles over to the sofa.* GREGERS *sits down on a chair next to him;* HJALMAR *is on the other side of* GREGERS. GINA *sits some distance from the table, sewing.* HEDVIG *is standing by her father.*]

GREGERS Do you remember, Lieutenant Ekdal, when Hjalmar and I used to come up and visit you summers and Christmas?

EKDAL You did? No; can't say as I do. But it's true I used to be a good hunter, if I do say so myself. I've killed bears, too. Nine of 'em.

GREGERS [*looks at him with compassion*] And now your hunting days are over.

EKDAL Oh—I wouldn't say that. I still go hunting once in a while. Well, yes, not in the old way, of course. For you see, the woods—the woods—the woods—! [*Drinks.*] Nice-looking woods up there now?

GREGERS Not as in your time. They have cut a great deal.

EKDAL Cut? [*In a lower voice and as if afraid.*] That's risky business, that is. It has consequences. The woods are vengeful.

HJALMAR [*filling his glass*] Here, father. Have some more.

GREGERS How can a man like you—such an outdoors man as you used to be— how can you stand living here in the middle of a musty city, within four walls?

EKDAL [*chuckles, glancing at* HJALMAR] Oh, it's not so bad here. Not bad at all.

GREGERS But surely—all the things your soul grew used to up there—? The cool, invigorating breezes? The free life in woods and mountains, among beasts and birds—?

EKDAL [*smiling*] Hjalmar, shall we show it to him?

HJALMAR [*quickly, a little embarrassed*] Oh no, father. Not tonight.

GREGERS What is it he wants to show me?

HJALMAR Oh, it's just—something. You can see it some other time.

GREGERS [*continues addressing* OLD EKDAL] You see, this is what I had in mind, Lieutenant. Why don't you come up to Høydal with me? I'll probably be going back shortly. I'm sure you could get some copying work to do up there as well. For down here you can't have a thing to cheer you up and keep you occupied.

EKDAL [*looks at him in astonishment*] Don't *I* have—!

GREGERS Yes, of course, you have Hjalmar. But then he has his own family. And a man like you, who have always loved the outdoors—

EKDAL [*striking the table*] Hjalmar, he *shall* see it!

HJALMAR But father, do you really think so? It's dark and—

EKDAL Nonsense. There's a moon. [*Getting up.*] I say he's got to see it. Let me out. Come and help me, Hjalmar!

HEDVIG Oh yes, father! Do!

HJALMAR [*getting up*] Oh well, all right.

GREGERS [*to* GINA] What is it?

GINA Oh, don't expect anything much.

[EKDAL *and* HJALMAR *have gone to the rear of the room. Each of them slides one of the double doors back.* HEDVIG *is helping the old man.* GREGERS *remains standing by the sofa.* GINA *keeps on sewing, paying no attention. Through the opened doors can be seen a big, elongated, irregular-shaped attic, with nooks and corners and a couple of chimneys standing free from the wall. Moonlight falls through several skylights, illuminating some parts of the room, while others are in deep shadow.*]

EKDAL [*to* GREGERS] You are welcome to come closer, sir.

GREGERS [*goes up to them*] What is this really?

EKDAL See for yourself. H'm.

HJALMAR [*somewhat embarrassed*] This is all father's, you understand.

GREGERS [*at the door, peering into the attic*] Do you keep chickens, Lieutenant?

EKDAL   Should say we do. They're roosting now. But you ought to see those chickens in daylight!

HEDVIG   And there is—

EKDAL   Hush, don't say anything yet.

GREGERS   And I see you've got pigeons, too.

EKDAL   Could be we have. We've got pigeons, all right! The roosts are up on the rafters, for pigeons like to be up high, you know.

HJALMAR   They aren't all of them just ordinary pigeons.

EKDAL   Ordinary! I should say not! We've got tumblers and even a couple of pouters. But come over here. Do you see that pen over by the wall?

GREGERS   Yes. What do you use that for?

EKDAL   That's where the rabbits are at night.

GREGERS   Oh? You have rabbits, too, do you?

EKDAL   Damn right we have rabbits! He asks if we have rabbits, Hjalmar! H'm. But now we're coming to the *real* thing. Here we are. Move, Hedvig. You stand here and look down—there; that's right. Now, do you see a basket with straw in it?

GREGERS   Yes, I do. And I see a bird.

EKDAL   H'm—A "bird."

GREGERS   Isn't it a duck?

EKDAL   [*offended*]   I'd say it's a duck!

HJALMAR   But what kind of duck, do you think?

HEDVIG   It's not just an ordinary duck.

EKDAL   Hush!

GREGERS   And it's not a muscovy duck, either.

EKDAL   No, Mr.—Werle; it's not a muscovy, for it's a wild duck!

GREGERS   Is it really? A wild duck?

EKDAL   That's what it is. The—"bird," as you called it. A wild duck. It's our wild duck.

HEDVIG   *My* wild duck. For it belongs to me.

GREGERS   And it lives here in the attic? It's thriving?

EKDAL   What's so odd about that? She's got a big pail of water to splash around in.

HJALMAR   Fresh water every other day.

GINA   [*turning to* HJALMAR]   Ekdal, please. I'm freezing.

EKDAL   H'm. All right; let's close up. Just as well not to disturb their night's rest, anyway. Help me Hedvig.

[HJALMAR *and* HEDVIG *slide the double doors shut.*]

EKDAL   You can have a good look at her some other time. [*Sits down in the armchair by the stove.*] I'm telling you, they are strange birds, those wild ducks.

GREGERS   But how did you ever catch it, Lieutenant?

EKDAL   I didn't. There's a certain man in this town we can thank for her.

GREGERS   [*struck by a thought*]   Would that man be my father?

EKDAL   Indeed it is. It's your father, sure enough. H'm.

HJALMAR   Funny you'd guess that, Gregers.

GREGERS   You told me before that you owed a great deal to my father, so I thought that perhaps—

GINA   But we didn't get the duck from Werle himself.

EKDAL   It's Håkon Werle we have to thank for her all the same, Gina. [*To* GREGERS.] He was out in a boat, see, and took a shot at her. But he doesn't see so well, your father doesn't. H'm. Anyway, she was only wounded.

GREGERS   I see. She got some buckshot in her.

HJALMAR   Yes. A little.

HEDVIG   Right under the wing, so she couldn't fly.

GREGERS   Then she went to the bottom, I suppose.

EKDAL   [*sleepily, his voice muffled*]   So it did. Always do that, wild ducks. Dive straight to the bottom—far as they can, sir. Bite themselves fast in the grasses and roots and weeds and all the other damn stuff down there. And never come up again.

GREGERS   But, Lieutenant, *your* wild duck did.

EKDAL   He had such a wonderfully clever dog, your father. And that dog—it went down and got the duck up.

GREGERS   [*to* HJALMAR]   And so it came to you?

HJALMAR   Not right away. First your father took it home with him, but it didn't seem to get on too well there, and then he told Pettersen to get rid of it.

EKDAL   [*half asleep*]   H'm—Pettersen—Ass—

HJALMAR   That's how we got it, for father knows Pettersen a little, and when he heard about the wild duck, he asked Pettersen to give it to him.

GREGERS   And now it seems perfectly contented in there in the attic.

HJALMAR   Yes, you would hardly believe how well it gets on. It's becoming fat. I think perhaps it's been in there so long that it has forgotten what wild life is like. And that makes all the difference.

GREGERS   I am sure you are right, Hjalmar. The thing to do is never to let it look at sea and sky again.—But I don't think I should stay any longer. I believe your father is asleep.

HJALMAR   Oh, as far as that is concerned—

GREGERS   Oh yes, one thing more. You said you had a room for rent? A vacant room?

HJALMAR   We do. What of it? Do you know anyone who—?

GREGERS   Could I get it?

HJALMAR   You?

GINA   Oh, Mr. Werle, I'm sure *you* don't want to—

GREGERS   Couldn't I have it? If I can, I'll move in first thing in the morning.

HJALMAR   Yes, indeed, with the greatest pleasure.

GINA   No, but Mr. Werle, that's not a room for you.

HJALMAR   Gina! How can you say that?

GINA   It's not large enough or light enough, and—

GREGERS   That doesn't matter, Mrs. Ekdal.

HJALMAR   I think it's quite a nice room myself, and decently furnished, too.

GINA   But remember those two downstairs.

GREGERS   Who are they?

GINA   There's one who used to be a private tutor.

HJALMAR   Molvik is his name. He studied to be a minister once.

GINA   And then there's a doctor, name of Relling.

GREGERS   Relling? I know him slightly. He used to practice up at Høydal.

GINA   They are a couple of real wild characters those two. Out all hours of the night, and when they come home they aren't always—y'know—

GREGERS   One gets used to that sort of thing. I hope I'll be like the wild duck.

GINA   H'm. Well, *I* think you ought to sleep on it first.

GREGERS   I take it you don't really want me in the house, Mrs. Ekdal.

GINA   Good Lord! How can you say a thing like that?

HJALMAR   Yes, Gina. It really does seem very odd of you. [*To* GREGERS.] Does this mean you'll be staying in town for a while?

GREGERS   [*putting on his overcoat*]   Yes, I think I'll stay.

HJALMAR   But not with your father? What do you intend to do?

GREGERS   If I knew that, Hjalmar, I'd be much better off. But when you're cursed with a name like "Gregers"—and then "Werle" after that—Did you ever hear of an uglier name?

HJALMAR   I don't think it's ugly at all.

GREGERS   Ugh! I feel like spitting in the face of anybody with a name like that. But since it's my cross in life to be Gregers Werle, such as I am—

HJALMAR   Ha-ha! If you weren't Gregers Werle, what would you like to be?

GREGERS   If I could choose, I'd like to be a really clever dog.

GINA   A dog!

HEDVIG   [involuntarily]   Oh no!

GREGERS   Yes, an exceptionally skillful dog—the kind that goes down to the bottom after wild ducks when they've dived down among the weeds and the grass down there in the mud.

HJALMAR   Honestly, Gregers. This makes no sense whatever.

GREGERS   I suppose it doesn't. But tomorrow morning, then, I'll be moving in. [To GINA.] You won't have any trouble with me; I'll do everything myself. [To HJALMAR.] The other things we can talk about tomorrow.—Goodnight, Mrs. Ekdal. [Nods to HEDVIG.] Goodnight!

GINA   Goodnight, Mr. Werle.

HEDVIG   Goodnight.

HJALMAR   [who has lighted a candle]   Wait a moment. I'll see you down. I'm sure it's all dark on the stairs.

[GREGERS and HJALMAR go out through the entrance door, right rear.]

GINA   [staring ahead, her sewing lowered in her lap]   Wasn't it funny all that talk about wanting to be a dog?

HEDVIG   Do you know, mother—I think he really meant something else.

GINA   What would that be?

HEDVIG   No, I couldn't say, but it was just like he had something else in mind all the time.

GINA   You think so? It sure was funny, though.

HJALMAR   [returning]   The lamp was still burning. [Blows out the candle and sits down.] Ah, at last it's possible to get a bite to eat. [Starts on the sandwiches.] Now do you see what I mean, Gina—about seizing the opportunity?

GINA   What opportunity?

HJALMAR   Well—it was lucky, wasn't it, that we got the room rented? And then to somebody like Gregers, a dear old friend.

GINA   Well, I don't know what to say to that.

HEDVIG   Oh mother, you'll see it will be fun.

HJALMAR   I must say you are strange. First you wanted nothing more than to get a lodger; then when we do, you don't like it.

GINA   I know, Ekdal. If only it had been somebody else. What do you think old Werle will say?

HJALMAR   He? It's none of his business.

GINA   But don't you see that something's bound to be wrong between the two of 'em, since the young one is moving out. Sure you know how those two are.

HJALMAR   That may be so, but—

GINA   And maybe Werle will think you are behind it!

HJALMAR   All right! Let him think that. Oh, by all means, Werle has done a great deal for me—I'm the first to admit it. But that doesn't mean I everlastingly have to let him run my life.

GINA   But Ekdal, dear, it could hurt Grandpa. Perhaps he'll lose what little he's making from working for Gråberg.

HJALMAR   I almost wish he would! Is it not humiliating for a man like me to see his gray-haired father treated like dirt? Ah, but soon now the time will be ripe. I feel it. [Takes another sandwich.] As sure as I have a mission in life, it shall be accomplished!

HEDVIG   Oh yes, father!

GINA   Shhh! Don't wake him up.

HJALMAR   [*in a lower voice*]   I say it again: I *will* accomplish it! The day will come, when—That's why it's such a good thing we got the room rented out, for that makes me more independent. And that's necessary for a man with a mission in life. [*Over by the armchair, with feeling.*] Poor old white-haired father. Trust your Hjalmar. He has broad enough shoulders—powerful shoulders, at any rate. Some day you'll wake up, and—[*to* GINA.] Or don't you believe that?

GINA   [*getting up*]   Sure I do, but let's first get him to bed.

HJALMAR   Yest, let us
    [*They tenderly lift the old man.*]

ACT III

> The studio. It is morning. Daylight comes in through the skylight, the blue cloth having been pulled aside.
> HJALMAR sits at the table retouching a photograph. Several other photographs are lying in front of him. After a while, GINA, in coat and hat, enters from outside. She is carrying a covered basket.

HJALMAR   Back already, Gina?

GINA   Yes. I'm in a hurry. [*Puts the basket down on a chair and takes off her coat and hat.*]

HJALMAR   Did you look in at Gregers's?

GINA   I did. It looks real nice in there. He fixed up the place real pretty, soon as he moved in.

HJALMAR   Oh?

GINA   Remember, he was to take care of everything himself? Well, he built a fire in the stove, but he hadn't opened the flue, so the whole room got filled with smoke. Phew! It smelled like—

HJALMAR   Oh dear—

GINA   Then do you know what he does? This really beats everything. He wanted to put out the fire, so he pours the water from the wash basin into the stove. The whole floor is sloppy with filth!

HJALMAR   I am sorry.

GINA   I've got the janitor's wife to clean up after him, pig as he is, but the room can't be lived in till this afternoon.

HJALMAR   Where is he now?

GINA   He said he was going out for a while.

HJALMAR   I went in there for a moment, too—right after you had left.

GINA   He told me. You've asked him for breakfast.

HJALMAR   Just a bit of a late morning meal. It's the first day and all. We can hardly do less. I am sure you have something.

GINA   I'll have to find something, at any rate.

HJALMAR   Be sure it's plenty, though. I think Relling and Molvik are coming, too. I ran into Relling on the stairs just now, and so of course I had to—

GINA   So we are to have those two as well.

HJALMAR   Good heavens, one or two more or less—can that make any differ-ence?

EKDAL   [*opens his door and looks in*]   Listen, Hjalmar—[*Sees* GINA.] Well, never mind.

GINA   Do you want something, Grandpa?

EKDAL   No. It doesn't matter. H'm! [*Goes back inside his room.*]

GINA   [*picking up her basket*]   Make sure he doesn't go out.

HJALMAR   Yes, I will.—Say, Gina—how about some herring salad? I believe Relling and Molvik made a night of it again last night.

GINA   If only they don't get here too soon.

HJALMAR   I'm sure they won't. Just take your time.

GINA   Well, all right. Then you can work some in the meantime.

HJALMAR   I *am* working! I'm working as hard as I can!

GINA   All I mean is you'd have it out of the way for later. [*Goes into the kitchen.*]

[HJALMAR *picks up the photograph and the brush and works for a while— slowly and with evident distaste.*]

EKDAL   [*peeks in, looks around, says in a low voice*]   Pst! Are you busy.

HJALMAR   Yes. I am struggling with these everlasting pictures—

EKDAL   All right, all right. If you're busy, then you're busy. H'm! [*Goes back inside his room. The door remains open.*]

HJALMAR   [*works in silence for a while, puts his brush down, walks over to* EKDAL's *door*]   Are *you* busy, father?

EKDAL   [*grumbling inside his room*]   When *you* are busy, *I* am busy! H'm!

HJALMAR   Oh all right. [*Returns to his work.*]

EKDAL   [*appears in his door again after a while*]   H'm, Hjalmar, listen—I'm not so *terribly* busy, you know.

HJALMAR   I thought you were writing.

EKDAL   Dammit all! Can't that Gråberg wait a day or two? Didn't think it was a matter of life and death.

HJALMAR   Of course not. And you aren't a slave, after all.

EKDAL   And there is this other job in there—

HJALMAR   Just what I was thinking. Do you want to go in there now? Shall I open the door for you?

EKDAL   Good idea.

HJALMAR   [*getting up*]   Then we'd have that job out of the way.

EKDAL   Exactly. It has to be ready for tomorrow, anyway. It *is* tomorrow, isn't it?

HJALMAR   Sure it's tomorrow.

[*They slide the double doors open. The morning sun is shining through the skylight. Some pigeons are flying around; others are cooing on their perches. From farther inside the room the chickens are heard clucking once in a while.*]

HJALMAR   All right, father. Guess you can go ahead.

EKDAL   [*entering the attic*]   Aren't you coming?

HJALMAR   Yes, do you know—I almost think I will. [*Notices* GINA *in the kitchen door.*] I? No, I don't have the time. I have to work. But then there is this thing—

[*He pulls a cord. A curtain comes down from within the attic. Its lower part is made out of a strip of old sailcloth; its upper part is a piece of stretched-out fish net. The attic floor is now no longer visible.*]

HJALMAR   [*returns to the table*]   Now! Maybe I can have peace for a few minutes.

GINA   Is he fooling around in there again?

HJALMAR   Would you rather he went down to Madam Eriksen? [*Sitting down.*] Do you want anything? I thought you said—

GINA   I just wanted to ask you if you think we can set the table in here?

HJALMAR   Yes. There aren't any appointments this early, are there?

GINA   No—only those two sweethearts who want their picture taken.

HJALMAR   Damn! Couldn't they come some other time!

GINA   Goodness, Ekdal, they'll be here after dinner, when you're asleep.

HJALMAR   Oh, in that case it's all right. Yes, let's eat in here.

GINA   Fine. But there's no hurry with the table. You're welcome to use it some more.

HJALMAR   Can't you see I *am* using it?

GINA   Then you'll be all done for afterwards, you know. [*Goes into the kitchen.*] [*Brief silence.*]

EKDAL   [*in the door to the attic, inside the fish net*]   Hjalmar!

HJALMAR   What?

EKDAL   Afraid we'll have to move the pail, after all.

HJALMAR   What else have I been saying all along?

EKDAL   H'm—h'm—h'm! [*Disappears inside again.*]

HJALMAR   [*keeps on working for a moment, glances over towards the attic, half rises, as* HEDVIG *enters from the kitchen. He quickly sits down again*] What do you want?

HEDVIG   Just to be with you, father.

HJALMAR   [*after a short while*]   Seems to me like you're snooping around. Have you been told to watch me, perhaps?

HEDVIG   No, of course not.

HJALMAR   What is mother doing?

HEDVIG   Mother is in the middle of the herring salad. [*Comes over to the table.*] Isn't there any little thing I can help you with, father?

HJALMAR   Oh no. It is better I do it all alone—as long as my strength lasts. There is no need for you to worry about anything, Hedvig, as long as your father is allowed to keep his health.

HEDVIG   Oh father. I won't have you talk that horrid way. [*She walks around a bit, stops by the opening to the inner room and looks in.*]

HJALMAR   What is he doing in there?

HEDVIG   Looks like a new ladder up to the water pail.

HJALMAR   He'll never manage that by himself! And here I am condemned to sit—!

HEDVIG   [*goes to him*]   Give me the brush, father. I can do it.

HJALMAR   I won't hear of it. You'll just be ruining your eyes.

HEDVIG   No, I won't. Give me the brush.

HJALMAR   [*getting up*]   It would only be for a minute or two—

HEDVIG   What possible harm could that do? [*Takes the brush.*] There now. [*Sits down.*] And here is one I can use as model.

HJALMAR   But don't ruin your eyes! Do you hear me? I will not take the responsibility. It's all yours. I'm just telling you.

HEDVIG   [*working*]   Yes, of course.

HJALMAR   You are really very good at it, Hedvig. It will only be for a few minutes, you understand.
[*He slips into the attic by the edge of the curtain.* HEDVIG *keeps on working.* HJALMAR *and* EKDAL *can be heard talking behind the curtain.*]

HJALMAR   [*appearing inside the net*]   Hedvig, please give me the pliers on the shelf. And the chisel. [*Turns around.*] See here, father. Just let me show you what I have in mind first.
[HEDVIG *fetches the tools from the shelf and gives them to him.*]

HJALMAR   Thank you. It was a good thing I went in.

[*He leaves the doorway. Sounds of carpentering and conversation are heard from inside.* HEDVIG *remains watching them. After a while there is a knock on the entrance door. She does not notice.*]

GREGERS [*bareheaded and coatless, enters, stops near the door*] H'm!

HEDVIG [*turns around and walks towards him*] Good morning! Won't you please come in?

GREGERS Thank you. [*Looks towards the attic.*] You seem to have workmen in the house.

HEDVIG Oh no. It's just father and Grandpa. I'll tell them you're here.

GREGERS Please don't. I'd rather wait a while. [*Sits down on the sofa.*]

HEDVIG It's such a mess in here—[*Begins removing the photographs.*]

GREGERS Never mind. Are they pictures you are retouching?

HEDVIG Yes. It is something I help father with.

GREGERS I hope you won't let me disturb you.

HEDVIG I won't.

[*She moves the things more within her reach and resumes work.* GREGERS *watches her in silence.*]

GREGERS Did the wild duck sleep well last night?

HEDVIG Yes, thank you. I think so.

GREGERS [*turning towards the attic*] In daylight it looks quite different from last night when there was a moon.

HEDVIG Yes, it varies so. In the morning it looks different than in the afternoon, and when it rains it looks different than when the sun is shining.

GREGERS You have noticed that?

HEDVIG Yes, of course.

GREGERS Do you too spend much time with the wild duck?

HEDVIG Yes, when I can.

GREGERS I suppose you don't have much spare time, though. You are going to school, of course?

HEDVIG Not any more. Father is afraid I'll ruin my eyes.

GREGERS Then he reads with you himself?

HEDVIG He has promised to, but he hasn't had the time yet.

GREGERS But isn't there anyone else who can help you?

HEDVIG Well, yes, there is Mr. Molvik, but he isn't always—you know—quite—

GREGERS You mean he is drunk sometimes.

HEDVIG I think so.

GREGERS Well, in that case you have time for many things. And in there, I suppose, it's like a world all its own?

HEDVIG Yes, quite. And there are so many strange things in there.

GREGERS There are?

HEDVIG Yes, there are big closets with books in them, and in many of the books there are pictures.

GREGERS I see.

HEDVIG And there is an old desk with drawers and drop-down leaves and a big clock with figures that come out. But the clock doesn't run any more.

GREGERS So time has stopped in there where the wild duck lives?

HEDVIG Yes. And there are old coloring sets and that sort of thing, and then all the books.

GREGERS I expect you read the books.

HEDVIG Yes, whenever I have a chance. But most of them are in English and I can't read that. But I look at the pictures. There is a great, big book that's called "Harrison's History of London." I think it is a hundred years old. There are ever so many pictures in it. In front it shows a picture of Death with an hourglass and a girl. I think that is horrible. But then there are all the pictures of churches and castles and streets and big ships that sail the seas.

GREGERS   Tell me—where do all those strange things come from?

HEDVIG   There was an old sea captain who used to live here. He brought them home. They called him The Flying Dutchman. And that's odd, I think, for he wasn't a Dutchman at all.

GREGERS   No?

HEDVIG   No. But finally he disappeared at sea, and all the things were left here.

GREGERS   Listen—when you sit in there looking at the pictures, don't you ever want to travel and see the real, big world for yourself?

HEDVIG   Oh no. I want to stay here at home always and help father and mother.

GREGERS   With the photographs?

HEDVIG   Not just with that. Best of all I'd like to learn how to engrave pictures like those in the English books.

GREGERS   H'm. And what does your father say to that?

HEDVIG   I don't think father likes the idea very much. He is funny about things like that. You know, he says I ought to learn basket-weaving and straw-plaiting. But I don't think that sounds like much of anything at all.

GREGERS   No, I don't think it does either.

HEDVIG   Though of course father is quite right in saying that if I had learned basket-weaving I could have made the new basket for the wild duck.

GREGERS   That's true. And that really ought to have been your job, you know.

HEDVIG   Yes. Because it is my wild duck.

GREGERS   So I hear.

HEDVIG   Oh yes. I own it. But father and Grandpa get to borrow it as often as they like.

GREGERS   So? And what do they do with it?

HEDVIG   Oh—they take care of it and build things for it and that sort of thing.

GREGERS   I see. For of course the wild duck is the noblest of all the animals in there.

HEDVIG   Yes, she is, for she is a real, wild bird. And then I feel sorrier for her than for any of the others, because she's all alone, poor thing.

GREGERS   No family, like the rabbits.

HEDVIG   No. And the chickens, they have so many they were little chicks together with. But she is all alone, with none of her own near by. And there is the strange thing about the wild duck. Nobody knows her and nobody knows where she is from.

GREGERS   And she has been down to the depths of the sea.

HEDVIG   [*glances quickly at him, suppresses a smile, asks*]   Why do you say "the depths of the sea"?

GREGERS   What should I say?

HEDVIG   You should say "the sea bottom" or "the bottom of the sea."

GREGERS   Can't I just as well say "the depths of the sea"?

HEDVIG   Yes, but I think it sounds so strange when other people say "the depths of the sea."

GREGERS   Why is that? Tell me.

HEDVIG   No, I won't, for it is so silly.

GREGERS   I don't think so. Please tell me why you smiled.

HEDVIG   It's because every time I think of what's in there—when it comes into my head all of a sudden, I mean—I always feel that the whole room and everything that's in it are the depths of the sea. But that's silly.

GREGERS   Don't say that.

HEDVIG   Yes, for it's just an old attic, you know.

GREGERS   [*looking intently at her*]   Are you sure?

HEDVIG   [surprised]   That it's an attic?

GREGERS   Yes. Are you sure it is?

[HEDVIG stares at him in silence, her mouth open in astonishment. GINA enters from the kitchen with linen, silverware, etc., to set the table.]

GREGERS   [getting up]   I am afraid I am too early for you.

GINA   Oh well. You have to be somewhere. Things are almost ready now, anyway. Clear the table, Hedvig.

[During the next scene HEDVIG clears the table and GINA sets it. GREGERS seats himself in the armchair and starts leafing through an album of photographs.]

GREGERS   I understand you know how to retouch, Mrs. Ekdal.

GINA   [looks at him out of the corner of her eye]   That's right.

GREGERS   That was fortunate.

GINA   How—fortunate?

GREGERS   I mean since Ekdal is a photographer.

HEDVIG   Mother knows how to take pictures, too.

GINA   Oh yes, I've had to learn that business, all right.

GREGERS   Perhaps it is you who are responsible for the daily routine?

GINA   Yes, when Ekdal himself doesn't have the time—

GREGERS   I suppose he busies himself a great deal with his old father?

GINA   Yes, and then it's not for a man like Ekdal to waste his time taking pictures of everybody and his grandmother.

GREGERS   I quite agree, but since he did choose this as his profession, shouldn't he—?

GINA   You know just as well as I do, Mr. Werle, that Ekdal isn't just one of your common, ordinary photographers.

GREGERS   Of course not, but—nevertheless—

[A shot is heard from the attic.]

GREGERS   [jumps up]   What was that?

GINA   Ugh! There they go, firing away again!

GREGERS   They shoot, too?

HEDVIG   They go hunting.

GREGERS   What? [Over by the door to the attic.] Do you go hunting, Hjalmar?

HJALMAR   [inside the curtain]   Have you arrived? I didn't know—I've been so busy—[To HEDVIG.] And you—not letting us know—! [Comes into the studio.]

GREGERS   Do you go shooting in the attic?

HJALMAR   [showing him a double-barreled pistol]   Oh, it's only this old thing.

GINA   You and Grandpa are going to have an accident with that pestol of yours one of these days.

HJALMAR   [irritated]   I believe I have told you that this kind of firearm is called a pistol.

GINA   I don't see that that makes it any better.

GREGERS   So you have taken up hunting, too, Hjalmar?

HJALMAR   Only a little rabbit hunting now and then. It's mostly for father's sake, you understand.

GINA   Menfolks are strange. They always need something to diverge themselves with.

HJALMAR   [grimly]   That's right. We always need something to divert ourselves with.

GINA   That's exactly what I'm saying.

HJALMAR   Oh well—! H'm! [To GREGERS.] Well, you see, we're fortunate in that the attic is situated so that nobody can hear the shots.

[*Puts the pistol on the top shelf.*] Don't touch the pistol, Hedvig! Remember, one barrel is loaded!

GREGERS [*peering through the net*] You have a hunting rifle, too, I see.

HJALMAR That's father's old gun. It doesn't work any more. There's something wrong with the lock. But it's rather fun to have it around all the same, for we take it apart and clean it once in a while and grease it and put it back together again. It's mostly father, of course, who amuses himself with things like that.

HEDVIG [*standing next to* GREGERS] Now you can get a good look at the wild duck.

GREGERS I was just looking at it. One wing is drooping a bit, isn't it?

HJALMAR Well that's not so strange. She was hit, you know.

GREGERS And she drags her foot a little. Or doesn't she?

HJALMAR Perhaps a little bit.

HEDVIG Yes, for that is the foot the dog seized her by.

HJALMAR But aside from that she has no other hurt or defect, and that's really quite remarkable when you consider that she has a charge of buckshot in her and has been between the teeth of a dog.

GREGERS [*with a glance at* HEDVIG] Yes, and been to the depths of the sea—for so long.

HEDVIG [*smiles*] Yes.

GINA [*busy at the table*] Oh yes, that precious wild duck. There sure is enough circumstance made over it.

HJALMAR H'm. Will you be done setting the table soon?

GINA In a minute. Hedvig, I need your help. [GINA *and* HEDVIG *go into the kitchen.*]

HJALMAR [*in a low voice*] You had better not watch father. He doesn't like it.

GREGERS [*leaves the attic door.*]

HJALMAR And I ought to close this before the others arrive. [*Shoos the birds away with his hands.*] Shoo! Shoo—you! [*Raising the curtain and sliding the doors back.*] This arrangement is my own invention. It is really quite amusing to fool around with these things and to fix them when they get broken. And it's absolutely necessary to have something like it, for Gina won't stand for rabbits and chickens in the studio.

GREGERS No, I suppose not. And perhaps the studio is your wife's department?

HJALMAR I generally leave the daily run of the business to her. That gives me a chance to retire into the living room and give my thoughts to more important things.

GREGERS What things, Hjalmar?

HJALMAR I have been wondering why you haven't asked me that before. Or maybe you haven't heard about the invention?

GREGERS Invention? No.

HJALMAR Really? You haven't? Oh well—up there in the woods and wilderness—

GREGERS So you have invented something!

HJALMAR Not quite yet, but I am working on it. As you can well imagine, when I decided to devote myself to photography it was not my intent to do nothing but take portraits of all sorts of ordinary people

GREGERS I suppose not. Your wife just said the same thing.

HJALMAR I made a pledge to myself that if I were to give my powers to this profession, I would raise it so high that it would become both an art and a science. That is how I decided to make some remarkable invention.

GREGERS   What is it? What does it do?

HJALMAR   Well, Gregers, you must not ask for details just yet. You see, it takes time. And don't think I am driven by vanity. I can truthfully say I am not working for my own sake. Far from it. It is my life's mission that is in my thoughts night and day.

GREGERS   What mission?

HJALMAR   The old man with the silver hair—can you forget him?

GREGERS   Yes, your poor father. But what exactly do you think you can do for him?

HJALMAR   I can resurrect his respect for himself by once again raising the name of Ekdal to fame and honor.

GREGERS   So that is your life's mission.

HJALMAR   Yes. I will rescue that shipwrecked man. For he was shipwrecked the moment the storm broke. During those terrible inquiries he was not himself. The pistol over yonder—the one we use to shoot rabbits with—it has played its part in the tragedy of the Ekdal family.

GREGERS   The pistol? Really?

HJALMAR   When sentence had been pronounced and he was to be confined— he had that pistol in his hand—

GREGERS   He tried to—!

HJALMAR   Yes, but didn't dare. He was a coward. So much of a wreck, so spiritually ruined was he already then. Can you understand it? He, an officer, the killer of nine bears, descended from two lieutenant colonels—I mean one after the other, of course—Can you understand it, Gregers?

GREGERS   I can indeed.

HJALMAR   Not I.—But the pistol came to figure in our family chronicle a second time. When he had begun to wear the garb of gray and sat there behind bolt and bar—oh, those were terrible days for me, believe me. I kept the shades down on both windows. When I looked out, I saw the sun shining as usual. I saw people in the street laughing and talking about nothing. I could not understand it. It seemed to me that all of existence ought to come to a standstill, as during an eclipse of the sun.

GREGERS   I felt that way when mother died.

HJALMAR   In such an hour Hjalmar Ekdal turned the pistol against himself—

GREGERS   You too were thinking of—?

HJALMAR   Yes.

GREGERS   But you did not pull the trigger?

HJALMAR   No. In the decisive moment I won a victory over myself. I remained alive. Take my word for it: it requires courage to go on living in a situation like that.

GREGERS   That depends on how you look at it.

HJALMAR   No, it doesn't. At any rate, it all turned out to be for the best. For soon now I will finish my invention, and when I do, Doctor Relling thinks, as I do myself, that father will be allowed to wear his uniform again. I shall claim that as my only reward.

GREGERS   So it is this business with the uniform that mostly—

HJALMAR   Yes, to be able to wear it again is what he dreams of and longs for. You have no idea how it cuts me to the quick to see him. Whenever we have a little family celebration here, like Gina's and my wedding anniversary or whatever it may be, then the old man appears in his lieutenant's uniform from happier days. But no sooner is there a knock on the door than he scuttles back to his own little room as fast as his old legs will carry him. He doesn't dare to show himself to strangers, you know. A sight like that lacerates a son's heart, Gregers!

GREGERS   About when do you think the invention will be ready?

HJALMAR   Heavens, you must not ask for details like that. An invention, you see, is something you don't altogether control yourself. It is very largely a matter of inspiration—a sudden idea—and it is next to impossible to tell beforehand when that may come.

GREGERS   But it is progressing?

HJALMAR   Certainly, it is progressing. It occupies my thoughts every day. It fills me. Every afternoon, after dinner, I shut myself up in the living room to ponder in peace. I just can't be hurried; it won't do any good. That is what Relling says, too.

GREGERS   And you don't think that all this business in the attic interferes too much, distracts you from your work?

HJALMAR   No, no, no. Quite the contrary. You must not say a thing like that. After all, I cannot everlastingly be pursuing the same exhausting train of thought. I need something else, something to occupy me during the waiting period. The inspiration, the sudden flash of insight, don't you see? —when it comes, it comes.

GREGERS   My dear Hjalmar, I almost think there is something of the wild duck in you.

HJALMAR   The wild duck? How do you mean?

GREGERS   You have plunged down through the sea and got yourself entangled in the grasses on the bottom.

HJALMAR   Are you perhaps referring to the well-nigh fatal shot that lodged in father's wing and hit me, too?

GREGERS   Not to that so much. I won't say you are crippled. But you are in a poisonous marsh, Hjalmar. You have contracted an insidious disease and gone to the bottom to die in the dark.

HJALMAR   I? Die in the dark? Honestly, Gregers. You really shouldn't say such things.

GREGERS   Don't you worry. I'll get you up again. For I, too, have got a mission in life. I found it yesterday.

HJALMAR   That may well be, but I shall ask you kindly to leave me out of it. I assure you that—aside from my easily explainable melancholia, of course— I am as contented a man as anybody could wish to be.

GREGERS   The fact that you are—that is one of the symptoms of the poisoning.

HJALMAR   No, really, Gregers. Please don't talk to me any more about disease and poison. I am not used to that sort of talk. In my house we never discuss unpleasant topics.

GREGERS   That I can well believe.

HJALMAR   No, for it isn't good for me. And there is no marshy air here, as you call it. The roof may be low in the poor photographer's home—I know very well it is—and my lot is lowly. But I am an inventor, and a provider as well. That is what raises me above my humble circumstances.—Ah! Here's lunch!

[GINA *and* HEDVIG *enter with bottles of beer, a decanter of brandy, glasses, and other appurtenances. At the same moment,* RELLING *and* MOLVIK *come through the entrance door. Neither one wears hat or coat.* MOLVIK *is dressed in black.*]

GINA   [*putting the things down on the table*]   Well, you two arrive just in time.

RELLING   Molvik thought he could smell herring salad, and then there was no holding him.—Good morning again, Ekdal.

HJALMAR   Gregers, may I introduce you to Mr. Molvik—And Doctor—that's right, you two already know each other, don't you.

GREGERS   Slightly.

RELLING   Oh yes, young Mr. Werle. We used to do some skirmishing up at the Høydal works. I take it you have just moved in?

GREGERS   This morning.

RELLING   Well, Molvik and I live downstairs, so you don't have far to go for doctor and minister if you need them.

GREGERS   Thank you; maybe I shall. We were thirteen at the table yesterday.

HJALMAR   Come now! Please don't start any of that unpleasantness again!

RELLING   Calm down, Ekdal. You are immune.

HJALMAR   I hope so, for my family's sake.—Sit down. Let's eat, drink, and be merry.

GREGERS   Aren't we going to wait for your father?

HJALMAR   No, he'll eat later in his own room. Do sit down!

   [*The men seat themselves and begin eating and drinking.* GINA *and* HEDVIG *wait on them.*]

RELLING   Molvik got pretty high last night, Mrs. Ekdal.

GINA   Again?

RELLING   Didn't you hear me bring him home?

GINA   Can't say I did.

RELLING   That's good, for Molvik was awful last night.

GINA   Is that true, Molvik?

MOLVIK   Let us consign last night's events to oblivion. They do not represent my better self.

RELLING   [*to* GREGERS]   It comes over him like an irresistible impulse. Then he has to go out and get drunk. You see, Molvik is demonic.

GREGERS   Demonic?

RELLING   That's right. Molvik is demonic.

GREGERS   H'm.

RELLING   And demonic natures aren't made to follow the straight and narrow path. They have to take off for the fields once in a while.—So you still stick it out up at that filthy old place?

GREGERS   So far.

RELLING   Did you ever collect on that claim you went around presenting?

GREGERS   Claim? [*Looks at him and understands.*] Oh I see.

HJALMAR   Have you been a bill collector, Gregers?

GREGERS   Oh nonsense.

RELLING   Oh yes, he has. He went around to all the cottages up there, trying to collect on something he called "the claim of the ideal."

GREGERS   I was young.

RELLING   You're right. You were very young. And the claim of the ideal—you never collected as long as I was up there.

GREGERS   Not since then, either.

RELLING   In that case, I suppose you have been wise enough to reduce the amount somewhat.

GREGERS   Never when I have to do with a real and genuine human being.

HJALMAR   I think that is reasonable enough.—Some butter, Gina.

RELLING   And a piece of bacon for Molvik.

MOLVIK   Ugh! Not bacon!

   [*There is a knock from inside the door to the attic.*]

HJALMAR   Go and open, Hedvig. Father wants to get out.

   [HEDVIG *opens the door a little.* OLD EKDAL *enters with the skin of a freshly flayed rabbit.* HEDVIG *closes the door after him.*]

EKDAL   Good morning, gentlemen! Good hunting today. Got me a big one.

HJALMAR   And you skinned it yourself, I see.

EKDAL   Salted it, too. It's nice, tender meat, rabbit is. It's sweet, y'know. Tastes like sugar. Good appetite, gentlemen! [*Goes into his room.*]

MOLVIK   [*getting up*]   Excuse me—I can't—Got to get downstairs—

RELLING   Drink soda water, you idiot!

MOLVIK   Uh—Uh—[*Hurries out, right rear.*]

RELLING   [*to* HJALMAR]   Let us drink to the old hunter.

HJALMAR   [*touching* RELLING's *glass with his own*]   For the sportsman on the brink of the grave—yes.

RELLING   For the gray-haired—[*Drinks.*] Tell me, is his hair gray or is it white?

HJALMAR   In between, I think. Though I don't think there are many hairs left on his head at all.

RELLING   Oh well. One can live happily with a wig, too. Ah, yes, Ekdal. You are really a very happy man. You have this beautiful ambition of yours to strive for—

HJALMAR   Believe me, I am striving.

RELLING   Then you have your excellent wife, shuffling about in slippered feet with that comfortable waddle of hers, making things nice and pleasant for you.

HJALMAR   Yes, Gina—[*Nods to her.*]—you are a good companion on life's journey.

GINA   Aw, you don't need to sit there and dissectate me!

RELLING   And your Hedvig, Ekdal.

HJALMAR   [*moved*]   Ah yes, the child! The child above all. Hedvig, come to me. [*Stroking her hair.*] What day is tomorrow?

HEDVIG   [*playfully shaking him*]   Oh, stop it, father!

HJALMAR   It's like a knife through my heart, when I consider how little we can do. Just a small celebration here in the attic.

HEDVIG   But that's just the way I like it!

RELLING   You wait till the invention is all done, Hedvig.

HJALMAR   Yes! Then you'll see, Hedvig. I have decided to secure your future. You shall be made comfortable for as long as you live. I will ask for something for you, something or other. That will be the impecunious inventor's sole reward.

HEDVIG   [*whispers, her arms around his neck*]   Oh you good, sweet father!

RELLING   [*to* GREGERS]   Well, now, don't you think it's nice for a change to sit down to a good table in a happy family circle?

HJALMAR   Yes, I really relish these hours at the table.

GREGERS   I, for one, don't like to breathe marsh air.

RELLING   Marsh air?

HJALMAR   Oh, don't start all that again!

GINA   I'll have you know there is no marsh air here, Mr. Werle. The place is aired every single day.

GREGERS   [*leaving the table*]   The stench I have in mind you don't get rid of by opening windows.

HJALMAR   Stench!

GINA   Yes, how do you like that, Ekdal!

RELLING   Begging your pardon—it wouldn't by any chance be you yourself who bring the stench with you from the Høydal mines?

GREGERS   It's just like you to call stench what I bring to this house.

RELLING   [*walks over to* GREGERS]   Listen here, Mr. Werle junior. I strongly suspect that you still carry the claim of the ideal around in your rear pocket.

GREGERS   I carry it in my heart.

RELLING   I don't care where the hell you carry it as long as you don't go bill collecting here while *I* am around.

GREGERS   And if I do so, nevertheless?

RELLING   Then you'll go head first down the stairs. Now you know!

HJALMAR   No, really, Relling—!

GREGERS   Go ahead! Throw me out!

GINA   [*interposing*]   No, we won't have any of that, Relling. But I will say this to you, Mr. Werle, that it seems like you are not the right person to come here and talk about stench after what you did to the stove in your room this morning.

[*There is a knock on the door.*]

HEDVIG   Mother, someone's knocking.

HJALMAR   Oh yes, let's have customers on top of everything else—!

GINA   I'll handle it. [*Opens the door, gives a start, steps back*]: Oh dear!

[WERLE, *in a fur coat, steps inside.*]

WERLE   I beg your pardon, but I am told my son is here.

GINA   [*swallowing hard*]   Yes sir.

HJALMAR   [*closer*]   Sir, wouldn't you like to—?

WERLE   Thanks. I just want a word with my son.

GREGERS   Well. Here I am.

WERLE   I want to talk with you in your room.

GREGERS   In my room—? Oh, all right. [*Is about to leave.*]

GINA   Good Lord, no! That's not a fit place!

WERLE   All right; out here in the hall, then. I want to see you alone.

HJALMAR   You may do that right here, Mr. Werle. Relling, come into the living room with me.

[HJALMAR *and* RELLING *go out, right front.* GINA *takes* HEDVIG *with her into the kitchen, left front.*]

GREGERS   [*after a brief silence*]   Well. We are alone.

WERLE   You dropped some hints last night. And since you have moved in with the Ekdals, I can only assume that you are planning something or other against me.

GREGERS   I plan to open Hjalmar Ekdal's eyes. He is to see his position as it really is. That's all.

WERLE   Is that the life mission you mentioned yesterday?

GREGERS   Yes. You have left me no other.

WERLE   So you feel it is I who have twisted your mind, Gregers?

GREGERS   You have twisted my whole life. I am not thinking of all that with mother. But it is you I can thank for the fact that I am being haunted and driven by a guilty conscience.

WERLE   Ah, I see. So your conscience is ailing.

GREGERS   I should have opposed you the time you were laying traps for Lieutenant Ekdal. I should have warned him, for I suspected how things were going.

WERLE   Yes, in that case you certainly ought to have said something.

GREGERS   I didn't have the courage. I was a coward—frightened. I felt an unspeakable fear of you—both then and for a long, long time afterwards.

WERLE   That fear appears to have left you now.

GREGERS   Yes, fortunately. What has been done to Old Ekdal, both by me and by—others, for that there is no remedy. But Hjalmar I can rescue from the web of lies and deceit in which he is suffocating.

WERLE   Do you think that is a good thing to do?

GREGERS   I am sure it is.

WERLE   I take it you think Mr. Photographer Ekdal is the kind of man who will be grateful for your friendly services?

GREGERS   Yes! He is that kind of man.

WERLE H'm. We'll see.

GREGERS Besides, if I am to continue living, I have to find a way to heal my sick conscience.

WERLE It will never get well. Your conscience has been sickly from the time you were a child. It's hereditary, Gregers. You have it from your mother. The only inheritance she left you.

GREGERS [with a contemptuous half smile] I see you still haven't forgotten your disappointment when you found out mother wasn't rich.

WERLE Let's not change the subject. Am I to think, then, that you are firmly resolved to guide Hjalmar Ekdal into the path you consider the right one?

GREGERS Yes. That is my firm intent.

WERLE In that case I could have saved myself coming all the way up here. For then I suppose there is no point in my asking you to move back home again?

GREGERS No.

WERLE And you don't want to join the firm?

GREGERS No.

WERLE Very well. But since I am to marry again, your part of the estate will have to be paid you.

GREGERS [quickly] No, I don't want that.

WERLE You don't want it?

GREGERS I dare not, for my conscience's sake.

WERLE [after a brief pause] Are you going back up to Høydal?

GREGERS No. I consider myself released from your service.

WERLE But what do you want to do with yourself?

GREGERS Accomplish my mission. Nothing else.

WERLE But afterwards? What are you going to live on?

GREGERS I have saved some of my salary.

WERLE How long do you think that will last?

GREGERS I think it will do for the time I have left.

WERLE What is that supposed to mean?

GREGERS I won't answer any more questions.

WERLE Well, goodbye, Gregers.

GREGERS Goodbye.

[WERLE leaves.]

HJALMAR [looks in] Did he leave?

GREGERS Yes.

[HJALMAR and RELLING enter from the living room, GINA and HEDVIG from the kitchen.]

RELLING Now that was a very successful breakfast.

GREGERS Put on your coat, Hjalmar. I want you to take a long walk with me.

HJALMAR Gladly. What did your father want? Did it have to do with me?

GREGERS Just come. We'll talk. I'll go and get my coat. [Goes out.]

GINA You shouldn't go with him, Ekdal.

RELLING No, don't. Stay here.

HJALMAR [taking his hat and coat] What! When an old friend feels the need to open his heart for me in private—!

RELLING But goddamit! Can't you see that the fellow is mad, cracked, insane!

GINA Yes, listen to Relling. His mother used to have physiological fits, too.

HJALMAR All the more reason why he needs a friend's alert eyes. [To GINA.] Be sure to have dinner ready at the usual time. Goodbye.

[Goes out.]

RELLING It's nothing less than a disaster that that man didn't go straight to hell down one of the shafts up at Høydal.

GINA Heavens—! Why do you say that?

RELLING [*mutters*] I have my reasons.

GINA Do you really think young Werle is crazy?

RELLING No, unfortunately. He is no madder than most people. He is sick, though.

GINA What do you think is wrong with him?

RELLING That I can tell you, Mrs. Ekdal. He suffers from an acute attack of moral integrity.

GINA Moral integrity?

HEDVIG Is that a disease?

RELLING Yes, it is a national disease, but it occurs only sporadically. [*Nods to* GINA.] That was a good meal, thank you. [*Goes out.*]

GINA [*troubled, walks up and down*] Ugh! That Gregers Werle—he's always been a weird fish.

HEDVIG [*by the table, looks at her searchingly*] I think this is very strange.

ACT IV

> *The studio. Photographs have just been taken. A cloth-covered camera on a tripod, a couple of chairs, and a small table are standing about in the middle of the floor. Afternoon light. The sun is about to disappear. After a while darkness begins to fall.* GINA *stands in the open entrance door with a small box and a wet glass plate in her hand. She is talking to someone not in sight.*

GINA Absolutely. When I promise something, I keep it. I'll have the first dozen ready for you on Monday.—Goodbye.

> [*Sounds of someone descending the stairs.* GINA *closes the door, puts the plate inside the box and the box into the camera.*]

HEDVIG [*enters from the kitchen*] Did they leave?

GINA [*putting things in order*] Yes, thank goodness. I finally got rid of them.

HEDVIG Can you understand why father isn't back yet?

GINA You're sure he is not down at Relling's?

HEDVIG No, he is not there. I just went down the kitchen stairs to ask.

GINA His food is getting cold and everything.

HEDVIG Yes. And father who is always so particular about having dinner on time.

GINA Oh well. You'll see he'll be back soon.

HEDVIG I wish he'd come. Everything seems so strange.

> [HJALMAR *enters from outside.*]

HEDVIG [*towards him*] Father! If you knew how we've been waiting for you!

GINA [*glancing at him*] You've been gone quite some time.

HJALMAR [*without looking at her*] Yes, I suppose I have.

> [*He starts taking his coat off.* GINA *and* HEDVIG *both go to help him. He turns them away.*]

GINA Maybe you and Werle had something to eat some place?

HJALMAR [*hanging up his coat*] No.

GINA [*toward the kitchen door*] I'll get your dinner.

HJALMAR Never mind. I don't feel like eating now.

HEDVIG [*coming closer*] Are you sick, father?

HJALMAR   Sick? No, I'm not sick—exactly. We had a strenuous walk, Gregers and I.

GINA   You shouldn't do that, Ekdal. You aren't used to it.

HJALMAR   H'm. There are many things in life a man has to get used to. [*Paces up and down.*] Anybody here while I've been gone?

GINA   Only that engaged couple.

HJALMAR   No new appointments?

GINA   No, not today.

HEDVIG   There will be some tomorrow, father, I am sure.

HJALMAR   I hope you are right, for tomorrow I plan to go to work in earnest.

HEDVIG   Tomorrow! But don't you remember what day is tomorrow?

HJALMAR   That's right. Well, then, the day after tomorrow. From now on I'll do everything myself. I want to assume the entire work load.

GINA   Whatever for, Ekdal? That's only making yourself miserable. I'll manage the pictures. You just go on with the invention.

HEDVIG   And the wild duck, father. And the chickens and the rabbits and—

HJALMAR   Don't ever mention all that junk to me again! Starting tomorrow, I'll never more set foot in the attic.

HEDVIG   But father, you promised that tomorrow we're having a celebration—

HJALMAR   H'm. That's right. Day after tomorrow then. That damn wild duck. I'd like to wring its neck!

HEDVIG   [*with a cry*]   The wild duck!

GINA   Now I've heard everything!

HEDVIG   [*shaking him*]   But father—it's *my* wild duck!

HJALMAR   That's why I won't do it. I don't have the heart—for your sake, Hedvig. But deep down I feel I ought to do it. I shouldn't harbor under my roof a creature that has been in those hands.

GINA   For heaven's sake! Even if Grandpa *did* get it from that awful Pettersen.

HJALMAR   [*walking up and down*]   There are certain demands—what shall I call them? Let me say ideal demands—certain claims, that a man disregards only at the peril of his soul.

HEDVIG   [*following after him*]   But think—the wild duck! That poor wild duck!

HJALMAR   [*halts*]   Didn't I tell you I'll spare it—for your sake? Not a hair on its head will be—h'm. Well, as I said, I'll spare it. After all, there are bigger tasks awaiting me. But you ought to go out for a little walk, Hedvig. The twilight is just right for you.

HEDVIG   I don't care to go out now.

HJALMAR   Yes, do. Seems to me you are squinting. The fumes in here aren't good for you. The air is close under this roof.

HEDVIG   All right. I'll run down the kitchen stairs and walk around a bit. My hat and coat? Oh yes, in my room. Father, please—don't do anything bad to the wild duck while I'm gone!

HJALMAR   Not a feather shall be plucked from its head. [*Clutches her to him.*] You and I, Hedvig—we two! Be on your way now.

[HEDVIG *nods goodbye to her parents and goes out through the kitchen door.*]

HJALMAR   [*pacing back and forth*]   Gina.

GINA   Yes?

HJALMAR   Starting tomorrow—or let's say the day after tomorrow—I'd like to keep account of the housekeeping expenses myself.

GINA   So you want to keep the accounts too, now?

HJALMAR   Keep track of what we take in, at any rate.

GINA   Lord knows, that's easily done!

HJALMAR   One wouldn't think so. It seems to me you make the money go incredibly far. [*Stops and looks at her.*] How do you do it?

GINA   It's because Hedvig and I need so little.

HJALMAR   Is it true that father is overpaid for the copying work he does for Werle?

GINA   I couldn't say about that. I don't know the rates.

HJALMAR   Well, what *does* he get? In round figures.—I want to know.

GINA   It differs. I guess it comes to about what he costs us, plus a little extra in spending money.

HJALMAR   What he costs us! And you haven't told me that!

GINA   No, I couldn't, for you were so happy because he got everything from you.

HJALMAR   And it has really been Werle all the time!

GINA   Oh well. He can afford it.

HJALMAR   Light the lamp!

GINA   [*lighting the lamp*]   And as far as that is concerned, how do we know it is Werle himself? It may be Gråberg—

HJALMAR   Really, Gina. You know that isn't so. Why do you say a thing like that?

GINA   I don't know. I just thought—

HJALMAR   H'm!

GINA   It wasn't me who got Grandpa all that copying to do. It was Bertha, when she took service there.

HJALMAR   It sounds to me like your voice is trembling.

GINA   [*putting the shade on the lamp*]   Does it?

HJALMAR   And your hands are shaking. Aren't they?

GINA   [*firmly*]   You might as well tell me straight, Ekdal. What has he been saying about me?

HJALMAR   Is it true—*can* it be true—that there was some kind of affair between you and Werle while you were in his house?

GINA   That's not so. Not then. He was after me, though. And Mrs. Werle thought there was something going on, and she made a fuss and a big hullaballoo about it, and she beat me and pulled me around—and so I quit.

HJALMAR   But afterwards—!

GINA   Well, then I went to live with mother. And you see—mother—she wasn't all the woman you thought she was, Ekdal. She talked to me about this, that, and the other. For Werle was a widower by that time—

HJALMAR   And then—?

GINA   You might as well know it, I guess. He didn't give up till he had his way.

HJALMAR   [*striking his hands together*]   And this is the mother of my child! How could you keep a thing like this from me?

GINA   Yes, I know it was wrong. I should have told you long ago, I suppose.

HJALMAR   You should have told me right away; that's what you should have. Then I would have known what sort of woman you were.

GINA   But would you have married me, irregardless?

HJALMAR   Of course, I wouldn't!

GINA   I didn't think so, and that's why I didn't dare to tell you. I had come to care for you, you know—a whole lot I cared for you. And I just couldn't see making myself as unhappy as all that—

HJALMAR   [*walking about*]   And this is my Hedvig's mother! And to know that everything I lay my eyes on here [*Kicks a chair.*]—my whole home—I owe to a favored predecessor! Oh, that seducer, that damn Werle!

GINA   Do you regret the fourteen-fifteen years we've had together?

HJALMAR   [*fronting her*]   Tell me if you haven't felt every day and every hour to be one long agony of repentance for that web of deceitful silence you

have woven around me, like a spider? Answer me! Haven't you lived here
in perpetual torture of guilt and remorse?

GINA   Bless you, Ekdal! I've been plenty busy with the house and the pictures—

HJALMAR   So you never cast a probing glance at your past?

GINA   No, to tell the truth, I had almost forgotten all those old stories.

HJALMAR   Oh, this dull, apathetic calm! There is something shocking about it.
Not even repentant—!

GINA   Just tell me this, Ekdal. What do you think would have become of you if
you hadn't got yourself a wife like me?

HJALMAR   Like you—!

GINA   Yes, for you know I have always been more practical and able to cope with
things than you. Of course, I am a couple of years older—

HJALMAR   What would have become of me!

GINA   For you've got to admit you weren't living exactly right when you first
met me.

HJALMAR   So you call that living wrong! Oh, what do you know about a man's
feelings when he sorrows and despairs—especially a man of my fiery temperament.

GINA   No, I guess I don't know. And I don't mean to execrete you for it, either,
for you turned into as decent a man as they come as soon as you got a house
and a family of your own to take care of. And now we were getting on so
nicely here, and Hedvig and I were just thinking that pretty soon we might
spend some money on clothes for ourselves.

HJALMAR   Yes, in the swamp of deceit!

GINA   That that fellow ever poked his nose inside here!

HJALMAR   I, too, thought our home a pleasant one. That was a mistake. Where
now do I gather the necessary inner resilience to bring my invention into
the world of reality? Perhaps it will die with me. If it does, it will be your
past, Gina, that has killed it.

GINA   [*on the verge of tears*]   Please, Ekdal—don't be saying such things! I that
have all my days only tried to make things nice and pleasant for you!

HJALMAR   I ask—what happens now to the breadwinner's dream? As I reclined
in there on the sofa, pondering the invention, it came to me that it was
going to drain me of my last drop of vitality. I knew that the day the patent
was issued and in my hands—that day would be my—my day of farewell.
And then it was my dream that you were to live on as the late inventor's
well-to-do widow.

GINA   [*wiping her tears*]   I won't have you talk that way, Ekdal. May the good
Lord never let me live the day when I'm your widow!

HJALMAR   Oh what difference does it all make! It is all over now, anyway. Everything!

[GREGERS *cautiously opens the entrance door and peers in.*]

GREGERS   May I come in?

HJALMAR   Yes, do.

GREGERS   [*goes up to them with a beaming, happy face, reaches out his hands to
them*]   Now, then—you dear people—! [*Looks from one to the other, whispers to* HJALMAR] It hasn't happened yet?

HJALMAR   [*loud*]   It has happened.

GREGERS   It has?

HJALMAR   I have lived through the bitterest moment of my life.

GREGERS   But also, I trust, its most exalted one.

HJALMAR   Anyway, it's done and over with.

GINA   May God forgive you, Mr. Werle.

GREGERS   [*greatly bewildered*]   But I don't understand—!

HJALMAR   What don't you understand?

GREGERS   As crucial a conversation as this—a conversation that is to be the foundation for a whole new way of life—a life, a partnership, in truth and frankness—

HJALMAR   I know. I know it very well.

GREGERS   I was so sure that when I came in here now I would be met with a splendor of revelation shining from both husband and wife. But all I see is this dull, heavy gloom—

GINA   So that's it. [*Removes the lamp shade.*]

GREGERS   You refuse to understand me, Mrs. Ekdal. Well, I suppose you need time. But you, Hjalmar? Surely, you must have felt a higher consecration in this great crisis.

HJALMAR   Of course I did. That is, in a way.

GREGERS   For surely nothing in the world can be compared to finding forgiveness in one's heart for her who has erred and lovingly lifting her up to one's own heights.

HJALMAR   Do you think a man so easily forgets the draught of wormwood I just drained?

GREGERS   An ordinary man, maybe not. But a man like you—!

HJALMAR   Oh, I know. But you must not rush me, Gregers. It takes time.

GREGERS   There is much of the wild duck in you, Hjalmar.

[RELLING *has entered.*]

RELLING   Ah! Here we go with the wild duck again!

HJALMAR   Mr. Werle's crippled prey—yes.

RELLING   Werle? Is it him you're talking about?

HJALMAR   About him—and about ourselves.

RELLING   [*in a low voice, to* GREGERS]   Damn you to hell!

HJALMAR   What are you saying?

RELLING   I am just expressing an ardent wish that this quack here would betake himself home. If he stays around he is likely to ruin both of you.

GREGERS   Those two cannot be ruined, Mr. Relling. Of Hjalmar I need say nothing. Him we know. But she, too, has surely in the depths of her being something reliable, something of integrity—

GINA   [*almost crying*]   Why didn't you leave me alone then?

RELLING   [*to* GREGERS]   Is it impertinent to ask exactly what you want in this house?

GREGERS   I want to lay the foundation for a true marriage.

RELLING   So you don't think the Ekdal's marriage is good enough as it is?

GREGERS   I daresay it is as good a marriage as most, unfortunately. But a true marriage it has yet to become.

HJALMAR   You have never had an eye for the claim of the ideal, Relling!

RELLING   Nonsense, boy!—Begging your pardon, Mr. Werle—how many— roughly—how many true marriages have you observed in your life?

GREGERS   Hardly a single one.

RELLING   Nor have I.

GREGERS   But I have seen a number of the other kind. And I have had occasion to witness what havoc a marriage like that can work in a pair of human beings.

HJALMAR   A man's whole moral foundation may crumble under his feet; that's the terrible thing.

RELLING   Well, I can't say I've ever been exactly married, so I can't judge about that. But I do know this, that the child belongs to marriage too. And you had better leave the child alone.

HJALMAR   Oh, Hedvig! My poor Hedvig!

RELLING Yes—keep Hedvig out of it, you two! You are grown-ups. In God's name, dò whatever fool things you like to your marriage. But I am warning you: be careful what you do to Hedvig. If you're not, there is no telling what may happen to her.

HJALMAR Happen to her!

RELLING Yes, she may bring a disaster upon herself—and perhaps on others, too.

GINA But how can you tell about that, Relling?

HJALMAR Are you saying there is some immediate danger to her eyes?

RELLING This has nothing whatever to do with her eyes. Hedvig is in a difficult age. She may do all sorts of crazy things.

GINA I know—she does already. She's taken to fooling around with the wood-stove in the kitchen. Playing fire, she calls it. Sometimes I'm scared she'll burn the whole house down.

RELLING There you are. I knew it.

GREGERS [*to* RELLING] But how do you explain a thing like that?

RELLING [*sullenly*] Her voice is changing, sir.

HJALMAR As long as the child has *me*—! As long as *my* head is above the ground! [*There is a knock on the door.*]

GINA Shhh, Ekdal. There are people outside. [MRS. SØRBY *enters, wearing hat and coat.*]

MRS. SØRBY Good evening!

GINA [*going to her*] Goodness! Is it you, Bertha!

MRS. SØRBY So it is. Maybe it's inconvenient—?

HJALMAR Oh by no means! A messenger from *that* house—!

MRS. SØRBY [*to* GINA] Frankly, I had hoped you'd be without your menfolks this time of day. I've just dropped in to have a word with you about something and say goodbye.

GINA You're going away?

MRS. SØRBY Tomorrow morning—to Høydal. Mr. Werle left this afternoon. [*Casually, to* GREGERS.] He asked me to say hello.

GINA Imagine—!

HJALMAR So Mr. Werle has left? And you are going after him?

MRS. SØRBY Yes. What do you say to that, Ekdal?

HJALMAR Look out, is all I say.

GREGERS I can explain. Father and Mrs. Sørby are getting married.

GINA Oh Bertha! At long last!

RELLING [*his voice trembling a little*] Surely, this cannot be true?

MRS. SØRBY Yes, my dear Relling, true it is.

RELLING You want to get married again?

MRS. SØRBY That's what it amounts to. Werle has got the license. We'll have a quiet little party up at the works.

GREGERS I suppose I should tender my felicitations like a good stepson.

MRS. SØRBY Thank you, if you really mean it. I hope this will be for the best for both Werle and myself.

RELLING I am sure you have every reason to think it will. Mr. Werle never gets drunk—at least not to my knowledge. Nor do I believe he is in the habit of beating up his wife, like the late lamented horse doctor.

MRS. SØRBY Let Sørby rest quietly in his grave. He had his good sides, too.

RELLING Mr. Industrialist Werle has better ones, I am sure.

MRS. SØRBY At least he has not thrown away what is best in himself. The man who does that must take the consequences.

RELLING Tonight I'll go out with Molvik.

MRS. SØRBY Don't do that, Relling. Don't—for my sake.

RELLING There's nothing else to do. [*To* HJALMAR.] Want to come along?

GINA   No, thank you. Ekdal doesn't go in for excapades like that.

HJALMAR   [*angrily, in a half whisper*]   For heaven's sake! Keep your mouth shut!

RELLING   Goodbye—Mrs. Werle! [*Goes out.*]

GREGERS   [*to* MRS. SØRBY]   It appears that you and Doctor Relling know each other quite well?

MRS. SØRBY   Yes, we've known each other for a good many years. At one time it looked as if we might have made a match of it.

GREGERS   I'm sure it was lucky for you that you didn't.

MRS. SØRBY   You may well say that. But I've always been wary of acting on impulse. A woman can't just throw herself away, you know.

GREGERS   Aren't you afraid I'll let my father know about this old acquaintance-ship?

MRS. SØRBY   Do you really believe I haven't told him myself?

GREGERS   Oh?

MRS. SØRBY   Your father knows every little thing people might say about me with any show of truth at all. I have told him everything. That was the first thing I did when I realized what his intentions were.

GREGERS   It seems to me you are more than usually frank.

MRS. SØRBY   I have always been frank. For us women that's the best policy.

HJALMAR   What do you say to that, Gina?

GINA   Oh, women differ. Some do it one way, others do it different.

MRS. SØRBY   Well, Gina, in my opinion I have followed the wiser course. And Werle hasn't kept back anything either. You see, that's what mainly brought us together. Now he can sit and talk to me as openly as a child. He has never been able to do that before. A healthy, vigorous man like him—all through his youth and all the best years of his life he had his ears drummed full with angry sermons. And very often sermons about sins he hadn't even committed—according to what I have been told.

GINA   That's the truth.

GREGERS   If you ladies want to pursue that topic any further, I had better absent myself.

MRS. SØRBY   You may just as well stay as far as that's concerned. I won't say another word. I just wanted you to know I haven't kept anything back or played him false in any way. Maybe people will say I am a very fortunate woman, and in a way of course that's true. But I don't think I am getting any more than I am giving. I'll certainly never desert him. And I can be of more service and use to him than anybody else, now that he'll soon be helpless.

HJALMAR   Will he be helpless?

GREGERS   [*to* MRS. SØRBY]   Don't say anything about that here.

MRS. SØRBY   It can't be kept secret any longer, much as he'd like to. He is going blind.

HJALMAR   [*struck*]   Blind? That's strange. He, too?

GINA   Lots of people go blind.

MRS. SØRBY   And I'm sure you can tell yourself what that must mean to a busi-nessman. Well, I'll try to be his eyes, the best I know how.—But I can't stay any longer. I have so much to do right now.—Oh yes, What I wanted to tell you, Ekdal, is that if Werle can be of any service to you, all you need to do is to get in touch with Gråberg.

GREGERS   That is an offer I am sure Hjalmar Ekdal will decline.

MRS. SØRBY   Really? It seems to me he hasn't always been so—

GINA   Yes, Bertha. Ekdal doesn't need to accept anything more from Mr. Werle.

HJALMAR   [*slowly, with weight*]   Tell your husband-to-be from me, that in the very near future I intend to go to Mr. Gråberg—

GREGERS   What! You want to do that!

HJALMAR   —I say, go to Mr. Gråberg, and demand an account of the sum I owe his employer. I desire to pay this debt of honor—ha-ha-ha!—let us call it a debt of honor! Enough! I shall pay it all, with five per cent interest.

GINA   But Ekdal—goodness! We don't have that kind of money!

HJALMAR   Be so good as to inform your fiancé that I am working incessantly on my invention. Please tell him that what sustains my mind during this exhausting enterprise is my ambition to free myself from a painful burden of debt. This is why I am an inventor. The entire proceeds from my invention are to be devoted to liberating myself from the obligation to remunerate your husband-to-be for his expenses on behalf of my family.

MRS. SØRBY   Something has happened here.

HJALMAR   Indeed, something has.

MRS. SØRBY   Well, goodbye. I had something else I wanted to talk to you about, Gina, but that will have to wait till some other time. Goodbye.

[HJALMAR and GREGERS *return her greeting silently.* GINA *sees her to the door.*]

HJALMAR   Not beyond the threshold, Gina!

[MRS. SØRBY *leaves.* GINA *closes the door.*]

HJALMAR   There, now, Gregers. I have that burdensome debt off my chest.

GREGERS   You soon will, at any rate.

HJALMAR   I believe my attitude must be deemed the proper one.

GREGERS   You are the man I have always taken you to be.

HJALMAR   In certain cases it is impossible to disregard the claims of the ideal. As provider for my family, I am bound, of course, to find my course of action difficult and painful. Believe me, it is no joke for a man situated as I am, without means, to assume a debt of many years' standing—a debt, you might say, covered by the sands of oblivion. But never mind. The man in me demands his rights.

GREGERS   [*placing his hand on his shoulder*]   Dear Hjalmar—wasn't it a good thing that I came?

HJALMAR   Yes.

GREGERS   That your whole situation was made clear to you—wasn't that a good thing?

HJALMAR   [*a bit impatiently*]   Of course it was. But there is one thing that shocks my sense of justice.

GREGERS   What is that?

HJALMAR   It is this that—But I don't know that I ought to speak so freely about your father—

GREGERS   Don't let that worry you. Say what you want.

HJALMAR   All right. Well, you see, there is something shocking in the notion that now it's he and not I who realizes the true marriage.

GREGERS   How can you say a thing like that!

HJALMAR   Well, it is. For your father and Mrs. Sørby are about to solemnify a union built on full mutual confidence, on complete, unconditional frankness on both sides. They conceal nothing from each other, there are no deceitful silences, there has been declared, if I may put it so, mutual absolution between them.

GREGERS   Well, what of it?

HJALMAR   Well, then—it's all there! All the difficult conditions you yourself said are prerequisites for the building of a true marriage.

GREGERS   But that's in quite a different way, Hjalmar. Surely, you won't compare either yourself or Gina with those two—? Oh I am sure you know what I mean.

HJALMAR   Yet I can't get away from the thought that in all this there is something that offends my sense of justice. It looks exactly as if there were no just order in the universe.

GINA Ekdal, for God's sake, don't talk like that!

GREGERS H'm. Let's not get involved in those issues.

HJALMAR Though, on the other hand, I do in a way discern fate's ruling finger, too. He is going blind.

GINA We don't know that yet.

HJALMAR There is no doubt about it. At least, we ought not to doubt it, for in that very fact lies the proof of just retribution. He did once hoodwink a trusting fellow being.

GREGERS I am afraid he has hoodwinked many.

HJALMAR And here comes the inexorable, the inscrutable, claiming Werle's own eyes.

GINA How you talk! I think it's scary.

HJALMAR It is salutary at times to contemplate the night side of existence.
[HEDVIG, *dressed for the outside, enters. She is happy, breathless.*]

GINA Back so soon?

HEDVIG Yes. I didn't feel like walking any farther. It was a good thing, too, for I met somebody as I was coming in.

HJALMAR Mrs. Sørby, I suppose.

HEDVIG Yes.

HJALMAR [*pacing the floor*] I hope you have seen her for the last time.
[*Silence.* HEDVIG, *troubled, looks from one to the other in order to gauge their mood.*]

HEDVIG [*approaching* HJALMAR, *ingratiatingly*] Father?

HJALMAR All right—what is it, Hedvig?

HEDVIG Mrs. Sørby had something for me.

HJALMAR [*halts*] For you?

HEDVIG Yes. Something for tomorrow.

GINA Bertha always brings you a little something for your birthday.

HJALMAR What is it?

HEDVIG No, you're not to find out now. Mother is to give it to me in the morning, when she brings me breakfast in bed.

HJALMAR What is all this mystification that I am to be kept in the dark about!

HEDVIG [*quickly*] I'll be glad to let you see it, father. It's a big letter. [*Takes the letter out of her coat pocket.*]

HJALMAR A letter too?

HEDVIG The letter is all there is. I suppose the other thing will come later. Just think—a letter! I never got a letter before. And it says "Miss" on the outside of it. [*Reads.*] "Miss Hedvig Ekdal." Just think—that's me!

HJALMAR Let me see that letter.

HEDVIG Here you are. [*Hands it to him.*]

HJALMAR It's Werle's handwriting.

GINA Are you sure, Ekdal?

HJALMAR See for yourself.

GINA How would I know?

HJALMAR Hedvig? May I open the letter? Read it?

HEDVIG If you like.

GINA Not tonight, Ekdal. It's supposed to be for tomorrow.

HEDVIG [*in a low voice*] Please let him read it! It's bound to be something nice, and then father will be in a good mood, and everything will be pleasant again.

HJALMAR You say I may open it?

HEDVIG Yes, please, father. I'd like to know what it is about, too.

HJALMAR   Good. [*Opens the envelope, reads the letter inside. Appears confused.*]
    What *is* this—?
GINA   What does it say?
HEDVIG   Please, father—tell us!
HJALMAR   Be quiet. [*Reads the letter again. He is pale, but his voice is controlled.*] It is a gift letter, Hedvig.
HEDVIG   Imagine! What is it I get?
HJALMAR   Read for yourself.
    [HEDVIG *goes over to the lamp and reads.*]
HJALMAR   [*in a low voice, clenches his fists*]   The eyes, the eyes! And now that
    letter!
HEDVIG   [*interrupting his reading*]   Seems to me like it's Grandpa who gets it.
HJALMAR   [*taking the letter away from her*]   You, Gina—can you make any
    sense out of this?
GINA   I don't know a blessed thing about it. Why don't you just tell me?
HJALMAR   Werle writes to Hedvig that her old grandfather no longer needs to
    trouble himself with the copying work he has been doing, but that he may
    go to the office every month and draw one hundred crowns—
GREGERS   Aha!
HEDVIG   One hundred crowns, mother! I read that.
GINA   That will be nice for Grandpa.
HJALMAR   —one hundred crowns for as long as he needs it. That means, of
    course, till he closes his eyes.
GINA   So *he* is all taken care of, poor soul.
HJALMAR   Then it comes. You can't have read that far, Hedvig. After his death,
    that money will be yours.
HEDVIG   Mine? All of it?
HJALMAR   He writes that the same amount has been set aside for you for the
    rest of your life. Are you listening, Gina?
GINA   Yes, I hear.
HEDVIG   Just think—all the money I'll be getting! [*Shaking* HJALMAR'S *arm.*]
    Father! Father! But aren't you glad?
HJALMAR   [*going away from her*]   Glad! [*Walking about.*] Oh what vistas, what
    perspectives, open up before me! It is Hedvig he is so generous to!
GINA   Well, she's the one with the birthday.
HEDVIG   And of course you will get it anyway, father! Don't you know I'll give
    it all to you and mother?
HJALMAR   To mother, yes! That's just it!
GREGERS   Hjalmar, this is a trap being prepared for you.
HJALMAR   You think this may be another trap?
GREGERS   When he was here this morning, he said, "Hjalmar Ekdal is not the
    man you think he is."
HJALMAR   Not the man—!
GREGERS   "You just wait and see," he said.
HJALMAR   You were to see me selling myself for money—!
HEDVIG   Mother, what *is* all this?
GINA   Go out and take your wraps off.
    [HEDVIG, *about to cry, goes out into the kitchen.*]
GREGERS   Well, Hjalmar—now we shall see who is right—he or I.
HJALMAR   [*slowly tearing the letter in two, putting the pieces down on the
    table*]   Here is my answer.
GREGERS   Just as I thought.
HJALMAR   [*to* GINA, *who is standing near the stove; in a low voice*]   No more
    concealment now. If everything was over between you and him when you—

came to care for me, as you call it, then why did he make it possible for us to get married?

GINA   I guess he thought he'd make free of the house.

HJALMAR   Just that? He wasn't worried about a certain possibility?

GINA   I don't know what you're talking about.

HJALMAR   I want to know—if your child has the right to live under my roof.

GINA   [*drawing herself up, her eyes flashing*]   You ask me that!

HJALMAR   Just tell me one thing. Is Hedvig mine or—?—Well?

GINA   [*looks at him with cold defiance*]   I don't know.

HJALMAR   [*with a slight tremble*]   You don't know!

GINA   How can I? A woman like me!

HJALMAR   [*quietly, turning away from her*]   In that case I have nothing more to do in this house.

GREGERS   Think it over, Hjalmar!

HJALMAR   [*putting his overcoat on*]   For a man like me there is nothing to think over.

GREGERS   Yes, there is ever so much to think over. You three must stay together if you are to attain to the sacrificial spirit of sublime forgivingness.

HJALMAR   I don't want to attain it! Never! Never! My hat! [*Takes his hat.*] My house is in ruins about me. [*Bursts out crying.*] Gregers! I have no child!

HEDVIG   [*who has opened the kitchen door*]   Father! What are you saying!

GINA   Oh dear!

HJALMAR   Don't come near me, Hedvig! Go far away from me. I can't stand looking at you. Oh those eyes—! Goodbye. [*Is about to go out.*]

HEDVIG   [*clings to him, cries*]   No! No! Don't leave me!

GINA   Look at the child, Ekdal! Look at the child!

HJALMAR   I will not! I cannot! I must get out—away from all this!
[*He tears himself loose from* HEDVIG *and exits.*]

HEDVIG   [*her eyes desperate*]   He's leaving us, mother! He's leaving us! He'll never come back!

GINA   Just don't cry, Hedvig. Father will be back. You wait.

HEDVIG   [*throws herself sobbing down on the sofa*]   No! No! He'll never come back to us any more!   ·

GREGERS   Do you believe I meant all for the best, Mrs. Ekdal?

GINA   Yes, I suppose you did, but God forgive you all the same.

HEDVIG   [*on the sofa*]   I want to die! What have I done to him, mother? You just have to get him back again!

GINA   Yes, yes, yes; only be quiet. I'll go out and look for him. [*Putting on her coat.*] Perhaps he's gone down to Relling's. But you're not to lie there, bawling like that. Promise?

HEDVIG   [*sobbing convulsively*]   All right, I'll stop, if only father comes home again.

GREGERS   [*to* GINA, *who is leaving*]   But would it not be better to let him fight his agony through by himself?

GINA   He can do that afterwards. First we've got to get the child quieted down. [*Goes out.*]

HEDVIG   [*sitting up, drying her eyes*]   Now you have to tell me what this is all about. Why doesn't father want me any more?

GREGERS   You must not ask that till you're big and grown-up.

HEDVIG   [*sobbing*]   But I just can't stay as miserable as this all the time till I'm grown up.—But I know what it is. Maybe I'm not really father's child.

GREGERS   [*uneasily*]   How could that be?

HEDVIG   Mother might have found me. And now perhaps father has found out about it. I have read about things like that.

GREGERS   Well, if it really were so—

HEDVIG   I think he could love me just as much, regardless. More, almost. The wild duck is a gift, too, and I love her very, very much.

GREGERS   [glad to turn the conversation]   Oh yes, the wild duck. Let's talk about the wild duck, Hedvig.

HEDVIG   That poor wild duck. He can't stand the sight of her, either. Just think, he wants to wring her neck!

GREGERS   Oh, I don't think he'll do that.

HEDVIG   No, but he said it. And I think that was horrid of father, for I pray for the wild duck every night, that she may be kept safe from death and all that's evil.

GREGERS   [looks at her]   Do you usually say prayers at night?

HEDVIG   Yes, I do.

GREGERS   Who taught you that?

HEDVIG   Myself, for father was terribly sick once and had leeches on his neck, and then he said that death was his dread companion.

GREGERS   And—?

HEDVIG   So I prayed for him when I went to bed. And I have done so ever since.

GREGERS   And now you pray for the wild duck, too?

HEDVIG   I thought it was best to mention her as well, for she was so sickly when we first got her.

GREGERS   Do you say morning prayers, too?

HEDVIG   Of course not.

GREGERS   Why is that so of course?

HEDVIG   Because it's light in the morning. There's not so much to be afraid of then.

GREGERS   And the wild duck you love so much—your father said he'd like to wring her neck?

HEDVIG   No, he said it would be better for him if he did, but he was going to spare her for my sake. And that was good of him.

GREGERS   [closer to her]   How would it be if you decided to sacrifice the wild duck for his sake?

HEDVIG   [getting up]   The wild duck!

GREGERS   What if you willingly gave up the dearest thing in the whole world for him?

HEDVIG   Do you think that would help?

GREGERS   Try it, Hedvig.

HEDVIG   [softly, with shining eyes]   Yes. I want to.

GREGERS   Do you think you have the right kind of strength for doing it?

HEDVIG   I shall ask Grandpa to shoot the wild duck for me.

GREGERS   Yes, do that. But not a word to your mother about this!

HEDVIG   Why not?

GREGERS   She doesn't understand us.

HEDVIG   The wild duck? I'll try it in the morning!

[GINA enters from the hall.]

HEDVIG   [towards her]   Did you find him, mother?

GINA   No, but I found out he's got Relling with him.

GREGERS   Are you sure?

GINA   Yes, the janitor's wife said so. Molvik's with them also.

GREGERS   Just now, when his soul so sorely needs to struggle in solitude—!

GINA   [taking off her coat]   Yes, men are funny. God knows where Relling is taking him! I ran over to Madam Eriksen's, but they aren't there.

HEDVIG   [struggling with her tears]   What if he never comes back!

GREGERS He'll come back. I'll get word to him tomorrow, and then you'll see *how* he comes back. You count on that, Hedvig, and get a good night's sleep. Goodnight. [*Goes out.*]

HEDVIG [*throws herself sobbing on* GINA's *neck*] Mother! Mother!

GINA [*patting her back, sighing*] Yes, Relling was right. This is what happens when crazy people come around pestering us with the claim of the ordeal.

ACT V

> The studio. Cold, gray morning light. There is wet snow on the big panes of the skylight.
> GINA, aproned, with broom and dust cloth in her hand, enters from the kitchen and goes towards the living room door. HEDVIG hurries in from the outside at the same moment.

GINA [*stops*] Well?

HEDVIG Yes, mother, I almost think he's down at Relling's—

GINA What did I tell you!

HEDVIG —for the janitor's wife said she heard Relling bring two others home with him last night.

GINA I knew it.

HEDVIG But what good does it do, if he doesn't come up here to us?

GINA I want to go down and have a talk with him, anyway.
[OLD EKDAL, *in dressing gown and slippers and with his lighted pipe, appears in the door to his room.*]

EKDAL Eh—Hjalmar—? Isn't Hjalmar here?

GINA No, he is out, Grandpa.

EKDAL So early? In this blizzard? Well, I can walk by myself in the morning, I can, if it comes to that.
[*He slides the attic door open.* HEDVIG *helps him. He enters. She closes the door behind him.*]

HEDVIG [*in a low voice*] Mother, what do you think will happen when poor Grandpa hears that father has left us?

GINA Silly! Grandpa mustn't hear anything about it, of course. It was a good thing he wasn't home last night, during all that hullaballoo.

HEDVIG Yes, but—
[GREGERS *enters.*]

GREGERS Well? Have you traced him yet?

GINA They say he's down at Relling's.

GREGERS At Relling's! Has he really been out with those two?

GINA It looks like it.

GREGERS But he is so badly in need of solitude—to find himself in earnest—

GINA Yes. I should think so, too.
[RELLING *enters.*]

HEDVIG [*goes towards him*] Is father with you?

GINA [*at the same time*] Is he down there?

RELLING He certainly is.

HEDVIG And you haven't told us!

RELLING I know. I am a big, bad beast. But I had this other big, bad beast to take care of, too—I mean the demonic one. And after that, I just fell asleep —sound asleep—

GINA   What does Ekdal say today?

RELLING   Not a thing.

HEDVIG   Doesn't he say anything at all?

RELLING   Not a blessed word.

GREGERS   I think I understand that.

GINA   But what is he doing?

RELLING   He is on the sofa, snoring.

GINA   Oh. Yes, Ekdal does snore a lot.

HEDVIG   He's asleep? Can he sleep now?

RELLING   It certainly looks that way.

GREGERS   That's reasonable enough, after the spiritual turmoil he's just been through—

GINA   And he isn't used to be out revelling nights, either.

HEDVIG   It may be a good thing that he is sleeping, mother.

GINA   That's what I am thinking. Anyway, we'd better not wake him up too soon. Thank you, Relling. First of all I've got to clean things up a bit and make the place look nice. Come and help me, Hedvig. [*They go into the living room.*]

GREGERS   [*turning to* RELLING]   Can you account for the present spiritual unrest in Hjalmar Ekdal?

RELLING   To tell you the truth, I haven't noticed any spiritual unrest in him.

GREGERS   What? At such a turning point—When his whole life is acquiring a new basis? How can you think that a personality like Hjalmar Ekdal—?

RELLING   Personality? He? If he ever had any tendency to sprout the kind of abnormal growth you call personality, I can assure you that all roots and tendrils were thoroughly extirpated in his boyhood.

GREGERS   That would indeed be strange, considering the loving upbringing he enjoyed.

RELLING   By those two crackpot, hysterical spinster aunts of his, you mean?

GREGERS   Let me tell you that they were women who never forgot the claim of the ideal—though I suppose you'll just be making fun of me again.

RELLING   No, I'm not in the mood. I do know about them, though. He has often enough held forth about "his soul's two mothers." Personally, I don't think he has much to be grateful to them for. Ekdal's misfortune is that he has always been looked upon as a shining light in his own circle.

GREGERS   And you don't think he is that? I mean, when it comes to depth of soul?

RELLING   I have never noticed it. That his father thought so is one thing. The old lieutenant has been an idiot all his days.

GREGERS   He has all his days been a man with a childlike mind. That is what you don't understand.

RELLING   All right. But after dear, sweet Hjalmar had taken up studying— after a fashion—right away he was the light of the future among his friends, too. He was handsome enough, the rascal—red and white, just the way little shop-girls like the fellows. And he had this sentimental temperament and this warm-hearted voice, and he could give such pretty declamations of other people's poetry and other people's thoughts—

GREGERS   [*indignantly*]   Is this Hjalmar Ekdal you are describing?

RELLING   Yes, if you please. For this is what he looks like on the inside, the idol you are prostrating yourself for.

GREGERS   I didn't know I was as blind as all that.

RELLING   Well—not far from it. For you are sick, too, you see.

GREGERS   That is true.

RELLING   Yes it is. And yours is a complicated case. First, there is this pesky integrity fever you're suffering from, and then something worse—you are forever walking around in a delirium of adoration, always looking for something to admire outside of yourself.

GREGERS   Yes, there certainly wouldn't be much point in looking for it within myself.

RELLING   But you are always so hideously wrong about all those big, wonderful flies you see and hear buzzing around you. Once again you have entered a cottage with your claim of the ideal. People here just can't pay.

GREGERS   If this is the way you think of Hjalmar Ekdal, what sort of pleasure can you derive from your constant association with him?

RELLING   Oh well. I am supposed to be a kind of doctor, believe it or not, so the least I can do is to look after the poor patients I share quarters with.

GREGERS   Ah, I see. Hjalmar Ekdal is sick, too?

RELLING   Most people are, worse luck.

GREGERS   And what treatment do you apply in Hjalmar's case?

RELLING   My usual one. I see to it that his vital lie is kept up.

GREGERS   Vital—lie? I am not sure I heard what you said.

RELLING   That's right. I said the vital lie. You see, that's the stimulating principle.

GREGERS   May I ask with what vital lie you have infected Hjalmar?

RELLING   You may not. I never reveal professional secrets to quacks. You are capable of messing him up for me even more than you have. But the method is proven. I have used it with Molvik, too. I have made him demonic. That's the suppurative I have applied to *his* neck.

GREGERS   But *isn't* he demonic?

RELLING   What the hell does it mean—being demonic? It's just some nonsense I thought of to save his life. If I hadn't, the poor, pitiful swine would have succumbed to self-hatred and despair many a year ago. Not to mention the old lieutenant! Though he has found his own cure.

GREGERS   Lieutenant Ekdal? What about him?

RELLING   What do you think? There he is, the old slayer of bears, chasing rabbits in a dark attic. And yet, there isn't a happier hunter alive than that old man when he is playing with all that junk. The four or five dried-out Christmas trees he has saved are the whole big, wild Høydal forest to him. The rooster and the chickens are wild fowl in the tree tops, and the rabbits bouncing about on the floor are bears he's grappling with —the frisky old sportsman.

GREGERS   Ah, yes—that unfortunate old Lieutenant Ekdal. He has certainly had to compromise the ideals of his youth.

RELLING   While I think of it, Mr. Werle—don't use the foreign word "ideals." We have available a good native one: "lies."

GREGERS   You think the two things are related

RELLING   About as closely as typhus and putrid fever.

GREGERS   Doctor Relling! I won't give up till I have rescued Hjalmar from your clutches!

RELLING   That might be his bad luck. Take his vital lie away from the average person, and you take his happiness, too. [*To* HEDVIG, *who enters from the living room.*] Well, now, little duck mother. I am going down to see if papa is still in bed pondering that wonderful invention of his. [*Goes out.*]

GREGERS   [*approaching* HEDVIG]   I can tell from looking at you that it has not yet been accomplished.

HEDVIG   What? Oh, that about the wild duck? No.

GREGERS   Your strength of purpose deserted you, I suppose, when the time for action had come.

HEDVIG   No, it wasn't that. But when I woke up this morning and remembered what we had talked about, it all seemed so strange.

GREGERS   Strange?

HEDVIG   Yes, I don't know—Last night, just at the time—I thought there was something very wonderful about it, but when I had slept and I thought about it again, it didn't seem like anything much.

GREGERS   I see. I could hardly expect you to grow up in this environment without injury to your soul.

HEDVIG   I don't care about that, if only father would come home again.

GREGERS   If only your eyes were opened to what gives life its worth—if only you possessed the true, joyful, brave, sacrificial spirit, then you'd see he'll return. But I still have faith in you, Hedvig. [*Goes out.*]
[HEDVIG *walks around aimlessly. She is about to enter the kitchen, when there is a knock on the inside of the door to the attic.* HEDVIG *opens the doors wide enough for old* EKDAL *to come out. She shuts them again.*]

EKDAL   H'm. Not much fun taking a walk by yourself, y'know.

HEDVIG   Wouldn't you like to go hunting, Grandpa?

EKDAL   It isn't hunting weather today. Too dark. Can hardly see a thing.

HEDVIG   Don't you ever want to shoot something beside rabbits?

EKDAL   Aren't the rabbits good enough, perhaps?

HEDVIG   Yes, but what about the wild duck?

EKDAL   Haw! So you're scared I'll shoot your wild duck? I'll never do that, Hedvig. Never.

HEDVIG   No, for I bet you don't know how. I've heard it's difficult to shoot wild ducks.

EKDAL   Don't know how! Should say I do!

HEDVIG   How would you do it, Grandpa?—I don't mean *my* wild duck, but another one.

EKDAL   Would try to get a shot in just below the breast; that's the best place. And try to shoot *against* the feathers, not *with*.

HEDVIG   Then they die?

EKDAL   Damn right they do—if you shoot right.—Well, better go in and dress up. H'm. Y'know. H'm—[*Goes into his own room.*]
[HEDVIG *waits a moment, glances towards the living room door, stands on tiptoe, takes the double-barreled pistol down from the shelf, looks at it.* GINA, *with broom and dust cloth, enters from the living room.* HEDVIG *quickly puts the pistol back, without* GINA'S *noticing.*]

GINA   Don't fool with father's things, Hedvig.

HEDVIG   [*leaving the shelf*]   I just wanted to straighten up some.

GINA   Why don't you go into the kitchen and see if the coffee is keeping hot? I am taking a tray with me when I go down.
[HEDVIG *goes into the kitchen.* GINA *starts putting the studio in order. After a short while, the door to the ouside is hesitantly opened and* HJALMAR *looks in. He is wearing a coat but no hat. He looks unkempt and unwashed. His eyes are dull and lusterless.*]

GINA   [*stands staring at him, still with the broom in her hand*]   Bless you, Ekdal—so you did come back, after all!

HJALMAR   [*enters, answers in a dull voice*]   I return—only to leave.

GINA   Yes, yes, I suppose. But good Lord! how you look!

HJALMAR   Look?

GINA   And your nice winter coat? I'd say that's done for.

HEDVIG   [*in the kitchen door*]   Mother, don't you want me to—[*sees* HJALMAR, *gives a shout of joy and runs towards him.*] Father! Father!

HJALMAR   [*turning away, with a gesture*]   Go away! Go away! [*To* GINA.]

Get her away from me, I say!

GINA   [*in a low voice*]   Go into the living room, Hedvig.

[HEDVIG *leaves silently.*]

HJALMAR   [*busy, pulling out the table drawer*]   I need my books with me. Where are my books?

GINA   Which books?

HJALMAR   My scientific works, of course—the technical journals I need for my invention.

GINA   [*looking on the shelf*]   Do you mean these over here, with no covers on them?

HJALMAR   Yes, yes, of course.

GINA   [*puts a pile of journals down on the table*]   Don't you want me to get Hedvig to cut them open for you?

HJALMAR   No. Nobody needs to cut any pages for me.

[*Brief silence.*]

GINA   So you are going to leave us, Ekdal?

HJALMAR   [*rummaging among the books*]   That goes without saying, I should think.

GINA   All right.

HJALMAR   [*violently*]   For you can hardly expect me to want to stay where my heart is pierced every single hour of the day!

GINA   God forgive you for thinking so bad of me!

HJALMAR   Proof—!

GINA   Seems to me, you're the one who should bring proof.

HJALMAR   After a past like yours? There are certain claims—I might call them the claims of the ideal—

GINA   What about Grandpa? What is *he* going to do, poor man?

HJALMAR   I know my duty. The helpless one goes with me. I'll go out and make arrangements—H'm [*Hesitantly.*] Has anybody found my hat on the stairs?

GINA   No. Have you lost your hat?

HJALMAR   I most certainly had it on when I came home last night; there isn't the slightest doubt about that. But now I can't find it.

GINA   Good Lord! Where did you go with those two drunks?

HJALMAR   Oh, don't ask about inessentials. Do you think I'm in a mood for remembering details?

GINA   I only hope you haven't got a cold, Ekdal [*Goes into the kitchen.*]

HJALMAR   [*speaking to himself, in a low voice, angrily, as he empties the drawer*]   You're a scoundrel, Relling!—A villain is what you are!— Miserable traitor!—I'd gladly see you assassinated—!

[*He puts aside some old letters, discovers the torn gift letter from the day before, picks it up and looks at the two pieces, puts them down quickly as* GINA *enters.*]

GINA   [*putting a tray with food down on the table*]   Here's a drop of coffee, if you want it. And some salt meat sandwiches.

HJALMAR   [*glancing at the tray*]   Salt meat? Never under this roof! True it is, I haven't taken solid nourishment for almost twenty-four hours, but that can't be helped.—My notes! My incipient memoirs! Where is my diary— all my important papers! [*Opens the door to the living room, but steps back.*] If she isn't there, too!

GINA   Heavens, Ekdal. She's got to be somewhere.

HJALMAR   Leave! [*He makes room.* HEDVIG, *scared, enters the studio. With his hand on the door knob; to* GINA.] During the last moments I spend in my former home I wish to be spared the sight of intruders—[*Enters the living room.*]

HEDVIG [*starts, asks her mother in a low and trembling voice*] Does that mean me?

GINA Stay in the kitchen, Hedvig, or no—go to your own room. [*To* HJALMAR, *as she enters the living room.*] Wait a minute, Ekdal. Don't make such a mess in the dresser. I know where everything is.

HEDVIG [*remains motionless for a moment, in helpless fright, presses her lips together not to cry, clenches her hands, whispers*] The wild duck!
[*She tiptoes over to the shelf and takes the pistol down, opens the doors to the inner attic, goes inside, closes behind her.* HJALMAR *and* GINA *are heard talking in the living room.*]

HJALMAR [*appears with some notebooks and a pile of old papers, which he puts down on the table*] The bag obviously won't be enough. There are thousands of things I need to take with me!

GINA [*entering with the bag*] Can't you leave most of it behind for the time being and just pick up a clean shirt and some underwear?

HJALMAR Phew—! These exhausting preparations—! [*Takes off his overcoat and throws it on the sofa.*]

GINA And there's the coffee getting cold too.

HJALMAR H'm. [*Without thinking, he takes a sip, and then another one.*]

GINA [*dusting off the back of chairs*] How are you ever going to find a large enough attic for the rabbits?

HJALMAR You mean I have to drag all those rabbits along, too?

GINA Grandpa can't do without his rabbits—you know that as well as I do.

HJALMAR He'll have to get used to that. I shall have to give up higher values in life than a bunch of rabbits.

GINA [*dusting off the shelf*] Shall I put the flute in for you?

HJALMAR No. No flute for me. But give me my pistol.

GINA You want that old pestol?

HJALMAR Yes. My loaded pistol.

GINA [*looking for it*] It's gone. He must have taken it inside with him.

HJALMAR Is he in the attic?

GINA Sure, he's in the attic.

HJALMAR H'm. The lonely grayhead—[*He eats a sandwich, empties his cup of coffee.*]

GINA If only we hadn't rented that room, you could have moved in there.

HJALMAR And stay under the same roof as—! Never! Never again!

GINA But couldn't you stay in the living room for a day or two? There you'd have everything to yourself.

HJALMAR Not within these walls!

GINA How about down at Relling's and Molvik's, then?

HJALMAR Don't mention their names to me! I get sick just thinking about them. Oh no—it's out into the wind and the snowdrifts for me—to walk from house to house seeking shelter for father and myself.

GINA But you have no hat, Ekdal! You've lost your hat, remember?

HJALMAR Oh, those two abominations! Rich in nothing but every vice! A hat must be procured. [*Takes another sandwich.*] Arrangements must be made. After all, I don't intend to catch my death. [*Looks for something on the tray.*]

GINA What are you looking for?

HJALMAR Butter.

GINA Just a moment. [*Goes out into the kitchen.*]

HJALMAR [*shouting after her*] Oh never mind. Dry bread is good enough for me.

GINA [*bringing a plate with butter*] Here. This is supposed to be freshly churned.

[*She pours him another cup of coffee. He sits down on the sofa, puts more butter on his bread, eats and drinks in silence.*]

HJALMAR   [*after a pause*]   Could I, without being disturbed by anyone—and I mean *anyone*—stay in the living room for a day or two?

GINA   You certainly can, if you want to.

HJALMAR   You see, I don't know how to get all of father's things moved out on such short notice.

GINA   And there is this, too, that first you'd have to tell him that you don't want to live together with the rest of us any more.

HJALMAR   [*pushing his cup away*]   Yes, yes—that, too. I shall have to go into all those intricate relationships once again, to explain—I must think, I must have air to breathe, I can't bear all the burdens in one single day.

GINA   Of course not. And in such awful weather too—

HJALMAR   [*moving* WERLE's *letter*]   I notice this piece of paper still lying around.

GINA   Well, *I* haven't touched it.

HJALMAR   Not that it concerns *me*—

GINA   I'm sure *I* don't expect to make use of it—

HJALMAR   Nevertheless, I suppose we shouldn't let it get completely lost. In all the fuss of moving, something might easily—

GINA   I'll take care of it, Ekdal.

HJALMAR   For the gift letter belongs to father, first of all. It's his affair whether he wants to make use of it or not.

GINA   [*with a sigh*]   Yes, poor old Grandpa—

HJALMAR   Just to make sure—Is there any glue?

GINA   [*walks over to the shelf*]   Here's a bottle.

HJALMAR   And a brush?

GINA   Here.   [*Brings him both.*]

HJALMAR   [*picks up a pair of scissors*]   Just a strip of paper on the back— [*Cuts and glues.*] Far be it from me to lay hands on somebody else's property—least of all the property of a poverty-stricken old man.—Well—not on—that other one's, either.—There, now! Leave it to dry for a while. And when it's dry, remove it. I don't want to see that document again— ever!

[GREGERS *enters.*]

GREGERS   [*a little surprised*]   What? So this is where you are, Hjalmar!

HJALMAR   [*quickly gets up*]   Sheer exhaustion drove me to sit down.

GREGERS   And I see you've had breakfast.

HJALMAR   The body, too, makes demands at times.

GREGERS   Well, what have you decided to do?

HJALMAR   For a man like me, there is only one way open. I am in the process of gathering up my most important possessions. Obviously, that takes time.

GINA   [*a trifle impatient*]   Do you want me to make the living room ready for you, or do you want me to pack the bag?

HJALMAR   [*after an irritated glance at* GREGERS]   Pack—and make the room ready.

GINA   [*picking up the bag*]   All right. I'll just put in the shirts and those other things. [*She goes into the living room, closing the door behind her.*]

GREGERS   [*after a short silence*]   I had no idea this would be the end of it. Is it really necessary for you to leave house and home?

HJALMAR   [*paces restlessly up and down*]   What do you want me to do? I am not made to be unhappy, Gregers. I require peace and security and comfort around me.

GREGERS   But you can have all that, Hjalmar. Just try. It seems to me there is a firm foundation to build upon now. Start all over again. And remember, you still have your invention to live for.

HJALMAR   Oh don't talk about that invention. It may take a long time yet.

GREGERS   So?

HJALMAR   Well, yes, for heaven's sake, what do you expect me to invent, anyway? The others have invented most of it already. It's getting more difficult every day.

GREGERS   But all the labor you have put into it—?

HJALMAR   It was that dissipated Relling who got me started on it.

GREGERS   Relling?

HJALMAR   Yes, it was he who first called attention to my talent for making some fabulous invention or other in photography.

GREGERS   I see. It was Relling—!

HJALMAR   Ah—I have been so wonderfully happy about it. Not so much about the invention itself, but because Hedvig believed in it—believed with all the strength and power of a child's soul.—That is, I *thought* she did— fool as I was.

GREGERS   Can you really think that Hedvig would be false to you?

HJALMAR   I can believe anything now. It is Hedvig who is in the way. She it is who is shutting the sun out of my entire life.

GREGERS   Hedvig? You mean Hedvig? How in the world is she going to be an obstacle?

HJALMAR   [*without answering*]   I have loved that child more than I can ever say. You have no idea how happy I was whenever I came back to my humble dwelling and she rushed towards me with her sweet, squinting eyes. Ha, credulous fool that I was! She was so unspeakably dear to me—and so I lulled myself into the dream that I was equally dear to her.

GREGERS   You call that a dream?

HJALMAR   How can I tell? I can't get anything out of Gina. Besides, she completely lacks any sense of the ideal aspects of the issue. But to you I can open up, Gregers. It is this terrible doubt—perhaps Hedvig has never really loved me.

GREGERS   Maybe you'll receive proof—[*Listens.*] Shh! What's that? The wild duck?

HJALMAR   It's just quacking. Father's in the attic.

GREGERS   He is! [*Joy lights his face.*] I tell you again, Hjalmar—maybe you will find proof that your poor, misunderstood Hedvig has always loved you!

HJALMAR   Pah! What proof could she give? I dare not trust to mere asseverations.

GREGERS   Surely, Hedvig doesn't know what deceit is.

HJALMAR   Ah, Gregers—that is just what I cannot be certain of. Who knows what Gina and this Mrs. Sørby may have been whispering and scheming? And Hedvig's ears are big enough, believe you me. Maybe that gift letter didn't come as such a surprise to her. It seemed to me I noticed something like that.

GREGERS   Good heavens, Hjalmar! What kind of spirit is this that's taken possession of you!

HJALMAR   I have had my eyes opened. You just wait. It may turn out that the gift letter was just the beginning. Mrs. Sørby has always been very fond of Hedvig, and now, of course, it's in her power to do anything she likes for the child. They can take her away from me what day and hour they choose.

GREGERS   Hedvig will never leave you, Hjalmar. Never.

HJALMAR   Don't be too sure. If they beckon her with their arms full—? And I who have loved her so infinitely much! I, whose greatest joy it was to take her tenderly by the hand and lead her, as one leads a frightened child through a dark and deserted room! Now I feel this painful certainty that the poor photographer in his attic has never really meant very much to her. She has only cleverly managed to keep on good terms with him while she bided her time.

GREGERS   You don't believe this, Hjalmar.

HJALMAR   That is just what is so terrible—I don't know what to believe—I'll never be able to find out! But do you really doubt that I am right? Ah, Gregers, you put too much trust in the claim of the ideal! If those others were to come now, with their ample offerings, and called to the child: Leave him; life awaits you here with us—

GREGERS   [*quickly*]   Yes, what then—?

HJALMAR   If then I were to ask her: Hedvig, are you willing to give your life for me? [*Laughs scornfully.*] Oh yes—you'd find out soon enough what answer I'd get!

[*A pistol shot is heard from within the attic.*]

GREGERS   [*with a shout of joy*]   Hjalmar!

HJALMAR   Must he go shooting today—!

GINA   [*enters*]   Can't say I like this, Ekdal—Grandpa in there all by himself, banging away.

HJALMAR   I'll take a look—

GREGERS   [*agitated, feelingly*]   Wait! Do you know what that was?

HJALMAR   Yes, of course, I do.

GREGERS   No, you don't. But *I* know. It was the proof!

HJALMAR   What proof?

GREGERS   It was a child's sacrifice. She has got your father to shoot the wild duck.

HJALMAR   Shoot the wild duck!

GINA   Heavens—!

HJALMAR   Whatever for?

GREGERS   She wanted to sacrifice to you what she held dearest in the whole world. For then she thought you'd love her again.

HJALMAR   [*softly, moved*]   Oh that child!

GINA   What she thinks of!

GREGERS   All she wanted was your love, Hjalmar. Without it, life didn't seem possible to her.

GINA   [*struggling with tears*]   *Now,* do you see, Ekdal?

HJALMAR   Gina, where is she?

GINA   [*sniffling*]   Poor thing, She is sitting out in the kitchen, I guess.

HJALMAR   [*walks to the kitchen door, flings it open, says*]   Hedvig—come! Come to me! [*Looks around.*] No. She isn't here.

GINA   Then she must be in her own room.

HJALMAR   [*offstage*]   No, she isn't there, either. [*Re-entering the studio.*] She must have gone out.

GINA   Yes, for you know you didn't want to see hide nor hair of her in the house.

HJALMAR   If only she'd come back soon—so I can tell her—Now I feel that everything will be all right, Gregers. Now I think we can start life over again.

GREGERS   [*quietly*]   I knew it. Restitution would come through the child.

[*Old* EKDAL *appears in the door to his room. He is in full uniform and is buckling on his sabre.*]

HJALMAR   [*surprised*]   Father! You're in there!

GINA   Do you go shooting in your room, now, Grandpa?

EKDAL   [*approaches indignantly*]   So you're off hunting by yourself, are you Hjalmar?

HJALMAR   [*tense, confused*]   You mean it wasn't you who fired that shot in the attic just now?

EKDAL   I? Fired? H'm.

GREGERS   [*shouts to* HJALMAR]   She has shot the wild duck herself!

HJALMAR   What *is* this? [*He hurriedly slides the attic doors open, looks in, gives a loud cry.*] Hedvig!

GINA   [*runs to the door*]   Oh God! What is it?

HJALMAR   [*going inside*]   She is lying on the floor!

GREGERS   Lying—! [*Follows* HJALMAR *inside.*]

GINA   [*at the same time*]   Hedvig! [*Enters the attic.*] No! No! No!

EKDAL   Ho-ho! So *she* has taken to hunting too, now!

[HJALMAR, GINA, *and* GREGERS *drag* HEDVIG *into the studio. Her trailing right hand clasps the pistol tightly.*]

HJALMAR   [*beside himself*]   The pistol went off! She's hit! Call for help! Help!

GINA   [*running out into the hallway, shouts down*]   Relling! Relling! Doctor Relling! Hurry up here, fast as you can!

[HJALMAR *and* GREGERS *put* HEDVIG *down on the sofa.*]

EKDAL   [*quietly*]   The woods avenge themselves.

HJALMAR   [*on his knees beside* HEDVIG]   She's coming to now. She is coming to. Oh yes, yes, yes—

GINA   [*having returned*]   Where's she hit? I can't see a thing.

[RELLING *enters hurriedly, followed by* MOLVIK. *The latter is without vest and tie, his tailcoat thrown open.*]

RELLING   What's the matter?

GINA   They say Hedvig has shot herself.

HJALMAR   Come and help us!

RELLING   Shot herself! [*He pulls the table back and begins to examine her.*]

HJALMAR   [*still on his knees, looking anxiously at* RELLING]   It can't be dangerous, can it, Relling? What, Relling? She hardly bleeds at all. It can't possibly be dangerous?

RELLING   How did this happen?

HJALMAR   Oh, I don't know—

GINA   She was going to shoot the wild duck.

RELLING   The wild duck?

HJALMAR   The pistol must have gone off.

RELLING   H'm. I see.

EKDAL   The woods avenge themselves. But I'm not afraid. [*Enters the attic and closes the doors behind him.*]

HJALMAR   Relling—why don't you say anything?

RELLING   The bullet has entered her chest.

HJALMAR   Yes, but she's coming to!

RELLING   Can't you see that Hedvig is dead?

GINA   [*bursts into tears*]   Oh, the child, the child—!

GREGERS   [*hoarsely*]   In the depths of the sea—

HJALMAR   [*jumps to his feet*]   She must live! I want her to live! For God's sake, Relling—just for a moment—just so I can tell her how unspeakably much I have loved her all the time!

RELLING   Her heart has been pierced. Internal hemorrhage. She died instantly.

HJALMAR   And I who chased her away from me like an animal! Frightened and lonely she crawled into the attic and died for love of me. [*Sobbing.*]

Never to be able to make up for it! Never to tell her—! [*Shakes his fists upwards.*] You! You above! If thou art at all—! Why hast thou done this unto me?

GINA   Shhh, shhh. You mustn't make such a fuss. We had no right to keep her, I suppose.

MOLVIK   The child is not dead. It sleepeth.

RELLING   Rubbish!

HJALMAR   [*quieting down, walks over to the sofa, looks at* HEDVIG, *his arms crossed*]   There she lies, so stiff and still.

RELLING   [*trying to release the pistol*]   She holds on so tightly, I can't—

GINA   No, no, Relling. Don't break her fingers. Let the pistol be.

HJALMAR   Let her have it with her.

GINA   Yes, let her. But the child isn't going to lie out here for a show. She is going into her own little room, right now. Give me a hand, Ekdal.

[HJALMAR *and* GINA *carry* HEDVIG *between them.*]

HJALMAR   [*carrying*]   Gina, Gina—do you think you can bear this?

GINA   The one has to help the other. Seems to me like now we both have a share in her.

MOLVIK   [*raising his arms, muttering*]   Praise be the Lord, to dust thou returnest, to dust thou returnest—

RELLING   [*whispers*]   Shut up, man! You're drunk.

[HJALMAR *and* GINA *carry* HEDVIG *through the kitchen door.* RELLING *closes the door behind them.* MOLVIK *slinks quietly out into the hall.*]

RELLING   [*goes up to* GREGERS]   Nobody is going to tell me this was an accident.

GREGERS   [*who has remained stunned, moving convulsively*]   Who is to say how this terrible thing happened?

RELLING   There were powder burns on her dress. She must have placed the muzzle against her chest and pulled the trigger.

GREGERS   Hedvig has not died in vain. Did you notice how grief released what is great in him?

RELLING   There is a touch of greatness in most of us when we stand in sorrow by a corpse. How long do you think that will last with him?

GREGERS   As if it won't last and grow throughout the rest of his days!

RELLING   Within a year little Hedvig won't be anything to him but an occasion for spouting pretty sentiments.

GREGERS   And you dare say that about Hjalmar Ekdal!

RELLING   Let's talk about this again when the first grass has withered on her grave. You'll hear all about "the child so early taken from the father's heart." You'll see him wallow in sentimentality and self-admiration and self-pity. You just wait!

GREGERS   If you are right and I am wrong, life isn't worth living.

RELLING   Oh, life would be fairly tolerable if only we'd be spared these blasted bill collectors who come around pestering us paupers with the claim of the ideal.

GREGERS   [*staring ahead*]   In that case I am glad my destiny is what it is.

RELLING   Beg your pardon—what *is* your destiny?

GREGERS   [*about to leave*]   To be the thirteenth man at the table.

RELLING   The hell it is.

GEORGE BERNARD SHAW
[1856–1950]

The "upstart son of a downstart father," George Bernard Shaw was born into an Irish Protestant family in Dublin four years before the American Civil War, and his ashes were scattered on his Ayot St. Lawrence estate in England five years after World War II. This incredible span of time was filled with an equally incredible range of activities. Critic, orator, gadfly, oracle, harlequin, prophet, essayist, novelist, dramatist, pamphleteer, Socialist agitator, pillar of the Fabian Society, successful Labour Party candidate for municipal office, romancer of famous actresses, and perhaps the world's most prolific letter writer, Bernard Shaw amazed the world with his energy and versatile genius. In keeping with his belief that the universe was purposefully driven by a "life force" to achieve higher qualities of life, Shaw wrote: "This is the true joy in life, the being used for a purpose recognized by yourself as a mighty one; the being thoroughly worn out before you are thrown on the scrap heap; the being a force of Nature instead of a feverish selfish little clod of ailments and grievances complaining that the world will not devote itself to making you happy."

The overwhelming success that came to Shaw as a result of his commitment came very slowly and grudgingly at first. Because the overt subjects of his early novels and plays were so controversial—divorce, prostitution, slum landlordism, and so on—they met strong opposition from the establishment, and it was not until the turn of the century, twenty-five years after he had emigrated to London, that people in substantial numbers began coming his way. In the 1880s, Shaw was one of a handful who saw and encouraged the death of the old Victorian order and who sought to prepare for the birth of a new order through a gradual and peaceful enlightening of the establishment. His forensic gifts were ideally suited for one who wished to educate men to change.

Unfortunately, his method for educating people was often misunderstood. Because of his talent for comic impersonation, ironic portrayal, and paradoxical statement, and his belief that "by laughter only can you destroy evil without malice and affirm good fellowship without mawkishness," he was often dismissed as a clown who could not be taken seriously. As Shaw himself explains, "When I first began to promulgate my opinions, I found that they appeared extravagant and even insane. In order to get a hearing, it was necessary for me to attain the footing of a privileged lunatic, with the license of a jester. Fortunately the matter was very easy. I found that I had only to say with perfect simplicity what I seriously meant just as it struck me, to make everybody laugh. My method is to take the utmost trouble to find the right thing to say, and then say it with the utmost levity. And all the time the real joke is that I am in earnest." The necessity to play the jester unfortunately trapped Shaw and considerably lessened his effectiveness as a revolutionary with all those who were unable to appreciate the seriousness of his wit, or the sanity of his method.

As a playwright, Shaw was especially adept at dialectical comedy, although it should be understood that his ultimate interest was not as much in the clash of ideas as in the clash of people who are animated by ideas. He was constantly amused and appalled by the degree to which ordinary people allowed their ideas to determine their behavior or to contradict their character. He seemingly never tired of portraying the obsessed and the hypocritical.

Cæsar and Cleopatra, written in 1898, is one of many Shaw plays that illustrate what Shaw considered to be the final conflict in life—"between the cruel will and the humane will." Chief among the over fifty plays that he wrote are *Widowers' Houses* (1892—his first), *Mrs. Warren's Profession* (1893), *Candida* (1894), *Man and Superman* (1903), *Major Barbara* (1905), *Androcles and the Lion* (1912), *Pygmalion* (1912), *Heartbreak House* (1913), *Back to Methuselah* (1921), *Saint Joan* (1923), *The Apple Cart* (1929), *The Simpleton of the Unexpected Isles* (1935), and *In Good King Charles's Golden Days* (1939).

CÆSAR
AND
CLEOPATRA
A History

GEORGE BERNARD SHAW

PROLOGUE

[In the doorway of the temple of Ra in Memphis. Deep gloom. An august personage with a hawk's head is mysteriously visible by his own light in the darkness within the temple. He surveys the modern audience with great contempt; and finally speaks the following words to them.]

Peace! Be silent and hearken unto me, ye quaint little islanders. Give ear, ye men with white paper on your breasts and nothing written thereon (to signify the innocency of your minds). Hear me, ye women who adorn yourselves alluringly and conceal your thoughts from your men, leading them to believe that ye deem them wondrous strong and masterful whilst in truth ye hold them in your hearts as children without judgment. Look upon my hawk's head; and know that I am Ra, who was once in Egypt a mighty god. Ye cannot kneel nor prostrate yourselves; for ye are packed in rows without freedom to move, obstructing one another's vision; neither do any of ye regard it as seemly to do aught until ye see all the rest do so too; wherefore it commonly happens that in great emergencies ye do nothing, though each telleth his fellow that something must be done. I ask you not for worship, but for silence. Let not your men speak nor your women cough; for I am come to draw you back two thousand years over the graves of sixty generations. Ye poor posterity, think not that ye

Cæsar and Cleopatra: A History by Bernard Shaw reprinted by permission of The Public Trustee and the Society of Authors, London, England.

are the first. Other fools before ye have seen the sun rise and set, and the moon change her shape and her hour. As they were so ye are; and yet not so great; for the pyramids my people built stand to this day; whilst the dustheaps on which ye slave, and which ye call empires, scatter in the wind even as ye pile your dead sons' bodies on them to make yet more dust.

Hearken to me then, oh ye compulsorily educated ones. Know that even as there is an old England and a new, and ye stand perplexed between the twain; so in the days when I was worshipped was there an old Rome and a new, and men standing perplexed between them. And the old Rome was poor and little, and greedy and fierce, and evil in many ways; but because its mind was little and its work was simple, it knew its own mind and did its own work; and the gods pitied it and helped it and strengthened it and shielded it; for the gods are patient with littleness. Then the old Rome, like the beggar on horseback, presumed on the favor of the gods, and said, "Lo! there is neither riches nor greatness in our littleness: the road to riches and greatness is through robbery of the poor and slaughter of the weak." So they robbed their own poor until they became great masters of that art, and knew by what laws it could be made to appear seemly and honest. And when they had squeezed their own poor dry, they robbed the poor of other lands, and added those lands to Rome until there came a new Rome, rich and huge. And I, Ra, laughed; for the minds of the Romans remained the same size whilst their dominion spread over the earth.

Now mark me, that ye may understand what ye are presently to see. Whilst the Romans still stood between the old Rome and the new, there arose among them a mighty soldier: Pompey the Great. And the way of the soldier is the way of death; but the way of the gods is the way of life; and so it comes that a god at the end of his way is wise and a soldier at the end of his way is a fool. So Pompey held by the old Rome, in which only soldiers could become great; but the gods turned to the new Rome, in which any man with wit enough could become what he would. And Pompey's friend Julius Cæsar was on the side of the gods; for he saw that Rome had passed beyond the control of the little old Romans. This Cæsar was a great talker and a politician: he bought men with words and with gold, even as ye are bought. And when they would not be satisfied with words and gold, and demanded also the glories of war, Cæsar in his middle age turned his hand to that trade; and they that were against him when he sought their welfare, bowed down before him when he became a slayer and a conqueror; for such is the nature of you mortals. And as for Pompey, the gods grew tired of his triumphs and his airs of being himself a god; for he talked of law and duty and other matters that concerned not a mere human worm. And the gods smiled on Cæsar; for he lived the life they had given him boldly, and was not forever rebuking us for our indecent ways of creation, and hiding our handiwork as a shameful thing. Ye know well what I mean; for this is one of your own sins.

And thus it fell out between the old Rome and the new, that Cæsar said, "Unless I break the law of old Rome, I cannot take my share in ruling her; and the gift of ruling that the gods gave me will perish without fruit." But Pompey said, "The law is above all; and if thou break it thou shalt die." Then said Cæsar, "I will break it: kill me who can." And he broke it. And Pompey went for him, as ye say, with a great army to slay him and uphold the old Rome. So Cæsar fled across the Adriatic sea; for the high gods had a lesson to teach him, which lesson they shall also teach you in due time if ye continue to forget them and to worship that cad among gods, Mammon. Therefore before they raised Cæsar to be master of the world, they were minded to throw him down into the dust, even beneath the feet of Pompey, and blacken his face before the nations. And Pompey they raised higher than ever, he and his laws and his high mind that aped the gods, so that his fall might be the more terrible. And Pompey followed Cæsar, and overcame him with all the majesty of old Rome, and stood over him and over the whole world even as ye stand over it with your fleet that covers thirty miles of the sea. And when Cæsar was brought down to utter nothingness, he made a last stand to die honorably, and did not despair; for he said, "Against me there is Pompey, and the old Rome, and the law and the legions: all all against me; but high above these are the gods; and Pompey is a fool." And the gods laughed and approved; and on the field of Pharsalia the impossible came to pass; the blood and iron ye pin your faith on fell before the spirit of man; for the spirit of man is the will of the gods; and Pompey's power crumbled in his hand, even as the power of imperial Spain crumbled when it was set against your fathers in the days when England was little, and knew her own mind, and had a mind to know instead of a circulation of newspapers. Wherefore look to it, lest some little people whom ye would enslave rise up and become in the hand of God the scourge of your boastings and your injustices and your lusts and stupidities.

And now, would ye know the end of Pompey, or will ye sleep while a god speaks? Heed my words well; for Pompey went where ye are gone, even to Egypt, where there was a Roman occupation even as there was but now a British one. And Cæsar pursued Pompey to Egypt: a Roman fleeing, and a Roman pursuing: dog eating dog. And the Egyptians said, "Lo: these Romans which have lent money to our kings and levied a distraint upon us with their arms, call for ever upon us to be loyal to them by betraying our own country to them. But now behold two Romes! Pompey's Rome and Cæsar's Rome! To which of the twain shall we pretend to be loyal?" So they turned in their perplexity to a soldier that had once served Pompey, and that knew the way of Rome and was full of her lusts. And they said to him, "Lo: in thy country dog eats dog; and both dogs are coming to eat us: what counsel hast thou to give us?" And this soldier, whose name was Lucius Septimius, and whom ye shall presently see before ye, replied, "Ye shall diligently consider which is the bigger dog of the two; and ye shall kill the other dog for his sake and thereby earn his favor." And the Egyptians said, "Thy counsel is expedient; but if we kill a man outside the law we set ourselves in the place of the gods; and this we dare not do. But thou, being a Roman, art accustomed to this kind of killing; for thou hast imperial instincts. Wilt thou therefore kill the lesser dog for us?" And he said, "I will; for I have made my home in Egypt; and I desire consideration and influence among you." And they said, "We knew well thou wouldst not do it for nothing: thou shalt have thy reward." Now when Pompey came, he came alone in a little galley, putting his trust in the law and the constitution. And it was plain to the people of Egypt that Pompey was now but a very small dog. So when he set his foot on the shore he was greeted by his old comrade Lucius Septimius, who welcomed him with one hand and with the other smote off his head, and kept it as it were a pickled cabbage to make a present to Cæsar. And mankind shuddered; but the gods laughed; for Septimius was but a knife that Pompey had sharpened; and when it turned against his own throat they said that Pompey had better have made Septimius a ploughman than so brave and readyhanded a slayer. Therefore again I bid you beware, ye who would all be Pompeys if ye dared; for war is a wolf that may come to your own door.

Are ye impatient with me? Do ye crave for a story of an unchaste woman? Hath the name of Cleopatra tempted ye hither? Ye foolish ones; Cleopatra is as yet but a child that is whipped by her nurse. And what I am about to shew you for the good of your souls is how Cæsar, seeking Pompey in Egypt, found Cleopatra; and how he received that present of a pickled cabbage that was once the head of Pompey; and what things happened between the old Cæsar

and the child queen before he left Egypt and battled his way back to Rome to
be slain there as Pompey was slain, by men in whom the spirit of Pompey still
lived. All this ye shall see; and ye shall marvel, after your ignorant manner, that
men twenty centuries ago were already just such as you, and spoke and lived
as ye speak and live, no worse and no better, no wiser and no sillier. And the
two thousand years that have past are to me, the god Ra, but a moment; nor
is this day any other than the day in which Cæsar set foot in the land of my
people. And now I leave you; for ye are a dull folk, and instruction is wasted
on you; and I had not spoken so much but that it is in the nature of a god to
struggle for ever with the dust and the darkness, and to drag from them, by the
force of his longing for the divine, more life and more light. Settle ye therefore
in your seats and keep silent; for ye are about to hear a man speak, and a great
man he was, as ye count greatness. And fear not that I shall speak to you again:
the rest of the story must ye learn from them that lived it. Farewell; and do not
presume to applaud me. [*The temple vanishes in utter darkness*].

[1912]

AN ALTERNATIVE TO THE PROLOGUE

*An October night on the Syrian border of Egypt towards the end of the XXXIII
Dynasty, in the year 706 by Roman computation, afterwards reckoned by Christian computation as 48 B.C. A great radiance of silver fire, the dawn of a moonlit night, is rising in the east. The stars and the cloudless sky are our own contemporaries, nineteen and a half centuries younger than we know them; but
you would not guess that from their appearance. Below them are two notable
drawbacks of civilization: a palace, and soldiers. The palace, an old, low, Syrian
building of whitened mud, is not so ugly as Buckingham Palace; and the officers in the courtyard are more highly civilized than modern English officers:
for example, they do not dig up the corpses of their dead enemies and mutilate
them, as we dug up Cromwell and the Mahdi. They are in two groups: one
intent on the gambling of their captain Belzanor, a warrior of fifty, who, with
his spear on the ground beside his knee, is stooping to throw dice with a sly-
looking young Persian recruit; the other gathered about a guardsman who has
just finished telling a naughty story (still current in English barracks) at which
they are laughing uproariously. They are about a dozen in number, all highly
aristocratic young Egyptian guardsmen, handsomely equipped with weapons and
armor, very unEnglish in point of not being ashamed of and uncomfortable
in their professional dress; on the contrary, rather ostentatiously and arrogantly
warlike, as valuing themselves on their military caste.*

*Belzanor is a typical veteran, tough and wilful; prompt, capable and crafty
where brute force will serve; helpless and boyish when it will not: an active
sergeant, an incompetent general, a deplorable dictator. Would, if influentially
connected, be employed in the two last capacities by a modern European State
on the strength of his success in the first. Is rather to be pitied just now in view
of the fact that Julius Cæsar is invading his country. Not knowing this, is intent
on his game with the Persian, whom, as a foreigner, he considers quite capable
of cheating him.*

*His subalterns are mostly handsome young fellows whose interest in the game
and the story symbolize with tolerable completeness the main interests in life
of which they are conscious. Their spears are leaning against the walls, or lying
on the ground ready to their hands. The corner of the courtyard forms a triangle
of which one side is the front of the palace, with a doorway, the other a wall*

with a gateway. The storytellers are on the palace side: the gamblers, on the gateway side. Close to the gateway, against the wall, is a stone block high enough to enable a Nubian sentinel, standing on it, to look over the wall. The yard is lighted by a torch stuck in the wall. As the laughter from the group round the storyteller dies away, the kneeling Persian, winning the throw, snatches up the stake from the ground.

BELZANOR   By Apis, Persian, thy gods are good to thee.

THE PERSIAN   Try yet again, O captain. Double or quits!

BELZANOR   No more. I am not in the vein.

THE SENTINEL   [*poising his javelin as he peers over the wall*]   Stand. Who goes there?
[*They all start, listening. A strange voice replies from without.*]

VOICE   The bearer of evil tidings.

BELZANOR   [*calling to the sentry*]   Pass him.

THE SENTINEL   [*grounding his javelin*]   Draw near, O bearer of evil tidings.

BELZANOR   [*pocketing the dice and picking up his spear*]   Let us receive this man with honor. He bears evil tidings.
[*The guardsmen seize their spears and gather about the gate, leaving a way through for the new comer.*]

PERSIAN   [*rising from his knee*]   Are evil tidings, then, so honorable?

BELZANOR   O barbarous Persian, hear my instruction. In Egypt the bearer of good tidings is sacrificed to the gods as a thank offering; but no god will accept the blood of the messenger of evil. When we have good tidings, we are careful to send them in the mouth of the cheapest slave we can find. Evil tidings are borne by young noblemen who desire to bring themselves into notice. [*They join the rest at the gate*].

THE SENTINEL   Pass, O young captain; and bow the head in the House of the Queen.

VOICE   Go anoint thy javelin with fat of swine, O Blackamoor: for before morning the Romans will make thee eat it to the very butt.
[*The owner of the voice, a fairhaired dandy, dressed in a different fashion from that affected by the guardsmen, but no less extravagantly, comes through the gateway laughing. He is somewhat battlestained; and his left forearm, bandaged, comes through a torn sleeve. In his right hand he carries a Roman sword in its sheath. He swaggers down the courtyard, the Persian on his right, Belzanor on his left, and the guardsmen crowding down behind him.*]

BELZANOR   Who are thou that laughest in the House of Cleopatra the Queen, and in the teeth of Belzanor, the captain of her guard?

THE NEW COMER   I am Bel Affris, descended from the gods.

BELZANOR   [*ceremoniously*]   Hail, cousin!

ALL   [*except the Persian*]   Hail, cousin!

PERSIAN   All the Queen's guards are descended from the gods, O stranger, save myself. I am Persian, and descended from many kings.

BEL AFFRIS   [*to the guardsmen*]   Hail, cousins! [*To the Persian, condescendingly*] Hail, mortal!

BELZANOR   You have been in battle, Bel Affris; and you are a soldier among soldiers. You will not let the Queen's women have the first of your tidings.

BEL AFFRIS   I have no tidings, except that we shall have our throats cut presently, women, soldiers, and all.

PERSIAN   [*to Belzanor*]   I told you so.

THE SENTINEL   [*who has been listening*]   Woe, alas!

BEL AFFRIS   [*calling to him*]   Peace, peace, poor Ethiop: destiny is with the gods who painted thee black. [*To Belzanor*] What has this mortal [*indicating the Persian*] told you?

BELZANOR   He says that the Roman Julius Cæsar, who has landed on our shores with a handful of followers, will make himself master of Egypt. He is afraid of the Roman soldiers. [*The guardsmen laugh with boisterous scorn*]. Peasants, brought up to scare crows and follow the plough! Sons of smiths and millers and tanners! And we nobles, consecrated to arms, descended from the gods!

PERSIAN   Belzanor: the gods are not always good to their poor relations.

BELZANOR   [*hotly, to the Persian*]   Man to man, are we worse than the slaves of Cæsar?

BEL AFFRIS   [*stepping between them*]   Listen, cousin. Man to man, we Egyptians are as gods above the Romans.

THE GUARDSMEN   [*exultantly*]   Aha!

BEL AFFRIS   But this Cæsar does not pit man against man: he throws a legion at you where you are weakest as he throws a stone from a catapult; and that legion is as a man with one head, a thousand arms, and no religion. I have fought against them; and I know.

BELZANOR   [*derisively*]   Were you frightened, cousin?

[*The guardsmen roar with laughter, their eyes sparkling at the wit of their captain.*]

BEL AFFRIS   No, cousin; but I was beaten. They were frightened (perhaps); but they scattered us like chaff.

[*The guardsmen, much damped, utter a growl of contemptuous disgust.*]

BELZANOR   Could you not die?

BEL AFFRIS   No: that was too easy to be worthy of a descendant of the gods. Besides, there was no time: all was over in a moment. The attack came just where we least expected it.

BELZANOR   That shews that the Romans are cowards.

BEL AFFRIS   They care nothing about cowardice, these Romans: they fight to win. The pride and honor of war are nothing to them.

PERSIAN   Tell us the tale of the battle. What befell?

THE GUARDSMEN   [*gathering eagerly round Bel Affris*]   Ay: the tale of the battle.

BEL AFFRIS   Know then, that I am a novice in the guard of the temple of Ra in Memphis, serving neither Cleopatra nor her brother Ptolemy, but only the high gods. We went a journey to inquire of Ptolemy why he had driven Cleopatra into Syria, and how we of Egypt should deal with the Roman Pompey, newly come to our shores after his defeat by Cæsar at Pharsalia. What, think ye, did we learn? Even that Cæsar is coming also in hot pursuit of his foe, and that Ptolemy has slain Pompey, whose severed head he holds in readiness to present to the conqueror. [*Sensation among the guardsmen*]. Nay, more: we found that Cæsar is already come; for we had not made half a day's journey on our way back when we came upon a city rabble flying from his legions, whose landing they had gone out to withstand.

BELZANOR   And ye, the temple guard! did ye not withstand these legions?

BEL AFFRIS   What man could, that we did. But there came the sound of a trumpet whose voice was as the cursing of a black mountain. Then saw we a moving wall of shields coming towards us. You know how the heart burns when you charge a fortified wall; but how if the fortified wall were to charge you?

THE PERSIAN   [*exulting in having told them so*]   Did I not say it?

BEL AFFRIS   When the wall came nigh, it changed into a line of men—common fellows enough, with helmets, leather tunics, and breastplates. Every man of them flung his javelin: the one that came my way drove through my shield as through a papyrus—lo there! [*he points to the bandage on his left arm*] and would have gone through my neck had I not stooped. They were charging at the double then, and were upon us with short swords almost as soon as their javelins. When a man is close to you with such a sword, you can do nothing with our weapons: they are all too long.

THE PERSIAN   What did you do?

BEL AFFRIS   Doubled my fist and smote my Roman on the sharpness of his jaw. He was but mortal after all: he lay down in a stupor; and I took his sword and laid it on. [*Drawing the sword*] Lo! a Roman sword with Roman blood on it!

THE GUARDSMEN   [*approvingly*]   Good! [*They take the sword and hand it round, examining it curiously*].

THE PERSIAN   And your men?

BEL AFFRIS   Fled. Scattered like sheep.

BELZANOR   [*furiously*]   The cowardly slaves! Leaving the descendants of the gods to be butchered!

BEL AFFRIS   [*with acid coolness*]   The descendants of the gods did not stay to be butchered, cousin. The battle was not to the strong; but the race was to the swift. The Romans who have no chariots, sent a cloud of horsemen in pursuit, and slew multitudes. Then our high priest's captain rallied a dozen descendants of the gods and exhorted us to die fighting. I said to myself: surely it is safer to stand than to lose my breath and be stabbed in the back; so I joined our captain and stood. Then the Romans treated us with respect; for no man attacks a lion when the field is full of sheep, except for the pride and honor of war, of which these Romans know nothing. So we escaped with our lives; and I am come to warn you that you must open your gates to Cæsar; for his advance guard is scarce an hour behind me; and not an Egyptian warrior is left standing between you and his legions.

THE SENTINEL   Woe, alas! [*He throws down his javelin and flies into the palace*].

BELZANOR   Nail him to the door, quick! [*The guardsmen rush for him with their spears; but he is too quick for them*]. Now this news will run through the palace like fire through stubble.

BEL AFFRIS   What shall we do to save the women from the Romans?

BELZANOR   Why not kill them?

PERSIAN   Because we should have to pay blood money for some of them. Better let the Romans kill them: it is cheaper.

BELZANOR   [*awestruck at his brain power*]   O subtle one! O serpent!

BEL AFFRIS   But your Queen?

BELZANOR   True: we must carry off Cleopatra.

BEL AFFRIS   Will ye not await her command?

BELZANOR   Command! a girl of sixteen! Not we. At Memphis ye deem her a Queen: here we know better. I will take her on the crupper of my horse. When we soldiers have carried her out of Cæsar's reach, then the priests and the nurses and the rest of them can pretend she is a queen again, and put their commands into her mouth.

PERSIAN   Listen to me, Belzanor.

BELZANOR   Speak, O subtle beyond thy years.

THE PERSIAN   Cleopatra's brother Ptolemy is at war with her. Let us sell her to him.

THE GUARDSMEN   O subtle one! O serpent!

BELZANOR   We dare not. We are descended from the gods; but Cleopatra is descended from the river Nile; and the lands of our fathers will grow no grain if the Nile rises not to water them. Without our father's gifts we should live the lives of dogs.

PERSIAN   It is true: the Queen's guard cannot live on its pay. But hear me further, O ye kinsmen of Osiris.

THE GUARDSMEN   Speak, O subtle one. Hear the serpent begotten!

PERSIAN   Have I heretofore spoken truly to you of Cæsar, when you thought I mocked you?

GUARDSMEN   Truly, truly.

BELZANOR   [*reluctantly admitting it*]   So Bel Affris says.

PERSIAN   Hear more of him, then. This Cæsar is a great lover of women: he makes them his friends and counsellors.

BELZANOR   Faugh! This rule of women will be the ruin of Egypt.

THE PERSIAN   Let it rather be the ruin of Rome! Cæsar grows old now: he is past fifty and full of labors and battles. He is too old for the young women; and the old women are too wise to worship him.

BEL AFFRIS   Take heed, Persian. Cæsar is by this time almost within earshot.

PERSIAN   Cleopatra is not yet a woman: neither is she wise. But she already troubles men's wisdom.

BELZANOR   Ay: that is because she is descended from the river Nile and a black kitten of the sacred White Cat. What then?

PERSIAN   Why, sell her secretly to Ptolemy, and then offer ourselves to Cæsar as volunteers to fight for the overthrow of her brother and the rescue of our Queen, the Great Granddaughter of the Nile.

THE GUARDSMEN   O serpent!

PERSIAN   He will listen to us if we come with her picture in our mouths. He will conquer and kill her brother, and reign in Egypt with Cleopatra for his Queen. And we shall be her guard.

GUARDSMEN   O subtlest of all the serpents! O admiration! O wisdom!

BEL AFFRIS   He will also have arrived before you have done talking, O word spinner.

BELZANOR   That is true. [*An affrighted uproar in the palace interrupts him*]. Quick: the flight has begun: guard the door. [*They rush to the door and form a cordon before it with their spears. A mob of women-servants and nurses surges out. Those in front recoil from the spears, screaming to those behind to keep back. Belzanor's voice dominates the disturbance as he shouts*] Back there. In again, unprofitable cattle.

THE GUARDSMEN   Back, unprofitable cattle.

BELZANOR   Send us out Ftatateeta, the Queen's chief nurse.

THE WOMEN   [*calling into the palace*] Ftatateeta, Ftatateeta. Come, come. Speak to Belzanor.

A WOMAN   Oh, keep back. You are thrusting me on the spearheads.

[*A huge grim woman, her face covered with a network of tiny wrinkles, and her eyes old, large, and wise; sinewy handed, very tall, very strong; with the mouth of a bloodhound and the jaws of a bulldog, appears on the threshold. She is dressed like a person of consequence in the palace, and confronts the guardsmen insolently.*]

FTATATEETA   Make way for the Queen's chief nurse.

BELZANOR   [*with solemn arrogance*]   Ftatateeta: I am Belzanor, the captain of the Queen's guard, descended from the gods.

FTATATEETA   [*retorting his arrogance with interest*]   Belzanor: I am Ftatateeta, the Queen's chief nurse; and your divine ancestors were proud to be painted on the wall in the pyramids of the kings whom my fathers served.

[*The women laugh triumphantly.*]

BELZANOR   [*with grim humor*]   Ftatateeta: daughter of a long-tongued, swivel-eyed chameleon, the Romans are at hand. [*A cry of terror from the women: they would fly but for the spears*] Not even the descendants of the gods can resist them; for they have each man seven arms, each carrying seven spears. The blood in their veins is boiling quicksilver; and their wives become mothers in three hours, and are slain and eaten the next day.

[*A shudder of horror from the women. Ftatateeta, despising them and scorning the soldiers, pushes her way through the crowd and confronts the spear points undismayed.*]

FTATATEETA   Then fly and save yourselves, O cowardly sons of the cheap clay gods that are sold to fish porters; and leave us to shift for ourselves.

BELZANOR   Not until you have first done our bidding, O terror of manhood. Bring out Cleopatra the Queen to us; and then go whither you will.

FTATATEETA   [*with a derisive laugh*]   Now I know why the gods have taken her out of our hands. [*The guardsmen start and look at one another*]. Know, thou foolish soldier, that the Queen has been missing since an hour past sundown.

BELZANOR   [*furiously*]   Hag: you have hidden her to sell to Cæsar or her brother. [*He grasps her by the left wrist, and drags her, helped by a few of the guard, to the middle of the courtyard, where, as they fling her on her knees, he draws a murderous looking knife*]. Where is she? Where is she? or— [*he threatens to cut her throat*].

FTATATEETA   [*savagely*]   Touch me, dog; and the Nile will not rise on your fields for seven times seven years of famine.

BELZANOR   [*frightened, but desperate*]   I will sacrifice: I will pay. Or stay. [*To the Persian*] You, O subtle one: your father's lands lie far from the Nile. Slay her.

PERSIAN   [*threatening her with his knife*]   Persia has but one god; yet he loves the blood of old women. Where is Cleopatra?

FTATATEETA   Persian: as Osiris lives, I do not know. I chid her for bringing evil days upon us by talking to the sacred cats of the priests, and carrying them in her arms. I told her she would be left alone here when the Romans came as a punishment for her disobedience. And now she is gone—run away— hidden. I speak the truth. I call Osiris to witness—

THE WOMEN   [*protesting officiously*]   She speaks the truth, Belzanor.

BELZANOR   You have frightened the child: she is hiding. Search—quick—into the palace—search every corner.

[*The guards, led by Belzanor, shoulder their way into the palace through the flying crowd of women, who escape through the courtyard gate.*]

FTATATEETA   [*screaming*]   Sacrilege! Men in the Queen's chambers! Sa—[*her voice dies away as the Persian puts his knife to her throat*].

BEL AFFRIS   [*laying a hand on Ftatateeta's left shoulder*]   Forbear her yet a moment, Persian. [*To Ftatateeta, very significantly*] Mother: your gods are asleep or away hunting; and the sword is at your throat. Bring us to where the Queen is hid, and you shall live.

FTATATEETA   [*contemptuously*]   Who shall stay the sword in the hand of a fool, if the high gods put it there? Listen to me, ye young men without understanding. Cleopatra fears me; but she fears the Romans more. There is but one power greater in her eyes than the wrath of the Queen's nurse and the cruelty of Cæsar; and that is the power of the Sphinx that sits in the desert watching the way to the sea. What she would have it know, she tells into the ears of the sacred cats; and on her birthday she sacrifices to it and decks it with poppies. Go ye therefore into the desert and seek Cleopatra in the shadow of the Sphinx; and on your heads see to it that no harm comes to her.

BEL AFFRIS   [*to the Persian*]   May we believe this, O subtle one?

PERSIAN   Which way come the Romans?

BEL AFFRIS   Over the desert, from the sea, by this very Sphinx.

PERSIAN   [*to Ftatateeta*]   O mother of guile! O aspic's tongue! You have made up this tale so that we two may go into the desert and perish on the spears of the Romans. [*Lifting his knife*] Taste death.

FTATATEETA . . Not from thee, baby.

[*She snatches his ankle from under him and flies stooping along the palace wall, vanishing in the darkness within its precinct. Bel Affris roars with laughter as the Persian tumbles. The guardsmen rush out of the palace with Belzanor and a mob of fugitives, mostly carrying bundles*].

PERSIAN   Have you found Cleopatra?

BELZANOR   She is gone. We have searched every corner.

THE NUBIAN SENTINEL   [*appearing at the door of the palace*]   Woe! Alas! Fly, fly!

BELZANOR   What is the matter now?

THE NUBIAN SENTINEL   The sacred white cat has been stolen.

ALL   Woe! woe!

[*General panic. They all fly with cries of consternation. The torch is thrown down and extinguished in the rush. The noise of the fugitives dies away. Darkness and dead silence*].

ACT I

The same darkness into which the temple of Ra and the Syrian palace vanished. The same silence. Suspense. Then the blackness and stillness break softly into silver mist and strange airs as the windswept harp of Memnon plays at the dawning of the moon. It rises full over the desert; and a vast horizon comes into relief, broken by a huge shape which soon reveals itself in the spreading radiance as a Sphinx pedestalled on the sands. The light still clears, until the upraised eyes of the image are distinguished looking straight forward and upward in infinite fearless vigil, and a mass of color between its great paws defines itself as a heap of red poppies on which a girl lies motionless, her silken vest heaving gently and regularly with the breathing of a dreamless sleeper, and her braided hair glittering in a shaft of moonlight like a bird's wing.

Suddenly there comes from afar a vaguely fearful sound (it might be the bellow of a Minotaur softened by great distance) and Memnon's music stops. Silence: then a few faint high-ringing trumpet notes. Then silence again. Then a man comes from the south with stealing steps, ravished by the mystery of the night, all wonder, and halts, lost in contemplation, opposite the left flank of the Sphinx, whose bosom, with its burden, is hidden from him by its massive shoulder.

THE MAN   Hail, Sphinx: salutation from Julius Cæsar! I have wandered in many lands, seeking the lost regions from which my birth into this world exiled me, and the company of creatures such as I myself. I have found flocks and pastures, men and cities, but no other Cæsar, no air native to me, no man kindred to me, none who can do my day's deed, and think my night's thought. In the little world yonder, Sphinx, my place is as high as yours in this great desert; only I wander, and you sit still; I conquer, and you endure;

I work and wonder, you watch and wait; I look up and am dazzled, look down and am darkened, look round and am puzzled, whilst your eyes never turn from looking out—out of the world—to the lost region—the home from which we have strayed. Sphinx, you and I, strangers to the race of men, are no strangers to one another: have I not been conscious of you and of this place since I was born? Rome is a madman's dream: this is my Reality. These starry lamps of yours I have seen from afar in Gaul, in Britain, in Spain, in Thessaly, signalling great secrets to some eternal sentinel below, whose post I never could find. And here at last is their sentinel—an image of the constant and immortal part of my life, silent, full of thoughts, alone in the silver desert. Sphinx, Sphinx: I have climbed mountains at night to hear in the distance the stealthy footfall of the winds that chase your sands in forbidden play—our invisible children, O Sphinx, laughing in whispers. My way hither was the way of destiny; for I am he of whose genius you are the symbol: part brute, part woman, and part god—nothing of man in me at all. Have I read your riddle, Sphinx?

THE GIRL [who has wakened, and peeped cautiously from her nest to see who is speaking] Old gentleman.

CÆSAR [starting violently, and clutching his sword] Immortal gods!

THE GIRL Old gentleman: dont run away.

CÆSAR [stupefied] "Old gentleman: dont run away"!!! This! to Julius Cæsar!

THE GIRL [urgently] Old gentleman.

CÆSAR Sphinx: you presume on your centuries. I am younger than you, though your voice is but a girl's voice as yet.

THE GIRL Climb up here, quickly; or the Romans will come and eat you.

CÆSAR [running forward past the Sphinx's shoulder, and seeing her] A child at its breast! a divine child!

THE GIRL Come up quickly. You must get up at its side and creep round.

CÆSAR [amazed] Who are you?

THE GIRL Cleopatra, Queen of Egypt.

CÆSAR Queen of the Gypsies, you mean.

CLEOPATRA You must not be disrespectful to me, or the Sphinx will let the Romans eat you. Come up. It is quite cosy here.

CÆSAR [to himself] What a dream! What a magnificent dream! Only let me not wake, and I will conquer ten continents to pay for dreaming it out to the end.
[He climbs to the Sphinx's flank, and presently reappears to her on the pedestal, stepping round to its right shoulder].

CLEOPATRA Take care. Thats right. Now sit down: you may have its other paw. [She seats herself comfortably on its left paw]. It is very powerful and will protect us; but [shivering, and with plaintive loneliness] it would not take any notice of me or keep me company. I am glad you have come: I was very lonely. Did you happen to see a white cat anywhere?

CÆSAR [sitting slowly down on the right paw in extreme wonderment] Have you lost one?

CLEOPATRA Yes: the sacred white cat: is it not dreadful? I brought him here to sacrifice him to the Sphinx; but when we got a little way from the city a black cat called him, and he jumped out of my arms and ran away to it. Do you think that the black cat can have been my great-great-great-grandmother?

CÆSAR [staring at her] Your great-great-great-grandmother! Well, why not? Nothing would surprise me on this night of nights.

CLEOPATRA I think it must have been. My great-grandmother's great-grandmother was a black kitten of the sacred white cat; and the river Nile made her his seventh wife. That is why my hair is so wavy. And I always want to be let do as I like, no matter whether it is the will of the gods or not: that is because my blood is made with Nile water.

CÆSAR   What are you doing here at this time of night? Do you live here?

CLEOPATRA   Of course not: I am the Queen; and I shall live in the palace at Alexandria when I have killed my brother, who drove me out of it. When I am old enough I shall do just what I like. I shall be able to poison the slaves and see them wriggle, and pretend to Ftatateeta that she is going to be put into the fiery furnace.

CÆSAR   Hm! Meanwhile why are you not at home and in bed?

CLEOPATRA   Because the Romans are coming to eat us all. You are not at home and in bed either.

CÆSAR   [*with conviction*]   Yes I am. I live in a tent; and I am now in that tent, fast asleep and dreaming. Do you suppose that I believe you are real, you impossible little dream witch?

CLEOPATRA   [*giggling and leaning trustfully towards him*]   You are a funny old gentleman. I like you.

CÆSAR   Ah, that spoils the dream. Why dont you dream that I am young?

CLEOPATRA   I wish you were; only I think I should be more afraid of you. I like men, especially young men with round strong arms; but I am afraid of them. You are old and rather thin and stringy; but you have a nice voice; and I like to have somebody to talk to, though I think you are a little mad. It is the moon that makes you talk to yourself in that silly way.

CÆSAR   What! you heard that, did you? I was saying my prayers to the great Sphinx.

CLEOPATRA   But this isnt the great Sphinx.

CÆSAR   [*much disappointed, looking up at the statue*]   What!

CLEOPATRA   This is only a dear little kitten of a Sphinx. Why, the great Sphinx is so big that it has a temple between its paws. This is my pet Sphinx. Tell me: do you think the Romans have any sorcerers who could take us away from the Sphinx by magic?

CÆSAR   Why? Are you afraid of the Romans?

CLEOPATRA   [*very seriously*]   Oh, they would eat us if they caught us. They are barbarians. Their chief is called Julius Cæsar. His father was a tiger and his mother a burning mountain; and his nose is like an elephant's trunk. [*Cæsar involuntarily rubs his nose*]. They all have long noses, and ivory tusks, and little tails, and seven arms with a hundred arrows in each; and they live on human flesh.

CÆSAR   Would you like me to shew you a real Roman?

CLEOPATRA   [*terrified*]   No. You are frightening me.

CÆSAR   No matter: this is only a dream—

CLEOPATRA   [*excitedly*]   It is not a dream: it is not a dream. See, see. [*She plucks a pin from her hair and jabs it repeatedly into his arm*].

CÆSAR   Ffff—Stop. [*Wrathfully*] How dare you?

CLEOPATRA   [*abashed*]   You said you were dreaming. [*Whimpering*] I only wanted to shew you—

CÆSAR   [*gently*]   Come, come: dont cry. A queen mustnt cry. [*He rubs his arm, wondering at the reality of the smart*]. Am I awake? [*He strikes his hand against the Sphinx to test its solidity. It feels so real that he begins to be alarmed, and says perplexedly*] Yes. I— [*quite panicstricken*] no: impossible: madness, madness! [*Desperately*] Back to camp—to camp. [*He rises to spring down from the pedestal*].

CLEOPATRA   [*flinging her arms in terror round him*]   No: you shant leave me. No, no, no: dont go. I'm afraid—afraid of the Romans.

CÆSAR [*as the conviction that he is really awake forces itself on him*] Cleopatra: can you see my face well?

CLEOPATRA Yes. It is so white in the moonlight.

CÆSAR Are you sure it is the moonlight that makes me look whiter than an Egyptian? [*Grimly*] Do you notice that I have a rather long nose?

CLEOPATRA [*recoiling, paralysed by a terrible suspicion*] Oh!

CÆSAR It is a Roman nose, Cleopatra.

CLEOPATRA Ah! [*With a piercing scream she springs up; darts round the left shoulder of the Sphinx; scrambles down to the sand; and falls on her knees in frantic supplication, shrieking*] Bite him in two, Sphinx: bite him in two. I meant to sacrifice the white cat—I did indeed—I [*Cæsar, who has slipped down from the pedestal, touches her on the shoulder*]—Ah! [*She buries her head in her arms*].

CÆSAR Cleopatra: shall I teach you a way to prevent Cæsar from eating you?

CLEOPATRA [*clinging to him piteously*] Oh do, do, do. I will steal Ftatateeta's jewels and give them to you. I will make the river Nile water your lands twice a year.

CÆSAR Peace, peace, my child. Your gods are afraid of the Romans: you see the Sphinx dare not bite me, nor prevent me carrying you off to Julius Cæsar.

CLEOPATRA [*in pleading murmurings*] You wont, you wont. You said you wouldnt.

CÆSAR Cæsar never eats women.

CLEOPATRA [*springing up full of hope*] What!

CÆSAR [*impressively*] But he eats girls [*she relapses*] and cats. Now you are a silly little girl; and you are descended from the black kitten. You are both a girl and a cat.

CLEOPATRA [*trembling*] And will he eat me?

CÆSAR Yes; unless you make him believe that you are a woman.

CLEOPATRA Oh, you must get a sorcerer to make a woman of me. Are you a sorcerer?

CÆSAR Perhaps. But it will take a long time; and this very night you must stand face to face with Cæsar in the palace of your fathers.

CLEOPATRA No, no. I darent.

CÆSAR Whatever dread may be in your soul—however terrible Cæsar may be to you—you must confront him as a brave woman and a great queen; and you must feel no fear. If your hand shakes: if your voice quavers; then—night and death! [*She moans*]. But if he thinks you worthy to rule, he will set you on the throne by his side and make you the real ruler of Egypt.

CLEOPATRA [*despairingly*] No: he will find me out: he will find me out.

CÆSAR [*rather mournfully*] He is easily deceived by women. Their eyes dazzle him; and he sees them not as they are, but as he wishes them to appear to him.

CLEOPATRA [*hopefully*] Then we will cheat him. I will put on Ftatateeta's head-dress; and he will think me quite an old woman.

CÆSAR If you do that he will eat you at one mouthful.

CLEOPATRA But I will give him a cake with my magic opal and seven hairs of the white cat baked in it; and—

CÆSAR [*abruptly*] Pah! you are a little fool. He will eat your cake and you too. [*He turns contemptuously from her*].

CLEOPATRA [*running after him and clinging to him*] Oh please, please! I will do whatever you tell me. I will be good. I will be your slave.
[*Again the terrible bellowing note sounds across the desert, now closer at hand. It is the bucina, the Roman war trumpet*].

CÆSAR Hark!

CLEOPATRA [*trembling*] What was that?

CÆSAR Cæsar's voice.

CLEOPATRA [*pulling at his hand*] Let us run away. Come. Oh, come.

CÆSAR You are safe with me until you stand on your throne to receive Cæsar. Now lead me thither.

CLEOPATRA [*only too glad to get away*] I will, I will. [*Again the bucina*]. Oh come, come, come: the gods are angry. Do you feel the earth shaking?

CÆSAR It is the tread of Cæsar's legions.

CLEOPATRA [*drawing him away*] This way, quickly. And let us look for the white cat as we go. It is he that has turned you into a Roman.

CÆSAR Incorrigible, oh, incorrigible! Away!

[*He follows her, the bucina sounding louder as they steal across the desert. The moonlight wanes: the horizon again shews black against the sky, broken only by the fantastic silhouette of the Sphinx. The sky itself vanishes in darkness, from which there is no relief until the gleam of a distant torch falls on great Egyptian pillars supporting the roof of a majestic corridor. At the further end of this corridor a Nubian slave appears carrying the torch. Cæsar, still led by Cleopatra, follows him. They come down the corridor, Cæsar peering keenly about at the strange architecture, and at the pillar shadows between which, as the passing torch makes them hurry noiselessly backwards, figures of men with wings and hawk's heads, and vast black marble cats, seem to flit in and out of ambush. Further along, the wall turns a corner and makes a spacious transept in which Cæsar sees, on his right, a throne, and behind the throne a door. On each side of the throne is a slender pillar with a lamp on it*].

CÆSAR What place is this?

CLEOPATRA This is where I sit on the throne when I am allowed to wear my crown and robes. [*The slave holds his torch to shew the throne*].

CÆSAR Order the slave to light the lamps.

CLEOPATRA [*shyly*] Do you think I may?

CÆSAR Of course. You are the Queen. [*She hesitates.*] Go on.

CLEOPATRA [*timidly, to the slave*] Light all the lamps.

FTATATEETA [*suddenly coming from behind the throne*] Stop. [*The slave stops. She turns sternly to Cleopatra, who quails like a naughty child*]. Who is this you have with you; and how dare you order the lamps to be lighted without my permission? [*Cleopatra is dumb with apprehension*].

CÆSAR Who is she?

CLEOPATRA Ftatateeta.

FTATATEETA [*arrogantly*] Chief nurse to—

CÆSAR [*cutting her short*] I speak to the Queen. Be silent. [*To Cleopatra*] Is this how your servants know their places? Send her away; and do you [*to the slave*] do as the Queen has bidden. [*The slave lights the lamps. Meanwhile Cleopatra stands hesitating, afraid of Ftatateeta*]. You are the Queen: send her away.

CLEOPATRA [*cajoling*] Ftatateeta, dear: you must go away—just for a little.

CÆSAR You are not commanding her to go away: you are begging her. You are no Queen. You will be eaten. Farewell. [*He turns to go*].

CLEOPATRA [*clutching him*] No, no, no. Dont leave me.

CÆSAR A Roman does not stay with queens who are afraid of their slaves.

CLEOPATRA I am not afraid. Indeed I am not afraid.

FTATATEETA We shall see who is afraid here. [*Menacingly*] Cleopatra—

CÆSAR On your knees, woman: am I also a child that you dare trifle with me? [*He points to the floor at Cleopatra's feet. Ftatateeta, half cowed, half savage, hesitates. Cæsar calls to the Nubian*] Slave. [*The Nubian comes to him*] Can you cut off a head? [*The Nubian nods and grins ecstatically, showing all his teeth. Cæsar takes his sword by the scabbard, ready to offer the hilt to the Nubian, and turns again to Ftatateeta, repeating his gesture*]. Have you remembered yourself, mistress?

>*Ftatateeta, crushed, kneels before Cleopatra, who can hardly believe her eyes.*

FTATATEETA [*hoarsely*] O Queen, forget not thy servant in the days of thy greatness.

CLEOPATRA [*blazing with excitement*] Go. Begone. Go away. [*Ftatateeta rises with stooped head, and moves backwards towards the door. Cleopatra watches her submission eagerly, almost clapping her hands, which are trembling. Suddenly she cries*] Give me something to beat her with.

[*She snatches a snake-skin from the throne and dashes after Ftatateeta, whirling it like a scourge in the air. Cæsar makes a bound and manages to catch her and hold her while Ftatateeta escapes*].

CÆSAR You scratch, kitten, do you?

CLEOPATRA [*breaking from him*] I will beat somebody. I will beat him. [*She attacks the slave.*] There, there, there! [*The slave flies for his life up the corridor and vanishes. She throws the snake-skin away and jumps on the step of the throne with her arms waving, crying*] I am a real Queen at last—a real, real Queen! Cleopatra the Queen! [*Cæsar shakes his head dubiously, the advantage of the change seeming open to question from the point of view of the general welfare of Egypt. She turns and looks at him exultantly. Then she jumps down from the steps, runs to him, and flings her arms round him rapturously, crying*] Oh, I love you for making me a Queen.

CÆSAR But queens love only kings.

CLEOPATRA I will make all the men I love kings. I will make you a king. I will have many young kings, with round, strong arms; and when I am tired of them I will whip them to death; but you shall always be my king: my nice, kind, wise, good old king.

CÆSAR Oh, my wrinkles, my wrinkles! And my child's heart! You will be the most dangerous of all Cæsar's conquests.

CLEOPATRA [*appalled*] Cæsar! I forgot Cæsar. [*Anxiously*] You will tell him that I am a Queen, will you not?—a real Queen. Listen! [*stealthily coaxing him*]: let us run away and hide until Cæsar is gone.

CÆSAR If you fear Cæsar, you are no true queen; and though you were to hide beneath a pyramid, he would go straight to it and lift it with one hand. And then—! [*he chops his teeth together*].

CLEOPATRA [*trembling*] Oh!

CÆSAR Be afraid if you dare. [*The note of the bucina resounds again in the distance. She moans with fear. Cæsar exults in it, exclaiming*] Aha! Cæsar approaches the throne of Cleopatra. Come: take your place. [*He takes her hand and leads her to the throne. She is too downcast to speak*]. Ho, there, Teetatota. How do you call your slaves?

CLEOPATRA [*spiritlessly, as she sinks on the throne and cowers there, shaking*] Clap your hands.

[*He claps his hands. Ftatateeta returns.*]

CÆSAR Bring the Queen's robes, and her crown, and her women; and prepare her.

CLEOPATRA [*eagerly—recovering herself a little*] Yes, the crown, Ftatateeta: I shall wear the crown.

FTATATEETA For whom must the Queen put on her state?

CÆSAR For a citizen of Rome. A king of kings, Totateeta.

CLEOPATRA [*stamping at her*] How dare you ask questions? Go and do as you are told. [*Ftatateeta goes out with a grim smile. Cleopatra goes on eagerly, to Cæsar*] Cæsar will know that I am a Queen when he sees my crown and robes, will he not?

CÆSAR   No. How shall he know that you are not a slave dressed up in the Queen's ornaments?

CLEOPATRA   You must tell him.

CÆSAR   He will not ask me. He will know Cleopatra by her pride, her courage, her majesty, and her beauty. [*She looks very doubtful*] Are you trembling?

CLEOPATRA   [*shivering with dread*]   No, I—I—[*in a very sickly voice*] No.
[*Ftatateeta and three women come in with the regalia.*]

FTATATEETA   Of all the Queen's women, these three alone are left. The rest are fled. [*They begin to deck Cleopatra, who submits, pale and motionless*].

CÆSAR   Good, good. Three are enough. Poor Cæsar generally has to dress himself.

FTATATEETA   [*contemptuously*]   The queen of Egypt is not a Roman barbarian. [*To Cleopatra*] Be brave, my nursling. Hold up your head before this stranger.

CÆSAR   [*admiring Cleopatra, and placing the crown on her head*]   Is it sweet or bitter to be a Queen, Cleopatra?

CLEOPATRA   Bitter.

CÆSAR   Cast out fear; and you will conquer Cæsar. Tota: are the Romans at hand?

FTATATEETA   They are at hand; and the guard has fled.

THE WOMEN   [*wailing subduedly*]   Woe to us!
[*The Nubian comes running down the hall.*]

NUBIAN   The Romans are in the courtyard.
[*He bolts through the door. With a shriek, the women fly after him. Ftatateeta's jaw expresses savage resolution: she does not budge. Cleopatra can hardly restrain herself from following them. Cæsar grips her wrist, and looks steadfastly at her. She stands like a martyr*].

CÆSAR   The Queen must face Cæsar alone. Answer "So be it."

CLEOPATRA   [*white*]   So be it.

CÆSAR   [*releasing her*]   Good.
[*A tramp and tumult of armed men is heard. Cleopatra's terror increases. The bucina sounds close at hand, followed by a formidable clangor of trumpets. This is too much for Cleopatra: she utters a cry and darts towards the door. Ftatateeta stops her ruthlessly.*]

FTATATEETA   You are my nursling. You have said "So be it"; and if you die for it, you must make the Queen's word good.
[*She hands Cleopatra to Cæsar, who takes her back, almost beside herself with apprehension, to the throne*].

CÆSAR   Now, if you quail—! [*He seats himself on the throne*].
[*She stands on the step, all but unconscious, waiting for death. The Roman soldiers troop in tumultuously through the corridor, headed by their ensign with his eagle, and their bucinator, a burly fellow with his instrument coiled round his body, its brazen bell shaped like the head of a howling wolf. When they reach the transept, they stare in amazement at the throne; dress into ordered rank opposite; draw their swords and lift them in the air with a shout of* Hail, Cæsar. *Cleopatra turns and stares wildly at Cæsar; grasps the situation; and, with a great sob of relief, falls into his arms.*]

ACT II

Alexandria. A hall on the first floor of the Palace, ending in a loggia approached by two steps. Through the arches of the loggia the Mediterranean can be seen, bright in the morning sun. The clean lofty walls, painted with a procession of the Egyptian theocracy, presented in profile as flat ornament, and the absence of mirrors, sham perspectives, stuffy upholstery and textiles, make the place handsome, wholesome, simple and cool, or, as a rich English manufacturer would express it, poor, bare, ridiculous and unhomely. For Tottenham Court Road civilization is to this Egyptian civilization as glass bead and tattoo civilization is to Tottenham Court Road.

The young king Ptolemy Dionysus (aged ten) is at the top of the steps, on his way in through the loggia, led by his guardian Pothinus, who has him by the hand. The court is assembled to receive him. It is made up of men and women (some of the women being officials) of various complexions and races, mostly Egyptian; some of them, comparatively fair, from lower Egypt, some, much darker, from upper Egypt; with a few Greeks and Jews. Prominent in a group on Ptolemy's right hand is Theodotus, Ptolemy's tutor. Another group, on Ptolemy's left, is headed by Achillas, the general of Ptolemy's troops. Theodotus is a little old man, whose features are as cramped and wizened as his limbs, except his tall straight forehead, which occupies more space than all the rest of his face. He maintains an air of magpie keenness and profundity, listening to what the others say with the sarcastic vigilance of a philosopher listening to the exercises of his disciples. Achillas is a tall handsome man of thirty-five, with a fine black beard curled like the coat of a poodle. Apparently not a clever man, but distinguished and dignified. Pothinus is a vigorous man of fifty, a eunuch, passionate, energetic and quick witted, but of common mind and character; impatient and unable to control his temper. He has fine tawny hair, like fur. Ptolemy, the King, looks much older than an English boy of ten; but he has the childish air, the habit of being in leading strings, the mixture of impotence and petulance, the appearance of being excessively washed, combed and dressed by other hands, which is exhibited by court-bred princes of all ages.   ,

All receive the King with reverences. He comes down the steps to a chair of state which stands a little to his right, the only seat in the hall. Taking his place before it, he looks nervously for instructions to Pothinus, who places himself at his left hand.

POTHINUS   The king of Egypt has a word to speak.

THEODOTUS   [*in a squeak which he makes impressive by sheer self-opinionativeness*]   Peace for the King's word!

PTOLEMY   [*without any vocal inflexions: he is evidently repeating a lesson*]   Take notice of this all of you. I am the first-born son of Auletes the Flute Blower who was your King. My sister Berenice drove him from his throne and reigned in his stead but—but—[*he hesitates*]—

POTHINUS   [*stealthily prompting*]—but the gods would not suffer—

PTOLEMY   Yes—the gods would not suffer—not suffer—[*He stops; then, crestfallen*] I forgot what the gods would not suffer.

THEODOTUS   Let Pothinus, the King's guardian, speak for the King.

POTHINUS   [*suppressing his impatience with difficulty*]   The King wished to say that the gods would not suffer the impiety of his sister to go unpunished.

PTOLEMY   [*hastily*]   Yes: I remember the rest of it. [*He resumes his monotone*]. Therefore the gods sent a stranger one Mark Antony a Roman captain of horsemen across the sands of the desert and he set my father again upon the throne. And my father took Berenice my sister and struck her head off. And now that my father is dead yet another of his daughters my sister Cleopatra would snatch the kingdom from me and reign in my place. But the gods would not suffer—[*Pothinus coughs admonitorily*]—the gods—the gods would not suffer—

POTHINUS   [*prompting*]—will not maintain—

PTOLEMY   Oh yes—will not maintain such iniquity they will give her head to the axe even as her sister's. But with the help of the witch Ftatateeta she hath cast a spell on the Roman Julius Cæsar to make him uphold her false pretence to rule in Egypt. Take notice then that I will not suffer—that I will not suffer—[*pettishly, to Pothinus*] What is it that I will not suffer?

POTHINUS   [*suddenly exploding with all the force and emphasis of political passion*]   The King will not suffer a foreigner to take from him the throne of our Egypt. [*A shout of applause*]. Tell the King, Achillas, how many soldiers and horsemen follow the Roman?

THEODOTUS   Let the King's general speak!

ACHILLAS   But two Roman legions, O King. Three thousand soldiers and scarce a thousand horsemen.

[*The court breaks into derisive laughter; and a great chattering begins, amid which Rufio, a Roman officer, appears in the loggia. He is a burly, black-bearded man of middle age, very blunt, prompt and rough, with small clear eyes, and plump nose and cheeks, which, however, like the rest of his flesh, are in ironhard condition.*]

RUFIO   [*from the steps*]   Peace, ho! [*The laughter and chatter cease abruptly*]. Cæsar approaches.

THEODOTUS   [*with much presence of mind*]   The King permits the Roman commander to enter!

[*Cæsar, plainly dressed, but wearing an oak wreath to conceal his baldness, enters from the loggia, attended by Britannus, his secretary, a Briton, about forty, tall, solemn, and already slightly bald, with a heavy, drooping, hazel-colored moustache trained so as to lose its ends in a pair of trim whiskers. He is carefully dressed in blue, with portfolio, inkhorn, and reed pen at his girdle. His serious air and sense of the importance of the business in hand is in marked contrast to the kindly interest of Cæsar, who looks at the scene, which is new to him, with the frank curiosity of a child, and then turns to the king's chair: Britannus and Rufio posting themselves near the steps at the other side.*]

CÆSAR   [*looking at Pothinus and Ptolemy*]   Which is the King? the man or the boy?

POTHINUS   I am Pothinus, the guardian of my lord the King.

CÆSAR   [*patting Ptolemy kindly on the shoulder*]   So you are the King. Dull work at your age, eh? [*To Pothinus*] Your servant, Pothinus. [*He turns away unconcernedly and comes slowly along the middle of the hall, looking from side to side at the courtiers until he reaches Achillas*]. And this gentleman?

THEODOTUS   Achillas, the King's general.

CÆSAR   [*to Achillas, very friendly*]   A general, eh? I am a general myself. But I began too old, too old. Health and many victories, Achillas!

ACHILLAS   As the gods will, Cæsar.

CÆSAR   [*turning to Theodotus*]   And you, sir, are—?

THEODOTUS   Theodotus, the King's tutor.

CÆSAR   You teach men how to be kings, Theodotus. That is very clever of you. [*Looking at the gods on the walls as he turns away from Theodotus and goes up again to Pothinus*] And this place?

POTHINUS   The council chamber of the chancellors of the King's treasury, Cæsar.

CÆSAR   Ah! that reminds me. I want some money.

POTHINUS   The King's treasury is poor, Cæsar.

CÆSAR   Yes: I notice that there is but one chair in it.

RUFIO   [*shouting gruffly*]   Bring a chair there, some of you, for Cæsar.

PTOLEMY   [*rising shyly to offer his chair*]   Cæsar—

CÆSAR   [*kindly*]   No, no, my boy: that is your chair of state. Sit down.
[*He makes Ptolemy sit down again. Meanwhile Rufio, looking about him, sees in the nearest corner an image of the god Ra, represented as a seated man with the head of a hawk. Before the image is a bronze tripod, about as large as a three-legged stool, with a stick of incense burning on it. Rufio, with Roman resourcefulness and indifference to foreign superstitions, promptly seizes the tripod; shakes off the incense; blows away the ash; and dumps it down behind Cæsar, nearly in the middle of the hall.*]

RUFIO   Sit on that, Cæsar.
[*A shiver runs through the court, followed by a hissing whisper of* Sacrilege!]

CÆSAR   [*seating himself*]   Now, Pothinus, to business. I am badly in want of money.

BRITANNUS   [*disapproving of these informal expressions*]   My master would say that there is a lawful debt due to Rome by Egypt, contracted by the King's deceased father to the Triumvirate; and that it is Cæsar's duty to his country to require immediate payment.

CÆSAR   [*blandly*]   Ah, I forgot. I have not made my companions known here. Pothinus: this is Britannus, my secretary. He is an islander from the western end of the world, a day's voyage from Gaul. [*Britannus bows stiffly*]. This gentleman is Rufio, my comrade in arms. [*Rufio nods*]. Pothinus: I want 1,600 talents.
[*The courtiers, appalled, murmur loudly, and Theodotus and Achillas appeal mutely to one another against so monstrous a demand.*]

POTHINUS   [*aghast*]   Forty million sesterces! Impossible. There is not so much money in the King's treasury.

CÆSAR   [*encouragingly*]   Only sixteen hundred talents, Pothinus. Why count it in sesterces? A sestertius is only worth a loaf of bread.

POTHINUS   And a talent is worth a racehorse. I say it is impossible. We have been at strife here, because the King's sister Cleopatra falsely claims his throne. The King's taxes have not been collected for a whole year.

CÆSAR   Yes they have, Pothinus. My officers have been collecting them all morning. [*Renewed whisper and sensation, not without some stifled laughter, among the courtiers*].

RUFIO   [*bluntly*]   You must pay, Pothinus. Why waste words? You are getting off cheaply enough.

POTHINUS [*bitterly*] Is it possible that Cæsar, the conqueror of the world, has time to occupy himself with such a trifle as our taxes?

CÆSAR My friend: taxes are the chief business of a conqueror of the world.

POTHINUS Then take warning, Cæsar. This day, the treasures of the temple and the gold of the King's treasury shall be sent to the mint to be melted down for our ransom in the sight of the people. They shall see us sitting under bare walls and drinking from wooden cups. And their wrath be on your head, Cæsar, if you force us to this sacrilege!

CÆSAR Do not fear, Pothinus: the people know how well wine tastes in wooden cups. In return for your bounty, I will settle this dispute about the throne for you, if you will. What say you?

POTHINUS If I say no, will that hinder you?

RUFIO [*defiantly*] No.

CÆSAR You say the matter has been at issue for a year, Pothinus. May I have ten minutes at it?

POTHINUS You will do your pleasure, doubtless.

CÆSAR Good! But first, let us have Cleopatra here.

THEODOTUS She is not in Alexandria: she is fled into Syria.

CÆSAR I think not. [*To Rufio*] Call Totateeta.

RUFIO [*calling*] Ho there, Teetatota.

[*Ftatateeta enters the loggia, and stands arrogantly at the top of the steps.*]

FTATATEETA Who pronounces the name of Ftatateeta, the Queen's chief nurse?

CÆSAR Nobody can pronounce it, Tota, except yourself. Where is your mistress?

[*Cleopatra, who is hiding behind Ftatateeta, peeps out at them, laughing. Cæsar rises.*]

CÆSAR Will the Queen favor us with her presence for a moment?

CLEOPATRA [*pushing Ftatateeta aside and standing haughtily on the brink of the steps*] Am I to behave like a Queen?

CÆSAR Yes.

[*Cleopatra immediately comes down to the chair of state; seizes Ptolemy; drags him out of his seat; then takes his place in the chair. Ftatateeta seats herself on the step of the loggia, and sits there, watching the scene with sibylline intensity.*]

PTOLEMY [*mortified, and struggling with his tears*] Cæsar: this is how she treats me always. If I am king why is she allowed to take everything from me?

CLEOPATRA You are not to be King, you little cry-baby. You are to be eaten by the Romans.

CÆSAR [*touched by Ptolemy's distress*] Come here, my boy, and stand by me. [*Ptolemy goes over to Cæsar, who, resuming his seat on the tripod, takes the boy's hand to encourage him. Cleopatra, furiously jealous, rises and glares at them.*]

CLEOPATRA [*with flaming cheeks*] Take your throne: I dont want it. [*She flings away from the chair, and approaches Ptolemy, who shrinks from her*]. Go this instant and sit down in your place.

CÆSAR Go, Ptolemy. Always take a throne when it is offered to you.

RUFIO I hope you will have the good sense to follow your own advice when we return to Rome, Cæsar.

[*Ptolemy slowly goes back to the throne, giving Cleopatra a wide berth, in evident fear of her hands. She takes his place beside Cæsar.*]

CÆSAR Pothinus—

CLEOPATRA [*interrupting him*] Are you not going to speak to me?

CÆSAR Be quiet. Open your mouth again before I give you leave; and you shall be eaten.

CLEOPATRA   I am not afraid. A queen must not be afraid. Eat my husband there, if you like: he is afraid.

CÆSAR   [starting]   Your husband! What do you mean?

CLEOPATRA   [pointing to Ptolemy]   That little thing.

[The two Romans and the Briton stare at one another in amazement.]

THEODOTUS   Cæsar: you are a stranger here, and not conversant with our laws. The kings and queens of Egypt may not marry except with their own royal blood. Ptolemy and Cleopatra are born king and consort just as they are born brother and sister.

BRITANNUS   [shocked]   Cæsar: this is not proper.

THEODOTUS   [outraged]   How!

CÆSAR   [recovering his self-possession]   Pardon him, Theodotus: he is a barbarian, and thinks that the customs of his tribe and island are the laws of nature.

BRITANNUS   On the contrary, Cæsar, it is these Egyptians who are barbarians; and you do wrong to encourage them. I say it is a scandal.

CÆSAR   Scandal or not, my friend, it opens the gate of peace. [He addresses Pothinus seriously]. Pothinus: hear what I propose.

RUFIO   Hear Cæsar there.

CÆSAR   Ptolemy and Cleopatra shall reign jointly in Egypt.

ACHILLAS   What of the King's younger brother and Cleopatra's younger sister?

RUFIO   [explaining]   There is another little Ptolemy, Cæsar: so they tell me.

CÆSAR   Well, the little Ptolemy can marry the other sister; and we will make them both a present of Cyprus.

POTHINUS   [impatiently]   Cyprus is of no use to anybody.

CÆSAR   No matter: you shall have it for the sake of peace.

BRITANNUS   [unconsciously anticipating a later statesman]   Peace with honor, Pothinus.

POTHINUS   [mutinously]   Cæsar: be honest. The money you demand is the price of our freedom. Take it; and leave us to settle our own affairs.

THE BOLDER COURTIERS   [encouraged by Pothinus's tone and Cæsar's quietness] Yes, yes. Egypt for the Egyptians!

[The conference now becomes an altercation, the Egyptians becoming more and more heated. Cæsar remains unruffled; but Rufio grows fiercer and doggeder, and Britannus haughtily indignant.]

RUFIO   [contemptuously]   Egypt for the Egyptians! Do you forget that there is a Roman army of occupation here, left by Aulus Gabinius when he set up your toy king for you?

ACHILLAS   [suddenly asserting himself]   And now under my command. I am the Roman general here, Cæsar.

CÆSAR   [tickled by the humor of the situation]   And also the Egyptian general, eh?

POTHINUS   [triumphantly]   That is so, Cæsar.

CÆSAR   [to Achillas]   So you can make war on the Egyptians in the name of Rome, and on the Romans—on me, if necessary—in the name of Egypt?

ACHILLAS   That is so, Cæsar.

CÆSAR   And which side are you on at present, if I may presume to ask, general?

ACHILLAS   On the side of the right and of the gods.

CÆSAR   Hm! How many men have you?

ACHILLAS   That will appear when I take the field.

RUFIO   [truculently]   Are your men Romans? If not, it matters not how many there are, provided you are no stronger than 500 to ten.

POTHINUS   It is useless to try to bluff us, Rufio. Cæsar has been defeated before and may be defeated again. A few weeks ago Cæsar was flying for his life before Pompey: a few months hence he may be flying for his life before Cato and Juba of Numidia, the African King.

ACHILLAS [*following up Pothinus's speech menacingly*] What can you do with 4,000 men?

THEODOTUS [*following up Achillas's speech with a raucous squeak*] And without money? Away with you.

ALL THE COURTIERS [*shouting fiercely and crowding towards Cæsar*] Away with you. Egypt for the Egyptians! Begone.

[*Rufio bites his beard, too angry to speak. Cæsar sits as comfortably as if he were at breakfast, and the cat were clamoring for a piece of Finnan-haddie.*]

CLEOPATRA Why do you let them talk to you like that, Cæsar? Are you afraid?

CÆSAR Why, my dear, what they say is quite true.

CLEOPATRA But if you go away, I shall not be Queen.

CÆSAR I shall not go away until you are Queen.

POTHINUS Achillas: if you are not a fool, you will take that girl whilst she is under your hand.

RUFIO [*daring them*] Why not take Cæsar as well, Achillas?

POTHINUS [*retorting the defiance with interest*] Well said, Rufio. Why not?

RUFIO Try, Achillas. [*Calling*] Guard there.

[*The loggia immediately fills with Cæsar's soldiers, who stand, sword in hand, at the top of the steps, waiting the word to charge from their centurion, who carries a cudgel. For a moment the Egyptians face them proudly: then they retire sullenly to their former places.*]

BRITANNUS You are Cæsar's prisoners, all of you.

CÆSAR [*benevolently*] Oh no, no, no. By no means. Cæsar's guests, gentlemen.

CLEOPATRA Wont you cut their heads off?

CÆSAR What! Cut off your brother's head?

CLEOPATRA Why not? He would cut off mine, if he got the chance. Wouldnt you, Ptolemy?

PTOLEMY [*pale and obstinate*] I would. I will, too, when I grow up.

[*Cleopatra is rent by a struggle between her newly-acquired dignity as a queen, and a strong impulse to put out her tongue at him. She takes no part in the scene which follows, but watches it with curiosity and wonder, fidgeting with the restlessness of a child, and sitting down on Cæsar's tripod when he rises.*]

POTHINUS Cæsar: if you attempt to detain us—

RUFIO He will succeed, Egyptian: make up your mind to that. We hold the palace, the beach, and the eastern harbor. The road to Rome is open; and you shall travel it if Cæsar chooses.

CÆSAR [*courteously*] I could do no less, Pothinus, to secure the retreat of my own soldiers. I am accountable for every life among them. But you are free to go. So are all here, and in the palace.

RUFIO [*aghast at this clemency*] What! Renegades and all?

CÆSAR [*softening the expression*] Roman army of occupation and all, Rufio.

POTHINUS [*bewildered*] But—but—but—

CÆSAR Well, my friend?

POTHINUS You are turning us out of our own palace into the streets; and you tell us with a grand air that we are free to go! It is for you to go.

CÆSAR Your friends are in the street, Pothinus. You will be safer there.

POTHINUS This is a trick. I am the king's guardian: I refuse to stir. I stand on my right here. Where is your right?

CÆSAR It is in Rufio's scabbard, Pothinus. I may not be able to keep it there if you wait too long.

[*Sensation.*]

POTHINUS [*bitterly*] And this is Roman justice!

THEODOTUS But not Roman gratitude, I hope.

CÆSAR Gratitude! Am I in your debt for any service, gentlemen?

THEODOTUS Is Cæsar's life of so little account to him that he forgets that we have saved it?

CÆSAR My life! Is that all?

THEODOTUS Your life. Your laurels. Your future.

POTHINUS It is true. I can call a witness to prove that but for us, the Roman army of occupation, led by the greatest soldier in the world, would now have Cæsar at its mercy. [*Calling through the loggia*] Ho, there, Lucius Septimius [*Cæsar starts, deeply moved*]: if my voice can reach you, come forth and testify before Cæsar.

CÆSAR [*shrinking*] No, no.

THEODOTUS Yes, I say. Let the military tribune bear witness.

[*Lucius Septimius, a clean shaven, trim athlete of about 40, with symmetrical features, resolute mouth, and handsome, thin Roman nose, in the dress of a Roman officer, comes in through the loggia and confronts Cæsar, who hides his face with his robe for a moment; then, mastering himself, drops it, and confronts the tribune with dignity.*]

POTHINUS Bear witness, Lucius Septimius. Cæsar came hither in pursuit of his foe. Did we shelter his foe?

LUCIUS As Pompey's foot touched the Egyptian shore, his head fell by the stroke of my sword.

THEODOTUS [*with viperish relish*] Under the eyes of his wife and child! Remember that, Cæsar! They saw it from the ship he had just left. We have given you a full and sweet measure of vengeance.

CÆSAR [*with horror*] Vengeance!

POTHINUS Our first gift to you, as your galley came into the roadstead, was the head of your rival for the empire of the world. Bear witness, Lucius Septimius: is it not so?

LUCIUS It is so. With this hand, that slew Pompey, I placed his head at the feet of Cæsar.

CÆSAR Murderer! So would you have slain Cæsar, had Pompey been victorious at Pharsalia.

LUCIUS Woe to the vanquished, Cæsar! When I served Pompey, I slew as good men as he, only because he conquered them. His turn came at last.

THEODOTUS [*flatteringly*] The deed was not yours, Cæsar, but ours—nay, mine; for it was done by my counsel. Thanks to us, you keep your reputation for clemency, and have your vengeance too.

CÆSAR Vengeance! Vengeance!! Oh, if I could stoop to vengeance, what would I not exact from you as the price of this murdered man's blood? [*They shrink back, appalled and disconcerted*]. Was he not my son-in-law, my ancient friend, for 20 years the master of great Rome, for 30 years the compeller of victory? Did not I, as a Roman, share his glory? Was the Fate that forced us to fight for the mastery of the world, of our making? Am I Julius Cæsar, or am I a wolf, that you fling to me the grey head of the old soldier, the laurelled conqueror, the mighty Roman, treacherously struck down by this callous ruffian, and then claim my gratitude for it! [*To Lucius Septimius*] Begone: you fill me with horror.

LUCIUS [*cold and undaunted*] Pshaw! You have seen severed heads before, Cæsar, and severed right hands too, I think; some thousands of them, in Gaul, after you vanquished Vercingetorix. Did you spare him, with all your clemency? Was that vengeance?

CÆSAR No, by the gods! would that it had been! Vengeance at least is human.

No, I say: those severed right hands, and the brave Vercingetorix basely strangled in a vault beneath the Capitol were [*with shuddering satire*] a wise severity, a necessary protection to the commonwealth, a duty of statesmanship—follies and fictions ten times bloodier than honest vengeance! What a fool was I then! To think that men's lives should be at the mercy of such fools! [*Humbly*] Lucius Septimius, pardon me: why should the slayer of Vercingetorix rebuke the slayer of Pompey? You are free to go with the rest. Or stay if you will: I will find a place for you in my service.

LUCIUS   The odds are against you, Cæsar. I go. [*He turns to go out through the loggia*].

RUFIO   [*full of wrath at seeing his prey escaping*]   That means that he is a Republican.

LUCIUS   [*turning defiantly on the loggia steps*]   And what are you?

RUFIO   A Cæsarian, like all Cæsar's soldiers.

CÆSAR   [*courteously*]   Lucius: believe me, Cæsar is no Cæsarian. Were Rome a true republic, then were Cæsar the first of Republicans. But you have made your choice. Farewell.

LUCIUS   Farewell. Come, Achillas, whilst there is yet time.

[*Cæsar, seeing that Rufio's temper threatens to get the worse of him, puts his hand on his shoulder and brings him down the hall out of harm's way, Britannus accompanying them and posting himself on Cæsar's right hand. This movement brings the three in a little group to the place occupied by Achillas, who moves haughtily away and joins Theodotus on the other side. Lucius Septimius goes out through the soldiers in the loggia. Pothinus, Theodotus and Achillas follow him with the courtiers, very mistrustful of the soldiers, who close up in their rear and go out after them, keeping them moving without much ceremony. The King is left in his chair, piteous, obstinate, with twitching face and fingers. During these movements Rufio maintains an energetic grumbling, as follows:—*]

RUFIO   [*as Lucius departs*]   Do you suppose he would let us go if he had our heads in his hands?

CÆSAR   I have no right to suppose that his ways are any baser than mine.

RUFIO   Psha!

CÆSAR   Rufio: if I take Lucius Septimius for my model, and become exactly like him, ceasing to be Cæsar, will you serve me still?

BRITANNUS   Cæsar: this is not good sense. Your duty to Rome demands that her enemies should be prevented from doing further mischief. [*Cæsar, whose delight in the moral eye-to-business of his British secretary is inexhaustible, smiles indulgently*].

RUFIO   It is no use talking to him, Britannus: you may save your breath to cool your porridge. But mark this, Cæsar. Clemency is very well for you; but what is it for your soldiers, who have to fight tomorrow the men you spared yesterday? You may give what orders you please; but I tell you that your next victory will be a massacre, thanks to your clemency. I, for one, will take no prisoners. I will kill my enemies in the field; and then you can preach as much clemency as you please: I shall never have to fight them again. And now, with your leave, I will see these gentry off the premises. [*He turns to go*].

CÆSAR   [*turning also and seeing Ptolemy*]   What! have they left the boy alone! Oh shame, shame!

RUFIO   [*taking Ptolemy's hand and making him rise*]   Come, your majesty!

PTOLEMY   [*to Cæsar, drawing away his hand from Rufio*]   Is he turning me out of my palace?

RUFIO   *[grimly]*   You are welcome to stay if you wish.

CÆSAR   *[kindly]*   Go, my boy. I will not harm you; but you will be safer away, among your friends. Here you are in the lion's mouth.

PTOLEMY   *[turning to go]*   It is not the lion I fear, but *[looking at Rufio]* the jackal. *[He goes out through the loggia]*.

CÆSAR   *[laughing approvingly]*   Brave boy!

CLEOPATRA   *[jealous of Cæsar's approbation, calling after Ptolemy]*   Little silly. You think that very clever.

CÆSAR   Britannus: attend the King. Give him in charge to that Pothinus fellow. *[Britannus goes out after Ptolemy]*.

RUFIO   *[pointing to Cleopatra]*   And this piece of goods? What is to be done with her? However, I suppose I may leave that to you. *[He goes out through the loggia]*.

CLEOPATRA   *[flushing suddenly and turning on Cæsar]*   Did you mean me to go with the rest?

CÆSAR   *[a little preoccupied, goes with a sigh to Ptolemy's chair, whilst she waits for his answer with red cheeks and clenched fists]*   You are free to do just as you please, Cleopatra.

CLEOPATRA   Then you do not care whether I stay or not?

CÆSAR   *[smiling]*   Of course I had rather you stayed.

CLEOPATRA   Much, much rather?

CÆSAR   *[nodding]*   Much, much rather.

CLEOPATRA   Then I consent to stay, because I am asked. But I do not want to, mind.

CÆSAR   That is quite understood. *[Calling]* Totateeta.

[Ftatateeta, still seated, turns her eyes on him with a sinister expression, but does not move.]

CLEOPATRA   *[with a splutter of laughter]*   Her name is not Totateeta: it is Ftatateeta. *[Calling]* Ftatateeta. *[Ftatateeta instantly rises and comes to Cleopatra]*.

CÆSAR   *[stumbling over the name]*   Tfatafeeta will forgive the erring tongue of a Roman. Tota: the Queen will hold her state here in Alexandria. Engage women to attend upon her; and do all that is needful.

FTATATEETA   Am I then the mistress of the Queen's household?

CLEOPATRA   *[sharply]*   No: *I* am the mistress of the Queen's household. Go and do as you are told, or I will have you thrown into the Nile this very afternoon, to poison the poor crocodiles.

CÆSAR   *[shocked]*   Oh no, no.

CLEOPATRA   Oh yes, yes. You are very sentimental, Cæsar; but you are clever; and if you do as I tell you, you will soon learn to govern.

[Cæsar, quite dumbfounded by this impertinence, turns in his chair and stares at her. Ftatateeta, smiling grimly, and shewing a splendid set of teeth, goes, leaving them alone together.]

CÆSAR   Cleopatra: I really think I must eat you, after all.

CLEOPATRA   *[kneeling beside him and looking at him with eager interest, half real, half affected to shew how intelligent she is]*   You must not talk to me now as if I were a child.

CÆSAR   You have been growing up since the sphinx introduced us the other night; and you think you know more than I do already.

CLEOPATRA   *[taken down, and anxious to justify herself]*   No: that would be very silly of me: of course I know that. But—*[suddenly]* are you angry with me?

CÆSAR   No.

CLEOPATRA   *[only half believing him]*   Then why are you so thoughtful?

CÆSAR   [*rising*] I have work to do, Cleopatra.

CLEOPATRA   [*drawing back*] Work! [*Offended*] You are tired of talking to me; and that is your excuse to get away from me.

CÆSAR   [*sitting down again to appease her*] Well, well: another minute. But then—work!

CLEOPATRA   Work! what nonsense! You must remember that you are a king now: I have made you one. Kings dont work.

CÆSAR   Oh! Who told you that, little kitten? Eh?

CLEOPATRA   My father was King of Egypt; and he never worked. But he was a great king, and cut off my sister's head because she rebelled against him and took the throne from him.

CÆSAR   Well; and how did he get his throne back again?

CLEOPATRA   [*eagerly, her eyes lighting up*] I will tell you. A beautiful young man, with strong round arms, came over the desert with many horsemen, and slew my sister's husband and gave my father back his throne. [*Wistfully*] I was only twelve then. Oh, I wish he would come again, now that I am queen. I would make him my husband.

CÆSAR   It might be managed, perhaps; for it was I who sent that beautiful young man to help your father.

CLEOPATRA   [*enraptured*] You know him!

CÆSAR   [*nodding*] I do.

CLEOPATRA   Has he come with you? [*Cæsar shakes his head: she is cruelly disappointed*]. Oh, I wish he had, I wish he had. If only I were a little older; so that he might not think me a mere kitten, as you do! But perhaps that is because you are old. He is many many years younger than you, is he not?

CÆSAR   [*as if swallowing a pill*] He is somewhat younger.

CLEOPATRA   Would he be my husband, do you think, if I asked him?

CÆSAR   Very likely.

CLEOPATRA   But I should not like to ask him. Could you not persuade him to ask me—without knowing that I wanted him to?

CÆSAR   [*touched by her innocence of the beautiful young man's character*] My poor child!

CLEOPATRA   Why do you say that as if you were sorry for me? Does he love anyone else?

CÆSAR   I am afraid so.

CLEOPATRA   [*tearfully*] Then I shall not be his first love.

CÆSAR   Not quite the first. He is greatly admired by women.

CLEOPATRA   I wish I could be the first. But if he loves me, I will make him kill all the rest. Tell me: is he still beautiful? Do his strong round arms shine in the sun like marble?

CÆSAR   He is in excellent condition—considering how much he eats and drinks.

CLEOPATRA   Oh, you must not say common, earthly things about him; for I love him. He is a god.

CÆSAR   He is a great captain of horsemen, and swifter of foot than any other Roman.

CLEOPATRA   What is his real name?

CÆSAR   [*puzzled*] His real name?

CLEOPATRA   Yes, I always call him Horus, because Horus is the most beautiful of our gods. But I want to know his real name.

CÆSAR   His name is Mark Antony.

CLEOPATRA   [*musically*] Mark Antony, Mark Antony, Mark Antony! What a beautiful name! [*She throws her arms round Cæsar's neck*]. Oh, how I love you for sending him to help my father! Did you love my father very much?

CÆSAR   No, my child; but your father, as you say, never worked. I always work.

So when he lost his crown he had to promise me 16,000 talents to get it back for him.

CLEOPATRA   Did he ever pay you?

CÆSAR   Not in full.

CLEOPATRA   He was quite right: it was too dear. The whole world is not worth 16,000 talents.

CÆSAR   That is perhaps true, Cleopatra. Those Egyptians who work paid as much of it as he could drag from them. The rest is still due. But as I most likely shall not get it, I must go back to my work. So you must run away for a little and send my secretary to me.

CLEOPATRA   [*coaxing*]   No: I want to stay and hear you talk about Mark Antony.

CÆSAR   But if I do not get to work, Pothinus and the rest of them will cut us off from the harbor; and then the way from Rome will be blocked.

CLEOPATRA   No matter: I dont want you to go back to Rome.

CÆSAR   But you want Mark Antony to come from it.

CLEOPATRA   [*springing up*]   Oh yes, yes, yes: I forgot. Go quickly and work, Cæsar; and keep the way over the sea open for my Mark Antony. [*She runs out through the loggia, kissing her hand to Mark Antony across the sea*].

CÆSAR   [*going briskly up the middle of the hall to the loggia steps*]   Ho, Britannus. [*He is startled by the entry of a wounded Roman soldier, who confronts him from the upper step*]. What now?

SOLDIER   [*pointing to his bandaged head*]   This, Cæsar; and two of my comrades killed in the market place.

CÆSAR   [*quiet, but attending*]   Ay. Why?

SOLDIER   There is an army come to Alexandria, calling itself the Roman army.

CÆSAR   The Roman army of occupation. Ay?

SOLDIER   Commanded by one Achillas.

CÆSAR   Well?

SOLDIER   The citizens rose against us when the army entered the gates. I was with two others in the market place when the news came. They set upon us. I cut my way out; and here I am.

CÆSAR   Good. I am glad to see you alive. [*Rufio enters the loggia hastily, passing behind the soldier to look out through one of the arches at the quay beneath*]. Rufio: we are besieged.

RUFIO   What! Already?

CÆSAR   Now or tomorrow: what does it matter? We shall be besieged.
   [*Britannus runs in.*]

BRITANNUS   Cæsar—

CÆSAR   [*anticipating him*]   Yes: I know. [*Rufio and Britannus come down the hall from the loggia at opposite sides, past Cæsar, who waits for a moment near the step to say to the soldier*]   Comrade: give the word to turn out on the beach and stand by the boats. Get your wound attended to. Go. [*The soldier hurries out. Cæsar comes down the hall between Rufio and Britannus*]   Rufio: we have some ships in the west harbor. Burn them.

RUFIO   [*staring*]   Burn them!!

CÆSAR   Take every boat we have in the east harbor, and seize the Pharos—that island with the lighthouse. Leave half our men behind to hold the beach and the quay outside this palace: that is the way home.

RUFIO   [*disapproving strongly*]   Are we to give up the city?

CÆSAR   We have not got it, Rufio. This palace we have; and—what is that building next door?

RUFIO   The theatre.

CÆSAR   We will have that too: it commands the strand. For the rest, Egypt for the Egyptians!

RUFIO   Well, you know best, I suppose. Is that all?

CÆSAR   That is all. Are those ships burnt yet?

RUFIO   Be easy: I shall waste no more time. [*He runs out*].

BRITANNUS   Cæsar: Pothinus demands speech of you. In my opinion he needs a lesson. His manner is most insolent.

CÆSAR   Where is he?

BRITANNUS   He waits without.

CÆSAR   Ho there! admit Pothinus.

> [*Pothinus appears in the loggia, and comes down the hall very haughtily to Cæsar's left hand.*]

CÆSAR   Well, Pothinus?

POTHINUS   I have brought you our ultimatum, Cæsar.

CÆSAR   Ultimatum! The door was open: you should have gone out through it before you declared war. You are my prisoner now. [*He goes to the chair and loosens his toga*].

POTHINUS   [*scornfully*]   I your prisoner! Do you know that you are in Alexandria, and that King Ptolemy, with an army outnumbering your little troop a hundred to one, is in possession of Alexandria?

CÆSAR   [*unconcernedly taking off his toga and throwing it on the chair*]   Well, my friend, get out if you can. And tell your friends not to kill any more Romans in the market place. Otherwise my soldiers, who do not share my celebrated clemency, will probably kill you. Britannus: pass the word to the guard; and fetch my armor. [*Britannus runs out. Rufio returns*]. Well?

RUFIO   [*pointing from the loggia to a cloud of smoke drifting over the harbor*]   See there! [*Pothinus runs eagerly up the steps to look out*].

CÆSAR   What, ablaze already! Impossible!

RUFIO   Yes, five good ships, and a barge laden with oil grappled to each. But it is not my doing: the Egyptians have saved me the trouble. They have captured the west harbor.

CÆSAR   [*anxiously*]   And the east harbor? The lighthouse, Rufio?

RUFIO   [*with a sudden splutter of raging ill usage, coming down to Cæsar and scolding him*]   Can I embark a legion in five minutes? The first cohort is already on the beach. We can do no more. If you want faster work, come and do it yourself.

CÆSAR   [*soothing him*]   Good, good. Patience, Rufio, patience.

RUFIO   Patience! Who is impatient here, you or I? Would I be here, if I could not oversee them from that balcony?

CÆSAR   Forgive me, Rufio; and [*anxiously*] hurry them as much as—

> [*He is interrupted by an outcry as of an old man in the extremity of misfortune. It draws near rapidly; and Theodotus rushes in, tearing his hair. and squeaking the most lamentable exclamations. Rufio steps back to stare at him, amazed at his frantic condition. Pothinus turns to listen.*]

THEODOTUS   [*on the steps, with uplifted arms*]   Horror unspeakable! Woe, alas! Help!

RUFIO   What now?

CÆSAR   [*frowning*]   Who is slain?

THEODOTUS   Slain! Oh, worse than the death of ten thousand men! Loss irreparable to mankind!

RUFIO   What has happened, man?

THEODOTUS   [*rushing down the hall between them*]   The fire has spread from your ships. The first of the seven wonders of the world perishes. The library of Alexandria is in flames.

RUFIO   Psha! [*Quite relieved, he goes up to the loggia and watches the preparations of the troops on the beach*].

CÆSAR   Is that all?

THEODOTUS   [*unable to believe his senses*]   All! Cæsar: will you go down to posterity as a barbarous soldier too ignorant to know the value of books?

CÆSAR   Theodotus: I am an author myself; and I tell you it is better that the Egyptians should live their lives than dream them away with the help of books.

THEODOTUS   [*kneeling, with genuine literary emotion: the passion of the pedant*]   Cæsar: once in ten generations of men, the world gains an immortal book.

CÆSAR   [*inflexible*]   If it did not flatter mankind, the common executioner would burn it.

THEODOTUS   Without history, death will lay you beside your meanest soldier.

CÆSAR   Death will do that in any case. I ask no better grave.

THEODOTUS   What is burning there is the memory of mankind.

CÆSAR   A shameful memory. Let it burn.

THEODOTUS   [*wildly*]   Will you destroy the past?

CÆSAR   Ay, and build the future with its ruins. [*Theodotus, in despair, strikes himself on the temples with his fists*]. But harken, Theodotus, teacher of kings: you who valued Pompey's head no more than a shepherd values an onion, and who now kneel to me, with tears in your old eyes, to plead for a few sheepskins scrawled with errors. I cannot spare you a man or a bucket of water just now; but you shall pass freely out of the palace. Now, away with you to Achillas; and borrow his legions to put out the fire. [*He hurries him to the steps*].

POTHINUS   [*significantly*]   You understand, Theodotus: I remain a prisoner.

THEODOTUS   A prisoner!

CÆSAR   Will you stay to talk whilst the memory of mankind is burning? [*Calling through the loggia*] Ho there! Pass Theodotus out. [*To Theodotus*] Away with you.

THEODOTUS   [*To Pothinus*]   I must go to save the library. [*He hurries out*].

CÆSAR   Follow him to the gate, Pothinus. Bid him urge your people to kill no more of my soldiers, for your sake.

POTHINUS   My life will cost you dear if you take it, Cæsar.

[*He goes out after Theodotus. Rufio, absorbed in watching the embarkation, does not notice the departure of the two Egyptians.*]

RUFIO   [*shouting from the loggia to the beach*]   All ready, there?

A CENTURION   [*from below*]   All ready. We wait for Cæsar.

CÆSAR   Tell them Cæsar is coming—the rogues! [*Calling*] Britannicus. [*This magniloquent version of his secretary's name is one of Cæsar's jokes. In later years it would have meant, quite seriously and officially, Conqueror of Britain*].

RUFIO   [*calling down*]   Push off, all except the longboat. Stand by it to embark, Cæsar's guard there. [*He leaves the balcony and comes down into the hall*]. Where are those Egyptians? Is this more clemency? Have you let them go?

CÆSAR   [*chuckling*]   I have let Theodotus go to save the library. We must respect literature, Rufio.

RUFIO   [*raging*]   Folly on folly's head! I believe if you could bring back all the dead of Spain, Gaul, and Thessaly to life, you would do it that we might have the trouble of fighting them over again.

CÆSAR   Might not the gods destroy the world if their only thought were to be at peace next year? [*Rufio, out of all patience, turns away in anger. Cæsar suddenly grips his sleeve, and adds slyly in his ear*] Besides, my friend:

every Egyptian we imprison means imprisoning two Roman soldiers to guard him. Eh?

RUFIO   Agh! I might have known there was some fox's trick behind your fine talking. [*He gets away from Cæsar with an ill-humored shrug, and goes to the balcony for another look at the preparations; finally goes out*].

CÆSAR   Is Britannus asleep? I sent him for my armor an hour ago. [*Calling*] Britannicus, thou British islander. Britannicus!
[*Cleopatra runs in through the loggia with Cæsar's helmet and sword, snatched from Britannus, who follows her with a cuirass and greaves. They come down to Cæsar, she to his left hand, Britannus to his right.*]

CLEOPATRA   I am going to dress you, Cæsar. Sit down. [*He obeys*]. These Roman helmets are so becoming! [*She takes off his wreath*]. Oh! [*She bursts out laughing at him*].

CÆSAR   What are you laughing at?

CLEOPATRA   Youre bald [*beginning with a big B, and ending with a splutter*].

CÆSAR   [*almost annoyed*]   Cleopatra! [*He rises, for the convenience of Britannus, who puts the cuirass on him*].

CLEOPATRA   So that is why you wear the wreath—to hide it.

BRITANNUS   Peace, Egyptian: they are the bays of the conqueror. [*He buckles the cuirass*].

CLEOPATRA   Peace, thou: islander! [*To Cæsar*] You should rub your head with strong spirits of sugar, Cæsar. That will make it grow.

CÆSAR   [*with a wry face*]   Cleopatra: do you like to be reminded that you are very young?

CLEOPATRA   [*pouting*]   No.

CÆSAR   [*sitting down again, and setting out his leg for Britannus, who kneels to put on his greaves*].   Neither do I like to be reminded that I am—middle aged. Let me give you ten of my superfluous years. That will make you 26, and leave me only—no matter. Is it a bargain?

CLEOPATRA   Agreed. 26, mind. [*She puts the helmet on him*]. Oh! How nice! You look only about 50 in it!

BRITANNUS   [*looking up severely at Cleopatra*]   You must not speak in this manner to Cæsar.

CLEOPATRA   Is it true that when Cæsar caught you on that island, you were painted all over blue?

BRITANNUS   Blue is the color worn by all Britons of good standing. In war we stain our bodies blue; so that though our enemies may strip us of our clothes and our lives, they cannot strip us of our respectability. [*He rises*].

CLEOPATRA   [*with Cæsar's sword*]   Let me hang this on. Now you look splendid. Have they made any statues of you in Rome?

CÆSAR   Yes, many statues.

CLEOPATRA   You must send for one and give it to me.

RUFIO   [*coming back into the loggia, more impatient than ever*]   Now Cæsar: have you done talking? The moment your foot is aboard there will be no holding our men back: the boats will race one another for the lighthouse.

CÆSAR   [*drawing his sword and trying the edge*]   Is this well set today, Britannicus? At Pharsalia it was as blunt as a barrel-hoop.

BRITANNUS   It will split one of the Egyptian's hairs today, Cæsar. I have set it myself.

CLEOPATRA   [*suddenly throwing her arms in terror round Cæsar*]   Oh, you are not really going into battle to be killed?

CÆSAR   No, Cleopatra. No man goes to battle to be killed.

CLEOPATRA   But they do get killed. My sister's husband was killed in battle. You must not go. Let him go [*pointing to Rufio. They all laugh at her*].

808,82
A 439
R 367m
D 568
S 717
B 346
S₀ 34
P-18B

Oh please, please dont go. What will happen to me if you never come back?

CÆSAR [*gravely*] Are you afraid?

CLEOPATRA [*shrinking*] No.

CÆSAR [*with quiet authority*] Go to the balcony; and you shall see us take the Pharos. You must learn to look on battles. Go. [*She goes, downcast, and looks out from the balcony*]. That is well. Now, Rufio. March.

CLEOPATRA [*suddenly clapping her hands*] Oh, you will not be able to go!

CÆSAR Why! What now?

CLEOPATRA They are drying up the harbor with buckets—a multitude of soldiers—over there [*pointing out across the sea to her left*]—they are dipping up the water.

RUFIO [*hastening to look*] It is true. The Egyptian army! Crawling over the edge of the west harbor like locusts. [*With sudden anger he turns on Cæsar*]. This is your accursed clemency, Cæsar. Theodotus has brought them—

CÆSAR [*delighted at his own cleverness*] I meant him to, Rufio. They have come to put out the fire. The library will keep them busy whilst we seize the lighthouse. Eh?

[*He rushes out buoyantly through the loggia, followed by Britannus*].

RUFIO [*disgustedly*] More foxing! Agh! [*He rushes off. A shout from the soldiers announces the appearance of Cæsar below*].

CENTURION [*below*] All aboard. Give way there. [*Another shout*].

CLEOPATRA [*waving her scarf through the loggia arch*] Goodbye, goodbye, dear Cæsar. Come back safe. Goodbye!

ACT III

The edge of the quay in front of the palace, looking out west over the east harbor of Alexandria to Pharos island, just to the end of which, and connected with it by a narrow mole, is the famous lighthouse, a gigantic square tower of white marble diminishing in size storey by storey to the top, on which stands a cresset beacon. The island is joined to the main land by the Heptastadium, a great mole or causeway five miles long bounding the harbor on the south.

In the middle of the quay a Roman sentinel stands on guard, pilum in hand, looking out to the lighthouse with strained attention, his left hand shading his eyes. The pilum is a stout wooden shaft 4½ feet long, with an iron spit about three feet long fixed in it. The sentinel is so absorbed that he does not notice the approach from the north end of the quay of four Egyptian market porters carrying rolls of carpet, preceded by Ftatateeta and Apollodorus the Sicilian. Apollodorus is a dashing young man of about 24, handsome and debonair, dressed with deliberate æstheticism in the most delicate purples and dove greys, with ornaments of bronze, oxydized silver, and stones of jade and agate. His sword, designed as carefully as a medieval cross, has a blued blade shewing through an openwork scabbard of purple leather and filigree. The porters, conducted by Ftatateeta, pass along the quay behind the sentinel to the steps of the palace, where they put down their bales and squat on the ground. Apollodorus does not pass along with them: he halts, amused by the preoccupation of the sentinel.

APOLLODORUS [*calling to the sentinel*] Who goes there, eh?

SENTINEL [*starting violently and turning with his pilum at the charge, revealing himself as a small, wiry, sandy-haired, conscientious young man with an elderly face*] Whats this? Stand. Who are you?

APOLLODORUS I am Apollodorus the Sicilian. Why, man, what are you dreaming of? Since I came through the lines beyond the theatre there, I have brought my caravan past three sentinels, all so busy staring at the lighthouse that not one of them challenged me. Is this Roman discipline?

SENTINEL We are not here to watch the land but the sea. Cæsar has just landed on the Pharos. [*Looking at Ftatateeta*] What have you here? Who is this piece of Egyptian crockery?

FTATATEETA Apollodorus: rebuke this Roman dog; and bid him bridle his tongue in the presence of Ftatateeta, the mistress of the Queen's household.

APOLLODORUS My friend: this is a great lady, who stands high with Cæsar.

SENTINEL [*not at all impressed, pointing to the carpets*] And what is all this truck?

APOLLODORUS Carpets for the furnishing of the Queen's apartments in the palace. I have picked them from the best carpets in the world; and the Queen shall choose the best of my choosing.

SENTINEL So you are the carpet merchant?

APOLLODORUS [*hurt*] My friend: I am a patrician.

SENTINEL A patrician! A patrician keeping a shop instead of following arms!

APOLLODORUS I do not keep a shop. Mine is a temple of the arts. I am a worshipper of beauty. My calling is to choose beautiful things for beautiful queens. My motto is Art for Art's sake.

SENTINEL That is not the password.

APOLLODORUS It is a universal password.

SENTINEL I know nothing about universal passwords. Either give me the password for the day or get back to your shop.

[*Ftatateeta, roused by his hostile tone, steals towards the edge of the quay with the step of a panther, and gets behind him.*]

APOLLODORUS How if I do neither?

SENTINEL Then I will drive this pilum through you.

APOLLODORUS At your service, my friend.

[*He draws his sword, and springs to his guard with unruffled grace*].

FTATATEETA [*suddenly seizing the sentinel's arms from behind*] Thrust your knife into the dog's throat, Apollodorus.

[*The chivalrous Apollodorus laughingly shakes his head; breaks ground away from the sentinel towards the palace; and lowers his point*].

SENTINEL [*struggling vainly*] Curse on you! Let me go. Help ho!

FTATATEETA [*lifting him from the ground*] Stab the little Roman reptile. Spit him on your sword.

[*A couple of Roman soldiers, with a centurion, come running along the edge of the quay from the north end. They rescue their comrade, and throw off Ftatateeta, who is sent reeling away on the left hand of the sentinel.*]

CENTURION [*an unattractive man of fifty, short in his speech and manners, with a vinewood cudgel in his hand*] How now? What is all this?

FTATATEETA [*to Apollodorus*] Why did you not stab him? There was time!

APOLLODORUS Centurion: I am here by order of the Queen to—

CENTURION [*interrupting him*] The Queen! Yes, yes: [*to the sentinel*] pass him in. Pass all these bazaar people in to the Queen, with their goods. But mind you pass no one out that you have not passed in—not even the Queen herself.

SENTINEL   This old woman is dangerous: she is as strong as three men. She wanted the merchant to stab me.

APOLLODORUS   Centurion: I am not a merchant. I am a patrician and a votary of art.

CENTURION   Is the woman your wife?

APOLLODORUS   [horrified]   No, no! [Correcting himself politely] Not that the lady is not a striking figure in her own way. But [emphatically] she is not my wife.

FTATATEETA   [to the centurion]   Roman: I am Ftatateeta, the mistress of the Queen's household.

CENTURION   Keep your hands off our men, mistress; or I will have you pitched into the harbor, though you were as strong as ten men. [To his men] To your posts: march!

[He returns with his men the way they came].

FTATATEETA   [looking malignantly after him]   We shall see whom Isis loves best: her servant Ftatateeta or a dog of a Roman.

SENTINEL   [to Apollodorus, with a wave of his pilum towards the palace]   Pass in there; and keep your distance. [Turning to Ftatateeta] Come within a yard of me, you old crocodile; and I will give you this [the pilum] in your jaws.

CLEOPATRA   [calling from the palace]   Ftatateeta, Ftatateeta.

FTATATEETA   [looking up, scandalized]   Go from the window, go from the window. There are men here.

CLEOPATRA   I am coming down.

FTATATEETA   [distracted]   No, no. What are you dreaming of? O ye gods, ye gods! Apollodorus: bid your men pick up your bales; and in with me quickly.

APOLLODORUS   Obey the mistress of the Queen's household.

FTATATEETA   [impatiently, as the porters stoop to lift the bales]   Quick, quick: she will be out upon us. [Cleopatra comes from the palace and runs across the quay to Ftatateeta]. Oh that ever I was born!

CLEOPATRA   [eagerly]   Ftatateeta: I have thought of something. I want a boat— at once.

FTATATEETA   A boat! No, no: you cannot, Apollodorus: speak to the Queen.

APOLLODORUS   [gallantly]   Beautiful queen: I am Apollodorus the Sicilian, your servant, from the bazaar. I have brought you the three most beautiful Persian carpets in the world to choose from.

CLEOPATRA   I have no time for carpets today. Get me a boat.

FTATATEETA   What whim is this? You cannot go on the water except in the royal barge.

APOLLODORUS   Royalty, Ftatateeta, lies not in the barge but in the Queen. [To Cleopatra] The touch of your majesty's foot on the gunwale of the meanest boat in the harbor will make it royal. [He turns to the harbor and calls seaward] Ho there, boatman! Pull in to the steps.

CLEOPATRA   Apollodorus: you are my perfect knight; and I will always buy my carpets through you. [Apollodorus bows joyously. An oar appears above the quay; and the boatman, a bullet-headed, vivacious, grinning fellow, burnt almost black by the sun, comes up a flight of steps from the water on the sentinel's right, oar in hand, and waits at the top]. Can you row, Apollodorus?

APOLLODORUS   My oars shall be your majesty's wings. Whither shall I row my Queen?

CLEOPATRA   To the lighthouse. Come. [She makes for the steps].

SENTINEL   [*opposing her with his pilum at the charge*]   Stand. You cannot pass.

CLEOPATRA   [*flushing angrily*]   How dare you? Do you know that I am the Queen?

SENTINEL   I have my orders. You cannot pass.

CLEOPATRA   I will make Cæsar have you killed if you do not obey me.

SENTINEL   He will do worse to me if I disobey my officer. Stand back.

CLEOPATRA   Ftatateeta: strangle him.

SENTINEL   [*alarmed—looking apprehensively at Ftatateeta, and brandishing his pilum*]   Keep off, there.

CLEOPATRA   [*running to Apollodorus*]   Apollodorus: make your slaves help us.

APOLLODORUS   I shall not need their help, lady. [*He draws his sword*]. Now, soldier: choose which weapon you will defend yourself with. Shall it be sword against pilum, or sword against sword?

SENTINEL   Roman against Sicilian, curse you. Take that. [*He hurls his pilum at Apollodorus, who drops expertly on one knee. The pilum passes whizzing over his head and falls harmless. Apollodorus, with a cry of triumph, springs up and attacks the sentinel, who draws his sword and defends himself, crying*] Ho there, guard. Help!

[*Cleopatra, half frightened, half delighted, takes refuge near the palace, where the porters are squatting among the bales. The boatman, alarmed, hurries down the steps out of harm's way, but stops, with his head just visible above the edge of the quay, to watch the fight. The sentinel is handicapped by his fear of an attack in the rear from Ftatateeta. His swordsmanship, which is of rough and ready sort, is heavily taxed, as he has occasionally to strike at her to keep her off between a blow and a guard with Apollodorus. The centurion returns with several soldiers. Apollodorus springs back towards Cleopatra as this reinforcement confronts him.*]

CENTURION   [*coming to the sentinel's right hand*]   What is this? What now?

SENTINEL   [*panting*]   I could do well enough by myself if it werent for the old woman. Keep her off me: that is all the help I need.

CENTURION   Make your report, soldier. What has happened?

FTATATEETA   Centurion: he would have slain the Queen.

SENTINEL   [*bluntly*]   I would, sooner than let her pass. She wanted to take boat, and go—so she said—to the lighthouse. I stopped her, as I was ordered to; and she set this fellow on me.

[*He goes to pick up his pilum and returns to his place with it*].

CENTURION   [*turning to Cleopatra*]   Cleopatra: I am loth to offend you; but without Cæsar's express order we dare not let you pass beyond the Roman lines.

APOLLODORUS   Well, Centurion; and has not the lighthouse been within the Roman lines since Cæsar landed there?

CLEOPATRA   Yes, yes. Answer that, if you can.

CENTURION   [*to Apollodorus*]   As for you, Apollodorus, you may thank the gods that you are not nailed to the palace door with a pilum for your meddling.

APOLLODORUS   [*urbanely*]   My military friend, I was not born to be slain by so ugly a weapon. When I fall, it will be [*holding up his sword*] by this white queen of arms, the only weapon fit for an artist. And now that you are convinced that we do not want to go beyond the lines, let me finish killing your sentinel and depart with the Queen.

CENTURION   [*as the sentinel makes an angry demonstration*]   Peace there, Cleopatra: I must abide by my orders, and not by the subtleties of this Sicilian. You must withdraw into the palace and examine your carpets there.

CLEOPATRA [*pouting*] I will not: I am the Queen. Cæsar does not speak to me as you do. Have Cæsar's centurions changed manners with his scullions?

CENTURION [*sulkily*] I do my duty. That is enough for me.

APOLLODORUS Majesty: when a stupid man is doing something he is ashamed of, he always declares that it is his duty.

CENTURION [*angry*] Apollodorus—

APOLLODORUS [*interrupting him with defiant elegance*] I will make amends for that insult with my sword at fitting time and place. Who says artist, says duellist. [*To Cleopatra*] Hear my counsel, star of the east. Until word comes to these soldiers from Cæsar himself, you are a prisoner. Let me go to him with a message from you, and a present; and before the sun has stooped half way to the arms of the sea, I will bring you back Cæsar's order of release.

CENTURION [*sneering at him*] And you will sell the Queen the present, no doubt.

APOLLODORUS Centurion: the Queen shall have from me, without payment, as the unforced tribute of Sicilian taste to Egyptian beauty, the richest of these carpets for her present to Cæsar.

CLEOPATRA [*exultantly, to the centurion*] Now you see what an ignorant common creature you are!

CENTURION [*curtly*] Well, a fool and his wares are soon parted. [*He turns to his men*] Two more men to this post here; and see that no one leaves the palace but this man and his merchandize. If he draws his sword again inside the lines, kill him. To your posts. March.

[*He goes out, leaving two auxiliary sentinels with the other.*]

APOLLODORUS [*with polite goodfellowship*] My friends: will you not enter the palace and bury our quarrel in a bowl of wine? [*He takes out his purse, jingling the coins in it*]. The Queen has presents for you all.

SENTINEL [*very sulky*] You heard our orders. Get about your business.

FIRST AUXILIARY Yes: you ought to know better. Off with you.

SECOND AUXILIARY [*looking longingly at the purse—this sentinel is a hooknosed man, unlike his comrade, who is squab faced*] Do not tantalize a poor man.

APOLLODORUS [*to Cleopatra*] Pearl of Queens: the centurion is at hand; and the Roman soldier is incorruptible when his officer is looking. I must carry your word to Cæsar.

CLEOPATRA [*who has been meditating among the carpets*] Are these carpets very heavy?

APOLLODORUS It matters not how heavy. There are plenty of porters.

CLEOPATRA How do they put the carpets into boats? Do they throw them down?

APOLLODORUS Not into small boats, majesty. It would sink them.

CLEOPATRA Not into that man's boat, for instance? [*pointing to the boatman*].

APOLLODORUS No. Too small.

CLEOPATRA But you can take a carpet to Cæsar in it if I send one?

APOLLODORUS Assuredly.

CLEOPATRA And you will have it carried gently down the steps and take great care of it?

APOLLODORUS Depend on me.

CLEOPATRA Great, great care?

APOLLODORUS More than of my own body.

CLEOPATRA You will promise me not to let the porters drop it or throw it about?

APOLLODORUS Place the most delicate glass goblet in the palace in the heart of the roll, Queen; and if it be broken, my head shall pay for it.

CLEOPATRA Good. Come, Ftatateeta. [*Ftatateeta comes to her. Apollodorus offers to squire them into the palace*]. No, Apollodorus, you must not come. I will choose a carpet for myself. You must wait here. [*She runs into the palace*].

APOLLODORUS [*to the porters*] Follow this lady [*indicating Ftatateeta*] and obey her.
[*The porters rise and take up their bales.*]

FTATATEETA [*addressing the porters as if they were vermin*] This way. And take your shoes off before you put your feet on those stairs.
[*She goes in, followed by the porters with the carpets. Meanwhile Apollodorus goes to the edge of the quay and looks out over the harbor. The sentinels keep their eyes on him malignantly.*]

APOLLODORUS [*addressing the sentinel*] My friend—

SENTINEL [*rudely*] Silence there.

FIRST AUXILIARY Shut your muzzle, you.

SECOND AUXILIARY [*in a half whisper, glancing apprehensively towards the north end of the quay*] Cant you wait a bit?

APOLLODORUS Patience, worthy three-headed donkey. [*They mutter ferociously; but he is not at all intimidated*]. Listen: were you set here to watch me, or to watch the Egyptians?

SENTINEL We know our duty.

APOLLODORUS Then why dont you do it? There is something going on over there [*pointing southwestward to the mole*].

SENTINEL [*sulkily*] I do not need to be told what to do by the like of you.

APOLLODORUS Blockhead. [*He begins shouting*] Ho there, Centurion. Hoiho!

SENTINEL Curse your meddling. [*Shouting*] Hoiho! Alarm! Alarm!

FIRST AND SECOND AUXILIARIES Alarm! alarm! Hoiho!
[*The Centurion comes running in with his guard.*]

CENTURION What now? Has the old woman attacked you again? [*Seeing Apollodorus*] Are you here still?

APOLLODORUS [*pointing as before*] See there. The Egyptians are moving. They are going to recapture the Pharos. They will attack by sea and land: by land along the great mole; by sea from the west harbor. Stir yourselves, my military friends: the hunt is up. [*A clangor of trumpets from several points along the quay*]. Aha! I told you so.

CENTURION [*quickly*] The two extra men pass the alarm to the south posts. One man keep guard here. The rest with me—quick.
[*The two auxiliary sentinels run off to the south. The centurion and his guard run off northward; and immediately afterwards the bucina sounds. The four porters come from the palace carrying a carpet, followed by Ftatateeta.*]

SENTINEL [*handling his pilum apprehensively*] You again!
[*The porters stop*].

FTATATEETA Peace, Roman fellow: you are now singlehanded. Apollodorus: this carpet is Cleopatra's present to Cæsar. It has rolled up in it ten precious goblets of the thinnest Iberian crystal, and a hundred eggs of the sacred blue pigeon. On your honor, let not one of them be broken.

APOLLODORUS On my head be it! [*To the porters*] Into the boat with them carefully.
[*The porters carry the carpet to the steps.*]

FIRST PORTER [*looking down at the boat*] Beware what you do, sir. Those eggs of which the lady speaks must weigh more than a pound apiece. This boat is too small for such a load.

BOATMAN [*excitedly rushing up the steps*] Oh thou injurious porter! Oh thou unnatural son of a she-camel! [*To Apollodorus*] My boat, sir, hath often carried five men. Shall it not carry your lordship and a bale of pigeon's eggs? [*To the porter*] Thou mangey dromedary, the gods shall punish thee for this envious wickedness.

FIRST PORTER [*stolidly*] I cannot quit this bale now to beat these; but another day I will lie in wait for thee.

APOLLODORUS [*going between them*] Peace there. If the boat were but a single plank, I would get to Cæsar on it.

FTATATEETA [*anxiously*] In the name of the gods, Apollodorus, run no risks with that bale.

APOLLODORUS Fear not, thou venerable grotesque: I guess its great worth. [*To the porters*] Down with it, I say; and gently; or ye shall eat nothing but stick for ten days.

[*The boatman goes down the steps, followed by the porters with the bale: Ftatateeta and Apollodorus watching from the edge.*]

APOLLODORUS Gently, my sons, my children—[*with sudden alarm*] gently, ye dogs. Lay it level in the stern—so—tis well.

FTATATEETA [*screaming down at one of the porters*] Do not step on it, do not step on it. Oh thou brute beast!

FIRST PORTER [*ascending*] Be not excited, mistress: all is well.

FTATATEETA [*panting*] All well! Oh, thou hast given my heart a turn! [*She clutches her side, gasping*].

[*The four porters have now come up and are waiting at the stairhead to be paid.*]

APOLLODORUS Here, ye hungry ones. [*He gives money to the first porter, who holds it in his hand to shew to the others. They crowd greedily to see how much it is, quite prepared, after the Eastern fashion, to protest to heaven against their patron's stinginess. But his liberality overpowers them*].

FIRST PORTER O bounteous prince!

SECOND PORTER O lord of the bazaar!

THIRD PORTER O favored of the gods!

FOURTH PORTER O father to all the porters of the market.

SENTINEL [*enviously, threatening them fiercely with his pilum*] Hence, dogs: off. Out of this. [*They fly before him northward along the quay*].

APOLLODORUS Farewell, Ftatateeta. I shall be at the lighthouse before the Egyptians. [*He descends the steps*].

FTATATEETA The gods speed thee and protect my nursling!

[*The sentry returns from chasing the porters and looks down at the boat, standing near the stairhead lest Ftatateeta should attempt to escape.*]

APOLLODORUS [*from beneath, as the boat moves off*] Farewell, valiant pilum pitcher.

SENTINEL Farewell, shopkeeper.

APOLLODORUS Ha, ha! Pull, thou brave boatman, pull. Soho-o-o-o-o! [*He begins to sing in barcarolle measure to the rhythm of the oars*]

My heart, my heart, spread out thy wings:
Shake off thy heavy load of love—

Give me the oars, O son of a snail.

SENTINEL [*threatening Ftatateeta*] Now mistress: back to your henhouse. In with you.

FTATATEETA [*falling on her knees and stretching her hands over the waters*] Gods of the seas, bear her safely to the shore!

SENTINEL Bear who safely? What do you mean?

FTATATEETA   [*looking darkly at him*]   Gods of Egypt and of Vengeance, let this Roman fool be beaten like a dog by his captain for suffering her to be taken over the waters.

SENTINEL   Accursed one: is she then in the boat? [*He calls over the sea*] Hoiho, there, boatman! Hoiho!

APOLLODORUS   [*singing in the distance*]

> My heart, my heart, be whole and free:
> Love is thine only enemy.

[*Meanwhile Rufio, the morning's fighting done, sits munching dates on a faggot of brushwood outside the door of the lighthouse, which towers gigantic to the clouds on his left. His helmet, full of dates, is between his knees; and a leathern bottle of wine is by his side. Behind him the great stone pedestal of the lighthouse is shut in from the open sea by a low stone parapet, with a couple of steps in the middle to the broad coping. A huge chain with a hook hangs down from the lighthouse crane above his head. Faggots like the one he sits on lie beneath it ready to be drawn up to feed the beacon. Cæsar is standing on the step at the parapet looking out anxiously, evidently ill at ease. Britannus comes out of the lighthouse door.*]

RUFIO   Well, my British islander. Have you been up to the top?

BRITANNUS   I have. I reckon it at 200 feet high.

RUFIO   Anybody up there?

BRITANNUS   One elderly Tyrian to work the crane; and his son, a well conducted youth of 14.

RUFIO   [*looking at the chain*]   What! An old man and a boy work that! Twenty men, you mean.

BRITANNUS   Two only, I assure you. They have counterweights, and a machine with boiling water in it which I do not understand: it is not of British design. They use it to haul up barrels of oil and faggots to burn in the brazier on the roof.

RUFIO   But—

BRITANNUS   Excuse me: I came down because there are messengers coming along the mole to us from the island. I must see what their business is. [*He hurries out past the lighthouse*].

CÆSAR   [*coming away from the parapet, shivering and out of sorts*] Rufio: this has been a mad expedition. We shall be beaten. I wish I knew how our men are getting on with that barricade across the great mole.

RUFIO   [*angrily*]   Must I leave my food and go starving to bring you a report?

CÆSAR   [*soothing him nervously*]   No, Rufio, no. Eat, my son, eat. [*He takes another turn, Rufio chewing dates meanwhile*]. The Egyptians cannot be such fools as not to storm the barricade and swoop down on us here before it is finished. It is the first time I have ever run an avoidable risk. I should not have come to Egypt.

RUFIO   An hour ago you were all for victory.

CÆSAR   [*apologetically*]   Yes: I was a fool—rash, Rufio—boyish.

RUFIO   Boyish! Not a bit of it. Here [*offering him a handful of dates*].

CÆSAR   What are these for?

RUFIO   To eat. Thats whats the matter with you. When a man comes to your age, he runs down before his midday meal. Eat and drink; and then have another look at our chances.

CÆSAR   [*taking the dates*]   My age! [*He shakes his head and bites a date*]. Yes, Rufio: I am an old man—worn out now—true, quite true. [*He gives way to melancholy contemplation, and eats another date*]. Achillas is still in his prime: Ptolemy is a boy. [*He eats another date, and plucks up a little*]. Well, every dog has his day; and I have had mine: I cannot complain. [*With sudden cheerfulness*] These dates are not bad, Rufio. [*Britannus returns, greatly excited, with a leathern bag. Cæsar is himself again in a moment*]. What now?

BRITANNUS   [*triumphantly*]   Our brave Rhodian mariners have captured a treasure. There! [*He throws the bag down at Cæsar's feet*]. Our enemies are delivered into our hands.

CÆSAR   In that bag?

BRITANNUS   Wait till you hear, Cæsar. This bag contains all the letters which have passed between Pompey's party and the army of occupation here.

CÆSAR   Well?

BRITTANUS   [*impatient of Cæsar's slowness to grasp the situation*]   Well, we shall now know who your foes are. The name of every man who has plotted against you since you crossed the Rubicon may be in these papers, for all we know.

CÆSAR   Put them in the fire.

BRITANNUS   Put them—[*he gasps*]!!!!

CÆSAR   In the fire. Would you have me waste the next three years of my life of proscribing and condemning men who will be my friends when I have proved that my friendship is worth more than Pompey's was—than Cato's is. O incorrigible British islander: am I a bull dog, to seek quarrels merely to shew how stubborn my jaws are?

BRITANNUS   But your honor—the honor of Rome—

CÆSAR   I do not make human sacrifices to my honor, as your Druids do. Since you will not burn these, at least I can drown them. [*He picks up the bag and throws it over the parapet into the sea*].

BRITANNUS   Cæsar: this is mere eccentricity. Are traitors to be allowed to go free for the sake of a paradox?

RUFIO   [*rising*]   Cæsar: when the islander has finished preaching, call me again. I am going to have a look at the boiling water machine. [*He goes into the lighthouse*].

BRITANNUS   [*with genuine feeling*]   O Cæsar, my great master, if I could but persuade you to regard life seriously, as men do in my country!

CÆSAR   Do they truly do so, Britannus?

BRITANNUS   Have you not been there? Have you not seen them? What Briton speaks as you do in your moments of levity? What Briton neglects to attend the services at the sacred grove? What Briton wears clothes of many colors as you do, instead of plain blue, as all solid, well esteemed men should? These are moral questions with us.

CÆSAR   Well, well, my friend: some day I shall settle down and have a blue toga, perhaps. Meanwhile, I must get on as best I can in my flippant Roman way. [*Apollodorus comes past the lighthouse*]. What now?

BRITANNUS   [*turning quickly, and challenging the stranger with official haughtiness*]   What is this? Who are you? How did you come here?

APOLLODORUS   Calm yourself, my friend: I am not going to eat you. I have come by boat, from Alexandria, with precious gifts for Cæsar.

CÆSAR   From Alexandria!

BRITANNUS   [*severely*]   This is Cæsar, sir.

RUFIO   [*appearing at the lighthouse door*]   Whats the matter now?

APOLLODORUS   Hail, great Cæsar! I am Apollodorus the Sicilian, an artist.

BRITANNUS   An artist! Why have they admitted this vagabond?

CÆSAR   Peace, man. Apollodorus is a famous patrician amateur.

BRITANNUS   [*disconcerted*]   I crave the gentleman's pardon. [*To Cæsar*] I understood him to say that he was a professional.

[*Somewhat out of countenance, he allows Apollodorus to approach Cæsar, changing places with him. Rufio, after looking Apollodorus up and down with marked disparagement, goes to the other side of the platform*].

CÆSAR   You are welcome, Apollodorus. What is your business?

APOLLODORUS   First, to deliver to you a present from the Queen of Queens.

CÆSAR   Who is that?

APOLLODORUS   Cleopatra of Egypt.

CÆSAR   [*taking him into his confidence in his most winning manner*] Apollodorus: this is no time for playing with presents. Pray you, go back to the Queen, and tell her that if all goes well I shall return to the palace this evening.

APOLLODORUS   Cæsar: I cannot return. As I approached the lighthouse, some fool threw a great leathern bag into the sea. It broke the nose of my boat; and I had hardly time to get myself and my charge to the shore before the poor little cockleshell sank.

CÆSAR   I am sorry, Apollodorus. The fool shall be rebuked. Well, well: what have you brought me? The Queen will be hurt if I do not look at it.

RUFIO   Have we time to waste on this trumpery? The Queen is only a child.

CÆSAR   Just so: that is why we must not disappoint her. What is the present, Apollodorus?

APOLLODORUS   Cæsar: it is a Persian carpet—a beauty! And in it are—so I am told—pigeons' eggs and crystal goblets and fragile precious things. I dare not for my head have it carried up that narrow ladder from the causeway.

RUFIO   Swing it up by the crane, then. We will send the eggs to the cook; drink our wine from the goblets; and the carpet will make a bed for Cæsar.

APOLLODORUS   The crane! Cæsar: I have sworn to tender this bale of carpet as I tender my own life.

CÆSAR   [*cheerfully*]   Then let them swing you up at the same time; and if the chain breaks, you and the pigeons' eggs will perish together.

[*He goes to the chain and looks up along it, examining it curiously*].

APOLLODORUS   [*to Britannus*]   Is Cæsar serious?

BRITANNUS   His manner is frivolous because he is an Italian; but he means what he says.

APOLLODORUS   Serious or not, he spake well. Give me a squad of soldiers to work the crane.

BRITANNUS   Leave the crane to me. Go and await the descent of the chain.

APOLLODORUS   Good. You will presently see me there [*turning to them all and pointing with an eloquent gesture to the sky above the parapet*] rising like the sun with my treasure.

[*He goes back the way he came. Britannus goes into the lighthouse.*]

RUFIO   [*ill-humoredly*]   Are you really going to wait here for this foolery, Cæsar?

CÆSAR   [*backing away from the crane as it gives signs of working*]   Why not?

RUFIO   The Egyptians will let you know why not if they have the sense to make a rush from the shore end of the mole before our barricade is finished. And here we are waiting like children to see a carpet full of pigeons' eggs.

[*The chain rattles, and is drawn up high enough to clear the parapet. It then swings round out of sight behind the lighthouse.*]

CÆSAR   Fear not, my son Rufio. When the first Egyptian takes his first step along the mole, the alarm will sound; and we two will reach the barricade from our end before the Egyptians reach it from their end—we two, Rufio: I, the old man, and you, his biggest boy. And the old man will be there first. So peace; and give me some more dates.

APOLLODORUS   [*from the causeway below*]   Soho, haul away. So-ho-o-o-o!

[*The chain is drawn up and comes round again from behind the lighthouse.*]

Apollodorus is swinging in the air with his bale of carpet at the end of it. He breaks into song as he soars above the parapet]

> Aloft, aloft, behold the blue
> That never shone in woman's eyes

Easy there: stop her. [*He ceases to rise*]. Further round!
[*The chain comes forward above the platform*].

RUFIO [*calling up*] Lower away there. [*The chain and its load begin to descend*].

APOLLODORUS [*calling up*] Gently—slowly—mind the eggs.

RUFIO [*calling up*] Easy there—slowly—slowly.
[*Apollodorus and the bale are deposited safely on the flags in the middle of the platform. Rufio and Cæsar help Apollodorus to cast off the chain from the bale.*]

RUFIO Haul up.
[*The chain rises clear of their heads with a rattle. Britannus comes from the lighthouse and helps them to uncord the carpet.*]

APOLLODORUS [*when the cords are loose*] Stand off, my friends: let Cæsar see.
[*He throws the carpet open*].

RUFIO Nothing but a heap of shawls. Where are the pigeons' eggs?

APOLLODORUS Approach, Cæsar; and search for them among the shawls.

RUFIO [*drawing his sword*] Ha, treachery! Keep back, Cæsar: I saw the shawl move: there is something alive there.

BRITANNUS [*drawing his sword*] It is a serpent.

APOLLODORUS Dares Cæsar thrust his hand into the sack where the serpent moves?

RUFIO [*turning on him*] Treacherous dog—

CÆSAR Peace. Put up your swords. Apollodorus: your serpent seems to breathe very regularly. [*He thrusts his hand under the shawls and draws out a bare arm*]. This is a pretty little snake.

RUFIO [*drawing out the other arm*] Let us have the rest of you.
[*They pull Cleopatra up by the wrists into a sitting position. Britannus, scandalized, sheathes his sword with a drive of protest.*]

CLEOPATRA [*gasping*] Oh, I'm smothered. Oh, Cæsar, a man stood on me in the boat; and a great sack of something fell upon me out of the sky; and then the boat sank; and then I was swung up into the air and bumped down.

CÆSAR [*petting her as she rises and takes refuge on his breast*] Well, never mind: here you are safe and sound at last.

RUFIO Ay; and now that she is here, where are we to do with her?

BRITANNUS She cannot stay here, Cæsar, without the companionship of some matron.

CLEOPATRA [*jealously, to Cæsar, who is obviously perplexed*] Arent you glad to see me?

CÆSAR Yes, yes; *I* am very glad. But Rufio is very angry; and Britannus is shocked.

CLEOPATRA [*contemptuously*] You can have their heads cut off, can you not?

CÆSAR They would not be so useful with their heads cut off as they are now, my sea bird.

RUFIO [*to Cleopatra*] We shall have to go away presently and cut some of your Egyptians' heads off. How will you like being left here with the chance of being captured by that little brother of yours if we are beaten?

CLEOPATRA But you mustnt leave me alone. Cæsar: you will not leave me alone, will you?

RUFIO   What! not when the trumpet sounds and all our lives depend on Cæsar's being at the barricade before the Egyptians reach it? Eh?

CLEOPATRA   Let them lose their lives: they are only soldiers.

CÆSAR   [*gravely*]   Cleopatra: when that trumpet sounds, we must take every man his life in his hand, and throw it in the face of Death. And of my soldiers who have trusted me there is not one whose hand I shall not hold more sacred than your head. [*Cleopatra is overwhelmed. Her eyes fill with tears*]. Apollodorus: you must take her back to the palace.

APOLLODORUS   Am I a dolphin, Cæsar, to cross the seas with young ladies on my back? My boat is sunk: all yours are either at the barricade or have returned to the city. I will hail one if I can: that is all I can do. [*He goes back to the causeway*].

CLEOPATRA   [*struggling with her tears*]   It does not matter. I will not go back. Nobody cares for me.

CÆSAR   Cleopatra—

CLEOPATRA   You want me to be killed.

CÆSAR   [*still more gravely*]   My poor child: your life matters little here to any-one but yourself.
[*She gives way altogether at this, casting herself down on the faggots weeping. Suddenly a great tumult is heard in the distance, bucinas and trumpets sounding through a storm of shouting. Britannus rushes to the parapet and looks along the mole. Cæsar and Rufio turn to one another with quick in-telligence*].

CÆSAR   Come, Rufio.

CLEOPATRA   [*scrambling to her knees and clinging to him*].   No no. Do not leave me, Cæsar. [*He snatches his skirt from her clutch*]. Oh!

BRITANNUS   [*from the parapet*]   Cæsar: we are cut off. The Egyptians have landed from the west harbor between us and the barricade!!!

RUFIO   [*running to see*]   Curses! It is true. We are caught like rats in a trap.

CÆSAR   [*ruthfully*]   Rufio, Rufio: my men at the barricade are between the sea party and the shore party. I have murdered them.

RUFIO   [*coming back from the parapet to Cæsar's right hand*]   Ay: that comes of fooling with this girl here.

APOLLODORUS   [*coming up quickly from the causeway*]   Look over the parapet, Cæsar.

CÆSAR   We have looked, my friend. We must defend ourselves here.

APOLLODORUS   I have thrown the ladder into the sea. They cannot get in without it.

RUFIO   Ay; and we cannot get out. Have you thought of that?

APOLLODORUS   Not get out! Why not? You have ships in the east harbor.

BRITANNUS   [*hopefully, at the parapet*]   The Rhodian galleys are standing in towards us already. [*Cæsar quickly joins Britannus at the parapet*].

RUFIO   [*to Apollodorus, impatiently*]   And by what road are we to walk to the galleys, pray?

APOLLODORUS   [*with gay, defiant rhetoric*]   By the road that leads everywhere— the diamond path of the sun and moon. Have you never seen the child's shadow play of The Broken Bridge? "Ducks and geese with ease get over"— eh? [*He throws away his cloak and cap, and binds his sword on his back*].

RUFIO   What are you talking about?

APOLLODORUS   I will shew you. [*Calling to Britannus*] How far off is the nearest galley?

BRITANNUS   Fifty fathom.

CÆSAR   No, no: they are further off than they seem in this clear air to your British eyes. Nearly quarter of a mile, Apollodorus.

APOLLODORUS   Good. Defend yourselves here until I send you a boat from that galley.

RUFIO   Have you wings, perhaps?

APOLLODORUS   Water wings, soldier. Behold!

[*He runs up the steps between Cæsar and Britannus to the coping of the parapet; springs into the air; and plunges head foremost into the sea.*]

CÆSAR   [*like a schoolboy—wildly excited*]   Bravo, bravo! [*Throwing off his cloak*] By Jupiter, I will do that too.

RUFIO   [*seizing him*]   You are mad. You shall not.

CÆSAR   Why not? Can I not swim as well as he?

RUFIO   [*frantic*]   Can an old fool dive and swim like a young one? He is twenty-five and you are fifty.

CÆSAR   [*breaking loose from Rufio*]   Old!!!

BRITANNUS   [*shocked*]   Rufio: you forget yourself.

CÆSAR   I will race you to the galley for a week's pay, father Rufio.

CLEOPATRA   But me! me!! me!!! what is to become of me?

CÆSAR   I will carry you on my back to the galley like a dolphin. Rufio: when you see me rise to the surface, throw her in: I will answer for her. And then in with you after her, both of you.

CLEOPATRA   No, no, NO. I shall be drowned.

BRITANNUS   Cæsar: I am a man and a Briton, not a fish. I must have a boat. I cannot swim.

CLEOPATRA   Neither can I.

CÆSAR   [*to Britannus*]   Stay here, then, alone, until I recapture the lighthouse: I will not forget you. Now, Rufio.

RUFIO   You have made up your mind to this folly?

CÆSAR   The Egyptians have made it up for me. What else is there to do? And mind where you jump: I do not want to get your fourteen stone in the small of my back as I come up. [*He runs up the steps and stands on the coping*].

BRITANNUS   [*anxiously*]   One last word, Cæsar. Do not let yourself be seen in the fashionable part of Alexandria until you have changed your clothes.

CÆSAR   [*calling over the sea*]   Ho, Apollodorus: [*he points skyward and quotes the barcarolle*]

The white upon the blue above—

APOLLODORUS   [*swimming in the distance*]

Is purple on the green below—

CÆSAR   [*exultantly*]   Aha! [*He plunges into the sea*].

CLEOPATRA   [*running excitedly to the steps*]   Oh, let me see. He will be drowned [*Rufio seizes her*]—Ah—ah—ah—ah! [*He pitches her screaming into the sea. Rufio and Britannus roar with laughter*].

RUFIO   [*looking down after her*].   He has got her. [*To Britannus*] Hold the fort, Briton. Cæsar will not forget you. [*He springs off*].

BRITANNUS   [*running to the steps to watch them as they swim*]   All safe, Rufio?

RUFIO   [*swimming*]   All safe.

CÆSAR   [*swimming further off*]   Take refuge up there by the beacon; and pile the fuel on the trap door, Britannus.

BRITANNUS   [*calling in reply*]   I will first do so, and then commend myself to my country's gods. [*A sound of cheering from the sea. Britannus gives full vent to his excitement*]. The boat has reached him: Hip, hip, hip, hurrah!

ACT IV

> *Cleopatra's sousing in the east harbor of Alexandria was in October 48 B.C. In March 47 she is passing the afternoon in her boudoir in the palace, among a bevy of her ladies, listening to a slave girl who is playing the harp in the middle of the room. The harpist's master, an old musician, with a lined face, prominent brows, white beard, moustache and eyebrows twisted and horned at the ends, and a consciously keen and pretentious expression, is squatting on the floor close to her on her right, watching her performance. Ftatateeta is in attendance near the door, in front of a group of female slaves. Except the harp player all are seated: Cleopatra in a chair opposite the door on the other side of the room; the rest on the ground. Cleopatra's ladies are all young, the most conspicuous being Charmian and Iras, her favorites. Charmian is a hatchet faced, terra cotta colored little goblin, swift in her movements, and neatly finished at the hands and feet. Iras is a plump, goodnatured creature, rather fatuous, with a profusion of red hair, and a tendency to giggle on the slightest provocation.*

CLEOPATRA   Can I—

FTATATEETA   [*insolently, to the player*]   Peace, thou! The Queen speaks. [*The player stops*].

CLEOPATRA   [*to the old musician*]   I want to learn to play the harp with my own hands. Cæsar loves music. Can you teach me?

MUSICIAN   Assuredly I and no one else can teach the queen. Have I not discovered the lost method of the ancient Egyptians, who could make a pyramid tremble by touching a bass string? All the other teachers are quacks: I have exposed them repeatedly.

CLEOPATRA   Good: you shall teach me. How long will it take?

MUSICIAN   Not very long: only four years. Your Majesty must first become proficient in the philosophy of Pythagoras.

CLEOPATRA   Has she [*indicating the slave*] become proficient in the philosophy of Pythagoras?

MUSICIAN   Oh, she is but a slave. She learns as a dog learns.

CLEOPATRA   Well, then, I will learn as a dog learns; for she plays better than you. You shall give me a lesson every day for a fortnight. [*The musician hastily scrambles to his feet and bows profoundly*]. After that, whenever I strike a false note you shall be flogged; and if I strike so many that there is not time to flog you, you shall be thrown into the Nile to feed the crocodiles. Give the girl a piece of gold; and send them away.

MUSICIAN   [*much taken aback*]   But true art will not be thus forced.

FTATATEETA   [*pushing him out*]   What is this? Answering the Queen, forsooth. Out with you.

[*He is pushed out by Ftatateeta, the girl following with her harp, amid the laughter of the ladies and slaves.*]

CLEOPATRA   Now, can any of you amuse me? Have you any stories or any news?

IRAS   Ftatateeta—

CLEOPATRA   Oh, Ftatateeta, Ftatateeta, always Ftatateeta. Some new tale to set me against her.

IRAS   No: this time Ftatateeta has been virtuous. [*All the ladies laugh—not the slaves*]. Pothinus has been trying to bribe her to let him speak with you.

CLEOPATRA   [*wrathfully*]   Ha! you all sell audiences with me, as if I saw whom you please, and not whom I please. I should like to know how much of her gold piece that harp girl will have to give up before she leaves the palace.

IRAS   We can easily find out that for you.

[*The ladies laugh.*]

CLEOPATRA   [*frowning*]   You laugh; but take care, take care. I will find out some day how to make myself served as Cæsar is served.

CHARMIAN   Old hooknose! [*They laugh again*].

CLEOPATRA   [*revolted*]   Silence. Charmian: do not you be a silly little Egyptian fool. Do you know why I allow you all to chatter impertinently just as you please, instead of treating you as Ftatateeta would treat you if she were Queen?

CHARMIAN   Because you try to imitate Cæsar in everything; and he lets everybody say what they please to him.

CLEOPATRA   No; but because I asked him one day why he did so; and he said "Let your women talk; and you will learn something from them." What have I to learn from them? I said. "What they are," said he; and oh! you should have seen his eye as he said it. You would have curled up, you shallow things. [*They laugh. She turns fiercely on Iras*]. At whom are you laughing—at me or at Cæsar?

IRAS   At Cæsar.

CLEOPATRA   If you were not a fool, you would laugh at me; and if you were not a coward you would not be afraid to tell me so. [*Ftatateeta returns*]. Ftatateeta: they tell me that Pothinus has offered you a bribe to admit him to my presence.

FTATATEETA   [*protesting*]   Now by my father's gods—

CLEOPATRA   [*cutting her short despotically*]   Have I not told you not to deny things? You would spend the day calling your father's gods to witness to your virtues if I let you. Go take the bribe; and bring in Pothinus. [*Ftatateeta is about to reply*]. Dont answer me. Go.

[*Ftatateeta goes out; and Cleopatra rises and begins to prowl to and fro between her chair and the door, meditating. All rise and stand.*]

IRAS   [*as she reluctantly rises*]   Heigho! I wish Cæsar were back in Rome.

CLEOPATRA   [*threateningly*]   It will be a bad day for you all when he goes. Oh, if I were not ashamed to let him see that I am as cruel at heart as my father, I would make you repent that speech! Why do you wish him away?

CHARMIAN   He makes you so terribly prosy and serious and learned and philosophical. It is worse than being religious, at our ages. [*The ladies laugh*].

CLEOPATRA   Cease that endless cackling, will you. Hold your tongues.

CHARMIAN   [*with mock resignation*]   Well, well: we must try to live up to Cæsar.

[*They laugh again. Cleopatra rages silently as she continues to prowl to and fro. Ftatateeta comes back with Pothinus, who halts on the threshold.*]

FTATATEETA   [*at the door*]   Pothinus craves the ear of the—

CLEOPATRA   There, there: that will do: let him come in. [*She resumes her seat. All sit down except Pothinus, who advances to the middle of the room. Ftatateeta takes her former place*]. Well, Pothinus: what is the latest news from your rebel friends?

POTHINUS   [*haughtily*]   I am no friend of rebellion. And a prisoner does not receive news.

CLEOPATRA   You are no more a prisoner than I am—than Cæsar is. These six months we have been besieged in this palace by my subjects. You are allowed to walk on the beach among the soldiers. Can I go further myself, or can Cæsar?

POTHINUS   You are but a child, Cleopatra, and do not understand these matters. [*The ladies laugh. Cleopatra looks inscrutably at him.*]

CHARMIAN   I see you do not know the latest news, Pothinus.

POTHINUS   What is that?

CHARMIAN   That Cleopatra is no longer a child. Shall I tell you how to grow much older, and much, much wiser in one day?

POTHINUS   I should prefer to grow wiser without growing older.

CHARMIAN   Well, go up to the top of the lighthouse; and get somebody to take you by the hair and throw you into the sea. [*The ladies laugh*].

CLEOPATRA   She is right, Pothinus: you will come to the shore with much conceit washed out of you. [*The ladies laugh. Cleopatra rises impatiently*]. Begone, all of you. I will speak with Pothinus alone. Drive them out, Ftatateeta. [*They run out laughing. Ftatateeta shuts the door on them*]. What are you waiting for?

FTATATEETA   It is not meet that the Queen remain alone with—

CLEOPATRA   [*interrupting her*]   Ftatateeta: must I sacrifice you to your father's gods to teach you that *I* am Queen of Egypt, and not you?

FTATATEETA   [*indignantly*]   You are like the rest of them. You want to be what these Romans call a New Woman.
[*She goes out, banging the door*].

CLEOPATRA   [*sitting down again*]   Now, Pothinus: why did you bribe Ftatateeta to bring you hither?

POTHINUS   [*studying her gravely*]   Cleopatra: what they tell me is true. You are changed.

CLEOPATRA   Do you speak with Cæsar every day for six months: and you will be changed.

POTHINUS   It is the common talk that you are infatuated with this old man?

CLEOPATRA   Infatuated? What does that mean? Made foolish, is it not? Oh no: I wish I were.

POTHINUS   You wish you were made foolish! How so?

CLEOPATRA   When I was foolish, I did what I liked, except when Ftatateeta beat me; and even then I cheated her and did it by stealth. Now that Cæsar has made me wise, it is no use my liking or disliking: I do what must be done, and have no time to attend to myself. That is not happiness; but it is greatness. If Cæsar were gone, I think I could govern the Egyptians; for what Cæsar is to me, I am to the fools around me.

POTHINUS   [*looking hard at her*]   Cleopatra: this may be the vanity of youth.

CLEOPATRA   No, no: it is not that I am so clever, but that the others are so stupid.

POTHINUS   [*musingly*]   Truly, that is the great secret.

CLEOPATRA   Well, now tell me what you came to say?

POTHINUS   [*embarrassed*]   I! Nothing.

CLEOPATRA   Nothing!

POTHINUS   At least—to beg for my liberty: that is all.

CLEOPATRA   For that you would have knelt to Cæsar. No, Pothinus: you came with some plan that depended on Cleopatra being a little nursery kitten. Now that Cleopatra is a Queen, the plan is upset.

POTHINUS   [*bowing his head submissively*]   It is so.

CLEOPATRA   [*exultant*]   Aha!

POTHINUS   [*raising his eyes keenly to hers*]   Is Cleopatra then indeed a Queen, and no longer Cæsar's prisoner and slave?

CLEOPATRA   Pothinus: we are all Cæsar's slaves—all we in this land of Egypt—whether we will or no. And she who is wise enough to know this will reign when Cæsar departs.

POTHINUS   You harp on Cæsar's departure.

CLEOPATRA   What if I do?

POTHINUS   Does he not love you?

CLEOPATRA   Love me! Pothinus: Cæsar loves no one. Who are those we love. Only those whom we do not hate: all people are strangers and enemies to us except those we love. But it is not so with Cæsar. He has no hatred in him: he makes friends with everyone as he does with dogs and children. His kindness to me is a wonder: neither mother, father, nor nurse have ever taken so much care for me, or thrown open their thoughts to me so freely.

POTHINUS   Well: is not this love?

CLEOPATRA   What! when he will do as much for the first girl he meets on his way back to Rome? Ask his slave, Britannus: he has been just as good to him. Nay, ask his very horse! His kindness is not for anything in me: it is in his own nature.

POTHINUS   But how can you be sure that he does not love you as men love women?

CLEOPATRA   Because I cannot make him jealous. I have tried.

POTHINUS   Hm! Perhaps I should have asked, then, do you love him?

CLEOPATRA   Can one love a god? Besides, I love another Roman: one whom I saw long before Cæsar—no god, but a man—one who can love and hate—one whom I can hurt and who would hurt me.

POTHINUS   Does Cæsar know this?

CLEOPATRA   Yes.

POTHINUS   And he is not angry?

CLEOPATRA   He promises to send him to Egypt to please me!

POTHINUS   I do not understand this man.

CLEOPATRA   [with superb contempt]   You understand Cæsar! How could you? [Proudly] I do—by instinct.

POTHINUS   [deferentially, after a moment's thought]   Your Majesty caused me to be admitted today. What message has the Queen for me?

CLEOPATRA   This. You think that by making my brother king, you will rule in Egypt because you are his guardian and he is a little silly.

POTHINUS   The Queen is pleased to say so.

CLEOPATRA   The Queen is pleased to say this also. That Cæsar will eat up you, and Achillas, and my brother, as a cat eats up mice; and that he will put on this land of Egypt as a shepherd puts on his garment. And when he has done that, he will return to Rome, and leave Cleopatra here as his viceroy.

POTHINUS   [breaking out wrathfully]   That he shall never do. We have a thousand men to his ten; and we will drive him and his beggarly legions into the sea.

CLEOPATRA   [with scorn, getting up to go]   You rant like any common fellow. Go, then, and marshal your thousands; and make haste; for Mithridates of Pergamos is at hand with reinforcements for Cæsar. Cæsar has held you at bay with two legions: we shall see what he will do with twenty.

POTHINUS   Cleopatra—

CLEOPATRA   Enough, enough: Cæsar has spoiled me for talking to weak things like you.

[She goes out. Pothinus, with a gesture of rage, is following, when Ftatateeta enters and stops him.]

POTHINUS   Let me go forth from this hateful place.

FTATATEETA   What angers you?

POTHINUS   The curse of all the gods of Egypt be upon her! She sold her country to the Roman, that she may buy it back from him with her kisses.

FTATATEETA   Fool: did she not tell you that she would have Cæsar gone?

POTHINUS   You listened?

FTATATEETA   I took care that some honest woman should be at hand whilst you were with her.

POTHINUS   Now by the gods—

FTATATEETA   Enough of your gods! Cæsar's gods are all powerful here. It is no use you coming to Cleopatra: you are only an Egyptian. She will not listen to any of her own race: she treats us all as children.

POTHINUS   May she perish for it!

FTATATEETA   [*balefully*]   May your tongue wither for that wish! Go! send for Lucius Septimius, the slayer of Pompey. He is a Roman: may be she will listen to him. Begone!

POTHINUS   [*darkly*]   I know to whom I must go now.

FTATATEETA   [*suspiciously*]   To whom, then?

POTHINUS   To a greater Roman than Lucius. And mark this, mistress. You thought, before Cæsar came, that Egypt should presently be ruled by you and your crew in the name of Cleopatra. I set myself against it—

FTATATEETA   [*interrupting him—wrangling*]   Ay; that it might be ruled by you and your crew in the name of Ptolemy.

POTHINUS   Better me, or even you, than a woman with a Roman heart; and that is what Cleopatra is now become. Whilst I live, she shall never rule. So guide yourself accordingly. [*He goes out*].

[*It is by this time drawing on to dinner time. The table is laid on the roof of the palace; and thither Rufio is now climbing, ushered by a majestic palace official, wand of office in hand, and followed by a slave carrying an inlaid stool. After many stairs they emerge at last into a massive colonnade on the roof. Light curtains are drawn between the columns on the north and east to soften the westering sun. The official leads Rufio to one of these shaded sections. A cord for pulling the curtains apart hangs down between the pillars.*]

THE OFFICIAL   [*bowing*]   The Roman commander will await Cæsar here.

[*The slave sets down the stool near the southernmost column, and slips out through the curtains.*]

RUFIO   [*sitting down, a little blown*]   Pouf! That was a climb. How high have we come?

THE OFFICIAL   We are on the palace roof, O Beloved of Victory!

RUFIO   Good! the Beloved of Victory has no more stairs to get up.

[*A second official enters from the opposite end, walking backwards.*]

THE SECOND OFFICIAL   Cæsar approaches.

[*Cæsar, fresh from the bath, clad in a new tunic of purple silk, comes in, beaming and festive, followed by two slaves carrying a light couch, which is hardly more than an elaborately designed bench. They place it near the northmost of the two curtained columns. When this is done they slip out through the curtains; and the two officials, formally bowing, follow them. Rufio rises to receive Cæsar.*]

CÆSAR   [*coming over to him*]   Why, Rufio! [*Surveying his dress with an air of admiring astonishment*]   A new baldrick! A new golden pommel to your sword! And you have had your hair cut! But not your beard—? impossible! [*He sniffs at Rufio's beard*]. Yes, perfumed, by Jupiter Olympus!

RUFIO   [*growling*]   Well: is it to please myself?

CÆSAR   [*affectionately*]   No, my son Rufio, but to please me—to celebrate my birthday.

RUFIO   [*contemptuously*]   Your birthday! You always have a birthday when there is a pretty girl to be flattered or an ambassador to be conciliated. We had seven of them in ten months last year.

CÆSAR [*contritely*] It is true, Rufio! I shall never break myself of these petty deceits.

RUFIO Who is to dine with us—besides Cleopatra?

CÆSAR Apollodorus the Sicilian.

RUFIO That popinjay!

CÆSAR Come! the popinjay is an amusing dog—tells a story; sings a song; and saves us the trouble of flattering the Queen. What does she care for old politicans and camp-fed bears like us? No, Apollodorus is good company, Rufio, good company.

RUFIO Well, he can swim a bit and fence a bit: he might be worse, if he only knew how to hold his tongue.

CÆSAR The gods forbid he should ever learn! Oh, this military life! this tedious, brutal life of action! That is the worst of us Romans: we are mere doers and drudgers: a swarm of bees turned into men. Give me a good talker—one with wit and imagination enough to live without continually doing something!

RUFIO Ay! a nice time he would have of it with you when dinner was over! Have you noticed that I am before my time?

CÆSAR Aha! I thought that meant something. What is it?

RUFIO Can we be overheard here?

CÆSAR Our privacy invites eavesdropping. I can remedy that. [*He claps his hands twice. The curtains are drawn, revealing the roof garden with a banqueting table set across in the middle for four persons, one at each end, and two side by side. The side next Cæsar and Rufio is blocked with golden wine vessels and basins. A gorgeous major-domo is superintending the laying of the table by a staff of slaves. The colonnade goes round the garden at both sides to the further end, where a gap in it, like a great gateway, leaves the view open to the sky beyond the western edge of the roof, except in the middle, where a life size image of Ra, seated on a huge plinth, towers up, with hawk head and crown of asp and disk. His altar, which stands at his feet, is a single white stone.*] Now everybody can see us, nobody will think of listening to us. [*He sits down on the bench left by the two slaves*].

RUFIO [*sitting down on his stool*] Pothinus wants to speak to you. I advise you to see him: there is some plotting going on here among the women.

CÆSAR Who is Pothinus?

RUFIO The fellow with hair like squirrel's fur—the little King's bear leader, whom you kept prisoner.

CÆSAR [*annoyed*] And has he not escaped?

RUFIO No.

CÆSAR [*rising imperiously*] Why not? You have been guarding this man instead of watching the enemy. Have I not told you always to let prisoners escape unless there are special orders to the contrary? Are there not enough mouths to be fed without him?

RUFIO Yes; and if you would have a little sense and let me cut his throat, you would save his rations. Anyhow he wont escape. Three sentries have told him they would put a pilum through him if they saw him again. What more can they do? He prefers to stay and spy on us. So would I if I had to do with generals subject to fits of clemency.

CÆSAR [*resuming his seat, argued down*] Hm! And so he wants to see me.

RUFIO Ay. I have brought him with me. He is waiting there [*jerking his thumb over his shoulder*] under guard.

CÆSAR And you want me to see him?

RUFIO [*obstinately*] I dont want anything. I daresay you will do what you like. Dont put it on to me.

CÆSAR [*with an air of doing it expressly to indulge Rufio*] Well, well: let us have him.

RUFIO [*calling*] Ho there, guard! Release your man and send him up. [*Beckoning*]. Come along!
[*Pothinus enters and stops mistrustfully between the two, looking from one to the other.*]

CÆSAR [*graciously*] Ah, Pothinus! You are welcome. And what is the news this afternoon?

POTHINUS Cæsar: I come to warn you of a danger, and to make you an offer.

CÆSAR Never mind the danger. Make the offer.

RUFIO Never mind the offer. Whats the danger?

POTHINUS Cæsar: you think that Cleopatra is devoted to you.

CÆSAR [*gravely*] My friend: I already know what I think. Come to your offer.

POTHINUS I will deal plainly. I know not by what strange gods you have been enabled to defend a palace and a few yards of beach against a city and an army. Since we cut you off from Lake Mareotis, and you dug wells in the salt sea sand and brought up buckets of fresh water from them, we have known that your gods are irresistible, and that you are a worker of miracles. I no longer threaten you—

RUFIO [*sarcastically*] Very handsome of you, indeed.

POTHINUS So be it: you are the master. Our gods sent the north west winds to keep you in our hands; but you have been too strong for them.

CÆSAR [*gently urging him to come to the point*] Yes, yes, my friend. But what then?

RUFIO Spit it out, man. What have you to say?

POTHINUS I have to say that you have a traitress in your camp. Cleopatra—

THE MAJOR-DOMO [*at the table, announcing*] The Queen! [*Cæsar and Rufio rise*].

RUFIO [*aside to Pothinus*] You should have spat it out sooner, you fool. Now it is too late.
[*Cleopatra, in gorgeous raiment, enters in state through the gap in the colonnade, and comes down past the image of Ra and past the table to Cæsar. Her retinue, headed by Ftatateeta, joins the staff at the table. Cæsar gives Cleopatra his seat, which she takes.*]

CLEOPATRA [*quickly, seeing Pothinus*] What is he doing here?

CÆSAR [*seating himself beside her, in the most amiable of tempers*] Just going to tell me something about you. You shall hear it. Proceed, Pothinus.

POTHINUS [*disconcerted*] Cæsar—[*he stammers*]

CÆSAR Well, out with it.

POTHINUS What I have to say is for your ear, not for the Queen's.

CLEOPATRA [*with subdued ferocity*] There are means of making you speak. Take care.

POTHINUS [*defiantly*] Cæsar does not employ those means.

CÆSAR My friend: when a man has anything to tell in this world, the difficulty is not to make him tell it, but to prevent him from telling it too often. Let me celebrate my birthday by setting you free. Farewell: we shall not meet again.

CLEOPATRA [*angrily*] Cæsar: this mercy is foolish.

POTHINUS [*to Cæsar*] Will you not give me a private audience? Your life may depend on it. [*Cæsar rises loftily*].

RUFIO [*aside to Pothinus*] Ass! Now we shall have some heroics.

CÆSAR [*oratorically*] Pothinus—

RUFIO [*interrupting him*] Cæsar: the dinner will spoil if you begin preaching your favorite sermon about life and death.

CLEOPATRA [*priggishly*] Peace, Rufio. I desire to hear Cæsar.

RUFIO [*bluntly*] Your Majesty has heard it before. You repeated it to Apollodorus last week; and he thought it was all your own. [*Cæsar's dignity collapses. Much tickled, he sits down again and looks roguishly at Cleopatra, who is furious. Rufio calls as before*] Ho there, guard! Pass the prisoner out. He is released. [*To Pothinus*] Now off with you. You have lost your chance.

POTHINUS [*his temper overcoming his prudence*] I will speak.

CÆSAR [*to Cleopatra*] You see. Torture would not have wrung a word from him.

POTHINUS Cæsar: you have taught Cleopatra the arts by which the Romans govern the world.

CÆSAR Alas! they cannot even govern themselves. What then?

POTHINUS What then? Are you so besotted with her beauty that you do not see that she is impatient to reign in Egypt alone, and that her heart is set on your departure?

CLEOPATRA [*rising*] Liar!

CÆSAR [*shocked*] What! Protestations! Contradictions!

CLEOPATRA [*ashamed, but trembling with suppressed rage*] No. I do not deign to contradict. Let him talk. [*She sits down again*].

POTHINUS From her own lips I have heard it. You are to be her catspaw: you are to tear the crown from her brother's head and set it on her own, delivering us all into her hand—delivering yourself also. And then Cæsar can return to Rome, or depart through the gate of death, which is nearer and surer.

CÆSAR [*calmly*] Well, my friend; and is not this very natural?

POTHINUS [*astonished*] Natural! Then you do not resent treachery?

CÆSAR Resent! O thou foolish Egyptian, what have I to do with resentment? Do I resent the wind when it chills me, or the night when it makes me stumble in darkness? Shall I resent youth when it turns from age, and ambition when it turns from servitude? To tell me such a story as this is but to tell me that the sun will rise tomorrow.

CLEOPATRA [*unable to contain herself*] But it is false—false. I swear it.

CÆSAR It is true, though you swore it a thousand times, and believed all you swore. [*She is convulsed with emotion. To screen her, he rises and takes Pothinus to Rufio, saying*] Come, Rufio: let us see Pothinus past the guard. I have a word to say to him. [*Aside to them*] We must give the Queen a moment to recover herself. [*Aloud*] Come. [*He takes Pothinus and Rufio out with him, conversing with them meanwhile*]. Tell your friends, Pothinus, that they must not think I am opposed to a reasonable settlement of the country's affairs—[*They pass out of hearing*].

CLEOPATRA [*in a stifled whisper*] Ftatateeta, Ftatateeta.

FTATATEETA [*hurrying to her from the table and petting her*] Peace, child: be comforted—

CLEOPATRA [*interrupting her*] Can they hear us?

FTATATEETA No, dear heart, no.

CLEOPATRA Listen to me. If he leaves the Palace alive, never see my face again.

FTATATEETA He? Poth—

CLEOPATRA [*striking her on the mouth*] Strike his life out as I strike his name from your lips. Dash him down from the wall. Break him on the stones. Kill, kill, kill him.

FTATATEETA [*shewing all her teeth*] The dog shall perish.

CLEOPATRA Fail in this, and you go out from before me for ever.

FTATATEETA [*resolutely*] So be it. You shall not see my face until his eyes are darkened.

[*Cæsar comes back, with Apollodorus, exquisitely dressed, and Rufio.*]

CLEOPATRA [to Ftatateeta] Come soon—soon. [Ftatateeta turns her meaning eyes for a moment on her mistress; then goes grimly away past Ra and out. Cleopatra runs like a gazelle to Cæsar] So you have come back to me, Cæsar. [Caressingly] I thought you were angry. Welcome, Apollodorus. [She gives him her hand to kiss, with her other arm about Cæsar].

APOLLODORUS Cleopatra grows more womanly beautiful from week to week.

CLEOPATRA Truth, Apollodorus?

APOLLODORUS Far, far short of the truth! Friend Rufio threw a pearl into the sea: Cæsar fished up a diamond.

CÆSAR Cæsar fished up a touch of rheumatism, my friend. Come: to dinner! to dinner! [They move towards the table].

CLEOPATRA [skipping like a young fawn] Yes, to dinner. I have ordered such a dinner for you, Cæsar!

CÆSAR Ay? What are we to have?

CLEOPATRA Peacocks' brains.

CÆSAR [as if his mouth watered] Peacocks' brains, Apollodorus!

APOLLODORUS Not for me. I prefer nightingales' tongues. [He goes to one of the two covers set side by side].

CLEOPATRA Roast boar, Rufio!

RUFIO [gluttonously] Good! [He goes to the seat next Apollodorus, on his left].

CÆSAR [looking at his seat, which is at the end of the table, to Ra's left hand] What has become of my leathern cushion?

CLEOPATRA [at the opposite end] I have got new ones for you.

THE MAJOR-DOMO These cushions, Cæsar, are of Maltese gauze, stuffed with rose leaves.

CÆSAR Rose leaves! Am I a caterpillar? [He throws the cushions away and seats himself on the leather mattress underneath].

CLEOPATRA What a shame! My new cushions!

THE MAJOR-DOMO [at Cæsar's elbow] What shall we serve to whet Cæsar's appetite?

CÆSAR What have you got?

THE MAJOR-DOMO Sea hedgehogs, black and white sea acorns, sea nettles, beccaficoes, purple shellfish—

CÆSAR Any oysters?

THE MAJOR-DOMO Assuredly.

CÆSAR British oysters?

THE MAJOR-DOMO [assenting] British oysters, Cæsar.

CÆSAR Oysters, then. [The Major-Domo signs to a slave at each order; and the slave goes out to execute it]. I have been in Britain—that western land of romance—the last piece of earth on the edge of the ocean that surrounds the world. I went there in search of its famous pearls. The British pearl was a fable; but in searching for it I found the British oyster.

APOLLODORUS All posterity will bless you for it. [To the Major-Domo] Sea hedgehogs for me.

RUFIO Is there nothing solid to begin with?

THE MAJOR-DOMO Fieldfares with asparagus—

CLEOPATRA [interrupting] Fattened fowls! have some fattened fowls, Rufio.

RUFIO Ay, that will do.

CLEOPATRA [greedily] Fieldfares for me.

THE MAJOR-DOMO Cæsar will deign to choose his wine? Sicilian, Lesbian, Chian—

RUFIO [contemptuously] All Greek.

APOLLODORUS Who would drink Roman wine when he could get Greek. Try the Lesbian, Cæsar.

CÆSAR   Bring me my barley water.

RUFIO   [*with intense disgust*]   Ugh! Bring me my Falernian. [*The Falernian is presently brought to him*].

CLEOPATRA   [*pouting*]   It is waste of time giving you dinners, Cæsar. My scullions would not condescend to your diet.

CÆSAR   [*relenting*]   Well, well: let us try the Lesbian. [*The Major-Domo fills Cæsar's goblet; then Cleopatra's and Apollodorus's*]. But when I return to Rome, I will make laws against these extravagances. I will even get the laws carried out.

CLEOPATRA   [*coaxingly*]   Never mind. Today you are to be like other people: idle, luxurious, and kind. [*She stretches her hand to him along the table*].

CÆSAR   Well, for once I will sacrifice my comfort—[*kissing her hand*] there! [*He takes a draught of wine*]. Now are you satisfied?

CLEOPATRA   And you no longer believe that I long for your departure for Rome?

CÆSAR   I no longer believe anything. My brains are asleep. Besides, who knows whether I shall return to Rome?

RUFIO   [*alarmed*]   How? Eh? What?

CÆSAR   What has Rome to shew me that I have not seen already? One year of Rome is like another, except that I grow older, whilst the crowd in the Appian Way is always the same age.

APOLLODORUS   It is no better here in Egypt. The old men, when they are tired of life, say "We have seen everything except the source of the Nile."

CÆSAR   [*his imagination catching fire*]   And why not see that? Cleopatra: will you come with me and track the flood to its cradle in the heart of the regions of mystery? Shall we leave Rome behind us—Rome, that has achieved greatness only to learn how greatness destroys nations of men who are not great! Shall I make you a new kingdom, and build you a holy city there in the great unknown?

CLEOPATRA   [*rapturously*]   Yes, yes. You shall.

RUFIO   Ay: now he will conquer Africa with two legions before we come to the roast boar.

APOLLODORUS   Come: no scoffing. This is a noble scheme: in it Cæsar is no longer merely the conquering soldier, but the creative poet-artist. Let us name the holy city, and consecrate it with Lesbian wine.

CÆSAR   Cleopatra shall name it herself.

CLEOPATRA   It shall be called Cæsar's Gift to his Beloved.

APOLLODORUS   No, no. Something vaster than that—something universal, like the starry firmament.

CÆSAR   [*prosaically*]   Why not simply The Cradle of the Nile?

CLEOPATRA   No: the Nile is my ancestor; and he is a god. Oh! I have thought of something. The Nile shall name it himself. Let us call upon him. [*To the Major-Domo*] Send for him. [*The three men stare at one another; but the Major-Domo goes out as if he had received the most matter-of-fact order*]. And [*to the retinue*] away with you all. [*The retinue withdraws, making obeisance. A priest enters, carrying a miniature sphinx with a tiny tripod before it. A morsel of incense is smoking in the tripod. The priest comes to the table and places the image in the middle of it. The light begins to change to the magenta purple of the Egyptian sunset, as if the god had brought a strange colored shadow with him. The three men are determined not to be impressed; but they feel curious in spite of themselves.*]

CÆSAR   What hocus-pocus is this?

CLEOPATRA You shall see. And it is not hocus-pocus. To do it properly, we should kill something to please him; but perhaps he will answer Cæsar without that if we spill some wine to him.

APOLLODORUS [*turning his head to look up over his shoulder at Ra*] Why not appeal to our hawkheaded friend here?

CLEOPATRA [*nervously*] Sh! He will hear you and be angry.

RUFIO [*phlegmatically*] The source of the Nile is out of his district, I expect.

CLEOPATRA No: I will have my city named by nobody but my dear little sphinx, because it was in its arms that Cæsar found me asleep. [*She languishes at Cæsar then turns curtly to the priest*]. Go. I am a priestess, and have power to take your charge from you. [*The priest makes a reverence and goes out*]. Now let us call on the Nile all together. Perhaps he will rap on the table.

CÆSAR What! table rapping! Are such superstitions still believed in this year 707 of the Republic?

CLEOPATRA It is no superstition: our priests learn lots of things from the tables. Is it not so, Apollodorus?

APOLLODORUS Yes: I profess myself a converted man. When Cleopatra is priestess, Apollodorus is a devotee. Propose the conjuration.

CLEOPATRA You must say with me "Send us thy voice, Father Nile."

ALL FOUR [*holding their glasses together before the idol*] Send us thy voice, Father Nile.
[*The death cry of a man in mortal terror and agony answers them. Appalled, the men set down their glasses, and listen. Silence. The purple deepens in the sky. Cæsar, glancing at Cleopatra, catches her pouring out her wine before the god, with gleaming eyes, and mute assurances of gratitude and worship. Apollodorus springs up and runs to the edge of the roof to peer down and listen.*]

CÆSAR [*looking piercingly at Cleopatra*] What was that?

CLEOPATRA [*petulantly*] Nothing. They are beating some slave.

CÆSAR Nothing.

RUFIO A man with a knife in him, I'll swear.

CÆSAR [*rising*] A murder!

APOLLODORUS [*at the back, waving his hand for silence*] S-sh! Silence. Did you hear that?

CÆSAR Another cry?

APOLLODORUS [*returning to the table*] No, a thud. Something fell on the beach, I think.

RUFIO [*grimly, as he rises*] Something with bones in it, eh?

CÆSAR [*shuddering*] Hush, hush, Rufio.
[*He leaves the table and returns to the colonnade: Rufio following at his left elbow, and Apollodorus at the other side*].

CLEOPATRA [*still in her place at the table*] Will you leave me, Cæsar? Apollodorus: are you going?

APOLLODORUS Faith, dearest Queen, my appetite is gone.

CÆSAR Go down to the courtyard, Apollodorus; and find out what has happened.
[*Apollodorus nods and goes out, making for the staircase by which Rufio ascended.*]

CLEOPATRA Your soldiers have killed somebody, perhaps. What does it matter?
[*The murmur of a crowd rises from the beach below. Cæsar and Rufio look at one another.*]

CÆSAR This must be seen to.
[*He is about to follow Apollodorus when Rufio stops him with a hand on his arm as Ftatateeta comes back by the far end of the roof, with dragging*]

steps, a drowsy satiety in her eyes and in the corners of the bloodhound lips. For a moment Cæsar suspects that she is drunk with wine. Not so Rufio: he knows well the red vintage that has inebriated her].

RUFIO [*in a low tone*]   There is some mischief between these two.

FTATATEETA   The Queen looks again on the face of her servant.

[*Cleopatra looks at her for a moment with an exultant reflection of her murderous expression. Then she flings her arms round her; kisses her repeatedly and savagely; and tears off her jewels and heaps them on her. The two men turn from the spectacle to look at one another. Ftatateeta drags herself sleepily to the altar; kneels before Ra; and remains there in prayer. Cæsar goes to Cleopatra, leaving Rufio in the colonnade.*]

CÆSAR [*with searching earnestness*]   Cleopatra: what has happened?

CLEOPATRA [*in mortal dread of him, but with her utmost cajolery*]   Nothing, dearest Cæsar. [*With sickly sweetness, her voice almost failing*]   Nothing. I am innocent. [*She approaches him affectionately*]   Dear Cæsar: are you angry with me? Why do you look at me so? I have been here with you all the time. How can I know what has happened?

CÆSAR [*reflectively*]   That is true.

CLEOPATRA [*greatly relieved, trying to caress him*]   Of course it is true. [*He does not respond to the caress*]   You know it is true, Rufio.

[*The murmur without suddenly swells to a roar and subsides.*]

RUFIO   I shall know presently. [*He makes for the altar in the burly trot that serves him for a stride, and touches Ftatateeta on the shoulder*].   Now, mistress: I shall want you. [*He orders her, with a gesture, to go before him*].

FTATATEETA [*rising and glowering at him*]   My place is with the Queen.

CLEOPATRA   She has done no harm, Rufio.

CÆSAR [*to Rufio*]   Let her stay.

RUFIO [*sitting down on the altar*]   Very well. Then my place is here too; and you can see what is the matter for yourself. The city is in a pretty uproar, it seems.

CÆSAR [*with grave displeasure*]   Rufio: there is a time for obedience.

RUFIO   And there is a time for obstinacy. [*He folds his arms doggedly*].

CÆSAR [*to Cleopatra*]   Send her away.

CLEOPATRA [*whining in her eagerness to propitiate him*]   Yes, I will. I will do whatever you ask me, Cæsar, always, because I love you. Ftatateeta: go away.

FTATATEETA   The Queen's word is my will. I shall be at hand for the Queen's call. [*She goes out past Ra, as she came*].

RUFIO [*following her*]   Remember, Cæsar, your bodyguard is also within call. [*He follows her out*].

[*Cleopatra, presuming upon Cæsar's submission to Rufio, leaves the table and sits down on the bench in the colonnade.*]

CLEOPATRA   Why do you allow Rufio to treat you so? You should teach him his place.

CÆSAR   Teach him to be my enemy, and to hide his thoughts from me as you are now hiding yours?

CLEOPATRA [*her fears returning*]   Why do you say that, Cæsar? Indeed, indeed, I am not hiding anything. You are wrong to treat me like this. [*She stifles a sob*].   I am only a child; and you turn into stone because you think some one has been killed. I cannot bear it. [*She purposely breaks down and weeps. He looks at her with profound sadness and complete coldness. She looks up to see what effect she is producing. Seeing that he is unmoved, she sits up, pretending to struggle with her emotion and to put it bravely away*].   But there: I know you hate tears: you shall not be troubled with them. I know you are not angry, but only sad; only I am so silly, I cannot help being hurt when you speak coldly. Of course you are quite right: it is dreadful to think of anyone being killed or even hurt; and I hope nothing really serious has—[*her voice dies away under his contemptuous penetration*].

CÆSAR What has frightened you into this? What have you done? [*A trumpet sounds on the beach below*]. Aha! that sounds like the answer.

CLEOPATRA [*sinking back trembling on the bench and covering her face with her hands*] I have not betrayed you, Cæsar: I swear it.

CÆSAR I know that. I have not trusted you. [*He turns from her, and is about to go out when Apollodorus and Britannus drag in Lucius Septimius to him. Rufio follows. Cæsar shudders*]. Again, Pompey's murderer!

RUFIO The town has gone mad, I think. They are for tearing the palace down and driving us into the sea straight away. We laid hold of this renegade in clearing them out of the courtyard.

CÆSAR Release him. [*They let go his arms*]. What has offended the citizens, Lucius Septimius?

LUCIUS What did you expect, Cæsar? Pothinus was a favorite of theirs.

CÆSAR What has happened to Pothinus? I set him free, here, not half an hour ago. Did they not pass him out?

LUCIUS Ay, through the gallery arch sixty feet above ground, with three inches of steel in his ribs. He is as dead as Pompey. We are quits now, as to killing—you and I.

CÆSAR [*shocked*] Assassinated!—our prisoner, our guest! [*He turns reproachfully on Rufio*] Rufio—

RUFIO [*emphatically—anticipating the question*] Whoever did it was a wise man and a friend of yours [*Cleopatra is greatly emboldened*]; but none of us had a hand in it. So it is no use to frown at me. [*Cæsar turns and looks at Cleopatra*].

CLEOPATRA [*violently—rising*] He was slain by order of the Queen of Egypt. I am not Julius Cæsar the dreamer, who allows every slave to insult him. Rufio has said I did well: now the others shall judge me too. [*She turns to the others*]. This Pothinus sought to make me conspire with him to betray Cæsar to Achillas and Ptolemy. I refused; and he cursed me and came privily to Cæsar to accuse me of his own treachery. I caught him in the act; and he insulted me—me, the Queen! to my face. Cæsar would not avenge me: he spoke him fair and set him free. Was I right to avenge myself? Speak, Lucius.

LUCIUS I do not gainsay it. But you will get little thanks from Cæsar for it.

CLEOPATRA Speak, Apollodorus. Was I wrong?

APOLLODORUS I have only one word of blame, most beautiful. You should have called upon me, your knight; and in a fair duel I should have slain the slanderer.

CLEOPATRA [*passionately*] I will be judged by your very slave, Cæsar. Britannus: speak. Was I wrong?

BRITANNUS Were treachery, falsehood, and disloyalty left unpunished, society must become like an arena full of wild beasts, tearing one another to pieces. Cæsar is in the wrong.

CÆSAR [*with quiet bitterness*] And so the verdict is against me, it seems.

CLEOPATRA [*vehemently*] Listen to me, Cæsar. If one man in all Alexandria can be found to say that I did wrong, I swear to have myself crucified on the door of the palace by my own slaves.

CÆSAR If one man in all the world can be found, now or forever, to know that you did wrong, that man will have either to conquer the world as I have, or be crucified by it [*The uproar in the streets again reaches them*]. Do you hear? These knockers at your gate are also believers in vengeance and in stabbing. You have slain their leader: it is right that they shall slay you. If you doubt it, ask your four counsellors here. And then in the name of that right [*he emphasizes the word with great scorn*] shall I not slay them for murdering their Queen, and be slain in my turn by their countrymen as the invader of their fatherland? Can Rome do less then than slay these slayers, too, to shew the world how Rome avenges her sons and her honor. And so, to the end of history, murder shall breed murder, always in the name of right and honor and peace, until the gods are tired of blood and create a race that can understand. [*Fierce uproar. Cleopatra becomes white with terror*]. Hearken, you who must not be insulted. Go near enough to catch their words: you will find them bitterer than the tongue of Pothinus. [*Loftily, wrapping himself up in an impenetrable dignity*] Let the Queen of Egypt now give her orders for vengeance, and take her measures for defence; for she has renounced Cæsar. [*He turns to go*].

CLEOPATRA   [*terrified, running to him and falling on her knees*]   You will not desert me, Cæsar. You will defend the palace.

CÆSAR   You have taken the powers of life and death upon you. I am only a dreamer.

CLEOPATRA   But they will kill me.

CÆSAR   And why not?

CLEOPATRA   In pity—

CÆSAR   Pity! What! has it come to this so suddenly, that nothing can save you now but pity? Did it save Pothinus?
[*She rises, wringing her hands, and goes back to the bench in despair. Apollodorus shews his sympathy with her by quietly posting himself behind the bench. The sky has by this time become the most vivid purple, and soon begins to change to a glowing pale orange, against which the colonnade and the great image shew darklier and darklier.*]

RUFIO   Cæsar: enough of preaching. The enemy is at the gate.

CÆSAR   [*turning on him and giving way to his wrath*]   Ay; and what has held him baffled at the gate all these months? Was it my folly, as you deem it, or your wisdom? In this Egyptian Red Sea of blood, whose hand has held all your heads above the waves? [*Turning on Cleopatra*] And yet, when Cæsar says to such an one, "Friend, go free," you, clinging for your little life to my sword, dare steal out and stab him in the back? And you, soldiers and gentlemen, and honest servants as you forget that you are, applaud this assassination, and say "Cæsar is in the wrong." By the gods, I am tempted to open my hand and let you all sink into the flood.

CLEOPATRA   [*with a ray of cunning hope*]   But, Cæsar, if you do, you will perish yourself.
[*Cæsar's eyes blaze.*]

RUFIO   [*greatly alarmed*]   Now, by great Jove, you filthy little Egyptian rat, that is the very word to make him walk out alone into the city and leave us here to be cut to pieces. [*Desperately, to Cæsar*] Will you desert us because we are a parcel of fools? I mean no harm by killing: I do it as a cat, by instinct. We are all dogs at your heels; but we have served you faithfully.

CÆSAR   [*relenting*]   Alas, Rufio, my son, my son: as dogs we are like to perish now in the streets.

APOLLODORUS   [*at his post behind Cleopatra's seat*]   Cæsar: what you say has an Olympian ring in it: it must be right; for it is fine art. But I am still on the side of Cleopatra. If we must die, she shall not want the devotion of a man's heart nor the strength of a man's arm.

CLEOPATRA   [*sobbing*]   But I dont want to die.

CÆSAR   [*sadly*]   Oh, ignoble, ignoble!

LUCIUS   [*coming forward between Cæsar and Cleopatra*]   Hearken to me, Cæsar. It may be ignoble; but I also mean to live as long as I can.

CÆSAR   Well, my friend, you are likely to outlive Cæsar. Is it any magic of mine, think you, that has kept your army and this whole city at bay for so long? Yesterday, what quarrel had they with me that they should risk their lives against me? But today we have flung them down their hero, murdered; and now every man of them is set upon clearing out this nest of assassins—for such we are and no more. Take courage then; and sharpen your sword. Pompey's head has fallen; and Cæsar's head is ripe.

APOLLODORUS   Does Cæsar despair?

CÆSAR   [*with infinite pride*]   He who has never hoped can never despair. Cæsar, in good or bad fortune, looks his fate in the face.

LUCIUS   Look it in the face, then; and it will smile as it always has on Cæsar.

CÆSAR   [*with involuntary haughtiness*]   Do you presume to encourage me?

LUCIUS   I offer you my services. I will change sides if you will have me.

CÆSAR   [*suddenly coming down to earth again, and looking sharply at him, divining that there is something behind the offer*]   What! At this point?

LUCIUS   [*firmly*]   At this point.

RUFIO   Do you suppose Cæsar is mad, to trust you?

LUCIUS   I do not ask him to trust me until he is victorious. I ask for my life, and for a command in Cæsar's army. And since Cæsar is a fair dealer, I will pay in advance.

CÆSAR   Pay! How?

LUCIUS   With a piece of good news for you.

[*Cæsar divines the news in a flash.*]

RUFIO   What news?

CÆSAR   [*with an elate and buoyant energy which makes Cleopatra sit up and stare*]   What news! What news, did you say, my son Rufio? The relief has arrived: what other news remains for us? Is it not so, Lucius Septimius? Mithridates of Pergamos is on the march.

LUCIUS   He has taken Pelusium.

CÆSAR   [*delighted*]   Lucius Septimius: you are henceforth my officer. Rufio: the Egyptians must have sent every soldier from the city to prevent Mithridates crossing the Nile. There is nothing in the streets now but mob—mob!

LUCIUS   It is so. Mithridates is marching by the great road to Memphis to cross above the Delta. Achillas will fight him there.

CÆSAR   [*all audacity*]   Achillas shall fight Cæsar there. See, Rufio. [*He runs to the table; snatches a napkin; and draws a plan on it with his finger dipped in wine, whilst Rufio and Lucius Septimius crowd about him to watch, all looking closely, for the light is now almost gone*]. Here is the palace [*pointing to his plan*]: here is the theatre. You [*to Rufio*] take twenty men and pretend to go by that street [*pointing it out*]; and whilst they are stoning you, out go the cohorts by this and this. My streets are right, are they, Lucius?

LUCIUS   Ay, that is the fig market—

CÆSAR   [*too much excited to listen to him*]   I saw them the day we arrived. Good! [*He throws the napkin on the table, and comes down again into the colonnade*]. Away, Britannus: tell Petronius that within an hour half our forces must take ship for the western lake. See to my horse and armor. [*Britannus runs out*] With the rest, I shall march round the lake and up the Nile to meet Mithridates. Away, Lucius; and give the word. [*Lucius hurries out after Britannus*]. Apollodorus: lend me your sword and your right arm for this campaign.

APOLLODORUS Ay, and my heart and life to boot.

CÆSAR [*grasping his hand*] I accept both. [*Mighty handshake*]. Are you ready for work?

APOLLODORUS Ready for Art—the Art of War [*he rushes out after Lucius, totally forgetting Cleopatra*].

RUFIO Come! this is something like business.

CÆSAR [*buoyantly*] Is it not, my only son? [*He claps his hands. The slaves hurry in to the table*]. No more of this mawkish revelling: away with all this stuff: shut it out of my sight and be off with you. [*The slaves begin to remove the table; and the curtains are drawn, shutting in the colonnade*]. You understand about the streets, Rufio?

RUFIO Ay, I think I do. I will get through them, at all events.
[*The bucina sounds busily in the courtyard beneath.*]

CÆSAR Come, then: we must talk to the troops and hearten them. You down to the beach: I to the courtyard. [*He makes for the staircase*].

CLEOPATRA [*rising from her seat, where she has been quite neglected all this time, and stretching out her hands timidly to him*] Cæsar.

CÆSAR [*turning*] Eh?

CLEOPATRA Have you forgotten me?

CÆSAR [*indulgently*] I am busy now, my child, busy. When I return your affairs shall be settled. Farewell; and be good and patient.
[*He goes, preoccupied and quite indifferent. She stands with clenched fists, in speechless rage and humiliation.*]

RUFIO That game is played and lost, Cleopatra. The woman always gets the worst of it.

CLEOPATRA [*haughtily*] Go. Follow your master.

RUFIO [*in her ear, with rough familiarity*] A word first. Tell your executioner that if Pothinus had been properly killed—in the throat—he would not have called out. Your man bungled his work.

CLEOPATRA [*enigmatically*] How do you know it was a man?

RUFIO [*startled, and puzzled*] It was not you: you were with us when it happened. [*She turns her back scornfully on him. He shakes his head, and draws the curtains to go out. It is now a magnificent moonlit night. The table has been removed. Ftatateeta is seen in the light of the moon and stars, again in prayer before the white altar-stone of Ra. Rufio starts; closes the curtains again softly; and says in a low voice to Cleopatra*] Was it she? with her own hand?

CLEOPATRA [*threateningly*] Whoever it was, let my enemies beware of her. Look to it, Rufio, you who dare make the Queen of Egypt a fool before Cæsar.

RUFIO [*looking grimly at her*] I will look to it, Cleopatra.
[*He nods in confirmation of the promise, and slips out through the curtains, loosening his sword in its sheath as he goes*].

ROMAN SOLDIERS [*in the courtyard below*] Hail, Cæsar! Hail, hail!
[*Cleopatra listens. The bucina sounds again, followed by several trumpets.*]

CLEOPATRA [*wringing her hands and calling*] Ftatateeta. Ftatateeta. It is dark; and I am alone. Come to me. [*Silence*] Ftatateeta. [*Louder*] Ftatateeta.
[*Silence. In a panic she snatches the cord and pulls the curtains apart*].
[*Ftatateeta is lying dead on the altar of Ra, with her throat cut. Her blood deluges the white stone.*]

ACT V

High noon. Festival and military pageant on the esplanade be-fore the palace. In the east harbor Cæsar's galley, so gorgeously decorated that it seems to be rigged with flowers, is alongside the quay, close to the steps Apollodorus descended when he em-barked with the carpet. A Roman guard is posted there in charge of a gangway, whence a red floorcloth is laid down the middle of the esplanade, turning off to the north opposite the central gate in the palace front, which shuts in the esplanade on the south side. The broad steps of the gate, crowded with Cleopatra's ladies, all in their gayest attire, are like a flower garden. The façade is lined by her guard, officered by the same gallants to whom Bel Affris announced the coming of Cæsar six months before in the old palace on the Syrian border. The north side is lined by Ro-man soldiers, with the townsfolk on tiptoe behind them, peering over their heads at the cleared esplanade, in which the officers stroll about, chatting. Among these are Belzanor and the Persian; also the centurion, vinewood cudgel in hand, battle worn, thick-booted, and much outshone, both socially and decoratively, by the Egyptian officers.

Apollodorus makes his way through the townsfolk and calls to the officers from behind the Roman line.

APOLLODORUS   Hullo! May I pass?

CENTURION   Pass Apollodorus the Sicilian there!

   [*The soldiers let him through*].

BELZANOR   Is Cæsar at hand?

APOLLODORUS   Not yet. He is still in the market place. I could not stand any more of the roaring of the soldiers! After half an hour of the enthusiasm of an army, one feels the need of a little sea air.

PERSIAN   Tell us the news. Hath he slain the priests?

APOLLODORUS   Not he. They met him in the market place with ashes on their heads and their gods in their hands. They placed the gods at his feet. The only one that was worth looking at was Apis: a miracle of gold and ivory work. By my advice he offered the chief priest two talents for it.

BELZANOR   [*appalled*]   Apis the all-knowing for two talents! What said the chief Priest?

APOLLODORUS   He invoked the mercy of Apis, and asked for five.

BELZANOR   There will be famine and tempest in the land for this.

PERSIAN   Pooh! Why did not Apis cause Cæsar to be vanquished by Achillas? Any fresh news from the war, Apollodorus?

APOLLODORUS   The little King Ptolemy was drowned.

BELZANOR   Drowned! How?

APOLLODORUS   With the rest of them. Cæsar attacked them from three sides at once and swept them into the Nile. Ptolemy's barge sank.

BELZANOR   A marvellous man, this Cæsar! Will he come soon, think you?

APOLLODORUS   He was settling the Jewish question when I left.

   [*A flourish of trumpets from the north, and commotion among the towns-folk, announces the approach of Cæsar.*]

PERSIAN   He has made short work of them. Here he comes.

   [*He hurries to his post in front of the Egyptian lines*].

BELZANOR [*following him*] Ho there! Cæsar comes.
[*The soldiers stand at attention, and dress their lines. Apollodorus goes to the Egyptian line.*]

CENTURION [*hurrying to the gangway guard*] Attention there! Cæsar comes.
[*Cæsar arrives in state with Rufio: Britannus following. The soldiers receive him with enthusiastic shouting.*]

CÆSAR I see my ship awaits me. The hour of Cæsar's farewell to Egypt has arrived. And now, Rufio, what remains to be done before I go?

RUFIO [*at his left hand*] You have not yet appointed a Roman governor for this province.

CÆSAR [*looking whimsically at him, but speaking with perfect gravity*] What say you to Mithridates of Pergamos, my reliever and rescuer, the great son of Eupator?

RUFIO Why, that you will want him elsewhere. Do you forget that you have some three or four armies to conquer on your way home?

CÆSAR Indeed! Well, what say you to yourself?

RUFIO [*incredulously*] I! I a governor! What are you dreaming of? Do you not know that I am only the son of a freedman?

CÆSAR [*affectionately*] Has not Cæsar called you his son? [*Calling to the whole assembly*] Peace awhile there; and hear me.

THE ROMAN SOLDIERS Hear Cæsar.

CÆSAR Hear the service, quality, rank and name of the Roman governor. By service, Cæsar's shield; by quality, Cæsar's friend; by rank, a Roman soldier. [*The Roman soldiers give a triumphant shout*]. By name, Rufio. [*They shout again*].

RUFIO [*kissing Cæsar's hand*] Ay: I am Cæsar's shield; but of what use shall I be when I am no longer on Cæsar's arm? Well,. no matter—[*He becomes husky, and turns away to recover himself*].

CÆSAR Where is that British Islander of mine?

BRITANNUS [*coming forward on Cæsar's right hand*] Here, Cæsar.

CÆSAR Who bade you, pray, thrust yourself into the battle of the Delta, uttering the barbarous cries of your native land, and affirming yourself a match for any four of the Egyptians, to whom you applied unseemly epithets?

BRITANNUS Cæsar: I ask you to excuse the language that escaped me in the heat of the moment.

CÆSAR And how did you, who cannot swim, cross the canal with us when we stormed the camp?

BRITANNUS Cæsar: I clung to the tail of your horse.

CÆSAR These are not the deeds of a slave, Britannicus, but of a free man.

BRITANNUS Cæsar: I was born free.

CÆSAR But they call you Cæsar's slave.

BRITANNUS Only as Cæsar's slave have I found real freedom.

CÆSAR [*moved*] Well said. Ungrateful that I am, I was about to set you free; but now I will not part from you for a million talents.
[*He claps him friendly on the shoulder. Britannus, gratified, but a trifle shamefaced, takes his hand and kisses it sheepishly*].

BELZANOR [*to the Persian*] This Roman knows how to make men serve him.

PERSIAN Ay: men too humble to become dangerous rivals to him.

BELZANOR O subtle one! O cynic!

CÆSAR [*seeing Apollodorus in the Egyptian corner, and calling to him*] Apollodorus: I leave the art of Egypt in your charge. Remember: Rome loves art and will encourage it ungrudgingly.

APOLLODORUS I understand, Cæsar. Rome will produce no art itself; but it will buy up and take away whatever the other nations produce.

CÆSAR What! Rome produce no art! Is peace not an art? is war not an art? is government not an art? is civilization not an art? All these we give you in exchange for a few ornaments. You will have the best of the bargain. [*Turning to Rufio*] And now, what else have I to do before I embark? [*Trying to recollect*] There is something I cannot remember: what can it be? Well, well: it must remain undone: we must not waste this favorable wind. Farewell, Rufio.

RUFIO Cæsar: I am loth to let you go to Rome without your shield. There are too many daggers there.

CÆSAR It matters not: I shall finish my life's work on my way back; and then I shall have lived long enough. Besides: I have always disliked the idea of dying: I had rather be killed. Farewell.

RUFIO [*with a sigh, raising his hands and giving Cæsar up as incorrigible*] Farewell. [*They shake hands*].

CÆSAR [*waving his hand to Apollodorus*] Farewell, Apollodorus, and my friends, all of you. Aboard!

[*The gangway is run out from the quay to the ship. As Cæsar moves towards it, Cleopatra, cold and tragic, cunningly dressed in black, without ornaments or decoration of any kind, and thus making a striking figure among the brilliantly dressed bevy of ladies as she passes through it, comes from the palace and stands on the steps. Cæsar does not see her until she speaks.*]

CLEOPATRA Has Cleopatra no part in this leavetaking?

CÆSAR [*enlightened*] Ah, I knew there was something. [*To Rufio*] How could you let me forget her, Rufio? [*Hastening to her*] Had I gone without seeing you, I should never have forgiven myself. [*He takes her hands, and brings her into the middle of the esplanade. She submits stonily*]. Is this mourning for me?

CLEOPATRA No.

CÆSAR [*remorsefully*] Ah, that was thoughtless of me! It is for your brother.

CLEOPATRA No.

CÆSAR For whom, then?

CLEOPATRA Ask the Roman governor whom you have left us.

CÆSAR Rufio?

CLEOPATRA Yes: Rufio. [*She points at him with deadly scorn*]. He who is to rule here in Cæsar's name, in Cæsar's way, according to Cæsar's boasted laws of life.

CÆSAR [*dubiously*] He is to rule as he can, Cleopatra. He has taken the work upon him, and will do it in his own way.

CLEOPATRA Not in your way, then?

CÆSAR [*puzzled*] What do you mean by my way?

CLEOPATRA Without punishment. Without revenge. Without judgment.

CÆSAR [*approvingly*] Ay: that is the right way, the great way, the only possible way in the end. [*To Rufio*] Believe it, Rufio, if you can.

RUFIO Why, I believe it, Cæsar. You have convinced me of it long ago. But look you. You are sailing for Numidia today. Now tell me: if you meet a hungry lion there, you will not punish it for wanting to eat you?

CÆSAR [*wondering what he is driving at*] No.

RUFIO Nor revenge upon it the blood of those it has already eaten.

CÆSAR No.

RUFIO Nor judge it for its guiltiness.

CÆSAR No.

RUFIO What, then, will you do to save your life from it?

CÆSAR [*promptly*] Kill it, man, without malice, just as it would kill me. What does this parable of the lion mean?

RUFIO Why, Cleopatra had a tigress that killed men at her bidding. I thought she might bid it kill you some day. Well, had I not been Cæsar's pupil, what pious things might I not have done to that tigress! I might have punished it. I might have revenged Pothinus on it.

CÆSAR [*interjects*] Pothinus!

RUFIO [*continuing*] I might have judged it. But I put all these follies behind me; and, without malice, only cut its throat. And that is why Cleopatra comes to you in mourning.

CLEOPATRA [*vehemently*] He has shed the blood of my servant Ftatateeta. On your head be it as upon his, Cæsar, if you hold him free of it.

CÆSAR [*energetically*] On my head be it, then; for it was well done. Rufio: had you set yourself in the seat of the judge, and with hateful ceremonies and appeals to the gods handed that woman over to some hired executioner to be slain before the people in the name of justice, never again would I have touched your hand without a shudder. But this was natural slaying: I feel no horror at it.

[*Rufio, satisfied, nods at Cleopatra, mutely inviting her to mark that.*]

CLEOPATRA [*pettish and childish in her impotence*] No: not when a Roman slays an Egyptian. All the world will now see how unjust and corrupt Cæsar is.

CÆSAR [*taking her hands coaxingly*] Come: do not be angry with me. I am sorry for that poor Totateeta. [*She laughs in spite of herself*]. Aha! you are laughing. Does that mean reconciliation?

CLEOPATRA [*angry with herself for laughing*] No, no, NO!! But it is so ridiculous to hear you call her Totateeta.

CÆSAR What! As much a child as ever, Cleopatra! Have I not made a woman of you after all?

CLEOPATRA Oh, it is you who are a great baby: you make me seem silly because you will not behave seriously. But you have treated me badly; and I do not forgive you.

CÆSAR Bid me farewell.

CLEOPATRA I will not.

CÆSAR [*coaxing*] I will send you a beautiful present from Rome.

CLEOPATRA [*proudly*] Beauty from Rome to Egypt indeed! What can Rome give me that Egypt cannot give me?

APOLLODORUS That is true, Cæsar. If the present is to be really beautiful, I shall have to buy it for you in Alexandria.

CÆSAR You are forgetting the treasures for which Rome is most famous, my friend. You cannot buy them in Alexandria.

APOLLODORUS What are they, Cæsar?

CÆSAR Her sons. Come, Cleopatra: forgive me and bid me farewell; and I will send you a man, Roman from head to heel and Roman of the noblest; not old and ripe for the knife; not lean in the arms and cold in the heart; not hiding a bald head under his conqueror's laurels; not stooped with the weight of the world on his shoulders; but brisk and fresh, strong and young, hoping in the morning, fighting in the day, and revelling in the evening. Will you take such an one in exchange for Cæsar?

CLEOPATRA [*palpitating*] His name, his name?

CÆSAR Shall it be Mark Antony? [*She throws herself into his arms*].

RUFIO You are a bad hand at a bargain, mistress, if you will swop Cæsar for Antony.

CÆSAR So now you are satisfied.

CLEOPATRA You will not forget.

CÆSAR I will not forget. Farewell: I do not think we shall meet again. Farewell.

[*He kisses her on the forehead. She is much affected and begins to sniff. He embarks*].

THE ROMAN SOLDIERS [*as he sets his foot on the gangway*] Hail, Cæsar; and farewell!

[*He reaches the ship and returns Rufio's wave of the hand.*]

APOLLODORUS [*to Cleopatra*] No tears, dearest Queen: they stab your servant to the heart. He will return some day.

CLEOPATRA I hope not. But I cant help crying, all the same.

[*She waves her handkerchief to Cæsar; and the ship begins to move*].

THE ROMAN SOLDIERS [*drawing their swords and raising them in the air*] Hail, Cæsar!

NOTES TO CÆSAR AND CLEOPATRA

Cleopatra's Cure for Baldness

For the sake of conciseness in a hurried situation I have made Cleopatra recommend rum. This, I am afraid, is an anachronism: the only real one in the play. To balance it, I give a couple of the remedies she actually believed in. They are quoted by Galen from Cleopatra's book on Cosmetic.

"For bald patches, powder red sulphuret of arsenic and take it up with oak gum, as much as it will bear. Put on a rag and apply, having soaped the place well first. I have mixed the above with a foam of nitre, and it worked well."

Several other receipts follow, ending with: "The following is the best of all, acting for fallen hairs, when applied with oil or pomatum; acts for falling off of eyelashes or for people getting bald all over. It is wonderful. Of domestic mice burnt, one part; of vine rag burnt, one part; of horse's teeth burnt, one part; of bear's grease one; of deer's marrow one; of reed bark one. To be pounded when dry, and mixed with plenty of honey til it gets the consistency of honey; then the bear's grease and marrow to be mixed (when melted), the medicine to be put in a brass flask, and the bald part rubbed til it sprouts."

Concerning these ingredients, my fellow-dramatist Gilbert Murray, who, as a Professor of Greek, has applied to classical antiquity the methods of high scholarship (my own method is pure divination), writes to me as follows: "Some of this I dont understand, and possibly Galen did not, as he quotes your heroine's own language. Foam of nitre is, I think, something like soapsuds. Reed bark is an odd expression. It might mean the outside membrane of a reed: I do not know what it ought to be called. In the burnt mice receipt I take it that you first mixed the solid powders with honey, and then added the grease. I expect Cleopatra preferred it because in most of the others you have to lacerate the skin, prick it, or rub it till it bleeds. I do not know what vine rag is. I translate literally."

Apparent Anachronisms

The only way to write a play which shall convey to the general public an impression of antiquity is to make the characters speak blank verse and abstain from reference to steam, telegraphy, or any of the material conditions of their existence. The more ignorant men are, the more convinced are they that their little parish and their little chapel is an apex to which civilization and philosophy has painfully struggled up the pyramid of time from a desert of savagery. Savagery, they think, became barbarism; barbarism became ancient civilization; ancient civilization became Pauline Christianity; Pauline Christianity became Roman Catholicism; Roman Catholicism became the Dark Ages; and the Dark Ages were finally enlightened by the Protestant instincts of the English race. The whole process is summed up as Progress with a capital P. And any elderly gentleman of Progressive temperament will testify that the improvement since he was a boy is enormous.

Now if we count the generations of Progressive elderly gentlemen since, say, Plato, and add together the successive enormous improvements to which each of them has testified, it will strike us at once as an unaccountable fact that the world, instead of having been improved in 67 generations out of all recognition, presents, on the whole, a rather less dignified appearance in Ibsen's Enemy of the People than in Plato's Republic. And in truth, the period of time covered by history is far too short to allow of any perceptible progress in the popular sense of Evolution of the Human Species. The notion that there has been any such Progress since Cæsar's time (less than 20 centuries) is too absurd for discussion. All the savagery, barbarism, dark ages and the rest of it of which we have any record as existing in the past, exists at the present moment. A British carpenter or stonemason may point out that he gets twice as much money for his labor as his father did in the same trade, and that his suburban house, with its bath, its cottage piano, its drawing room suite, and its album of photographs, would have shamed the plainness of his grandmother's. But the descendants of feudal barons, living in squalid lodgings on a salary of fifteen shillings a week instead of in castles on princely revenues, do not congratulate the world on the change. Such changes, in fact, are not to the point. It has been known, as far back as our records go, that man running wild in the woods is different from man kennelled in a city slum; that a dog seems to understand a shepherd better than a hewer of wood and drawer of water can understand an astronomer; and that breeding, gentle nurture, and luxurious food and shelter will produce a kind of man with whom the common laborer is socially incompatible. The same thing is true of horses and dogs. Now there is clearly room for great changes in the world by increasing the percentage of individuals who are carefully bred and gently nurtured, even to finally making the most of every man and woman born. But that possibility existed in the days of the Hittites as much as it does today. It does not give the slightest real support to the common assumption that the civilized contemporaries of the Hittites were unlike their civilized descendants today.

This would appear the tritest commonplace if it were not that the ordinary citizen's ignorance of the past combines with his idealization of the present to mislead and flatter him. Our latest book on the new railway across Asia describes the dulness of the Siberian farmer and the vulgar pursepride of the Siberian man of business without the least consciousness that the string of contemptuous instances given might have been saved by writing simply "Farmers and provincial plutocrats in Siberia are exactly what they are in England." The latest professor descanting on the civilization of the Western Empire in the fifth century feels bound to assume, in the teeth of his own researches, that the Christian was one sort of animal and the Pagan another. It might as well be assumed as indeed it generally is assumed by implication, that a murder committed with a poisoned arrow is different from a murder committed with a Mauser rifle. All such notions are illusions. Go back to the first syllable of recorded time, and there you will find your Christian and your Pagan, your yokel and your poet, helot and hero, Don Quixote and Sancho, Tamino and Papageno, Newton and bushman unable to count eleven, all alive and contemporaneous, and all convinced that they are the heirs of all the ages and the privileged recipients of THE truth (all others damnable heresies) , just as you have them today, flourishing in countries each of which is the bravest and best that ever sprang at Heaven's command from out the azure main.

Again, there is the illusion of "increased command over Nature," meaning that cotton is cheap and that ten miles of country road on a bicycle have replaced four on foot. But even if man's increased command over Nature included any increased command over himself (the only sort of command relevant to his evolution into a higher being) , the fact remains that it is only by running away from the increased command over Nature to country places where Nature is still in primitive command over Man that he can recover from the effects of the smoke, the stench, the foul air, the overcrowding, the racket, the ugliness, the dirt which the cheap cotton costs us. If manufacturing activity means Progress, the town must be more advanced than the country; and the field laborers and village artisans of today must be much less changed from servants of Job than the proletariat of modern London from the proletariat of Cæsar's Rome. Yet the cockney proletarian is so inferior to the village laborer that it is only by steady recruiting from the country that London is kept alive. This does not seem as if the change since Job's time were Progress in the popular sense: quite the reverse. The common stock of discoveries in physics has accumulated a little: that is all.

One more illustration. Is the Englishman prepared to admit that the American is his superior as a human being? I ask this question because the scarcity of labor in America relatively to the demand for it has led to a development of machinery there, and a consequent "increase of command over Nature" which makes many of our English methods appear almost medieval to the up-to-date Chicagoan. This means that the American has an advantage over the Englishman of exactly the same nature that the Englishman has over the contemporaries of Cicero. Is the Englishman prepared to draw the same conclusion in both cases? I think not. The American, of course, will draw it cheerfully; but I must then ask him whether, since a modern negro has a greater "command over Nature" than Washington had, we are also to accept the conclusion, involved in his former one, that humanity has progressed from Washington to the *fin de siècle* negro.

Finally, I would point out that if life is crowned by its success and devotion in industrial organization and ingenuity, we had better worship the ant and the bee (as moralists urge us to do in our childhood) , and humble ourselves before the arrogance of the birds of Aristophanes.

My reason then for ignoring the popular conception of Progress in Cæsar and Cleopatra is that there is no reason to suppose that any Progress has taken place since their time. But even if I shared the popular delusion, I do not see that I could have made any essential difference in the play. I can only imitate humanity as I know it. Nobody knows whether Shakespear thought that ancient Athenian joiners, weavers, or bellows menders were any different from Elizabethan ones; but it is quite certain that he could not have made them so, unless, indeed, he had played the literary man and made Quince say, not "Is all our company here?" but "Bottom: was not that Socrates that passed us at the Piræus with Glaucon and Polemarchus on his way to the house of Kephalus?" And so on.

Cleopatra

Cleopatra was only sixteen when Cæsar went to Egypt; but in Egypt sixteen is a riper age than it is in England. The childishness I have ascribed to her, as far as it is childishness of character and not lack of experience, is not a matter of years. It may be observed in our own climate at the present day in many women of fifty. It is a mistake to suppose that the difference between wisdom and folly has anything to do with the difference between physical age and physical youth. Some women are younger at seventy than most women at seventeen.

It must be borne in mind, too, that Cleopatra was a queen, and was therefore not the typical Greek-cultured, educated Egyptian lady of her time. To represent her by any such type would be as absurd as to represent George IV by a type founded on the attainments of Sir Isaac Newton. It is true that an ordinarily well educated Alexandrian girl of her time would no more have believed bogey stories about the Romans than the daughter of a modern Oxford professor would believe them about the Germans (though, by the way, it is possible to talk great nonsense at Oxford about foreigners when we are at war with them). But I do not feel bound to believe that Cleopatra was well educated. Her father, the illustrious Flute Blower, was not at all a parent of the Oxford professor type. And Cleopatra was a chip of the old block.

Britannus

I find among those who have read this play in manuscript a strong conviction that an ancient Briton could not possibly have been like a modern one. I see no reason to adopt this curious view. It is true that the Roman and Norman conquests must have for a time disturbed the normal British type produced by the climate. But Britannus, born before these events, represents the unadulterated Briton who fought Cæsar and impressed Roman observers much as we should expect the ancestors of Mr Podsnap to impress the cultivated Italians of their time.

I am told that it is not scientific to treat national character as a product of climate. This only shews the wide difference between common knowledge and the intellectual game called science. We have men of exactly the same stock, and speaking the same language, growing in Great Britain, in Ireland, and in America. The result is three of the most distinctly marked nationalities under the sun. Racial characteristics are quite another matter. The difference between a Jew and a Gentile has nothing to do with the difference between an Englishman and a German. The characteristics of Britannus are local characteristics, not race characteristics. In an ancient Briton they would, I take it, be exaggerated, since modern Britain, disforested, drained, urbanified and consequently cosmopolized, is presumably less characteristically British than Cæsar's Britain.

And again I ask does anyone who, in the light of a competent knowledge of his own age, has studied history from contemporary documents, believe that 67 generations of promiscuous marriage have made any appreciable difference in the human fauna of these isles? Certainly I do not.

Julius Cæsar

As to Cæsar himself, I have purposely avoided the usual anachronism of going to Cæsar's books, and concluding that the style is the man. That is only true of authors who have the specific literary genius, and have practised long enough to attain complete self-expression in letters. It is not true even on these conditions in an age when literature is conceived as a game of style, and not as a vehicle of self-expression by the author. Now Cæsar was an amateur stylist writing books of travel and campaign histories in a style so impersonal that the authenticity of the later volumes is disputed. They reveal some of his qualities just as the Voyage of a Naturalist Round the World reveals some of Darwin's, without expressing his private personality. An Englishman reading them would say that Cæsar was a man of great common sense and good taste, meaning thereby a man without originality or moral courage.

In exhibiting Cæsar as a much more various person than the historian of the Gallic wars, I hope I have not been too much imposed on by the dramatic illusion to which all great men owe part of their reputation and some of the whole of it. I admit that reputations gained in war are specially questionable. Able civilians taking up the profession of arms, like Cæsar and Cromwell, in middle age, have snatched all its laurels from opponent commanders bred to it, apparently because capable persons engaged in military pursuits are so scarce that the existence of two of them at the same time in the same hemisphere is extremely rare. The capacity of any conqueror is therefore more likely than not to be an illusion produced by the incapacity of his adversary. At all events, Cæsar might have won his battles without being wiser than Charles XII or Nelson or Joan of Arc, who were, like most modern "self-made" millionaires, half-witted geniuses, enjoying the worship accorded by all races to certain forms of insanity. But Cæsar's victories were only advertisements for an eminence that would never have become popular without them. Cæsar is greater off the battle field than on it. Nelson off his quarterdeck was so quaintly out of the question that when his head was injured at the battle of the Nile, and his conduct became for some years openly scandalous, the difference was not important enough to be noticed. It may, however, be said that peace hath her illusory reputations no less than war. And it is certainly true that in civil life mere capacity for work—the power of killing a dozen secretaries under you, so to speak, as a life-or-death courier kills horses—enables men with common ideas and superstitions to distance all competitors in the strife of political ambition. It was this power of work that astonished Cicero as the most prodigious of Cæsar's gifts, as it astonished later observers in Napoleon before it wore him out. How if Cæsar were nothing but a Nelson and a Gladstone combined! a prodigy of vitality without any special quality of mind! nay, with ideas that were worn out before he was born, as Nelson's and Gladstone's were! I have considered that possibility too, and rejected it. I cannot cite all the stories about Cæsar which seem to me to shew that he was genuinely original; but let me at least point out that I have been careful to attribute nothing but originality to him. Originality gives a man an air of frankness, generosity, and magnanimity by enabling him to estimate the value of truth, money, or success in any particular instance quite independently of convention and moral generalization. He therefore will not, in the ordinary Treasury bench fashion, tell a lie which everybody knows to be a lie (and consequently expects him as a matter of good taste to tell.) His lies are not found out: they pass for candors. He understands the paradox of money, and gives it away when he can get most for it: in other words, when its value is least, which is just when a common man tries hardest to get it. He knows that the real moment of success is not the moment apparent to the crowd. Hence, in order to produce an impression of complete disinterestedness and magnanimity, he has only to act with entire selfishness; and this is perhaps the only sense in which a man can be said to be *naturally* great. It is in this sense that I have represented Cæsar as great. Having virtue, he has no need of goodness. He is neither forgiving, frank, nor generous, because a man who is too great to resent has nothing to forgive; a man who says things that other people are afraid to say need be no more frank than Bismarck was; and there is no generosity in giving things you do not want to people of whom you intend to make use. This distinction between virtue and goodness is not understood in England: hence the poverty of our drama in heroes. Our stage attempts at them are mere goody-goodies. Goodness, in its popular British sense of self-denial, implies that man is vicious by nature, and that supreme goodness is supreme martyrdom. Not sharing that pious opinion, I have not given countenance to it in any of my plays. In this I follow the precedent of the ancient myths, which represent the hero as vanquishing his enemies, not in fair fight, but with enchanted sword, superequine horse and magical invulnerability, the possession of which, from the vulgar moralistic point of view, robs his exploits of any merit whatever.

As to Cæsar's sense of humor, there is no more reason to assume that he lacked it than to assume that he was deaf or blind. It is said that on the occasion of his assassination by a conspiracy of moralists (it is always your moralist who makes assassination a duty, on the scaffold or off it) , he defended himself until the good Brutus struck him, when he exclaimed "What! you too, Brutus!" and disdained further fight. If this be true, he must have been an incorrigible comedian. But even if we waive this story, or accept the traditional sentimental interpretation of it, there is still abundant evidence of his lightheartedness and adventurousness. Indeed it is clear from his whole history that what has been called his ambition was an instinct for exploration. He had much more of Columbus and Franklin in him than of Henry V.

However, nobody need deny Cæsar a share, at least, of the qualities I have attributed to him. All men, much more Julius Cæsars, possess all qualities in some degree. The really interesting question is whether I am right in assuming that the way to produce an impression of greatness is by exhibiting a man, not as mortifying his nature by doing his duty, in the manner which our system of putting little men into great positions (not having enough great men in our influential families to go round) forces us to inculcate, but as simply doing what he naturally wants to do. For this raises the question whether our world has not been wrong in its moral theory for the last 2,500 years or so. It must be a constant puzzle to many of us that the Christian era, so excellent in its intentions, should have been practically such a very discreditable episode in the history of the race. I doubt if this is altogether due to the vulgar and sanguinary sensationalism of our religious legends, with their substitution of gross physical torments and public executions for the passion of humanity. Islam, substituting voluptuousness for torment (a merely superficial difference, it is true) has done no better. It may have been the failure of Christianity to emancipate itself from expiatory theories of moral responsibility, guilt, innocence, reward, punishment, and the rest of it, that baffled its intention of changing the world. But these are bound up in all philosophies of creation as opposed to cosmism. They may therefore be regarded as the price we pay for popular religion.

ANTON CHEKHOV
[1860–1904]

The son of an ex-serf, Anton Chekhov began his writing career with short, realistic tales of the common life that he had experienced among the country and town folk of Czarist Russia. Though he sometimes practiced medicine among the peasantry, his stories sold well enough for him to refrain from the medical practice he had qualified for. He led a relatively quiet life, highlighted by his travels, literary successes, and friendships with famous people. He was known and admired by such opposite temperaments as Tolstoi and Gorki, both of whom perceived in Chekhov a simplicity and gentleness that struck them as almost a kind of saintliness. Gorki, for instance, wrote that "in Anton Chekhov's presence everyone involuntarily felt in himself a desire to be simple, more truthful, more one's self."

Whether Chekhov's quietly merry and retiring temperament was the result of delicate health (he had contracted tuberculosis while studying at the University of Moscow) or of a delicate spirituality, it is surprising that this least dramatic of men should have become a dramatist. He at first professed a disdain for everything theatrical, but wound up married to the theater in more ways than one. Two years before his death, he married the Moscow Art Theatre's ablest actress, Olga Knipper, who often remained in Moscow while Chekhov worked on *The Cherry Orchard* in the country, their marriage largely carried on by correspondence.

The Cherry Orchard, Chekhov's last play, was produced by the famous Stanislavsky in Moscow in 1904. When the strong-minded Stanislavsky played his sprightly comedy as a slow-moving tragedy, Chekhov characteristically said little to Stanislavsky in person, though he grumbled persistently in letters to his wife and friends. *The Cherry Orchard* is a remarkable play for many reasons, one being that it is the play of a man who possessed such strength and health of mind that he could write a gay comedy celebrating life's absurdity even as he knew he was dying.

The Cherry Orchard was preceded by a few minor plays and a trio of major plays—*The Sea Gull* (1896), *Uncle Vanya* (1899), and *The Three Sisters* (1901) —that combine with *The Cherry Orchard* to form an imposing quartet of dramatic achievement.

THE
CHERRY ORCHARD
A Comedy in Four Acts

ANTON CHEKHOV

Translated by Robert Corrigan

CAST

LYUBOV ANDREYEVNA RANEVSKY, *owner of the cherry orchard*
ANYA, *her daughter, age 17*
VARYA, *her adopted daughter, age 24*
LEONID ANDREYEVICH GAEV, *Lyubov's brother*
YERMOLAY ALEXEYEVICH LOPAHIN, *a business man*
PYOTR SERGEYEVICH TROFIMOV, *a student*
BORIS BORISOVICH SEMYONOV-PISHCHIK, *a landowner*

CHARLOTTA IVANOVNA, *a governess*
SEMYON PANTALEYEVICH EPIHODOV, *a clerk on the Ranevsky estate*
DUNYASHA, *a maid*
FEERS, *an old servant, age 87*
YASHA, *a young servant*
A TRAMP
THE STATION MASTER
A POST-OFFICE CLERK
GUESTS *and* SERVANTS

The action takes place on the estate of Madame Ranevsky.

From *Six Plays of Chekhov* edited and translated by Robert W. Corrigan. Rinehart Edition. Copyright © 1962 by Robert W. Corrigan. Reprinted by permission of Holt, Rinehart and Winston, Inc.

ACT I

A room which used to be the children's room and is still called the nursery. Several doors, one leading into ANYA's *room. It is early in the morning and the sun is rising. It is early in May, but there is a morning frost. The windows are closed but through them can be seen the blossoming cherry trees. Enter* DUNYASHA, *carrying a candle, and* LOPAHIN *with a book in his hand.*

LOPAHIN The train's arrived, thank God. What time is it?

DUNYASHA It's nearly two. [*Blows out the candle.*] It's daylight already.

LOPAHIN The train must have been at least two hours late. [*Yawns and stretches.*] And what a fool I am! I make a special trip out here to meet them at the station, and then I fall asleep. . . . Just sat down in the chair and dropped off. What a nuisance. Why didn't you wake me up?

DUNYASHA I thought you'd gone. [*Listens.*] I think they're coming.

LOPAHIN [*Also listens.*] No . . . I should've been there to help them with their luggage and other things . . . [*Pause.*] Lyubov Andreyevna has been abroad for five years. I wonder what she's like now. She used to be such a kind and good person. So easy to get along with and always considerate. Why, I remember when I was fifteen, my father—he had a store in town then—hit me in the face and it made my nose bleed. . . . We'd come out here for something or other, and he was drunk. Oh, I remember it as if it happened yesterday. . . . She was so young and beautiful . . . Lyubov Andreyevna brought me into this very room—the nursery, and she fixed my nose and she said to me, "Don't cry, little peasant, it'll be better by the time you get married.". . . [*Pause.*] "Little peasant". . . She was right, my father was a peasant. And look at me now—going about in a white waistcoat and brown shoes, like a crown in peacock's feathers. Oh, I am rich all right, I've got lots of money, but when you think about it, I'm still just a peasant. [*Turning over pages of the book.*] Here, I've been reading this book, and couldn't understand a word of it. Fell asleep reading it. [*Pause.*]

DUNYASHA The dogs have been awake all night: they know their mistress is coming.

LOPAHIN Why, what's the matter with you, Dunyasha?

DUNYASHA My hands are shaking. I think I'm going to faint.

LOPAHIN You've become too delicate and refined, Dunyasha. You get yourself all dressed up like a lady, and you fix your hair like one, too. You shouldn't do that, you know. You must remember your place.

[*Enter* EPIHODOV *with a bouquet of flowers; he wears a jacket and brightly polished high boots which squeak loudly. As he enters he drops the flowers.*]

EPIHODOV [*Picks up the flowers.*] The gardener sent these. He says they're to go in the dining room. [*Hands the flowers to* DUNYASHA.]

LOPAHIN And bring me some kvass.

DUNYASHA All right.

EPIHODOV It's chilly outside this morning, three degrees of frost, and here the cherry trees are all in bloom. I can't say much for this climate of ours, you know. [*Sighs.*] No, I really can't. It doesn't contribute to—well, you know, things . . . And what do you think, Yermolay Alexeyevich, the day before yesterday I bought myself a pair of boots and they squeak so much . . . well, I mean to say, they're impossible. . . . What can I use to fix them?

LOPAHIN Oh, be quiet! And don't bother me!

EPIHODOV Every day something unpleasant happens to me. But I don't complain; I'm used to it, why I even laugh. [*Enter* DUNYASHA: *she serves* LOPAHIN *with kvass.*] Well, I have to be going. [*Bumps into a chair which falls over.*] There, you see! [*Triumphantly.*] You can see for yourself what I mean, you see . . . so to speak . . . It's absolutely amazing! [*Goes out.*]

DUNYASHA   I must tell you a secret, Yermolay Alexeyevich. Epihodov proposed to me.

LOPAHIN   Really!

DUNYASHA   I don't know what to do. . . . He's a quiet man, but then sometimes he starts talking, and then you can't understand a word he says. It sounds nice, and he says it with so much feeling, but it doesn't make any sense. I think I like him a little, and he's madly in love with me. But the poor man, he's sort of unlucky! Do you know, something unpleasant seems to happen to him every day. That's why they tease him and call him "two-and-twenty misfortunes."

LOPAHIN   [*Listens.*]   I think I hear them coming. . . .

DUNYASHA   Coming! . . . Oh, what's the matter with me. . . . I feel cold all over.

LOPAHIN   Yes, they're really coming! Let's go and meet them at the door. I wonder if she'll recognize me? We haven't seen each other for five years.

DUNYASHA   [*Agitated.*]   I'm going to faint . . . Oh, I'm going to faint! . . .

[*The sound of two carriages driving up to the house can be heard.* LOPAHIN *and* DUNYASHA *hurry out. The stage is empty. Then there are sounds of people arriving in the next room.* FEERS, *who has gone to meet the train, enters the room leaning on a cane. He crosses the stage as rapidly as he can. He is dressed in an old-fashioned livery coat and a top hat and is muttering to himself, though it is impossible to make out what he is saying. The noises off-stage become louder.*]

VOICE   [*Off-stage.*]   Let's go through here.

[*Enter* LYUBOV ANDREYEVNA, ANYA, *and* CHARLOTTA IVANOVNA, *leading a small dog, all in traveling clothes,* VARYA, *wearing an overcoat and a kerchief over her head,* GAEV, SEMYONOV-PISHCHIK, LOPAHIN, DUNYASHA, *carrying a bundle and parasol, and other servants with luggage.*]

ANYA   Let's go through here. Do you remember what room this is, Mamma?

LYUBOV   [*Joyfully, through her tears.*]   The nursery!

VARYA   How cold it is! My hands are numb. [*To* LYUBOV.] Your rooms are the same as always, Mamma dear, the white one, and the lavender one.

LYUBOV   The nursery, my dear, beautiful room! . . . I used to sleep here when I was little. [*Cries.*] And here I am again, like a little child . . . [*She kisses her brother, then* VARYA, *then her brother again.*] And Varya hasn't changed a bit, looking like a nun. And I recognized Dunyasha, too. [*Kisses* DUNYASHA.]

GAEV   The train was two hours late. Just think of it! Such efficiency!

CHARLOTTA   [*To* PISHCHIK.]   And my dog eats nuts, too.

PISHCHIK   [*Astonished.*]   Think of that!

[*They all go out except* ANYA *and* DUNYASHA.]

DUNYASHA   We've waited and waited for you . . . [*Helps* ANYA *to take off her hat and coat.*]

ANYA   I haven't slept for four nights . . . I'm freezing.

DUNYASHA   It was Lent when you left, and it was snowing and freezing; but it's spring now. Darling! [*She laughs and kisses her.*] Oh, how I've missed you! I could hardly stand it. My pet, my precious . . . But I must tell you . . . I can't wait another minute . . .

ANYA   [*Without enthusiasm.*]   What time is it? . . .

DUNYASHA   Epihodov, the clerk, proposed to me right after Easter.

ANYA   You never talk about anything else . . . [*Tidies her hair.*] I've lost all my hairpins. . . . [*She's so tired she can hardly keep on her feet.*]

DUNYASHA I really don't know what to think. He loves me . . . he loves me very much!

ANYA [*Looking through the door into her room, tenderly.*] My own room, my own windows, just as if I'd never left them! I'm home again! Tomorrow I'm going to get up and run right to the garden! Oh, if only I could fall asleep! I couldn't sleep all the way back, I've been so worried.

DUNYASHA Pyotr Sergeyevich came the day before yesterday.

ANYA [*Joyfully.*] Petya!

DUNYASHA We put him in the bathhouse, he's probably asleep now. He said he didn't want to inconvenience you. [*Looks at her watch.*] I should have gotten him up, but Varya told me not to. "Don't you dare get him up," she said.

[*Enter* VARYA *with a bunch of keys at her waist.*]

VARYA Dunyasha, get some coffee, and hurry! Mamma wants some.

DUNYASHA I'll get it right away. [*Goes out.*]

VARYA Thank God, you're back! You're home again. [*Embracing her.*] My little darling's come home! How are you, my precious?

ANYA If you only knew what I've had to put up with!

VARYA I can just imagine . . .

ANYA You remember, I left just before Easter and it was cold then. And Charlotta never stopped talking the whole time, talking and those silly tricks of hers. Why did you make me take Charlotta?

VARYA But you couldn't go all alone, darling. At seventeen!

ANYA When we got to Paris it was cold and snowing. My French was terrible. Mamma was living on the fifth floor, and the place was filled with people —some French ladies, and an old priest with a little book, and the room was full of cigarette smoke. It was so unpleasant. All of a sudden I felt so sorry for Mamma that I put my arms around her neck and hugged her and wouldn't let go I was so upset. Later Mamma cried and was very kind.

VARYA [*Tearfully.*] I can't stand to hear it! . . .

ANYA She had already sold her villa at Mentone, and she had nothing left, not a thing. And I didn't have any money left either, not a penny. In fact, I barely had enough to get to Paris. And Mamma didn't understand it at all. On the way, we'd eat at the best restaurants and she'd order the most expensive dishes and tip the waiters a rouble each. Charlotta's the same way. And Yasha expected a full-course dinner for himself; it was horrible. You know, Yasha is Mamma's valet, now, we brought him with us.

VARYA Yes, I've seen the scoundrel.

ANYA Well, how's everything here? Have you paid the interest on the mortgage?

VARYA With what?

ANYA Oh dear! Oh dear!

VARYA The time runs out in August, and then it will be up for sale.

ANYA Oh dear!

LOPAHIN [*Puts his head through the door and moos like a cow.*] Moo-o. . . . [*Disappears.*]

VARYA [*Tearfully.*] I'd like to hit him . . . [*Clenches her fist.*]

ANYA [*Her arms round* VARYA, *dropping her voice.*] Varya, has he proposed to you? [VARYA *shakes her head.*] But he loves you. . . . Why don't you talk to him, what are you waiting for?

VARYA Nothing will come of it. He's too busy to have time to think of me . . . He doesn't notice me at all. It's easier when he isn't around, it makes me miserable just to see him. Everybody talks of our wedding and congratulates me, but in fact there's nothing to it; it's all a dream. [*In a different tone.*] You've got a new pin, it looks like a bee.

ANYA [*Sadly.*] Mamma bought it for me. [*She goes into her room and then with childlike gaiety.*] Did you know that in Paris I went up in a balloon?

VARYA My darling's home again! My precious one's home. [DUNYASHA *returns with a coffeepot and prepares coffee. Standing by* ANYA'*s door.*] You know, all day long, as I go about the house doing my work, I'm always dreaming. If only we could marry you to some rich man, I'd be more at peace. Then they could go away; first I'd go to the cloisters, and then I'd go on a pilgrimage to Kiev, and then Moscow . . . I'd spend my life just walking from one holy place to another. On and on. Oh, what a wonderful life that would be!

ANYA The birds are singing in the garden. What time is it?

VARYA It must be nearly three. Time you went to bed, darling. [*Goes into* ANYA'*s room.*] Oh, what a wonderful life!
[*Enter* YASHA, *with a blanket and a small bag.*]

YASHA [*Crossing the stage, in an affectedly genteel voice.*] May I go through here?

DUNYASHA My, how you've changed since you've been abroad, Yasha. I hardly recognized you.

YASHA Hm! And who are you?

DUNYASHA When you went away, I was no bigger than this . . . [*Shows her height from the floor.*] I'm Dunyasha, Fyodor's daughter. You don't remember me!

YASHA Hm! You're quite a little peach! [*Looks around and embraces her; she screams and drops a saucer.* YASHA *goes out quickly.*]

VARYA [*In the doorway, crossly.*] What's happening in here?

DUNYASHA [*Tearfully.*] I've broken a saucer.

VARYA That's good luck.

ANYA [*Coming out of her room.*] We ought to warn Mamma that Petya's here.

VARYA I gave strict orders not to wake him up.

ANYA [*Pensively.*] Six years ago father died, and then a month later Grisha was drowned in the river. He was such a beautiful little boy—and only seven! Mamma couldn't stand it so she went away . . . and never looked back. [*Shivers.*] How well I understand her! If she only knew! [*Pause.*] And, Petya was Grisha's tutor, he might remind her . . .
[*Enter* FEERS, *wearing a jacket and a white waistcoat.*]

FEERS [*Goes over and is busy with the samovar.*] The mistress will have her coffee in here. [*Puts on white gloves.*] Is it ready? [*To* DUNYASHA, *severely.*] Where's the cream?

DUNYASHA Oh, I forgot! [*Goes out quickly.*]

FEERS [*Fussing around the coffeepot.*] That girl's hopeless. . . . [*Mutters.*] They've come from Paris . . . Years ago the master used to go to Paris . . . Used to go by carriage . . . [*Laughs.*]

VARYA Feers, what are you laughing at?

FEERS What would you like? [*Happily.*] The mistress has come home! Home at last! I don't mind if I die now . . . [*Weeps with joy.*]
[*Enter* LYUBOV, LOPAHIN, GAEV *and* SEMYONOV-PISHCHIK, *the latter in a long peasant coat of fine cloth and full trousers tucked inside high boots.* GAEV, *as he comes in, moves his arms and body as if he were playing billiards.*]

LYUBOV How does it go now? Let me think . . . The red off the side and into the middle pocket!

GAEV That's right! Then I put the white into the corner pocket! . . . Years ago we used to sleep in this room, and now I'm fifty-one, strange as it may seem.

LOPAHIN   Yes, time flies.

GAEV   What?

LOAPHIN   Time flies, I say.

GAEV   This place smells of patchouli . . .

ANYA   I'm going to bed. Goodnight, Mamma. [*Kisses her.*]

LYUBOV   My precious child! [*Kisses her hands.*] Are you glad you're home? I still can't get used to it.

ANYA   Goodnight, Uncle.

GAEV   [*Kisses her face and hands.*]   God bless you. You're so much like your mother! [*To his sister.*] You looked exactly like her at her age, Lyuba.

ANYA   [*Shakes hands with* LOPAHIN *and* PISHCHIK, *goes out and shuts the door after her.*]

LYUBOV   She's very tired.

PISHCHIK   It's been a long trip for her.

VARYA   [*To* LOPAHIN *and* PISHCHIK.]   Well, gentlemen? It's nearly three o'clock, time to say good-bye.

LYUBOV   [*Laughs.*] You haven't changed a bit, Varya. [*Draws* VARYA *to her and kisses her.*] Let me have some coffee, then we'll all turn in. [FEERS *places a cushion under her feet.*] Thank you, my dear. I've got into the habit of drinking coffee. I drink it day and night. Thank you, my dear old friend. [*Kisses* FEERS.]

VARYA   I'd better see if they brought all the luggage in. [*Goes out.*]

LYUBOV   Is it really me sitting here? [*Laughing.*] I'd like to dance and wave my arms about. [*Covering her face with her hands.*] But am I just dreaming? God, how I love it here—my own country! Oh, I love it so much, I could hardly see anything from the train, I was crying so hard. [*Through tears.*] Here, but I must drink my coffee. Thank you, Feers, thank you, my dear old friend. I'm so glad you're still alive.

FEERS   The day before yesterday.

GAEV   He doesn't hear very well.

LOPAHIN   I've got to leave for Kharkov a little after four. What a nuisance! It's so good just to see you, and I want to talk with you . . . You look as lovely as ever.

PISHCHIK   [*Breathing heavily.*] Prettier. In her fancy Parisian clothes . . . She's simply ravishing!

LOPAHIN   Your brother here—Leonid Andreyevich—says that I'm nothing but a hick from the country, a tight-fisted peasant, but it doesn't bother me. Let him say what he likes. All I want is that you trust me as you always have. Merciful God! My father was your father's serf, and your grandfather's, too, but you've done so much for me that I've forgotten all that. I love you as if you were my own sister . . . more than that even.

LYUBOV   I just can't sit still, I can't for the life of me! [*She jumps up and walks about in great excitement.*] I'm so happy, it's too much for me. It's all right, you can laugh at me. I know I'm being silly . . . My wonderful old bookcase! [*Kisses bookcase.*] And my little table!

GAEV   You know, the old Nurse died while you were away.

LYUBOV   [*Sits down and drinks coffee.*]   Yes, you wrote to me about it. May she rest in peace.

GAEV   Anastasy died, too. And Petrushka quit and is working in town for the chief of police. [*Takes a box of gumdrops out of his pocket and puts one in his mouth.*]

PISHCHIK   My daughter, Dashenka, sends you her greetings.

LOPAHIN   I feel like telling you some good news, something to cheer you up. [*Looks at his watch.*] I'll have to leave in a minute, so there's not much time to talk. But briefly it's this. As you know, the cherry orchard is going to be sold to pay your debts. They've set August 22nd as the date for the auction, but you can sleep in peace and not worry about it; there's a way out. Here's my plan, so please pay close attention. Your estate is only twenty miles from town, and the railroad is close by. Now, if the cherry orchard and the land along the river were subdivided and leased for the building of summer cottages, you'd have a yearly income of at least twenty-five thousand roubles.

GAEV   Such nonsense!

LYUBOV   I'm afraid I don't quite understand, Yermolay Alexeyevich.

LOPAHIN   You'd divide the land into one acre lots and rent them for at least twenty-five roubles a year. I'll bet you, that if you advertise it now there won't be a lot left by the fall; they'll be snapped up almost at once. You see, you're saved! And really, I must congratulate you; it's a perfect setup. The location is marvelous and the river's deep enough for swimming. Of course, the land will have to be cleared and cleaned up a bit. For instance, all those old buildings will have to be torn down . . . And this house, too . . . but then it's not really good for anything any more. . . . And then, the old cherry orchard will have to be cut down . . .

LYUBOV   Cut down? My good man, forgive me, but you don't seem to understand. If there's one thing that's interesting and really valuable in this whole part of the country, it's our cherry orchard.

LOPAHIN   The only valuable thing about it is that it's very large. It only produces a crop every other year and then who wants to buy it?

GAEV   Why, this orchard is even mentioned in the Encyclopedia.

LOPAHIN   [*Looking at his watch.*]   If you don't decide now, and do something about it before August, the cherry orchard as well as the estate will be auctioned off. So make up your minds! There's no other way out, I promise you. There's no other way.

FEERS   In the old days, forty or fifty years ago, the cherries were dried, preserved, pickled, made into jam, and sometimes. . . .

GAEV   Be quiet, Feers.

FEERS   And sometimes, whole wagon-loads of dried cherries were shipped to Moscow and Kharkov. We used to make a lot of money on them then! And the dried cherries used to be soft, juicy, sweet, and very good . . . They knew how to do it then . . . they had a way of cooking them . . .

LYUBOV   And where is that recipe now?

FEERS   They've forgotten it. Nobody can remember it.

PISHCHIK   [*To* LYUBOV.]   What's it like in Paris. Did you eat frogs?

LYUBOV   I ate crocodiles.

PISHCHIK   Well, will you imagine that!

LOPAHIN   Until recently only rich people and peasants lived in the country, but now lots of people come out for the summer. Almost every town, even the small ones, is surrounded with summer places. And probably within the next twenty years there'll be more and more of these people. Right now, all they do is sit on the porch and drink tea, but later on they might begin to grow a few things, and then your cherry orchard would be full of life again . . . rich and prosperous.

GAEV   [*Indignantly.*]   Such a lot of nonsense!

[*Enter* VARYA *and* YASHA.]

VARYA   There were two telegrams for you, Mamma dear. [*Takes out the keys and opens the old bookcase, making a great deal of noise.*] Here they are.

LYUBOV They're from Paris. [*Tears them up without reading them.*] I'm through with Paris.

GAEV Do you know, Lyuba, how old this bookcase is? Last week I pulled out the bottom drawer, and I found the date it was made burned in the wood. Just think, it's exactly a hundred years old. What do you think of that, eh? We ought to celebrate its anniversary. I know it's an inanimate object, but still—it's a bookcase!

PISHCHIK [*Astonished.*] A hundred years! Can you imagine that!

GAEV Yes . . . That's quite something [*Feeling round the bookcase with his hands.*] Dear, most honored bookcase! I salute you! For one hundred years you have served the highest ideals of goodness and justice. For one hundred years you have made us aware of the need for creative work; several generations of our family have had their courage sustained and their faith in a brighter future fortified by your silent call; you have fostered in us the ideals of public service and social consciousness. [*Pause.*]

LOPAHIN Yes . . .

LYUBOV You haven't changed a bit, Leonid.

GAEV [*Slightly embarrassed.*] I shoot it off the corner into the middle pocket! . . .

LOPAHIN [*Looks at his watch.*] Well, I've got to go.

YASHA [*Brings medicine to* LYUBOV.] Would you like to take your pills now; it's time.

PISHCHIK You shouldn't take medicine, my dear . . . they don't do you any good . . . or harm either. Let me have them. [*Takes the box from her, pours the pills into the palm of his hand, blows on them, puts them all into his mouth and drinks them down with kvass.*] There!

LYUBOV [*Alarmed.*] You're out of your mind!

PISHCHIK I took all the pills.

LOPAHIN What a stomach! [*All laugh.*]

FEERS His honor was here during Holy Week, and he ate half a bucket of pickles. [*Mutters.*]

LYUBOV What's he saying?

VARYA He's been muttering like that for three years now. We're used to it.

YASHA It's his age. . . .

[CHARLOTTA IVANOVNA, *very thin, and tightly laced in a white dress, with a lorgnette at her waist, passes across the stage.*]

LOPAHIN Excuse me, Charlotta Ivanovna, for not greeting you. I didn't have a chance. [*Tries to kiss her hand.*]

CHARLOTTA [*Withdrawing her hand.*] If I let you kiss my hand, then you'd want to kiss my elbow next, and then my shoulder.

LOPAHIN This just isn't my lucky day. [*All laugh.*] Charlotta Ivanovna, do a trick for us.

CHARLOTTA Not now. I want to go to bed. [*Goes out.*]

LOPAHIN I'll be back in three weeks. [*Kisses* LYUBOV's *hand.*] It's time I'm going so I'll say good-bye. [*To* GAEV.] Au revoir. [*Embraces* PISHCHIK.] Au revoir. [*Shakes hands with* VARYA, *then with* FEERS *and* YASHA.] I don't want to go, really. [*To* LYUBOV.] Think over the idea of the summer cottages and if you decide anything, let me know, and I'll get you a loan of at least fifty thousand. So think it over seriously.

VARYA [*Crossly.*] Won't you ever go?

LOPAHIN I'm going, I'm going. [*Goes out.*]

GAEV What a boor! I beg your pardon . . . Varya's going to marry him, he's Varya's fiancé.

VARYA Please don't talk like that, Uncle.

LYUBOV   Well, Varya, I'd be delighted. He's a good man.

PISHCHIK   He's a man . . . you have to say that . . . a most worthy fellow . . . My Dashenka says so too . . . she says all sorts of things. . . . [*He drops asleep and snores, but wakes up again at once.*] By the way, my dear, will you lend me two hundred and forty roubles? I've got to pay the interest on the mortgage tomorrow . . .

VARYA   [*In alarm.*]   We haven't got it, really we haven't!

LYUBOV   It's true, I haven't got a thing.

PISHCHIK   It'll turn up. [*Laughs.*] I never lose hope. There are times when I think everything's lost, I'm ruined, and then—suddenly!—a railroad is built across my land, and they pay me for it! Something's bound to happen, if not today, then tomorrow, or the next day. Perhaps Dashenka will win two thousand—she's got a lottery ticket.

LYUBOV   Well, we've finished our coffee; now we can go to bed.

FEERS   [*Brushing* GAEV, *admonishing him.*]   You've got on the trousers again! What am I going to do with you?

VARYA   [*In a low voice.*]   Anya's asleep. [*Quietly opens a window.*] The sun's rising and see how wonderful the trees are! And the air smells so fragrant! The birds are beginning to sing.

GAEV   [*Coming to the window.*]   The orchard is all white. You haven't forgotten, Lyuba? How straight that lane is . . . just like a ribbon. And how it shines on moonlight nights. Do you remember? You haven't forgotten, have you?

LYUBOV   [*Looks through the window at the orchard.*]   Oh, my childhood, my innocent childhood! I used to sleep here, and I'd look out at the orchard and every morning when I woke up I was so happy. The orchard was exactly the same, nothing's changed. [*Laughs happily.*] All, all white! Oh, my orchard! After the dark, gloomy autumn and the cold winter, you are young again and full of joy; the angels have not deserted you! If only this burden could be taken from me, if only I could forget my past!

GAEV   Yes, and now the orchard's going to be sold to pay our debts, how strange it all is.

LYUBOV   Look, there's Mother walking through the orchard . . . dressed all in white! [*Laughs happily.*] It is Mother!

GAEV   Where?

VARYA   Oh, please, Mamma dear!

LYUBOV   You're right, it's no one, I only imagined it. Over there, you see, on the right, by the path that goes to the arbor, there's a small white tree that's bending so it looks just like a woman.

[*Enter* TROFIMOV. *He is dressed in a shabby student's uniform, and wears glasses.*]

What a wonderful orchard! Masses of white blossoms, the blue sky . . .

TROFIMOV   Lyubov Andreyevna! [*She turns to him.*] I'll just say hello and leave at once. [*Kisses her hand warmly.*] They told me to wait until morning, but I couldn't wait any longer. [LYUBOV *looks at him, puzzled.*]

VARYA   [*Through tears.*]   This is Petya Trofimov.

TROFIMOV   Petya Trofimov, I was Grisha's tutor. Have I changed that much? [LYUBOV *puts her arms round him and weeps quietly.*]

GAEV   [*Embarrassed.*]   Now, now, Lyuba . . .

VARYA   [*Weeps.*]   Didn't I tell you to wait until tomorrow, Petya?

LYUBOV   My Grisha . . . my little boy . . . Oh, Grisha . . . my son . . .

VARYA   Don't cry, Mamma darling. There's nothing we can do, it was God's will.

TROFIMOV   [*Gently, with emotion.*]   Don't, don't . . . please.

LYUBOV [*Weeping quietly.*] My little boy was lost . . . drowned . . . Why? Why, my friend? [*More quietly.*] Anya's asleep in there, and here I'm crying and making a scene. But tell me, Petya, what's happened to your good looks? You've aged so.

TROFIMOV A peasant woman on the train called me "that moth-eaten man."

LYUBOV You used to be such an attractive boy, a typical young student. But now your hair is thin and you wear glasses. Are you still a student? [*She walks to the door.*]

TROFIMOV I expect I'll be a student as long as I live.

LYUBOV [*Kisses her brother, then* VARYA.] Well, go to bed now. You have aged, too, Leonid.

PISHCHIK [*Following her.*] Yes, I suppose it's time to get to bed. Oh, my gout! I'd better spend the night here, and in the morning, Lyubov Andreyevna, my dear, I'd like to borrow the two hundred and forty roubles.

GAEV Don't you ever stop?

PISHCHIK Just two hundred and forty roubles . . . To pay the interest on my mortgage.

LYUBOV I haven't any money, my friend.

PISHCHIK Oh, I'll pay you back, my dear. It's not much, after all.

LYUBOV Oh, all right. Leonid will give it to you. You give him the money, Leonid.

GAEV Why, of course; glad to. As much as he wants!

LYUBOV What else can we do? He needs it. He'll pay it back.
 [LYUBOV, TROFIMOV, PISHCHIK *and* FEERS *go out.* GAEV, VARYA *and* YASHA *remain.*]

GAEV My sister hasn't lost her habit of throwing money away. [*To* YASHA.] Get out of the way, you smell like a barnyard.

YASHA [*With a sneer.*] And you haven't changed either, have you Leonid Andreyevich?

GAEV What's that? [*To* VARYA.] What did he say?

VARYA [*To* YASHA.] Your mother came out from town yesterday to see you, and she's been waiting out in the servant's quarters ever since.

YASHA I wish she wouldn't bother me.

VARYA Oh, you ought to be ashamed of yourself.

YASHA What's she in such a hurry for? She could have come tomorrow. [YASHA *goes out.*]

VARYA Mamma hasn't changed a bit. She'd give away everything we had, if she could.

GAEV Yes . . . You know, when many things are prescribed to cure a disease, that means it's incurable. I've been wracking my brains to find an answer, and I've come up with several solutions, plenty of them—which means there aren't any. It would be wonderful if we could inherit some money, or if our Anya were to marry some very rich man, or if one of us went to Yaroslavl and tried our luck with our old aunt, the Countess. You know she's very rich.

VARYA [*Weeping.*] If only God would help us.

GAEV Oh, stop blubbering! The Countess is very rich, but she doesn't like us . . . To begin with, my sister married a lawyer, and not a nobleman . . . [ANYA *appears in the doorway.*] She married a commoner . . . and since then no one can say she's behaved in the most virtuous way possible. She's good, kind, and lovable, and I love her very much, but no matter how much you may allow for extenuating circumstances, you've got to admit that her morals have not been beyond reproach. You can sense it in everything she does . . .

VARYA [*In a whisper.*] Anya's standing in the doorway.

GAEV What? [*A pause.*] Isn't that strange, something's gotten into my right eye . . . I'm having a terrible time seeing. and last Thursday, when I was in the District Court . . . [ANYA *comes in.*]

VARYA Anya, why aren't you asleep?

ANYA I don't feel like sleeping. I just can't.

GAEV My dear little girl! [*Kisses* ANYA's *face and hands.*] My child! [*Tearfully.*] You're not just my niece, you're an angel, my whole world. Please believe me, believe . . .

ANYA I believe you, Uncle. Everyone loves you, respects you . . . but, dear Uncle, you shouldn't talk so much, just try to keep quiet. What were you saying just now about mother, about your own sister? What made you say that?

GAEV Yes, yes! [*He takes her hand and puts it over his face.*] You're quite right, it was a horrible thing to say! My God! My God! And that speech I made to the bookcase . . . so stupid! As soon as I finished it, I realized how stupid it was.

VARYA It's true, Uncle dear, you oughtn't to talk so much. Just keep quiet, that's all.

ANYA If you keep quiet, you'll find life is more peaceful.

GAEV I'll be quiet. [*Kisses* ANYA's *and* VARYA's *hands.*] I'll be quiet. But I must tell you something about all this business, it's important. Last Thursday I went to the District Court, and I got talking with some friends, and from what they said it looks as if it might be possible to get a second mortgage so we can pay the interest to the bank.

VARYA If only God would help us!

GAEV I'm going again on Tuesday to talk with them some more. [*To* VARYA.] Oh, stop crying. [*To* ANYA.] Your mother's going to talk with Lopahin, and he certainly won't refuse her. And after you've had a little rest, you can go to Yaroslavl to see your grandmother, the Countess. You see, we'll attack the problem from three sides, and—it's as good as solved! We'll pay the interest, I'm sure of it. [*He eats a gumdrop.*] On my honor, on anything you like, I swear the estate'll not be sold! [*Excited.*] I'll bet my happiness on it! Here's my hand, you can call me a worthless liar if I allow the auction to take place. I swear it with all my soul!

ANYA [*Calmer, with an air of happiness.*] How good you are, Uncle, and how sensible! [*Embracing him.*] I'm not afraid anymore. I feel so happy and at peace.

[*Enter* FEERS.]

FEERS [*Reproachfully.*] Leonid Andreyevich, aren't you ashamed of yourself? When are you going to bed?

GAEV In a minute. Now you go away, Feers. I can get ready for bed myself. Come along, children, time for bed. We'll talk about it some more to-morrow, you must go to bed now. [*Kisses* ANYA *and* VARYA.] You know, I'm a man of the 'eighties. People don't think much of that period these days, but still I can say that I've suffered a great deal in my lifetime because of my convictions. There's a reason why the peasants love me. You have to know the peasants! You have to know . . .

ANYA You're beginning again, Uncle!

VARYA Yes, you'd better keep quiet, Uncle dear.

FEERS [*Sternly.*] Leonid Andreyevich!

GAEV I'm coming, I'm coming! Go to bed now! Bank the white into the side pocket. There's a shot for you . . . [*Goes out;* FEERS *hobbles after him.*]

ANYA I feel better now, although I don't want to go to Yaroslavl. I don't like the Countess at all, but then, thanks to Uncle, we really don't have to worry at all. [*She sits down.*]

VARYA   I've got to get some sleep. I'm going. Oh, by the way, we had a terrible scene while you were gone. You know, there are only a few old servants left out in the servants' quarters: just Yefmushka, Polya, Yevstignay, and Karp. Well, they let some tramp sleep out there, and at first I didn't say anything about it. But then later, I heard people saying that I had given orders to feed them nothing but beans. Because I was stingy, you see . . . Yevstignay was the cause of it all. "Well," I think to myself, "if that's how things are, just you wait!" So I called Yevstignay in. [*Yawns.*] So he came. "What's all this, Yevstignay," I said to him, "you're such a fool." [*She walks up to* ANYA.] Anichka! [*A pause.*] She's asleep! . . . [*Takes her arm.*] Let's go to bed! Come! [*Leads her away.*] My darling's fallen asleep! Come . . . [*They go towards the door. The sound of a shepherd's pipe is heard from far away, beyond the orchard.* TROFIMOV *crosses the stage, but, seeing* VARYA *and* ANYA, *stops.*] Sh-sh! She's asleep . . . asleep . . . Come along, come along.

ANYA   [*Softly, half-asleep.*]   I'm so tired. . . . I can hear the bells ringing all the time . . . Uncle . . . dear . . . Mamma and Uncle. . . .

VARYA   Come, darling, come. . . . [*They go into* ANYA's *room.*]

TROFIMOV   [*Deeply moved.*]   Oh, Anya . . . my sunshine! My spring!

CURTAIN

ACT II

An old abandoned chapel in a field. Beside it are a well, an old bench, and some tombstones. A road leads to the Ranevsky estate. On one side a row of poplars casts a shadow; at that point the cherry orchard begins. In the distance, a line of telegraph poles can be seen, and beyond them, on the horizon, is the outline of a large town, visible only in very clear weather. It's nearly sunset. CHARLOTTA, YASHA *and* DUNYASHA *are sitting on the bench;* EPIHODOV *is standing near by, playing a guitar; everyone is lost in thought.* CHARLOTTA *is wearing an old hunting cap; she has taken a shotgun off her shoulder and is adjusting the buckle on the strap.*

CHARLOTTA   [*Thoughtfully.*]   I don't know how old I am. For you see, I haven't got a passport . . . but I keep pretending that I'm still very young. When I was a little girl, my father and mother traveled from fair to fair giving performances—oh, very good ones. And I used to do the "salto-mortale" and all sorts of other tricks, too. When Papa and Mamma died, a German lady took me to live with her and sent me to school. So when I grew up I became a governess. But where I come from and who I am, I don't know. Who my parents were—perhaps they weren't even married—I don't know. [*Taking a cucumber from her pocket and beginning to eat it.*] I don't know anything. [*Pause.*] I'm longing to talk to someone, but there isn't anybody. I haven't anybody . . .

EPIHODOV   [*Plays the guitar and sings.*]   "What care I for the noisy world? . . . What care I for friends and foes?" How pleasant it is to play the mandolin!

DUNYASHA That's a guitar, nôt a mandolin. [*She looks at herself in a little mirror and powders her face.*]

EPIHODOV To a man who's madly in love this is a mandolin. [*Sings quietly.*] "If only my heart were warmed by the fire of love requited." . . . [YASHA *joins in.*]

CHARLOTTA How dreadfully these people sing! . . . Ach! Like a bunch of jackals.

DUNYASHA [*To* YASHA.] You're so lucky to have been abroad!

YASHA Of course I am. Naturally. [*Yawns, then lights a cigar.*]

EPIHODOV Stands to reason. Abroad everything's reached its maturity . . . I mean to say, everything's been going on for such a long time.

YASHA Obviously.

EPIHODOV Now, I'm a cultured man, I read all kinds of extraordinary books, you know, but somehow I can't seem to figure out where I'm going, what it is I really want, I mean to say—whether to live or to shoot myself. Nevertheless, I always carry a revolver on me. Here it is. [*Shows the revolver.*]

CHARLOTTA That's finished, so now I'm going. [*Slips the strap of the gun over her shoulder.*] Yes, Epihodov, you are a very clever man, and frightening, too; the women must be wild about you! Brr! [*Walks off.*] All these clever people are so stupid, I haven't anyone to talk to. I'm so lonely, always alone, I have nobody and . . . and who I am and what I'm here for, nobody knows . . . [*Wanders out.*]

EPIHODOV Frankly, and I want to keep to the point, I have to admit that Fate, so to speak, treats me absolutely without mercy, like a small ship is buffeted by the storm, as it were. I mean to say, suppose I'm mistaken, then why for instance should I wake up this morning and suddenly see a gigantic spider sitting on my chest? Like this . . . [*Showing the size with both hands.*] Or if I pick up a jug to have a drink of kvass, there's sure to be something horrible, like a cockroach, inside it. [*Pause.*] Have you read Buckle? [*Pause.*] May I trouble you for a moment, Dunyasha? I'd like to speak with you.

DUNYASHA Well, go ahead.

EPIHODOV I'd very much like to speak with you alone. [*Sighs.*]

DUNYASHA [*Embarrassed.*] Oh, all right . . . But first bring me my little cape . . . It's hanging by the cupboard. It's getting terribly chilly . . .

EPIHODOV Very well, I'll get it. . . . Now I know what to do with my revolver. [*Takes his guitar and goes off playing it.*]

YASHA Two-and-twenty misfortunes! Just between you and me, he's a stupid fool. [*Yawns.*]

DUNYASHA I hope to God he doesn't shoot himself. [*Pause.*] He makes me so nervous and I'm always worrying about him. I came to live here when I was still a little girl. Now I no longer know how to live a simple life, and my hands are as white . . . as white as a lady's. I've become such a delicate and sensitive creature. I'm afraid of everything . . . so frightened. If you deceive me, Yasha, I don't know what will happen to my nerves.

YASHA [*Kisses her.*] You sweet little peach! Just remember, a girl must always control herself. Personally I think nothing is worse than a girl who doesn't behave herself.

DUNYASHA I love you so much, so passionately! You're so intelligent, you can talk about anything. [*Pause.*]

YASHA [*Yawns.*] Yes, I suppose so . . . In my opinion, it's like this: if a girl loves someone it means she's immoral. [*Pause.*] I enjoy smoking a cigar in the fresh air . . . [*Listens.*] Someone's coming. It's the ladies and gentlemen.

. . . [DUNYASHA *impulsively embraces him.*] Go to the house now, as though you'd been swimming down at the river. No, this way or they'll see you. I wouldn't want them to think I was interested in you.

DUNYASHA [*Coughing softly.*] That cigar has given me such a headache . . . [*Goes out.*]

[YASHA *remains sitting by the shrine. Enter* LYUBOV, GAEV *and* LOPAHIN.]

LOPAHIN You've got to make up your minds once and for all; there's no time to lose. After all, it's a simple matter. Will you lease your land for the cottages, or won't you? You can answer in one word: yes or no? Just one word!

LYUBOV Who's been smoking such wretched cigars? [*Sits down.*]

GAEV How very convenient everything is with the railroad nearby. [*Sits down.*] Well, here we are—we've been to town, had lunch and we're home already. I put the red into the middle pocket! I'd like to go in . . . just for one game. . . .

LYUBOV You've got lots of time.

LOPAHIN Just one word! [*Beseechingly.*] Please give me an answer!

GAEV [*Yawns.*] What did you say?

LYUBOV [*Looking into her purse.*] Yesterday I had lots of money, but today there's practically none left. My poor Varya feeds us all milk soups to economize; the old servants in the kitchen have nothing but dried peas, and here I am wasting money senselessly, I just don't understand it. . . . [*She drops her purse, scattering gold coins.*] Now I've dropped it again. . . . [*Annoyed.*]

YASHA Allow me, madam, I'll pick them right up. [*Picks up the money.*]

LYUBOV Thank you, Yasha . . . And why did we go out for lunch today? And that restaurant of yours . . . the food was vile, the music ghastly, and the tablecloths smelled of soap. And Leonid, why do you drink so much? And eat so much? And talk so much? Today at the restaurant you were at it again, and it was all so pointless. About the seventies, and the decadents. And to whom? Really, talking to the waiters about the decadents!

LOPAHIN Yes, that's too much.

GAEV [*Waving his hand.*] I know I'm hopeless. [*To* YASHA, *irritably.*] Why are you always bustling about in front of me?

YASHA [*Laughs.*] The minute you open your mouth I start laughing.

GAEV [*To his sister.*] Either he goes, or I do. . . .

LYUBOV Get along, Yasha, you'd better leave us now.

YASHA [*Hands the purse to* LYUBOV.] I'm going. [*He can hardly restrain his laughter.*] Right this minute. . . . [*Goes out.*]

LOPAHIN You know, that rich merchant Deriganov is thinking of buying your estate. They say he's coming to the auction himself.

LYUBOV Where did you hear that?

LOPAHIN That's what they say in town.

GAEV Our Aunt in Yaroslavl has promised to send us some money, but when and how much we don't know.

LOPAHIN How much will she send? A hundred thousand? Two hundred?

LYUBOV Well, hardly . . . Ten or fifteen thousand, perhaps. And we should be thankful for that.

LOPAHIN Forgive me for saying it, but really, in my whole life I've never met such unrealistic, unbusinesslike, queer people as you. You're told in plain language that your estate's going to be sold, and you don't seem to understand it at all.

LYUBOV But what are we to do? Please, tell us.

LOPAHIN I keep on telling you. Every day I tell you the same thing. You must lease the cherry orchard and the rest of the land for summer cottages, and you must do it now, as quickly as possible. It's almost time for the auction. Please, try to understand! Once you definitely decide to lease it for the cottages, you'll be able to borrow as much money as you like, and you'll be saved.

LYUBOV   Summer cottages and vacationers! Forgive me, but it's so vulgar.

GAEV   I agree with you entirely.

LOPAHIN   Honestly, I'm going to burst into tears, or scream, or faint. I can't stand it any more! It's more than I can take! [*To* GAEV.] And you're an old woman!

GAEV   What did you say?

LOPAHIN   I said, you're an old woman!

LYUBOV   [*Alarmed.*]   No, don't go, please stay. I beg you! Perhaps we can think of something.

LOPAHIN   What's there to think of?

LYUBOV   Please don't go! I feel so much more cheerful when you're here. [*Pause.*] I keep expecting something horrible to happen . . . as though the house were going to collapse on top of us.

GAEV   [*In deep thought.*]   I bank it off the cushions, and then into the middle pocket. . . .

LYUBOV   We've sinned too much. . . .

LOPAHIN   Sinned! What sins have you . . .

GAEV   [*Putting a gumdrop into his mouth.*]   They say I've eaten up my fortune in gumdrops. [*Laughs.*]

LYUBOV   Oh, my sins! Look at the way I've always wasted money. It's madness. And then I married a man who had nothing but debts. And he was a terrible drinker . . . Champagne killed him! And then, as if I hadn't enough misery, I fell in love with someone else. We went off together, and just at that time—it was my first punishment, a blow that broke my heart—my little boy was drowned right here in this river . . . so I went abroad. I went away for good, never to return, never to see this river again . . . I just shut my eyes and ran away in a frenzy of grief, but *he* . . . he followed me. It was so cruel and brutal of him! I bought a villa near Mentone because he fell ill there, and for three years, day and night, I never had any rest. He was very sick, and he completely exhausted me; my soul dried up completely. Then, last year when the villa had to be sold to pay the debts, I went to Paris, and there he robbed me of everything I had and left me for another woman. . . . I tried to poison myself. . . . It was all so stupid, so shameful! And then suddenly I felt an urge to come back to Russia, to my own country, to my little girl . . . [*Dries her tears.*] Oh, Lord, Lord, be merciful, forgive my sins! Don't punish me any more! [*Takes a telegram out of her pocket.*] This came from Paris today. He's asking my forgiveness, he's begging me to return. [*Tears up the telegram.*] Sounds like music somewhere. [*Listens.*]

GAEV   That's our famous Jewish orchestra. Don't you remember, four violins, a flute, and a bass?

LYUBOV   Are they still playing? Sometime we should have a dance and they could play for us.

LOPAHIN   [*Listens.*] I can't hear anything . . . [*Sings quietly.*] "And the Germans, if you pay, will turn Russians into Frenchmen, so they say" . . . [*Laughs.*] I saw a wonderful play last night. It was so funny.

LYUBOV   It probably wasn't funny at all. Instead of going to plays, you should take a good look at yourself. Just think how dull your life is, and how much nonsense you talk!

LOPAHIN   That's true, I admit it! Our lives are stupid . . . [*Pause.*] My father was a peasant, an idiot. He knew nothing and he taught me nothing. He only beat me when he was drunk, and always with a stick. And as a matter of fact, I'm just as much an idiot myself. I don't know anything and my handwriting's awful. I'm ashamed for people to see it—it's like a pig's.

LYUBOV   You ought to get married, my friend.

LOPAHIN   Yes . . . That's true.

LYUBOV   You ought to marry our Varya. She's a fine girl.

LOPAHIN   Yes.

LYUBOV   She comes from simple people, and she works hard all day long without stopping. But the main thing is she loves you, and you've liked her for a long time yourself.

LOPAHIN   Well. . . . I think it's a fine idea . . . She's a nice girl. [*Pause.*]

GAEV   I've been offered a job at the bank. Six thousand a year. Did I tell you?

LYUBOV   Yes, you did. You'd better stay where you are.
    [FEERS *enters, bringing an overcoat.*]

FEERS   [*To* GAEV.]   Please put it on, sir, you might catch cold.

GAEV   [*Puts on the overcoat.*]   Oh, you *are* a nuisance.

FEERS   You must stop this! You went off this morning without letting me know. [*Looks him over.*]

LYUBOV   How you've aged, Feers!

FEERS   What can I do for you, Madam?

LOPAHIN   She says you've aged a lot.

FEERS   I've lived for a long time. They were planning to marry me before your father was born. [*Laughs.*] Why, I was already head butler at the time of the emancipation, but I wouldn't take my freedom, I stayed on with the master and mistress. . . . [*Pause.*] I remember everyone was happy at the time, but what they were happy about, they didn't know themselves.

LOPAHIN   That was the good life all right! All the peasants were flogged!

FEERS   [*Not having heard him.*]   That's right! The peasants belonged to their masters, and the masters belonged to the peasants; but now everything's all confused, and people don't know what to make of it.

GAEV   Be quiet, Feers. Tomorrow I've got to go to town. I've been promised an introduction to some general or other who might lend us some money for the mortgage.

LOPAHIN   Nothing will come of it. And how would you pay the interest, anyway?

LYUBOV   He's talking nonsense again. There aren't any generals.
    [*Enter* TROFIMOV, ANYA *and* VARYA.]

GAEV   Here come the children.

ANYA   There's Mamma.

LYUBOV   Come here, my dears. Oh, my darling children. . . . [*Embraces* ANYA *and* VARYA.] If you only knew how much I love you! Here now, sit down beside me. [*All sit down.*]

LOPAHIN   Our perennial student is always with the girls.

TROFIMOV   It's none of your business.

LOPAHIN   He'll soon be fifty, and he's still a student.

TROFIMOV   Oh, stop your stupid jokes.

LOPAHIN   What's bothering you? My, you *are* a strange fellow!

TROFIMOV   Why do you keep pestering me?

LOPAHIN   [*Laughs.*]   Just let me ask you one question: what's your opinion of me?

TROFIMOV   My opinion of you, Yermolay Alexeyevich, is this: you're a rich man, and soon you'll be a millionaire. For the same reason that wild beasts are necessary to maintain nature's economic laws, you are necessary, too—each of you devours everything that gets in his way.

[*Everybody laughs.*]

VARYA   You'd better talk about the planets, Petya.

LYUBOV   No, let's go on with the conversation we had yesterday.

TROFIMOV   What was that?

GAEV   About pride.

TROFIMOV   We talked for a long time yesterday, but we didn't agree on anything. The proud man, the way you use the word, has some mysterious quality about him. Perhaps you're right in a way, but if we look at it simply, without trying to be too subtle, you have to ask yourself why should we be proud at all? Why be proud when you realize that Man, as a species, is poorly constructed physiologically, and is usually coarse, stupid, and profoundly unhappy, too? We ought to put an end to such vanity and just go to work. That's right, we ought to work.

GAEV   You'll die just the same, no matter what you do.

TROFIMOV   Who knows? And anyway, what does it mean—to die? It could be that man has a hundred senses, and when he dies only the five that are known perish, while the other ninety-five go on living.

LYUBOV   How clever you are, Petya!

LOPAHIN   [*Ironically.*]   Oh, very clever!

TROFIMOV   Humanity is continually advancing, is continually seeking to perfect its powers. Someday all the things which we can't understand now, will be made clear. But if this is to happen, we've got to work, work with all our might to help those who are searching for truth. Up until now, here in Russia only a few have begun to work. Nearly all of the intelligentsia that I know have no commitment, they don't do anything, and are as yet incapable of work. They call themselves "the intelligentsia," but they still run roughshod over their servants, and they treat the peasants like animals, they study without achieving anything, they read only childish drivel, and they don't do a thing. As for their knowledge of science, it's only jargon, and they have no appreciation of art either. They are all so serious, and they go about with solemn looks on their faces; they philosophize and talk about important matters; and yet before our very eyes our workers are poorly fed, they live in the worst kind of squalor, sleeping not on beds, but on the floor thirty to forty in a room—with roaches, odors, dampness, and depravity everywhere. It's perfectly clear that all our moralizing is intended to deceive not only ourselves, but others as well. Tell me, where are the nursery schools we're always talking about, where are the libraries? We only write about them in novels, but in actuality there aren't any. There's nothing but dirt, vulgarity, and decadent Orientalism. . . . I'm afraid of those serious faces, I don't like them; I'm afraid of serious talk. It would be better if we'd just keep quiet.

LOPAHIN   Well, let me tell you that *I'm* up before five every morning, and I work from morning till night. I always have money, my own and other people's, and I have lots of opportunities to see what the people around me are like. You only have to start doing something to realize how few honest, decent people there are. Sometimes, when I can't sleep, I start thinking about it. God's given us immense forests, and wide-open fields, and unlimited horizons—living in such a world we ought to be giants!

YUBOV   But why do you want giants? They're all right in fairy tales, anywhere else they're terrifying.

[EPIHODOV *crosses the stage in the background, playing his guitar.*]

LYUBOV [*Pensively.*] There goes Epihodov. . . .

ANYA [*Pensively.*] There goes Epihodov. . . .

GAEV The sun's gone down, my friends.

TROFIMOV Yes.

GAEV [*In a subdued voice, as if reciting a poem.*] Oh, glorious Nature, shining with eternal light, so beautiful, yet so indifferent to our fate . . . you, whom we call Mother, the wellspring of Life and Death, you live and you destroy. . . .

VARYA [*Imploringly.*] Uncle, please!

ANYA You're doing it again, Uncle!

TROFIMOV You'd better bank the red into middle pocket.

GAEV All right, I'll keep quiet.

[*They all sit deep in thought; the only thing that can be heard is the muttering of* FEERS. *Suddenly there is a sound in the distance, as if out of the sky, like the sound of a harp string breaking, gradually and sadly dying away.*]

LYUBOV What was that?

LOPAHIN I don't know. Sounded like a cable broke in one of the mines. But it must've been a long way off.

GAEV Perhaps it was a bird . . . a heron, maybe.

TROFIMOV Or an owl. . . .

LYUBOV [*Shudders.*] Whatever it was, it sounded unpleasant . . . [*A pause.*]

FEERS It was the same way before the disaster: the owl hooted and the samovar was humming.

GAEV What disaster?

FEERS Before they freed us. [*A pause.*]

LYUBOV We'd better get started, my friends. It's getting dark and we should get home. [*To* ANYA.] You're crying, my darling! What's wrong? [*She embraces her.*]

ANYA Nothing, Mamma. It's nothing.

TROFIMOV Someone's coming.

[*Enter* A TRAMP *in a battered white hunting cap and an overcoat; he's slightly drunk.*]

TRAMP Excuse me, but can I get to the station through here?

GAEV Yes, just follow the road.

TRAMP Much obliged to you, sir. [*Coughs.*] It's a beautiful day today. [*Declaiming.*] "Oh, my brother, my suffering brother! . . . Come to the Volga, whose groans . . ." [*To* VARYA.] Mademoiselle, could a poor starving Russian trouble you for just enough to . . . [VARYA *cries out, frightened.*]

LOPAHIN [*Angrily.*] Really, this is too much!

LYUBOV [*At a loss what to do.*] Here, take this . . . here you are. [*Looks in her purse.*] I haven't any silver . . . but that's all right, here's a gold one. . . .

TRAMP Thank you very much! [*Goes off. Laughter.*]

VARYA [*Frightened.*] I'm going. . . . I'm going . . . Oh, Mamma, you know there's not even enough to eat in the house, and you gave him all that!

LYUBOV Well, what can you do with a silly woman like me? I'll give you everything I've got as soon as we get home. Yermolay Alexeyevich, you'll lend me some more, won't you?

LOPAHIN Why of course I will.

LYUBOV Come, it's time to go now. By the way, Varya, we've just about arranged your marriage. Congratulations!

VARYA [*Through her tears.*] Don't joke about things like that, Mother!

LOPAHIN Go to a nunnery, Okhmelia! . . .

GAEV Look at how my hands are trembling. I haven't had a game for so long.

LOPAHIN Okhmelia, nymph, remember me in your prayers!

LYUBOV Come along, everybody. It's almost supper time.

VARYA That man frightened me so. My heart's still pounding.

LOPAHIN My friends, just one thing, please just a word: the cherry orchard's to be sold on the 22nd of August. Remember that! Think of what. . . .

[*All go out except* TROFIMOV *and* ANYA.]

ANYA [*Laughs.*] We can thank the tramp for a chance to be alone! He frightened Varya so.

TROFIMOV Varya's afraid—she's afraid we might fall in love—so she follows us about all day long. She's so narrow-minded, she can't understand that we're above falling in love. To free ourselves of all that's petty and ephemeral, all that prevents us from being free and happy, that's the whole aim and meaning of our life. Forward! We march forward irresistibly towards that bright star shining there in the distance! Forward! Don't fall behind, friends!

ANYA [*Raising her hands.*] How beautifully you talk! [*A pause.*] It's wonderful here today.

TROFIMOV Yes, the weather's marvelous.

ANYA What have you done to me, Petya? Why don't I love the cherry orchard like I used to? I used to love it so very much I used to think that there wasn't a better place in all the world than our orchard.

TROFIMOV The whole of Russia is our orchard. The earth is great and beautiful and there are many wonderful places in it. [*A pause.*] Just think, Anya: Your grandfather, and your great grandfather, and all your ancestors were serf owners—they owned living souls. Don't you see human beings staring at you from every tree in the orchard, from every leaf and every trunk? Don't you hear their voices? . . . They owned living souls—and it has made you all different persons, those who came before you, and you who are living now, so that your mother, your uncle and you yourself don't even notice that you're living on credit, at the expense of other people, people you don't admit any further than your kitchen. We're at least two hundred years behind the times; we have no real values, no sense of our past, we just philosophize and complain of how depressed we feel, and drink vodka. Yet it's obvious that if we're ever to live in the present, we must first atone for our past and make a clean break with it, and we can only atone for it by suffering, by extraordinary, unceasing work. You've got to understand that, Anya.

ANYA The house we live in hasn't really been ours for a long time. I'll leave it, I promise you.

TROFIMOV Yes, leave it, and throw away the keys. Be free as the wind.

ANYA [*In rapture.*] How beautifully you say things.

TROFIMOV You must believe me, Anya, you must. I'm not thirty yet, I'm young, and I'm still a student, but I've suffered so much already. As soon as winter comes, I'll be hungry and sick and nervous, poor as a beggar. Fate has driven me everywhere! And yet, my soul is always—every moment of every day and every night—it's always full of such marvelous hopes and visions. I have a premonition of happiness, Anya, I can sense it's coming. . . .

ANYA [*Pensively.*] The moon's coming up.

[EPIHODOV *is heard playing the same melancholy tune on his guitar. The moon comes up. Somewhere near the poplars* VARYA *is looking for* ANYA *and calling.*]

VARYA [*Off-stage.*] Anya! Where are you?

TROFIMOV   Yes, the moon is rising. [*A pause.*] There it is—happiness—it's com-
ing nearer and nearer. Already, I can hear its footsteps. And if we never see
it, if we never know it, what does it matter? Others will see it!
[VARYA's *voice.*]   Anya! Where are you?
TROFIMOV   It's Varya again! [*Angrily.*] It's disgusting!
ANYA   Well? Let's go to the river. It's lovely there.
TROFIMOV   Yes, let's. [TROFIMOV *and* ANYA *go out.*]
[VARYA's *voice.*]   Anya! Anya!

CURTAIN

ACT III

*The drawing room separated by an arch from the ballroom. The
same Jewish orchestra that was mentioned in Act II, is playing
off-stage. The chandelier is lighted. It is evening. In the ballroom
they are dancing the Grand-rond.* SEMYONOV-PISHCHIK *is heard
calling: "Promenade à une paire!" Then they all enter the drawing room.* PISHCHIK *and* CHARLOTTA IVANOVNA *are the first couple,
followed by* TROFIMOV *and* LYUBOV, ANYA *and a* POST-OFFICE CLERK,
VARYA *and* THE STATION MASTER, *etc.* VARYA *is crying softly and
wipes away her tears as she dances.* DUNYASHA *is in the last couple.*
PISHCHIK *shouts: "Grand rond balancez!" and "Les cavaliers à
genoux et remerciez vos dames!"* FEERS, *wearing a dress coat,
crosses the room with soda water on a tray.* PISHCHIK *and* TRO-
FIMOV *come back into the drawing room.*

PISHCHIK   I've got this high blood-pressure—I've had two strokes already, you
know—and it makes dancing hard word for me; but, as they say, if you're
one of a pack, you wag your tail, whether you bark or not. Actually I'm as
strong as a horse. My dear father—may he rest in peace—had a little joke.
He used to say that the ancient line of Semyonov-Pishchik was descended
from the very same horse that Caligula made a member of the Senate.
[*Sitting down.*] But my trouble is, I haven't any money. A starving dog can
think of nothing but food . . . [*Starts to snore, but wakes up almost at
once.*] That's just like me—I can't think of anything but money . . .
TROFIMOV   You know, you're right, there *is* something horsy about you.
PISHCHIK   Well, a horse is a fine animal, you can sell a horse. . . .
[*The sound of someone playing billiards is heard in the next room.* VARYA
appears under the arch to the ballroom.]
TROFIMOV   [*Teasing her.*]   Madame Lopahin! Madame Lopahin!
VARYA   [*Angrily.*]   The "moth-eaten man!"
TROFIMOV   Yes, I am a moth-eaten man, and I'm proud of it.
VARYA   [*Thinking bitterly.*]   Now we've hired an orchestra—but how are we
going to pay for it? [*Goes out.*]
TROFIMOV   [*To* PISHCHIK.]   If all the energy you've spent during your life
looking for money to pay the interest on your debts had been used for
something useful, you'd have probably turned the world upside down by
now.
PISHCHIK   The philosopher Nietzsche, the greatest, the most famous—a man of
the greatest intelligence, in fact—says its quite all right to counterfeit.
TROFIMOV   Oh, you've read Nietzsche?

PISHCHIK   Of course not, Dashenka told me. But right now I'm in such an im-
possible position that I could forge a few notes. The day after tomorrow
I've got to pay 310 roubles. I've borrowed 130 already. . . . [*Feels in his
pockets, in alarm.*] The money's gone! I've lost the money. [*Tearfully.*]
Where's the money? [*Joyfully.*] Oh, here it is, inside the lining! I'm so upset,
I'm sweating all over! . . . [*Enter* LYUBOV *and* CHARLOTTA.]

LYUBOV   [*Humming the "Lezginka."*]   What's taking Leonid so long? What's
he doing in town? [*To* DUNYASHA.] Dunyasha, offer the musicians some tea.

TROFIMOV   The auction was probably postponed.

LYUBOV   The orchestra came at the wrong time, and the party started at the
wrong time . . . Oh, well . . . never mind . . . [*She sits down and hums
quietly.*]

CHARLOTTA   [*Hands a deck of cards to* PISHCHIK.]   Here's a deck of cards—think
of any card.

PISHCHIK   I've thought of one.

CHARLOTTA   Now shuffle the deck. That's right. Now give it to me, my dear
Monsieur Pishchik. *"Ein, zwei, drei!"* Why look! There it is, in your coat
pocket.

PISHCHIK   [*Takes the card out of his coat pocket.*]   The eight of spades, that's
right! [*In astonishment.*] Isn't that amazing!

CHARLOTTA   [*Holding the deck of cards on the palm of her hand, to* TROFIMOV.]
Quickly, which card's on the top?

TROFIMOV   Well . . . ahh . . . the queen of spades.

CHARLOTTA   You're right, here it is! Now, which card?

PISHCHIK   The ace of hearts.

CHARLOTTA   Right again! [*She claps her hand over the pack of cards, which
disappears.*] What beautiful weather we're having today!
[*A woman's voice, as if coming from underneath the floor, answers her.*]

VOICE   Oh yes, indeed, the weather's perfectly marvelous!

CHARLOTTA   [*Addressing the voice.*]   How charming you are! I'm fond of you!

VOICE   And I like you very much, too.

STATION MASTER   [*Applauding.*]   Bravo, Madame ventriloquist! Bravo!

PISHCHIK   [*Astonished.*]   Isn't that amazing! Charlotta Ivanovna, you're absolutely wonderful! I'm completely in love with you!

CHARLOTTA   [*Shrugging her shoulders.*]   In love? What do you know about love?
"Guter Mensch, aber schlechter Musikant."

TROFIMOV   [*Slaps* PISHCHIK *on the shoulder.*]   He's just an old horse, he is!

CHARLOTTA   Your attention please! Here's one more trick. [*She takes a shawl
from a chair.*] Now there's this very nice shawl . . . [*Shakes it out.*] Who'd
like to buy it?

PISHCHIK   [*Amazed.*]   Imagine that!

CHARLOTTA   *"Ein, zwei, drei!"*
[*She lifts up the shawl and* ANYA *is standing behind it;* ANYA *curtsies, runs
to her mother, gives her a hug, and runs back to the ballroom. Everybody's
delighted.*]

LYUBOV   [*Clapping.*]   Bravo, bravo!

CHARLOTTA   Once more. *"Ein, zwei, drei!"*
[*Lifts the shawl again; behind it is* VARYA, *who bows.*]

PISHCHIK   [*Amazed.*]   Isn't that amazing!

CHARLOTTA   It's all over!
[*She throws the shawl over* PISHCHIK, *curtsies, and runs into the ballroom.*]

PISHCHIK   [*Going after her.*]   You little rascal! . . . Have you ever seen anything like her? What a girl . . . [*Goes out.*]

LYUBOV   Leonid's still not here. I can't understand what's keeping him all this time in town. Anyway, by now everything's been settled; either the estate's been sold or the auction didn't take place. Why does he wait so long to let us know?

VARYA [*Trying to comfort her.*] Uncle's bought it, I'm sure he did.

TROFIMOV [*Sarcastically.*] Why of course he did!

VARYA Our great-aunt sent him power of attorney to buy it in her name, and transfer the mortgage to her. She's done it for Anya's sake . . . God will look after us, I'm sure of it—Uncle will buy the estate.

LYUBOV Your great-aunt sent us fifteen thousand to buy the estate in her name —she doesn't trust us—but that's not enough to even pay the interest. [*She covers her face with her hands.*] My fate is being decided today, my fate. . . .

TROFIMOV [*To* VARYA, *teasingly.*] Madame Lopahin!

VARYA [*Crossly.*] The perpetual student! Why, you've been thrown out of the University twice already!

LYUBOV But why get so cross, Varya? He's only teasing you about Lopahin, there's no harm in that, is there? If you want to, why don't you marry him; he's a fine man, and he's interesting, too. Of course, if you don't want to, don't. No one's trying to force you, darling.

VARYA I'm very serious about this. Mother . . . and I want to be frank with you . . . he's a good man and I like him.

LYUBOV Then marry him. What are you waiting for? I don't understand you at all.

VARYA But, Mother, I can't propose to him myself, can I? It's been two years now since everybody began talking to me about him, and everybody's talking, but he doesn't say a word, or when he does, he just jokes with me. I understand, of course. He's getting rich and his mind's busy with other things, and he hasn't any time for me. If only I had some money, even a little, just a hundred roubles, I'd leave everything and go away, the farther the better. I'd go into a convent.

TROFIMOV How beautiful!

VARYA [*To* TROFIMOV.] Of course, a student like you has to be so intelligent! [*Quietly and tearfully.*] How ugly you've become, Petya, how much older you look! [*To* LYUBOV, *her tearfulness gone.*] The only thing I can't stand, Mother, is not having any work to do. I've got to stay busy.
[*Enter* YASHA.]

YASHA [*With difficulty restraining his laughter.*] Epihodov's broken a cue! . . . [*Goes out.*]

VARYA But what's Epihodov doing here? Who let him play billiards? I don't understand these people. . . . [*Goes out.*]

LYUBOV Please don't tease her, Petya. Don't you see she's upset already?

TROFIMOV Oh, she's such a busy-body—always sticking her nose into other people's business. She hasn't left Anya and me alone all summer. She's afraid we might fall in love. What difference should it make to her? Besides, I didn't give her any reason to think so. I don't believe in such trivialities. We're above love!

LYUBOV And I suppose I'm below love. [*Uneasily.*] Why isn't Leonid back? If only I knew whether the estate's been sold or not. It's such an incredible calamity that for some reason I don't know what to think, I feel so helpless. I think I'm going to scream this very minute . . . I'll do something silly. Help me, Petya. Talk to me, say something!

TROFIMOV What difference does it make whether the estate's sold today or not? It was gone a long time ago. You can't turn back, the path's lost. You mustn't worry, and above all you mustn't deceive yourself. For once in your life you must look the truth straight in the face.

LYUBOV What truth? *You* know what truth is and what it isn't, but I've lost such visionary powers. I don't see anything. You're able to solve all your problems so decisively—but, tell me, my dear boy, isn't that because you're young, because life is still hidden from your young eyes, because you can't believe anything horrible will ever happen to you and you don't expect it to? Oh, yes, you're more courageous and honest and serious than we are, but put yourself in our position, try to be generous—if only a little bit— and have pity on me. I was born here, you know, and my father and mother lived here, and my grandfather, too, and I love this house—I can't conceive of life without the cherry orchard, and if it really has to be sold, then sell me with it . . . [*Embraces* TROFIMOV, *kisses him on the forehead.*] You know, my little boy was drowned here. . . . [*Weeps.*] Have pity on me, my dear, kind friend.

TROFIMOV You know that I sympathize with you from the bottom of my heart.

LYUBOV But you should say it differently . . . differently. [*Takes out her hand-kerchief and a telegram falls on to the floor.*] There's so much on my mind today, you can't imagine. It's so noisy around here that my soul trembles with every sound, and I'm shaking all over—yet I can't go to my room because the silence of being alone frightens me. . . . Don't blame me, Petya. . . . I love you as if you were my own son. I'd gladly let Anya marry you, honestly I would, but, my dear boy, you must study, you've got to graduate. You don't do anything, Fate tosses you from one place to another—it's so strange—Well, it is, isn't it? Isn't it? And you should do something about your beard, make it grow somehow. . . . [*Laughs.*] You look so funny!

TROFIMOV [*Picks up the telegram.*] I don't care how I look. That's so super-ficial.

LYUBOV This telegram's from Paris. I get one every day . . . Yesterday, today. That beast is sick again, and everything's going wrong for him. . . . He wants me to forgive him, he begs me to return, and, really, I suppose I should go to Paris and stay with him for awhile. You're looking very stern, Petya, but what am I to do, my dear boy, what am I to do? He's sick, and lonely, and unhappy, and who'll take care of him, who'll stop him from making a fool of himself, and give him his medicine at the right time? And anyway, why should I hide it, or keep quiet about it? I love him; yes, I love him. I do, I do. . . . He's a stone around my neck, and I'm sinking to the bottom with him—but I love him and I can't live without him. [*She presses* TROFIMOV's *hand.*] Don't think I'm evil, Petya, don't say anything, please don't. . . .

TROFIMOV [*With strong emotion.*] Please—forgive my frankness, but that man's swindling you!

LYUBOV No, no, no, you mustn't talk like that. . . .
[*Puts her hands over her ears.*]

TROFIMOV But he's a scoundrel, and you're the only one who doesn't know it! He's a despicable, worthless scoundrel. . . .

LYUBOV [*Angry, but in control of herself.*] You're twenty-six or twenty-seven years old, but you're talking like a schoolboy!

TROFIMOV Say whatever you want!

LYUBOV You should be a man at your age, you ought to understand what it means to be in love. And you should be in love. . . . Tell me, why haven't you fallen in love! [*Angrily.*] Yes, yes! Oh, you're not so "pure," your purity is a perversion, you're nothing but a ridiculous prude, a freak. . . .

TROFIMOV [*Horrified.*] What is she saying?

LYUBOV "I'm above love!" You're not above love, you're useless, as Feers would say. Imagine not having a mistress at your age! . . .

TROFIMOV [*Horrified.*] This is terrible! What's she saying? [*Goes quickly towards the ballroom, clutching his head between his hands.*] This is dreadful. . . . I can't stand it, I'm going. . . . [*Goes out, but returns at once.*] Everything's over between us!
[*Goes out through the door into the hall.*]

LYUBOV [*Calls after him.*] Petya, wait! You funny boy, I was only joking! Petya!
[*Someone can be heard running quickly downstairs and suddenly falling down with a crash.* ANYA *and* VARYA *scream, and then begin laughing.*] What's happened?
[ANYA *runs in.*]

ANYA [*Laughing.*] Petya fell down the stairs. [*Runs out.*]

LYUBOV What a strange boy he is!
[*The* STATION MASTER *stands in the middle of the ballroom and begins to recite "The Sinner" by Alexey Tolstoy. The others listen to him, but he's hardly had time to recite more than a little bit when a waltz is played, and he stops. Everyone dances.* TROFIMOV, ANYA, VARYA *come in from the hall.*] Poor Petya . . . there, my dear boy . . . Please forgive me . . . Come, let's dance . . . [*She dances with* PETYA. ANYA *and* VARYA *dance. Enter* FEERS, *then* YASHA. FEERS *leans on his cane by the side door.* YASHA *looks at the dancers from the drawing room.*]

YASHA How are you, old boy?

FEERS Not too well . . . We used to have generals, barons, and admirals at our parties . . . long ago, but now we send for the post-office clerk and the station master, and even they don't want to come it seems. I seem to be getting weaker somehow . . . My old master, the mistress' grandfather, used to make everyone take sealing wax no matter what was wrong with them. I've been taking it every day for the last twenty years, maybe even longer. Perhaps that's why I'm still alive.

YASHA How you bore me, old man! [*Yawns.*] Why don't you just go away and die . . . It's about time.

FEERS Eh, you! . . . You're useless . . . [*Mutters.*]
[TROFIMOV *and* LYUBOV *dancing, come into the drawing room.*]

LYUBOV Thank you. I think I'll sit down for a bit. [*Sits down.*] I'm tired.
[*Enter* ANYA.]

ANYA [*Agitated.*] There's a man in the kitchen who's been saying that the cherry orchard was sold today.

LYUBOV Sold? To whom?

ANYA He didn't say. He's gone.
[*She and* TROFIMOV *dance into the ballroom.*]

YASHA There was some old man gossiping there. A stranger.

FEERS Leonid Andreyevich isn't back yet, he hasn't come yet. And he's only got his light overcoat on; he'll probably catch a cold. Oh, these youngsters!

LYUBOV I've got to know, or I think I'll die. Yasha, go and find out who bought it.

YASHA But the old guy went away a long time ago. [*Laughs.*]

LYUBOV [*With a touch of annoyance.*] What are you laughing at? What's so humorous?

YASHA Epihodov's so funny—he's so stupid. Two-and-twenty misfortunes!

LYUBOV Feers, if the estate's sold, where will you go?

FEERS I'll go wherever you tell me to go.

LYUBOV Why are you looking like that? Aren't you well? You ought to be in bed.

FEERS Yes . . . [*With a faint smile.*] But if I went to bed, who'd take care of the guests and keep things going? There's no one in the house but me.

YASHA [*To* LYUBOV.] Lyubov Andreyevna! I want to ask you something! If you go back to Paris, will you please take me with you? I couldn't stand staying here. [*Looking round and speaking in a low voice.*] I don't have to say it, you can see for yourself how uncivilized everything is here. The people are immoral, it's frightfully dull, and the food is terrible. And then there's that Feers walking about the place and muttering all sorts of stupid things. Take me with you, please!

[*Enter* PISHCHIK.]

PISHCHIK May I have this dance, beautiful lady . . . [LYUBOV *gets up to dance.*] I'll have that 180 roubles from you yet, you enchantress . . . Yes, I will . . . [*Dances.*] Just 180 roubles, that's all . . .

[*They go into the ballroom.*]

YASHA [*Sings quietly.*] "Don't you understand the passion in my soul? . . . [*In the ballroom a woman in a grey top hat and check trousers starts jumping and throwing her arms about; shouts of: "Bravo, Charlotta Ivanovna!"*]

DUNYASHA [*Stops to powder her face.*] Anya told me to dance: there are so many men and not enough ladies; but I get so dizzy from dancing and it makes my heart beat so fast. Feers Nikolayevich, the post-office clerk said something to me just now that completely took my breath away.

[*The music stops.*]

FEERS What did he say?

DUNYASHA You're like a flower, he said.

YASHA [*Yawns.*] What ignorance! . . .

[*Goes out.*]

DUNYASHA Like a flower . . . I'm so sensitive, I love it when people say beautiful things to me.

FEERS You'll be having your head turned if you're not careful.

[*Enter* EPIHODOV.]

EPIHODOV Avdotya Fyodorovna, you act as if you don't want to see me . . . as if I were some kind of insect. [*Sighs.*] Such is life!

DUNYASHA What do you want?

EPIHODOV But then, you may be right. [*Sighs.*] Of course, if one looks at it from a certain point of view—if I may so express myself, and please excuse my frankness, you've driven me into such a state . . . Oh, I know what my fate is; every day some misfortune's sure to happen to me, but I've long since been accustomed to that, so I look at life with a smile. You gave me your word, and though I . . .

DUNYASHA Please, let's talk later, just let me alone now. I'm lost in a dream. [*Plays with her fan.*]

EPIHODOV Some misfortune happens to me every day, but I—how should I put it—I just smile, I even laugh.

[VARYA *enters from the ballroom.*]

VARYA Are you still here, Semyon? Your manners are abominable, really! [*To* DUNYASHA.] You'd better go now, Dunyasha. [*To* EPIHODOV.] First you play billiards and break a cue, and now you're going about the drawing room, like one of the guests.

EPIHODOV Permit me to inform you, but you have no right to attack me like this.

VARYA I'm not attacking, I'm telling you. You just wander from one place to another, instead of doing your work. We've hired a clerk, but why no one knows.

EPIHODOV [*Offended.*] Whether I work, wander, eat, or play billiards, the only people who are entitled to judge my actions are those who are older than me and have some idea of what they're talking about.

VARYA How dare you say that to me? [*Beside herself in anger.*] You dare to say that? Are you suggesting that I don't know what I'm talking about? Get out of here! Right now!

EPIHODOV [*Cowed.*] I wish you'd express yourself more delicately.

VARYA [*Beside herself.*] Get out this minute! Get out! [*He goes to the door, she follows him.*] Two-and-twenty misfortunes! Get out of here! I don't want ever to see you again!

EPIHODOV [*Goes out; his voice is heard from outside the door.*] I'm going to complain.

VARYA Oh, you're coming back, are you? [*She seizes the stick which* FEERS *left by the door.*] Well, come along, come in . . . I'll show you! So, you're coming back . . . are you? There, take that . . .
[*Swings the stick, and at that moment* LOPAHIN *comes in.*]

LOPAHIN [*Whom the stick did not, in fact, touch.*] Thank you very much!

VARYA [*Angry and ironically.*] I'm sorry!

LOPAHIN Don't mention it. I'm much obliged to you for the kind reception.

VARYA That's quite all right. [*Walks away and then looks around and asks gently.*] I haven't hurt you, have I?

LOPAHIN No, not at all. . . . But there's going to be a huge bump, though.

VOICES [*In the ballroom.*] Lopahin's here! Yermolay Alexeyevich!

PISHCHIK There he is! You can see him, do you hear him? . . . [*Embraces* LOPAHIN.] You smell of cognac, my good fellow! . . . Well we're having a party here, too.
[*Enter* LYUBOV.]

LYUBOV It's you, Yermolay Alexeyevich? What's taken you to long? Where's Leonid?

LOPAHIN Leonid Andreyevich's here, he'll be along in a minute.

LYUBOV [*Agitated.*] Well, what happened? Was there an auction? Tell me!

LOPAHIN [*Embarrassed, afraid of betraying his joy.*] The auction was over by four o'clock . . . We missed our train and had to wait until nine-thirty. [*Sighs heavily.*] Ugh! I feel a little dizzy . . .
[*Enter* GAEV; *he carries packages in his right hand and wipes away his tears with his left.*]

LYUBOV Leonid, what happened? Leonid? [*Impatiently, with tears.*] Tell me quickly, for God's sake! . . .

GAEV [*Doesn't answer, but waves his hand. To* FEERS, *crying.*] Here, take these . . . it's some anchovies and Kerch herrings . . . I haven't eaten all day . . . What I've been through!
[*Through the open door leading to the ballroom a game of billards can be heard and* YASHA's *voice is heard.*]

YASHA Seven and eighteen.

GAEV [*His expression changes and he stops crying.*] I'm very tired. Come, Feers, I want to change my things.
[*Goes out through the ballroom, followed by* FEERS.]

PISHCHIK Well, what happened at the auction? Come on, tell us!

LYUBOV Has the cherry orchard been sold?

LOPAHIN It has.

LYUBOV Who bought it?

LOPAHIN I did.
[*A pause.* LYUBOV *is overcome; only the fact that she is standing beside a table and a chair keeps her from falling.* VARYA *takes the keys from her belt, throws them on the floor in the middle of the room and goes out.*]
I bought it. Wait a moment, ladies and gentlemen, please. I'm so mixed up, I don't quite know what to say . . . [*Laughs.*] When we got to the auction, Deriganov was already there. Leonid had only fifteen thousand roubles,

and immediately Deriganov bid thirty thousand over and above the mortgage. I saw how things were, so I stepped in and raised it to forty. He bid forty-five, I went to fifty-five; he kept on raising five thousand and I raised it ten thousand. Well, finally it ended—I bid ninety thousand over and above the mortgage, and it went to me. The cherry orchard's mine now! All right, tell me I'm drunk, tell me I'm crazy and that I'm just imagining all this. . . . [*Stamps his feet.*] Don't laugh at me! If only my father and grandfather could rise from their graves and see all that's happened . . . how their Yermolay, their ignorant, beaten Yermolay, the little boy that ran around in his bare feet in the winter . . . if only they could see that he's bought this estate, the most beautiful place in the world! Yes, he's bought the very estate where his father and grandfather were slaves and where they weren't even admitted to the kitchen! I must be asleep, I'm dreaming, it only seems to be true . . . it's all just my imagination, my imagination must be confused . . . [*Picks up the keys, smiling gently.*] She threw these down because she wanted to show that she's not the mistress here anymore. [*Jingles the keys.*] Well, never mind. [*The orchestra is heard tuning up.*] Hey there! you musicians, play something for us! I want some music! My friends, come along and soon you'll see Yermolay Lopahin take an axe to the cherry orchard, you'll see the trees come crashing to the ground! We're going to build hundreds of summer cottages, and our children and our grandchildren will see a whole new world growing up here . . . So play, let's have some music!
[*The band plays.* LYUBOV *has sunk into a chair and is crying bitterly. Reproachfully.*]
Why, why didn't you listen to me? My poor, dear lady, you'll never get it back now. [*With tears.*] Oh, if only all this could be over soon, if only we could change this unhappy and disjointed life of ours somehow!
PISHCHIK   [*Taking his arm, in a low voice.*]   She's crying. Come into the ballroom, let her be by herself . . . Come on . . .
[*Takes his arm and leads him away to the ballroom.*]
LOPAHIN   What's the matter! Where's the music? Come on, play! Play! Everything will be as *I* want it now. [*Ironically.*] Here comes the new owner, here comes the owner of the cherry orchard! [*He tips over a little table accidentally and nearly upsets the candelabra.*] Don't worry about it, I can pay for everything!
[*Goes out with* PISHCHIK. *There is no one left in the ballroom or drawing room, but* LYUBOV, *who sits huddled up in a chair, crying bitterly. The orchestra continues to play quietly.* ANYA *and* TROFIMOV *enter quickly;* ANYA *goes up to her mother and kneels beside her,* TROFIMOV *remains at the entrance to the ballroom.*]
ANYA   Mamma! . . . Mamma, you're crying. Dear, kind, good Mamma, my precious one, I love you! God bless you, Mamma! The cherry orchard's sold, that's true, it's gone, but don't cry, Mamma, you still have your life ahead of you, you still have your good, innocent heart. You must come with me, Mamma, away from here! We'll plant a new orchard, even more wonderful than this one—and when you see it, you'll understand everything, and your heart will be filled with joy, like the sun in the evening; and then you'll smile again, Mamma! Come, dearest one, come with me! . . .

CURTAIN

ACT IV

> *The same setting as for Act I. There are no pictures on the walls,*
> *or curtains at the windows; most of the furniture is gone and the*
> *few remaining pieces are stacked in a corner, as if for sale. There*
> *is a sense of desolation. Beside the door, suitcases and other lug-*
> *gage have been piled together. The voices of* VARYA *and* ANYA *can*
> *be heard through the door on the left, which is open.* LOPAHIN
> *stands waiting;* YASHA *is holding a tray with glasses of champagne.*
> *In the hall* EPIHODOV *is tying up a large box. Off-stage there is a*
> *low hum of voices; the peasants have called to say good-bye.* GAEV's
> *voice from off-stage.*

GAEV Thank you, friends, thank you.

YASHA The peasants have come to say good-bye. In my opinion, Yermolay Alexeyevich, they're good people, but they don't know much.
[*The hum subsides.* LYUBOV *and* GAEV *enter from the hall;* LYUBOV *is not crying but her face is pale and it quivers. She is unable to speak.*]

GAEV You gave them everything you had, Lyuba. You shouldn't have done that. You really shouldn't.

LYUBOV I couldn't help it! I couldn't help it! [*Both go out.*]

LOPAHIN [*Calls after them through the door.*] Please, have some champagne, please do! Just a little glass before you go. I didn't think to bring some from town, and at the station I could find only this one bottle. Please have some. [*A pause.*] You don't want any, my friends? [*Walks away from the door.*] If I'd known that, I wouldn't have brought it. . . . Well, then I won't have any either. [YASHA *carefully puts the tray on a chair.*] Have a drink, Yasha, nobody else wants any.

YASHA To the travelers! And to those staying behind. [*Drinks.*] This champagne isn't the real thing, believe me.

LOPAHIN What do you mean, eight roubles a bottle. [*A pause.*] God, it's cold in here.

YASHA The stoves weren't lit today. What difference does it make since we're leaving? [*Laughs.*]

LOPAHIN Why are you laughing?

YASHA Because I feel good.

LOPAHIN It's October already, but it's still sunny and clear, just like summer. Good building weather. [*Looks at his watch, then at the door.*] Ladies and gentlemen, the train leaves in forty-seven minutes. We've got to start in twenty minutes. So hurry up.
[TROFIMOV, *wearing an overcoat, comes in from outdoors.*]

TROFIMOV It's time we get started. The horses are ready. God knows where my goloshes are, they've disappeared. [*Calls through the door.*] Anya, my goloshes aren't here; I can't find them.

LOPAHIN I've got to go to Kharkov. I'm taking the same train. I'll be spending the winter in Kharkov: I've stayed around here too long, and it drives me crazy having nothing to do. I can't be without work: I just don't know what to do with my hands; they hang there, as if they didn't belong to me.

TROFIMOV We'll be gone soon, then you can start making money again.

LOPAHIN Have a drink.

TROFIMOV No, thanks.

LOPAHIN So, you're going to Moscow?

TROFIMOV Yes, I'll go with them to town, and then, tomorrow I'll leave for Moscow.

LOPAHIN   I suppose the professors are waiting for you to come before they begin classes.

TROFIMOV   That's none of your business.

LOPAHIN   How many years have you been studying at the university?

TROFIMOV   Can't you say something new for a change, that's getting pretty old. [*Looks for his goloshes.*] By the way, since we probably won't see each other again, let me give you a bit of advice, as we say good-bye: stop waving your arms! Try to get rid of that habit of making wide, sweeping gestures. And another thing, all this talk about building estates, these calculations about summer tourists that are going to buy property, all these predictions—they're all sweeping gestures, too. . . . You know, in spite of everything, I like you. You've got beautiful delicate fingers, like an artist's, you've a fine, sensitive soul. . . .

LOPAHIN   [*Embraces him.*]   Good-bye, my friend. Thanks for everything. I can give you some money for your trip, if you need it.

TROFIMOV   What for? I don't need it.

LOPAHIN   But you haven't got any!

TROFIMOV   Yes, I have, thank you. I got some money for a translation. Here it is, in my pocket. [*Anxiously.*] But I can't find my goloshes.

VARYA   [*From the other room.*]   Here, take the nasty things!
[*She throws a pair of rubber goloshes into the room.*]

TROFIMOV   What are you so angry about, Varya? Hm . . . but these aren't my goloshes!

LOPAHIN   I sowed three thousand acres of poppies last spring, and I've made forty thousand on it. And when they were in bloom, what a picture it was! What I mean to say is that I've made the forty thousand, so now I can lend you some money. Why be so stuck up? So I'm a peasant . . . I speak right out.

TROFIMOV   Your father was a peasant, mine was a druggist. What's that got to do with it? [LOPAHIN *takes out his wallet.*] Forget it, put it away . . . Even if you offered me two hundred thousand, I wouldn't take it. I'm a free man. And all that you rich men—and poor men too—all that you value so highly doesn't have the slightest power over me—it's all just so much fluff floating about in the air. I'm strong and I'm proud! I can get along without you, I can pass you by. Humanity is advancing towards the highest truth, the greatest happiness that it's possible to achieve on earth, and I'm one of the avant-garde!

LOPAHIN   Will you get there?

TROFIMOV   Yes. [*A pause.*] I'll get there myself, or show others the way to get there.
[*The sound of an axe hitting a tree is heard in the distance.*]

LOPAHIN   Well, my friend, it's time to go. Good-bye. We show off in front of one another, and all the time life is slipping by. When I work all day long, without resting, I'm happier and sometimes I even think I know why I exist. But how many people there are in Russia, my friend, who exist for no reason at all. But, never mind, it doesn't matter. They say Leonid Andreyevich has a job at the bank, at six thousand a year. That won't last long; he's too lazy. . . .

ANYA   [*In the doorway.*]   Mamma begs you not to let them cut down the orchard until we've left.

TROFIMOV   Really, haven't you got any tact?
[*Goes out through the hall.*]

LOPAHIN   All right, I'll take care of it. . . . These people!
[*Follows* TROFIMOV.]

ANYA Has Feers been taken to the hospital?

YASHA I told them to take him this morning. He's gone, I think.

ANYA [*To* EPIHODOV, *who passes through the ballroom.*] Semyon Pantaleye-vich, will you please find out whether Feers has been taken to the hospital?

YASHA [*Offended.*] I told Yegor this morning. Why ask a dozen times?

EPIHODOV That old Feers—frankly speaking, I mean—he's beyond repair, it's time he joined his ancestors. As for me, I can only envy him. [*He places a suitcase on top of a cardboard hatbox and squashes it.*] There you are, you see! . . . I might have known it!
[*Goes out.*]

YASHA [*Sardonically.*] Two-and-twenty misfortunes!

VARYA [*From behind the door.*] Has Feers been taken to the hospital?

ANYA Yes.

VARYA Why wasn't the letter to the doctor taken then?

ANYA I'll send someone after them with it . . .
[*Goes out.*]

VARYA [*From the adjoining room.*] Where's Yasha? Tell him his mother is here and wants to say good-bye to him.

YASHA [*Waves his hand.*] This is too much! I'll lose my patience.
[*While the foregoing action has been taking place,* DUNYASHA *has been busy with the luggage; now that* YASHA *is alone, she comes up to him.*]

DUNYASHA If only you'd look at me just once, Yasha! You're going . . . you're leaving me! . . . [*She cries and throws her arms round his neck.*]

YASHA What are you crying for? [*Drinks champagne.*] In a week I'll be in Paris again. Tomorrow we'll get on the train—and off we'll go—gone! I can't believe it. *"Vive la France!"* I can't stand it here and could never live here—nothing ever happens. I've seen enough of all this ignorance. I've had enough of it. [*Drinks.*] What are you crying for? Behave yourself properly, then you won't cry.

DUNYASHA [*Looking into a handmirror and powdering her nose.*] Please, write to me from Paris. You know how much I've loved you, Yasha. Oh, I've loved you so much! I'm very sensitive, Yasha!

YASHA Sshh, someone's coming. [*Pretends to be busy with a suitcase, humming quietly.*]
[*Enter* LYUBOV ANDREYEVNA, GAEV, ANYA *and* CHARLOTTA IVANOVNA.]

GAEV We've got to leave soon. There isn't much time left. [*Looks at* YASHA.] What a smell! Who's been eating herring?

LYUBOV We'll have to leave in the carriage in ten minutes. [*Looks about the room.*] Good-bye, dear house, the home of our fathers. Winter will pass and spring will come again, and then you won't be here any more, you'll be torn down. How much these walls have seen! [*Kisses her daughter passion-ately.*] My little treasure, how radiant you look, your eyes are shining like diamonds. Are you glad? Very glad?

ANYA Oh, yes, very glad, Mamma! Our new life is just beginning!

GAEV [*Gaily.*] Really, everything's all right now. Before the cherry orchard was sold we were all worried and upset, but as soon as things were settled once and for all, we all calmed down and even felt quite cheerful. I'm working in a bank now, a real financier. . . . The red into the side pocket . . . And say what you like, Lyuba, you're looking much better. No doubt about it.

LYUBOV Yes, that's true, my nerves are better. [*Someone helps her on with her hat and coat.*] I'm sleeping better, too. Take out my things, Yasha, it's time. [*To* ANYA.] My little darling, we'll be seeing each other again soon. I'm going to Paris—I'll live on the money which your Grandmother sent us to buy the estate—God bless Grandmamma!—but that money won't last very long either.

ANYA You'll come back soon, Mamma . . . won't you? I'll study and pass my exams and then I'll work and help you. We'll read together, Mamma . . . all sort of things . . . won't we? [*She kisses her mother's hands.*] We'll read during the long autumn evenings. We'll read lots of books, and a new wonderful world will open up before us . . . [*Dreamily.*] Mamma, come back soon . . .

LYUBOV I'll come back, my precious. [*Embraces her.*]

[*Enter* LOPAHIN. CHARLOTTA *quietly sings to herself.*]

GAEV Happy Charlotta! She's singing.

CHARLOTTA [*Picks up a bundle that looks like a baby in a blanket.*] Bye-bye, little baby. [*A sound like a baby crying is heard.*] Hush, be quiet, my darling, be a good little boy. [*The "crying" continues.*] Oh, my baby, you poor thing! [*Throws the bundle down.*] Are you going to find me another job? If you don't mind, I've got to have one.

LOPAHIN We'll find you one, Charlotta Ivanovna, don't worry.

GAEV Everybody's leaving us, Varya's going away . . . all of a sudden nobody wants us.

CHARLOTTA There's no place for me to live in town. I'll have to go. [*Hums.*] Oh, well, what do I care. [*Enter* PISHCHIK.]

LOPAHIN Look what's here!

PISHCHIK [*Gasping for breath.*] Oohhh, let me get my breath . . . I'm worn out . . . My good friends. . . . Give me some water . . .

GAEV I suppose you want to borrow some money? I'm going . . . Excuse me . . . [*Goes out.*]

PISHCHIK I haven't seen you for a long time . . . my beautiful lady . . . [*To* LOPAHIN.] You're here, too . . . glad to see you . . . you're a man of great intelligence . . . here . . . take this . . . [*Gives money to* LOPAHIN.] Four hundred roubles . . . I still owe you eight hundred and forty. . . .

LOPAHIN [*Shrugging his shoulders in amazement.*] It's like a dream. . . . Where did you get it?

PISHCHIK Wait a minute . . . I'm so hot . . . A most extraordinary thing happened. Some Englishman came along and discovered some kind of white clay on my land. . . . [*To* LYUBOV.] Here's four hundred for you also, my dear . . . enchantress . . . [*Gives her the money.*] You'll get the rest later. [*Takes a drink of water.*] A young man on the train was just telling me that some great philosopher advises people to jump off roofs. You just jump off, he says, and that settles the whole problem. [*Amazed at what he has just said.*] Imagine that! More water, please

LOPAHIN What Englishmen?

PISHCHIK I leased the land to them for twenty-four years. . . . And now you must excuse me, I'm in a hurry and have to get on. I'm going to Znoikov's, then to Kardamonov's . . . I owe them all money. [*Drinks.*] Your health. I'll come again on Thursday . . .

LYUBOV We're just leaving for town, and tomorrow I'm going abroad.

PISHCHIK What's that? [*In agitation.*] Why to town? Oh, I see . . . this furniture and the suitcases. . . . Well, never mind . . . [*Tearfully.*] What difference does it make. . . . These Englishmen, you know, they're very intelligent . . . Never mind. . . . I wish you all the best, God bless you. Never mind, everything comes to an end eventually. [*Kisses* LYUBOV's *hand.*] And when you hear that my end has come, just think of a horse, and say: "There used to be a man like that once . . . his name was Semyonov-Pishchik—God bless him!" Wonderful weather we're having. Yes . . . [*Goes out embarrassed, but returns at once and stands in the doorway.*] Dashenka sends her greetings. [*Goes out.*]

LYUBOV   Well, we can get started now. I'm leaving with two worries on my mind. One is Feers—he's sick. [*Glances at her watch.*] We've still got five minutes. . . .

ANYA   Mamma, Feers has been taken to the hospital. Yasha sent him this morning.

LYUBOV   The other is Varya. She's used to getting up early and working, and now, with nothing to do, she's like a fish out of water. She's gotten so thin and pale, and she cries a lot, the poor dear. [*A pause.*] You know very well, Yermolay Alexeyevich, that I've been hoping you two would get married . . . and everything pointed to it. [*Whispers to* ANYA *and motions to* CHARLOTTA, *and they both go out.*] She loves you, and you're fond of her, too . . . I just don't know, I don't know why you seem to avoid each other. I don't understand it.

LOPAHIN   Neither do I, I admit it. The whole thing's so strange. . . . If there's still time, I'm ready to. . . . Let's settle it at once—and get it over with! Without you here, I don't feel I'll ever propose to her.

LYUBOV   That's an excellent idea! You won't need more than a minute. I'll call her at once.

LOPAHIN   And there's champagne here, too, we'll celebrate. [*Looks at the glasses.*] They're empty, someone's drunk it all. [YASHA *coughs.*] They must have poured it down.

LYUBOV   [*With animation.*]   Oh, I'm so glad. I'll call her, and we'll leave you alone. Yasha, *"allez!"* [*Through the door.*] Varya, come here for a minute, leave what you're doing and come here! Varya! [*Goes out with* YASHA.]

LOPAHIN   [*Looking at his watch.*]   Yes. . . .
   [*A pause. Whispering and suppressed laughter are heard behind the door, then* VARYA *comes in and starts fussing with the luggage. At last she says:*]

VARYA   That's strange, I can't find it. . . .

LOPAHIN   What are you looking for?

VARYA   I packed it myself, and I can't remember . . . [*A pause.*]

LOPAHIN   Where are you going to now, Varvara Mihailovna?

VARYA   I? To the Rogulins. I've taken a job as their housekeeper.

LOPAHIN   That's in Yashnevo, isn't it? Almost seventy miles from here. [*A pause.*] So this is the end of life in this house. . . .

VARYA   [*Still fussing with the luggage.*]   Where could it be? Perhaps I put it in the trunk? Yes, life in this house has come to an end . . . there won't be any more. . . .

LOPAHIN   And I'm going to Kharkov. . . . On the next train. I've got a lot of work to do there. I'm leaving Epihodov here. . . . I've hired him.

VARYA   Really! . . .

LOPAHIN   Remember, last year at this time it was snowing already, but now it's still so bright and sunny. Though it's cold . . . Three degrees of frost.

VARYA   I haven't looked. [*A pause.*] Besides, our thermometer's broken. . . .
   [*A pause. A voice is heard from outside the door.*]

VOICE   Yermolay Alexeyevich!

LOPAHIN   [*As if he had been waiting for it.*]   I'm coming! Right away! [*Goes out quickly.*]
   [VARYA *sits on the floor, with her head on a bundle of clothes, crying quietly. The door opens,* LYUBOV *enters hesitantly.*]

LYUBOV   Well? [*A pause.*] We must be going.

VARYA   [*Stops crying and wipes her eyes.*]   Yes, Mamma, it's time we got started. I'll just have time to get to the Rogulins today, if we don't miss the train.

LYUBOV   [*Calls through the door.*]   Anya, put your things on. [*Enter* ANYA, *fol-*

lowed by GAEV *and* CHARLOTTA. GAEV *wears a heavy overcoat with a hood. Servants and coachmen come into the room.* EPIHODOV *is picking up the luggage.*] Now we can begin our journey!

ANYA [*Joyfully.*]   Our journey!

GAEV   My friends, my dear, beloved friends! As I leave this house forever, how can I be silent, how can I refrain from expressing to you, as I say good-bye for the last time, the feelings which now overwhelm me. . . .

ANYA [*Begging.*]   Uncle!

VARYA   Uncle, please don't!

GAEV [*Downcast.*]   I put the red into the corner and then . . . I'll keep quiet. [*Enter* TROFIMOV *and* LOPAHIN.]

TROFIMOV   Well, ladies and gentlemen, it's time we get started.

LOPAHIN   Epihodov, my coat!

LYUBOV   I'll just stay for one more minute. It seems as if I'd never seen the walls and ceilings of this house before, and now I look at them with such longing, such love. . . .

GAEV   I remember when I was six—it was Trinity Sunday . . . I was sitting here at this window watching father on his way to church. . . .

LYUBOV   Have they taken everything out?

LOPAHIN   It looks like it. [*To* EPIHODOV, *as he puts on his coat.*] Be sure to take care of everything, Epihodov.

EPIHODOV [*In a husky voice.*]   Don't worry, Yermolay Alexeyevich!

LOPAHIN   What is wrong with your voice?

EPIHODOV   I just had some water, and it went down the wrong throat.

YASHA [*With contempt.*]   What a fool!

LYUBOV   After we leave, there won't be a soul here. . . .

LOPAHIN   Not until spring. [VARYA *pulls an umbrella from a bundle of clothes;* LOPAHIN *pretends to be afraid.*] What are you doing that for? . . . I didn't mean to. . . .

TROFIMOV   Ladies and gentlemen, hurry up, it's time. The train will be here soon.

VARYA   Petya, here are your goloshes beside the suitcase. [*Tearfully.*] How dirty and old they are! . . .

TROFIMOV [*Puts them on.*]   Hurry up, ladies and gentlemen!

GAEV [*Greatly embarrassed, afraid of breaking into tears.*]   The train, the station . . . The red off the white into the middle pocket. . . .

LYUBOV   Let us go!

LOPAHIN   Are we all here? No one left? [*Locks the door on the left.*] There are some things stored in there, best to keep it locked up. Come along!

ANYA   Good-bye, old house! Good-bye, old life!

TROFIMOV   Welcome to the new life! . . . [*Goes out with* ANYA.]
[VARYA *looks around the room and goes out slowly.* YASHA *and* CHARLOTTA, *with her little dog, follow.*]

LOPAHIN   And so, until the spring. Come, my friends. . . . *Au revoir!* [*Goes out.*]
[LYUBOV *and* GAEV *alone. They seem to have been waiting for this moment, and now they embrace each other and cry quietly, with restraint, so as not to be heard.*]

GAEV [*In despair.*]   Sister, my sister. . . .

LYUBOV   Oh, my orchard, my beloved, my beautiful orchard! My life, my youth, my happiness . . . good-bye! . . . Good-bye!

ANYA [*Off-stage, calling gaily.*]   Mamma! . . .

TROFIMOV [*Off-stage, gaily and excitedly.*]   Yoo-hoo! . . .

LYUBOV   Just one last time—to look at these walls, these windows. . . . Mother loved to walk in this room. . . .

GAEV   Sister, my sister . . .

ANYA [*Off-stage.*] Mamma!

TROFIMOV [*Off-stage.*] Yoo-hoo!

LYUBOV We're coming . . . [*They go out.*]

[*The stage is empty. The sound of doors being locked and then of carriages driving off. Silence. In the stillness the dull sounds of an axe striking on a tree can be heard. They sound mournful and sad. Footsteps are heard and from the door on the right* FEERS *enters. He is dressed, as usual, in a coat and white waistcoat, and is wearing slippers. He is ill.*]

FEERS [*Walks up to the middle door and tries the handle.*] Locked. They've gone . . . [*Sits down on a sofa.*] They've forgotten me. Never mind. . . . I'll sit here for a bit. I don't suppose Leonid Andreyevich put on his fur coat, he probably wore his light one. [*Sighs, preoccupied.*] I didn't take care of it . . . These young people! . . . [*Mutters something unintelligible.*] My life's slipped by as if I'd never lived. . . . [*Lies down.*] I'll lie down a bit. You haven't got any strength left, nothing's left, nothing. . . . Oh, you . . . you old good-for-nothing! . . . [*Lies, motionless.*]

[*A distant sound that seems to come out of the sky, like a breaking harp, slowly and sadly dying away. Then all is silent, except for the sound of an axe striking a tree in the orchard far away.*]

CURTAIN

ARTHUR MILLER
[1915–   ]

Throughout his successful career as a dramatist Arthur Miller has probed deeply into the nature of personal guilt, social guilt, and the nexus between the two. Many of Miller's themes are traceable to his Jewish heritage, a heritage of intense moral seriousness about the relationship of the individual to society. It is partly because of his own background, Miller says, that "I couldn't ever write a totally nihilistic work."

Miller was born and raised in New York, the son of a well-to-do Austrian-American father and an American mother. For most of his youth he remained an indifferent student, although he enjoyed reading on his own. He particularly revered Dostoevski's *The Brothers Karamazov,* which first awakened in him the desire to become a writer. After graduating from high school in the midst of the Great Depression, Miller worked at a number of menial jobs in New York for several years. But in 1933 he entered the University of Michigan as a student of journalism. There, under the guidance of Kenneth Rowe, he began his apprenticeship as a playwright. Miller returned to New York after his graduation in 1938, and worked through the war years as a reporter and radio script-writer. The experience of writing half-hour radio plays, he says, sharpened his respect for "the right phrase" and for concentrated dramatic effect: "the economy of words in a good radio play was everything."

Miller's first great success as a playwright came in 1947 with *All My Sons,* the story of a corrupt manufacturer of war materials who is indirectly responsible for the death of his son. The form of this play was the intense realism of the Ibsen tradition, but Miller's later plays generally depend for their full effect on nonrealistic (usually expressionistic) elements. In his masterpiece, *Death of a Salesman* (1949), Miller moves freely from "real" events to the "expression" of events being remembered and imagined by the protagonist (a man worn out by his life-long pursuit of the American dream of "Success," who begins to crack up as he vaguely perceives his spiritual failure). In this play Miller's imaginative stage conception allows the same "set" to serve many purposes, such as the correlation of past and present action. In other plays—*A View from the Bridge* (1955) and *After the Fall* (1963) —Miller makes effective use of a narrator who speaks directly to the audience.

Miller's concern with contemporary social and political issues—reflected in *All My Sons*—has continued to dominate most of his later work. *The Crucible* (1953), a tragedy which deals with the Salem witch trials of the seventeenth century, is an implicit indictment of the McCarthyism of the early 1950's. *After the Fall* (which, unfortunately, was widely interpreted as mere "autobiography," particularly in regard to Miller's marriage to Marilyn Monroe) probes into several areas of social responsibility. The play registers a protest against the arbitrary, destructive power of the House Un-American Activities Committee (at whose hearing Miller himself had earlier refused to testify), and it keeps before the audience's mind the spectre of the six million Jews executed during the Nazi regime.

None of Miller's dramas, however, constitute "social protest" in an abstract sense: all are organized around individual protagonists who are interesting in themselves. *Death of a Salesman* and *A View from the Bridge* present "common men" as protagonists, but each is "common" only in a socio-economic sense, for each is conceived in psychological depth. Miller has argued at length that such characters have the potential of tragic heroism, and that they should not be denied the kind of "respect" usually reserved for the traditional tragic heroes who fall from "high degree."

Miller now lives near Roxbury, Connecticut, where he continues to write for the New York stage. His most recent plays are *Incident at Vichy* (1964) and *The Price* (1968).

A VIEW
FROM THE BRIDGE

ARTHUR MILLER

CHARACTERS

LOUIS
MIKE
ALFIERI
EDDIE
CATHERINE
BEATRICE
MARCO
TONY

RODOLPHO
FIRST IMMIGRATION OFFICER
SECOND IMMIGRATION OFFICER
MR. LIPARI
MRS. LIPARI
TWO "SUBMARINES"
NEIGHBORS

ACT I

The street and house front of a tenement building. The front is skeletal entirely. The main acting area is the living room-dining room of EDDIE'S *apartment. It is a worker's flat, clean, sparse, homely. There is a rocker down front; a round dining table at center, with chairs; and a portable phonograph.*

A View from the Bridge by Arthur Miller, Copyright 1955, © 1957 by Arthur Miller. Reprinted by permission of The Viking Press, Inc.

> *At back are a bedroom door and an opening to the kitchen; none of these interiors are seen.*
> *At the right, forestage, a desk. This is* MR. ALFIERI'S *law office.*
> *There is also a telephone booth. This is not used until the last scenes, so it may be covered or left in view.*
> *A stairway leads up to the apartment, and then farther up to the next story, which is not seen.*
> *Ramps, representing the street, run upstage and off to right and left.*
> *As the curtain rises,* LOUIS *and* MIKE, *longshoremen, are pitching coins against the building at left.*
> *A distant foghorn blows.*
> *Enter* ALFIERI, *a lawyer in his fifties turning gray; he is portly, good-humored, and thoughtful. The two pitchers nod to him as he passes. He crosses the stage to his desk, removes his hat, runs his fingers through his hair, and grinning, speaks to the audience.*

ALFIERI You wouldn't have known it, but something amusing has just happened. You see how uneasily they nod to me? That's because I am a lawyer. In this neighborhood to meet a lawyer or a priest on the street is unlucky. We're only thought of in connection with disasters, and they'd rather not get too close.

I often think that behind that suspicious little nod of theirs lie three thousand years of distrust. A lawyer means the law, and in Sicily, from where their fathers came, the law has not been a friendly idea since the Greeks were beaten.

I am inclined to notice the ruins in things, perhaps because I was born in Italy. . . . I only came here when I was twenty-five. In those days, Al Capone, the greatest Carthaginian of all, was learning his trade on these pavements, and Frankie Yale himself was cut precisely in half by a machine gun on the corner of Union Street, two blocks away. Oh, there were many here who were justly shot by unjust men. Justice is very important here.

But this is Red Hook, not Sicily. This is the slum that faces the bay on the seaward side of Brooklyn Bridge. This is the gullet of New York swallowing the tonnage of the world. And now we are quite civilized, quite American. Now we settle for half, and I like it better. I no longer keep a pistol in my filing cabinet.

And my practice is entirely unromantic.

My wife has warned me, so have my friends; they tell me the people in this neighborhood lack elegance, glamour. After all, who have I dealt with in my life? Longshoremen and their wives, and fathers and grandfathers, compensation cases, evictions, family squabbles—the petty troubles of the poor—and yet . . . every few years there is still a case, and as the

The play in this printed form is designed for the reading public only. All dramatic rights therein are fully protected by copyright and no public or private performance—professional or amateur—may be given without the written permission of the author and the payment of royalty. As the courts have also ruled that the public reading of a play constitutes a public performance, no such reading may be given except under conditions above stated. Communications should be addressed to the author's representative, Ashley Famous Agency, Inc., 1301 Avenue of the Americas, New York, N. Y. 10019.

parties tell me what the trouble is, the flat air in my office suddenly washes in with the green scent of the sea, the dust in this air is blown away and the thought comes that in some Cæsar's year, in Calabria perhaps or on the cliff at Syracuse, another lawyer, quite differently dressed, heard the same complaint and sat there as powerless as I, and watched it run its bloody course.

[EDDIE *has appeared and has been pitching coins with the men and is highlighted among them. He is forty—a husky, slightly overweight longshoreman.*]

This one's name was Eddie Carbone, a longshoreman working the docks from Brooklyn Bridge to the breakwater where the open sea begins. [ALFIERI *walks into darkness.*]

EDDIE [*moving up steps into doorway*] Well, I'll see ya, fellas.

[CATHERINE *enters from kitchen, crosses down to window, looks out.*]

LOUIS You workin' tomorrow?

EDDIE Yeah, there's another day yet on that ship. See ya, Louis.

[EDDIE *goes into the house, as light rises in the apartment.*]

[CATHERINE *is waving to* LOUIS *from the window and turns to him.*]

CATHERINE Hi, Eddie!

[EDDIE *is pleased and therefore shy about it; he hangs up his cap and jacket.*]

EDDIE Where you goin' all dressed up?

CATHERINE [*running her hands over her skirt*] I just got it. You like it?

EDDIE Yeah, it's nice. And what happened to your hair?

CATHERINE You like it? I fixed it different. [*Calling to kitchen.*] He's here, B.!

EDDIE Beautiful. Turn around, lemme see in the back. [*She turns for him.*] Oh, if your mother was alive to see you now! She wouldn't believe it.

CATHERINE You like it, huh?

EDDIE You look like one of them girls that went to college. Where you goin'?

CATHERINE [*taking his arm*] Wait'll B. comes in, I'll tell you something. Here, sit down. [*She is walking him to the armchair. Calling offstage.*] Hurry up, will you, B.?

EDDIE [*sitting*] What's goin' on?

CATHERINE I'll get you a beer, all right?

EDDIE Well, tell me what happened. Come over here, talk to me.

CATHERINE I want to wait till B. comes in. [*She sits on her heels beside him.*] Guess how much we paid for the skirt.

EDDIE I think it's too short, ain't it?

CATHERINE [*standing*] No! not when I stand up.

EDDIE Yeah, but you gotta sit down sometimes.

CATHERINE Eddie, it's the style now. [*She walks to show him.*] I mean, if you see me walkin' down the street—

EDDIE Listen, you been givin' me the willies the way you walk down the street, I mean it.

CATHERINE Why?

EDDIE Catherine, I don't want to be a pest, but I'm tellin' you you're walkin' wavy.

CATHERINE I'm walkin' wavy?

EDDIE Now don't aggravate me, Katie, you are walkin' wavy! I don't like the looks they're givin' you in the candy store. And with them new high heels on the sidewalk—clack, clack, clack. The heads are turnin' like windmills.

CATHERINE But those guys look at all the girls, you know that.

EDDIE You ain't "all the girls."

CATHERINE [*almost in tears because he disapproves*] What do you want me to do? You want me to—

EDDIE   Now don't get mad, kid.

CATHERINE   Well, I don't know what you want from me.

EDDIE   Katie, I promised your mother on her deathbed. I'm responsible for you. You're a baby, you don't understand these things. I mean like when you stand here by the window, wavin' outside.

CATHERINE   I was wavin' to Louis!

EDDIE   Listen, I could tell you things about Louis which you wouldn't wave to him no more.

CATHERINE   [*trying to joke him out of his warning*]   Eddie, I wish there was one guy you couldn't tell me things about!

EDDIE   Catherine, do me a favor, will you? You're gettin' to be a big girl now, you gotta keep yourself more, you can't be so friendly, kid. [*Calls.*] Hey, B., what're you doin' in there? [*To* CATHERINE.] Get her in here, will you? I got news for her.

CATHERINE   [*starting out*]   What?

EDDIE   Her cousins landed.

CATHERINE   [*clapping her hands together*]   No! [*She turns instantly and starts for the kitchen.*] B.! Your cousins!

[BEATRICE *enters, wiping her hands with a towel.*]

BEATRICE   [*in the face of* CATHERINE'*s shout*]   What?

CATHERINE   Your cousins got in!

BEATRICE   [*astounded, turns to* EDDIE]   What are you talkin' about? Where?

EDDIE   I was just knockin' off work before and Tony Bereli come over to me; he says the ship is in the North River.

BEATRICE   [*her hands are clasped at her breast; she seems half in fear, half in unutterable joy*]   They're all right?

EDDIE   He didn't see them yet, they're still on board. But as soon as they get off he'll meet them. He figures about ten o'clock they'll be here.

BEATRICE   [*sits, almost weak from tension*]   And they'll let them off the ship all right? That's fixed, heh?

EDDIE   Sure, they give them regular seamen papers and they walk off with the crew. Don't worry about it, B., there's nothin' to it. Couple of hours they'll be here.

BEATRICE   What happened? They wasn't supposed to be till next Thursday.

EDDIE   I don't know; they put them on any ship they can get them out on. Maybe the other ship they was supposed to take there was some danger— What you cryin' about?

BEATRICE   [*astounded and afraid*]   I'm—I just—I can't believe it! I didn't even buy a new tablecloth; I was gonna wash the walls—

EDDIE   Listen, they'll think it's a millionaire's house compared to the way they live. Don't worry about the walls. They'll be thankful. [*To* CATHERINE.] Whyn't you run down buy a tablecloth. Go ahead, here. [*He is reaching into his pocket.*]

CATHERINE   There's no stores open now.

EDDIE   [*to* BEATRICE]   You was gonna put a new cover on the chair.

BEATRICE   I know—well, I thought it was gonna be next week! I was gonna clean the walls, I was gonna wax the floors. [*She stands disturbed.*]

CATHERINE   [*pointing upward*]   Maybe Mrs. Dondero upstairs—

BEATRICE   [*of the tablecloth*]   No, hers is worse than this one. [*Suddenly.*] My God, I don't even have nothin' to eat for them! [*She starts for the kitchen.*]

EDDIE   [*reaching out and grabbing her arm*]   Hey, hey! Take it easy.

BEATRICE   No, I'm just nervous, that's all. [*To* CATHERINE.] I'll make the fish.

EDDIE   You're savin' their lives, what're you worryin' about the tablecloth? They probably didn't see a tablecloth in their whole life where they come from.

BEATRICE   [*looking into his eyes*] I'm just worried about you, that's all I'm worried.

EDDIE   Listen, as long as they know where they're gonna sleep.

BEATRICE   I told them in the letters. They're sleepin' on the floor.

EDDIE   Beatrice, all I'm worried about is you got such a heart that I'll end up on the floor with you, and they'll be in our bed.

BEATRICE   All right, stop it.

EDDIE   Because as soon as you see a tired relative, I end up on the floor.

BEATRICE   When did you end up on the floor?

EDDIE   When your father's house burned down I didn't end up on the floor?

BEATRICE   Well, their house burned down!

EDDIE   Yeah, but it didn't keep burnin' for two weeks!

BEATRICE   All right, look, I'll tell them to go someplace else. [*She starts into the kitchen.*]

EDDIE   Now wait a minute. Beatrice! [*She halts. He goes to her.*] I just don't want you bein' pushed around, that's all. You got too big a heart. [*He touches her hand.*] What're you so touchy?

BEATRICE   I'm just afraid if it don't turn out good you'll be mad at me.

EDDIE   Listen, if everybody keeps his mouth shut, nothin' can happen. They'll pay for their board.

BEATRICE   Oh, I told them.

EDDIE   Then what the hell. [*Pause. He moves.*] It's an honor, B. I mean it. I was just thinkin' before, comin' home, suppose my father didn't come to this country, and I was starvin' like them over there . . . and I had people in America could keep me a couple of months? The man would be honored to lend me a place to sleep.

BEATRICE   [*there are tears in her eyes. She turns to* CATHERINE] You see what he is? [*She turns and grabs* EDDIE's *face in her hands.*] Mmm! You're an angel! God'll bless you. [*He is gratefully smiling.*] You'll see, you'll get a blessing for this!

EDDIE   [*laughing*] I'll settle for my own bed.

BEATRICE   Go, Baby, set the table.

CATHERINE   We didn't tell him about me yet.

BEATRICE   Let him eat first, then we'll tell him. Bring everything in.
     [*She hurries* CATHERINE *out.*]

EDDIE   [*sitting at the table*] What's all that about? Where's she goin'?

BEATRICE   Noplace. It's very good news, Eddie. I want you to be happy.

EDDIE   What's goin' on?
     [CATHERINE *enters with plates, forks.*]

BEATRICE   She's got a job.
     [*Pause.* EDDIE *looks at* CATHERINE, *then back to* BEATRICE.]

EDDIE   What job? She's gonna finish school.

CATHERINE   Eddie, you won't believe it—

EDDIE   No—no, you gonna finish school. What kinda job, what do you mean? All of a sudden you—

CATHERINE   Listen a minute, it's wonderful.

EDDIE   It's not wonderful. You'll never get nowheres unless you finish school. You can't take no job. Why didn't you ask me before you take a job?

BEATRICE   She's askin' you now, she didn't take nothin' yet.

CATHERINE   Listen a minute! I came to school this morning and the principal called me out of the class, see? To go to his office.

EDDIE   Yeah?

CATHERINE   So I went in and he says to me he's got my records, y'know? And there's a company wants a girl right away. It ain't exactly a secretary, it's a stenographer first, but pretty soon you get to be secretary. And he says to me that I'm the best student in the whole class—

BEATRICE You hear that?

EDDIE Well why not? Sure she's the best.

CATHERINE I'm the best student, he says, and if I want, I should take the job and the end of the year he'll let me take the examination and he'll give me the certificate. So I'll save practically a year!

EDDIE [*strangely nervous*] Where's the job? What company?

CATHERINE It's a big plumbing company over Nostrand Avenue.

EDDIE Nostrand Avenue and where?

CATHERINE It's someplace by the Navy Yard.

BEATRICE Fifty dollars a week, Eddie.

EDDIE [*to* CATHERINE, *surprised*] Fifty?

CATHERINE I swear.

[*Pause.*]

EDDIE What about all the stuff you wouldn't learn this year, though?

CATHERINE There's nothin' more to learn, Eddie, I just gotta practice from now on. I know all the symbols and I know the keyboard. I'll just get faster, that's all. And when I'm workin' I'll keep gettin' better and better, you see?

BEATRICE Work is the best practice anyway.

EDDIE That ain't what I wanted, though.

CATHERINE Why! It's a great big company—

EDDIE I don't like that neighborhood over there.

CATHERINE It's a block and half from the subway, he says.

EDDIE Near the Navy Yard plenty can happen in a block and a half. And a plumbin' company! That's one step over the water front. They're practically longshoremen.

BEATRICE Yeah, but she'll be in the office, Eddie.

EDDIE I know she'll be in the office, but that ain't what I had in mind.

BEATRICE Listen, she's gotta go to work sometime.

EDDIE Listen, B., she'll be with a lotta plumbers? And sailors up and down the street? So what did she go to school for?

CATHERINE But it's fifty a week, Eddie.

EDDIE Look, did I ask you for money? I supported you this long I support you a little more. Please, do me a favor, will ya? I want you to be with different kind of people. I want you to be in a nice office. Maybe a lawyer's office someplace in New York in one of them nice buildings. I mean if you're gonna get outa here then get out; don't go practically in the same kind of neighborhood.

[*Pause.* CATHERINE *lowers her eyes.*]

BEATRICE Go, Baby, bring in the supper. [CATHERINE *goes out.*] Think about it a little bit, Eddie. Please. She's crazy to start work. It's not a little shop, it's a big company. Some day she could be a secretary. They picked her out of the whole class. [*He is silent, staring down at the tablecloth, fingering the pattern.*] What are you worried about? She could take care of herself. She'll get out of the subway and be in the office in two minutes.

EDDIE [*somehow sickened*] I know that neighborhood, B., I don't like it.

BEATRICE Listen, if nothin' happened to her in this neighborhood it ain't gonna happen noplace else. [*She turns his face to her.*] Look, you gotta get used to it, she's no baby no more. Tell her to take it. [*He turns his head away.*] You hear me? [*She is angering.*] I don't understand you; she's seventeen years old, you gonna keep her in the house all her life?

EDDIE [*insulted*] What kinda remark is that?

BEATRICE [*with sympathy but insistent force*] Well, I don't understand when it ends. First it was gonna be when she graduated high school, so she graduated high school. Then it was gonna be when she learned stenographer, so she learned stenographer. So what're we gonna wait for now? I mean it, Eddie, sometimes I don't understand you; they picked her out of the whole class, it's an honor for her.

[CATHERINE *enters with food, which she silently sets on the table. After a moment of watching her face,* EDDIE *breaks into a smile, but it almost seems that tears will form in his eyes.*]

EDDIE With your hair that way you look like a madonna, you know that? You're the madonna type. [*She doesn't look at him, but continues ladling out food onto the plates.*] You wanna go to work, heh, Madonna?

CATHERINE [*softly*] Yeah.

EDDIE [*with a sense of her childhood, her babyhood, and the years*] All right, go to work. [*She looks at him, then rushes and hugs him.*] Hey, hey! Take it easy! [*He holds her face away from him to look at her.*] What're you cryin' about? [*He is affected by her, but smiles his emotion away.*]

CATHERINE [*sitting at her place*] I just—[*Bursting out.*] I'm gonna buy all new dishes with my first pay! [*They laugh warmly.*] I mean it. I'll fix up the whole house! I'll buy a rug!

EDDIE And then you'll move away.

CATHERINE No, Eddie!

EDDIE [*grinning*] Why not? That's life. And you'll come visit on Sundays, then once a month, then Christmas and New Year's, finally.

CATHERINE [*grasping his arm to reassure him and to erase the accusation*] No, please!

EDDIE [*smiling but hurt*] I only ask you one thing—don't trust nobody. You got a good aunt but she's got too big a heart, you learned bad from her. Believe me.

BEATRICE Be the way you are, Katie, don't listen to him.

EDDIE [*to* BEATRICE—*strangely and quickly resentful*] You lived in a house all your life, what do you know about it? You never worked in your life.

BEATRICE She likes people. What's wrong with that?

EDDIE Because most people ain't people. She's goin' to work: plumbers; they'll chew her to pieces if she don't watch out. [*To* CATHERINE.] Believe me, Katie, the less you trust, the less you be sorry.

[EDDIE *crosses himself and the women do the same, and they eat.*]

CATHERINE First thing I'll buy is a rug, heh, B.?

BEATRICE I don't mind. [*To* EDDIE.] I smelled coffee all day today. You unloadin' coffee today?

EDDIE Yeah, a Brazil ship.

CATHERINE I smelled it too. It smelled all over the neighborhood.

EDDIE That's one time, boy, to be a longshoreman is a pleasure. I could work coffee ships twenty hours a day. You go down in the hold, y'know? It's like flowers, that smell. We'll bust a bag tomorrow, I'll bring you some.

BEATRICE Just be sure there's no spiders in it, will ya? I mean it. [*She directs this to* CATHERINE, *rolling her eyes upward.*] I still remember that spider coming out of that bag he brung home. I nearly died.

EDDIE You call that a spider? You oughta see what comes outa the bananas sometimes.

BEATRICE Don't talk about it!

EDDIE I seen spiders could stop a Buick.

BEATRICE   [*clapping her hands over her ears*]   All right, shut up!

EDDIE   [*laughing and taking a watch out of his pocket*]   Well, who started with spiders?

BEATRICE   All right, I'm sorry, I didn't mean it. Just don't bring none home again. What time is it?

EDDIE   Quarter nine. [*Puts watch back in his pocket. They continue eating in silence.*]

CATHERINE   He's bringin' them ten o'clock, Tony?

EDDIE   Around, yeah. [*He eats.*]

CATHERINE   Eddie, suppose somebody asks if they're livin' here. [*He looks at her as though already she had divulged something publicly. Defensively.*] I mean if they ask.

EDDIE   Now look, Baby, I can see we're gettin' mixed up again here.

CATHERINE   No, I just mean . . . people'll see them goin' in and out.

EDDIE   I don't care who sees them goin' in and out as long as you don't see them goin' in and out. And this goes for you too, B. You don't see nothin' and you don't know nothin'.

BEATRICE   What do you mean? I understand.

EDDIE   You don't understand; you still think you can talk about this to somebody just a little bit. Now lemme say it once and for all, because you're makin' me nervous again, both of you. I don't care if somebody comes in the house and sees them sleepin' on the floor, it never comes out of your mouth who they are or what they're doin' here.

BEATRICE   Yeah, but my mother'll know—

EDDIE   Sure she'll know, but just don't you be the one who told her, that's all. This is the United States government you're playin' with now, this is the Immigration Bureau. If you said it you knew it, if you didn't say it you didn't know it.

CATHERINE   Yeah, but Eddie, suppose somebody—

EDDIE   I don't care what question it is. You—don't—know—nothin'. They got stool pigeons all over this neighborhood they're payin' them every week for information, and you don't know who they are. It could be your best friend. You hear? [*To* BEATRICE.] Like Vinny Bolzano, remember Vinny?

BEATRICE   Oh, yeah. God forbid.

EDDIE   Tell her about Vinny. [*To* CATHERINE.] You think I'm blowin' steam here? [*To* BEATRICE.] Go ahead, tell her. [*To* CATHERINE.] You was a baby then. There was a family lived next door to her mother, he was about sixteen—

BEATRICE   No, he was no more than fourteen, cause I was to his confirmation in Saint Agnes. But the family had an uncle that they were hidin' in the house, and he snitched to the Immigration.

CATHERINE   The kid snitched?

EDDIE   On his own uncle!

CATHERINE   What, was he crazy?

EDDIE   He was crazy after, I tell you that, boy.

BEATRICE   Oh, it was terrible. He had five brothers and the old father. And they grabbed him in the kitchen and pulled him down the stairs—three flights his head was bouncin' like a coconut. And they spit on him in the street, his own father and his brothers. The whole neighborhood was cryin'.

CATHERINE   Ts! So what happened to him?

BEATRICE   I think he went away. [*To* EDDIE.] I never seen him again, did you?

EDDIE   [*rises during this, taking out his watch*]   Him? You'll never see him no more, a guy do a thing like that? How's he gonna show his face? [*To* CATHERINE, *as he gets up uneasily.*] Just remember, kid, you can quicker get back a million dollars that was stole than a word that you gave away. [*He is standing now, stretching his back.*]

CATHERINE Okay, I won't say a word to nobody, I swear.

EDDIE Gonna rain tomorrow. We'll be slidin' all over the decks. Maybe you oughta put something on for them, they be here soon.

BEATRICE I only got fish, I hate to spoil it if they ate already. I'll wait, it only takes a few minutes; I could broil it.

CATHERINE What happens, Eddie, when that ship pulls out and they ain't on it, though? Don't the captain say nothin'?

EDDIE [*slicing an apple with his pocket knife*] Captain's pieced off, what do you mean?

CATHERINE Even the captain?

EDDIE What's the matter, the captain don't have to live? Captain gets a piece, maybe one of the mates, piece for the guy in Italy who fixed the papers for them, Tony here'll get a little bite. . . .

BEATRICE I just hope they get work here, that's all I hope.

EDDIE Oh, the syndicate'll fix jobs for them; till they pay 'em off they'll get them work every day. It's after the pay-off, then they'll have to scramble like the rest of us.

BEATRICE Well, it be better than they got there.

EDDIE Oh sure, well, listen. So you gonna start Monday, heh, Madonna?

CATHERINE [*embarrassed*] I'm supposed to, yeah.

[EDDIE *is standing facing the two seated women. First* BEATRICE *smiles, then* CATHERINE, *for a powerful emotion is on him, a childish one and a knowing fear, and the tears show in his eyes—and they are shy before the avowal.*]

EDDIE [*sadly smiling, yet somehow proud of her*] Well . . . I hope you have good luck. I wish you the best. You know that, kid.

CATHERINE [*rising, trying to laugh*] You sound like I'm goin' a million miles!

EDDIE I know. I guess I just never figured on one thing.

CATHERINE [*smiling*] What?

EDDIE That you would ever grow up. [*He utters a soundless laugh at himself, feeling his breast pocket of his shirt.*] I left a cigar in my other coat, I think. [*He starts for the bedroom.*]

CATHERINE Stay there! I'll get it for you.

[*She hurries out. There is a slight pause, and* EDDIE *turns to* BEATRICE, *who has been avoiding his gaze.*]

EDDIE What are you mad at me lately?

BEATRICE Who's mad? [*She gets up, clearing the dishes.*] I'm not mad. [*She picks up the dishes and turns to him.*] You're the one is mad. [*She turns and goes into the kitchen as* CATHERINE *enters from the bedroom with a cigar and a pack of matches.*]

CATHERINE Here! I'll light it for you! [*She strikes a match and holds it to his cigar. He puffs. Quietly.*] Don't worry about me, Eddie, heh?

EDDIE Don't burn yourself. [*Just in time she blows out the match.*] You better go in help her with the dishes.

CATHERINE [*turns quickly to the table, and, seeing the table cleared, she says, almost guiltily*] Oh! [*She hurries into the kitchen, and as she exits there.*] I'll do the dishes, B.!

[*Alone,* EDDIE *stands looking toward the kitchen for a moment. Then he takes out his watch, glances at it, replaces it in his pocket, sits in the armchair, and stares at the smoke flowing out of his mouth.*

The lights go down, then come up on ALFIERI, *who has moved onto the forestage.*]

ALFIERI He was as good a man as he had to be in a life that was hard and even. He worked on the piers when there was work, he brought home his pay, and he lived. And toward ten o'clock of that night, after they had eaten, the cousins came.

[*The lights fade on* ALFIERI *and rise on the street. Enter* TONY, *escorting* MARCO *and* RODOLPHO, *each with a valise.* TONY *halts, indicates the house. They stand for a moment looking at it.*]

MARCO   [*he is a square-built peasant of thirty-two, suspicious, tender, and quiet-voiced*]   Thank you.

TONY   You're on your own now. Just be careful, that's all. Ground floor.

MARCO   Thank you.

TONY   [*indicating the house*]   I'll see you on the pier tomorrow. You'll go to work.

[MARCO *nods.* TONY *continues on walking down the street.*]

RODOLPHO   This will be the first house I ever walked into in America! Imagine! She said they were poor!

MARCO   Ssh! Come. [*They go to door.*]

[MARCO *knocks. The lights rise in the room.* EDDIE *goes and opens the door. Enter* MARCO *and* RODOLPHO, *removing their caps.* BEATRICE *and* CATHERINE *enter from the kitchen. The lights fade in the street.*]

EDDIE   You Marco?

MARCO   Marco.

EDDIE   Come on in! [*He shakes* MARCO'S *hand.*]

BEATRICE   Here, take the bags!

MARCO   [*nods, looks to the women and fixes on* BEATRICE. *Crosses to* BEATRICE]   Are you my cousin? [*She nods. He kisses her hand.*]

BEATRICE   [*above the table, touching her chest with her hand*]   Beatrice. This is my husband, Eddie. [*All nod.*] Catherine, my sister Nancy's daughter. [*The brothers nod.*]

MARCO   [*indicating* RODOLPHO]   My brother. Rodolpho. [RODOLPHO *nods.* MARCO *comes with a certain formal stiffness to* EDDIE.] I want to tell you now Eddie —when you say go, we will go.

EDDIE   Oh, no . . . [*Takes* MARCO'S *bag.*]

MARCO   I see it's a small house, but soon, maybe, we can have our own house.

EDDIE   You're welcome, Marco, we got plenty of room here. Katie, give them supper, heh? [*Exits into bedroom with their bags.*]

CATHERINE   Come here, sit down. I'll get you some soup.

MARCO   [*as they go to the table*]   We ate on the ship. Thank you. [*To* EDDIE, *calling off to bedroom.*] Thank you.

BEATRICE   Get some coffee. We'll all have coffee. Come sit down.

[RODOLPHO *and* MARCO *sit, at the table.*]

CATHERINE   [*wondrously*]   How come he's so dark and you're so light, Rodolpho?

RODOLPHO   [*ready to laugh*]   I don't know. A thousand years ago, they say, the Danes invaded Sicily.

[BEATRICE *kisses* RODOLPHO. *They laugh as* EDDIE *enters.*]

CATHERINE   [*to* BEATRICE]   He's practically blond!

EDDIE   How's the coffee doin'?

CATHERINE   [*brought up*]   I'm gettin' it. [*She hurries out to kitchen.*]

EDDIE   [*sits on his rocker*]   Yiz have a nice trip?

MARCO   The ocean is always rough. But we are good sailors.

EDDIE   No trouble gettin' here?

MARCO   No. The man brought us. Very nice man.

RODOLPHO   [*to* EDDIE]   He says we start to work tomorrow. Is he honest?

EDDIE [*laughing*] No. But as long as you owe them money, they'll get you plenty of work. [*To* MARCO.] Yiz ever work on the piers in Italy?

MARCO Piers? Ts!—no.

RODOLPHO [*smiling at the smallness of his town*] In our town there are no piers, only the beach, and little fishing boats.

BEATRICE So what kinda work did yiz do?

MARCO [*shrugging shyly, even embarrassed*] Whatever there is, anything.

RODOLPHO Sometimes they build a house, or if they fix the bridge—Marco is a mason and I bring him the cement. [*He laughs.*] In harvest time we work in the fields . . . if there is work. Anything.

EDDIE Still bad there, heh?

MARCO Bad, yes.

RODOLPHO [*laughing*] It's terrible! We stand around all day in the piazza listening to the fountain like birds. Everybody waits only for the train.

BEATRICE What's on the train?

RODOLPHO Nothing. But if there are many passengers and you're lucky you make a few lire to push the taxi up the hill.
[*Enter* CATHERINE; *she listens.*]

BEATRICE You gotta push a taxi?

RODOLPHO [*laughing*] Oh, sure! It's a feature in our town. The horses in our town are skinnier than goats. So if there are too many passengers we help to push the carriages up to the hotel. [*He laughs.*] In our town the horses are only for show.

CATHERINE Why don't they have automobile taxis?

RODOLPHO There is one. We push that too. [*They laugh.*] Everything in our town, you gotta push!

BEATRICE [*to* EDDIE] How do you like that!

EDDIE [*to* MARCO] So what're you wanna do, you gonna stay here in this country or you wanna go back?

MARCO [*surprised*] Go back?

EDDIE Well, you're married, ain't you?

MARCO Yes. I have three children.

BEATRICE Three! I thought only one.

MARCO Oh, no. I have three now. Four years, five years, six years.

BEATRICE Ah . . . I bet they're cryin' for you already, heh?

MARCO What can I do? The older one is sick in his chest. My wife—she feeds them from her own mouth. I tell you the truth, if I stay there they will never grow up. They eat the sunshine.

BEATRICE My God. So how long you want to stay?

MARCO With your permission, we will stay maybe a—

EDDIE She don't mean in this house, she means in the country.

MARCO Oh. Maybe four, five, six years, I think.

RODOLPHO [*smiling*] He trusts his wife.

BEATRICE Yeah, but maybe you'll get enough, you'll be able to go back quicker.

MARCO I hope. I don't know. [*To* EDDIE.] I understand it's not so good here either.

EDDIE Oh, you guys'll be all right—till you pay them off, anyway. After that, you'll have to scramble, that's all. But you'll make better here than you could there.

RODOLPHO How much? We hear all kinds of figures. How much can a man make? We work hard, we'll work all day, all night—
[MARCO *raises a hand to hush him.*]

EDDIE [*he is coming more and more to address* MARCO *only*] On the average a whole year? Maybe—well, it's hard to say, see. Sometimes we lay off, there's no ships three four weeks.

MARCO   Three, four weeks!—Ts!

EDDIE   But I think you could probably—thirty, forty a week, over the whole twelve months of the year.

MARCO   [*rises, crosses to* EDDIE]   Dollars.

EDDIE   Sure dollars.

[MARCO *puts an arm round* RODOLPHO *and they laugh.*]

MARCO   If we can stay here a few months, Beatrice—

BEATRICE   Listen, you're welcome, Marco—

MARCO   Because I could send them a little more if I stay here.

BEATRICE   As long as you want, we got plenty a room.

MARCO   [*his eyes are showing tears*]   My wife—[*To* EDDIE.] My wife—I want to send right away maybe twenty dollars—

EDDIE   You could send them something next week already.

MARCO   [*he is near tears*]   Eduardo . . . [*He goes to* EDDIE, *offering his hand.*]

EDDIE   Don't thank me. Listen, what the hell, it's no skin off me. [*To* CATHERINE.] What happened to the coffee?

CATHERINE   I got it on. [*To* RODOLPHO.] You married too? No.

RODOLPHO   [*rises*]   Oh, no . . .

BEATRICE   [*to* CATHERINE]   I told you he—

CATHERINE   I know, I just thought maybe he got married recently.

RODOLPHO   I have no money to get married. I have a nice face, but no money. [*He laughs.*]

CATHERINE   [*to* BEATRICE]   He's a real blond!

BEATRICE   [*to* RODOLPHO]   You want to stay here too, heh? For good?

RODOLPHO   Me? Yes, forever! Me, I want to be an American. And then I want to go back to Italy when I am rich, and I will buy a motorcycle. [*He smiles.* MARCO *shakes him affectionately.*]

CATHERINE   A motorcycle!

RODOLPHO   With a motorcycle in Italy you will never starve any more.

BEATRICE   I'll get you coffee. [*She exits to the kitchen.*]

EDDIE   What you do with a motorcycle?

MARCO   He dreams, he dreams.

RODOLPHO   [*to* MARCO]   Why? [*To* EDDIE.] Messages! The rich people in the hotel always need someone who will carry a message. But quickly, and with a great noise. With a blue motorcycle I would station myself in the court-yard of the hotel, and in a little while I would have messages.

MARCO   When you have no wife you have dreams.

EDDIE   Why can't you just walk, or take a trolley or sump'm?

[*Enter* BEATRICE *with coffee.*]

RODOLPHO   Oh, no, the machine, the machine is necessary. A man comes into a great hotel and says, I am a messenger. Who is this man? He disappears walking, there is no noise, nothing. Maybe he will never come back, maybe he will never deliver the message. But a man who rides up on a great machine, this man is responsible, this man exists. He will be given messages. [*He helps* BEATRICE *set out the coffee things.*] I am also a singer, though.

EDDIE   You mean a regular—?

RODOLPHO   Oh, yes. One night last year Andreola got sick. Baritone. And I took his place in the garden of the hotel. Three arias I sang without a mistake! Thousand-lire notes they threw from the tables, money was falling like a storm in the treasury. It was magnificent. We lived six months on that night, eh, Marco?

[MARCO *nods doubtfully.*]

MARCO   Two months.

[EDDIE *laughs.*]

BEATRICE   Can't you get a job in that place?

RODOLPHO   Andreola got better. He's a baritone, very strong.

[BEATRICE *laughs.*]

MARCO   [*regretfully, to* BEATRICE]   He sang too loud.

RODOLPHO   Why too loud?

MARCO   Too loud. The guests in that hotel are all Englishmen. They don't like too loud.

RODOLPHO   [*to* CATHERINE]   Nobody ever said it was too loud!

MARCO   I say. It was too loud. [*To* BEATRICE.] I knew it as soon as he started to sing. Too loud.

RODOLPHO   Then why did they throw so much money?

MARCO   They paid for your courage. The English like courage. But once is enough.

RODOLPHO   [*to all but* MARCO]   I never heard anybody say it was too loud.

CATHERINE   Did you ever hear of jazz?

RODOLPHO   Oh, sure! I *sing* jazz.

CATHERINE   [*rises*]   You could sing jazz?

RODOLPHO   Oh, I sing Napolidan, jazz, bel canto—I sing "Paper Doll," you like "Paper Doll"?

CATHERINE   Oh, sure, I'm crazy for "Paper Doll." Go ahead, sing it.

RODOLPHO   [*takes his stance after getting a nod of permission from* MARCO, *and with a high tenor voice begins singing*]

> "I'll tell you boys it's tough to be alone,
> And it's tough to love a doll that's not your own.
> I'm through with all of them,
> I'll never fall again,
> Hey, boy, what you gonna do?
> I'm gonna buy a paper doll that I can call my own,
> A doll that other fellows cannot steal.

[EDDIE *rises and moves upstage.*]

> And then those flirty, flirty guys
> With their flirty, flirty eyes
> Will have to flirt with dollies that are real—"

EDDIE   Hey, kid—hey, wait a minute—

CATHERINE   [*enthralled*]   Leave him finish, it's beautiful! [*To* BEATRICE.] He's terrific! It's terrific, Rodolpho.

EDDIE   Look, kid; you don't want to be picked up, do ya?

MARCO   No—no! [*He rises.*]

EDDIE   [*indicating the rest of the building*]   Because we never had no singers here . . . and all of a sudden there's a singer in the house, y'know what I mean?

MARCO   Yes, yes. You'll be quiet, Rodolpho.

EDDIE   [*he is flushed*]   They got guys all over the place, Marco. I mean.

MARCO   Yes. He'll be quiet. [*To* RODOLPHO.] You'll be quiet.

[RODOLPHO *nods.* EDDIE *has risen, with iron control, even a smile. He moves to* CATHERINE.]

EDDIE   What's the high heels for, Garbo?

CATHERINE   I figured for tonight—

EDDIE   Do me a favor, will you? Go ahead.

[*Embarrassed now, angered,* CATHERINE *goes out into the bedroom.* BEATRICE *watches her go and gets up; in passing, she gives* EDDIE *a cold look, restrained only by the strangers, and goes to the table to pour coffee.*]

EDDIE [*striving to laugh, and to* MARCO, *but directed as much to* BEATRICE] All actresses they want to be around here.

RODOLPHO [*happy about it*] In Italy too! All the girls.

[CATHERINE *emerges from the bedroom in low-heel shoes, comes to the table.* RODOLPHO *is lifting a cup.*]

EDDIE [*he is sizing up* RODOLPHO, *and there is a concealed suspicion*] Yeah, heh?

RODOLPHO Yes! [*Laughs, indicating* CATHERINE.] Especially when they are so beautiful!

CATHERINE You like sugar?

RODOLPHO Sugar? Yes! I like sugar very much!

[EDDIE *is downstage, watching as she pours a spoonful of sugar into his cup, his face puffed with trouble, and the room dies. Lights rise on* ALFIERI.]

ALFIERI Who can ever know what will be discovered? Eddie Carbone had never expected to have a destiny. A man works, raises his family, goes bowling, eats, gets old, and then he dies. Now, as the weeks passed, there was a future, there was a trouble that would not go away.

[*The lights fade on* ALFIERI, *then rise on* EDDIE *standing at the doorway of the house.* BEATRICE *enters on the street. She sees* EDDIE, *smiles at him. He looks away. She starts to enter the house when* EDDIE *speaks.*]

EDDIE It's after eight.

BEATRICE Well, it's a long show at the Paramount.

EDDIE They must've seen every picture in Brooklyn by now. He's supposed to stay in the house when he ain't working. He ain't supposed to go advertising himself.

BEATRICE Well that's his trouble, what do you care? If they pick him up they pick him up, that's all. Come in the house.

EDDIE What happened to the stenography? I don't see her practice no more.

BEATRICE She'll get back to it. She's excited, Eddie.

EDDIE She tell you anything?

BEATRICE [*comes to him, now the subject is opened*] What's the matter with you? He's a nice kid, what do you want from him?

EDDIE That's a nice kid? He gives me the heeby-jeebies.

BEATRICE [*smiling*] Ah, go on, you're just jealous.

EDDIE Of *him?* Boy, you don't think much of me.

BEATRICE I don't understand you. What's so terrible about him?

EDDIE You mean it's all right with you? That's gonna be her husband?

BEATRICE Why? He's a nice fella, hard workin', he's a good-lookin' fella.

EDDIE He sings on the ships, didja know that?

BEATRICE What do you mean, he sings?

EDDIE Just what I said, he sings. Right on the deck, all of a sudden, a whole song comes out of his mouth—with motions. You know what they're callin' him now? Paper Doll they're callin' him, Canary. He's like a weird. He comes out on the pier, one-two-three, it's a regular free show.

BEATRICE Well, he's a kid; he don't know how to behave himself yet.

EDDIE And with that wacky hair; he's like a chorus girl or sump'm.

BEATRICE So he's blond, so—

EDDIE I just hope that's his regular hair, that's all I hope.

BEATRICE You crazy or sump'm? [*She tries to turn him to her.*]

EDDIE [*he keeps his head turned away*] What's so crazy? I don't like his whole way.

BEATRICE   Listen, you never seen a blond guy in your life? What about Whitey Balso?

EDDIE   [*turning ot her victoriously*]   Sure, but Whitey don't sing; he don't do like that on the ships.

BEATRICE   Well, maybe that's the way they do in Italy.

EDDIE   Then why don't his brother sing? Marco goes around like a man; nobody kids Marco. [*He moves from her, halts. She realizes there is a campaign solidified in him.*] I tell you the truth I'm surprised I have to tell you all this. I mean I'm surprised, B.

BEATRICE   [*she goes to him with purpose now*]   Listen, you ain't gonna start nothin' here.

EDDIE   I ain't startin' nothin', but I ain't gonna stand around lookin' at that. For that character I didn't bring her up. I swear, B., I'm surprised at you; I sit there waitin' for you to wake up but everything is great with you.

BEATRICE   No, everything ain't great with me.

EDDIE   No?

BEATRICE   No. But I got other worries.

EDDIE   Yeah. [*He is already weakening.*]

BEATRICE   Yeah, you want me to tell you?

EDDIE   [*in retreat*]   Why? What worries you got?

BEATRICE   When am I gonna be a wife again, Eddie?

EDDIE   I ain't been feelin' good. They bother me since they came.

BEATRICE   It's almost three months you don't feel good; they're only here a couple of weeks. It's three months, Eddie.

EDDIE   I don't know, B. I don't want to talk about it.

BEATRICE   What's the matter, Eddie, you don't like me, heh?

EDDIE   What do you mean, I don't like you? I said I don't feel good, that's all.

BEATRICE   Well, tell me, am I doing something wrong? Talk to me.

EDDIE   [*Pause. He can't speak, then*]   I can't. I can't talk about it.

BEATRICE   Well tell me what—

EDDIE   I got nothin' to say about it!

[*She stands for a moment; he is looking off; she turns to go into the house.*]

EDDIE   I'll be all right, B.; just lay off me, will ya? I'm worried about her.

BEATRICE   The girl is gonna be eighteen years old, it's time already.

EDDIE   B., he's taking her for a ride!

BEATRICE   All right, that's her ride. What're you gonna stand over her till she's forty? Eddie, I want you to cut it out now, you hear me? I don't like it! Now come in the house.

EDDIE   I want to take a walk, I'll be in right away.

BEATRICE   They ain't goin' to come any quicker if you stand in the street. It ain't nice, Eddie.

EDDIE   I'll be in right away. Go ahead. [*He walks off.*]

[*She goes into the house.* EDDIE *glances up the street, sees* LOUIS *and* MIKE *coming, and sits on an iron railing.* LOUIS *and* MIKE *enter.*]

LOUIS   Wanna go bowlin' tonight?

EDDIE   I'm too tired. Goin' to sleep.

LOUIS   How's your two submarines?

EDDIE   They're okay.

LOUIS   I see they're gettin' work allatime.

EDDIE   Oh yeah, they're doin' all right.

MIKE   That's what we oughta do. We oughta leave the country and come in under the water. Then we get work.

EDDIE   You ain't kiddin'.

LOUIS   Well, what the hell. Y'know?

EDDIE   Sure.

LOUIS   [*sits on railing beside* EDDIE]   Believe me, Eddie, you got a lotta credit comin' to you.

EDDIE   Aah, they don't bother me, don't cost me nutt'n.

MIKE   That older one, boy, he's a regular bull. I seen him the other day liftin' coffee bags over the Matson Line. They leave him alone he woulda load the whole ship by himself.

EDDIE   Yeah, he's a strong guy, that guy. Their father was a regular giant, supposed to be.

LOUIS   Yeah, you could see. He's a regular slave.

MIKE   [*grinning*]   That blond one, though—[EDDIE *looks at him.*] He's got a sense of humor. [LOUIS *snickers.*]

EDDIE   [*searchingly*]   Yeah. He's funny—

MIKE   [*starting to laugh*]   Well he ain't exackly funny, but he's always like makin' remarks like, y'know? He comes around, everybody's laughin'. [LOUIS *laughs.*]

EDDIE   [*uncomfortably, grinning*]   Yeah, well . . . he's got a sense of humor.

MIKE   [*laughing*]   Yeah, I mean, he's always makin' like remarks, like, y'know?

EDDIE   Yeah, I know. But he's a kid yet, y'know? He—he's just a kid, that's all.

MIKE   [*getting hysterical with* LOUIS]   I know. You take one look at him— everybody's happy. [LOUIS *laughs.*] I worked one day with him last week over the Moore-MacCormack Line, I'm tellin' you they was all hysterical. [LOUIS *and he explode in laughter.*]

EDDIE   Why? What'd he do?

MIKE   I don't know . . . he was just humorous. You never can remember what he says, y'know? But it's the way he says it. I mean he gives you a look sometimes and you start laughin'!

EDDIE   Yeah. [*Troubled.*] He's got a sense of humor.

MIKE   [*gasping*]   Yeah.

LOUIS   [*rising*]   Well, we see ya, Eddie.

EDDIE   Take it easy.

LOUIS   Yeah. See ya.

MIKE   If you wanna come bowlin' later we're goin' Flatbush Avenue.

[*Laughing, they move to exit, meeting* RODOLPHO *and* CATHERINE *entering on the street. Their laughter rises as they see* RODOLPHO, *who does not understand but joins in.* EDDIE *moves to enter the house as* LOUIS *and* MIKE *exit.* CATHERINE *stops him at the door.*]

CATHERINE   Hey, Eddie—what a picture we saw! Did we laugh!

EDDIE   [*he can't help smiling at sight of her*]   Where'd you go?

CATHERINE   Paramount. It was with those two guys, y'know? That—

EDDIE   Brooklyn Paramount?

CATHERINE   [*with an edge of anger, embarrassed before* RODOLPHO]   Sure, the Brooklyn Paramount. I told you we wasn't goin' to New York.

EDDIE   [*retreating before the threat of her anger*]   All right, I only asked you. [*To* RODOLPHO.] I just don't want her hangin' around Times Square, see? It's full of tramps over there.

RODOLPHO   I would like to go to Broadway once, Eddie. I would like to walk with her once where the theaters are and the opera. Since I was a boy I see pictures of those lights.

EDDIE   [*his little patience waning*]   I want to talk to her a minute, Rodolpho. Go inside, will you?

RODOLPHO   Eddie, we only walk together in the streets. She teaches me.

CATHERINE   You know what he can't get over? That there's no fountains in Brooklyn!

EDDIE   [*smiling unwillingly*]   Fountains? [RODOLPHO *smiles at his own naïveté.*]

CATHERINE   In Italy he says, every town's got fountains, and they meet there. And you know what? They got oranges on the trees where he comes from, and lemons. Imagine—on the trees? I mean it's interesting. But he's crazy for New York.

RODOLPHO   [*attempting familiarity*]   Eddie, why can't we go once to Broadway—?

EDDIE   Look, I gotta tell her something—

RODOLPHO   Maybe you can come too. I want to see all those lights. [*He sees no response in* EDDIE's *face. He glances at* CATHERINE.] I'll walk by the river before I go to sleep. [*He walks off down the street.*]

CATHERINE   Why don't you talk to him, Eddie? He blesses you, and you don't talk to him hardly.

EDDIE   [*enveloping her with his eyes*]   I bless you and you don't talk to me. [*He tries to smile.*]

CATHERINE   *I* don't talk to you? [*She hits his arm.*] What do you mean?

EDDIE   I don't see you no more. I come home you're runnin' around some-place—

CATHERINE   Well, he wants to see everything, that's all, so we go. . . . You mad at me?

EDDIE   No. [*He moves from her, smiling sadly.*] It's just I used to come home, you was always there. Now, I turn around, you're a big girl. I don't know how to talk to you.

CATHERINE   Why?

EDDIE   I don't know, you're runnin', you're runnin', Katie. I don't think you listening any more to me.

CATHERINE   [*going to him*]   Ah, Eddie, sure I am. What's the matter? You don't like him?
[*Slight pause.*]

EDDIE   [*turns to her*]   *You* like him, Katie?

CATHERINE   [*with a blush but holding her ground*]   Yeah. I like him.

EDDIE   [*his smile goes*]   You like him.

CATHERINE   [*looking down*]   Yeah. [*Now she looks at him for the consequences, smiling but tense. He looks at her like a lost boy.*] What're you got against him? I don't understand. He only blesses you.

EDDIE   [*turns away*]   He don't bless me, Katie.

CATHERINE   He does! You're like a father to him!

EDDIE   [*turns to her*]   Katie.

CATHERINE   What, Eddie?

EDDIE   You gonna marry him?

CATHERINE   I don't know. We just been . . . goin' around, that's all. [*Turns to him.*] What're you got against him, Eddie? Please, tell me. What?

EDDIE   He don't respect you.

CATHERINE   Why?

EDDIE   Katie . . . if you wasn't an orphan, wouldn't he ask your father's permission before he run around with you like this?

CATHERINE   Oh, well, he didn't think you'd mind.

EDDIE   He knows I mind, but it don't bother him if I mind, don't you see that?

CATHERINE   No, Eddie, he's got all kinds of respect for me. And you too! We walk across the street he takes my arm—he almost bows to me! You got him all wrong, Eddie; I mean it, you—

EDDIE   Katie, he's only bowin' to his passport.

CATHERINE   His passport!

EDDIE   That's right. He marries you he's got the right to be an American citizen. That's what's goin' on here.

[*She is puzzled and surprised.*]

You understand what I'm tellin' you? The guy is lookin' for his break, that's all he's lookin' for.

CATHERINE   [*pained*]   Oh, no, Eddie, I don't think so.

EDDIE   You don't think so! Katie, you're gonna make me cry here. Is that a workin' man? What does he do with his first money? A snappy new jacket he buys, records, a pointy pair new shoes and his brother's kids are starvin' over there with tuberculosis? That's a hit-and-run guy, baby; he's got bright lights in his head, Broadway. Them guys don't think of nobody but theirself! You marry him and the next time you see him it'll be for divorce!

CATHERINE   [*steps toward him*]   Eddie, he never said a word about his papers or—

EDDIE   You mean he's supposed to tell you that?

CATHERINE   I don't think he's even thinking about it.

EDDIE   What's better for him to think about! He could be picked up any day here and he's back pushin' taxis up the hill!

CATHERINE   No, I don't believe it.

EDDIE   Katie, don't break my heart, listen to me.

CATHERINE   I don't want to hear it.

EDDIE   Katie, listen . . .

CATHERINE   He loves me!

EDDIE   [*with deep alarm*]   Don't say that, for God's sake! This is the oldest racket in the country—

CATHERINE   [*desperately, as though he had made his imprint*]   I don't believe it! [*She rushes to the house.*]

EDDIE   [*following her*]   They been pullin' this since the Immigration Law was put in! They grab a green kid that don't know nothin' and they—

CATHERINE   [*sobbing*]   I don't believe it and I wish to hell you'd stop it!

EDDIE   Katie!

[*They enter the apartment. The lights in the living room have risen and* BEATRICE *is there. She looks past the sobbing* CATHERINE *at* EDDIE, *who, in the presence of his wife, makes an awkward gesture of eroded command, indicating* CATHERINE.]

EDDIE   Why don't you straighten her out?

BEATRICE   [*inwardly angered at his flowing emotion, which in itself alarms her*]   When are you going to leave her alone?

EDDIE   B., the guy is no good!

BEATRICE   [*suddenly, with open fright and fury*]   You going to leave her alone? Or you gonna drive me crazy?

[*He turns, striving to retain his dignity, but nevertheless in guilt walks out of the house, into the street and away.* CATHERINE *starts into a bedoom.*]

Listen, Catherine.

[CATHERINE *halts, turns to her sheepishly.*]

What are you going to do with yourself?

CATHERINE   I don't know.

BEATRICE   Don't tell me you don't know; you're not a baby any more, what are you going to do with yourself?

CATHERINE   He won't listen to me.

BEATRICE   I don't understand this. He's not your father, Catherine. I don't understand what's going on here.

CATHERINE   [*as one who herself is trying to rationalize a buried impulse*]   What am I going to do, just kick him in the face with it?

BEATRICE Look, honey, you wanna get married, or don't you wanna get married? What are you worried about, Katie?

CATHERINE [*quietly, trembling*] I don't know B. It just seems wrong if he's against it so much.

BEATRICE [*never losing her aroused alarm*] Sit down, honey, I want to tell you something. Here, sit down. Was there ever any fella he liked for you? There wasn't, was there?

CATHERINE But he says Rodolpho's just after his papers.

BEATRICE Look, he'll say anything. What does he care what he says? If it was a prince came here for you it would be no different. You know that, don't you?

CATHERINE Yeah, I guess.

BEATRICE So what does that mean?

CATHERINE [*slowly turns her head to* BEATRICE] What?

BEATRICE It means you gotta be your own self more. You still think you're a little girl, honey. But nobody else can make up your mind for you any more, you understand? You gotta give him to understand that he can't give you orders no more.

CATHERINE Yeah, but how am I going to do that? He thinks I'm a baby.

BEATRICE Because *you* think you're a baby. I told you fifty times already, you can't act the way you act. You still walk around in front of him in your slip—

CATHERINE Well I forgot.

BEATRICE Well you can't do it. Or like you sit on the edge of the bathtub talkin' to him when he's shavin' in his underwear.

CATHERINE When'd I do that?

BEATRICE I seen you in there this morning.

CATHERINE Oh . . . well, I wanted to tell him something and I—

BEATRICE I know, honey. But if you act like a baby and he be treatin' you like a baby. Like when he comes home sometimes you throw yourself at him like when you was twelve years old.

CATHERINE Well I like to see him and I'm happy so I—

BEATRICE Look, I'm not tellin' you what to do honey, but—

CATHERINE No, you could tell me, B.! Gee, I'm all mixed up. See, I—He looks so sad now and it hurts me.

BEATRICE Well look Katie, if it's goin' to hurt you so much you're gonna end up an old maid here.

CATHERINE No!

BEATRICE I'm tellin' you, I'm not makin' a joke. I tried to tell you a couple of times in the last year or so. That's why I was so happy you were going to go out and get work, you wouldn't be here so much, you'd be a little more independent. I mean it. It's wonderful for a whole family to love each other, but you're a grown woman and you're in the same house with a grown man. So you'll act different now, heh?

CATHERINE Yeah, I will. I'll remember.

BEATRICE Because it ain't only up to him, Katie, you understand? I told him the same thing already.

CATHERINE [*quickly*] What?

BEATRICE That he should let you go. But, you see, if only I tell him, he thinks I'm just bawlin' him out, or maybe I'm jealous or somethin', you know?

CATHERINE [*astonished*] He said you was jealous?

BEATRICE No, I'm just sayin' maybe that's what he thinks. [*She reaches over to* CATHERINE's *hand; with a strained smile.*] You think I'm jealous of you, honey?

CATHERINE   No! It's the first I thought of it.

BEATRICE   [*with a quiet sad laugh*]   Well you should have thought of it before
. . . but I'm not. We'll be all right. Just give him to understand; you
don't have to fight, you're just—You're a woman, that's all, and you got a
nice boy, and now the time came when you said good-by. All right?

CATHERINE   [*strangely moved at the prospect*]   All right. . . . If I can.

BEATRICE   Honey . . . you gotta.

[CATHERINE, *sensing now an imperious demand, turns with some fear, with
a discovery, to* BEATRICE. *She is at the edge of tears, as though a familiar
world had shattered.*]

CATHERINE   Okay.

[*Lights out on them and up on* ALFIERI, *seated behind his desk.*]

ALFIERI   It was at this time that he first came to me. I had represented his
father in an accident case some years before, and I was acquainted with
the family in a casual way. I remember him now as he walked through my
doorway—

[*Enter* EDDIE *down right ramp.*]

His eyes were like tunnels; my first thought was that he had committed a
crime.

[EDDIE *sits beside the desk, cap in hand, looking out.*]

But soon I saw it was only a passion that had moved into his body, like
a stranger. [ALFIERI *pauses, looks down at his desk, then to* EDDIE *as though
he were continuing a conversation with him.*] I don't quite understand
what I can do for you. Is there a question of law somewhere?

EDDIE   That's what I want to ask you.

ALFIERI   Because there's nothing illegal about a girl falling in love with an
immigrant.

EDDIE   Yeah, but what about it if the only reason for it is to get his papers?

ALFIERI   First of all you don't know that.

EDDIE   I see it in his eyes; he's laughin' at her and he's laughin' at me.

ALFIERI   Eddie, I'm a lawyer. I can only deal in what's provable. You understand that, don't you? Can you prove that?

EDDIE   *I know what's in his mind, Mr. Alfieri!*

ALFIERI   Eddie, even if you could prove that—

EDDIE   Listen . . . will you listen to me a minute? My father always said you
was a smart man. I want you to listen to me.

ALFIERI   I'm only a lawyer, Eddie.

EDDIE   Will you listen a minute? I'm talkin' about the law. Lemme just bring
out what I mean. A man, which he comes into the country illegal, don't
it stand to reason he's gonna take every penny and put it in the sock?
Because they don't know from one day to another, right?

ALFIERI   All right.

EDDIE   He's spendin'. Records he buys now. Shoes. Jackets. Y'understand me?
This guy ain't worried. This guy is *here.* So it must be that he's got it all
laid out in his mind already—he's stayin'. Right?

ALFIERI   Well? What about it?

EDDIE   All right. [*He glances at* ALFIERI, *then down to the floor.*] I'm talking
to you confidential, ain't I?

ALFIERI   Certainly.

EDDIE   I mean it don't go no place but here. Because I don't like to say this
about anybody. Even my wife I didn't exactly say this.

ALFIERI   What is it?

EDDIE   [*takes a breath and glances briefly over each shoulder*]   The guy ain't
right, Mr. Alfieri.

ALFIERI   What do you mean?

EDDIE   I mean he ain't right.

ALFIERI   I don't get you.

EDDIE   [shifts to another position in the chair]   Dja ever get a look at him?

ALFIERI   Not that I know of, no.

EDDIE   He's a blond guy. Like . . . platinum. You know what I mean?

ALFIERI   No.

EDDIE   I mean if you close the paper fast—you could blow him over.

ALFIERI   Well that doesn't mean—

EDDIE   Wait a minute, I'm tellin' you sump'm. He sings, see. Which is—I mean it's all right, but sometimes he hits a note, see. I turn around. I mean— high. You know what I mean?

ALFIERI   Well, that's a tenor.

EDDIE   I know a tenor, Mr. Alfieri. This ain't no tenor. I mean if you came in the house and you didn't know who was singin', you wouldn't be lookin' for him you be lookin' for her.

ALFIERI   Yes, but that's not—

EDDIE   I'm tellin' you sump'm, wait a minute. Please, Mr. Alfieri. I'm tryin' to bring out my thoughts here. Couple of nights ago my niece brings out a dress which it's too small for her, because she shot up like a light this last year. He takes the dress, lays it on the table, he cuts it up; one-two-three, he makes a new dress. I mean he looked so sweet there, like an angel— you could kiss him he was so sweet.

ALFIERI   Now look, Eddie—

EDDIE   Mr. Alfieri, they're laughin' at him on the piers. I'm ashamed. Paper Doll they call him. Blondie now. His brother thinks it's because he's got a sense of humor, see—which he's got—but that ain't what they're laughin'. Which they're not goin' to come out with it because they know he's my relative, which they have to see me if they make a crack, y'know? But I know what they're laughin' at, and when I think of that guy layin' his hands on her I could—I mean it's eatin' me out, Mr. Alfieri, because I struggled for that girl. And now he comes in my house and—

ALFIERI   Eddie, look—I have my own children. I understand you. But the law is very specific. The law does not . . .

EDDIE   [with a fuller flow of indignation]   You mean to tell me that there's no law that a guy which he ain't right can go to work and marry a girl and—?

ALFIERI   You have no recourse in the law, Eddie.

EDDIE   Yeah, but if he ain't right, Mr. Alfieri, you mean to tell me—

ALFIERI   There is nothing you can do, Eddie, believe me.

EDDIE   Nothin'.

ALFIERI   Nothing at all. There's only one legal question here.

EDDIE   What?

ALFIERI   The manner in which they entered the country. But I don't think you want to do anything about that, do you?

EDDIE   You mean—?

ALFIERI   Well, they entered illegally.

EDDIE   Oh, Jesus, no, I wouldn't do nothin' about that, I mean—

ALFIERI   All right, then, let me talk now, eh?

EDDIE   Mr. Alfieri, I can't believe what you tell me. I mean there must be some kinda law which—

ALFIERI   Eddie, I want you to listen to me. [Pause.] You know, sometimes God mixes up the people. We all love somebody, the wife, the kids—every man's got somebody that he loves, heh? But sometimes . . . there's too much. You know? There's too much, and it goes where it mustn't. A man works hard, he brings up a child, sometimes it's a niece, sometimes even a daughter, and he never realizes it, but through the years—there is too much love for the daughter, there is too much love for the niece. Do you understand what I'm saying to you?

EDDIE [*sardonically*]   What do you mean, I shouldn't look out for her good?

ALFIERI   Yes, but these things have to end, Eddie, that's all. The child has to grow up and go away, and the man has to learn to forget. Because after all, Eddie—what other way can it end? [*Pause.*] Let her go. That's my advice. You did your job, now it's her life; wish her luck, and let her go. [*Pause.*] Will you do that? Because there's no law, Eddie; make up your mind to it; the law is not interested in this.

EDDIE   You mean to tell me, even if he's a punk? If he's—

ALFIERI   There's nothing you can do.

[EDDIE *stands.*]

EDDIE   Well, all right, thanks. Thanks very much.

ALFIERI   What are you going to do?

EDDIE [*with a helpless but ironic gesture*]   What can I do? I'm a patsy, what can a patsy do? I worked like a dog twenty years so a punk could have her, so that's what I done. I mean, in the worst times, in the worst, when there wasn't a ship comin' in the harbor, I didn't stand around lookin' for relief —I hustled. When there was empty piers in Brooklyn I went to Hoboken, Staten Island, the West Side, Jersey, all over—because I made a promise. I took out of my own mouth to give to her. I took out of my wife's mouth. I walked hungry plenty days in this city! [*It begins to break through.*] And now I gotta sit in my own house and look at a son-of-a-bitch punk like that—which he came out of nowhere! I give him my house to sleep! I take the blankets off my bed for him, and he takes and puts his dirty filthy hands on her like a goddam thief!

ALFIERI [*rising*]   But, Eddie, she's a woman now.

EDDIE   He's stealing from me!

ALFIERI   She wants to get married, Eddie. She can't marry you, can she?

EDDIE [*furiously*]   What're you talkin' about, marry me! I don't know what the hell you're talkin' about!

[*Pause.*]

ALFIERI   I gave you my advice, Eddie. That's it.

[EDDIE *gathers himself. A pause.*]

EDDIE   Well, thanks. Thanks very much. It just—it's breakin' my heart, y'know. I—

ALFIERI   I understand. Put it out of your mind. Can you do that?

EDDIE   I'm—[*He feels the threat of sobs, and with a helpless wave.*] I'll see you around. [*He goes out up the right ramp.*]

ALFIERI [*sits on desk*]   There are times when you want to spread an alarm, but nothing has happened. I knew, I knew then and there—I could have finished the whole story that afternoon. It wasn't as though there was a mystery to unravel. I could see every step coming, step after step, like a dark figure walking down a hall toward a certain door. I knew where he was heading for, I knew where he was going to end. And I sat here many afternoons asking myself why, being an intelligent man, I was so powerless to stop it. I even went to a certain old lady in the neighborhood, a very wise old woman, and I told her, and she only nodded, and said, "Pray for him . . ." And so I—waited here.

[*As lights go out on* ALFIERI, *they rise in the apartment where all are finishing dinner.* BEATRICE *and* CATHERINE *are clearing the table.*]

CATHERINE   You know where they went?

BEATRICE   Where?

CATHERINE   They went to Africa once. On a fishing boat.

[EDDIE *glances at her.*]

It's true, Eddie.

[BEATRICE *exits into the kitchen with dishes.*]

EDDIE   I didn't say nothin'. [*He goes to his rocker, picks up a newspaper.*]

CATHERINE   And I was never even in Staten Island.

EDDIE   [*sitting with the paper*]   You didn't miss nothin'.

[*Pause.* CATHERINE *takes dishes out.*]

How long that take you, Marco—to get to Africa?

MARCO   [*rising*]   Oh . . . two days. We go all over.

RODOLPHO   [*rising*]   Once we went to Yugoslavia.

EDDIE   [*to* MARCO]   They pay all right on them boats?

[BEATRICE *enters. She and* RODOLPHO *stack the remaining dishes.*]

MARCO   If they catch fish they pay all right. [*Sits on a stool.*]

RODOLPHO   They're family boats, though. And nobody in our family owned one. So we only worked when one of the families was sick.

BEATRICE   Y'know, Marco, what I don't understand—there's an ocean full of fish and yiz are all starvin'.

EDDIE   They gotta have boats, nets, you need money.

[CATHERINE *enters.*]

BEATRICE   Yeah, but couldn't they like fish from the beach? You see them down Coney Island—

MARCO   Sardines.

EDDIE   Sure. [*Laughing.*] How you gonna catch sardines on a hook?

BEATRICE   Oh, I didn't know they're sardines. [*To* CATHERINE.] They're sardines!

CATHERINE   Yeah, they follow them all over the ocean, Africa, Yugoslavia . . . [*She sits and begins to look through a movie magazine.* RODOLPHO *joins her.*]

BEATRICE   [*to* EDDIE]   It's funny, y'know. You never think of it, that sardines are swimming in the ocean! [*She exits to kitchen with dishes.*]

CATHERINE   I know. It's like oranges and lemons on a tree. [*To* EDDIE.] I mean you ever think of oranges and lemons on a tree?

EDDIE   Yeah, I know. It's funny. [*To* MARCO.] I heard that they paint the oranges to make them look orange.

[BEATRICE *enters.*]

MARCO   [*he has been reading a letter*]   Paint?

EDDIE   Yeah, I heard that they grow like green.

MARCO   No, in Italy the oranges are orange.

RODOLPHO   Lemons are green.

EDDIE   [*resenting his instruction*]   I know lemons are green, for Christ's sake, you see them in the store they're green sometimes. I said oranges they paint, I didn't say nothin' about lemons.

BEATRICE   [*sitting; diverting their attention*]   Your wife is gettin' the money all right, Marco?

MARCO   Oh, yes. She bought medicine for my boy.

BEATRICE   That's wonderful. You feel better, heh?

MARCO   Oh, yes! But I'm lonesome.

BEATRICE   I just hope you ain't gonna do like some of them around here. They're here twenty-five years, some men, and they didn't get enough to-gether to go back twice.

MARCO   Oh, I know. We have many families in our town, the children never saw the father. But I will go home. Three, four years, I think.

BEATRICE   Maybe you should keep more here. Because maybe she thinks it comes so easy you'll never get ahead of yourself.

MARCO   Oh, no, she saves. I send everything. My wife is very lonesome.
   [*He smiles shyly.*]
BEATRICE   She must be nice. She pretty? I bet, heh?
MARCO   [*blushing*]   No, but she understand everything.
RODOLPHO   Oh, he's got a clever wife!
EDDIE   I betcha there's plenty surprises sometimes when those guys get back there, heh?
MARCO   Surprises?
EDDIE   [*laughing*]   I mean, you know—they count the kids and there's a couple extra than when they left?
MARCO   No—no . . . The women wait, Eddie. Most. Most. Very few surprises.
RODOLPHO   It's more strict in our town.
   [EDDIE *looks at him now.*]
   It's not so free.
EDDIE   [*rises, paces up and down*]   It ain't so free here either, Rodolpho, like you think. I seen greenhorns sometimes get in trouble that way—they think just because a girl don't go around with a shawl over her head that she ain't strict, y'know? Girl don't have to wear black dress to be strict. Know what I mean?
RODOLPHO   Well, I always have respect—
EDDIE   I know, but in your town you wouldn't just drag off some girl without permission, I mean. [*He turns.*] You know what I mean, Marco? It ain't that much different here.
MARCO   [*cautiously*]   Yes.
BEATRICE   Well, he didn't exactly drag her off though, Eddie.
EDDIE   I know, but I seen some of them get the wrong idea sometimes. [*To* RODOLPHO.] I mean it might be a little more free here but it's just as strict.
RODOLPHO   I have respect for her, Eddie. I do anything wrong?
EDDIE   Look, kid, I ain't her father, I'm only her uncle—
BEATRICE   Well then, be an uncle then.
   [EDDIE *looks at her, aware of her criticizing force.*]
   I *mean.*
MARCO   No, Beatrice, if he does wrong you must tell him. [*To* EDDIE.] What does he do wrong?
EDDIE   Well, Marco, till he came here she was never out on the street twelve o'clock at night.
MARCO   [*to* RODOLPHO]   You come home early now.
BEATRICE   [*to* CATHERINE]   Well, you said the movie ended late, didn't you?
CATHERINE   Yeah.
BEATRICE   Well, tell him, honey. [*To* EDDIE.] The movie ended late.
EDDIE   Look, B., I'm just sayin'—he thinks she always stayed out like that.
MARCO   You come home early now, Rodolpho.
RODOLPHO   [*embarrassed*]   All right, sure. But I can't stay in the house all the time, Eddie.
EDDIE   Look, kid, I'm not only talkin' about her. The more you run around like that the more chance you're takin'. [*To* BEATRICE.] I mean suppose he gets hit by a car or something. [*To* MARCO.] Where's his papers, who is he? Know what I mean?
BEATRICE   Yeah, but who is he in the daytime, though? It's the same chance in the daytime.
EDDIE   [*holding back a voice full of anger*]   Yeah, but he don't have to go lookin' for it, Beatrice. If he's here to work, then he should work; if he's here for a good time then he could fool around! [*To* MARCO.] But I understood, Marco, that you was both comin' to make a livin' for your family. You understand me, don't you, Marco? [*He goes to his rocker.*]

MARCO   I beg your pardon, Eddie.

EDDIE   I mean, that's what I understood in the first place, see.

MARCO   Yes. That's why we came.

EDDIE   [*sits on his rocker*]   Well, that's all I'm askin'.

[EDDIE *reads his paper. There is a pause, an awkwardness. Now* CATHERINE *gets up and puts a record on the phonograph—"Paper Doll."*]

CATHERINE   [*flushed with revolt*]   You wanna dance, Rodolpho?

[EDDIE *freezes.*]

RODOLPHO   [*in deference to* EDDIE]   No, I—I'm tired.

BEATRICE   Go ahead, dance, Rodolpho.

CATHERINE   Ah, come on. They got a beautiful quartet, these guys. Come.

[*She has taken his hand and he stiffly rises, feeling* EDDIE's *eyes on his back, and they dance.*]

EDDIE   [*to* CATHERINE]   What's that, a new record?

CATHERINE   It's the same one. We bought it the other day.

BEATRICE   [*to* EDDIE]   They only bought three records. [*She watches them dance;* EDDIE *turns his head away.* MARCO *just sits there, waiting. Now* BEATRICE *turns to* EDDIE.] Must be nice to go all over in one of them fishin' boats. I would like that myself. See all them other countries?

EDDIE   Yeah.

BEATRICE   [*to* MARCO]   But the women don't go along, I bet.

MARCO   No, not on the boats. Hard work.

BEATRICE   What're you got, a regular kitchen and everything?

MARCO   Yes, we eat very good on the boats—especially when Rodolpho comes along; everybody gets fat.

BEATRICE   Oh, he cooks?

MARCO   Sure, very good cook. Rice, pasta, fish, everything.

[EDDIE *lowers his paper.*]

EDDIE   He's a cook, too! [*Looking at* RODOLPHO.] He sings, he cooks . . .

[RODOLPHO *smiles thankfully.*]

BEATRICE   Well it's good, he could always make a living.

EDDIE   It's wonderful. He sings, he cooks, he could make dresses . . .

CATHERINE   They get some high pay, them guys. The head chefs in all the big hotels are men. You read about them.

EDDIE   That's what I'm sayin'.

[CATHERINE *and* RODOLPHO *continue dancing.*]

CATHERINE   Yeah, well, I mean.

EDDIE   [*to* BEATRICE]   He's lucky, believe me. [*Slight pause. He looks away, then back to* BEATRICE.] That's why the water front is no place for him. [*They stop dancing.* RODOLPHO *turns off phonograph.*] I mean like me—I can't cook, I can't sing, I can't make dresses, so I'm on the water front. But if I could cook, if I could sing, if I could make dresses, I wouldn't be on the water front. [*He has been unconsciously twisting the newspaper into a tight roll. They are all regarding him now; he senses he is exposing the issue and he is driven on.*] I would be someplace else. I would be like in a dress store. [*He has bent the rolled paper and it suddenly tears in two. He suddenly gets up and pulls his pants up over his belly and goes to* MARCO.] What do you say, Marco, we go to the bouts next Saturday night. You never seen a fight, did you?

MARCO   [*uneasily*]   Only in the moving pictures.

EDDIE   [*going to* RODOLPHO]   I'll treat yiz. What do you say, Danish? You wanna come along? I'll buy the tickets.

RODOLPHO   Sure. I like to go.

CATHERINE   [*goes to* EDDIE; *nervously happy now*]   I'll make some coffee, all right?

EDDIE   Go ahead, make some! Make it nice and strong. [*Mystified, she smiles and exits to kitchen. He is weirdly elated, rubbing his fists into his palms. He strides to* MARCO.] You wait, Marco, you see some real fights here. You ever do any boxing?

MARCO   No, I never.

EDDIE   [*to* RODOLPHO]   Betcha you have done some, heh?

RODOLPHO   No.

EDDIE   Well, come on, I'll teach you.

BEATRICE   What's he got to learn that for?

EDDIE   Ya can't tell, one a these days somebody's liable to step on his foot or sump'm. Come on, Rodolpho, I show you a couple a passes. [*He stands below table.*]

BEATRICE   Go ahead, Rodolpho. He's a good boxer, he could teach you.

RODOLPHO   [*embarrassed*]   Well, I don't know how to—[*He moves down to* EDDIE.]

EDDIE   Just put your hands up. Like this, see? That's right. That's very good, keep your left up, because you lead with the left, see, like this. [*He gently moves his left into* RODOLPHO's *face.*] See? Now what you gotta do is you gotta block me, so when I come in like that you—[RODOLPHO *parries his left.*] Hey, that's very good! [RODOLPHO *laughs.*] All right, now come into me. Come on.

RODOLPHO   I don't want to hit you, Eddie.

EDDIE   Don't pity me, come on. Throw it, I'll show you how to block it. [RO-DOLPHO *jabs at him, laughing. The others join.*] 'At's it. Come on again. For the jaw right here. [RODOLPHO *jabs with more assurance.*] Very good!

BEATRICE   [*to* MARCO]   He's very good!

[EDDIE *crosses directly upstage of* RODOLPHO.]

EDDIE   Sure, he's great! Come on, kid, put sump'm behind it, you can't hurt me. [RODOLPHO, *more seriously, jabs at* EDDIE's *jaw and grazes it.*] Attaboy. [CATHERINE *comes from the kitchen, watches.*] Now I'm gonna hit you, so block me, see?

CATHERINE   [*with beginning alarm*]   What are they doin'?

[*They are lightly boxing now.*]

BEATRICE   [*she senses only the comradeship in it now*]   He's teachin' him; he's very good!

EDDIE   Sure, he's terrific! Look at him go! [RODOLPHO *lands a blow.*] 'At's it! Now, watch out, here I come, Danish! [*He feints with his left hand and lands with his right. It mildly staggers* RODOLPHO. MARCO *rises.*]

CATHERINE   [*rushing to* RODOLPHO]   Eddie!

EDDIE   Why? I didn't hurt him. Did I hurt you, kid? [*He rubs the back of his hand across his mouth.*]

RODOLPHO   No, no, he didn't hurt me. [*To* EDDIE *with a certain gleam and a smile.*] I was only surprised.

BEATRICE   [*pulling* EDDIE *down into the rocker*]   That's enough, Eddie; he did pretty good, though.

EDDIE   Yeah. [*Rubbing his fists together.*] He could be very good, Marco. I'll teach him again.

[MARCO *nods at him dubiously.*]

RODOLPHO   Dance, Catherine. Come. [*He takes her hand; they go to phonograph and start it. It plays "Paper Doll."*]

[RODOLPHO *takes her in his arms. They dance.* EDDIE *in thought sits in his chair, and* MARCO *takes a chair, places it in front of* EDDIE, *and looks down at it.* BEATRICE *and* EDDIE *watch him.*]

MARCO   Can you lift this chair?

EDDIE   What do you mean?

MARCO   From here. [*He gets on one knee with one hand behind his back, and grasps the bottom on one of the chair legs but does not raise it.*]

EDDIE   Sure, why not? [*He comes to the chair, kneels, grasps the leg, raises the chair one inch, but it leans over to the floor.*] Gee, that's hard, I never knew that. [*He tries again, and again fails.*] It's on an angle, that's why, heh?

MARCO   Here.

[MARCO *kneels, grasps, and with strain slowly raises the chair higher and higher, getting to his feet now.* RODOLPHO *and* CATHERINE *have stopped dancing as* MARCO *raises the chair over his head.*

MARCO *is face to face with* EDDIE, *a strained tension gripping his eyes and jaw, his neck stiff, the chair raised like a weapon over* EDDIE'S *head—and he transforms what might appear like a glare of warning into a smile of triumph, and* EDDIE'S *grin vanishes as he absorbs his look.*]

CURTAIN

ACT II

[*Light rises on* ALFIERI *at his desk.*]

ALFIERI   On the twenty-third of that December a case of Scotch whisky slipped from a net while being unloaded—as a case of Scotch whisky is inclined to do on the twenty-third of December on Pier Forty-one. There was no snow, but it was cold, his wife was out shopping. Marco was still at work. The boy had not been hired that day; Catherine told me later that this was the first time they had been alone together in the house.

[*Light is rising on* CATHERINE *in the apartment.* RODOLPHO *is watching as she arranges a paper pattern on cloth spread on the table.*]

CATHERINE   You hungry?

RODOLPHO   Not for anything to eat. [*Pause.*] I have nearly three hundred dollars. Catherine?

CATHERINE   I heard you.

RODOLPHO   You don't like to talk about it any more?

CATHERINE   Sure, I don't mind talkin' about it.

RODOLPHO   What worries you, Catherine?

CATHERINE   I been wantin' to ask you about something. Could I?

RODOLPHO   All the answers are in my eyes, Catherine. But you don't look in my eyes lately. You're full of secrets. [*She looks at him. She seems withdrawn.*] What is the question?

CATHERINE   Suppose I wanted to live in Italy.

RODOLPHO   [*smiling at the incongruity*]   You going to marry somebody rich?

CATHERINE   No, I mean live there—you and me.

RODOLPHO   [*his smile vanishing*]   When?

CATHERINE   Well . . . when we get married.

RODOLPHO   [*astonished*]   You want to be an Italian?

CATHERINE   No, but I could live there without being Italian. Americans live there.

RODOLPHO   Forever?

CATHERINE   Yeah.

RODOLPHO   [*crosses to rocker*]   You're fooling.

CATHERINE   No, I mean it.

RODOLPHO   Where do you get such an idea?

CATHERINE   Well, you're always saying it's so beautiful there, with the mountains and the ocean and all the—

RODOLPHO   You're fooling me.

CATHERINE   I mean it.

RODOLPHO   [*goes to her slowly*]   Catherine, if I ever brought you home with no money, no business, nothing, they would call the priest and the doctor and they would say Rodolpho is crazy.

CATHERINE   I know, but I think we would be happier there.

RODOLPHO   Happier! What would you eat? You can't cook the view!

CATHERINE   Maybe you could be a singer, like in Rome or—

RODOLPHO   Rome! Rome is full of singers.

CATHERINE   Well, I could work then.

RODOLPHO   Where?

CATHERINE   God, there must be jobs somewhere!

RODOLPHO   There's nothing! Nothing, nothing, nothing. Now tell me what you're talking about. How can I bring you from a rich country to suffer in a poor country? What are you talking about? [*She searches for words.*] I would be a criminal stealing your face. In two years you would have an old, hungry face. When my brother's babies cry they give them water, water that boiled a bone. Don't you believe that?

CATHERINE   [*quietly*]   I'm afraid of Eddie here.

[*Slight pause.*]

RODOLPHO   [*steps closer to her*]   We wouldn't live here. Once I am a citizen I could work anywhere and I would find better jobs and we would have a house, Catherine. If I were not afraid to be arrested I would start to be something wonderful here!

CATHERINE   [*steeling herself*]   Tell me something. I mean just tell me, Rodolpho —would you still want to do it if it turned out we had to go live in Italy? I mean just if it turned out that way.

RODOLPHO   This is your question or his question?

CATHERINE   I would like to know, Rodolpho. I mean it.

RODOLPHO   To go there with nothing.

CATHERINE   Yeah.

RODOLPHO   No. [*She looks at him wide-eyed.*] No.

CATHERINE   You wouldn't?

RODOLPHO   No; I will not marry you to live in Italy. I want you to be my wife, and I want to be a citizen. Tell him that, or I will. Yes. [*He moves about angrily.*] And tell him also, and tell yourself, please, that I am not a beggar, and you are not a horse, a gift, a favor for a poor immigrant.

CATHERINE   Well, don't get mad!

RODOLPHO   I am furious! [*Goes to her.*] Do you think I am so desperate? My brother is desperate, not me. You think I would carry on my back the rest of my life a woman I didn't love just to be an American? It's so wonderful? You think we have no tall buildings in Italy? Electric lights? No wide streets? No flags? No automobiles? Only work we don't have. I want to be an American so I can work, that is the only wonder here—work! How can you insult me, Catherine?

CATHERINE   I didn't mean that—

RODOLPHO   My heart dies to look at you. Why are you so afraid of him?

CATHERINE   [*near tears*]   I don't know!

RODOLPHO   Do you trust me, Catherine? You?

CATHERINE   It's only that I—He was good to me, Rodolpho. You don't know him; he was always the sweetest guy to me. Good. He razzes me all the time but he don't mean it. I know. I would—just feel ashamed if I made him sad. 'Cause I always dreamt that when I got married he would be happy at the wedding, and laughin'—and now he's—mad all the time and nasty— [*She is weeping.*] Tell him you'd live in Italy—just tell him, and maybe he would start to trust you a little, see? Because I want him to be happy; I mean—I like him, Rodolpho—and I can't stand it!

RODOLPHO Oh, Catherine—oh, little girl.

CATHERINE I love you, Rodolpho, I love you.

RODOLPHO Then why are you afraid? That he'll spank you?

CATHERINE Don't, don't laugh at me! I've been here all my life. . . . Every day I saw him when he left in the morning and when he came home at night. You think it's so easy to turn around and say to a man he's nothin' to you no more?

RODOLPHO I know, but—

CATHERINE You don't know; nobody knows! I'm not a baby, I know a lot more than people think I know. Beatrice says to be a woman, but—

RODOLPHO Yes.

CATHERINE Then why don't she be a woman? If I was a wife I would make a man happy instead of goin' at him all the time. I can tell a block away when he's blue in his mind and just wants to talk to somebody quiet and nice. . . . I can tell when he's hungry or wants a beer before he even says anything. I know when his feet hurt him, I mean I *know* him and now I'm supposed to turn around and make a stranger out of him? I don't know why I have to do that, I mean.

RODOLPHO Catherine. If I take in my hands a little bird. And she grows and wishes to fly. But I will not let her out of my hands because I love her so much, is that right for me to do? I don't say you must hate him; but anyway you must go, mustn't you? Catherine?

CATHERINE [*softly*] Hold me.

RODOLPHO [*clasping her to him*] Oh, my little girl.

CATHERINE Teach me. [*She is weeping.*] I don't know anything, teach me, Rodolpho, hold me.

RODOLPHO There's nobody here now. Come inside. Come. [*He is leading her toward the bedrooms.*] And don't cry any more.
[*Light rises on the street. In a moment* EDDIE *appears. He is unsteady, drunk. He mounts the stairs. He enters the apartment, looks around, takes out a bottle from one pocket, puts it on the table. Then another bottle from another pocket, and a third from an inside pocket. He sees the pattern and cloth, goes over to it and touches it, and turns toward upstage.*]

EDDIE Beatrice? [*He goes to the open kitchen door and looks in.*] Beatrice? Beatrice?
[CATHERINE *enters from bedroom; under his gaze she adjusts her dress.*]

CATHERINE You got home early.

EDDIE Knocked off for Christmas early. [*Indicating the pattern.*] Rodolpho makin' you a dress?

CATHERINE No. I'm makin' a blouse.
[RODOLPHO *appears in the bedroom doorway.* EDDIE *sees him and his arm jerks slightly in shock.* RODOLPHO *nods to him testingly.*]

RODOLPHO Beatrice went to buy presents for her mother.
[*Pause.*]

EDDIE Pack it up. Go ahead. Get your stuff and get outa here. [CATHERINE *instantly turns and walks toward the bedroom, and* EDDIE *grabs her arm.*] Where you goin'?

CATHERINE [*trembling with fright*] I think I have to get out of here, Eddie.

EDDIE   No, you ain't goin' nowheres, he's the one.

CATHERINE   I think I can't stay here no more. [*She frees her arm, steps back toward the bedroom.*] I'm sorry, Eddie. [*She sees the tears in his eyes.*] Well, don't cry. I'll be around the neighborhood; I'll see you. I just can't stay here no more. You know I can't. [*Her sobs of pity and love for him break her composure.*] Don't you know I can't? You know that, don't you? [*She goes to him.*] Wish me luck. [*She clasps her hands prayerfully.*] Oh, Eddie, don't be like that!

EDDIE   You ain't goin' nowheres.

CATHERINE   Eddie, I'm not gonna be a baby any more! You—
   [*He reaches out suddenly, draws her to him, and as she strives to free herself he kisses her on the mouth.*]

RODOLPHO   Don't! [*He pulls on* EDDIE's *arm.*] Stop that! Have respect for her!

EDDIE   [*spun round by* RODOLPHO]   You want something?

RODOLPHO   Yes! She'll be my wife. That is what I want. My wife!

EDDIE   But what're you gonna be?

RODOLPHO   I show you what I be!

CATHERINE   Wait outside; don't argue with him!

EDDIE   Come on, show me! What're you gonna be? Show me!

RODOLPHO   [*with tears of rage*]   Don't say that to me!
   [RODOLPHO *flies at him in attack.* EDDIE *pins his arms, laughing, and suddenly kisses him.*]

CATHERINE   Eddie! Let go, ya hear me! I'll kill you! Leggo of him!
   [*She tears at* EDDIE's *face and* EDDIE *releases* RODOLPHO. EDDIE *stands there with tears rolling down his face as he laughs mockingly at* RODOLPHO. *She is staring at him in horror.* RODOLPHO *is rigid. They are like animals that have torn at one another and broken up without a decision, each waiting for the other's mood.*]

EDDIE   [*to* CATHERINE]   You see? [*To* RODOLPHO.] I give you till tomorrow, kid. Get outa here. Alone. You hear me? Alone.

CATHERINE   I'm going with him, Eddie. [*She starts toward* RODOLPHO.]

EDDIE   [*indicating* RODOLPHO *with his head*]   Not with that. [*She halts, frightened. He sits, still panting for breath, and they watch him helplessly as he leans toward them over the table.*] Don't make me do nuttin', Catherine. Watch your step, submarine. By rights they oughta throw you back in the water. But I got pity for you. [*He moves unsteadily toward the door, always facing* RODOLPHO.] Just get outa here and don't lay another hand on her unless you wanna go out feet first. [*He goes out of the apartment.*]
   [*The lights go down, as they rise on* ALFIERI.]

ALFIERI   On December twenty-seventh I saw him next. I normally go home well before six, but that day I sat around looking out my window at the bay, and when I saw him walking through my doorway, I knew why I had waited. And if I seem to tell this like a dream, it was that way. Several moments arrived in the course of the two talks we had when it occurred to me how—almost transfixed I had come to feel. I had lost my strength somewhere. [EDDIE *enters, removing his cap, sits in the chair, looks thoughtfully out.*] I looked in his eyes more than I listened—in fact, I can hardly remember the conversation. But I will never forget how dark the room became when he looked at me; his eyes were like tunnels. I kept wanting to call the police, but nothing had happened. Nothing at all had really happened. [*He breaks off and looks down at the desk. Then he turns to* EDDIE.] So in other words, he won't leave?

EDDIE   My wife is talkin' about renting a room upstairs for them. An old lady on the top floor is got an empty room.

ALFIERI   What does Marco say?

EDDIE   He just sits there. Marco don't say much.

ALFIERI   I guess they didn't tell him, heh? What happened?

EDDIE   I don't know; Marco don't say much.

ALFIERI   What does your wife say?

EDDIE   [*unwilling to pursue this*] Nobody's talkin' much in the house. So what about that?

ALFIERI   But you didn't prove anything about him. It sounds like he just wasn't strong enough to break your grip.

EDDIE   I'm tellin' you I know—he ain't right. Somebody that don't want it can break it. Even a mouse, if you catch a teeny mouse and you hold it in your hand, that mouse can give you the right kind of fight. He didn't give me the right kind of fight, I know it, Mr. Alfieri, the guy ain't right.

ALFIERI   What did you do that for, Eddie?

EDDIE   To show her what he is! So she would see, once and for all! Her mother'll turn over in the grave! [*He gathers himself almost peremptorily.*] So what do I gotta do now? Tell me what to do.

ALFIERI   She actually said she's marrying him?

EDDIE   She told me, yeah. So what do I do?
    [*Slight pause.*]

ALFIERI   This is my last word, Eddie, take it or not, that's your business. Morally and legally you have no rights, you cannot stop it; she is a free agent.

EDDIE   [*angering*] Didn't you hear what I told you?

ALFIERI   [*with a tougher tone*] I heard what you told me, and I'm telling you what the answer is. I'm not only telling you now, I'm warning you—the law is nature. The law is only a word for what has a right to happen. When the law is wrong it's because it's unnatural, but in this case it is natural and a river will drown you if you buck it now. Let her go. And bless her. [*A phone booth begins to glow on the opposite side of the stage; a faint, lonely blue.* EDDIE *stands up, jaws clenched.*] Somebody had to come for her, Eddie, sooner or later. [EDDIE *starts turning to go and* ALFIERI *rises with new anxiety.*] You won't have a friend in the world, Eddie! Even those who understand will turn against you, even the ones who feel the same will despise you! [EDDIE *moves off.*] Put it out of your mind! Eddie! [*He follows into the darkness, calling desperately.*]
    [EDDIE *is gone. The phone is glowing in light now. Light is out on* ALFIERI. EDDIE *has at the same time appeared beside the phone.*]

EDDIE   Give me the number of the Immigration Bureau. Thanks. [*He dials.*] I want to report something. Illegal immigrants. Two of them. That's right. Four-forty-one Saxon Street, Brooklyn, yeah. Ground floor. Heh? [*With greater difficulty.*] I'm just around the neighborhood, that's all. Heh?
    [*Evidently he is being questioned further, and he slowly hangs up. He leaves the phone just as* LOUIS *and* MIKE *come down the street.*]

LOUIS   Go bowlin', Eddie?

EDDIE   No, I'm due home.

LOUIS   Well, take it easy.

EDDIE   I'll see yiz.
    [*They leave him, exiting right, and he watches them go. He glances about, then goes up into the house. The lights go on in the apartment.* BEATRICE *is taking down Christmas decorations and packing them in a box.*]

EDDIE   Where is everybody? [BEATRICE *does not answer.*] I says where is everybody?

BEATRICE   [*looking up at him, wearied with it, and concealing a fear of him*] I decided to move them upstairs with Mrs. Dondero.

EDDIE   Oh, they're all moved up there already?

BEATRICE   Yeah.

EDDIE   Where's Catherine? She up there?

BEATRICE   Only to bring pillow cases.

EDDIE   She ain't movin' in with them.

BEATRICE   Look, I'm sick and tired of it. I'm sick and tired of it!

EDDIE   All right, all right, take it easy.

BEATRICE   I don't wanna hear no more about it, you understand? Nothin'!

EDDIE   What're you blowin' off about? Who brought them in here?

BEATRICE   All right, I'm sorry; I wish I'd a drop dead before I told them to come. In the ground I wish I was.

EDDIE   Don't drop dead, just keep in mind who brought them in here, that's all. [*He moves about restlessly.*] I mean I got a couple of rights here. [*He moves, wanting to beat down her evident disapproval of him.*] This is my house here not their house.

BEATRICE   What do you want from me? They're moved out; what do you want now?

EDDIE   I want my respect!

BEATRICE   So I moved them out, what more do you want? You got your house now, you got your respect.

EDDIE   [*he moves about biting his lip*]   I don't like the way you talk to me, Beatrice.

BEATRICE   I'm just tellin' you I done what you want!

EDDIE   I don't like it! The way you talk to me and the way you look at me. This is my house. And she is my niece and I'm responsible for her.

BEATRICE   So that's why you done that to him?

EDDIE   I done what to him?

BEATRICE   What you done to him in front of her; you know what I'm talkin' about. She goes around shakin' all the time, she can't go to sleep! That's what you call responsible for her?

EDDIE   [*quietly*]   The guy ain't right, Beatrice. [*She is silent.*] Did you hear what I said?

BEATRICE   Look, I'm finished with it. That's all. [*She resumes her work.*]

EDDIE   [*helping her to pack the tinsel*]   I'm gonna have it out with you one of these days, Beatrice.

BEATRICE   Nothin' to have out with me, it's all settled. Now we gonna be like it never happened, that's all.

EDDIE   I want my respect, Beatrice, and you know what I'm talkin' about.

BEATRICE   What?
[*Pause.*]

EDDIE   [*finally his resolution hardens*]   What I feel like doin' in the bed and what I don't feel like doin'. I don't want no—

BEATRICE   When'd I say anything about that?

EDDIE   You said, you said, I ain't deaf. I don't want no more conversations about that, Beatrice. I do what I feel like doin' or what I don't feel like doin'.

BEATRICE   Okay.
[*Pause.*]

EDDIE   You used to be different, Beatrice. You had a whole different way.

BEATRICE   *I'm* no different.

EDDIE   You didn't used to jump me all the time about everything. The last year or two I come in the house I don't know what's gonna hit me. It's a shootin' gallery in here and I'm the pigeon.

BEATRICE   Okay, okay.

EDDIE   Don't tell me okay, okay, I'm tellin' you the truth. A wife is supposed to believe the husband. If I tell you that guy ain't right don't tell me he is right.

BEATRICE   But how do you know?

EDDIE   Because I know. I don't go around makin' accusations. He give me the heeby-jeebies the first minute I seen him. And I don't like you sayin' I don't want her marryin' anybody. I broke my back payin' her stenography lessons so she could go out and meet a better class of people. Would I do that if I didn't want her to get married? Sometimes you talk like I was a crazy man or sump'm.

BEATRICE   But she likes him.

EDDIE   Beatrice, she's a baby, how is she gonna know what she likes?

BEATRICE   Well, you kept her a baby, you wouldn't let her go out. I told you a hundred times.
[*Pause.*]

EDDIE   All right. Let her go out, then.

BEATRICE   She don't wanna go out now. It's too late, Eddie.
[*Pause.*]

EDDIE   Suppose I told her to go out. Suppose I—

BEATRICE   They're going to get married next week, Eddie.

EDDIE   [*his head jerks around to her*]   She said that?

BEATRICE   Eddie, if you want my advice, go to her and tell her good luck. I think maybe now that you had it out you learned better.

EDDIE   What's the hurry next week?

BEATRICE   Well, she's been worried about him bein' picked up; this way he could start to be a citizen. She loves him, Eddie. [*He gets up, moves about uneasily, restlessly.*] Why don't you give her a good word? Because I still think she would like you to be a friend, y'know? [*He is standing, looking at the floor.*] I mean like if you told her you'd go to the wedding.

EDDIE   She asked you that?

BEATRICE   I know she would like it. I'd like to make a party here for her. I mean there oughta be some kinda send-off. Heh? I mean she'll have trouble enough in her life, let's start it off happy. What do you say? Cause in her heart she still loves you, Eddie. I know it. [*He presses his fingers against his eyes.*] What're you, cryin'? [*She goes to him, holds his face.*] Go . . . whyn't you go tell her you're sorry?
[CATHERINE *is seen on the upper landing of the stairway, and they hear her descending.*]
There . . . she's comin' down. Come on, shake hands with her.

EDDIE   [*moving with suppressed suddenness*]   No, I can't, I can't talk to her.

BEATRICE   Eddie, give her a break; a wedding should be happy!

EDDIE   I'm goin', I'm goin' for a walk.
[*He goes upstage for his jacket.* CATHERINE *enters and starts for the bedroom door.*]

BEATRICE   Katie? . . . Eddie, don't go, wait a minute. [*She embraces* EDDIE's *arm with warmth.*] Ask him, Katie. Come on, honey.

EDDIE   It's all right, I'm—[*He starts to go and she holds him.*]

BEATRICE   No, she wants to ask you. Come on, Katie, ask him. We'll have a party! What're we gonna do, hate each other? Come on!

CATHERINE   I'm gonna get married, Eddie. So if you wanna come, the wedding be on Saturday.
[*Pause.*]

EDDIE   Okay. I only wanted the best for you, Katie. I hope you know that.

CATHERINE   Okay. [*She starts out again.*]

EDDIE   Catherine? [*She turns to him.*] I was just tellin' Beatrice . . . if you wanna go out, like . . . I mean I realize maybe I kept you home too much. Because he's the first guy you ever knew, y'know? I mean now that you got a job, you might meet some fellas, and you get a different idea, y'know? I mean you could always come back to him, you're still only kids, the both of yiz. What's the hurry? Maybe you'll get around a little bit, you grow up a little more, maybe you'll see different in a couple of months. I mean you be surprised, it don't have to be him.

CATHERINE   No, we made it up already.

EDDIE   [with increasing anxiety]   Katie, wait a minute.

CATHERINE   No, I made up my mind.

EDDIE   But you never knew no other fella, Katie! How could you make up your mind?

CATHERINE   Cause I did. I don't want nobody else.

EDDIE   But, Katie, suppose he gets picked up.

CATHERINE   That's why we gonna do it right away. Soon as we finish the wedding he's goin' right over and start to be a citizen. I made up my mind, Eddie. I'm sorry. [To BEATRICE.] Could I take two more pillow cases for the other guys?

BEATRICE   Sure, go ahead. Only don't let her forget where they came from.

[CATHERINE goes into a bedroom.]

EDDIE   She's got other boarders up there?

BEATRICE   Yeah, there's two guys that just came over.

EDDIE   What do you mean, came over?

BEATRICE   From Italy. Lipari the butcher—his nephew. They come from Bari, they just got here yesterday. I didn't even know till Marco and Rodolpho moved up there before.

[CATHERINE enters, going toward exit with two pillow cases.]

It'll be nice, they could all talk together.

EDDIE   Catherine! [She halts near the exit door. He takes in BEATRICE too.] What're you, got no brains? You put them up there with two other submarines?

CATHERINE   Why?

EDDIE   [in a driving fright and anger]   Why! How do you know they're not trackin' these guys? They'll come up for them and find Marco and Rodolpho! Get them out of the house!

BEATRICE   But they been here so long already—

EDDIE   How do you know what enemies Lipari's got? Which they'd love to stab him in the back?

CATHERINE   Well what'll I do with them?

EDDIE   The neighborhood is full of rooms. Can't you stand to live a couple of blocks away from him? Get them out of the house!

CATHERINE   Well maybe tomorrow night I'll—

EDDIE   Not tomorrow, do it now. Catherine, you never mix yourself with somebody else's family! These guys get picked up, Lipari's liable to blame you or me and we got his whole family on our head. They got a temper, that family.

[Two men in overcoats appear outside, start into the house.]

CATHERINE   How'm I gonna find a place tonight?

EDDIE   Will you stop arguin' with me and get them out! You think I'm always tryin' to fool you or sump'm? What's the matter with you, don't you believe I could think of your good? Did I ever ask sump'm for myself? You think I got no feelin's? I never told you nothin' in my life that wasn't for your good. Nothin'! And look at the way you talk to me! Like I was an enemy!

Like I—[*A knock on the door. His head swerves. They all stand motionless. Another knock.* EDDIE, *in a whisper, pointing upstage.*] Go up the fire escape, get them out over the back fence.

[CATHERINE *stands motionless, uncomprehending.*]

FIRST OFFICER [*in the hall*] Immigration! Open up in there!

EDDIE Go, go. Hurry up! [*She stands a moment staring at him in a realized horror.*] Well, what're you lookin' at!

FIRST OFFICER Open up!

EDDIE [*calling toward door*] Who's that there?

FIRST OFFICER Immigration, open up.

[EDDIE *turns, looks at* BEATRICE. *She sits. Then he looks at* CATHERINE. *With a sob of fury* CATHERINE *streaks into a bedroom. Knock is repeated.*]

EDDIE All right, take it easy, take it easy. [*He goes and opens the door. The* OFFICER *steps inside.*] What's all this?

FIRST OFFICER Where are they?

[SECOND OFFICER *sweeps past and, glancing about, goes into the kitchen.*]

EDDIE Where's who?

FIRST OFFICER Come on, come on, where are they? [*He hurries into the bedrooms.*]

EDDIE Who? We got nobody here. [*He looks at* BEATRICE, *who turns her head away. Pugnaciously, furious, he steps toward* BEATRICE.] What's the matter with *you?*

[FIRST OFFICER *enters from the bedroom, calls to the kitchen.*]

FIRST OFFICER Dominick?

[*Enter* SECOND OFFICER *from kitchen.*]

SECOND OFFICER Maybe it's a different apartment.

FIRST OFFICER There's only two more floors up there. I'll take the front, you go up the fire escape. I'll let you in. Watch your step up there.

SECOND OFFICER Okay, right, Charley. [FIRST OFFICER *goes out apartment door and runs up the stairs.*] This is Four-forty-one, isn't it?

EDDIE That's right.

[SECOND OFFICER *goes out into the kitchen.* EDDIE *turns to* BEATRICE. *She looks at him now and sees his terror.*]

BEATRICE [*weakened with fear*] Oh, Jesus, Eddie.

EDDIE What's the matter with *you?*

BEATRICE [*pressing her palms against her face*] Oh, my God, my God.

EDDIE What're you, accusin' me?

BEATRICE [*her final thrust is to turn toward him instead of running from him*] My God, what did you do?

[*Many steps on the outer stair draw his attention. We see the* FIRST OFFICER *descending, with* MARCO, *behind him* RODOLPHO, *and* CATHERINE *and the two strange immigrants, followed by* SECOND OFFICER. BEATRICE *hurries to door.*]

CATHERINE [*backing down stairs, fighting with* FIRST OFFICER; *as they appear on the stairs*] What do yiz want from them? They work, that's all. They're boarders upstairs, they work on the piers.

BEATRICE [*to* FIRST OFFICER] Ah, Mister, what do you want from them, who do they hurt?

CATHERINE [*pointing to* RODOLPHO] They ain't no submarines, he was born in Philadelphia.

FIRST OFFICER Step aside, lady.

CATHERINE What do you mean? You can't just come in a house and—

FIRST OFFICER All right, take it easy. [*To* RODOLPHO.] What street were you born in Philadelphia?

CATHERINE   What do you mean, what street? Could you tell me what street you were born?

FIRST OFFICER   Sure. Four blocks away, One-eleven Union Street. Let's go fellas.

CATHERINE   [*fending him off* RODOLPHO]   No, you can't!' Now, get outa here!

FIRST OFFICER   Look, girlie, if they're all right they'll be out tomorrow. If they're illegal they go back where they came from. If you want, get yourself a lawyer, although I'm tellin' you now you're wasting your money. Let's get them in the car, Dom. [*To the men.*] Andiamo, Andiamo, let's go.
   [*The men start, but* MARCO *hangs back.*]

BEATRICE   [*from doorway*]   Who're they hurtin', for God's sake, what do you want from them? They're starvin' over there, what do you want! Marco!
   [MARCO *suddenly breaks from the group and dashes into the room and faces* EDDIE; BEATRICE *and* FIRST OFFICER *rush in as* MARCO *spits into* EDDIE'S *face.*
      CATHERINE *runs into hallway and throws herself into* RODOLPHO'S *arms.*
   EDDIE, *with an enraged cry, lunges for* MARCO.]

EDDIE   Oh, you mother's—!
   [FIRST OFFICER *quickly intercedes and pushes* EDDIE *from* MARCO, *who stands there accusingly.*]

FIRST OFFICER   [*between them, pushing* EDDIE *from* MARCO]   Cut it out!

EDDIE   [*over the* FIRST OFFICER'S *shoulder, to* MARCO]   I'll kill you for that, you son of a bitch!

FIRST OFFICER   Hey! [*Shakes him.*] Stay in here now, don't come out, don't bother him. You hear me? Don't come out, fella.
   [*For an instant there is silence Then* FIRST OFFICER *turns and takes* MARCO'S *arm and then gives a last, informative look at* EDDIE. *As he and* MARCO *are going out into the hall,* EDDIE *erupts.*]

EDDIE   I don't forget that, Marco! You hear what I'm sayin'?
   [*Out in the hall,* FIRST OFFICER *and* MARCO *go down the stairs. Now, in the street,* LOUIS, MIKE, *and several neighbors including the butcher,* LIPARI—*a stout, intense, middle-aged man—are gathering around the stoop.* LIPARI, *the butcher, walks over to the two strange men and kisses them. His wife, keening, goes and kisses their hands.* EDDIE *is emerging from the house shouting after* MARCO. BEATRICE *is trying to restrain him.*]

EDDIE   That's the thanks I get? Which I took the blankets off my bed for yiz? You gonna apologize to me, Marco! *Marco!*

FIRST OFFICER   [*in the doorway with* MARCO]   All right, lady, let them go. Get in the car, fellas, it's over there.
   [RODOLPHO *is almost carrying the sobbing* CATHERINE *off up the street, left.*]

CATHERINE   He was born in Philadelphia! What do you want from him?

FIRST OFFICER   Step aside, lady, come on now . . .
   [*The* SECOND OFFICER *has moved off with the two strange men.* MARCO, *taking advantage of the* FIRST OFFICER'S *being occupied with* CATHERINE, *suddenly frees himself and points back at* EDDIE.]

MARCO   That one! I accuse that one!
   [EDDIE *brushes* BEATRICE *aside and rushes out to the stoop.*]

FIRST OFFICER   [*grabbing him and moving him quickly off up the left street*]   Come on!

MARCO   [*as he is taken off, pointing back at* EDDIE]   That one! He killed my children! That one stole the food from my children!
   [MARCO *is gone. The crowd has turned to* EDDIE.]

EDDIE   [*to* LIPARI *and wife*]   He's crazy! I give them the blankets off my bed. Six months I kept them like my own brothers!
   [LIPARI, *the butcher, turns and starts up left with his arm around his wife.*]

EDDIE   Lipari! [*He follows* LIPARI *up left.*] For Christ's sake, I kept them, I give them the blankets off my bed!

[LIPARI *and wife exit.* EDDIE *turns and starts crossing down right to* LOUIS *and* MIKE.]

EDDIE   Louis! *Louis!*

[LOUIS *barely turns, then walks off and exits down right with* MIKE. *Only* BEATRICE *is left on the stoop.* CATHERINE *now returns, blank-eyed, from off-stage and the car.* EDDIE *calls after* LOUIS *and* MIKE.]

EDDIE   He's gonna take that back. He's gonna take that back or I'll kill him! You hear me? I'll kill him! I'll kill him! [*He exits up street calling.*]

[*There is a pause of darkness before the lights rise, on the reception room of a prison.* MARCO *is seated;* ALFIERI, CATHERINE, *and* RODOLPHO *standing.*]

ALFIERI   I'm waiting, Marco, what do you say?

RODOLPHO   Marco never hurt anybody.

ALFIERI   I can bail you out until your hearing comes up. But I'm not going to do it, you understand me? Unless I have your promise. You're an honorable man, I will believe your promise. Now what do you say?

MARCO   In my country he would be dead now. He would not live this long.

ALFIERI   All right, Rodolpho—you come with me now.

RODOLPHO   No! Please, mister. Marco—promise the man. Please, I want you to watch the wedding. How can I be married and you're in here? Please, you're not going to do anything; you know you're not.

[MARCO *is silent.*]

CATHERINE   [*kneeling left of* MARCO] Marco, don't you understand? He can't bail you out if you're gonna do something bad. To hell with Eddie. Nobody is gonna talk to him again if he lives to a hundred. Everybody knows you spit in his face, that's enough, isn't it? Give me the satisfaction—I want you at the wedding. You got a wife and kids, Marco. You could be workin' till the hearing comes up, instead of layin' around here.

MARCO   [*to* ALFIERI] I have no chance?

ALFIERI   [*crosses to behind* MARCO] No, Marco. You're going back. The hearing is a formality, that's all.

MARCO   But him? There is a chance, eh?

ALFIERI   When she marries him he can start to become an American. They permit that, if the wife is born here.

MARCO   [*looking at* RODOLPHO] Well—we did something. [*He lays a palm on* RODOLPHO's *arm and* RODOLPHO *covers it.*]

RODOLPHO   Marco, tell the man.

MARCO   [*pulling his hand away*] What will I tell him? He knows such a promise is dishonorable.

ALFIERI   To promise not to kill is not dishonorable.

MARCO   [*looking at* ALFIERI] No?

ALFIERI   No.

MARCO   [*gesturing with his head—this is a new idea*] Then what is done with such a man?

ALFIERI   Nothing. If he obeys the law, he lives. That's all.

MARCO   [*rises, turns to* ALFIERI] The law? All the law is not in a book.

ALFIERI   Yes. In a book. There is no other law.

MARCO   [*his anger rising*] He degraded my brother. My blood. He robbed my children, he mocks my work. I work to come here, mister!

ALFIERI   I know, Marco—

MARCO   There is no law for that? Where is the law for that?

ALFIERI   There is none.

MARCO   [*shaking his head, sitting*]   I don't understand this country.

ALFIERI   Well? What is your answer? You have five or six weeks you could work. Or else you sit here. What do you say to me?

MARCO   [*lowers his eyes. It almost seems he is ashamed*]   All right.

ALFIERI   You won't touch him. This is your promise.

[*Slight pause.*]

MARCO   Maybe he wants to apologize to me.

[MARCO *is staring away.* ALFIERI *takes one of his hands.*]

ALFIERI   This is not God, Marco. You hear? Only God makes justice.

MARCO   All right.

ALFIERI   [*nodding, not with assurance*]   Good! Catherine, Rodolpho, Marco, let us go.

[CATHERINE *kisses* RODOLPHO *and* MARCO, *then kisses* ALFIERI's *hand.*]

CATHERINE   I'll get Beatrice and meet you at the church. [*She leaves quickly.*]

[MARCO *rises.* RODOLPHO *suddenly embraces him.* MARCO *pats him on the back and* RODOLPHO *exits after* CATHERINE. MARCO *faces* ALFIERI.]

ALFIERI   Only God, Marco.

[MARCO *turns and walks out.* ALFIERI *with a certain processional tread leaves the stage. The lights dim out.*

   The lights rise in the apartment. EDDIE *is alone in the rocker, rocking back and forth in little surges. Pause. Now* BEATRICE *emerges from a bedroom. She is in her best clothes, wearing a hat.*]

BEATRICE   [*with fear, going to* EDDIE]   I'll be back in about an hour, Eddie. All right?

EDDIE   [*quietly, almost inaudibly, as though drained*]   What, have I been talkin' to myself?

BEATRICE   Eddie, for God's sake, it's her wedding.

EDDIE   Didn't you hear what I told you? You walk out that door to that wedding you ain't comin' back here, Beatrice.

BEATRICE   Why! What do you want?

EDDIE   I want my respect. Didn't you ever hear of that? From my wife?

[CATHERINE *enters from bedroom.*]

CATHERINE   It's after three; we're supposed to be there already, Beatrice. The priest won't wait.

BEATRICE   Eddie. It's her wedding. There'll be nobody there from her family. For my sister let me go. I'm goin' for my sister.

EDDIE   [*as though hurt*]   Look, I been arguin' with you all day already, Beatrice, and I said what I'm gonna say. He's gonna come here and apologize to me or nobody from this house is goin' into that church today. Now if that's more to you than I am, then go. But don't come back. You be on my side or on their side, that's all.

CATHERINE   [*suddenly*]   Who the hell do you think you are?

BEATRICE   Sssh!

CATHERINE   You got no more right to tell nobody nothin'! Nobody! The rest of your life, nobody!

BEATRICE   Shut up, Katie! [*She turns* CATHERINE *around.*]

CATHERINE   You're gonna come with me!

BEATRICE   I can't Katie, I can't . . .

CATHERINE   How can you listen to him? This rat!

BEATRICE   [*shaking* CATHERINE]   Don't you call him that!

CATHERINE   [*clearing from* BEATRICE]   What're you scared of? He's a rat! He belongs in the sewer!

BEATRICE   Stop it!

CATHERINE [*weeping*] He bites people when they sleep! He comes when nobody's lookin' and poisons decent people. In the garbage he belongs!
[EDDIE *seems about to pick up the table and fling it at her.*]

BEATRICE No, Eddie! Eddie! [*To* CATHERINE.] Then we all belong in the garbage. You, and me too. Don't say that. Whatever happened we all done it,
and don't you ever forget it, Catherine. [*She goes to* CATHERINE.] Now go,
go to your wedding, Katie, I'll stay home. Go. God bless you, God bless
your children.
[*Enter* RODOLPHO.]

RODOLPHO Eddie?

EDDIE Who said you could come in here? Get outa here!

RODOLPHO Marco is coming, Eddie.
[*Pause.* BEATRICE *raises her hands in terror.*]
He's praying in the church. You understand? [*Pause.* RODOLPHO *advances
into the room.*] Catherine, I think it is better we go. Come with me.

CATHERINE Eddie, go away, please.

BEATRICE [*quietly*] Eddie. Let's go someplace. Come. You and me.
[*He has not moved.*]
I don't want you to be here when he comes. I'll get your coat.

EDDIE Where? Where am I goin'? This is my house.

BEATRICE [*crying out*] What's the use of it! He's crazy now, you know the way
they get, what good is it! You got nothin' against Marco, you always liked
Marco!

EDDIE I got nothin' against Marco? Which he called me a rat in front of the
whole neighborhood? Which he said I killed his children! Where you been?

RODOLPHO [*quite suddenly, stepping up to* EDDIE] It is my fault, Eddie. Everything. I wish to apologize. It was wrong that I do not ask your permission.
I kiss your hand. [*He reaches for* EDDIE's *hand, but* EDDIE *snaps it away from
him.*]

BEATRICE Eddie, he's apologizing!

RODOLPHO I have made all our troubles. But you have insult me too. Maybe
God understand why you did that to me. Maybe you did not mean to insult
me at all—

BEATRICE Listen to him! Eddie, listen what he's tellin' you!

RODOLPHO I think, maybe when Marco comes, if we can tell him we are comrades now, and we have no more argument between us. Then maybe Marco
will not—

EDDIE Now, listen—

CATHERINE Eddie, give him a chance!

BEATRICE What do you want! Eddie, what do you want!

EDDIE I want my name! He didn't take my name; he's only a punk. Marco's
got my name—[*to* RODOLPHO] and you can run tell him, kid, that he's gonna
give it back to me in front of this neighborhood, or we have it out. [*Hoisting
up his pants.*] Come on, where is he? Take me to him.

BEATRICE Eddie, listen—

EDDIE I heard enough! Come on, let's go!

BEATRICE Only blood is good? He kissed your hand!

EDDIE What he does don't mean nothin' to nobody! [*To* RODOLPHO.] Come on!

BEATRICE [*barring his way to the stairs*] What's gonna mean somethin'? Eddie,
listen to me. Who could give you your name? Listen to me, I love you, I'm
talkin' to you, I love you; if Marco'll kiss your hand outside, if he goes on
his knees, what is he got to give you? That's not what you want.

EDDIE Don't bother me!

BEATRICE You want somethin' else, Eddie, and you can never have her!

CATHERINE [*in horror*] B.!

EDDIE [*shocked, horrified, his fists clenching*] Beatrice!

[MARCO *appears outside, walking toward the door from a distant point.*]

BEATRICE [*crying out, weeping*] The truth is not as bad as blood, Eddie! I'm tellin' you the truth—tell her good-by forever!

EDDIE [*crying out in agony*] That's what you think of me—that I would have such a thought? [*His fists clench his head as though it will burst.*]

MARCO [*calling near the door outside*] Eddie Carbone!

[EDDIE *swerves about; all stand transfixed for an instant. People appear outside.*]

EDDIE [*as though flinging his challenge*] Yeah, Marco! Eddie Carbone. Eddie Carbone. Eddie Carbone. [*He goes up the stairs and emerges from the apartment.* RODOLPHO *streaks up and out past him and runs to* MARCO.]

RODOLPHO No, Marco, please! Eddie, please, he has children! You will kill a family!

BEATRICE Go in the house! Eddie, go in the house!

EDDIE [*he gradually comes to address the people*] Maybe he come to apologize to me. Heh, Marco? For what you said about me in front of the neighborhood? [*He is incensing himself and little bits of laughter even escape him as his eyes are murderous and he cracks his knuckles in his hands with a strange sort of relaxation.*] He knows that ain't right. To do like that? To a man? Which I put my roof over their head and my food in their mouth? Like in the Bible? Strangers I never seen in my whole life? To come out of the water and grab a girl for a passport? To go and take from your own family like from the stable—and never a word to me? And now accusations in the bargain! [*Directly to* MARCO.] Wipin' the neighborhood with my name like a dirty rag! I want my name, Marco. [*He is moving now, carefully, toward* MARCO.] Now gimme my name and we go together to the wedding.

BEATRICE *and* CATHERINE [*keening*] Eddie! Eddie, don't! Eddie!

EDDIE No, Marco knows what's right from wrong. Tell the people, Marco, tell them what a liar you are! [*He has his arms spread and* MARCO *is spreading his.*] Come on, liar, you know what you done! [*He lunges for* MARCO *as a great hushed shout goes up from the people.*]

[MARCO *strikes* EDDIE *beside the neck.*]

MARCO Animal! You go on your knees to me!

[EDDIE *goes down with the blow and* MARCO *starts to raise a foot to stomp him when* EDDIE *springs a knife into his hand and* MARCO *steps back.* LOUIS *rushes in toward* EDDIE.]

LOUIS Eddie, for Christ's sake!

[EDDIE *raises the knife and* LOUIS *halts and steps back.*]

EDDIE You lied about me, Marco. Now say it. Come on now, say it!

MARCO Anima-a-a-l!

[EDDIE *lunges with the knife.* MARCO *grabs his arm, turning the blade inward and pressing it home as the women and* LOUIS *and* MIKE *rush in and separate them, and* EDDIE, *the knife still in his hand, falls to his knees before* MARCO. *The two women support him for a moment, calling his name again and again.*]

CATHERINE Eddie I never meant to do nothing bad to you.

EDDIE Then why—Oh, B.!

BEATRICE Yes, yes!

EDDIE My B.!

[*He dies in her arms, and* BEATRICE *covers him with her body.* ALFIERI,

*who is in the crowd, turns out to the audience. The lights have gone
down, leaving him in a glow, while behind him the dull prayers of the
people and the keening of the women continue.*]

ALFIERI Most of the time now we settle for half and I like it better. But the
truth is holy, and even as I know how wrong he was, and his death useless,
I tremble, for I confess that something perversely pure calls to me from
his memory—not purely good, but himself purely, for he allowed himself
to be wholly known and for that I think I will love him more than all my
sensible clients. And yet, it is better to settle for half, it must be! And so I
mourn him—I admit it—with a certain . . . alarm.

CURTAIN

TENNESSEE WILLIAMS
[1914–   ]

Born Thomas Lanier Williams, and called "Tennessee" because he was descended from pioneering Tennessee stock, Tennessee Williams grew up in Columbus, Mississippi, as the son of a shoe salesman. His mother, a descendant of Southern aristocracy, along with her father, an Episcopal clergyman with a taste for literature and cocktails, were most responsible for the shaping of the author's mind. From the very first, Tennessee Williams lived in a divided world —the stiflingly unsuccessful world of his father's business contradicting the more cultured and sophisticated world of his grandfather's rectory. It was in that rectory that Williams observed those genteel Southern women whose anguish over the encroachments of a cruder way of life was to inspire a number of his plays.

Biographical details most relevant to *The Glass Menagerie* are to be found in Williams' teen-age sojourn in the city of St. Louis, where his family had moved from Mississippi. In moving to St. Louis where his father was a clerk, Williams experienced a great wrench in his life and learned the hard lesson of shabby gentility. It was in St. Louis, writes Kenneth Tynan, "in a stuffy, back-street apartment, that his world split, amoeba-like, into two irreconcilable halves—the soft, feminine world of the room that he and his sister filled with little glass animals, and the cruel, male world of the alley outside, where cats fought and coupled to a persistent screaming." After a short stay at the University of Missouri, Williams was forced by the depression to take a job in a shoe factory, a job he so detested that after three years he had a heart attack and a complete physical breakdown. Upon recovery, he took a B.A. at the University of Iowa in 1938. Small, local successes with his early literary efforts undoubtedly encouraged him to leave home and break with the future of shabby gentility offered by his father's clerkship and the job at the shoe factory. Then began the long epic of tormented wandering that has been Tennessee Williams' life ever since.

The Glass Menagerie, produced in New York in 1945, was his first success, and remains his most popular play. It was followed by a series of plays most of which have been converted into films, among them being *A Streetcar Named Desire* (1947), *Summer and Smoke* (1948), *The Rose Tattoo* (1950), *Cat on a Hot Tin Roof* (1954), *Orpheus Descending* (1957), *Sweet Bird of Youth* (1959), *Suddenly Last Summer* (1959), and *Night of the Iguana* (1962).

THE
GLASS MENAGERIE

TENNESSEE WILLIAMS

CHARACTERS

AMANDA WINGFIELD, *the mother*
LAURA WINGFIELD, *her daughter*
TOM WINGFIELD, *her son*
JIM O'CONNOR, *the gentleman caller*

SCENE: *An Alley in St. Louis*

PART I. *Preparation for a Gentleman Caller.*
PART II. *The Gentleman calls.*

TIME: *Now and the Past.*

SCENE ONE

The Wingfield apartment is in the rear of the building, one of those vast hive-like conglomerations of cellular living-units that flower as warty growths in overcrowded urban centers of lower

Copyright 1945 by Tennessee Williams and Edwina D. Williams. Reprinted by permission of Random House, Inc.

middle-class population and are symptomatic of the impulse of this largest and fundamentally enslaved section of American society to avoid fluidity and differentiation and to exist and function as one interfused mass of automatism.

The apartment faces an alley and is entered by a fire-escape, a structure whose name is a touch of accidental poetic truth, for all of these huge buildings are always burning with the slow and implacable fires of human desperation. The fire-escape is included in the set—that is, the landing of it and steps descending from it.

The scene is memory and is therefore nonrealistic. Memory takes a lot of poetic license. It omits some details; others are exaggerated, according to the emotional value of the articles it touches, for memory is seated predominantly in the heart. The interior is therefore rather dim and poetic.

At the rise of the curtain, the audience is faced with the dark, grim rear wall of the Wingfield tenement. This building, which runs parallel to the footlights, is flanked on both sides by dark, narrow alleys which run into murky canyons of tangled clotheslines, garbage cans and the sinister lattice-work of neighboring fire-escapes. It is up and down these side alleys that exterior entrances and exits are made, during the play. At the end of TOM'S *opening commentary, the dark tenement wall slowly reveals [by means of a transparency] the interior of the ground floor Wingfield apartment.*

Downstage is the living room, which also serves as a sleeping room for LAURA, *the sofa unfolding to make her bed. Upstage, center, and divided by a wide arch or second proscenium with transparent faded portieres [or second curtain], is the dining room. In an old-fashioned what-not in the living room are seen scores of transparent glass animals. A blown-up photograph of the father hangs on the wall of the living room, facing the audience, to the left of the archway. It is the face of a very handsome young man in a doughboy's First World War cap. He is gallantly smiling, ineluctably smiling, as if to say, "I will be smiling forever."*

The audience hears and sees the opening scene in the dining room through both the transparent fourth wall of the building and the transparent gauze portieres of the dining-room arch. It is during this revealing scene that the fourth wall slowly ascends, out of sight. This transparent exterior wall is not brought down again until the very end of the play, during TOM'S *final speech.*

The narrator is an undisguised convention of the play. He takes whatever license with dramatic convention as is convenient to his purposes.

TOM *enters dressed as a merchant sailor from alley, stage left, and strolls across the front of the stage to the fire-escape. There he stops and lights a cigarette. He addresses the audience.*

TOM   Yes, I have tricks in my pocket, I have things up my sleeve. But I am the opposite of a stage magician. He gives you illusion that has the appearance of truth. I give you truth in the pleasant disguise of illusion. To begin with, I turn back time. I reverse it to that quaint period, the thirties, when the huge middle class of America was matriculating in a school for the blind. Their eyes had failed them, or they had failed their eyes, and so they were having their fingers pressed forcibly down on the fiery Braille alphabet of a dissolving economy. In Spain there was revolution. Here there was only shouting and confusion. In Spain there was Guernica.[1] Here there were disturbances of labor, sometimes pretty violent, in otherwise peaceful cities such as Chicago, Cleveland, Saint Louis . . . This is the social background of the play.

[MUSIC]

The play is memory. Being a memory play, it is dimly lighted, it is sentimental, it is not realistic. In memory everything seems to happen to music. That explains the fiddle in the wings. I am the narrator of the play, and also a character in it. The other characters are my mother, Amanda, my sister, Laura, and a gentleman caller who appears in the final scenes. He is the most realistic character in the play, being an emissary from a world of reality that we were somehow set apart from. But since I have a poet's weakness for symbols, I am using this character also as a symbol; he is the long delayed but always expected something that we live for. There is a fifth character in the play who doesn't appear except in this larger-than-life photograph over the mantel. This is our father who left us a long time ago. He was a telephone man who fell in love with long distances; he gave up his job with the telephone company and skipped the light fantastic out of town . . . The last we heard of him was a picture post-card from Mazatlan, on the Pacific coast of Mexico, containing a message of two words—"Hello—Good-bye!" and no address. I think the rest of the play will explain itself. . . .
[AMANDA's *voice becomes audible through the portieres*]

[LEGEND ON SCREEN: * "OÙ SONT LES NEIGES"[2]]

[*He divides the portieres and enters the upstage area*]

[AMANDA *and* LAURA *are seated at a drop-leaf table. Eating is indicated by gestures without food or utensils.* AMANDA *faces the audience.* TOM *and* LAURA *are seated in profile*]

[*The interior has lit up softly and through the scrim we see* AMANDA *and* LAURA *seated at the table in the upstage area*]

AMANDA   [*Calling*]   Tom?
TOM   Yes, Mother.
AMANDA   We can't say grace until you come to the table!
TOM   Coming, Mother. [*He bows slightly and withdraws, reappearing a few moments later in his place at the table*]
AMANDA   [*To her son*]   Honey, don't *push* with your *fingers.* If you have to push with something, the thing to push with is a crust of bread. And chew —chew! Animals have sections in their stomachs which enable them to digest food without mastication, but human beings are supposed to chew their food before they swallow it down. Eat food leisurely, son, and really

---

[1] A town in northern Spain bombed by the Germans in 1937 during the Spanish Civil War and the name of a famous painting by Picasso on the event.

* For playwright's explanation of screen legends see Production Notes following play.

[2] "Where are the Snows [of Yesteryear]," a famous line from a poem by the medieval French poet Villon (1431–1480?).

enjoy it. A well-cooked meal has lots of delicate flavors that have to be held in the mouth for appreciation. So chew your food and give your salivary glands a chance to function!

[TOM *deliberately lays his imaginary fork down and pushes his chair back from the table*]

TOM   I haven't enjoyed one bite of this dinner because of your constant directions on how to eat it. It's you that make me rush through meals with your hawk-like attention to every bite I take. Sickening—spoils my appetite— all this discussion of animals' secretion—salivary glands—mastication!

AMANDA   [*Lightly*]   Temperament like a Metropolitan star! [*He rises and crosses downstage*] You're not excused from the table.

TOM   I'm getting a cigarette.

AMANDA   You smoke too much.

[LAURA *rises*]

LAURA   I'll bring in the blanc mange.

[*He remains standing with his cigarette by the portieres during the following*]

AMANDA   [*Rising*]   No, sister, no, sister—you be the lady this time and I'll be the darky.

LAURA   I'm already up.

AMANDA   Resume your seat, little sister—I want you to stay fresh and pretty
    —for gentlemen callers!

LAURA   I'm not expecting any gentlemen callers.

AMANDA   [*Crossing out to kitchenette. Airily*]   Sometimes they come when they are least expected! Why, I remember one Sunday afternoon in Blue Mountain—[*Enters kitchenette*]

TOM   I know what's coming!

LAURA   Yes. But let her tell it.

TOM   Again?

LAURA   She loves to tell it.

[AMANDA *returns with bowl of dessert*]

AMANDA   One Sunday afternoon in Blue Mountain—your mother received— *seventeen!*—gentlemen callers! Why, sometimes there weren't chairs enough to accommodate them all. We had to send the nigger over to bring in folding chairs from the parish house.

TOM   [*Remaining at portieres*]   How did you entertain those gentlemen callers?

AMANDA   I understood the art of conversation!

TOM   I bet you could talk.

AMANDA   Girls in those days *knew* how to talk, I can tell you.

TOM   Yes?

[IMAGE: AMANDA AS A GIRL ON A PORCH, GREETING CALLERS]

AMANDA   They knew how to entertain their gentlemen callers. It wasn't enough for a girl to be possessed of a pretty face and a graceful figure— although I wasn't slighted in either respect. She also needed to have a nimble wit and a tongue to meet all occasions.

TOM   What did you talk about?

AMANDA   Things of importance going on in the world! Never anything coarse or common or vulgar. [*She addresses* TOM *as though he were seated in the vacant chair at the table though he remains by portieres. He plays this scene as though he held the book*] My callers were gentlemen—all! Among my callers were some of the most prominent young planters of the Mississippi Delta—planters and sons of planters!

[TOM *motions for music and a spot of light on* AMANDA]

[*Her eyes lift, her face glows, her voice becomes rich and elegiac*]

[*SCREEN LEGEND: "OÙ SONT LES NEIGES"*]

There was young Champ Laughlin who later became vice-president of the Delta Planters Bank. Hadley Stevenson who was drowned in Moon Lake and left his widow one hundred and fifty thousand in Government bonds. There were the Cutrere brothers, Wesley and Bates. Bates was one of my bright particular beaux! He got in a quarrel with that wild Wainwright boy. They shot it out on the floor of Moon Lake Casino. Bates was shot through the stomach. Died in the ambulance on his way to Memphis. His widow was also well-provided for, came into eight or ten thousand acres, that's all. She married him on the rebound—never loved her—carried my picture on him the night he died! And there was that boy that every girl in the Delta had set her cap for! That beautiful, brilliant young Fitzhugh boy from Greene County!

TOM   What did he leave his widow?

AMANDA   He never married! Gracious, you talk as though all of my old admirers had turned up their toes to the daisies!

TOM   Isn't this the first you've mentioned that still survives?

AMANDA   That Fitzhugh boy went North and made a fortune—came to be known as the Wolf of Wall Street! He had the Midas touch, whatever he touched turned to gold! And I could have been Mrs. Duncan J. Fitzhugh, mind you! But—I picked your *father*!

LAURA   [*Rising*]   Mother, let me clear the table.

AMANDA   No, dear, you go in front and study your typewriter chart. Or practice your shorthand a little. Stay fresh and pretty!—It's almost time for our gentlemen callers to start arriving. [*She flounces girlishly toward the kitchenette*] How many do you suppose we're going to entertain this afternoon?

[TOM *throws down the paper and jumps up with a groan*]

LAURA   [*Alone in the dining room*]   I don't believe we're going to receive any, Mother.

AMANDA   [*Reappearing, airily*]   What? No one—not one? You must be joking! [LAURA *nervously echoes her laugh. She slips in a fugitive manner through the half-open portieres and draws them gently behind her. A shaft of very clear light is thrown on her face against the faded tapestry of the curtains. MUSIC: "THE GLASS MENAGERIE" UNDER FAINTLY. Lightly*] Not one gentleman caller? It can't be true! There must be a flood, there must have been a tornado!

LAURA   It isn't a flood, it's not a tornado, Mother. I'm just not popular like you were in Blue Mountain. . . . [TOM *utters another groan.* LAURA *glances at him with a faint, apologetic smile. Her voice catching a little*] Mother's afraid I'm going to be an old maid.

THE SCENE DIMS OUT WITH "GLASS MENAGERIE" MUSIC

SCENE TWO

"*Laura, Haven't You Ever Liked Some Boy?*"
On the dark stage the screen is lighted with the image of blue roses.
Gradually LAURA'S *figure becomes apparent and the screen goes out.*

The music subsides.
LAURA *is seated in the delicate ivory chair at the small claw-foot table.*
She wears a dress of soft violet material for a kimono—her hair tied back from her forehead with a ribbon.
She is washing and polishing her collection of glass.
AMANDA *appears on the fire-escape steps. At the sound of her ascent,* LAURA *catches her breath, thrusts the bowl of ornaments away and seats herself stiffly before the diagram of the typewriter keyboard as though it held her spellbound. Something has happened to* AMANDA. *It is written in her face as she climbs to the landing: a look that is grim and hopeless and a little absurd.*
She has on one of those cheap or imitation velvety-looking cloth coats with imitation fur collar. Her hat is five or six years old, one of those dreadful cloche hats that were worn in the late twenties and she is clasping an enormous black patent-leather pocketbook with nickel clasps and initials. This is her full-dress outfit, the one she usually wears to the D.A.R.
Before entering she looks through the door.
She purses her lips, opens her eyes wide, rolls them upward and shakes her head.
Then she slowly lets herself in the door. Seeing her mother's expression LAURA *touches her lips with a nervous gesture.*

LAURA   Hello, Mother, I was—[*She makes a nervous gesture toward the chart on the wall.* AMANDA *leans against the shut door and stares at* LAURA *with a martyred look*]

AMANDA   Deception? Deception? [*She slowly removes her hat and gloves, continuing the sweet suffering stare. She lets the hat and gloves fall on the floor—a bit of acting*]

LAURA   [*Shakily*]   How was the D.A.R. meeting? [AMANDA *slowly opens her purse and removes a dainty white handkerchief which she shakes out delicately and delicately touches to her lips and nostrils*] Didn't you go to the D.A.R. meeting, Mother?

AMANDA   [*Faintly, almost inaudibly*]—No.—No. [*Then more forcibly*] I did not have the strength—to go to the D.A.R. In fact, I did not have the courage! I wanted to find a hole in the ground and hide myself in it forever!
[*She crosses slowly to the wall and removes the diagram of the typewriter keyboard. She holds it in front of her for a second, staring at it sweetly and sorrowfully—then bites her lips and tears it in two pieces*]

LAURA   [*Faintly*]   Why did you do that, Mother? [AMANDA *repeats the same procedure with the chart of the Gregg Alphabet*] Why are you—

AMANDA   Why? Why? How old are you, Laura?

LAURA   Mother, you know my age.

AMANDA   I thought that you were an adult; it seems that I was mistaken.
[*She crosses slowly to the sofa and sinks down and stares at* LAURA]

LAURA   Please don't stare at me, Mother.
[AMANDA *closes her eyes and lowers her head. Count ten*]

AMANDA   What are we going to do, what is going to become of us, what is the future?
[*Count ten*]

LAURA   Has something happened, Mother? [AMANDA *draws a long breath and takes out the handkerchief again. Dabbing process*] Mother, has—something happened?

AMANDA I'll be all right in a minute. I'm just bewildered—[*Count five*]—by life. . . .

LAURA Mother, I wish that you would tell me what's happened!

AMANDA As you know, I was supposed to be inducted into my office at the D.A.R. this afternoon. *IMAGE: A SWARM OF TYPEWRITERS.* But I stopped off at Rubicam's Business College to speak to your teachers about your having a cold and ask them what progress they thought you were making down there.

LAURA Oh. . . .

AMANDA I went to the typing instructor and introduced myself as your mother. She didn't know who you were. Wingfield, she said. We don't have any such student enrolled at the school! I assured her she did, that you had been going to classes since early in January. "I wonder," she said, "if you could be talking about that terribly shy little girl who dropped out of school after only a few days' attendance?" "No," I said, "Laura, my daughter, has been going to school every day for the past six weeks!" "Excuse me," she said. She took the attendance book out and there was your name, unmistakably printed, and all the dates you were absent until they decided that you had dropped out of school. I still said, "No, there must have been some mistake! There must have been some mix-up in the records!" And she said, "No— I remember her perfectly now. Her hands shook so that she couldn't hit the right keys! The first time we gave a speed-test, she broke down completely—was sick at the stomach and almost had to be carried into the washroom! After that morning she never showed up any more. We phoned the house but never got any answer"—while I was working at Famous and Barr,[3] I suppose, demonstrating those—Oh! I felt so weak I could barely keep on my feet! I had to sit down while they got me a glass of water! Fifty dollars' tuition, all of our plans—my hopes and ambitions for you— just gone up the spout, just gone up the spout like that. [LAURA *draws a long breath and gets awkwardly to her feet. She crosses to the victrola and winds it up*] What are you doing?

LAURA Oh! [*She releases the handle and returns to her seat*]

AMANDA Laura, where have you been going when you've gone out pretending that you were going to business college?

LAURA I've just been going out walking.

AMANDA That's not true.

LAURA It is. I just went walking.

AMANDA Walking? Walking? In winter? Deliberately courting pneumonia in that light coat? Where did you walk to, Laura?

LAURA All sorts of places—mostly in the park.

AMANDA Even after you'd started catching that cold?

LAURA It was the lesser of two evils, Mother. [*IMAGE: WINTER SCENE IN PARK*] I couldn't go back up. I—threw up—on the floor!

AMANDA From half past seven till after five every day you mean to tell me you walked around in the park, because you wanted to make me think that you were still going to Rubicam's Business College?

LAURA It wasn't as bad as it sounds. I went inside places to get warmed up.

AMANDA Inside where?

LAURA I went in the art museum and the bird-houses at the Zoo. I visited the penguins every day! Sometimes I did without lunch and went to the movies.

---

[3] A St. Louis department store.

Lately I've been spending most of my afternoons in the Jewel-box, that big glass house where they raise the tropical flowers.

AMANDA   You did all this to deceive me, just for deception? [LAURA *looks down*] Why?

LAURA   Mother, when you're disappointed, you get that awful suffering look on your face, like the picture of Jesus' mother in the museum!

AMANDA   Hush!

LAURA   I couldn't face it.

[*Pause. A whisper of strings*]

[LEGEND: "THE CRUST OF HUMILITY"]

AMANDA   [*Hopelessly fingering the huge pocketbook*]   So what are we going to do the rest of our lives? Stay home and watch the parades go by? Amuse ourselves with the glass menagerie, darling? Eternally play those worn-out phonograph records your father left as a painful reminder of him? We won't have a business career—we've given that up because it gave us nervous indigestion! [*Laughs wearily*] What is there left but dependency all our lives? I know so well what becomes of unmarried women who aren't prepared to occupy a position. I've seen such pitiful cases in the South—barely tolerated spinsters living upon the grudging patronage of sister's husband or brother's wife!—stuck away in some little mouse-trap of a room—encouraged by one in-law to visit another—little birdlike women without any nest—eating the crust of humility all their life! Is that the future that we've mapped out for ourselves? I swear it's the only alternative I can think of! It isn't a very pleasant alternative, is it? Of course—some girls *do marry*. [LAURA *twists her hands nervously*] Haven't you ever liked some boy?

LAURA   Yes. I liked one once. [*Rises*] I came across his picture a while ago.

AMANDA   [*With some interest*]   He gave you his picture?

LAURA   No, it's in the year-book.

AMANDA   [*Disappointed*]   Oh—a high-school boy.

[SCREEN IMAGE: JIM AS HIGH-SCHOOL HERO BEARING A SILVER CUP]

LAURA   Yes. His name was Jim. [LAURA *lifts the heavy annual from the claw-foot table*] Here he is in *The Pirates of Penzance*.[4]

AMANDA   [*Absently*]   The what?

LAURA   The operetta the senior class put on. He had a wonderful voice and we sat across the aisle from each other Mondays, Wednesdays and Fridays in the Aud. Here he is with the silver cup for debating! See his grin?

AMANDA   [*Absently*]   He must have had a jolly disposition.

LAURA   He used to call me—Blue Roses.

[IMAGE: BLUE ROSES]

AMANDA   Why did he call you such a name as that?

LAURA   When I had that attack of pleurosis—he asked me what was the matter when I came back. I said pleurosis—he thought that I said Blue Roses! So that's what he always called me after that. Whenever he saw me, he'd holler, "Hello, Blue Roses!" I didn't care for the girl that he went out with. Emily Meisenbach. Emily was the best-dressed girl at Soldan. She never struck me,

---

[4] An operetta by Gilbert and Sullivan (1879).

though, as being sincere . . . It says in the Personal Section—they're en-engaged. That's—six years ago! They must be married by now.

AMANDA Girls that aren't cut out for business careers usually wind up married to some nice man. [*Gets up with a spark of revival*] Sister, that's what you'll do!

[LAURA *utters a startled, doubtful laugh. She reaches quickly for a piece of glass*]

LAURA But, Mother—

AMANDA Yes? [*Crossing to photograph*]

LAURA [*In a tone of frightened apology*] I'm—crippled!

[*IMAGE: SCREEN*]

AMANDA Nonsense! Laura, I've told you never, never to use that word. Why, you're not crippled, you just have a little defect—hardly noticeable, even! When people have some slight disadvantage like that, they cultivate other things to make up for it—develop charm—and vivacity—and—*charm!* That's all you have to do! [*She turns again to the photograph*] One thing your father had *plenty of*—was *charm!*

[TOM *motions to the fiddle in the wings*]

THE SCENE FADES OUT WITH MUSIC

SCENE THREE

[*LEGEND ON SCREEN: "AFTER THE FIASCO—"*]

[TOM *speaks from the fire-escape landing*]

TOM After the fiasco at Rubicam's Business College, the idea of getting a gentleman caller for Laura began to play a more important part in Mother's calculations. It became an obsession. Like some archetype of the universal unconscious, the image of the gentleman caller haunted our small apartment. . . . [*IMAGE: YOUNG MAN AT DOOR WITH FLOWERS*] An evening at home rarely passed without some allusion to this image, this spectre, this hope. . . . Even when he wasn't mentioned, his presence hung in Mother's preoccupied look and in my sister's frightened, apologetic manner—hung like a sentence passed upon the Wingfields! Mother was a woman of action as well as words. She began to take logical steps in the planned direction. Late that winter and in the early spring—realizing that extra money would be needed to properly feather the nest and plume the bird— she conducted a vigorous campaign on the telephone, roping in subscribers to one of those magazines for matrons called *The Homemaker's Companion*, the type of journal that features the serialized sublimations of ladies of letters who think in terms of delicate cup-like breasts, slim, tapering waists, rich, creamy thighs, eyes like wood-smoke in autumn, fingers that soothe and caress like strains of music, bodies as powerful as Etruscan sculpture.

[*SCREEN IMAGE: GLAMOR MAGAZINE COVER*]

[AMANDA *enters with phone on long extension cord. She is spotted in the dim stage*]

AMANDA Ida Scott? This is Amanda Wingfield! We *missed* you at the D.A.R.

last Monday! I said to myself: She's probably suffering with that sinus condition! How is that sinus condition? Horrors! Heaven have mercy!—You're a Christian martyr, yes, that's what you are, a Christian martyr! Well, I just now happened to notice that your subscription to the *Companion*'s about to expire! Yes, it expires with the next issue, honey!—just when that wonderful new serial by Bessie Mae Hopper is getting off to such an exciting start. Oh, honey, it's something that you can't miss! You remember how *Gone With the Wind* [5] took everybody by storm? You simply couldn't go out if you hadn't read it. All everybody *talked* was Scarlett O'Hara. Well, this is a book that critics already compare to *Gone With the Wind*. It's the *Gone With the Wind* of the post-World War generation!—What?—Burning? —Oh, honey, don't let them burn, go take a look in the oven and I'll hold the wire! Heavens—I think she's hung up!

DIM OUT

[LEGEND ON SCREEN: "YOU THINK I'M IN LOVE
WITH CONTINENTAL SHOEMAKERS?"]

[Before the stage is lighted, the violent voices of TOM *and* AMANDA *are heard]*

[They are quarreling behind the portieres. In front of them stands LAURA *with clenched hands and panicky expression]*

[A clear pool of light on her figure throughout this scene]
TOM   What in Christ's name am I—
AMANDA   *[Shrilly]*   Don't you use that—
TOM   Supposed to do!
AMANDA   Expression! Not in my—
TOM   Ohhh!
AMANDA   Presence! Have you gone out of your senses?
TOM   I have, that's true, *driven* out!
AMANDA   What is the matter with you, you—big—big—IDIOT!
TOM   Look—I've got *no thing,* no single thing—
AMANDA   Lower your voice!
TOM   In my life here that I can call my OWN! Everything is—
AMANDA   Stop that shouting!
TOM   Yesterday you confiscated my books! You had the nerve to—
AMANDA   I took that horrible novel back to the library—yes! That hideous book by that insane Mr. Lawrence. [6] *[*TOM *laughs wildly]* I cannot control the output of diseased minds or people who cater to them—*[*TOM *laughs still more wildly]* BUT I WON'T ALLOW SUCH FILTH BROUGHT INTO MY HOUSE! No, no, no, no, no!
TOM   House, house! Who pays rent on it, who makes a slave of himself to—
AMANDA   *[Fairly screeching]*   Don't you DARE to—
TOM   No, no, I mustn't say things! *I've* got to just—
AMANDA   Let me tell you—
TOM   I don't want to hear any more! *[He tears the portieres open. The upstage area is lit with a turgid smoky red glow]*
   *[*AMANDA's *hair is in metal curlers and she wears a very old bathrobe, much too large for her slight figure, a relic of the faithless Mr. Wingfield]*

---

[5] An extremely popular novel by Margaret Mitchell (1936).
[6] D. H. Lawrence (1885–1930), English poet and novelist.

[*An upright typewriter and a wild disarray of manuscripts is on the drop-leaf table. The quarrel was probably precipitated by* AMANDA'*s interruption of his creative labor. A chair lying overthrown on the floor*]

[*Their gesticulating shadows are cast on the ceiling by the fiery glow*]

AMANDA   You *will* hear more, you—

TOM   No, I won't hear more, I'm going out!

AMANDA   You come right back in—

TOM   Out, out out! Because I'm—

AMANDA   Come back here, Tom Wingfield! I'm not through talking to you!

TOM   Oh, go—

LAURA   [*Desperately*]—Tom!

AMANDA   You're going to listen, and no more insolence from you! I'm at the end of my patience! [*He comes back toward her*]

TOM   What do you think I'm at? Aren't I suppose to have any patience to reach the end of, Mother? I know, I know. It seems unimportant to you, what I'm *doing*—what I *want* to do—having a little *difference* between them! You don't think that—

AMANDA   I think you've been doing things that you're ashamed of. That's why you act like this. I don't believe that you go every night to the movies. Nobody goes to the movies night after night. Nobody in their right minds goes to the movies as often as you pretend to. People don't go to the movies at nearly midnight, and movies don't let out at two A.M. Come in stumbling. Muttering to yourself like a maniac! You get three hours' sleep and then go to work. Oh, I can picture the way you're doing down there. Moping, doping, because you're in no condition.

TOM   [*Wildly*]   No, I'm in no condition!

AMANDA   What right have you got to jeopardize your job? Jeopardize the security of us all? How do you think we'd manage if you were—

TOM   Listen! You think I'm crazy *about* the *warehouse*? [*He bends fiercely toward her slight figure*] You think I'm in love with the Continental Shoe-makers? You think I want to spend fifty-five *years* down there in that—*celotex interior!* with—*fluorescent—tubes!* Look! I'd rather somebody picked up a crowbar and battered out my brains—than go back mornings! I *go!* Every time you come in yelling that God damn *"Rise and Shine!" "Rise and Shine!"* I say to myself, "How *lucky dead* people are!" But I get up. I *go!* For sixty-five dollars a month I give up all that I dream of doing and being *ever!* And you say self—*self's* all I ever think of. Why, listen, if self is what I thought of, Mother, I'd be where he is—GONE! [*Pointing to father's picture*] As far as the system of transportation reaches! [*He starts past her. She grabs his arm*] Don't grab at me, Mother!

AMANDA   Where are you going?

TOM   I'm going to the *movies!*

AMANDA   I don't believe that lie!

TOM   [*Crouching toward her, overtowering her tiny figure. She backs away, gasping*]   I'm going to opium dens! Yes, opium dens, dens of vice and crimi-nals' hang-outs, Mother. I've joined the Hogan gang, I'm a hired assassin, I carry a Tommy gun in a violin case! I run a string of cat-houses in the Val-ley! They call me Killer, Killer Wingfield, I'm leading a double-life, a sim-ple, honest warehouse worker by day, by night, a dynamic *czar* of the *un-derworld, Mother.* I go to gambling casinos, I spin away fortunes on the roulette table! I wear a patch over one eye and a false mustache, sometimes I put on green whiskers. On those occasions they call me—*El Diablo!* Oh, I could tell you things to make you sleepless! My enemies plan to dynamite this place. They're going to blow us all sky-high some night! I'll be glad, very happy, and so will you! You'll go up, up on a broomstick, over Blue Mountain with seventeen gentlemen callers! You ugly—babbling old—witch. . . . [*He goes through a series of violent, clumsy movements, seizing his overcoat, lunging to the door, pulling it fiercely open. The women watch him, aghast. His arm catches in the sleeve of the coat as he struggles to pull it on. For a moment he is pinioned by the bulky garment. With an outraged groan he tears the coat off again, splitting the shoulder of it, and hurls it across the room. It strikes against the shelf of* LAURA'S *glass collection, there is a tinkle of shattering glass.* LAURA *cries out as if wounded*]

[MUSIC LEGEND: "THE GLASS MENAGERIE"]

LAURA   [*Shrilly*]   My glass!—menagerie. . . . [*She covers her face and turns away*]
[*But* AMANDA *is still stunned and stupefied by the "ugly witch" so that she barely notices this occurrence. Now she recovers her speech*]
AMANDA   [*In an awful voice*]   I won't speak to you—until you apologize!
[*She crosses through portieres and draws them together behind her.* TOM *is left with* LAURA. LAURA *clings weakly to the mantel with her face averted.* TOM *stares at her stupidly for a moment. Then he crosses to shelf. Drops awkwardly on his knees to collect the fallen glass, glancing at* LAURA *as if he would speak but couldn't*]

"*The Glass Menagerie*" steals in as

THE SCENE DIMS OUT

SCENE FOUR

The interior is dark. Faint light in the alley.
A deep-voiced bell in a church is tolling the hour of five as the scene commences.
TOM *appears at the top of the alley. After each solemn boom of the bell in the tower, he shakes a little noise-maker or rattle as if to express the tiny spasm of man in contrast to the sustained power and dignity of the Almighty. This and the unsteadiness of his advance make it evident that he has been drinking.*
As he climbs the few steps to the fire-escape landing light steals up inside. LAURA *appears in nightdress, observing* TOM'S *empty bed in the front room.*
TOM *fishes in his pockets for door key, removing a motley assortment of articles in the search, including a perfect shower of movie-ticket stubs and an empty bottle. At last he finds the key, but just as he is about to insert it, it slips from his fingers. He strikes a match and crouches below the door.*

TOM   [*Bitterly*]   One crack—and it falls through!
[LAURA *opens the door.*]
LAURA   Tom! Tom, what are you doing?
TOM   Looking for a door key.
LAURA   Where have you been all this time?

TOM   I have been to the movies.

LAURA   All this time at the movies?

TOM   There was a very long program. There was a Garbo picture and a Mickey Mouse and a travelogue and a newsreel and a preview of coming attractions. And there was an organ solo and a collection for the milk-fund—simultaneously—which ended up in a terrible fight between a fat lady and an usher!

LAURA   [*Innocently*]   Did you have to stay through everything?

TOM   Of course! And, oh, I forgot! There was a big stage show! The headliner on this stage show was Malvolio the Magician. He performed wonderful tricks, many of them, such as pouring water back and forth between pitchers. First it turned to wine and then it turned to beer and then it turned to whiskey. I know it was whiskey it finally turned into because he needed somebody to come up out of the audience to help him, and I came up—both shows! It was Kentucky Straight Bourbon. A very generous fellow, he gave souvenirs. [*He pulls from his back pocket a shimmering rainbow-colored scarf*] He gave me this. This is his magic scarf. You can have it, Laura. You wave it over a canary cage and you get a bowl of goldfish. You wave it over the goldfish bowl and they fly away canaries. . . . But the wonderfullest trick of all was the coffin trick. We nailed him into a coffin and he got out of the coffin without removing one nail. [*He has come inside*] There is a trick that would come in handy for me—get me out of this 2 by 4 situation! [*Flops onto bed and starts removing shoes*]

LAURA   Tom—Shhh!

TOM   What're you shushing me for?

LAURA   You'll wake up Mother.

TOM   Goody, goody! Pay 'er back for all those "Rise an' Shines." [*Lies down, groaning*] You know it don't take much intelligence to get yourself into a nailed-up coffin, Laura. But who in hell ever got himself out of one without removing one nail?

[*As if in answer, the father's grinning photograph lights up*]

SCENE DIMS OUT

[*Immediately following: The church bell is heard striking six. At the sixth stroke the alarm clock goes off in* AMANDA's *room, and after a few moments we hear her calling: "Rise and Shine! Rise and Shine! Laura, go tell your brother to rise and shine!"*]

TOM   [*Sitting up slowly*]   I'll rise—but I won't shine.

[*The light increases*]

AMANDA   Laura, tell your brother his coffee is ready.

[LAURA *slips into front room*]

LAURA   Tom it's nearly seven. Don't make Mother nervous. [*He stares at her stupidly. Beseechingly*] Tom, speak to Mother this morning. Make up with her, apologize, speak to her!

TOM   She won't to me. It's her that started not speaking.

LAURA   If you just say you're sorry she'll start speaking.

TOM   Her not speaking—is that such a tragedy?

LAURA   Please—please!

AMANDA   [*Calling from kitchenette*]   Laura, are you going to do what I asked you to do, or do I have to get dressed and go out myself?

LAURA   Going, going—soon as I get on my coat! [*She pulls on a shapeless felt hat with nervous, jerky movement, pleadingly glancing at* TOM. *Rushes awkwardly for coat. The coat is one of* AMANDA's, *inaccurately made-over, the sleeves too short for* LAURA] Butter and what else?

AMANDA   [*Entering upstage*]   Just butter. Tell them to charge it.

LAURA   Mother, they make such faces when I do that.

AMANDA   Sticks and stones can break our bones, but the expression on Mr. Garfinkel's face won't harm us! Tell your brother his coffee is getting cold.

LAURA   [*At door*]   Do what I asked you, will you, will you, Tom?

[*He looks sullenly away*]

AMANDA   Laura, go now or just don't go at all!

LAURA   [*Rushing out*]   Going—going! [*A second later she cries out.* TOM *springs up and crosses to door.* AMANDA *rushes anxiously in.* TOM *opens the door*]

TOM   Laura?

LAURA   I'm all right. I slipped, but I'm all right.

AMANDA   [*Peering anxiously after her*]   If anyone breaks a leg on those fire-escape steps, the landlord ought to be sued for every cent he possesses! [*She shuts door. Remembers she isn't speaking and returns to other room.*]

[*As* TOM *enters listlessly for his coffee, she turns her back to him and stands rigidly facing the window on the gloomy gray vault of the areaway. Its light on her face with its aged but childish features is cruelly sharp, satirical as a Daumier print*]

[*MUSIC UNDER: "AVE MARIA"*]

[*Tom glances sheepishly but sullenly at her averted figure and slumps at the table. The coffee is scalding hot; he sips it and gasps and spits it back in the cup. At his gasp,* AMANDA *catches her breath and half turns. Then catches herself and turns back to window*]

[TOM *blows on his coffee, glancing sidewise at his mother. She clears her throat.* TOM *clears his. He starts to rise. Sinks back down again, scratches his head, clears his throat again.* AMANDA *coughs.* TOM *raises his cup in both hands to blow on it, his eyes staring over the rim of it at his mother for several moments. Then he slowly sets the cup down and awkwardly and hesitantly rises from the chair*]

TOM   [*Hoarsely*]   Mother. I—I apologize, Mother. [AMANDA *draws a quick, shuddering breath. Her face works grotesquely. She breaks into childlike tears*] I'm sorry for what I said, for everything that I said, I didn't mean it.

AMANDA   [*Sobbingly*]   My devotion has made me a witch and so I make myself hateful to my children!

TOM   No, you *don't.*

AMANDA   I worry so much, don't sleep, it makes me nervous!

TOM   [*Gently*]   I understand that.

AMANDA   I've had to put up a solitary battle all these years. But you're my right-hand bower! Don't fall down, don't fail!

TOM   [*Gently*]   I try, Mother.

AMANDA   [*With great enthusiasm*]   Try and you will SUCCEED!

[*The notion makes her breathless*] Why, you—you're just *full* of natural endowments! Both of my children—they're *unusual* children! Don't you think I know it? I'm so—*proud!* Happy and—feel I've—so much to be thankful for but—Promise me one thing, son!

TOM   What, Mother?

AMANDA   Promise, son, you'll—never be a drunkard!

TOM   [*Turns to her grinning*]   I will never be a drunkard, Mother.

AMANDA   That's what frightened me so, that you'd be drinking! Eat a bowl of Purina!

TOM   Just coffee, Mother.

AMANDA   Shredded wheat biscuit?

TOM   No. No, Mother, just coffee.

AMANDA   You can't put in a day's work on an empty stomach. You've got ten minutes—don't gulp! Drinking too-hot liquids makes cancer of the stomach. . . . Put cream in.

TOM   No, thank you.

AMANDA   To cool it.

TOM   No! No, thank you, I want it black.

AMANDA   I know, but it's not good for you. We have to do all that we can to build ourselves up. In these trying times we live in, all that we have to cling to is—each other. . . . That's why it's so important to—Tom, I—I sent out your sister so I could discuss something with you. If you hadn't spoken I would have spoken to you. [*Sits down*]

TOM   [*Gently*]   What is it, Mother, that you want to discuss?

AMANDA   *Laura!*

[TOM *puts his cup down slowly*]

[LEGEND ON SCREEN: "LAURA"]

[MUSIC: "THE GLASS MENAGERIE"]

TOM   —Oh.—Laura . . .

AMANDA   [*Touching his sleeve*]   You know how Laura is. So quiet but—still water runs deep! She notices things and I think she—broods about them. [TOM *looks up*] A few days ago I came in and she was crying.

TOM   What about?

AMANDA   You.

TOM   Me?

AMANDA   She has an idea that you're not happy here.

TOM   What gave her that idea?

AMANDA   What gives her any idea? However, you do act strangely. I—I'm not criticizing, understand *that!* I know your ambitions do not lie in the ware-house, that like everybody in the whole wide world—you've had to—make sacrifices, but—Tom—Tom—life's not easy, it calls for—Spartan endurance! There's so many things in my heart that I cannot describe to you! I've never told you but I—*loved* your father. . . .

TOM   [*Gently*]   I know that, Mother.

AMANDA   And you—when I see you taking after his ways! Staying out late—and—well, you *had* been drinking the night you were in that—terrifying condition! Laura says that you hate the apartment and that you go out nights to get away from it! Is that true, Tom?

TOM   No. You say there's so much in your heart that you can't describe to me. That's true of me, too. There's so much in my heart that I can't describe to *you!* So let's respect each other's—

AMANDA   But, why—*why,* Tom—are you always so *restless?* Where do you *go* to, nights?

TOM   I—go to the movies.

AMANDA   Why do you go to the movies so much, Tom?

TOM   I go to the movies because—I like adventure. Adventure is something I don't have much of at work, so I go to the movies.

AMANDA   But, Tom, you go to the movies *entirely* too *much!*

TOM   I like a lot of adventure.

[AMANDA *looks baffled, then hurt. As the familiar inquisition resumes he becomes hard and impatient again.* AMANDA *slips back into her querulous attitude toward him*]

[*IMAGE ON SCREEN: SAILING VESSEL WITH JOLLY ROGER*]

AMANDA   Most young men find adventure in their careers.

TOM   Then most young men are not employed in a warehouse.

AMANDA   The world is full of young men employed in warehouses and offices and factories.

TOM   Do all of them find adventure in their careers?

AMANDA   They do or they do without it! Not everybody has a craze for adventure.

TOM   Man is by instinct a lover, a hunter, a fighter, and none of those instincts are given much play at the warehouse!

AMANDA   Man is by instinct! Don't quote instinct to me! Instinct is something that people have got away from! It belongs to animals! Christian adults don't want it!

TOM   What do Christian adults want, then, Mother?

AMANDA   Superior things! Things of the mind and the spirit! Only animals have to satisfy instincts! Surely your aims are somewhat higher than theirs! Than monkeys—pigs—

TOM   I reckon they're not.

AMANDA   You're joking. However, that isn't what I wanted to discuss.

TOM   [*rising*]   I haven't much time.

AMANDA   [*Pushing his shoulders*]   Sit down.

TOM   You want me to punch in red at the warehouse, Mother?

AMANDA   You have five minutes. I want to talk about Laura.

[*LEGEND: "PLANS AND PROVISIONS"*]

TOM   All right! What about Laura?

AMANDA   We have to be making plans and provisions for her. She's older than you, two years, and nothing has happened. She just drifts along doing nothing. It frightens me terribly how she just drifts along.

TOM   I guess she's the type that people call home girls.

AMANDA   There's no such type, and if there is, it's a pity! That is unless the home is hers, with a husband!

TOM   What?

AMANDA   Oh, I can see the handwriting on the wall as plain as I see the nose in front of my face! It's terrifying! More and more you remind me of your father! He was out all hours without explanation—Then *left! Good-bye!* And me with the bag to hold. I saw that letter you got from the Merchant Marine. I know what you're dreaming of. I'm not standing here blindfolded. Very well, then. Then *do* it! But not till there's somebody to take your place.

TOM   What do you mean?

AMANDA   I mean that as soon as Laura has got somebody to take care of her, married, a home of her own, independent—why, then you'll be free to go wherever you please, on land, on sea, whichever way the wind blows you! But until that time you've got to look out for your sister. I don't say me because I'm old and don't matter! I say for your sister because she's young and dependent! I put her in business college—a dismal failure! Frightened her so it made her sick to her stomach. I took her over to the Young People's League at the church. Another fiasco. She spoke to nobody, nobody spoke to her. Now all she does is fool with those pieces of glass and play those wornout records. What kind of a life is that for a girl to lead?

TOM   What can I do about it?

AMANDA   Overcome selfishness! Self, self, self is all that you ever think of!

[TOM *springs up and crosses to get his coat. It is ugly and bulky. He pulls on a cap with earmuffs*] Where is your muffler? Put your wool muffler on! [*He snatches it angrily from the closet and tosses it around his neck and pulls both ends tight*] Tom! I haven't said what I had in mind to ask you.

TOM I'm too late to—

AMANDA [*Catching his arm—very importunately. Then shyly*] Down at the warehouse, aren't there some—nice young men?

TOM No!

AMANDA There *must* be—*some* . . .

TOM Mother—
[*Gesture*]

AMANDA Find out one that's clean-living—doesn't drink and—ask him out for Sister!

TOM What?

AMANDA For *Sister!* To *meet! Get acquainted!*

TOM [*Stamping to door*] Oh, my go-osh!

AMANDA Will you? [*He opens door. Imploringly*] Will you? [*He starts down*] Will you? *Will* you, dear?

TOM [*Calling back*] YES!

[AMANDA *closes the door hesitantly and with a troubled but faintly hopeful expression*]

[*SCREEN IMAGE: GLAMOR MAGAZINE COVER*]

[*Spot* AMANDA *at phone*]

AMANDA Ella Cartwright? This is Amanda Wingfield! How are you, honey? How is that kidney condition? [*Count five*] Horrors! [*Count five*] You're a Christian martyr, yes, honey, that's what you are, a Christian martyr! Well, I just happened to notice in my little red book that your subscription to the *Companion* has just run out! I knew that you wouldn't want to miss out on the wonderful serial starting in this new issue. It's by Bessie Mae Hopper, the first thing she's written since *Honeymoon for Three.* Wasn't that a strange and interesting story? Well, this one is even lovelier, I believe. It has a sophisticated, society background. It's all about the horsey set on Long Island!

FADE OUT

SCENE FIVE

[*LEGEND ON SCREEN: "ANNUNCIATION." Fade with music.*]

> It is early dusk of a spring evening. Supper has just been finished in the Wingfield apartment. AMANDA and LAURA *in light-colored dresses are removing dishes from the table, in the upstage area, which is shadowy, their movements formalized almost as a dance or ritual, their moving forms as pale and silent as moths.*
> TOM, *in white shirt and trousers, rises from the table and crosses toward the fire-escape.*

AMANDA [*As he passes her*] Son, will you do me a favor?

TOM What?

AMANDA   Comb your hair! You look so pretty when your hair is combed! [TOM *slouches on sofa with evening paper. Enormous caption "Franco Triumphs"*] There is only one respect in which I would like you to emulate your father.

TOM   What respect is that?

AMANDA   The care he always took of his appearance. He never allowed himself to look untidy. [*He throws down the paper and crosses to fire-escape*] Where are you going?

TOM   I'm going out to smoke.

AMANDA   You smoke too much. A pack a day at fifteen cents a pack. How much would that amount to in a month? Thirty times fifteen is how much, Tom? Figure it out and you will be astounded at what you could save. Enough to give you a night-school course in accounting at Washington U! Just think what a wonderful thing that would be for you, son!

[TOM *is unmoved by the thought*]

TOM   I'd rather smoke. [*He steps out on landing, letting the screen door slam*]

AMANDA   [*Sharply*]   I know! That's the tragedy of it. . . . [*Alone, she turns to look at her husband's picture*]

[*DANCE MUSIC: "ALL THE WORLD IS WAITING FOR THE SUNRISE!"*]

TOM   [*To the audience*]   Across the alley from us was the Paradise Dance Hall. On evenings in spring the windows and doors were open and the music came outdoors. Sometimes the lights were turned out except for a large glass sphere that hung from the ceiling. It would turn slowly about and filter the dusk with delicate rainbow colors. Then the orchestra played a waltz or a tango, something that had a slow and sensuous rhythm. Couples would come outside, to the relative privacy of the alley. You could see them kissing behind ash-pits and telephone poles. This was the compensation for lives that passed like mine, without any change or adventure. Adventure and change were imminent in this year. They were waiting around the corner for all these kids. Suspended in the mist over Berchtesgaden,[7] caught in the folds of Chamberlain's umbrella [8]—In Spain there was Guernica! But here there was only hot swing music and liquor, dance halls, bars, and movies, and sex that hung in the gloom like a chandelier and flooded the world with brief, deceptive rainbows. . . . All the world was waiting for bombardments!

[AMANDA *turns from the picture and comes outside*]

AMANDA   [*Sighing*]   A fire-escape landing's a poor excuse for a porch. [*She spreads a newspaper on a step and sits down, gratefully and demurely as if she were settling into a swing on a Mississippi veranda*] What are you looking at?

TOM   The moon.

AMANDA   Is there a moon this evening?

TOM   It's rising over Garfinkel's Delicatessen.

AMANDA   So it is! A little silver slipper of a moon. Have you made a wish on it yet?

TOM   Um-hum.

AMANDA   What did you wish for?

TOM   That's a secret.

AMANDA   A secret, huh? Well, I won't tell mine either. I will be just as mysterious as you.

---

[7] Hitler's mountain retreat in southern Bavaria.

[8] A popular symbol of Sir Neville Chamberlain, British Prime Minister in the late thirties who was known as an appeaser of Hitler.

TOM   I bet I can guess what yours is.

AMANDA   Is my head so transparent?

TOM   You're not a sphinx.

AMANDA   No, I don't have secrets. I'll tell you what I wished for on the moon. Success and happiness for my precious children! I wish for that whenever there's a moon, and when there isn't a moon, I wish for it, too.

TOM   I thought perhaps you wished for a gentleman caller.

AMANDA   Why do you say that?

TOM   Don't you remember asking me to fetch one?

AMANDA   I remember suggesting that it would be nice for your sister if you brought home some nice young man from the warehouse. I think that I've made that suggestion more than once.

TOM   Yes, you have made it repeatedly.

AMANDA   Well?

TOM   We are going to have one.

AMANDA   *What?*

TOM   A gentleman caller!

THE ANNUNCIATION IS CELEBRATED WITH MUSIC

[AMANDA *rises*]

[IMAGE ON SCREEN: CALLER WITH BOUQUET]

AMANDA   You mean you have asked some nice young man to come over?

TOM   Yep. I've asked him to dinner.

AMANDA   You really did?

TOM   I did!

AMANDA   You did, and did he—*accept?*

TOM   He did!

AMANDA   Well, well—well, well! That's—lovely!

TOM   I thought that you would be pleased.

AMANDA   It's definite, then?

TOM   Very definite.

AMANDA   Soon?

TOM   Very soon.

AMANDA   For heaven's sake, stop putting on and tell me some things, will you?

TOM   What things do you want me to tell you?

AMANDA   *Naturally* I would like to know when he's *coming!*

TOM   He's coming tomorrow.

AMANDA   *Tomorrow?*

TOM   Yep. Tomorrow.

AMANDA   But, Tom!

TOM   Yes, Mother?

AMANDA   Tomorrow gives me no time!

TOM   Time for what?

AMANDA   Preparations! Why didn't you phone me at once, as soon as you asked him, the minute that he accepted? Then, don't you see, I could have been getting ready!

TOM   You don't have to make any fuss.

AMANDA   Oh, Tom, Tom, Tom, of course I have to make a fuss! I want things nice, not sloppy! Not thrown together. I'll certainly have to do some fast thinking, won't I?

TOM   I don't see why you have to think at all.

AMANDA   You just don't know. We can't have a gentleman caller in a pigsty! All my wedding silver has to be polished, the monogrammed table linen ought to be laundered! The windows have to be washed and fresh curtains put up. And how about clothes? We have to *wear* something, don't we?

TOM   Mother, this boy is no one to make a fuss over!

AMANDA   Do you realize he's the first young man we've introduced to your sister? It's terrible, dreadful, disgraceful that poor little sister has never received a single gentleman caller! Tom, come inside! [*She opens the screen door*]

TOM   What for?

AMANDA   I want to ask you some things.

TOM   If you're going to make such a fuss, I'll call it off, I'll tell him not to come!

AMANDA   You certainly won't do anything of the kind. Nothing offends people worse than broken engagements. It simply means I'll have to work like a Turk! We won't be brilliant, but we will pass inspection. Come on inside. [TOM *follows, groaning*] Sit down.

TOM   Any particular place you would like me to sit?

AMANDA   Thank heavens I've got that new sofa! I'm also making payments on a floor lamp I'll have sent out! And put the chintz covers on, they'll brighten things up! Of course I'd hoped to have these walls re-papered. . . . What is the young man's name?

TOM   His name is O'Connor.

AMANDA   That, of course, means fish—tomorrow is Friday! I'll have that salmon loaf—with Durkee's dressing! What does he do? He works at the warehouse?

TOM   Of course! How else would I—

AMANDA   Tom, he—doesn't drink?

TOM   Why do you ask me that?

AMANDA   Your father *did!*

TOM   Don't get started on that!

AMANDA   He *does* drink, then?

TOM   Not that I know of!

AMANDA   Make sure, be certain! The last thing I want for my daughter's a boy who drinks!

TOM   Aren't you being a little bit premature? Mr. O'Connor has not yet appeared on the scene!

AMANDA   But will tomorrow. To meet your sister, and what do I know about his character? Nothing! Old maids are better off than wives of drunkards!

TOM   Oh, my God!

AMANDA   Be still!

TOM   [*Leaning forward to whisper*]   Lots of fellows meet girls whom they don't marry!

AMANDA   Oh, talk sensibly, Tom—and don't be sarcastic! [*She has gotten a hairbrush*]

TOM   What are you doing?

AMANDA   I'm brushing that cow-lick down! What is this young man's position at the warehouse?

TOM   [*Submitting grimly to the brush and the interrogation*]   This young man's position is that of a shipping clerk, Mother.

AMANDA   Sounds to me like a fairly responsible job, the sort of a job *you* would be in if you just had more *get-up*. What is his salary? Have you any idea?

TOM   I would judge it to be approximately eighty-five dollars a month.

AMANDA   Well—not princely, but—

TOM   Twenty more than I make.

AMANDA   Yes, how well I know! But for a family man, eighty-five dollars a month is not much more than you can just get by on. . . .

TOM   Yes, but Mr. O'Connor is not a family man.

AMANDA   He might be, mightn't he? Some time in the future?

TOM   I see. Plans and provisions.

AMANDA   You are the only young man that I know of who ignores the fact that the future becomes the present, the present the past, and the past turns into everlasting regret if you don't plan for it!

TOM   I will think that over and see what I can make of it.

AMANDA   Don't be supercilious with your mother! Tell me some more about this —what do you call him?

TOM   James D. O'Connor. The D. is for Delaney.

AMANDA   Irish on *both* sides! *Gracious!* And doesn't drink?

TOM   Shall I call him up and ask him right this minute?

AMANDA   The only way to find out about those things is to make discreet inquiries at the proper moment. When I was a girl in Blue Mountain and it was suspected that a young man drank, the girl whose attentions he had been receiving, if any girl *was*, would sometimes speak to the minister of his church, or rather her father would if her father was living, and sort of feel him out on the young man's character. That is the way such things are discreetly handled to keep a young woman from making a tragic mistake!

TOM   Then how did you happen to make a tragic mistake?

AMANDA   That innocent look of your father's had everyone fooled! He *smiled,* the world was *enchanted!* No girl can do worse than put herself at the mercy of a handsome appearance! I hope that Mr. O'Connor is not too good-looking.

TOM   No, he's not too good-looking. He's covered with freckles and hasn't too much of a nose.

AMANDA   He's not right-down homely, though?

TOM   Not right-down homely. Just medium homely, I'd say.

AMANDA   Character's what to look for in a man.

TOM   That's what I've always said, Mother.

AMANDA   You've never said anything of the kind and I suspect you would never give it a thought.

TOM   Don't be so suspicious of me.

AMANDA   At least I hope he's the type that's up and coming.

TOM   I think he really goes in for self-improvement.

AMANDA   What reason have you to think so?

TOM   He goes to night school.

AMANDA   [*Beaming*]   Splendid! What does he do, I mean study?

TOM   Radio engineering and public speaking!

AMANDA   Then he has visions of being advanced in the world! Any young man who studies public speaking is aiming to have an executive job some day! And radio engineering? A thing for the future! Both of these facts are very illuminating. Those are the sort of things that a mother should know concerning any young man who comes to call on her daughter. Seriously or—not.

TOM   One little warning. He doesn't know about Laura. I didn't let on that we had dark ulterior motives. I just said, why don't you come and have dinner with us? He said okay and that was the whole conversation.

AMANDA   I bet it was! You're eloquent as an oyster. However, he'll know about Laura when he gets here. When he sees how lovely and sweet and pretty she is, he'll thank his lucky stars he was asked to dinner.

TOM   Mother, you mustn't expect too much of Laura.

AMANDA   What do you mean?

TOM   Laura seems all those things to you and me because she's ours and we love her. We don't even notice she's crippled any more.

AMANDA   Don't say crippled! You know that I never allow that word to be used!
TOM   But face facts, Mother. She is and—that's not all—
AMANDA   What do you mean "not all"?
TOM   Laura is very different from other girls.
AMANDA   I think the difference is all to her advantage.
TOM   Not quite all—in the eyes of others—strangers—she's terribly shy and lives in a world of her own and those things make her seem a little peculiar to people outside the house.
AMANDA   Don't say peculiar.
TOM   Face the facts. She is.

THE DANCE-HALL MUSIC CHANGES TO A TANGO THAT HAS A MINOR
AND SOMEWHAT OMINOUS TONE

AMANDA   In what way is she peculiar—may I ask?
TOM   [*Gently*]   She lives in a world of her own—a world of—little glass ornaments, Mother. . . . [*Gets up.* AMANDA *remains holding brush, looking at him, troubled*] She plays old phonograph records and—that's about all—[*He glances at himself in the mirror and crosses to door*]
AMANDA   [*Sharply*]   Where are you going?
TOM   I'm going to the movies. [*Out screen door*]
AMANDA   Not to the movies, every night to the movies! [*Follows quickly to screen door*] I don't believe you always go to the movies! [*He is gone.* AMANDA *looks worriedly after him for a moment. Then vitality and optimism return and she turns from the door. Crossing to portieres*] Laura! Laura! [LAURA *answers from kitchenette*]
LAURA   Yes, Mother.
AMANDA   Let those dishes go and come in front! [LAURA *appears with dish towel. Gaily*] Laura, come here and make a wish on the moon!
LAURA   [*Entering*]   Moon—moon?
AMANDA   A little silver slipper of a moon. Look over your left shoulder, Laura, and make a wish! [LAURA *looks faintly puzzled as if called out of sleep.* AMANDA *seizes her shoulders and turns her at an angle by the door*] No! Now, darling, *wish!*
LAURA   What shall I wish for, Mother?
AMANDA   [*Her voice trembling and her eyes suddenly filling with tears*]   Happiness! Good Fortune!
[*The violin rises and the stage dims out*]

SCENE SIX

[*IMAGE: HIGH SCHOOL HERO*]

TOM   And so the following evening I brought Jim home to dinner. I had known Jim slightly in high school. In high school Jim was a hero. He had tremendous Irish good nature and vitality with the scrubbed and polished look of white chinaware. He seemed to move in a continual spotlight. He was a star in basketball, captain of the debating club, president of the senior class and the glee club and he sang the male lead in the annual light operas. He was always running or bounding, never just walking. He seemed always at the point of defeating the law of gravity. He was shooting with such velocity through his adolescence that you would logically expect him to arrive at nothing short of the White House by the time he was thirty. But Jim apparently ran into more interference after his graduation from Soldan. His speed had definitely slowed. Six years after he left high school he was holding a job that wasn't much better than mine.

[IMAGE: CLERK]

He was the only one at the warehouse with whom I was on friendly terms. I was valuable to him as someone who could remember his former glory, who had seen him win basketball games and the silver cup in debating. He knew of my secret practice of retiring to a cabinet of the washroom to work on poems when business was slack in the warehouse. He called me Shakespeare. And while the other boys in the warehouse regarded me with suspicious hostility, Jim took a humorous attitude toward me. Gradually his attitude affected the others, their hostility wore off and they also began to smile at me as people smile at an oddly fashioned dog who trots across their path at some distance.

I knew that Jim and Laura had known each other at Soldan, and I had heard Laura speak admiringly of his voice. I didn't know if Jim remembered her or not. In high school Laura had been as unobtrusive as Jim had been astonishing. If he did remember Laura, it was not as my sister, for when I asked him to dinner, he grinned and said, "You know, Shakespeare, I never thought of you as having folks!"

He was about to discover that I did. . . .

LIGHT UP STAGE

[*LEGEND ON SCREEN: "THE ACCENT OF A COMING FOOT"*]

[*Friday evening. It is about five o'clock of a late spring evening which comes "scattering poems in the sky"*]

[*A delicate lemony light is in the Wingfield apartment*]

[AMANDA *has worked like a Turk in preparation for the gentleman caller. The results are astonishing. The new floor lamp with its rose-silk shade is in place, a colored paper lantern conceals the broken light fixture in the ceiling, new billowing white curtains are at the windows, chintz covers are on chairs and sofa, a pair of new sofa pillows make their initial appearance*]

[*Open boxes and tissue paper are scattered on the floor*]

[LAURA *stands in the middle with lifted arms while* AMANDA *crouches before her, adjusting the hem of the new dress, devout and ritualistic. The dress is colored and designed by memory. The arrangement of* LAURA's *hair is changed; it is softer and more becoming. A fragile, unearthly prettiness has come out in* LAURA: *she is like a piece of translucent glass touched by light, given a momentary radiance, not actual, not lasting*]

AMANDA [*Impatiently*] Why are you trembling?
LAURA Mother, you've made me so nervous!
AMANDA How have I made you nervous?
LAURA By all this fuss! You make it seem so important!
AMANDA I don't understand you, Laura. You couldn't be satisfied with just

sitting home, and yet whenever I try to arrange something for you, you seem to resist it. [*She gets up*] Now take a look at yourself. No, wait! Wait just a moment—I have an idea!

LAURA   What is it now?

[AMANDA *produces two powder puffs which she wraps in handkerchiefs and stuffs in* LAURA'*s bosom*]

LAURA   Mother, what are you doing?

AMANDA   They call them "Gay Deceivers"!

LAURA   I won't wear them!

AMANDA   You will!

LAURA   Why should I?

AMANDA   Because, to be painfully honest, your chest is flat.

LAURA   You make it seem like we were setting a trap.

AMANDA   All pretty girls are a trap, a pretty trap, and men expect them to be.

[*LEGEND: "A PRETTY TRAP."*] Now look at yourself, young lady. This is the prettiest you will ever be! I've got to fix myself now! You're going to be surprised by your mother's appearance! [*She crosses through portieres, humming gaily*]

[LAURA *moves slowly to the long mirror and stares solemnly at herself*]

[*A wind blows the white curtains inward in a slow, graceful motion and with a faint, sorrowful sighing*]

AMANDA   [*Off stage*]   It isn't dark enough yet. [*She turns slowly before the mirror with a troubled look.*]

[*LEGEND ON SCREEN: "THIS IS MY SISTER: CELEBRATE HER WITH STRINGS!" MUSIC.*]

AMANDA   [*Laughing, off*]   I'm going to show you something. I'm going to make a spectacular appearance!

LAURA   What is it, Mother?

AMANDA   Possess your soul in patience—you will see! Something I've resurrected from that old trunk! Styles haven't changed so terribly much after all. . . . [*She parts the portieres*] Now just look at your mother! [*She wears a girlish frock of yellowed voile with a blue silk sash. She carries a bunch of jonquils —the legend of her youth is nearly revived. Feverishly*] This is the dress in which I led the cotillion. Won the cakewalk twice at Sunset Hill, wore one spring to the Governor's ball in Jackson! See how I sashayed around the ballroom, Laura? [*She raises her skirt and does a mincing step around the room*] I wore it on Sundays for my gentlemen callers! I had it on the day I met your father—I had malaria fever all that spring. The change of climate from East Tennessee to the Delta [9]—weakened resistance—I had a little temperature all the time—not enough to be serious—just enough to make me restless and giddy! Invitations poured in—parties all over the Delta!—"Stay in bed," said Mother, "you have fever!"—but I just wouldn't.—I took quinine but kept on going, going!—Evenings, dances!—Afternoons, long, long rides! Picnics—lovely!—So lovely, that country in May.—All lacy with dogwood, literally flooded with jonquils!—That was the spring I had the craze for jonquils. Jonquils became an absolute obsession. Mother said, "Honey, there's no more room for jonquils." And still I kept on bringing in more jonquils. Whenever, wherever I saw them, I'd say, "Stop! Stop! I see jon-

---

[9] The rich cotton-growing area of the state of Mississippi.

quils!" I made the young men help me gather the jonquils! It was a joke, Amanda and her jonquils! Finally there were no more vases to hold them, every available space was filled with jonquils. No vases to hold them? All right, I'll hold them myself! And then I—[*She stops in front of the picture.* MUSIC] met your father! Malaria fever and jonquils and then—this—boy. . . . [*She switches on the rose-colored lamp*] I hope they get here before it starts to rain. [*She crosses upstage and places the jonquils in bowl on table*] I gave your brother a little extra change so he and Mr. O'Connor could take the service car home.

LAURA   [*With altered look*]   What did you say his name was?

AMANDA   O'Connor.

LAURA   What is his first name?

AMANDA   I don't remember. Oh, yes, I do. It was—Jim!

    [LAURA *sways slightly and catches hold of a chair*]

[*LEGEND ON SCREEN: "NOT JIM!"*]

LAURA   [*Faintly*]   Not—Jim!

AMANDA   Yes, that was it, it was Jim! I've never known a Jim that wasn't nice!

[*MUSIC: OMINOUS*]

LAURA   Are you sure his name is Jim O'Connor?

AMANDA   Yes. Why?

LAURA   Is he the one that Tom used to know in high school?

AMANDA   He didn't say so. I think he just got to know him at the warehouse.

LAURA   There was a Jim O'Connor we both knew in high school—[*Then, with effort*] If that is the one that Tom is bringing to dinner—you'll have to excuse me, I won't come to the table.

AMANDA   What sort of nonsense is this?

LAURA   You asked me once if I'd ever liked a boy. Don't you remember I showed you this boy's picture?

AMANDA   You mean the boy you showed me in the year book?

LAURA   Yes, that boy.

AMANDA   Laura, Laura, were you in love with that boy?

LAURA   I don't know, Mother. All I know is I couldn't sit at the table if it was him!

AMANDA   It won't be him! It isn't the least bit likely. But whether it is or not, you will come to the table. You will not be excused.

LAURA   I'll have to be, Mother.

AMANDA   I don't intend to humor your silliness. Laura. I've had too much from you and your brother, both! So just sit down and compose yourself till they come. Tom has forgotten his key so you'll have to let them in, when they arrive.

LAURA   [*Panicky*]   Oh, Mother—*you* answer the door!

AMANDA   [*Lightly*]   I'll be in the kitchen—busy!

LAURA   Oh, Mother, please answer the door, don't make me do it!

AMANDA   [*Crossing into kitchenette*]   I've got to fix the dressing for the salmon. Fuss, fuss—silliness!—over a gentleman caller!

    [*Door swings shut.* LAURA *is left alone*]

[*LEGEND: "TERROR!"*]

[*She utters a low moan and turns off the lamp—sits stiffly on the edge of the sofa, knotting her fingers together*]

[*LEGEND ON SCREEN: "THE OPENING OF A DOOR!"*]

[TOM *and* JIM *appear on the fire-escape steps and climb to landing. Hearing their approach,* LAURA *rises with a panicky gesture. She retreats to the portieres*]

[*The doorbell.* LAURA *catches her breath and touches her throat. Low drums*]

AMANDA   [*Calling*]   Laura, sweetheart! The door!
    [LAURA *stares at it without moving*]
JIM   I think we just beat the rain.
TOM   Uh-huh. [*He rings again, nervously.* JIM *whistles and fishes for a cigarette*]
AMANDA   [*Very, very gaily*]   Laura, that is your brother and Mr. O'Connor! Will you let them in, darling?
    [LAURA *crosses toward kitchenette door*]
LAURA   [*Breathlessly*]   Mother—you go to the door!
    [AMANDA *steps out of kitchenette and stares furiously at* LAURA. *She points imperiously at the door*]
LAURA   Please, please!
AMANDA   [*In a fierce whisper*]   What is the matter with you, you silly thing?
LAURA   [*Desperately*]   Please, you answer it, *please!*
AMANDA   I told you I wasn't going to humor you, Laura. Why have you chosen this moment to lose your mind?
LAURA   Please, please, please, you go!
AMANDA   You'll have to go to the door because I can't!
LAURA   [*Despairingly*]   I can't either!
AMANDA   *Why?*
LAURA   I'm *sick!*
AMANDA   I'm sick, too—of your nonsense! Why can't you and your brother be normal people? Fantastic whims and behavior! [TOM *gives a long ring.*] Preposterous goings on! Can you give me one reason—[*Calls out lyrically*] COMING! JUST ONE SECOND!—why you should be afraid to open a door? Now you answer it, Laura!
LAURA   Oh, oh, oh . . . [*She returns through the portieres. Darts to the victrola and winds it frantically and turns it on*]
AMANDA   Laura Wingfield, you march right to that door!
LAURA   Yes—yes, Mother!
    [*A faraway, scratchy rendition of "Dardanella" softens the air and gives her strength to move through it. She slips to the door and draws it cautiously open*]

[TOM *enters with the caller,* JIM O'CONNOR]
TOM   Laura, this is Jim. Jim, this is my sister, Laura.
JIM   [*Stepping inside*]   I didn't know that Shakespeare had a sister!
LAURA   [*Retreating stiff and trembling from the door*]   How—how do you do?
JIM   [*Heartily extending his hand*]   Okay!
    [LAURA *touches it hesitantly with hers*]
JIM   Your hand's *cold,* Laura!
LAURA   Yes, well—I've been playing the victrola. . . .
JIM   Must have been playing classical music on it! You ought to play a little hot swing music to warm you up!
LAURA   Excuse me—I haven't finished playing the victrola. . . .

[*She turns awkwardly and hurries into the front room. She pauses a second by the victrola. Then catches her breath and darts through the portieres like a frightened deer*]

JIM [*Grinning*] What was the matter?

TOM Oh—with Laura? Laura is—terribly shy.

JIM Shy, huh? It's unusual to meet a shy girl nowadays. I don't believe you ever mentioned you had a sister.

TOM Well, now you know. I have one. Here is the *Post Dispatch*. You want a piece of it?

JIM Uh-huh.

TOM What piece? The comics?

JIM Sports! [*Glances at it*] Ole Dizzy Dean [10] is on his bad behavior.

TOM [*Disinterest*] Yeah? [*Lights cigarette and crosses back to fire-escape door*]

JIM Where are *you* going?

TOM I'm going out on the terrace.

JIM [*Goes after him*] You know, Shakespeare—I'm going to sell you a bill of goods!

TOM What goods?

JIM A course I'm taking.

TOM Huh?

JIM In public speaking! You and me, we're not the warehouse type.

TOM Thanks—that's good news. But what has public speaking got to do with it?

JIM It fits you for—executive positions!

TOM Awww.

JIM I tell you it's done a helluva lot for me.

[*IMAGE: EXECUTIVE AT DESK*]

TOM In what respect?

JIM In every! Ask yourself what is the difference between you an' me and men in the office down front? Brains?—No!—Ability?—No! Then what? Just one little thing—

TOM What is that one little thing?

JIM Primarily it amounts to—social poise! Being able to square up to people and hold your own on any social level!

AMANDA [*Off stage*] Tom?

TOM Yes, Mother?

AMANDA Is that you and Mr. O'Connor?

TOM Yes, Mother?

AMANDA Well, you just make yourselves comfortable in there.

TOM Yes, Mother.

AMANDA Ask Mr. O'Connor if he would like to wash his hands.

JIM Aw, no—no—thank you—I took care of that at the warehouse. Tom—

TOM Yes?

JIM Mr. Mendoza was speaking to me about you.

TOM Favorably?

JIM What do you think?

TOM Well—

JIM You're going to be out of a job if you don't wake up.

TOM I am waking up—

JIM You show no signs.

TOM The signs are interior.

[10] A well-known baseball pitcher of the St. Louis Cardinals.

[IMAGE ON SCREEN: THE SAILING VESSEL WITH
JOLLY ROGER AGAIN]

TOM   I'm planning to change. [*He leans over the rail speaking with quiet exhilaration. The incandescent marquees and signs of the first-run movie houses light his face from across the alley. He looks like a voyager*] I'm right at the point of committing myself to a future that doesn't include the warehouse and Mr. Mendoza or even a night-school course in public speaking.

JIM   What are you gassing about?

TOM   . I'm tired of the movies.

JIM   Movies!

TOM   Yes, movies! Look at them—[*A wave toward the marvels of Grand Avenue*] All of those glamorous people—having adventures—hogging it all, globbling the whole thing up! You know what happens? People go to the *movies* instead of *moving!* Hollywood characters are supposed to have all the adventures for everybody in America, while everybody in America sits in a dark room and watches them have them! Yes, until there's a war. That's when adventure becomes available to the masses! *Everyone's* dish, not only Gable's! [11] Then the people in the dark room come out of the dark room to have some adventures themselves—Goody, goody!—It's our turn now, to go to the South Sea Island—to make a safari—to be exotic, far-off!—But I'm not patient. I don't want to wait till then. I'm tired of the *movies* and I am *about* to *move!*

JIM   [*Incredulously*]   Move?

TOM   Yes.

JIM   When?

TOM   Soon!

JIM   Where? Where?

[THEME THREE MUSIC SEEMS TO ANSWER THE QUESTION,
WHILE TOM THINKS IT OVER. HE SEARCHES AMONG
HIS POCKETS]

TOM   I'm starting to boil inside. I know I seem dreamy, but inside—well, I'm boiling! Whenever I pick up a shoe, I shudder a little thinking how short life is and what I am doing!—Whatever that means, I know it doesn't mean shoes—except as something to wear on a traveler's feet! [*Finds paper*] Look—

JIM   What?

TOM   I'm a member.

JIM   [*Reading*]   The Union of Merchant Seamen.

TOM   I paid my dues this month, instead of the light bill.

JIM   You will regret it when they turn the lights off.

TOM   I won't be here.

JIM   How about your mother?

TOM   I'm like my father. The bastard son of a bastard! See how he grins? And he's been absent going on sixteen years!

JIM   You're just talking, you drip. How does your mother feel about it?

TOM   Shhh!—Here comes Mother! Mother is not acquainted with my plans!

AMANDA   [*Enters portieres*]   Where are you all?

TOM   On the terrace, Mother.

---

[11] Clark Gable, well-known motion picture actor.

[*They start inside. She advances to them.* TOM *is distinctly shocked at her appearance. Even* JIM *blinks a little. He is making his first contact with girlish Southern vivacity and in spite of the night-school course in public speaking is somewhat thrown off the beam by the unexpected outlay of social charm*]

[*Certain responses are attempted by* JIM *but are swept aside by* AMANDA'S *gay laughter and chatter.* TOM *is embarrassed but after the first shock* JIM *reacts very warmly. Grins and chuckles, is altogether won over*]

[*IMAGE: AMANDA AS A GIRL*]

AMANDA [*Coyly smiling, shaking her girlish ringlets*] Well, well, well, so this is Mr. O'Connor. Introductions entirely unnecessary. I've heard so much about you from my boy. I finally said to him, Tom—good gracious! —why don't you bring this paragon to supper? I'd like to meet this nice young man at the warehouse!—Instead of just hearing him sing your praises so much! I don't know why my son is so standoffish—that's not Southern behavior! Let's sit down and—I think we could stand a little more air in here! Tom, leave the door open. I felt a nice fresh breeze a moment ago. Where has it gone to? Mmm, so warm already! And not quite summer, even. We're going to burn up when summer really gets started. However, we're having—we're having a very light supper. I think light things are better fo' this time of year. The same as light clothes are. Light clothes an' light food are what warm weather calls fo'. You know our blood gets so thick during th' winter—it takes a while fo' us to *adjust* ou'selves!—when the season changes . . . It's come so quick this year. I wasn't prepared. All of a sudden—heavens! Already summer!—I ran to the trunk an' pulled out this light dress—Terribly old! Historical almost! But feels so good—so good an' co-ol, y'know. . . .

TOM Mother—

AMANDA Yes, honey?

TOM How about—supper?

AMANDA Honey, you go ask Sister if supper is ready! You know that Sister is in full charge of supper! Tell her you hungry boys are waiting for it. [*To* JIM] Have you met Laura?

JIM She—

AMANDA Let you in? Oh, good, you've met already! It's rare for a girl as sweet an' pretty as Laura to be domestic! But Laura is, thank heavens, not only pretty but also very domestic. I'm not at all. I never was a bit. I never could make a thing but angel-food cake. Well, in the South we had so many servants. Gone, gone, gone. All vestige of gracious living! Gone completely! I wasn't prepared for what the future brought me. All of my gentlemen callers were sons of planters and so of course I assumed that I would be married to one and raise my family on a large piece of land with plenty of servants. But man proposes—and woman accepts the proposal! —To vary that old, old saying a little bit—I married no planter! I married a man who worked for the telephone company!—That gallantly smiling gentleman over there! [*Points to the picture*] A telephone man who—fell in love with long-distance!—Now he travels and I don't even know where! —But what am I going on for about my—tribulations? Tell me yours—I hope you don't have any! Tom?

TOM [*Returning*] Yes, Mother?

AMANDA Is supper nearly ready?

TOM It looks to me like supper is on the table.

AMANDA Let me look—[*She rises prettily and looks through portieres*] Oh, lovely!—But where is Sister?

TOM Laura is not feeling well and she says that she thinks she'd better not come to the table.

AMANDA What?—Nonsense!—Laura? Oh, Laura!

LAURA [*Off stage, faintly*] Yes, Mother.

AMANDA You really must come to the table. We won't be seated until you come to the table! Come in, Mr. O'Connor. You sit over there, and I'll— Laura? Laura Wingfield! You're keeping us waiting, honey! We can't say grace until you come to the table!

[*The back door is pushed weakly open and* LAURA *comes in. She is obviously quite faint, her lips trembling, her eyes wide and staring. She moves unsteadily toward the table*]

[LEGEND: "TERROR!"]

[*Outside a summer storm is coming abruptly. The white curtains billow inward at the windows and there is a sorrowful murmur and deep blue dusk*]

[LAURA *suddenly stumbles—she catches at a chair with a faint moan*]

TOM Laura!

AMANDA Laura! [*There is a clap of thunder*] [*LEGEND: "AH!"*] [*Despairingly*] Why, Laura, you *are* sick, darling! Tom, help your sister into the living room, dear! Sit in the living room, Laura—rest on the sofa. Well! [*To the gentleman caller*] Standing over the hot stove made her ill!—I told her that it was just too warm this evening, but—[TOM *comes back in.* LAURA *is on the sofa*] Is Laura all right now?

TOM Yes.

AMANDA What *is* that? Rain? A nice cool rain has come up! [*She gives the gentleman caller a frightened look*] I think we may—have grace—now . . . [TOM *looks at her stupidly*] Tom, honey—you say grace!

TOM Oh . . . "For these and all thy mercies—" [*They bow their heads,* AMANDA *stealing a nervous glance at* JIM. *In the living room* LAURA, *stretched on the sofa, clenches her hand to her lips, to hold back a shuddering sob*] God's Holy Name be praised—

THE SCENE DIMS OUT

SCENE SEVEN

A SOUVENIR.

Half an hour later. Dinner is just being finished in the upstage area which is concealed by the drawn portieres.

As the curtain rises LAURA *is still huddled upon the sofa, her feet drawn under her, her head resting on a pale blue pillow, her eyes wide and mysteriously watchful. The new floor lamp with its shade of rose-colored silk gives a soft, becoming light to her face, bringing out the fragile, unearthly prettiness which*

usually escapes attention. There is a steady murmur of rain,
but it is slackening and stops soon after the scene begins; the
air outside becomes pale and luminous as the moon breaks out.
A moment after the curtain rises, the lights in both rooms
flicker and go out.

JIM   Hey, there, Mr. Light Bulb!
[AMANDA *laughs nervously*]

[*LEGEND: "SUSPENSION OF A PUBLIC SERVICE"*]

AMANDA   Where was Moses when the lights went out? Ha-ha. Do you know
the answer to that one, Mr. O'Connor?
JIM   No, Ma'am, what's the answer?
AMANDA   In the dark! [JIM *laughs appreciatively*] Everybody sit still. I'll light
the candles. Isn't it lucky we have them on the table? Where's a match?
Which of you gentlemen can provide a match?
JIM   Here.
AMANDA   Thank you, sir.
JIM   Not at all, Ma'am!
AMANDA   I guess the fuse has burnt out. Mr. O'Connor, can you tell a burnt-
out fuse? I know I can't and Tom is a total loss when it comes to me-
chanics. [*SOUND: GETTING UP: VOICES RECEDE A LITTLE TO
KITCHENETTE*] Oh, be careful you don't bump into something. We
don't want our gentleman caller to break his neck. Now wouldn't that be
a fine howdy-do?
JIM   Ha-ha! Where is the fuse-box?
AMANDA   Right here next to the stove. Can you see anything?
JIM   Just a minute.
AMANDA   Isn't electricity a mysterious thing? Wasn't it Benjamin Franklin
who tied a key to a kite? We live in such a mysterious universe, don't we?
Some people say that science clears up all the mysteries for us. In my
opinion it only creates more! Have you found it yet?
JIM   No, Ma'am. All these fuses look okay to me.
AMANDA   Tom!
TOM   Yes, Mother?
AMANDA   That light bill I gave you several days ago. The one I told you we
got the notices about?
TOM   Oh—Yeah.

[*LEGEND: "HA!"*]

AMANDA   You didn't neglect to pay it by any chance?
TOM   Why, I—
AMANDA   Didn't! I might have known it!
JIM   Shakespeare probably wrote a poem on that light bill, Mrs. Wingfield.
AMANDA   I might have known better than to trust him with it! There's such
a high price for negligence in this world!
JIM   Maybe the poem will win a ten dollar prize.
AMANDA   We'll just have to spend the remainder of the evening in the nine-
teenth century, before Mr. Edison made the Mazda lamp!
JIM   Candlelight is my favorite kind of light.
AMANDA   That shows you're romantic! But that's no excuse for Tom. Well,
we got through dinner. Very considerate of them to let us get through

dinner before they plunged us into everlasting darkness, wasn't it, Mr. O'Connor?

JIM   Ha-ha!

AMANDA   Tom, as a penalty for your carelessness you can help me with the dishes.

JIM   Let me give you a hand.

AMANDA   Indeed you will not!

JIM   I ought to be good for something.

AMANDA   Good for something? [*Her tone is rhapsodic*] You? Why, Mr. O'Connor, nobody, *nobody's* given me this much entertainment in years—as you have!

JIM   Aw, now, Mrs. Wingfield!

AMANDA   I'm not exaggerating, not one bit! But Sister is all by her lonesome. You go keep her company in the parlor! I'll give you this lovely old candelabrum that used to be on the altar at the church of the Heavenly Rest. It was melted a little out of shape when the church burnt down. Lightning struck it one spring. Gypsy Jones was holding a revival at the time and he intimated that the church was destroyed because the Episcopalians gave card parties.

JIM   Ha-ha.

AMANDA   And how about you coaxing Sister to drink a little wine? I think it would be good for her! Can you carry both at once?

JIM   Sure. I'm Superman!

AMANDA   Now, Thomas, get into this apron!

[*The door of kitchenette swings closed on* AMANDA's *gay laughter; the flickering light approaches the portieres*]

[LAURA *sits up nervously as he enters. Her speech at first is low and breathless from the almost intolerable strain of being alone with a stranger*]

[*THE LEGEND: "I DON'T SUPPOSE YOU REMEMBER ME AT ALL!"*]

[*In her first speeches in this scene, before* JIM's *warmth overcomes her paralyzing shyness,* LAURA's *voice is thin and breathless as though she has just run up a steep flight of stairs*]

[JIM's *attitude is gently humorous. In playing this scene it should be stressed that while the incident is apparently unimportant, it is to* LAURA *the climax of her secret life*]

JIM   Hello, there, Laura.

LAURA   [*Faintly*]   Hello. [*She clears her throat*]

JIM   How are you feeling now? Better?

LAURA   Yes. Yes, thank you.

JIM   This is for you. A little dandelion wine. [*He extends it toward her with extravagant gallantry*]

LAURA   Thank you.

JIM   Drink it—but don't get drunk! [*He laughs heartily.* LAURA *takes the glass uncertainly; laughs shyly*] Where shall I set the candles?

LAURA   Oh—oh, anywhere . . .

JIM   How about here on the floor? Any objections?

LAURA   No.

JIM   I'll spread a newspaper under to catch the drippings. I like to sit on the floor. Mind if I do?

LAURA   Oh, no.

JIM   Give me a pillow?

LAURA   What?

JIM   A pillow!

LAURA   Oh . . . [*Hands him one quickly*]

JIM   How about you? Don't you like to sit on the floor?

LAURA   Oh—yes.

JIM   Why don't you, then?

LAURA   I—will.

JIM   Take a pillow! [LAURA *does. Sits on the other side of the candelabrum.* JIM *crosses his legs and smiles engagingly at her*] I can't hardly see you sitting way over there.

LAURA   I can—see you.

JIM   I know, but that's not fair, I'm in the limelight. [LAURA *moves her pillow closer*] Good! Now I can see you! Comfortable?

LAURA   Yes.

JIM   So am I. Comfortable as a cow. Will you have some gum?

LAURA   No, thank you.

JIM   I think that I will indulge, with your permission. [*Musingly unwraps it and holds it up*] Think of the fortune made by the guy that invented the first piece of chewing gum. Amazing, huh? The Wrigley Building is one of the sights of Chicago.—I saw it summer before last when I went up to the Century of Progress.[12] Did you take in the Century of Progress?

LAURA   No, I didn't.

JIM   Well, it was quite a wonderful exposition. What impressed me most was the Hall of Science. Gives you an idea of what the future will be in America, even more wonderful than the present time is! [*Pause. Smiling at her*] Your brother tells me you're shy. Is that right, Laura?

LAURA   I—don't know.

JIM   I judge you to be an old-fashioned type of girl. Well, I think that's a pretty good type to be. Hope you don't think I'm being too personal—do you?

LAURA   [*Hastily, out of embarrassment*] I believe I *will* take a piece of gum, if you—don't mind. [*Clearing her throat*] Mr. O'Connor, have you—kept up with your singing?

JIM   Singing? Me?

LAURA   Yes. I remember what a beautiful voice you had.

JIM   When did you hear me sing?

[*VOICE OFF STAGE IN THE PAUSE*]

VOICE   [*Off stage*]

> O blow, ye winds, heigh-ho,
> A-roving I will go!
>   I'm off to my love
>   With a boxing glove—
> Ten thousand miles away!

JIM   You say you've heard me sing?

LAURA   Oh, yes! Yes, very often . . . I—don't suppose you remember me— at all?

JIM   [*Smiling doubtfully*] You know I have an idea I've seen you before. I

---

[12] The title given to the theme of the Chicago World's Fair of 1933.

had that idea soon as you opened the door. It seemed almost like I was about to remember your name. But the name that I started to call you—wasn't a name! And so I stopped myself before I said it.

LAURA   Wasn't it—Blue Roses?

JIM   [*Springs up. Grinning*] Blue Roses! My gosh, yes—Blue Roses! That's what I had on my tongue when you opened the door! Isn't it funny what tricks your memory plays? I didn't connect you with high school somehow or other. But that's where it was; it was high school. I didn't even know you were Shakespeare's sister! Gosh, I'm sorry.

LAURA   I didn't expect you to. You—barely knew me!

JIM   But we did have a speaking acquaintance, huh?

LAURA   Yes, we—spoke to each other.

JIM   When did you recognize me?

LAURA   Oh, right away!

JIM   Soon as I came in the door?

LAURA   When I heard your name I thought it was probably you. I knew that Tom used to know you a little in high school. So when you came in the door—Well, then I was—sure.

JIM   Why didn't you *say* something, then?

LAURA   [*Breathlessly*] I didn't know what to say, I was—too surprised!

JIM   For goodness' sakes! You know, this sure is funny!

LAURA   Yes! Yes, isn't it, though . . .

JIM   Didn't we have a class in something together?

LAURA   Yes, we did.

JIM   What class was that?

LAURA   It was—singing—Chorus!

JIM   Aw!

LAURA   I sat across the aisle from you in the Aud.

JIM   Aw.

LAURA   Mondays, Wednesdays and Fridays.

JIM   Now I remember—you always came in late.

LAURA   Yes, it was so hard for me, getting upstairs. I had that brace on my leg—it clumped so loud!

JIM   I never heard any clumping.

LAURA   [*Wincing at the recollection*] To me it sounded like—thunder!

JIM   Well, well, well, I never even noticed.

LAURA   And everybody was seated before I came in. I had to walk in front of all those people. My seat was in the back row. I had to go clumping all the way up the aisle with everyone watching!

JIM   You shouldn't have been self-conscious.

LAURA   I know, but I was. It was always such a relief when the singing started.

JIM   Aw, yes, I've placed you now! I used to call you Blue Roses. How was it that I got started calling you that?

LAURA   I was out of school a little while with pleurosis. When I came back you asked me what was the matter. I said I had pleurosis—you thought I said Blue Roses. That's what you always called me after that!

JIM   I hope you didn't mind.

LAURA   Oh, no—I liked it. You see, I wasn't acquainted with many—people. . . .

JIM   As I remember you sort of stuck by yourself.

LAURA   I—I—never have had much luck at—making friends.

JIM   I don't see why you wouldn't.

LAURA   Well, I—started out badly.

JIM   You mean being—

LAURA   Yes, it sort of—stood between me—

JIM   You shouldn't have let it!

LAURA   I know, but it did, and—

JIM   You were shy with people!

LAURA   I tried not to be but never could—

JIM   Overcome it?

LAURA   No, I—I never could!

JIM   I guess being shy is something you have to work out of kind of gradually.

LAURA   [Sorrowfully]   Yes—I guess it—

JIM   Takes time!

LAURA   Yes—

JIM   People are not so dreadful when you know them. That's what you have to remember! And everybody has problems, not just you, but practically everybody has got some problems. You think of yourself as having the only problems, as being the only one who is disappointed. But just look around you and you will see lots of people as disappointed as you are. For instance, I hoped when I was going to high school that I would be further along at this time, six years later, than I am now—You remember that wonderful write-up I had in the *Torch?*

LAURA   Yes! [*She rises and crosses to table*]

JIM   It said I was bound to succeed in anything I went into! [LAURA *returns with the annual*] Holy Jeez! The *Torch!*
      [*He accepts it reverently. They smile across it with mutual wonder.* LAURA *crouches beside him and they begin to turn through it.* LAURA'S *shyness is dissolving in his warmth*]

LAURA   Here you are in *Pirates of Penzance!*

JIM   [*Wistfully*]   I sang the baritone lead in that operetta.

LAURA   [*Rapidly*]   So—beautifully!

JIM   [*Protesting*]   Aw—

LAURA   Yes, yes—beautifully—beautifully!

JIM   You heard me?

LAURA   All three times!

JIM   No!

LAURA   Yes!

JIM   All three performances?

LAURA   [*Looking down*]   Yes.

JIM   Why?

LAURA   I—wanted to ask you to—autograph my program.

JIM   Why didn't you ask me to?

LAURA   You were always surrounded by your own friends so much that I never had a chance to.

JIM   You should have just—

LAURA   Well, I—thought you might think I was—

JIM   Thought I might think you was—what?

LAURA   Oh—

JIM   [*With reflective relish*]   I was beleaguered by females in those days.

LAURA   You were terribly popular!

JIM   Yeah—

LAURA   You had such a—friendly way—

JIM   I was spoiled in high school.

LAURA   Everybody—liked you!

JIM   Including you?

LAURA   I—yes, I—I did, too—[*She gently closes the book in her lap*]

JIM   Well, well, well!—Give me that program, Laura. [*She hands it to him.*

He signs it with a flourish] There you are—better late than never!

LAURA   Oh, I—what a—surprise!

JIM   My signature isn't worth very much right now. But some day—maybe—it will increase in value! Being disappointed is one thing and being discouraged is something else. I am disappointed but I am not discouraged. I'm twenty-three years old. How old are you?

LAURA   I'll be twenty-four in June.

JIM   That's not old age!

LAURA   No, but—

JIM   You finished high school?

LAURA   [*With difficulty*]   I didn't go back.

JIM   You mean you dropped out?

LAURA   I made bad grades in my final examinations. [*She rises and replaces the book and the program. Her voice strained*] How is—Emily Meisenbach getting along?

JIM   Oh, that kraut-head!

LAURA   Why do you call her that?

JIM   That's what she was.

LAURA   You're not still—going with her?

JIM   I never see her.

LAURA   It said in the Personal Section that you were—engaged!

JIM   I know, but I wasn't impressed by that—propaganda!

LAURA   It wasn't—the truth?

JIM   Only in Emily's optimistic opinion!

LAURA   Oh—

[LEGEND: "WHAT HAVE YOU DONE SINCE HIGH SCHOOL?"]

[JIM *lights a cigarette and leans indolently back on his elbows smiling at* LAURA *with a warmth and charm which lights her inwardly with altar candles. She remains by the table and turns in her hands a piece of glass to cover her tumult*]

JIM   [*After several reflective puffs on a cigarette*]   What have you done since high school? [*She seems not to hear him*] Huh? [LAURA *looks up*] I said what have you done since high school, Laura?

LAURA   Nothing much.

JIM   You must have been doing something these six long years.

LAURA   Yes.

JIM   Well, then, such as what?

LAURA   I took a business course at business college—

JIM   How did that work out?

LAURA   Well, not very—well—I had to drop out, it gave me—indigestion—[JIM *laughs gently*]

JIM   What are you doing now?

LAURA   I don't do anything—much. Oh, please don't think I sit around doing nothing! My glass collection takes up a good deal of time. Glass is something you have to take good care of.

JIM   What did you say—about glass?

LAURA   Collection I said—I have one—[*She clears her throat and turns away again, acutely shy*]

JIM   [*Abruptly*]   You know what I judge to be the trouble with you? Inferiority complex! Know what that is? That's what they call it when someone low-rates himself! I understand it because I had it, too. Although my case was not so aggravated as yours seems to be. I had it until I took up public speaking, developed my voice, and learned that I had an aptitude for science. Before that time I never thought of myself as being outstanding in any way whatsoever! Now I've never made a regular study of it, but I have a friend who says I can analyze people better than doctors that make a profession of it. I don't claim that to be necessarily true, but I can sure guess a person's psychology, Laura! [*Takes out his gum*] Excuse me, Laura. I always take it out when the flavor is gone. I'll use this scrap of paper to wrap it in. I know how it is to get it stuck on a shoe. Yep—that's what I judge to be your principal trouble. A lack of confidence in yourself as a person. You don't have the proper amount of faith in yourself. I'm basing that fact on a number of your remarks and also on certain observations I've made. For instance that clumping you thought was so awful in high school. You say that you even dreaded to walk into class. You see what you did? You dropped out of school, you gave up an education because of a clump, which as far as I know was practically non-existent! A little physical defect is what you have. Hardly noticeable even! Magnified thousands of times by imagination! You know what my strong advice to you is? Think of yourself as *superior* in some way?

LAURA   In what way would I think?

JIM   Why, man alive, Laura! Just look about you a little. What do you see? A world full of common people! All of 'em born and all of 'em going to die! Which of them has one-tenth of your good points! Or mine! Or anyone else's, as far as that goes—Gosh! Everybody excels in some one thing. Some in many! [*Unconsciously glances at himself in the mirror*] All you've got to do is discover in *what!* Take me, for instance. [*He adjusts his tie at the mirror*] My interest happens to lie in electro-dynamics. I'm taking a course in radio engineering at night school, Laura, on top of a fairly responsible job at the warehouse. I'm taking that course and studying public speaking.

LAURA   Ohhhh.

JIM   Because I believe in the future of television! [*Turning back to her*] I wish to be ready to go up right along with it. Therefore I'm planning to get in on the ground floor. In fact I've already made the right connections and all that remains is for the industry itself to get under way! Full steam—[*His eyes are starry*] Knowledge—Zzzzzp! Money—Zzzzzp!—Power! That's the cycle democracy is built on! [*His attitude is convincingly dynamic. LAURA stares at him, even her shyness eclipsed in her absolute wonder. He suddenly grins*] I guess you think I think a lot of myself!

LAURA   No—o-o-o, I—

JIM   Now how about you? Isn't there something you take more interest in than anything else?

LAURA   Well, I do—as I said—have my—glass collection—
[*A peal of girlish laughter from the kitchen*]

JIM   I'm not right sure I know what you're talking about. What kind of glass is it?

LAURA   Little articles of it, they're ornaments mostly! Most of them are little animals made out of glass, the tiniest little animals in the world. Mother calls them a glass menagerie! Here's an example of one, if you'd like to see it! This one is one of the oldest. It's nearly thirteen. [*MUSIC: "THE GLASS MENAGERIE"*] [*He stretches out his hand*] Oh, be careful—if you breathe, it breaks!

JIM   I'd better not take it. I'm pretty clumsy with things.

LAURA   Go on, I trust you with him! [*Places it in his palm*] There now—you're holding him gently! Hold him over the light, he loves the light! You see how the light shines through him?

JIM   It sure does shine!

LAURA   I shouldn't be partial, but he is my favorite one.

JIM   What kind of a thing is this one supposed to be?

LAURA   Haven't you noticed the single horn on his forehead?

JIM   A unicorn, huh?

LAURA   Mmm-hmmm!

JIM   Unicorns, aren't they extinct in the modern world?

LAURA   I know!

JIM   Poor little fellow, he must feel sort of lonesome.

LAURA   [*Smiling*]   Well, if he does he doesn't complain about it. He stays on a shelf with some horses that don't have horns and all of them seem to get along nicely together.

JIM   How do you know?

LAURA   [*Lightly*]   I haven't heard any arguments among them!

JIM   [*Grinning*]   No arguments, huh? Well, that's a pretty good sign! Where shall I set him?

LAURA   Put him on the table. They all like a change of scenery once in a while!

JIM   [*Stretching*]   Well, well, well, well— Look how big my shadow is when I stretch!

LAURA   Oh, oh, yes—it stretches across the ceiling!

JIM   [*Crossing to door*]   I think it's stopped raining. [*Opens fire-escape door*] Where does the music come from?

LAURA   From the Paradise Dance Hall across the alley.

JIM   How about cutting the rug a little, Miss Wingfield?

LAURA   Oh, I—

JIM   Or is your program filled up? Let me have a look at it. [*Grasps imaginary card*] Why, every dance is taken! I'll just have to scratch some out. [*WALTZ MUSIC: "LA GOLONDRINA"*] Ahhh, a waltz! [*He executes some sweeping turns by himself then holds his arms toward* LAURA]

LAURA   [*Breathlessly*]   I—can't dance!

JIM   There you go, that inferiority stuff!

LAURA   I've never danced in my life!

JIM   Come on, try!

LAURA   Oh, but I'd step on you!

JIM   I'm not made out of glass.

LAURA   How—how—how do we start?

JIM   Just leave it to me. You hold your arms out a little.

LAURA   Like this?

JIM   A little bit higher. Right. Now don't tighten up, that's the main thing about it—relax.

LAURA   [*Laughing breathlessly*]   It's hard not to.

JIM   Okay.

LAURA   I'm afraid you can't budge me.

JIM   What do you bet I can't? [*He swings her into motion*]

LAURA   Goodness, yes, you can!

JIM   Let yourself go, now, Laura, just let yourself go.

LAURA   I'm—

JIM   Come on!

LAURA   Trying!

JIM   Not so stiff—Easy does it!

LAURA   I know but I'm—

JIM   Loosen th' backbone! There now, that's a lot better.

LAURA   Am I?

JIM   Lots, lots better! [*He moves her about the room in a clumsy waltz*]

LAURA Oh, my!

JIM Ha-ha!

LAURA Oh, my goodness!

JIM Ha-ha-ha! [*They suddenly bump into the table.* JIM *stops*] What did we hit on?

LAURA Table.

JIM Did something fall off it? I think—

LAURA Yes.

JIM I hope that it wasn't the little glass horse with the horn!

LAURA Yes.

JIM Aw, aw, aw. Is it broken?

LAURA Now it is just like all the other horses.

JIM It's lost its—

LAURA Horn! It doesn't matter. Maybe it's a blessing in disguise.

JIM You'll never forgive me. I bet that that was your favorite piece of glass.

LAURA I don't have favorites much. It's no tragedy, Freckles. Glass breaks so easily. No matter how careful you are. The traffic jars the shelves and things fall off them.

JIM Still I'm awfully sorry that I was the cause.

LAURA [*Smiling*] I'll just imagine he had an operation. The horn was removed to make him feel less—freakish! [*They both laugh*] Now he will feel more at home with the other horses, the ones that don't have horns . . .

JIM Ha-ha, that's very funny! [*Suddenly serious*] I'm glad to see that you have a sense of humor. You know—you're—well—very different! Surprisingly different from anyone else I know! [*His voice becomes soft and hesitant with a genuine feeling*] Do you mind me telling you that? [LAURA *is abashed beyond speech*] I mean it in a nice way . . . [LAURA *nods shyly, looking away*] You make me feel sort of—I don't know how to put it! I'm usually pretty good at expressing things, but—This is something that I don't know how to say! [LAURA *touches her throat and clears it—turns the broken unicorn in her hands*] [*Even softer*] Has anyone ever told you that you were pretty? [*PAUSE: MUSIC*] [LAURA *looks up slowly, with wonder, and shakes her head*] Well, you are! In a very different way from anyone else. And all the nicer because of the difference, too. [*His voice becomes low and husky.* LAURA *turns away, nearly faint with the novelty of her emotions*] I wish that you were my sister. I'd teach you to have some confidence in yourself. The different people are not like other people, but being different is nothing to be ashamed of. Because other people are not such wonderful people. They're one hundred times one thousand. You're one times one! They walk all over the earth. You just stay here. They're common as—weeds, but —you—well, you're—*Blue Roses!*

[*IMAGE ON SCREEN: BLUE ROSES*]

MUSIC CHANGES

LAURA But blue is wrong for—roses . . .

JIM It's right for you—You're—pretty!

LAURA In what respect am I pretty?

JIM In all respects—believe me! Your eyes—your hair—are pretty! Your hands are pretty! [*He catches hold of her hand*] You think I'm making this up because I'm invited to dinner and have to be nice. Oh, I could do that! I could put on an act for you, Laura, and say lots of things without being very sincere. But this time I am. I'm talking to you sincerely. I happened to notice you had this inferiority complex that keeps you from feeling comfortable with people. Somebody needs to build your confidence up and make you proud instead of shy and turning away and—blushing—Somebody ought to—Ought to—*kiss* you, Laura! [*His hand slips slowly up her arm to her shoulder*] [*MUSIC SWELLS TUMULTUOUSLY*] [*He suddenly turns her about and kisses her on the lips*] [*When he releases her* LAURA *sinks on the sofa with a bright, dazed look*] [JIM *backs away and fishes in his pocket for a cigarette*] [*LEGEND ON SCREEN: "SOUVENIR"*] Stumble-john! [*He lights the cigarette, avoiding her look*] [*There is a peal of girlish laughter from* AMANDA *in the kitchen*] [LAURA *slowly raises and opens her hand. It still contains the little broken glass animal. She looks at it with a tender, bewildered expression*] Stumble-john! I shouldn't have done that—That was way off the beam. You don't smoke, do you? [*She looks up, smiling, not hearing the question*] [*He sits beside her a little gingerly. She looks at him speechlessly—waiting*] [*He coughs decorously and moves a little farther aside as he considers the situation and senses her feelings, dimly, with perturbation*] [*Gently*] Would you—care for a—mint? [*She doesn't seem to hear him but her look grows brighter even*] Peppermint—Life Saver? My pocket's a regular drug store—wherever I go . . . [*He pops a mint in his mouth. Then gulps and decides to make a clean breast of it. He speaks slowly and gingerly*] Laura, you know, if I had a sister like you, I'd do the same thing as Tom. I'd bring out fellows and—introduce her to them. The right type of boys of a type to—appreciate her. Only—well—he made a mistake about me. Maybe I've got no call to be saying this. That may not have been the idea in having me over. But what if it was? There's nothing wrong about that. The only trouble is that in my case—I'm not in a situation to—do the right thing. I can't take down your number and say I'll phone. I can't call up next week and—ask for a date. I thought I had better explain the situation in case you misunderstood it and—hurt your feelings. . . . [*Pause*] [*Slowly, very slowly,* LAURA's *look changes, her eyes returning slowly from his to the ornament in her palm*] [AMANDA *utters another gay laugh in the kitchen*]

LAURA [*Faintly*] You—won't—call again?

JIM No, Laura, I can't. [*He rises from the sofa*] As I was just explaining, I've—got strings on me, Laura, I've—been going steady! I go out all the time with a girl named Betty. She's a home-girl like you, and Catholic, and Irish, and in a great many ways we—get along fine. I met her last summer on a moonlight boat trip up the river to Alton, on the *Majestic*. Well—right away from the start it was—love! [*LEGEND: LOVE!*] [LAURA *sways slightly forward and grips the arm of the sofa. He fails to notice, now enrapt in his own comfortable being*] Being in love has made a new man of me! [*Leaning stiffly forward, clutching the arm of the sofa,* LAURA *struggles visibly with her storm. But* JIM *is oblivious, she is a long way off*] The power of love is really pretty tremendous! Love is something that—changes the whole world, Laura! [*The storm abates a little and* LAURA *leans back. He notices her again*] It happened that Betty's aunt took sick, she got a wire and had to go to Centralia. So Tom—when he asked me to dinner—I naturally just accepted the invitation, not knowing that you—that he—that I—[*He stops awkwardly*] Huh—I'm a stumble-john! [*He flops back on the sofa*] [*The holy candles in the altar of* LAURA's *face have been snuffed out. There is a look of almost infinite desolation*] [JIM *glances at her uneasily*] I wish that you would—say something. [*She bites her lip which was trembling and then bravely smiles. She opens her hand again on the broken glass ornament. Then she gently takes his hand and raises it level with her own. She care-*

fully places the unicorn in the palm of his hand, then pushes his fingers closed upon it] What are you—doing that for? You want me to have him?—Laura? [*She nods*] What for?

LAURA A—souvenir . . .

[*She rises unsteadily and crouches beside the victrola to wind it up*]

[*LEGEND ON SCREEN: "THINGS HAVE A WAY OF TURNING OUT SO BADLY!"*]

[*OR IMAGE: "GENTLEMAN CALLER WAVING GOODBYE!—GAILY"*]

[*At this moment* AMANDA *rushes brightly back in the front room. She bears a pitcher of fruit punch in an old-fashioned cut-glass pitcher and a plate of macaroons. The plate has a gold border and poppies painted on it*]

AMANDA Well, well, well! Isn't the air delightful after the shower? I've made you children a little liquid refreshment. [*Turns gaily to the gentleman caller*] Jim, do you know that song about lemonade?

> "Lemonade, lemonade
>   Made in the shade and stirred with a spade—
>   Good enough for any old maid!"

JIM [*Uneasily*] Ha-ha! No—I never heard it.

AMANDA Why, Laura! You look so serious!

JIM We were having a serious conversation.

AMANDA Good! Now you're better acquainted!

JIM [*Uncertainly*] Ha-ha! Yes.

AMANDA You modern young people are much more serious-minded than my generation. I was so gay as a girl!

JIM You haven't changed, Mrs. Wingfield.

AMANDA Tonight I'm rejuvenated! The gaiety of the occasion, Mr. O'Connor! [*She tosses her head with a peal of laughter. Spills lemonade*] Oooo! I'm baptizing myself!

JIM Here—let me—

AMANDA [*Setting the pitcher down*] There now. I discovered we had some maraschino cherries. I dumped them in, juice and all!

JIM You shouldn't have gone to that trouble, Mrs. Wingfield.

AMANDA Trouble, trouble? Why it was loads of fun! Didn't you hear me cutting up in the kitchen? I bet your ears were burning! I told Tom how outdone with him I was for keeping you to himself so long a time! He should have brought you over much, much sooner! Well, now that you've found your way, I want you to be a very frequent caller! Not just occasional but all the time. Oh, we're going to have a lot of gay times together! I see them coming! Mmm, just breathe that air! So fresh, and the moon's so pretty! I'll skip back out—I know where my place is when young folks are having a—serious conversation!

JIM Oh, don't go out, Mrs. Wingfield. The fact of the matter is I've got to be going.

AMANDA Going, now? You're joking! Why, it's only the shank of the evening, Mr. O'Connor!

JIM Well, you know how it is.

AMANDA You mean you're a young workingman and have to keep workingmen's hours. We'll let you off early tonight. But only on the condition that next time you stay later. What's the best night for you? Isn't Saturday night the best night for you workingmen?

JIM   I have a couple of time-clocks to punch, Mrs. Wingfield. One at morning, another one at night!

AMANDA   My, but you *are* ambitious! You work at night, too?

JIM   No, Ma'am, not work but—Betty! [*He crosses deliberately to pick up his hat. The band at the Paradise Dance Hall goes into a tender waltz*]

AMANDA   Betty? Betty? Who's—Betty! [*There is an ominous cracking sound in the sky*]

JIM   Oh, just a girl. The girl I go steady with! [*He smiles charmingly. The sky falls*]

[*LEGEND: "THE SKY FALLS"*]

AMANDA   [*A long-drawn exhalation*]   Ohhhh . . . Is it a serious romance, Mr. O'Connor?

JIM   We're going to be married the second Sunday in June.

AMANDA   Ohhhh—how nice! Tom didn't mention that you were engaged to be married.

JIM   The cat's not out of the bag at the warehouse yet. You know how they are. They call you Romeo and stuff like that. [*He stops at the oval mirror to put on his hat. He carefully shapes the brim and the crown to give a discreetly dashing effect*] It's been a wonderful evening, Mrs. Wingfield. I guess this is what they mean by Southern hospitality.

AMANDA   It really wasn't anything at all.

JIM   I hope it don't seem like I'm rushing off. But I promised Betty I'd pick her up at the Wabash depot, an' by the time I get my jalopy down there her train'll be in. Some women are pretty upset if you keep 'em waiting.

AMANDA   Yes, I know— The tyranny of women! [*Extends her hand*] Good-bye, Mr. O'Connor. I wish you luck—and happiness—and success! All three of them, and so does Laura!—Don't you, Laura?

LAURA   Yes!

JIM   [*Taking her hand*]   Good-bye, Laura. I'm certainly going to treasure that souvenir. And don't you forget the good advice I gave you. [*Raises his voice to a cheery shout*] So long, Shakespeare! Thanks again, ladies—Good night!

[*He grins and ducks jauntily out*]

[*Still bravely grimacing, AMANDA closes the door on the gentleman caller. Then she turns back to the room with a puzzled expression. She and LAURA don't dare to face each other. LAURA crouches beside the victrola to wind it*]

AMANDA   [*Faintly*]   Things have a way of turning out so badly. I don't believe that I would play the victrola. Well, well—well—Our gentleman caller was engaged to be married! Tom!

TOM   [*From back*]   Yes, Mother?

AMANDA   Come in here a minute. I want to tell you something awfully funny.

TOM   [*Enters with macaroon and a glass of the lemonade*]   Has the gentleman caller gotten away already?

AMANDA   The gentleman caller has made an early departure. What a wonderful joke you played on us!

TOM   How do you mean?

AMANDA   You didn't mention that he was engaged to be married.

TOM   Jim? Engaged?

AMANDA   That's what he just informed us.

TOM   I'll be jiggered! I didn't know about that.

AMANDA   That seems very peculiar.

TOM   What's peculiar about it?

AMANDA   Didn't you call him your best friend down at the warehouse?

TOM   He is, but how did I know?

AMANDA   It seems extremely peculiar that you wouldn't know your best friend was going to be married!

TOM   The warehouse is where I work, not where I know things about people!

AMANDA   You don't know things anywhere! You live in a dream; you manufacture illusions! [*He crosses to door*] Where are you going?

TOM   I'm going to the movies.

AMANDA   That's right, now that you've had us make such fools of ourselves. The effort, the preparations, all the expense! The new floor lamp, the rugs, the clothes for Laura! All for what? To entertain some other girl's fiancé! Go to the movies, go! Don't think about us, a mother deserted, an unmarried sister who's crippled and has no job! Don't let anything interfere with your selfish pleasure! Just go, go, go—to the movies!

TOM   All right, I will! The more you shout about my selfishness to me the quicker I'll go, and I won't go to the movies!

AMANDA   Go, then! Then go to the moon—you selfish dreamer!

[TOM *smashes his glass on the floor. He plunges out on the fire-escape, slamming the door.* LAURA *screams—cut by door*]

[*Dance-hall music up.* TOM *goes to the rail and grips it desperately, lifting his face in the chill white moonlight penetrating the narrow abyss of the alley*]

[*LEGEND ON SCREEN: "AND SO GOOD-BYE . . ."*]

[TOM'S *closing speech is timed with the interior pantomime. The interior scene is played as though viewed through soundproof glass.* AMANDA *appears to be making a comforting speech to* LAURA *who is huddled upon the sofa. Now that we cannot hear the mother's speech, her silliness is gone and she has dignity and tragic beauty.* LAURA'S *dark hair hides her face until at the end of the speech she lifts it to smile at her mother.* AMANDA'S *gestures are slow and graceful, almost dancelike, as she comforts the daughter. At the end of her speech she glances a moment at the father's picture—then withdraws through the portieres. At close of* TOM'S *speech,* LAURA *blows out the candles, ending the play*]

TOM   I didn't go to the moon, I went much further—for time is the longest distance between two places—Not long after that I was fired for writing a poem on the lid of a shoe-box. I left Saint Louis. I descended the steps of this fire-escape for a last time and followed, from then on, in my father's footsteps, attempting to find in motion what was lost in space—I traveled around a great deal. The cities swept about me like dead leaves, leaves that were brightly colored but torn away from the branches. I would have stopped, but I was pursued by something. It always came upon me unawares, taking me altogether by surprise. Perhaps it was a familiar bit of music. Perhaps it was only a piece of transparent glass—Perhaps I am walking along a street at night, in some strange city, before I have found companions. I pass the lighted window of a shop where perfume is sold. The window is filled with pieces of colored glass, tiny transparent bottles in delicate colors, like bits of a shattered rainbow. Then all at once my sister touches my shoulder. I turn around and look into her eyes . . . Oh, Laura, Laura, I tried to leave you behind me, but I am more faithful than I intended to be! I reach for a cigarette, I cross the street, I run into the movies

or a bar, I buy a drink, I speak to the nearest stranger—anything that can blow your candles out! [LAURA *bends over the candles*]—for nowadays the world is lit by lightning! Blow out your candles, Laura—and so good-bye. . . .
[*She blows the candles out*]

THE SCENE DISSOLVES

PRODUCTION NOTES

Being a "memory play," *The Glass Menagerie* can be presented with unusual freedom of convention. Because of its considerably delicate or tenuous material, atmospheric touches and subtleties of direction play a particularly important part. Expressionism and all other unconventional techniques in drama have only one valid aim, and that is a closer approach to truth. When a play employs unconventional techniques, it is not, or certainly shouldn't be, trying to escape its responsibility of dealing with reality, or interpreting experience, but is actually or should be attempting to find a closer approach, a more penetrating and vivid expression of things as they are. The straight realistic play with its genuine frigidaire and authentic ice-cubes, its characters that speak exactly as its audience speaks, corresponds to the academic landscape and has the same virtue of a photographic likeness. Everyone should know nowadays the unimportance of the photographic in art: that truth, life, or reality is an organic thing which the poetic imagination can represent or suggest, in essence, only through transformation, through changing into other forms than those which were merely present in appearance.

These remarks are not meant as comments only on this particular play. They have to do with a conception of a new, plastic theatre which must take the place of the exhausted theatre of realistic conventions if the theatre is to resume vitality as a part of our culture.

The Screen Device

There is *only one important difference between the original and acting version of the play* and that is the *omission* in the latter of the device which I tentatively included in my *original* script. This device was the use of a screen on which were projected magic-lantern slides bearing images or titles. I do not regret the omission of this device from the present Broadway production. The extraordinary power of Miss Taylor's [13] performance made it suitable to have the utmost simplicity in the physical production. But I think it may be interesting to some readers to see how this device was conceived. So I am putting it into the published manuscript. These images and legends, projected from behind, were cast on a section of wall between the front-room and dining-room areas, which should be indistinguishable from the rest when not in use.

The purpose of this will probably be apparent. It is to give accent to certain values in each scene. Each scene contains a particular point (or several) which is structurally the most important. In an episodic play, such as this, the basic structure or narrative line may be obscured from the audience; the effect may

---

[13] Who first played the part of Amanda.

seem fragmentary rather than architectural. This may not be the fault of the play so much as a lack of attention in the audience. The legend or image upon the screen will strengthen the effect of what is merely allusion in the writing and allow the primary point to be made more simply and lightly than if the entire responsibility were on the spoken lines. Aside from this structural value, I think the screen will have a definite emotional appeal, less definable but just as important. An imaginative producer or director may invent many other uses for this device than those indicated in the present script. In fact the possibilities of the device seem much larger to me than the instance of this play can possibly utilize.

The Music

Another extra-literary accent in this play is provided by the use of music. A single recurring tune, "The Glass Menagerie," is used to give emotional emphasis to suitable passages. This tune is like circus music, not when you are on the grounds or in the immediate vicinity of the parade, but when you are at some distance and very likely thinking of something else. It seems under those circumstances to continue almost interminably and it weaves in and out of your preoccupied consciousness; then it is the lightest, most delicate music in the world and perhaps the saddest. It expresses the surface vivacity of life with the underlying strain of immutable and inexpressible sorrow. When you look at a piece of delicately spun glass you think of two things: how beautiful it is and how easily it can be broken. Both of those ideas should be woven into the recurring tune, which dips in and out of the play as if it were carried on a wind that changes. It serves as a thread of connection and allusion between the narrator with his separate point in time and space and the subject of his story. Between each episode it returns as reference to the emotion, nostalgia, which is the first condition of the play. It is primarily Laura's music and therefore comes out most clearly when the play focuses upon her and the lovely fragility of glass which is her image.

The Lighting

The lighting in the play is not realistic. In keeping with the atmosphere of memory, the stage is dim. Shafts of light are focused on selected areas or actors, sometimes in contradistinction to what is the apparent center. For instance, in the quarrel scene between Tom and Amanda, in which Laura has no active part, the clearest pool of light is on her figure. This is also true of the supper scene, when her silent figure on the sofa should remain the visual center. The light upon Laura should be distinct from the others, having a peculiar pristine clarity such as light used in early religious portraits of female saints or madonnas. A certain correspondence to light in religious paintings, such as El Greco's, where the figures are radiant in atmosphere that is relatively dusky, could be effectively used throughout the play. (It will also permit a more effective use of the screen.) A free, imaginative use of light can be of enormous value in giving a mobile, plastic quality to plays of a more or less static nature.

T.W.

BERTOLT BRECHT
[1898–1956]

Bertolt Brecht, the son of a factory executive, was born in Augsburg, Bavaria. He was one of countless young Germans whose view of life was changed immeasurably by the experience of the First World War: Brecht's service in a field hospital made him aware of a horrible discrepancy between war itself and the sort of propaganda which justifies it. As a young man, he aimed at a medical career, and he pursued advanced studies at Munich and Berlin before turning to the theater. As a mature playwright, he meant to be a kind of doctor of society itself, prescribing large doses of pacifist and socialist ideology.

During the 1920s Brecht belonged to a group of avant-garde, leftist artists in Berlin. His early plays—such as *In the City's Thickets* (1922) and *One is Another* (1927)—depicted the ironic incongruities of human life in general, and the rat-race of bourgeois life in particular. These plays were radically expressionistic, but Brecht defended them as legitmate departures from the illusionistic "realism" of middle-class dramas portraying middle-class problems with middle-class solutions. In 1928, Brecht collaborated with the brilliant composer Kurt Weill on *The Three-Penny Opera;* this enduringly-successful work was an adaptation of John Gay's eighteenth-century comedy, *The Beggar's Opera,* but Brecht made the play a strikingly contemporary reflection of the confusion—moral, social, and economic—of post-war Germany.

When Hitler came to power in 1933, Brecht was forced to flee Germany. He did not return until 1949 when he became a citizen of East Berlin, professing loyalty to the Communist regime. In the intervening years Brecht lived in Russia, France, Norway, the United States (1941–1947), and Switzerland. Until the end of the Second World War he turned out a steady stream of anti-Nazi poems, plays (*The Private Life of the Master Race,* 1938; *The Fears and Miseries of the Third Reich,* 1944), and direct propaganda. But Brecht often had larger political purposes: *Saint Joan of the Stockyards* (1937) is a direct espousal of Marxism; *Mother Courage* (1941) is an implicit manifesto of pacifism.

Brecht conceived of the stage as a didactic medium. He developed a theory of "epic theater," a theater of "learning," in which the audience is not to be merely entertained or diverted, but moved to social action. Emotions should be frustated so that the audience perceives intellectually the necessity for transforming society; the effect should be one of "alienation" rather than pleasure. This theory has consequences for dramatic production: the atmosphere should be closer to that of the classroom than the "realistic" theater; the play's structure should be disconnected (thus limiting emotional involvement); narrator's songs, pantomimes, and special effects should interrupt the action; the acting should be deliberately artificial.

Paradoxically, Brecht's talent as a dramatist undercuts his own theory: his characteristic voice is that of the poet rather than the propagandist. His grim ironies and brilliant sense of the comic create dramatic situations which involve the audience emotionally—with an interest that extends far beyond the "lesson" of the stage-parable. Moreover, Brecht created many characters who—like Azdak in *The Caucasian Chalk Circle* (1948)—charm us with a personality uniquely their own.

Like Azdak, Brecht was something of an eccentric, and his career in East Berlin (from 1949 until his death in 1956) was not free of occasional conflicts with the Communist authorities. *The Caucasian Chalk Circle* suggests a basis for such conflict, for in the play Brecht the artist and individualist has triumphed over Brecht the ideologist and activist.

THE CAUCASIAN CHALK CIRCLE

BERTOLT BRECHT
Adapted by Eric Bentley

CHARACTERS

OLD MAN *on the right*
PEASANT WOMAN *on the right*
YOUNG PEASANT
A VERY YOUNG WORKER
OLD MAN *on the left*
PEASANT WOMAN *on the left*
AGRICULTURIST KATO
GIRL TRACTORIST
WOUNDED SOLDIER
THE DELEGATE *from the capital*
THE SINGER
GEORGI ABASHWILI, *the Governor*
NATELLA, *the Governor's wife*
MICHAEL, *their son*
SHALVA, *an adjutant*
ARSEN KAZBEKI, *a fat prince*

MESSENGER *from the Capital*
NIKO MIKADZE *and* MIKA LOLADZE,
doctors
SIMON SHASHAVA, *a soldier*
GRUSHA VASHNADZE, *a kitchen maid*
OLD PEASANT *with the milk*
CORPORAL *and* PRIVATE
PEASANT *and his wife*
LAVRENTI VASHNADZE, *Grusha's brother*
ANIKO, *his wife*
PEASANT WOMAN, *for a while Grusha's
mother-in-law*
JUSSUP, *her son*
MONK
AZDAK, *village recorder*
SHAUWA, *a policeman*

Copyright 1947, 1948, 1961, 1963 by Eric Bentley; Prologue © Copyright 1959 by Eric Bentley; Introduction © Copyright 1965 by Eric Bentley. Originally published in the volume *Parables for the Theatre: Two Plays by Bertolt Brecht* by the University of Minnesota Press. Reprinted by permission.

GRAND DUKE	STABLEBOY
DOCTOR	POOR OLD PEASANT WOMAN
INVALID	IRAKLI, *her brother-in-law, a bandit*
LIMPING MAN	THREE WEALTHY FARMERS
BLACKMAILER	ILLO SHUBOLADZE *and* SANDRO OBOLADZE,
LUDOVICA	*lawyers*
INNKEEPER, *her father-in-law*	OLD MARRIED COUPLE

SOLDIERS, SERVANTS, PEASANTS, BEGGARS, MUSICIANS, MERCHANTS, NOBLES, ARCHITECTS

The time and the place: After a prologue, set in 1945, we move back perhaps 1000 years.

The action of The Caucasian Chalk Circle *centers on Nuka (or Nukha), a town in Azerbaijan. However, the capital referred to in the prologue is not Baku (capital of Soviet Azerbaijan) but Tiflis (or Tbilisi), capital of Georgia. When Azdak, later, refers to "the capital" he means Nuka itself, though whether Nuka was ever capital of Georgia I do not know: in what reading I have done on the subject I have only found Nuka to be the capital of a Nuka Khanate.*

The word "Georgia" has not been used in this English version because of its American associations; instead, the alternative name "Grusinia" (in Russian, Gruziya) has been used.

The reasons for resettling the old Chinese story in Transcaucasia are not far to seek. The play was written when the Soviet chief of state, Joseph Stalin, was a Georgian, as was his favorite poet, cited in the Prologue, Mayakovsky. And surely there is a point in having this story acted out at the place where Europe and Asia meet, a place incomparably rich in legend and history. Here Jason found the Golden Fleece. Here Noah's Ark touched ground. Here the armies of both Genghis Khan and Tamerlane wrought havoc.

—E.B.

PROLOGUE

Summer, 1945.

Among the ruins of a war-ravaged Caucasian village the members of two kolkhoz villages, mostly WOMEN *and* OLDER MEN, *are sitting in a circle, smoking and drinking wine. With them is a* DELEGATE *of the State Reconstruction Commission from Nuka.*

PEASANT WOMAN [*left*] [*pointing*] In those hills over there we stopped three Nazi tanks, but the apple orchard was already destroyed.

OLD MAN [*right*] Our beautiful dairy farm: a ruin.

GIRL TRACTORIST I laid the fire, Comrade.

[*Pause.*]

DELEGATE   Nuka, Azerbaijan S.S.R. Delegation received from the goat-breeding Kolkhoz "Rosa Luxemburg." This is a collective farm which moved eastwards on orders from the authorities at the approach of Hitler's armies. They are now planning to return. Their delegates have looked at the village and the land and found a lot of destruction. [*Delegates on the right nod.*] But the neighboring fruit farm—Kolkhoz [*to the left*] "Galinsk"—proposes to use the former grazing land of Kolkhoz "Rosa Luxemburg" for orchards and vineyards. This land lies in a valley where grass doesn't grow very well. As a delegate of the Reconstruction Commission in Nuka I request that the two Kolkhoz villages decide between themselves whether Kolkhoz "Rosa Luxemburg" shall return or not.

OLD MAN   [*right*]   First of all, I want to protest against the time limit on discussion. We of Kolkhoz "Rosa Luxemburg" have spent three days and three nights getting here. And now discussion is limited to half a day.

WOUNDED SOLDIER   [*left*]   Comrade, we haven't as many villages as we used to have. We haven't as many hands. We haven't as much time.

GIRL TRACTORIST   All pleasures have to be rationed. Tobacco is rationed, and wine. Discussion should be rationed.

OLD MAN   [*right*]   [*sighing*]   Death to the fascists! But I will come to the point and explain why we want our valley back. There are a great many reasons, but I'll begin with one of the simplest. Makinä Abakidze, unpack the goat cheese. [*A peasant woman from right takes from a basket an enormous cheese wrapped in a cloth. Applause and laughter.*] Help yourselves, Comrades, start in!

OLD MAN   [*left*]   [*suspiciously*]   Is this a way of influencing us?

OLD MAN   [*right*]   [*amid laughter*]   How could it be a way of influencing you, Surab, you valley-thief? Everyone knows you'll take the cheese and the valley, too. [*Laughter.*] All I expect from you is an honest answer. Do you like the cheese?

OLD MAN   [*left*]   The answer is: yes.

OLD MAN   [*right*]   Really. [*Bitterly.*]   I ought to have known you know nothing about cheese.

OLD MAN   [*left*]   Why not? When I tell you I like it?

OLD MAN   [*right*]   Because you can't like it. Because it's not what it was in the old days. And why not? Because our goats don't like the new grass as they did the old. Cheese is not cheese because grass is not grass, that's the thing. Please put that in your report.

OLD MAN   [*left*]   But your cheese is excellent.

OLD MAN   [*right*]   It isn't excellent. It's just passable. The new grazing land is no good, whatever the young people may say. One can't live there. It doesn't even smell of morning in the morning. [*Several people laugh.*]

DELEGATE   Don't mind their laughing; they understand you. Comrades, why does one love one's country? Because the bread tastes better there, the air smells better, voices sound stronger, the sky is higher, the ground is easier to walk on. Isn't that so?

OLD MAN   [*right*]   The valley has belonged to us from all eternity.

SOLDIER   [*left*]   What does *that* mean—from all eternity? Nothing belongs to anyone from all eternity. When you were young you didn't even belong to yourself. You belonged to the Kazbeki princes.

OLD MAN   [*right*]   Doesn't it make a difference, though, what kind of trees stand next to the house you are born in? Or what kind of neighbors you have? Doesn't that make a difference? We want to go back just to have you as our neighbors, valley-thieves! Now you can all laugh again.

OLD MAN [*left*] [*laughing*] Then why don't you listen to what your neighbor, Kato Wachtang, our agriculturist, has to say about the valley?

PEASANT WOMAN [*right*] We've not said all we have to say about our valley. By no means. Not all the houses are destroyed. As for the dairy farm, at least the foundation wall is still standing.

DELEGATE You can claim State support—here and there—you know that. I have suggestions here in my pocket.

PEASANT WOMAN [*right*] Comrade Specialist, we haven't come here to haggle. I can't take your cap and hand you another, and say "This one's better." The other one might *be* better, but you *like* yours better.

GIRL TRACTORIST A piece of land is not a cap—not in our country, Comrade.

DELEGATE Don't get mad. It's true we have to consider a piece of land as a tool to produce something useful, but it's also true that we must recognize love for a particular piece of land. As far as I'm concerned, I'd like to find out more exactly what you [*to those on the left*] want to do with the valley.

OTHERS Yes, let Kato speak.

KATO [*rising; she's in military uniform*] Comrades, last winter, while we were fighting in these hills here as Partisans, we discussed how, once the Germans were expelled, we could build up our fruit culture to ten times its original size. I've prepared a plan for an irrigation project. By means of a cofferdam on our mountain lake, 300 hectares of unfertile land can be irrigated. Our Kolkhoz could not only cultivate more fruit, but also have vineyards. The project, however, would pay only if the disputed valley of Kolkhoz "Rosa Luxemburg" were also included. Here are the calculations. [*She hands* DELEGATE *a briefcase.*]

OLD MAN [*right*] Write into the report that our Kolkhoz plans to start a new stud farm.

GIRL TRACTORIST Comrades, the project was conceived during days and nights when we had to take cover in the mountains. We were often without ammunition for our half-dozen rifles. Even finding a pencil was difficult. [*Applause from both sides.*]

OLD MAN [*right*] Our thanks to the Comrades of Kolkhoz "Galinsk" and all those who've defended our country! [*They shake hands and embrace.*]

PEASANT WOMAN [*left*] In doing this our thought was that our soldiers—both your men and our men—should return to a still more productive homeland.

GIRL TRACTORIST As the poet Mayakovsky said: "The home of the Soviet people shall also be the home of Reason!"

[*The delegates excluding the* OLD MAN *have got up, and with the* DELEGATE *specified proceed to study the* AGRICULTURIST's *drawings. Exclamations such as:*] "Why is the altitude of fall 22 meters?"—"This rock will have to be blown up"—"Actually, all they need is cement and dynamite"—"They force the water to come down here, that's clever!"

A VERY YOUNG WORKER [*right*] [*to* OLD MAN, *right*] They're going to irrigate all the fields between the hills, look at that, Aleko!

OLD MAN [*right*] I'm not going to look. I knew the project would be good. I won't have a pistol pointed at me!

DELEGATE But they only want to point a pencil at you! [*Laughter.*]

OLD MAN [*right*] [*gets up gloomily, and walks over to look at the drawings*] These valley-thieves know only too well that we in this country are suckers for machines and projects.

PEASANT WOMAN [*right*] Aleko Bereshwili, you have a weakness for new projects. That's well known.

DELEGATE   What about my report? May I write that you will all support the cession of your old valley in the interests of this project when you get back to your Kolkhoz?

PEASANT WOMAN   [*right*]   I will. What about you, Aleko?

OLD MAN   [*right*]   [*bent over drawings*]   I suggest that you give us copies of the drawings to take along.

PEASANT WOMAN   [*right*]   Then we can sit down and eat. Once he has the drawings and he's ready to discuss them, the matter is settled. I know him. And it will be the same with the rest of us.
[*Delegates laughingly embrace again.*]

OLD MAN   [*left*]   Long live the Kolkhoz "Rosa Luxemburg" and much luck to your horse-breeding project!

PEASANT WOMAN   [*left*]   In honor of the visit of the delegates from Kolkhoz "Rosa Luxemburg" and of the Specialist, the plan is that we all hear a presentation of the Singer Arkadi Tscheidse.
[*Applause.* GIRL TRACTORIST *has gone off to bring the* SINGER.]

PEASANT WOMAN   [*right*]   Comrades, your entertainment had better be good. It's going to cost us a valley.

PEASANT WOMAN   [*left*]   Arkadi Tscheidse knows about our discussion. He's promised to perform something that has a bearing on the problem.

KATO   We wired Tiflis three times. The whole thing nearly fell through at the last minute because his driver had a cold.

PEASANT WOMAN   [*left*]   Arkadi Tscheidse knows 21,000 lines of verse.

OLD MAN   [*left*]   He's hard to get. You and the Planning Commission should persuade him to come north more often, Comrade.

DELEGATE   We are more interested in economics, I'm afraid.

OLD MAN   [*left*]   [*smiling*]   You arrange the redistribution of vines and tractors, why not songs?
[*Enter the* SINGER *Arkadi Tscheidse, led by* GIRL TRACTORIST. *He is a well-built man of simple manners, accompanied by* FOUR MUSICIANS *with their instruments. The artists are greeted with applause.*]

GIRL TRACTORIST   This is the Comrade Specialist, Arkadi.
[*The* SINGER *greets them all.*]

DELEGATE   Honored to make your acquaintance. I heard about your songs when I was a boy at school. Will it be one of the old legends?

SINGER   A very old one. It's called "The Chalk Circle" and comes from the Chinese. But we'll do it, of course, in a changed version. Comrades, it's an honor for me to entertain you after a difficult debate. We hope you will find that the voice of the old poet also sounds well in the shadow of Soviet tractors. It may be a mistake to mix different wines, but old and new wisdom mix admirably. Now I hope we'll get something to eat before the performance begins—it would certainly help.

VOICES   Surely. Everyone into the Club House!
[*While everyone begins to move,* DELEGATE *turns to* GIRL TRACTORIST.]

DELEGATE   I hope it won't take long. I've got to get back tonight.

GIRL TRACTORIST   How long will it last, Arkadi? The Comrade Specialist must get back to Tiflis tonight.

SINGER   [*casually*]   It's actually two stories. An hour or two.

GIRL TRACTORIST   [*confidentially*]   Couldn't you make it shorter?

SINGER   No.

VOICE   Arkadi Tscheidse's performance will take place here in the square after the meal.
[*And they all go happily to eat.*]

1
THE NOBLE CHILD

As the lights go up, the SINGER *is seen sitting on the floor, a black sheepskin cloak round his shoulders, and a little, well-thumbed notebook in his hand. A small group of listeners—the chorus—sits with him. The manner of his recitation makes it clear that he has told his story over and over again. He mechanically fingers the pages, seldom looking at them. With appropriate gestures, he gives the signal for each scene to begin.*

SINGER

In olden times, in a bloody time,
There ruled in a Caucasian city—
Men called it City of the Damned—
A Governor.
His name was Georgi Abashwili.
He was rich as Croesus
He had a beautiful wife
He had a healthy baby.
No other governor in Grusinia
Had so many horses in his stable
So many beggars on his doorstep
So many soldiers in his service
So many petitioners in his courtyard.
Georgi Abashwili—how shall I describe him to you?
He enjoyed his life.
On the morning of Easter Sunday
The Governor and his family went to church.
[*At the left a large doorway, at the right an even larger gateway.* BEGGARS *and* PETITIONERS *pour from the gateway, holding up thin* CHILDREN, *crutches, and petitions. They are followed by* IRONSHIRTS, *and then, expensively dressed, the* GOVERNOR'S FAMILY.]

BEGGARS AND PETITIONERS
—Mercy! Mercy, Your Grace! The taxes are too high.
—I lost my leg in the Persian War, where can I get . . .
—My brother is innocent, Your Grace, a misunderstanding . . .
—The child is starving in my arms!
—Our petition is for our son's discharge from the army, our last remaining son!
—Please, Your Grace, the water inspector takes bribes.
[*One servant collects the petitions. Another distributes coins from a purse. Soldiers push the crowd back, lashing at them with thick leather whips.*]

SOLDIER   Get back! Clear the church door!
[*Behind the* GOVERNOR, *his* WIFE, *and the* ADJUTANT, *the* GOVERNOR'S CHILD *is brought through the gateway in an ornate carriage.*]

CROWD
—The baby!
—I can't see it, don't shove so hard!
—God bless the child, Your Grace!

SINGER   [*while the crowd is driven back with whips*]
>   For the first time on that Easter Sunday, the people saw the Governor's heir.
>
>   Two doctors never moved from the noble child, apple of the Governor's eye.
>
>   Even the mighty Prince Kazbeki bows before him at the church door.
>   [*The* FAT PRINCE *steps forwards and greets the* FAMILY.]

FAT PRINCE   Happy Easter, Natella Abashwili! What a day! When it was raining last night, I thought to myself, gloomy holidays! But this morning the sky was gay. I love a gay sky, a simple heart, Natella Abashwili. And little Michael is a governor from head to foot! Tititi! [*He tickles the* CHILD.]

GOVERNOR'S WIFE   What do you think, Arsen, at last Georgi has decided to start building the east wing. All those wretched slums are to be torn down to make room for the garden.

FAT PRINCE   Good news after so much bad! What's the latest on the war, Brother Georgi? [*The* GOVERNOR *indicates a lack of interest.*] Strategical retreat, I hear. Well, minor reverses are to be expected. Sometimes things go well, sometimes not. Such is war. Doesn't mean a thing, does it?

GOVERNOR'S WIFE   He's coughing. Georgi, did you hear? [*She speaks sharply to the* DOCTORS, *two dignified men standing close to the little carriage.*] He's coughing!

FIRST DOCTOR   [*to the* SECOND]   May I remind you, Niko Mikadze, that I was against the lukewarm bath? [*To the* GOVERNOR'S WIFE:] There's been a little error over warming the bath water, Your Grace.

SECOND DOCTOR   [*equally polite*]   Mika Loladze, I'm afraid I can't agree with you. The temperature of the bath water was exactly what our great, beloved Mishiko Oboladze prescribed. More likely a slight draft during the night, Your Grace.

GOVERNOR'S WIFE   But do pay more attention to him. He looks feverish, Georgi.

FIRST DOCTOR   [*bending over the* CHILD]   No cause for alarm, Your Grace. The bath water will be warmer. It won't occur again.

SECOND DOCTOR   [*with a venomous glance at the* FIRST]   I won't forget that, my dear Mika Loladze. No cause for concern, Your Grace.

FAT PRINCE   Well, well, well! I always say: "A pain in my liver? Then the doctor gets fifty strokes on the soles of his feet." We live in a decadent age. In the old days one said: "Off with his head!"

GOVERNOR'S WIFE   Let's go into church. Very likely it's the draft here.
>   [*The procession of* FAMILY *and* SERVANTS *turns into the doorway. The* FAT PRINCE *follows, but the* GOVERNOR *is kept back by the* ADJUTANT, *a handsome young man. When the crowd of* PETITIONERS *has been driven off, a young dust-stained* RIDER, *his arm in a sling, remains behind.*]

ADJUTANT   [*pointing at the* RIDER, *who steps forward*]   Won't you hear the messenger from the capital, Your Excellency? He arrived this morning. With confidential papers.

GOVERNOR   Not before Service, Shalva. But did you hear Brother Kazbeki wish me a happy Easter? Which is all very well, but I don't believe it did rain last night.

ADJUTANT   [*nodding*]   We must investigate.

GOVERNOR   Yes, at once. Tomorrow.
>   [*They pass through the doorway. The* RIDER, *who has waited in vain for an audience, turns sharply round and, muttering a curse, goes off. Only one of the palace guards—*SIMON SHASHAVA—*remains at the door.*]

SINGER

The city is still.
Pigeons strut in the church square.
A soldier of the Palace Guard
Is joking with a kitchen maid
As she comes up from the river with a bundle.

[*A girl*—GRUSHA VASHNADZE—*comes through the gateway with a bundle made of large green leaves under her arm.*]

SIMON   What, the young lady is not in church? Shirking?

GRUSHA   I was dressed to go. But they needed another goose for the banquet. And they asked me to get it. I know about geese.

SIMON   A goose? [*He feigns suspicion.*] I'd like to see that goose. [GRUSHA *does not understand.*] One must be on one's guard with women. "I only went for a fish," they tell you, but it turns out to be something else.

GRUSHA   [*walking resolutely toward him and showing him the goose*]   There! If it isn't a fifteen-pound goose stuffed full of corn, I'll eat the feathers.

SIMON   A queen of a goose! The Governor himself will eat it. So the young lady has been down to the river again?

GRUSHA   Yes, at the poultry farm.

SIMON   Really? At the poultry farm, down by the river . . . not higher up maybe? Near those willows?

GRUSHA   I only go to the willows to wash the linen.

SIMON   [*insinuatingly*]   Exactly.

GRUSHA   Exactly what?

SIMON   [*winking*]   Exactly that.

GRUSHA   Why shouldn't I wash the linen by the willows?

SIMON   [*with exaggerated laughter*]   "Why shouldn't I wash the linen by the willows!" That's good, really good!

GRUSHA   I don't understand the soldier. What's so good about it?

SIMON   [*slyly*]   "If something I know someone learns, she'll grow hot and cold by turns!"

GRUSHA   I don't know what I could learn about those willows.

SIMON   Not even if there was a bush opposite? That one could see everything from? Everything that goes on there when a certain person is—"washing linen"?

GRUSHA   What does go on? Won't the soldier say what he means and have done?

SIMON   Something goes on. Something can be seen.

GRUSHA   Could the soldier mean I dip my toes in the water when it's hot? There's nothing else.

SIMON   There's more. Your toes. And more.

GRUSHA   More what? At most my foot?

SIMON   Your foot. And a little more. [*He laughs heartily.*]

GRUSHA   [*angrily*]   Simon Shashava, you ought to be ashamed of yourself! To sit in a bush on a hot day and wait till a girl comes and dips her legs in the river! And I bet you bring a friend along too! [*She runs off.*]

SIMON   [*shouting after her*]   I didn't bring any friend along!

[*As the* SINGER *resumes his tale, the* SOLDIER *steps into the doorway as though to listen to the service.*]

SINGER

The city lies still
But why are there armed men?
The Governor's palace is at peace
But why is it a fortress?

And the Governor returned to his palace
And the fortress was a trap
And the goose was plucked and roasted
But the goose was not eaten this time
And noon was no longer the hour to eat:
Noon was the hour to die.

[*From the doorway at the left the* FAT PRINCE *quickly appears, stands still, looks around. Before the gateway at the right two* IRONSHIRTS *are squatting and playing dice. The* FAT PRINCE *sees them, walks slowly past, making a sign to them. They rise: one goes through the gateway, the other goes off at the right. Muffled voices are heard from various directions in the rear: "To your posts!" The palace is surrounded. The* FAT PRINCE *quickly goes off. Church bells in the distance. Enter, through the doorway, the Governor's family and procession, returning from church.*]

GOVERNOR'S WIFE [*passing the* ADJUTANT] It's impossible to live in such a slum. But Georgi, of course, will only build for his little Michael. Never for me! Michael is all! All for Michael!

[*The procession turns into the gateway. Again the* ADJUTANT *lingers behind. He waits. Enter the wounded* RIDER *from the doorway. Two* IRONSHIRTS *of the Palace Guard have taken up positions by the gateway.*]

ADJUTANT [*to the* RIDER] The Governor does not wish to receive military news before dinner—especially if it's depressing, as I assume. In the afternoon His Excellency will confer with prominent architects. They're coming to dinner too. And here they are! [*Enter three gentlemen through the doorway.*] Go to the kitchen and eat, my friend. [*As the* RIDER *goes, the* ADJUTANT *greets the* ARCHITECTS.] Gentlemen, His Excellency expects you at dinner. He will devote all his time to you and your great new plans. Come!

ONE OF THE ARCHITECTS We marvel that His Excellency intends to build. There are disquieting rumors that the war in Persia has taken a turn for the worse.

ADJUTANT All the more reason to build! There's nothing to those rumors anyway. Persia is a long way off, and the garrison here would let itself be hacked to bits for its Governor. [*Noise from the palace. The shrill scream of a woman. Someone is shouting orders. Dumbfounded, the* ADJUTANT *moves toward the gateway. An* IRONSHIRT *steps out, points his lance at him.*] What's this? Put down that lance, you dog.

ONE OF THE ARCHITECTS It's the Princes! Don't you know the Princes met last night in the capital? And they're against the Grand Duke and his Governors? Gentlemen, we'd better make ourselves scarce. [*They rush off. The* ADJUTANT *remains helplessly behind.*]

ADJUTANT [*furiously to the Palace Guard*] Down with those lances! Don't you see the Governor's life is threatened?

[*The* IRONSHIRTS *of the Palace Guard refuse to obey. They stare coldly and indifferently at the* ADJUTANT *and follow the next events without interest.*]

SINGER
O blindness of the great!
They go their way like gods,
Great over bent backs,
Sure of hired fists,
Trusting in the power
Which has lasted so long.
But long is not forever.

O change from age to age!

Thou hope of the people!

[*Enter the* GOVERNOR, *through the gateway, between two* SOLDIERS *armed to the teeth. He is in chains. His face is gray.*]

Up, great sir, deign to walk upright!

From your palace the eyes of many foes follow you!

And now you don't need an architect, a carpenter will do.

You won't be moving into a new palace

But into a little hole in the ground.

Look about you once more, blind man!

[*The arrested man looks round.*]

Does all you had please you?

Between the Easter Mass and the Easter meal

You are walking to a place whence no one returns.

[*The* GOVERNOR *is led off. A horn sounds an alarm. Noise behind the gateway.*]

When the house of a great one collapses

Many little ones are slain.

Those who had no share in the *good* fortunes of the mighty

Often have a share in their *mis*fortunes.

The plunging wagon

Drags the sweating oxen down with it

Into the abyss.

[*The* SERVANTS *come rushing through the gateway in panic.*]

SERVANTS [*among themselves*]

—The baskets!

—Take them all into the third courtyard! Food for five days!

—The mistress has fainted! Someone must carry her down.

—She must get away.

—What about us? We'll be slaughtered like chickens, as always.

—Goodness, what'll happen? There's bloodshed already in the city, they say.

—Nonsense, the Governor has just been asked to appear at a Princes' meeting. All very correct. Everything'll be ironed out. I heard this on the best authority . . .

[*The two* DOCTORS *rush into the courtyard.*]

FIRST DOCTOR [*trying to restrain the other*] Niko Mikadze, it is your duty as a doctor to attend Natella Abashwili.

SECOND DOCTOR My duty! It's yours!

FIRST DOCTOR Whose turn is it to look after the child today, Niko Mikadze, yours or mine?

SECOND DOCTOR Do you really think, Mika Loladze, I'm going to stay a minute longer in this accursed house on that little brat's account? [*They start fighting. All one hears is:* "You neglect your duty!" *and* "Duty, my foot!" *Then the* SECOND DOCTOR *knocks the* FIRST *down.*] Go to hell! [*Exit.*]

[*Enter the soldier,* SIMON SHASHAVA. *He searches in the crowd for* GRUSHA.]

SIMON Grusha! There you are at last! What are you going to do?

GRUSHA Nothing. If worst comes to worst, I've a brother in the mountains. How about you?

SIMON Forget about me. [*Formally again*] Grusha Vashnadze, your wish to know my plans fills me with satisfaction. I've been ordered to accompany Madam Abashwili as her guard.

GRUSHA But hasn't the Palace Guard mutinied?

SIMON   [*seriously*]   That's a fact.

GRUSHA   Isn't it dangerous to go with her?

SIMON   In Tiflis, they say: Isn't the stabbing dangerous for the knife?

GRUSHA   You're not a knife, you're a man, Simon Shashava, what has that woman to do with you?

SIMON   That woman has nothing to do with me. I have my orders, and I go.

GRUSHA   The soldier is pigheaded: he is running into danger for nothing—nothing at all. I must get into the third courtyard, I'm in a hurry.

SIMON   Since we're both in a hurry we shouldn't quarrel. You need time for a good quarrel. May I ask if the young lady still has parents?

GRUSHA   No, just a brother.

SIMON   As time is short—my second question is this: Is the young lady as healthy as a fish in water?

GRUSHA   I may have a pain in the right shoulder once in a while. Otherwise I'm strong enough for my job. No one has complained. So far.

SIMON   That's well known. When it's Easter Sunday, and the question arises who'll run for the goose all the same, she'll be the one. My third question is this: Is the young lady impatient? Does she want apples in winter?

GRUSHA   Impatient? No. But if a man goes to war without any reason and then no message comes—that's bad.

SIMON   A message will come. And now my final question . . .

GRUSHA   Simon Shashava, I must get to the third courtyard at once. My answer is yes.

SIMON   [*very embarrassed*]   Haste, they say, is the wind that blows down the scaffolding. But they also say: The rich don't know what haste is. I'm from . . .

GRUSHA   Kutsk . . .

SIMON   The young lady has been inquiring about me? I'm healthy, I have no dependents, I make ten piasters a month, as paymaster twenty piasters, and I'm asking—very sincerely—for your hand.

GRUSHA   Simon Shashava, it suits me well.

SIMON   [*taking from his neck a thin chain with a little cross on it*]   My mother gave me this cross, Grusha Vashnadze. The chain is silver. Please wear it.

GRUSHA   Many thanks, Simon.

SIMON   [*hangs it round her neck*]   It would be better to go to the third courtyard now. Or there'll be difficulties. Anyway, I must harness the horses. The young lady will understand?

GRUSHA   Yes, Simon.

[*They stand undecided.*]

SIMON   I'll just take the mistress to the troops that have stayed loyal. When the war's over, I'll be back. In two weeks. Or three. I hope my intended won't get tired, awaiting my return.

GRUSHA

Simon Shashava, I shall wait for you.
Go calmly into battle, soldier
The bloody battle, the bitter battle
From which not everyone returns:
When you return I shall be there.
I shall be waiting for you under the green elm
I shall be waiting for you under the bare elm
I shall wait until the last soldier has returned
And longer
When you come back from the battle

No boots will stand at my door
The pillow beside mine will be empty
And my mouth will be unkissed.
When you return, when you return
You will be able to say: It is just as it was.

SIMON   I thank you, Grusha Vashnadze. And good-bye!

[*He bows low before her. She does the same before him. Then she runs quickly off without looking round. Enter the* ADJUTANT *from the gateway.*]

ADJUTANT   [*harshly*]   Harness the horses to the carriage! Don't stand there doing nothing, scum!

[SIMON SHASHAVA *stands to attention and goes off. Two* SERVANTS *crowd from the gateway, bent low under huge trunks. Behind them, supported by her women, stumbles* NATELLA ABASHWILI. *She is followed by a* WOMAN *carrying the* CHILD.]

GOVERNOR'S WIFE   I hardly know if my head's still on. Where's Michael? Don't hold him so clumsily. Pile the trunks onto the carriage. No news from the city, Shalva?

ADJUTANT   None. All's quiet so far, but there's not a minute to lose. No room for all those trunks in the carriage. Pick out what you need. [*Exit quickly.*]

GOVERNOR'S WIFE   Only essentials! Quick, open the trunks! I'll tell you what I need. [*The trunks are lowered and opened. She points at some brocade dresses.*] The green one! And, of course, the one with the fur trimming. Where are Niko Mikadze and Mika Loladze? I've suddenly got the most terrible migraine again. It always starts in the temples. [*Enter* GRUSHA.] Taking your time, eh? Go and get the hot water bottles this minute! [GRUSHA *runs off, returns later with hot water bottles; the* GOVERNOR'S WIFE *orders her about by signs.*] Don't tear the sleeves.

A YOUNG WOMAN   Pardon, madam, no harm has come to the dress.

GOVERNOR'S WIFE   Because I stopped you. I've been watching you for a long time. Nothing in your head but making eyes at Shalva Tzereteli. I'll kill you, you bitch! [*She beats the* YOUNG WOMAN.]

ADJUTANT   [*appearing in the gateway*]   Please make haste, Natella Abashwili. Firing has broken out in the city.
[*Exit.*]

GOVERNOR'S WIFE   [*letting go of the* YOUNG WOMAN]   Oh dear, do you think they'll lay hands on us? Why should they? Why? [*She herself begins to rummage in the trunks.*] How's Michael? Asleep?

WOMAN WITH THE CHILD   Yes, madam.

GOVERNOR'S WIFE   Then put him down a moment and get my little saffron-colored boots from the bedroom. I need them for the green dress. [*The* WOMAN *puts down the* CHILD *and goes off.*] Just look how these things have been packed! No love! No understanding! If you don't give them every order yourself . . . At such moments you realize what kind of servants you have! They gorge themselves at your expense, and never a word of gratitude! I'll remember this.

ADJUTANT   [*entering, very excited*]   Natella, you must leave at once!

GOVERNOR'S WIFE   Why? I've got to take this silver dress—it cost a thousand piasters. And that one there, and where's the wine-colored one?

ADJUTANT   [*trying to pull her away*]   Riots have broken out! We must leave at once. Where's the baby?

GOVERNOR'S WIFE   [*calling to the* YOUNG WOMAN *who was holding the baby*]   Maro, get the baby ready! Where on earth are you?

ADJUTANT   [*leaving*]   We'll probably have to leave the carriage behind and go ahead on horseback.

[*The* GOVERNOR'S WIFE *rummages again among her dresses, throws some onto the heap of chosen clothes, then takes them off again. Noises, drums are heard. The* YOUNG WOMAN *who was beaten creeps away. The sky begins to grow red.*]

GOVERNOR'S WIFE [*rummaging desperately*] I simply cannot find the wine-colored dress. Take the whole pile to the carriage. Where's Asja? And why hasn't Maro come back? Have you all gone crazy?

ADJUTANT [*returning*] Quick! Quick!

GOVERNOR'S WIFE [*to the* FIRST WOMAN] Run! Just throw them into the carriage!

ADJUTANT We're not taking the carriage. And if you don't come now, I'll ride off on my own.

GOVERNOR'S WIFE [*as the* FIRST WOMAN *can't carry everything*] Where's that bitch Asja? [*The* ADJUTANT *pulls her away.*] Maro, bring the baby! [*To the* FIRST WOMAN] Go and look for Masha. No, first take the dresses to the carriage. Such nonsense! I wouldn't dream of going on horseback!

[*Turning round, she sees the red sky, and starts back rigid. The fire burns. She is pulled out by the* ADJUTANT. *Shaking, the* FIRST WOMAN *follows with the dresses.*]

MARO [*from the doorway with the boots*] Madam! [*She sees the trunks and dresses and runs toward the* CHILD, *picks it up, and holds it a moment.*] They left it behind, the beasts. [*She hands it to* GRUSHA.] Hold it a moment. [*She runs off, following the* GOVERNOR'S WIFE.]

[*Enter* SERVANTS *from the gateway.*]

COOK Well, so they've actually gone. Without the food wagons, and not a minute too early. It's time for us to clear out.

GROOM This'll be an unhealthy neighborhood for quite a while. [*To one of the* WOMEN:] Suliko, take a few blankets and wait for me in the foal stables.

GRUSHA What have they done with the Governor?

GROOM [*gesturing throat cutting*] Ffffft.

A FAT WOMAN [*seeing the gesture and becoming hysterical*] Oh dear, oh dear, oh dear, oh dear! Our master Georgi Abashwili! A picture of health he was, at the morning Mass—and now! Oh, take me away, we've all lost, we must die in sin like our master, Georgi Abashwili!

OTHER WOMAN [*soothing her*] Calm down, Nina! You'll be taken to safety. You've never hurt a fly.

FAT WOMAN [*being led out*] Oh dear, oh dear, oh dear! Quick! Let's all get out before they come, before they come!

A YOUNG WOMAN Nina takes it more to heart than the mistress, that's a fact. They even have to have their weeping done for them.

COOK We'd better get out, all of us.

ANOTHER WOMAN [*glancing back*] That must be the East Gate burning.

YOUNG WOMAN [*seeing the* CHILD *in* GRUSHA's *arms*] The baby! What are you doing with it?

GRUSHA It got left behind.

YOUNG WOMAN She simply left it there. Michael, who was kept out of all the drafts!

[*The* SERVANTS *gather round the* CHILD.]

GRUSHA He's waking up.

GROOM Better put him down, I tell you. I'd rather not think what'd happen to anybody who was found with that baby.

COOK That's right. Once they get started, they'll kill each other off, whole families at a time. Let's go.

[*Exeunt all but* GRUSHA, *with the* CHILD *on her arm, and* TWO WOMEN.]

TWO WOMEN   Didn't you hear? Better put him down.

GRUSHA   The nurse asked me to hold him a moment.

OLDER WOMAN   She's not coming back, you simpleton.

YOUNGER WOMAN   Keep your hands off it.

OLDER WOMAN   [*amiably*]   Grusha, you're a good soul, but you're not very bright, and you know it. I tell you, if he had the plague he couldn't be more dangerous.

GRUSHA   [*stubbornly*]   He hasn't got the plague. He looks at me! He's human!

OLDER WOMAN   Don't look at *him*. You're a fool—the kind that always gets put upon. A person need only say, "Run for the salad, you have the longest legs," and you run. My husband has an ox cart—you can come with us if you hurry! Lord, by now the whole neighborhood must be in flames.

[*Both women leave, sighing. After some hesitation,* GRUSHA *puts the sleeping* CHILD *down, looks at it for a moment, then takes a brocade blanket from the heap of clothes and covers it. Then both women return, dragging bundles.* GRUSHA *starts guiltily away from the* CHILD *and walks a few steps to one side.*]

YOUNGER WOMAN   Haven't you packed anything yet? There isn't much time, you know. The Ironshirts will be here from the barracks.

GRUSHA   Coming!

[*She runs through the doorway. Both women go to the gateway and wait. The sound of horses is heard. They flee screaming. Enter the* FAT PRINCE *with drunken* IRONSHIRTS. *One of them carries the Governor's head on a lance.*]

FAT PRINCE   Here! In the middle! [*One soldier climbs onto the other's back, takes the head, holds it tentatively over the door.*] That's not the middle. Farther to the right. That's it. What I do, my friends, I do well. [*While with hammer and nail, the soldier fastens the head to the wall by its hair:*] This morning at the church door I said to Georgi Abashwili: "I love a gay sky." Actually, I prefer the lightning that comes out of a gay sky. Yes, indeed. It's a pity they took the brat along, though, I need him, urgently.

[*Exit with* IRONSHIRTS *through the gateway. Trampling of horses again. Enter* GRUSHA *through the doorway looking cautiously about her. Clearly she has waited for the* IRONSHIRTS *to go. Carrying a bundle, she walks toward the gateway. At the last moment, she turns to see if the* CHILD *is still there. Catching sight of the head over the doorway, she screams. Horrified, she picks up her bundle again, and is about to leave when the* SINGER *starts to speak. She stands rooted to the spot.*]

SINGER

As she was standing between courtyard and gate,
She heard or she thought she heard a low voice calling.
The child called to her,
Not whining, but calling quite sensibly,
Or so it seemed to her.
"Woman," it said, "help me."
And it went on, not whining, but saying quite sensibly:
"Know, woman, he who hears not a cry for help
But passes by with troubled ears will never hear
The gentle call of a lover nor the blackbird at dawn
Nor the happy sigh of the tired grape-picker as the Angelus rings."
[*She walks a few steps toward the* CHILD *and bends over it.*]

Hearing this she went back for one more look at the child:
Only to sit with him for a moment or two,
Only till someone should come,
His mother, or anyone.
[*Leaning on a trunk, she sits facing the* CHILD.]
Only till she would have to leave, for the danger was too great,
The city was full of flame and crying.
[*The light grows dimmer, as though evening and night were coming on.*]
Fearful is the seductive power of goodness!
[GRUSHA *now settles down to watch over the* CHILD *through the night. Once, she lights a small lamp to look at it. Once, she tucks it in with a coat. From time to time she listens and looks to see whether someone is coming.*]
And she sat with the child a long time,
Till evening came, till night came, till dawn came.
She sat too long, too long she saw
The soft breathing, the small clenched fists,
Till toward morning the seduction was complete
And she rose, and bent down and, sighing, took the child
And carried it away.
[*She does what the* SINGER *says as he describes it.*]
As if it was stolen goods she picked it up.
As if she was a thief she crept away.

2

THE FLIGHT INTO
THE NORTHERN MOUNTAINS

SINGER
> When Grusha Vashnadze left the city
> On the Grusinian highway
> On the way to the Northern Mountains
> She sang a song, she bought some milk.

CHORUS
> How will this human child escape
> The bloodhounds, the trap-setters?
> Into the deserted mountains she journeyed
> Along the Grusinian highway she journeyed
> She sang a song, she bought some milk.
> [GRUSHA VASHNADZE *walks on. On her back she carries the* CHILD *in a sack, in one hand is a large stick, in the other a bundle. She sings.*]

THE SONG OF THE FOUR GENERALS

> Four generals
> Set out for Iran.
> With the first one, war did not agree.
> The second never won a victory.

For the third the weather never was right.
For the fourth the men would never fight.
Four generals
And not a single man!
Sosso Robakidse
Went marching to Iran
With him the war did so agree
He soon had won a victory.
For him the weather was always right.
For him the men would always fight.
Sosso Robakidse,
He is our man!

[*A peasant's cottage appears.*]

GRUSHA [*to the* CHILD] Noontime is meal time. Now we'll sit hopefully in the grass, while the good Grusha goes and buys a little pitcher of milk. [*She lays the* CHILD *down and knocks at the cottage door. An* OLD MAN *opens it.*] Grandfather, could I have a little pitcher of milk? And a corn cake, maybe?

OLD MAN Milk? We have no milk. The soldiers from the city have our goats. Go to the soldiers if you want milk.

GRUSHA But grandfather, you must have a little pitcher of milk for a baby?

OLD MAN And for a God-bless-you, eh?

GRUSHA Who said anything about a God-bless-you? [*She shows her purse.*] We'll pay like princes. "Head in the clouds, backside in the water." [*The peasant goes off, grumbling, for milk*] How much for the milk?

OLD MAN Three piasters. Milk has gone up.

GRUSHA Three piasters for this little drop? [*Without a word the* OLD MAN *shuts the door in her face.*] Michael, did you hear that? Three piasters! We can't afford it! [*She goes back, sits down again, and gives the* CHILD *her breast.*] Suck. Think of the three piasters. There's nothing there, but you *think* you're drinking, and that's something. [*Shaking her head, she sees that the* CHILD *isn't sucking any more. She gets up, walks back to the door, and knocks again.*] Open, grandfather, we'll pay. [*Softly.*] May lightning strike you! [*When the* OLD MAN *appears:*] I thought it would be half a piaster. But the baby must be fed. How about one piaster for that little drop?

OLD MAN Two.

GRUSHA Don't shut the door again. [*She fishes a long time in her bag.*] Here are two piasters. The milk better be good. I still have two days' journey ahead of me. It's a murderous business you have here—and sinful, too!

OLD MAN Kill the soldiers if you want milk.

GRUSHA [*giving the* CHILD *some milk*] This is an expensive joke. Take a sip, Michael, it's a week's pay. Around here they think we earned our money just sitting on our behinds. Oh, Michael, Michael, you're a nice little load for a girl to take on! [*Uneasy, she gets up, puts the* CHILD *on her back, and walks on. The* OLD MAN, *grumbling, picks up the pitcher and looks after her unmoved.*]

SINGER
As Grusha Vashnadze went northward
The Princes' Ironshirts went after her.

CHORUS
How will the barefoot girl escape the Ironshirts,
The bloodhounds, the trap-setters?

They hunt even by night.
Pursuers never tire.
Butchers sleep little.
[*Two* IRONSHIRTS *are trudging along the highway.*]

CORPORAL   You'll never amount to anything, blockhead, your heart's not in
it. Your senior officer sees this in little things. Yesterday, when I made the
fat gal, yes, you grabbed her husband as I commanded, and you did kick
him in the belly, at my request, but did you *enjoy* it, like a loyal Private,
or were you just doing your duty? I've kept an eye on you blockhead,
you're a hollow reed and a tinkling cymbal, you won't get promoted.
[*They walk a while in silence.*] Don't think I've forgotten how insubordi-
nate you are, either. Stop limping! I forbid you to limp! You limp because I sold the horses, and I sold the horses because I'd never have got
that price again. You limp to show me you don't like márching. I know
you. It won't help. You wait. Sing!

TWO IRONSHIRTS   [*singing*]
Sadly to war I went my way
Leaving my loved one at her door.
My friends will keep her honor safe
Till from the war I'm back once more.

CORPORAL   Louder!

TWO IRONSHIRTS   [*singing*]
When 'neath a headstone I shall be
My love a little earth will bring:
"Here rest the feet that oft would run to me
And here the arms that oft to me would cling."
[*They begin to walk again in silence.*]

CORPORAL   A good soldier has his heart and soul in it. When he receives an
order, he gets a hard-on, and when he drives his lance into the enemy's
guts, he comes. [*He shouts for joy.*] He lets himself be torn to bits for his
superior officer, and as he lies dying he takes note that his corporal is
nodding approval, and that is reward enough, it's his dearest wish. *You*
won't get any nod of approval, but you'll croak all right. Christ, how'm
I to get my hands on the Governor's bastard with the help of a fool like
you! [*They stay on stage behind.*]

SINGER
When Grusha Vashnadze came to the River Sirra
Flight grew too much for her, the helpless child too heavy.
In the cornfields the rosy dawn
Is cold to the sleepless one, only cold.
The gay clatter of the milk cans in the farmyard where the smoke rises
Is only a threat to the fugitive.
She who carries the child feels its weight and little more.
[GRUSHA *stops in front of a farm. A fat* PEASANT WOMAN *is carrying a milk
can through the door.* GRUSHA *waits until she has gone in, then approaches
the house cautiously.*]

GRUSHA   [*to the* CHILD]   Now you've wet yourself again, and you know I've
no linen. Michael, this is where we part company. It's far enough from
the city. They wouldn't want you *so* much that they'd follow you all
this way, little good-for-nothing. The peasant woman is kind, and can't
you just smell the milk? [*She bends down to lay the* CHILD *on the threshold.*] So farewell, Michael, I'll forget how you kicked me in the back all
night to make me walk faster. And you can forget the meager fare—it was

meant well. I'd like to have kept you—your nose is so tiny—but it can't be. I'd have shown you your first rabbit, I'd have trained you to keep dry, but now I must turn around. My sweetheart the soldier might be back soon, and suppose he didn't find me? You can't ask that, can you? [*She creeps up to the door and lays the* CHILD *on the threshold. Then, hiding behind a tree, she waits until the* PEASANT WOMAN *opens the door and sees the bundle.*]

PEASANT WOMAN   Good heavens, what's this? Husband!

PEASANT   What is it? Let me finish my soup.

PEASANT WOMAN   [*to the* CHILD] Where's your mother then? Haven't you got one? It's a boy. Fine linen. He's from a good family, you can see that. And they just leave him on our doorstep. Oh, these are times!

PEASANT   If they think we're going to feed it, they're wrong. You can take it to the priest in the village. That's the best we can do.

PEASANT WOMAN   What'll the priest do with him? He needs a mother. There, he's waking up. Don't you think we could keep him, though?

PEASANT   [*shouting*] No!

PEASANT WOMAN   I could lay him in the corner by the armchair. All I need is a crib. I can take him into the fields with me. See him laughing? Husband, we have a roof over our heads. We can do it. Not another word out of you! [*She carries the* CHILD *into the house. The* PEASANT *follows protesting.* GRUSHA *steps out from behind the tree, laughs, and hurries off in the opposite direction.*]

SINGER

Why so cheerful, making for home?

CHORUS

Because the child has won new parents with a laugh,
Because I'm rid of the little one, I'm cheerful.

SINGER

And why so sad?

CHORUS

Because I'm single and free, I'm sad
Like someone who's been robbed
Someone who's newly poor.
[*She walks for a short while, then meets the two* IRONSHIRTS *who point their lances at her.*]

CORPORAL   Lady, you are running straight into the arms of the Armed Forces. Where are you coming from? And when? Are you having illicit relations with the enemy? Where is he hiding? What movements is he making in your rear? How about the hills? How about the valleys? How are your stockings held in position? [GRUSHA *stands there frightened.*] Don't be scared, we always withdraw, if necessary . . . what, blockhead? I always withdraw. In that respect at least, I can be relied on. Why are you staring like that at my lance? In the field no soldier drops his lance, that's a rule. Learn it by heart, blockhead. Now, lady, where are you headed?

GRUSHA   To meet my intended, one Simon Shashava, of the Palace Guard in Nuka.

CORPORAL   Simon Shashava? Sure, I know him. He gave me the key so I could look you up once in a while. Blockhead, we are getting to be unpopular. We must make her realize we have honorable intentions. Lady, behind apparent frivolity I conceal a serious nature, so let me tell you officially: I want a child from you. [GRUSHA *utters a little scream.*] Blockhead, she understands me. Uh-huh, isn't it a sweet shock? "Then first I must take

the noodles out of the oven, Officer. Then first I must change my torn
shirt, Colonel." But away with jokes, away with my lance! We are looking
for a baby. A baby from a good family. Have you heard of such a baby,
from the city, dressed in fine linen, and suddenly turning up here?

GRUSHA   No, I haven't heard a thing. [*Suddenly she turns round and runs back,
panic-stricken. The* IRONSHIRTS *glance at each other, then follow her, cursing.*]

SINGER

Run, kind girl! The killers are coming!
Help the helpless babe, helpless girl!
And so she runs!

CHORUS

In the bloodiest times
There are kind people.
[*As* GRUSHA *rushes into the cottage, the* PEASANT WOMAN *is bending over the*
CHILD's *crib.*]

GRUSHA   Hide him. Quick! The Ironshirts are coming! I laid him on your doorstep. But he isn't mine. He's from a good family.

PEASANT WOMAN   Who's coming? What Ironshirts?

GRUSHA   Don't ask questions. The Ironshirts that are looking for it.

PEASANT WOMAN   They've no business in my house. But I must have a little
talk with you, it seems.

GRUSHA   Take off the fine linen. It'll give us away.

PEASANT WOMAN   Linen, my foot! In this house I make the decisions! *"You
can't vomit in* my *room!"* Why did you abandon it? It's a sin.

GRUSHA   [*looking out of the window*]   Look, they're coming out from behind
those trees! I shouldn't have run away, it made them angry. Oh, what shall
I do?

PEASANT WOMAN   [*looking out of the window and suddenly starting with fear*]
Gracious! Ironshirts!

GRUSHA   They're after the baby.

PEASANT WOMAN   Suppose they come in!

GRUSHA   You mustn't give him to them. Say he's yours.

PEASANT WOMAN   Yes.

GRUSHA   They'll run him through if you hand him over.

PEASANT WOMAN   But suppose they ask for it? The silver for the harvest is
in the house.

GRUSHA   If you let them have him, they'll run him through, right here in this
room! You've got to say he's yours!

PEASANT WOMAN   Yes. But what if they don't believe me?

GRUSHA   You must be firm.

PEASANT WOMAN   They'll burn the roof over our heads.

GRUSHA   That's why you must say he's yours. His name's Michael. But I
shouldn't have told you. [*The* PEASANT WOMAN *nods.*] Don't nod like that.
And don't tremble—they'll notice.

PEASANT WOMAN   Yes.

GRUSHA   And stop saying yes, I can't stand it. [*She shakes the* WOMAN.] Don't you
have any children?

PEASANT WOMAN   [*muttering*]   He's in the war.

GRUSHA   Then maybe *he's* an Ironshirt? Do you want *him* to run children
through with a lance? You'd bawl him out. "No fooling with lances in my
house!" you'd shout, "is that what I've reared you for? Wash your neck
before you speak to your mother!"

PEASANT WOMAN   That's true, he couldn't get away with anything around here!

GRUSHA   So you'll say he's yours?

PEASANT WOMAN   Yes.

GRUSHA   Look! They're coming!

[*There is a knocking at the door. The women don't answer. Enter* IRON-SHIRTS. *The* PEASANT WOMAN *bows low.*]

CORPORAL   Well, here she is. What did I tell you? What a nose I have! I *smelt* her. Lady, I have a question for you. Why did you run away? What did you think I would do to you? I'll bet it was something unchaste. Confess!

GRUSHA   [*while the* PEASANT WOMAN *bows again and again.*]   I'd left some milk on the stove, and I suddenly remembered it.

CORPORAL   Or maybe you imagined I looked at you unchastely? Like there could be something between us? A carnal glance, know what I mean?

GRUSHA   I didn't see it.

CORPORAL   But it's possible, huh? You admit that much. After all, I might be a pig. I'll be frank with you: I could think of all sorts of things if we were alone. [*To the* PEASANT WOMAN:] Shouldn't you be busy in the yard? Feeding the hens?

PEASANT WOMAN   [*falling suddenly to her knees*]:   Soldier, I didn't know a thing about it. Please don't burn the roof over our heads.

CORPORAL   What are you talking about?

PEASANT WOMAN   I had nothing to do with it. She left it on my doorstep, I swear it!

CORPORAL   [*suddenly seeing the* CHILD *and whistling*]:   Ah, so there's a little something in the crib! Blockhead, I smell a thousand piasters. Take the old girl outside and hold on to her. It looks like I have a little cross-examining to do. [*The* PEASANT WOMAN *lets herself be led out by the* PRIVATE, *without a word.*] So, you've *got* the child I wanted from you! [*He walks toward the crib.*]

GRUSHA   Officer, he's mine. He's not the one you're after.

CORPORAL   I'll just take a look. [*He bends over the crib.*]

[GRUSHA *looks round in despair.*]

GRUSHA   He's mine! He's mine!

CORPORAL   Fine linen!

[GRUSHA *dashes at him to pull him away. He throws her off and again bends over the crib. Again looking round in despair, she sees a log of wood, seizes it, and hits the* CORPORAL *over the head from behind. The* CORPORAL *collapses. She quickly picks up the* CHILD *and rushes off.*]

SINGER

And in her flight from the Ironshirts
After twenty-two days of journeying
At the foot of the Janga-Tau Glacier
Grusha Vashnadze decided to adopt the child.

CHORUS

The helpless girl adopted the helpless child.

[GRUSHA *squats over a half-frozen stream to get the* CHILD *water in the hollow of her hand.*]

GRUSHA

Since no one else will take you, son,
I must take you.
Since no one else will take you, son,
You must take me.
O black day in a lean, lean year,

The trip was long, the milk was dear,
My legs are tired, my feet are sore:
But I wouldn't be without you any more.
I'll throw your silken shirt away
And wrap you in rags and tatters.
I'll wash you, son, and christen you in glacier water.
We'll see it through together.
[*She has taken off the child's fine linen and wrapped it in a rag.*]

SINGER

When Grusha Vashnadze
Pursued by the Ironshirts
Came to the bridge on the glacier
Leading to the villages of the Eastern Slope
She sang the Song of the Rotten Bridge
And risked two lives.
[*A wind has risen. The bridge on the glacier is visible in the dark. One rope is broken and half the bridge is hanging down the abyss.* MERCHANTS, *two men and a woman, stand undecided before the bridge as* GRUSHA *and the* CHILD *arrive. One man is trying to catch the hanging rope with a stick.*]

FIRST MAN   Take your time, young woman. You won't get across here anyway.

GRUSHA   But I *have* to get the baby to the east side. To my brother's place.

MERCHANT WOMAN   Have to? How d'you mean, "have to"? I have to get there, too—because I have to buy carpets in Atum—carpets a woman had to sell because her husband had to die. But can *I* do what I have to? Can she? Andrei's been fishing for that rope for hours. And I ask you, how are we going to fasten it, even if he gets it up?

FIRST MAN   [*listening*]   Hush, I think I hear something.

GRUSHA   The bridge isn't quite rotted through. I think I'll try it.

MERCHANT WOMAN   *I* wouldn't—if the devil himself were after me. It's suicide.

FIRST MAN   [*shouting*]   Hi!

GRUSHA   Don't shout! [*To the* MERCHANT WOMAN] Tell him not to shout.

FIRST MAN   But there's someone down there calling. Maybe they've lost their way.

MERCHANT WOMAN   Why shouldn't he shout? Is there something funny about you? Are they after you?

GRUSHA   All right, I'll tell. The Ironshirts are after me. I knocked one down.

SECOND MAN   Hide our merchandise!
[*The* WOMAN *hides a sack behind a rock.*]

FIRST MAN   Why didn't you say so right away? [*To the others:*] If they catch her they'll make mincemeat out of her!

GRUSHA   Get out of my way. I've got to cross that bridge.

SECOND MAN   You can't. The precipice is two thousand feet deep.

FIRST MAN   Even with the rope it'd be no use. We could hold it up with our hands. But then we'd have to do the same for the Ironshirts.

GRUSHA   Go away.
[*There are calls from the distance*] "Hi, up there!"

MERCHANT WOMAN   They're getting near. But you can't take the child on that bridge. It's sure to break. And look!
[GRUSHA *looks down into the abyss. The* IRONSHIRTS *are heard calling again from below.*]

SECOND MAN   Two thousand feet!

GRUSHA   But those men are worse.

FIRST MAN   You can't do it. Think of the baby. Risk your life but not a child's.

SECOND MAN   With the child she's that much heavier!

MERCHANT WOMAN   Maybe she's *really* got to get across. Give *me* the baby. I'll hide it. Cross the bridge alone!

GRUSHA   I won't. We belong together. [*To the* CHILD] "Live together, die together." [*She sings.*]

THE SONG OF THE ROTTEN BRIDGE

> Deep is the abyss, son,
> I see the weak bridge sway
> But it's not for us, son,
> To choose the way.
>
> The way I know
> Is the one you must tread,
> And all you will eat
> Is my bit of bread.
>
> Of every four pieces
> You shall have three.
> Would that I knew
> How big they will be!

Get out of my way, I'll try it without the rope.

MERCHANT WOMAN   You are tempting God!

[*There are shouts from below.*]

GRUSHA   Please, throw that stick away, or they'll get the rope and follow me. [*Pressing the* CHILD *to her, she steps onto the swaying bridge. The* MERCHANT WOMAN *screams when it looks as though the bridge is about to collapse. But* GRUSHA *walks on and reaches the far side.*]

FIRST MAN   She made it!

MERCHANT WOMAN   [*who has fallen on her knees and begun to pray, angrily*] I still think it was a sin.

[*The* IRONSHIRTS *appear; the* CORPORAL'*s head is bandaged.*]

CORPORAL   Seen a woman with a child?

FIRST MAN   [*while the* SECOND MAN *throws the stick into the abyss*]   Yes, there! But the bridge won't carry you!

CORPORAL   You'll pay for this, blockhead!

[GRUSHA, *from the far bank, laughs and shows the* CHILD *to the* IRONSHIRTS. *She walks on. The wind blows.*]

GRUSHA   [*turning to the* CHILD] You mustn't be afraid of the wind. He's a poor thing too. He has to push the clouds along and he gets quite cold doing it. [*Snow starts falling.*] And the snow isn't so bad, either, Michael. It covers the little fir trees so they won't die in winter. Let me sing you a little song. [*She sings.*]

THE SONG OF THE CHILD

> Your father is a bandit
> A harlot the mother who bore you.
> Yet honorable men
> Shall kneel down before you.
> Food to the baby horses
> The tiger's son will take.
> The mothers will get milk
> From the son of the snake.

3

IN THE NORTHERN MOUNTAINS

SINGER

> Seven days the sister, Grusha Vashnadze,
> Journeyed across the glacier
> And down the slopes she journeyed.
> "When I enter my brother's house," she thought,
> "He will rise and embrace me."
> "Is that you, sister?" he will say,
> "I have long expected you.
> This is my dear wife,
> And this is my farm, come to me by marriage,
> With eleven horses and thirty-one cows. Sit down.
> Sit down with your child at our table and eat."
> The brother's house was in a lovely valley.
> When the sister came to the brother,
> She was ill from walking.
> The brother rose from the table.

[*A fat peasant couple rise from the table.* LAVRENTI VASHNADZE *still has a napkin round his neck, as* GRUSHA, *pale and supported by a* SERVANT, *enters with the* CHILD.]

LAVRENTI   Where've *you* come from, Grusha?

GRUSHA   [*feebly*]   Across the Janga-Tu Pass, Lavrenti.

SERVANT   I found her in front of the hay barn. She has a baby with her.

SISTER-IN-LAW   Go and groom the mare.

[*Exit the* SERVANT.]

LAVRENTI   This is my wife Aniko.

SISTER-IN-LAW   I thought you were in service in Nuka.

GRUSHA   [*barely able to stand*]   Yes, I was.

SISTER-IN-LAW   Wasn't it a good job? We were told it was.

GRUSHA   The Governor got killed.

LAVRENTI   Yes, we heard there were riots. Your aunt told us. Remember, Aniko?

SISTER-IN-LAW   Here with us, it's very quiet. City people always want something going on. [*She walks toward the door, calling:*] Sosso, Sosso, don't take the cake out of the oven yet, d'you hear? Where on earth are you? [*Exit, calling.*]

LAVRENTI   [*quietly, quickly*]   Is there a father? [*As she shakes her head*] I thought not. We must think up something. She's religious.

SISTER-IN-LAW   [*returning*]   Those servants! [*To* GRUSHA] You have a child.

GRUSHA   It's mine. [*She collapses.* LAVRENTI *rushes to her assistance.*]

SISTER-IN-LAW   Heavens, she's ill—what are we going to do?

LAVRENTI   [*escorting her to a bench near the stove*]   Sit down, sit. I think it's just weakness. Aniko.

SISTER-IN-LAW   As long as it's not scarlet fever!

LAVRENTI   She'd have spots if it was. It's only weakness. Don't worry, Aniko [*To* GRUSHA:] Better, sitting down?

SISTER-IN-LAW   Is the child hers?

GRUSHA   Yes, mine.

LAVRENTI   She's on her way to her husband.

SISTER-IN-LAW   I see. Your meat's getting cold. [LAVRENTI *sits down and begins to eat.*] Cold food's not good for you, the fat mustn't get cold, you know your stomach's your weak spot. [*To* GRUSHA] If your husband's not in the city, where is he?

LAVRENTI   She got married on the other side of the mountain, she says.

SISTER-IN-LAW   On the other side of the mountain. I see. [*She also sits down to eat.*]

GRUSHA   I think I should lie down somewhere, Lavrenti.

SISTER-IN-LAW   If it's consumption we'll all get it. [*She goes on cross-examining her.*] Has your husband got a farm?

GRUSHA   He's a soldier.

LAVRENTI   But he's coming into a farm—a small one—from his father.

SISTER-IN-LAW   Isn't he in the war? Why not?

GRUSHA   [*with effort*]   Yes, he's in the war.

SISTER-IN-LAW   Then why d'you want to go to the farm?

LAVRENTI   When he comes back from the war, he'll return to his farm.

SISTER-IN-LAW   But you're going there now?

LAVRENTI   Yes, to wait for him.

SISTER-IN-LAW   [*calling shrilly*]   Sosso, the cake!

GRUSHA   [*murmuring feverishly*]   A farm—a soldier—waiting—sit down, eat.

SISTER-IN-LAW   It's scarlet fever.

GRUSHA   [*starting up*]   Yes, he's got a farm!

LAVRENTI   I think it's just weakness, Aniko. Would you look after the cake yourself, dear?

SISTER-IN-LAW   But when will he come back if war's broken out again as people say? [*She waddles off, shouting:*] Sosso! Where on earth are you? Sosso!

LAVRENTI   [*getting up quickly and going to* GRUSHA]   You'll get a bed in a minute. She has a good heart. But wait till after supper.

GRUSHA   [*holding out the* CHILD *to him*]   Take him.

LAVRENTI   [*taking it and looking around*]   But you can't stay here long with the child. She's religious, you see.

GRUSHA *collapses.* LAVRENTI *catches her.*

SINGER
    The sister was so ill,
    The cowardly brother had to give her shelter.
    Summer departed, winter came.
    The winter was long, the winter was short.
    People mustn't know anything.
    Rats mustn't bite.
    Spring mustn't come.
    [GRUSHA *sits over the weaving loom in a workroom. She and the* CHILD, *who is squatting on the floor, are wrapped in blankets. She sings.*]
    [*Enter* LAVRENTI. *He sit down beside his sister.*]

                    THE SONG OF THE CENTER
            And the lover started to leave
            And his betrothed ran pleading after him
            Pleading and weeping, weeping and teaching:
            "Dearest mine, dearest mine
            When you go to war as now you do
            When you fight the foe as soon you will
            Don't lead with the front line
            And don't push with the rear line
            At the front is red fire
            In the rear is red smoke
            Stay in the war's center
            Stay near the standard bearer

The first always die
The last are also hit
Those in the center come home."

Michael, we must be clever. If we make ourselves as small as cockroaches, the sister-in-law will forget we're in the house, and then we can stay till the snow melts.

[*Enter* LAVRENTI. *He sits down beside his sister.*]

LAVRENTI Why are you sitting there muffled up like coachmen, you two? Is it too cold in the room?

GRUSHA [*hastily removing one shawl*] It's not too cold, Lavrenti.

LAVRENTI If it's too cold, you shouldn't be sitting here with the child. Aniko would never forgive herself! [*Pause*] I hope our priest didn't question you about the child?

GRUSHA He did, but I didn't tell him anything.

LAVRENTI That's good. I wanted to speak to you about Aniko. She has a good heart but she's very, very sensitive. People need only mention our farm and she's worried. She takes everything hard, you see. One time our milk-maid went to church with a hole in her stocking. Ever since, Aniko has worn two pairs of stockings in church. It's the old family in her. [*He listens.*] Are you sure there are no rats around? If there are rats, you couldn't live here. [*There are sounds as of dripping from the roof.*] What's that, dripping?

GRUSHA It must be a barrel leaking.

LAVRENTI Yes, it must be a barrel. You've been here six months, haven't you? Was I talking about Aniko? [*They listen again to the snow melting.*] You can't imagine how worried she gets about your soldier-husband. "Suppose he comes back and can't find her!" she says and lies awake. "He can't come before the spring," I tell her. The dear woman! [*The drops begin to fall faster.*] When d'you think he'll come? What do *you* think? [GRUSHA *is silent.*] Not before the spring, you agree? [GRUSHA *is silent.*] You don't believe he'll come at all? [GRUSHA *is silent.*] But when the spring comes and the snow melts here and on the passes, you can't stay on. They may come and look for you. There's already talk of an illegitimate child. [*The "glockenspiel" of the falling drops has grown faster and steadier.*] Grusha, the snow is melting on the roof. Spring is here.

GRUSHA Yes.

LAVRENTI [*eagerly*] I'll tell you what we'll do. You need a place to go, and, because of the child [*he sighs*], you have to have a husband, so people won't talk. Now I've made cautious inquiries to see if we can find you a husband. Grusha, I *have* one. I talked to a peasant woman who has a son. Just the other side of the mountain. A small farm. And she's willing.

GRUSHA But I *can't* marry! I must wait for Simon Shashava.

LAVRENTI Of course. That's all been taken care of. You don't need a man in bed—you need a man on paper. And I've found you one. The son of this peasant woman is going to die. Isn't that wonderful? He's at his last gasp. And all in line with our story—a husband from the other side of the mountain! And when you met him he was at the last gasp. So you're a widow. What do you say?

GRUSHA It's true I could use a document with stamps on it for Michael.

LAVRENTI Stamps make all the difference. Without something in writing the Shah couldn't prove he's a Shah. And you'll have a place to live.

GRUSHA How much does the peasant woman want?

LAVRENTI Four hundred piasters.

GRUSHA Where will you find it?

LAVRENTI [*guiltily*] Aniko's milk money.

GRUSHA No one would know us there. I'll do it.

LAVRENTI [*getting up*] I'll let the peasant woman know.
[*Quick exit.*]

GRUSHA Michael, you make a lot of work. I came by you as the pear tree comes by sparrows. And because a Christian bends down and picks up a crust of bread so nothing will go to waste. Michael, it would have been better had I walked quickly away on that Easter Sunday in Nuka in the second courtyard. Now I *am* a fool.

SINGER
The bridegroom was on his deathbed when the bride arrived.
The bridegroom's mother was waiting at the door, telling her to hurry.
The bride brought a child along.
The witness hid it during the wedding.
[*On one side the bed. Under the mosquito net lies a very sick man.* GRUSHA *is pulled in at a run by her future mother-in-law. They are followed by* LAVRENTI *and the* CHILD.]

MOTHER-IN-LAW Quick! Quick! Or he'll die on us before the wedding. [*To* LAVRENTI] I was never told she had a child already.

LAVRENTI What difference does it make? [*Pointing toward the dying man.*] It can't matter to him—in his condition.

MOTHER-IN-LAW To him? But I'll never survive the shame! We are honest people. [*She begins to weep.*] My Jussup doesn't have to marry a girl with a child!

LAVRENTI All right, make it another two hundred piasters. You'll have it in writing that the farm will go to you: but she'll have the right to live here for two years.

MOTHER-IN-LAW [*drying her tears*] It'll hardly cover the funeral expenses. I hope she'll really lend a hand with the work. And what's happened to the monk? He must have slipped out through the kitchen window. We'll have the whole village on our necks when they hear Jussup's end is come! Oh dear! I'll go get the monk. But he mustn't see the child!

LAVRENTI I'll take care he doesn't. But why only a monk? Why not a priest?

MOTHER-IN-LAW Oh, he's just as good. I only made one mistake: I paid half his fee in advance. Enough to send him to the tavern. I only hope . . .
[*She runs off.*]

LAVRENTI She saved on the priest, the wretch! Hired a cheap monk.

GRUSHA You *will* send Simon Shashava to see me if he turns up after all?

LAVRENTI Yes. [*Pointing at the* SICK PEASANT.] Won't you take a look at him? [GRUSHA, *taking* MICHAEL *to her, shakes her head.*] He's not moving an eyelid. I hope we aren't too late.
[*They listen. On the opposite side enter neighbors who look around and take up positions against the walls, thus forming another wall near the bed, yet leaving an opening so that the bed can be seen. They start murmuring prayers. Enter the* MOTHER-IN-LAW *with a* MONK. *Showing some annoyance and surprise, she bows to the guests.*]

MOTHER-IN-LAW I hope you won't mind waiting a few moments? My son's bride has just arrived from the city. An emergency wedding is about to be celebrated. [*To the* MONK *in the bedroom*] I might have known you couldn't keep your trap shut. [*To* GRUSHA] The wedding can take place at once. Here's the license. Me and the bride's brother [LAVRENTI *tries to hide in the background, after having quietly taken* MICHAEL *back from* GRUSHA. *The* MOTHER-IN-LAW *waves him away.*] are the witnesses.

[GRUSHA *has bowed to the* MONK. *They go to the bed. The* MOTHER-IN-LAW *lifts the mosquito net. The* MONK *starts reeling off the marriage ceremony in Latin. Meanwhile the* MOTHER-IN-LAW *beckons to* LAVRENTI *to get rid of the* CHILD, *but fearing that it will cry he draws its attention to the ceremony.* GRUSHA *glances once at the* CHILD, *and* LAVRENTI *waves the* CHILD's *hand in a greeting.*]

MONK   Are you prepared to be a faithful, obedient, and good wife to this man, and to cleave to him until death you do part?

GRUSHA   [*looking at the* CHILD]   I am.

MONK   [*to the* SICK PEASANT]   Are you prepared to be a good and loving husband to your wife until death you do part? [*As the* SICK PEASANT *does not answer, the* MONK *looks inquiringly around.*]

MOTHER-IN-LAW   Of course he is! Didn't you hear him say yes?

MONK   All right. We declare the marriage contracted! How about extreme unction?

MOTHER-IN-LAW   Nothing doing! The wedding cost quite enough. Now I must take care of the mourners. [*To* LAVRENTI] Did we say seven hundred?

LAVRENTI   Six hundred. [*He pays.*] Now I don't want to sit with the guests and get to know people. So farewell, Grusha, and if my widowed sister comes to visit me, she'll get a welcome from my wife, or I'll show my teeth. [*Nods, gives the* CHILD *to* GRUSHA, *and leaves. The mourners glance after him without interest.*]

MONK   May one ask where this child comes from?

MOTHER-IN-LAW   Is there a child? I don't see a child. And you don't see a child either—you understand? Or it may turn out I saw all sorts of things in the tavern! Now come on!
[*After* GRUSHA *has put the* CHILD *down and told him to be quiet, they move over left;* GRUSHA *is introduced to the neighbors.*]
This is my daughter-in-law. She arrived just in time to find dear Jussup still alive.

ONE WOMAN   He's been ill now a whole year, hasn't he? When our Vassili was drafted he was there to say good-bye.

ANOTHER WOMAN   Such things are terrible for a farm. The corn all ripe and the farmer in bed! It'll really be a blessing if he doesn't suffer too long, I say.

FIRST WOMAN   [*confidentially*]   You know why we thought he'd taken to his bed? Because of the draft! And now his end is come!

MOTHER-IN-LAW   Sit yourselves down, please! And have some cakes!
[*She beckons to* GRUSHA *and both women go into the bedroom, where they pick up the cake pans off the floor. The guests, among them the* MONK, *sit on the floor and begin conversing in subdued voices.*]

ONE PEASANT   [*to whom the* MONK *has handed the bottle which he has taken from his soutane*]   There's a child, you say! How can that have happened to Jussup?

A WOMAN   She was certainly lucky to get herself married, with him so sick!

MOTHER-IN-LAW   They're gossiping already. And wolfing down the funeral cakes at the same time! If he doesn't die today, I'll have to bake some more tomorrow!

GRUSHA   I'll bake them for you.

MOTHER-IN-LAW   Yesterday some horsemen rode by, and I went out to see who it was. When I came in again he was lying there like a corpse! So I sent for you. It can't take much longer. [*She listens.*]

MONK   Dear wedding and funeral guests! Deeply touched, we stand before a bed of death and marriage. The bride gets a veil; the groom, a shroud:

how varied, my children, are the fates of men! Alas! One man dies and has a roof over his head, and the other is married and the flesh turns to dust from which it was made. Amen.

MOTHER-IN-LAW He's getting his own back. I shouldn't have hired such a cheap one. It's what you'd expect. A more expensive monk would behave himself. In Sura there's one with a real air of sanctity about him, but of course he charges a fortune. A fifty piaster monk like that has no dignity, and as for piety, just fifty piasters' worth and no more! When I came to get him in the tavern he'd just made a speech, and he was shouting: "The war is over, beware of the peace!" We must go in.

GRUSHA [*giving* MICHAEL *a cake*] Eat this cake, and keep nice and still, Michael.

[*The two women offer cakes to the guests. The dying man sits up in bed. He puts his head out from under the mosquito net, stares at the two women, then sinks back again. The* MONK *takes two bottles from his soutane and offers them to the peasant beside him. Enter three* MUSICIANS *who are greeted with a sly wink by the* MONK.]

MOTHER-IN-LAW [*to the* MUSICIANS] What are you doing here? With instruments?

ONE MUSICIAN Brother Anastasius here [*pointing at the* MONK] told us there was a wedding on.

MOTHER-IN-LAW What? You brought them? Three more on my neck! Don't you know there's a dying man in the next room?

MONK A very tempting assignment for a musician: something that could be either a subdued Wedding March or a spirited Funeral Dance.

MOTHER-IN-LAW Well, you might as well play. Nobody can stop you eating in any case.

[*The musicians play a potpourri. The women serve cakes.*]

MONK The trumpet sounds like a whining baby. And you, little drum, what have you got to tell the world?

DRUNKEN PEASANT [*beside the* MONK, *sings*]
There was a young woman who said:
I thought I'd be happier, wed.
But my husband is old
And remarkably cold
So I sleep with a candle instead.

[*The* MOTHER-IN-LAW *throws the* DRUNKEN PEASANT *out. The music stops. The guests are embarrassed.*]

GUESTS [*loudly*]
—Have you heard? The Grand Duke is back! But the Princes are against him.
—They say the Shah of Persia has lent him a great army to restore order in Grusinia.
—But how is that possible? The Shah of Persia is the enemy . . .
—The enemy of Grusinia, you donkey, not the enemy of the Grand Duke!
—In any case, the war's over, so our soldiers are coming back.

[GRUSHA *drops a cake pan.* GUESTS *help her pick up the cake.*]

AN OLD WOMAN [*to* GRUSHA] Are you feeling bad? It's just excitement about dear Jussup. Sit down and rest a while, my dear. [GRUSHA *staggers.*]

GUESTS Now everything'll be the way it was. Only the taxes'll go up because now we'll have to pay for the war.

GRUSHA [*weakly*] Did someone say the soldiers are back?

A MAN I did.

GRUSHA It can't be true.

FIRST MAN   [to a woman]   Show her the shawl. We bought it from a soldier. It's from Persia.

GRUSHA   [looking at the shawl]   They are here. [She gets up, takes a step, kneels down in prayer, takes the silver cross and chain out of her blouse, and kisses it.]

MOTHER-IN-LAW   [while the guests silently watch GRUSHA]   What's the matter with you? Aren't you going to look after our guests? What's all this city nonsense got to do with us?

GUESTS   [resuming conversation while GRUSHA remains in prayer]
—You can buy Persian saddles from the soldiers too. Though many want crutches in exchange for them.
—The leaders on one side can win a war, the soldiers on both sides lose it.
—Anyway, the war's over. It's something they can't draft you any more.
[The dying man sits bolt upright in bed. He listens.]
—What we need is two weeks of good weather.
—our pear trees are hardly bearing a thing this year.

MOTHER-IN-LAW   [offering cakes]   Have some more cakes and welcome! There are more!
[The MOTHER-IN-LAW goes to the bedroom with the empty cake pans. Unaware of the dying man, she is bending down to pick up another tray when he begins to talk in a hoarse voice.]

PEASANT   How many more cakes are you going to stuff down their throats? D'you think I can shit money?
[The MOTHER-IN-LAW starts, stares at him aghast, while he climbs out from behind the mosquito net.]

FIRST WOMAN   [talking kindly to GRUSHA in the next room]   Has the young wife got someone at the front?

A MAN   It's good news that they're on their way home, huh?

PEASANT   Don't stare at me like that! Where's this wife you've saddled me with?
[Receiving no answer, he climbs out of bed and in his nightshirt staggers into the other room. Trembling, she follows him with the cake pan.]

GUESTS   [seeing him and shrieking]   Good God! Jussup!
[Everyone leaps up in alarm. The women rush to the door. GRUSHA, still on her knees, turns round and stares at the man.]

PEASANT   A funeral supper! You'd enjoy that, wouldn't you? Get out before I throw you out! [As the guests stampede from the house, gloomily to GRUSHA] I've upset the apple cart, huh? [Receiving no answer, he turns round and takes a cake from the pan which his mother is holding.]

SINGER
O confusion! The wife discovers she has a husband.
By day there's the child, by night there's the husband.
The lover is on his way both day and night.
Husband and wife look at each other.
The bedroom is small.
[Near the bed the PEASANT is sitting in a high wooden bathtub, naked, the MOTHER-IN-LAW is pouring water from a pitcher. Opposite, GRUSHA cowers with MICHAEL, who is playing at mending straw mats.]

PEASANT   [to his mother]   That's her work, not yours. Where's she hiding out now?

MOTHER-IN-LAW   [calling]   Grusha! The peasant wants you!

GRUSHA   [to MICHAEL]   There are still two holes to mend.

PEASANT   [when GRUSHA approaches]   Scrub my back!

GRUSHA   Can't the peasant do it himself?

PEASANT   "Can't the peasant do it himself?" Get the brush! To hell with you!

Are you the wife here? Or are you a visitor? [*To the* MOTHER-IN-LAW] It's too cold!

MOTHER-IN-LAW   I'll run for hot water.

GRUSHA   Let me go.

PEASANT   You stay here. [*The* MOTHER-IN-LAW *exits.*] Rub harder. And no shirking. You've seen a naked fellow before. That child didn't come out of thin air.

GRUSHA   The child was not conceived in joy, if that's what the peasant means.

PEASANT   [*turning and grinning*] You don't look the type. [GRUSHA *stops scrubbing him, starts back. Enter the* MOTHER-IN-LAW.]

PEASANT   A nice thing you've saddled me with! A simpleton for a wife!

MOTHER-IN-LAW   She just isn't cooperative.

PEASANT   Pour—but go easy! Ow! Go easy, I said. [*To* GRUSHA] Maybe you did something wrong in the city . . . I wouldn't be surprised. Why else should you be here? But I won't talk about that. I've not said a word about the illegitimate object you brought into my house either. But my patience has limits! It's against nature. [*To the* MOTHER-IN-LAW] More! [*To* GRUSHA] And even if your soldier does come back, you're married.

GRUSHA   Yes.

PEASANT   But your soldier won't come back. Don't you believe it.

GRUSHA   No.

PEASANT   You're cheating me. You're my wife and you're not my wife. Where you lie, nothing lies, and yet no other woman can lie there. When I go to work in the morning I'm tired—when I lie down at night I'm awake as the devil. God has given you sex—and what d'you do? I don't have ten piasters to buy myself a woman in the city. Besides, it's a long way. Woman weeds the fields and opens up her legs, that's what our calendar says. D'you hear?

GRUSHA   [*quietly*] Yes. I didn't mean to cheat you out of it.

PEASANT   She didn't mean to cheat me out of it! Pour some more water! [*The* MOTHER-IN-LAW *pours.*] Ow!

SINGER

As she sat by the stream to wash the linen
She saw his image in the water
And his face grew dimmer with the passing moons.
As she raised herself to wring the linen
She heard his voice from the murmuring maple
And his voice grew fainter with the passing moons.
Evasions and sighs grew more numerous,
Tears and sweat flowed.
With the passing moons the child grew up.

[GRUSHA *sits by a stream, dipping linen into the water. In the rear, a few children are standing.*]

GRUSHA   [*to* MICHAEL] You can play with them, Michael, but don't let them boss you around just because you're the littlest. [MICHAEL *nods and joins the children. They start playing.*]

BIGGEST BOY   Today it's the Heads-Off Game. [*To a* FAT BOY] You're the Prince and you laugh. [*To* MICHAEL] You're the Governor. [*To a* GIRL] You're the Governor's wife and you cry when his head's cut off. And I do the cutting. [*He shows his wooden sword.*] With this. First, they lead the Governor into the yard. The Prince walks in front. The Governor's wife comes last.

[*They form a procession. The* FAT BOY *is first and laughs. Then comes* MICHAEL, *then the* BIGGEST BOY, *and then the* GIRL, *who weeps.*]

MICHAEL   [*standing still*] Me cut off head!

BIGGEST BOY   That's my job. You're the littlest. The Governor's the easy part. All you do is kneel down and get your head cut off—simple.
MICHAEL   Me want sword!
BIGGEST BOY   It's mine! [*He gives* MICHAEL *a kick.*]
GIRL   [*shouting to* GRUSHA]   He won't play his part!
GRUSHA   [*laughing*]   Even the little duck is a swimmer, they say.
BIGGEST BOY   You can be the Prince if you can laugh. [MICHAEL *shakes his head.*]
FAT BOY   I laugh best. Let him cut off the head just once. Then you do it, then me.

[*Reluctantly, the* BIGGEST BOY *hands* MICHAEL *the wooden sword and kneels down. The* FAT BOY *sits down, slaps his thigh, and laughs with all his might. The* GIRL *weeps loudly.* MICHAEL *swings the big sword and "cuts off" the head. In doing so, he topples over.*]

BIGGEST BOY   Hey! I'll show you how to cut heads off!

[MICHAEL *runs away. The children run after him.* GRUSHA *laughs, following them with her eyes. On looking back, she sees* SIMON SHASHAVA *standing on the opposite bank. He wears a shabby uniform.*]

GRUSHA   Simon!
SIMON   Is that Grusha Vashnadze?
GRUSHA   Simon!
SIMON   [*formally*]   A good morning to the young lady. I hope she is well.
GRUSHA   [*getting up gaily and bowing low*]   A good morning to the soldier. God be thanked he has returned in good health.
SIMON   They found better fish, so they didn't eat me, said the haddock.
GRUSHA   Courage, said the kitchen boy. Good luck, said the hero.
SIMON   How are things here? Was the winter bearable? The neighbor considerate?
GRUSHA   The winter was a trifle rough, the neighbor as usual, Simon.
SIMON   May one ask if a certain person still dips her toes in the water when rinsing the linen?
GRUSHA   The answer is no. Because of the eyes in the bushes.
SIMON   The young lady is speaking of soldiers. Here stands a paymaster.
GRUSHA   A job worth twenty piasters?
SIMON   And lodgings.
GRUSHA   [*with tears in her eyes*]   Behind the barracks under the date trees.
SIMON   Yes, there. A certain person has kept her eyes open.
GRUSHA   She has, Simon.
SIMON   And has not forgotten? [GRUSHA *shakes her head.*] So the door is still on its hinges as they say? [GRUSHA *looks at him in silence and shakes her head again.*] What's this? Is anything not as it should be?
GRUSHA   Simon Shashava, I can never return to Nuka. Something has happened.
SIMON   What can have happened?
GRUSHA   For one thing, I knocked an Ironshirt down.
SIMON   Grusha Vashnadze must have had her reasons for that.
GRUSHA   Simon Shashava, I am no longer called what I used to be called.
SIMON   [*after a pause*]   I do not understand.
GRUSHA   When do women change their names, Simon? Let me explain. Nothing stands between us. Everything is just as it was. You must believe that.
SIMON   Nothing stands between us and yet there's something?
GRUSHA   How can I explain it so fast and with the stream between us? Couldn't you cross the bridge there?
SIMON   Maybe it's no longer necessary.

GRUSHA It is very necessary. Come over on this side, Simon, Quick!

SIMON Does the young lady wish to say someone has come too late?

[GRUSHA *looks up at him in despair, her face streaming with tears.* SIMON *stares before him. He picks up a piece of wood and starts cutting it.*]

SINGER

So many words are said, so many left unsaid.

The soldier has come.

Where he comes from, he does not say.

Hear what he thought and did not say:

"The battle began, gray at dawn, grew bloody at noon.

The first man fell in front of me, the second behind me, the third at my side.

I trod on the first, left the second behind, the third was run through by the captain.

One of my brothers died by steel, the other by smoke.

My neck caught fire, my hands froze in my gloves, my toes in my socks.

I fed on aspen buds, I drank maple juice, I slept on stone, in water."

SIMON I see a cap in the grass. Is there a little one already?

GRUSHA There is, Simon. There's no keeping *that* from you. But please don't worry, it is not mine.

SIMON When the wind once starts to blow, they say, it blows through every cranny. The wife need say no more. [GRUSHA *looks into her lap and is silent.*]

SINGER

There was yearning but there was no waiting.

The oath is broken. Neither could say why.

Hear what she thought but did not say:

"While you fought in the battle, soldier,

The bloody battle, the bitter battle

I found a helpless infant

I had not the heart to destroy him

I had to care for a creature that was lost

I had to stoop for breadcrumbs on the floor

I had to break myself for that which was not mine

That which was other people's.

Someone must help!

For the little tree needs water

The lamb loses its way when the shepherd is asleep

And its cry is unheard!"

SIMON Give me back the cross I gave you. Better still, throw it in the stream. [*He turns to go.*]

GRUSHA [*getting up*] Simon Shashava, don't go away! He isn't mine! He isn't mine! [*She hears the children calling.*] What's the matter, children?

VOICES Soldiers! And they're taking Michael away!

[GRUSHA *stands aghast as two* IRONSHIRTS, *with* MICHAEL *between them, come toward her.*]

ONE OF THE IRONSHIRTS Are you Grusha? [*She nods.*] Is this your child?

GRUSHA Yes. [SIMON *goes.*] Simon!

IRONSHIRT We have orders, in the name of the law, to take this child, found in your custody, back to the city. It is suspected that the child is Michael Abashwili, son and heir of the late Governor Georgi Abashwili, and his wife, Natella Abashwili. Here is the document and the seal. [*They lead the* CHILD *away.*]

GRUSHA [*running after them, shouting*] Leave him here. Please! He's mine!

SINGER

The Ironshirts took the child, the beloved child.
The unhappy girl followed them to the city, the dreaded city.
She who had borne him demanded the child.
She who had raised him faced trial.
Who will decide the case?
To whom will the child be assigned?
Who will the judge be? A good judge? A bad?
The city was in flames.
In the judge's seat sat Azdak.[1]

4
THE STORY OF THE JUDGE

SINGER

Hear the story of the judge
How he turned judge, how he passed judgment, what kind of judge he was.
On that Easter Sunday of the great revolt, when the Grand Duke was over-
thrown
And his Governor Abashwili, father of our child, lost his head
The Village Scrivener Azdak found a fugitive in the
woods and hid him in his hut.
[AZDAK, *in rags and slightly drunk, is helping an old beggar into his cottage.*]

AZDAK   Stop snorting, you're not a horse. And it won't do you any good with the police to run like a snotty nose in April. Stand still, I say. [*He catches the* OLD MAN, *who has marched into the cottage as if he'd like to go through the walls.*] Sit down. Feed. Here's a hunk of cheese. [*From under some rags, in a chest, he fishes out some cheese, and the* OLD MAN *greedily begins to eat.*] Haven't eaten in a long time, huh? [*The* OLD MAN *growls.*] Why were you running like that, asshole? The cop wouldn't even have seen you.

OLD MAN   Had to! Had to!

AZDAK   Blue funk? [*The* OLD MAN *stares, uncomprehending.*] Cold feet? Panic? Don't lick your chops like a Grand Duke. Or an old sow. I can't stand it. We have to accept respectable stinkers as God made them, but not you! I once heard of a senior judge who farted at a public dinner to show an independent spirit! Watching you eat like that gives me the most awful ideas. Why don't you say something? [*Sharply.*] Show me your hand. Can't you hear? [*The* OLD MAN *slowly puts out his hand.*] White! So you're not a beggar at all! A fraud, a walking swindle! And I'm hiding you from the cops like you were an honest man! Why were you running like that if you're a landowner? For that's what you are. Don't deny it! I see it in your guilty face! [*He gets up.*] Get out! [*The* OLD MAN *looks at him uncertainly.*] What are you waiting for, peasant-flogger?

OLD MAN   Pursued. Need undivided attention. Make proposition . . .

AZDAK   Make what? A proposition? Well, if that isn't the height of insolence. He's making me a proposition! The bitten man scratches his fingers bloody, and the leech that's biting him makes him a proposition! Get out, I tell you!

---

[1] The name Azdak should be accented on the second syllable.—E. B.

OLD MAN Understand point of view! Persuasion! Pay hundred thousand piasters one night! Yes?

AZDAK What, you think you can buy me? For a hundred thousand piasters? Let's say a hundred and fifty thousand. Where are they?

OLD MAN Have not them here. Of course. Will be sent. Hope do not doubt.

AZDAK Doubt very much. Get out!

[*The* OLD MAN *gets up, waddles to the door. A* VOICE *is heard offstage.*]

VOICE Azdak!

[*The* OLD MAN *turns, waddles to the opposite corner, stands still.*]

AZDAK [*calling out*] I'm not in! [*He walks to door.*] So *you're* sniffing around here again, Shauwa?

SHAUWA [*reproachfully*] You caught another rabbit, Azdak. And you'd promised me it wouldn't happen again!

AZDAK [*severely*] Shauwa, don't talk about things you don't understand. The rabbit is a dangerous and destructive beast. It feeds on plants, especially on the species of plants known as weeds. It must therefore be exterminated.

SHAUWA Azdak, don't be so hard on me. I'll lose my job if I don't arrest you. I know you have a good heart.

AZDAK I do not have a good heart! How often must I tell you I'm a man of intellect?

SHAUWA [*slyly*] I know, Azdak. You're a superior person. You say so yourself. I'm just a Christian and an ignoramus. So I ask you: When one of the Prince's rabbits is stolen, and I'm a policeman, what should I do with the offending party?

AZDAK Shauwa, Shauwa, shame on you. You stand and ask me a question, than which nothing could be more seductive. It's like you were a woman—let's say that bad girl Nunowna, and you showed me your thigh—Nunowna's thigh, that would be—and asked me: "What shall I do with my thigh, it itches?" Is she as innocent as she pretends? Of course not. I catch a rabbit, but you catch a man. Man is made in God's image. Not so a rabbit, you know that. I'm a rabbit-eater, but you're a man-eater, Shauwa. And God will pass judgment on you. Shauwa, go home and repent. No, stop, there's something . . . [*He looks at the* OLD MAN *who stands trembling in the corner.*] No, it's nothing. Go home and repent. [*He slams the door behind* SHAUWA.] Now you're surprised, huh? Surprised I didn't hand you over? I couldn't hand over a bedbug to that animal. It goes against the grain. Now don't tremble because of a cop! So old and still so scared? Finish your cheese, but eat it like a poor man, or else they'll still catch you. Must I even explain how a poor man behaves? [*He pushes him down, and then gives him back the cheese.*] That box is the table. Lay your elbows on the table. Now, encircle the cheese on the plate like it might be snatched from you at any moment— what right have you to be safe, huh?—now, hold your knife like an undersized sickle, and give your cheese a troubled look because, like all beautiful things, it's already fading away. [AZDAK *watches him.*] They're after you, which speaks in your favor, but how can we be sure they're not mistaken about you? In Tiflis one time they hanged a landowner, a Turk, who could prove he quartered his peasants instead of merely cutting them in half, as is the custom, and he squeezed twice the usual amount of taxes out of them, his zeal was above suspicion. And yet they hanged him like a common criminal—because he was a Turk—a thing he couldn't do much about. What injustice! He got onto the gallows by a sheer fluke. In short, I don't trust you.

SINGER
   Thus Azdak gave the old beggar a bed,

And learned that old beggar was the old butcher, the Grand Duke himself,
And was ashamed.
He denounced himself and ordered the policeman to
   take him to Nuka, to court, to be judged.

[*In the court of justice three* IRONSHIRTS *sit drinking. From a beam hangs a man in judge's robes. Enter* AZDAK, *in chains, dragging* SHAUWA *behind him.*]

AZDAK [*shouting*] I've helped the Grand Duke, the Grand Thief, the Grand Butcher, to escape! In the name of justice I ask to be severely judged in public trial!

FIRST IRONSHIRT Who's this queer bird?

SHAUWA That's our Village Scrivener, Azdak.

AZDAK I am contemptible! I am a traitor! A branded criminal! Tell them, flatfoot, how I insisted on being tied up and brought to the capital. Because I sheltered the Grand Duke, the Grand Swindler, by mistake. And how I found out afterwards. See the marked man denounce himself! Tell them how I forced you to walk half the night with me to clear the whole thing up.

SHAUWA And all by threats. That wasn't nice of you, Azdak.

AZDAK Shut your mouth, Shauwa. You don't understand. A new age is upon us! It'll go thundering over you. You're finished. The police will be wiped out—poof! Everything will be gone into, everything will be brought into the open. The guilty will give themselves up. Why? They couldn't escape the people in any case. [*To* SHAUWA:] Tell them how I shouted all along Shoemaker Street [*with big gestures, looking at the* IRONSHIRTS] "In my ignorance I let the Grand Swindler escape! So tear me to pieces, brothers!" I wanted to get it in first.

FIRST IRONSHIRT And what did your brothers answer?

SHAUWA They comforted him in Butcher Street, and they laughed themselves sick in Shoemaker Street. That's all.

AZDAK But with you it's different. I can see you're men of iron. Brothers, where's the judge? I must be tried.

FIRST IRONSHIRT [*pointing at the hanged man*] There's the judge. And please stop "brothering" us. It's rather a sore spot this evening.

AZDAK "There's the judge." An answer never heard in Grusinia before. Townsman, where's His Excellency the Governor? [*Pointing to the ground.*] There's His Excellency, stranger. Where's the Chief Tax Collector? Where's the official Recruiting Officer? The Patriarch? The Chief of Police? There, there, there—all there. Brothers, I expected no less of you.

SECOND IRONSHIRT What? *What* was it you expected, funny man?

AZDAK What happened in Persia, brother, what happened in Persia?

SECOND IRONSHIRT What did happen in Persia?

AZDAK Everybody was hanged. Viziers, tax collectors. Everybody. Forty years ago now. My grandfather, a remarkable man by the way, saw it all. For three whole days. Everywhere.

SECOND IRONSHIRT And who ruled when the Vizier was hanged?

AZDAK A peasant ruled when the Vizier was hanged.

SECOND IRONSHIRT And who commanded the army?

AZDAK A soldier, a soldier.

SECOND IRONSHIRT And who paid the wages?

AZDAK A dyer. A dyer paid the wages.

SECOND IRONSHIRT Wasn't it a weaver, maybe?

FIRST IRONSHIRT And why did all this happen, Persian?

AZDAK Why did all this happen? Must there be a special reason? Why do you scratch yourself, brother? War! Too long a war! And no justice! My grandfather brought back a song that tells how it was. I will sing it for you. With my friend the policeman. [*To* SHAUWA] And hold the rope tight. It's very suitable. [*He sings, with* SHAUWA *holding the rope tight around him.*]

THE SONG OF INJUSTICE IN PERSIA

Why don't our sons bleed any more? Why don't our
  daughters weep?
Why do only the slaughterhouse cattle have blood in
  their veins?
Why do only the willows shed tears on Lake Urmia?
The king must have a new province, the peasant must
  give up his savings.
That the roof of the world might be conquered, the
  roof of the cottage is torn down.
Our men are carried to the ends of the earth, so that
  great ones can eat at home.
The soldiers kill each other, the marshals salute each
  other.
They bite the widow's tax money to see if it's good,
  their swords break.
The battle was lost, the helmets were paid for.
Refrain: Is it so? Is it so?

SHAUWA [*refrain*] Yes, yes, yes, yes, yes it's so.
AZDAK Want to hear the rest of it? [*The* FIRST IRONSHIRT *nods.*]
SECOND IRONSHIRT [*to* SHAUWA] Did he teach you that song?
SHAUWA Yes, only my voice isn't very good.
SECOND IRONSHIRT No. [*To* AZDAK] Go on singing.
AZDAK The second verse is about the peace. [*He sings.*]

The offices are packed, the streets overflow with
  officials.
The rivers jump their banks and ravage the fields.
Those who cannot let down their own trousers rule
  countries.
They can't count up to four, but they devour eight
  courses.
The corn farmers, looking round for buyers, see only
  the starving.
The weavers go home from their looms in rags.
Refrain: Is it so? Is it so?

SHAUWA [*refrain*] Yes, yes, yes, yes, yes it's so.
AZDAK

That's why our sons don't bleed any more, that's why
  our daughters don't weep.
That's why only the slaughterhouse cattle have blood
  in their veins,
And only the willows shed tears by Lake Urmia
  toward morning.

FIRST IRONSHIRT Are you going to sing that song here in town?
AZDAK Sure. What's wrong with it?
FIRST IRONSHIRT Have you noticed that the sky's getting red? [*Turning round,* AZDAK *sees the sky red with fire.*] It's the people's quarters on the outskirts of town. The carpet weavers have caught the "Persian Sickness," too. And

they've been asking if Prince Kazbeki isn't eating too many courses. This morning they strung up the city judge. As for us we beat them to pulp. We were paid one hundred piasters per man, you understand?

AZDAK [*after a pause*] I understand. [*He glances shyly round and, creeping away, sits down in a corner, his head in his hands.*]

IRONSHIRTS [*to each other*] If there ever was a troublemaker it's him.

—He must've come to the capital to fish in the troubled waters.

SHAUWA Oh, I don't think he's a really bad character, gentlemen. Steals a few chickens here and there. And maybe a rabbit.

SECOND IRONSHIRT [*approaching* AZDAK] Came to fish in the troubled waters, huh?

AZDAK [*looking up*] I don't know why I came.

SECOND IRONSHIRT Are you in with the carpet weavers maybe? [AZDAK *shakes his head.*] How about that song?

AZDAK From my grandfather. A silly and ignorant man.

SECOND IRONSHIRT Right. And how about the dyer who paid the wages?

AZDAK [*muttering*] That was in Persia.

FIRST IRONSHIRT And this denouncing of yourself? Because your didn't hang the Grand Duke with your own hands?

AZDAK Didn't I tell you I let him run? [*He creeps farther away and sits on the floor.*]

SHAUWA I can swear to that: he let him run.

[*The* IRONSHIRTS *burst out laughing and slap* SHAUWA *on the back.* AZDAK *laughs loudest. They slap* AZDAK *too, and unchain him. They all start drinking as the* FAT PRINCE *enters with a young man.*]

FIRST IRONSHIRT [*to* AZDAK, *pointing at the* FAT PRINCE] There's your "new age" for you! [*More laughter.*]

FAT PRINCE Well, my friends, what is there to laugh about? Permit me a serious word. Yesterday morning the Princes of Grusinia overthrew the warmongering government of the Grand Duke and did away with his Governors. Unfortunately the Grand Duke himself escaped. In this fateful hour our carpet weavers, those eternal troublemakers, had the effrontery to stir up a rebellion and hang the universally loved city judge, our dear Illo Orbeliani. Ts—ts—ts. My friends, we need peace, peace, peace in Grusinia! And justice! So I've brought along my dear nephew Bizergan Kazbeki. He'll be the new judge, hm? A very gifted fellow. What do you say? I want your opinion. Let the people decide!

SECOND IRONSHIRT Does this mean *we* elect the judge?

FAT PRINCE Precisely. Let the people propose some very gifted fellow! Confer among yourselves, my friends. [*The* IRONSHIRTS *confer.*] Don't worry, my little fox. The job's yours. And when we catch the Grand Duke we won't have to kiss this rabble's ass any longer.

IRONSHIRTS [*among themselves*]

—Very funny: they're wetting their pants because they haven't caught the Grand Duke.

When the outlook isn't so bright, they say: "My friends!" and "Let the people decide!"

—Now he even wants justice for Grusinia! But fun is fun as long as it lasts! [*Pointing at* AZDAK.] *He* knows all about justice. Hey, rascal, would you like this nephew fellow to be the judge?

AZDAK Are you asking me? You're not asking *me?!*

FIRST IRONSHIRT Why not? Anything for a laugh!

AZDAK You'd like to test him to the marrow, correct? Have you a criminal on hand? An experienced one? So the candidate can show what he knows?

SECOND IRONSHIRT Let's see. We do have a couple of doctors downstairs. Let's use them.

AZDAK Oh, no, that's no good, we can't take real criminals till we're sure the judge will be appointed. He may be dumb, but he must be appointed, or the law is violated. And the law is a sensitive organ. It's like the spleen, you mustn't hit it—that would be fatal. Of course you can hang those two without violating the law, because there was no judge in the vicinity. But judgment, when pronounced, must be pronounced with absolute gravity—it's all such nonsense. Suppose, for instance, a judge jails a woman—let's say she's stolen a corn cake to feed her child—and this judge isn't wearing his robes—or maybe he's scratching himself while passing sentence and half his body is uncovered—a man's thigh *will* itch once in a while—the sentence this judge passes is a disgrace and the law is violated. In short it would be easier for a judge's robe and a judge's hat to pass judgment than for a man with no robe and no hat. If you don't treat it with respect, the law just disappears on you. Now you don't try out a bottle of wine by offering it to a dog; you'd only lose your wine.

FIRST IRONSHIRT Then what do you suggest, hairsplitter?

AZDAK I'll be the defendant.

FIRST IRONSHIRT You? [*He bursts out laughing.*]

FAT PRINCE What have you decided?

FIRST IRONSHIRT We've decided to stage a rehearsal. Our friend here will be the defendant. Let the candidate be the judge and sit there.

FAT PRINCE It isn't customary, but why not? [*To the* NEPHEW] A mere formality, my little fox. What have I taught you? Who got there first—the slow runner or the fast?

NEPHEW The silent runner, Uncle Arsen.

[*The* NEPHEW *takes the chair. The* IRONSHIRTS *and the* FAT PRINCE *sit on the steps. Enter* AZDAK, *mimicking the gait of the Grand Duke.*]

AZDAK [*in the Grand Duke's accent*] Is any here knows me? Am Grand Duke.

IRONSHIRTS
—*What* is he?
—The Grand Duke. He knows him, too.
—Fine. So get on with the trial.

AZDAK Listen! Am accused instigating war? Ridiculous! Am saying ridiculous! That enough? If not, have brought lawyers. Believe five hundred. [*He points behind him, pretending to be surrounded by lawyers.*] Requisition all available seats for lawyers! [*The* IRONSHIRTS *laugh; the* FAT PRINCE *joins in.*]

NEPHEW [*to the* IRONSHIRTS] You really wish me to try this case? I find it rather unusual. From the taste angle, I mean.

FIRST IRONSHIRT Let's go!

FAT PRINCE [*smiling*] Let him have it, my little fox!

NEPHEW All right. People of Grusinia versus Grand Duke. Defendant, what have you got to say for yourself?

AZDAK Plenty. Naturally, have read war lost. Only started on the advice of patriots. Like Uncle Arsen Kazbeki. Call Uncle Arsen as witness.

FAT PRINCE [*to the* IRONSHIRTS, *delightedly*] What a madcap!

NEPHEW Motion rejected. One cannot be arraigned for declaring a war, which every ruler has to do once in a while, but only for running a war badly.

AZDAK Rubbish! Did not run it at all! Had it run! Had it run by Princes! Naturally, they messed it up.

NEPHEW Do you by any chance deny having been commander-in-chief?

AZDAK Not at all! Always *was* commander-in-chief. At birth shouted at wet nurse. Was trained drop turds in toilet, grew accustomed to command. Always commanded officials rob my cash box. Officers flog soldiers only on command. Landowners sleep with peasants' wives only on strictest command. Uncle Arsen here grew his belly at *my* command!

IRONSHIRTS [*clapping*] He's good! Long live the Grand Duke!

FAT PRINCE Answer him, my little fox: I'm with you.

NEPHEW I shall answer him according to the dignity of the law. Defendant, preserve the dignity of the law!

AZDAK Agreed. Command you proceed with trial!

NEPHEW It is not your place to command me. You claim that the Princes forced you to declare war. How can you claim, then, that they—er—"messed it up"?

AZDAK Did not send enough people. Embezzled funds. Sent sick horses. During attack, drinking in whorehouse. Call Uncle Arsen as witness.

NEPHEW Are you making the outrageous suggestion that the Princes of this country did not fight?

AZDAK No. Princes fought. Fought for war contracts.

FAT PRINCE [*jumping up*] That's too much! This man talks like a carpet weaver!

AZDAK Really? Told nothing but truth.

FAT PRINCE Hang him! Hang him!

FIRST IRONSHIRT [*pulling the* PRINCE *down*] Keep quiet! Go on, Excellency!

NEPHEW Quiet! I now render a verdict: You must be hanged! By the neck! Having lost war!

AZDAK Young man, seriously advise not fall publicly into jerky clipped speech. Cannot be watchdog if howl like wolf. Got it? If people realize Princes speak same language as Grand Duke, may hang Grand Duke *and Princes,* huh? By the way, must overrule verdict. Reason? War lost, but not for Princes. Princes won their war. Got 3,863,000 piasters for horses not delivered, 8,240,000 piasters for food supplies not produced. Are therefore victors. War lost only for Grusinia, which is not present in this court.

FAT PRINCE I think that will do, my friends. [*To* AZDAK] You can withdraw, funny man. [*To the* IRONSHIRTS] You may now ratify the new judge's appointment, my friends.

FIRST IRONSHIRT Yes, we can. Take down the judge's gown. [*One* IRONSHIRT *climbs on the back of the other, pulls the gown off the hanged man.*] [*To the* NEPHEW] Now you run away so the right ass can get on the right chair. [*To* AZDAK] Step forward! Go to the judge's seat! Now sit in it! [AZDAK *steps up, bows, and sits down.*] The judge was always a rascal! Now the rascal shall be a judge! [*The judge's gown is placed round his shoulders, the hat on his head.*] And what a judge!

SINGER
And there was civil war in the land.
The mighty were not safe.
And Azdak was made a judge by the Ironshirts.
And Azdak remained a judge for two years.

SINGER AND CHORUS
When the towns were set afire
And rivers of blood rose higher and higher,
Cockroaches crawled out of every crack.
And the court was full of schemers
And the church of foul blasphemers.
In the judge's cassock sat Azdak.
[AZDAK *sits in the judge's chair, peeling an apple.* SHAUWA *is sweeping out*

the hall. On one side an INVALID *in a wheelchair. Opposite, a young man accused of blackmail. An* IRONSHIRT *stands guard, holding the Ironshirts' banner.*]

AZDAK   In consideration of the large number of cases, the Court today will hear two cases at a time. Before I open the proceedings, a short announcement—I accept. [*He stretches out his hand. The* BLACKMAILER *is the only one to produce any money. He hands it to* AZDAK.] I reserve the right to punish one of the parties for contempt of court. [*He glances at the* IN-VALID.] You [*to the* DOCTOR] are a doctor, and you [*to the* INVALID] are bringing a complaint against him. Is the doctor responsible for your condition?

INVALID   Yes. I had a stroke on his account.

AZDAK   That would be professional negligence.

INVALID   Worse than negligence. I gave this man money for his studies. So far, he hasn't paid me back a cent. It was when I heard he was treating a patient free that I had my stroke.

AZDAK   Rightly. [*To a* LIMPING MAN] And what are *you* doing here?

LIMPING MAN   I'm the patient, Your Honor.

AZDAK   He treated your leg for nothing?

LIMPING MAN   The wrong leg! My rheumatism was in the left leg, he operated on the right. That's why I limp.

AZDAK   And you were treated free?

INVALID   A five-hundred-piaster operation free! For nothing! For a God-bless-you! And I paid for this man's studies! [*To the* DOCTOR] Did they teach you to operate free?

DOCTOR   Your Honor, it is the custom to demand the fee before the operation, as the patient is more willing to pay before an operation than after. Which is only human. In the case in question I was convinced, when I started the operation, that my servant had already received the fee. In this I was mistaken.

INVALID   He was mistaken! A good doctor doesn't make mistakes! He examines before he operates!

AZDAK   That's right: [*To* SHAUWA] Public Prosecutor, what's the other case about?

SHAUWA   [*busily sweeping*]   Blackmail.

BLACKMAILER   High Court of Justice, I'm innocent. I only wanted to find out from the landowner concerned if he really *had* raped his niece. He informed me very politely that this was not the case, and gave me the money only so I could pay for my uncle's studies.

AZDAK   Hm. [*To the* DOCTOR] You, on the other hand, can cite no extenuating circumstances for your offense, huh?

DOCTOR   Except that to err is human.

AZDAK   And you are aware that in money matters a good doctor is a highly responsible person? I once heard of a doctor who got a thousand piasters for a sprained finger by remarking that sprains have something to do with blood circulation, which after all a less good doctor might have overlooked, and who, on another occasion made a real gold mine out of a somewhat disordered gall bladder. He treated it with such loving care. You have no excuse, Doctor. The corn merchant Uxu had his son study medicine to get some knowledge of trade, our medical schools are so good. [*To the* BLACKMAILER] What's the landowner's name?

SHAUWA   He doesn't want it mentioned.

AZDAK   In that case I will pass judgment. The Court considers the blackmail proved. And you [*to the* INVALID] are sentenced to a fine of one thousand piasters. If you have a second stroke, the doctor will have to treat you free. Even if he has to amputate. [*To the* LIMPING MAN] As compensation, you will receive a bottle of rubbing alcohol. [*To the* BLACKMAILER] You are sentenced to hand over half the proceeds of your deal to the Public Prosecutor to keep the landowner's name secret. You are advised, moreover, to study medicine—you seem well suited to that calling. [*To the* DOCTOR] You have perpetrated an unpardonable error in the practice of your profession: you are acquitted. Next cases!

SINGER AND CHORUS
Men won't do much for a shilling.
For a pound they may be willing.
For twenty pounds the verdict's in the sack.
As for the many, all too many,
Those who've only got a penny—
They've one single, sole recourse: Azdak:

[*Enter* AZDAK *from the caravansary on the highroad, followed by an old bearded* INNKEEPER. *The judge's chair is carried by a* STABLEMAN *and* SHAUWA. *An* IRONSHIRT, *with a banner, takes up his position.*]

AZDAK Put me down. Then we'll get some air, maybe even a good stiff breeze from the lemon grove there. It does justice good to be done in the open: the wind blows her skirts up and you can see what she's got. Shauwa, we've been eating too much. These official journeys are exhausting. [*To the* INNKEEPER] It's a question of your daughter-in-law?

INNKEEPER Your Worship, it's a question of the family honor. I wish to bring an action on behalf of my son, who's away on business on the other side the mountain. This is the offending stableman, and here's my daughter-in-law.

[*Enter the* DAUGHTER-IN-LAW, *a voluptuous wench. She is veiled.*]

AZDAK [*sitting down*] I accept. [*Sighing, the* INNKEEPER *hands him some money.*] Good. Now the formalities are disposed of. This is a case of rape?

INNKEEPER Your Honor, I caught the fellow in the act. Ludovica was in the straw on the stable floor.

AZDAK Quite right, the stable. Lovely horses! I specially liked the little roan.

INNKEEPER The first thing I did, of course, was to question Ludovica. On my son's behalf.

AZDAK [*seriously*] I said I specially liked the little roan.

INNKEEPER [*coldly*] Really? Ludovica confessed the stableman took her against her will.

AZDAK Take your veil off, Ludovica. [*She does so.*] Ludovica, you please the Court. Tell us how it happened.

LUDOVICA [*well schooled*] When I entered the stable to see the new foal the stableman said to me on his own accord: "It's hot today!" and laid his hand on my left breast. I said to him: "Don't do that!" But he continued to handle me indecently, which provoked my anger. Before I realized his sinful intentions, he got much closer. It was all over when my father-in-law entered and accidentally trod on me.

INNKEEPER [*explaining*] On my son's behalf.

AZDAK [*to the* STABLEMAN] You admit you started it?

STABLEMAN Yes.

AZDAK Ludovica, you like to eat sweet things?

LUDOVICA Yes, sunflower seeds!

AZDAK You like to lie a long time in the bathtub?

LUDOVICA Half an hour or so.

AZDAK Public Prosecutor, drop your knife—there on the ground. [SHAUWA *does so.*] Ludovica, pick up that knife. [LUDOVICA, *swaying her hips, does so.*] See that? [*He points at her.*] The way it moves? The rape is now proven. By eating too much—sweet things, especially—by lying too long in warm water, by laziness and too soft a skin, you have raped that unfortunate man. Think you can run around with a behind like that and get away with it in court? This is a case of intentional assault with a dangerous weapon! You are sentenced to hand over to the Court the little roan which your father liked to ride "on his son's behalf." And now, come with me to the stables, so the Court can inspect the scene of the crime, Ludovica.

SINGER AND CHORUS
> When the sharks the sharks devour
> Little fishes have their hour.
> For a while the load is off their back.
> On Grusinia's highways faring
> Fixed-up scales of justice bearing
> Strode the poor man's magistrate: Azdak.
>
> And he gave to the forsaken
> All that from the rich he'd taken.
> And a bodyguard of roughnecks was Azdak's.
> And our good and evil man, he
> Smiled upon Grusinia's Granny.
> His emblem was a tear in sealing wax.
>
> All mankind should love each other
> But when visiting your brother
> Take an ax along and hold it fast.
> Not in theory but in practice
> Miracles are wrought with axes
> And the age of miracles is not past.

[AZDAK'S *judge's chair is in a tavern. Three rich* FARMERS *stand before* AZDAK. SHAUWA *brings him wine. In a corner stands an* OLD PEASANT WOMAN. *In the open doorway, and outside, stand villagers looking on. An* IRONSHIRT *stands guard with a banner.*]

AZDAK   The Public Prosecutor has the floor.

SHAUWA   It concerns a cow. For five weeks, the defendant has had a cow in her stable, the property of the farmer Suru. She was also found to be in possession of a stolen ham, and a number of cows belonging to Shutoff were killed after he asked the defendant to pay the rent on a piece of land.

FARMERS
    —It's a matter of my ham, Your Honor.
    —It's a matter of my cow, Your Honor.
    —It's a matter of my land, Your Honor.

AZDAK   Well, Granny, what have *you* got to say to all this?

OLD WOMAN   Your Honor, one night toward morning, five weeks ago, there was a knock at my door, and outside stood a bearded man with a cow. "My dear woman," he said, "I am the miracle-working Saint Banditus and because your son has been killed in the war, I bring you this cow as a souvenir. Take good care of it."

FARMERS
    —The robber, Irakli, Your Honor!
    —Her brother-in-law, Your Honor!
    —The cow-thief!

—The incendiary!

—He must be beheaded!

[*Outside, a woman screams. The crowd grows restless, retreats. Enter the* BANDIT *Irakli with a huge ax.*]

BANDIT   A very good evening, dear friends! A glass of vodka!

FARMERS   [*crossing themselves*]   Irakli!

AZDAK   Public Prosecutor, a glass of vodka for our guest. And who are you?

BANDIT   I'm a wandering hermit, Your Honor. Thanks for the gracious gift. [*He empties the glass which* SHAUWA *has brought.*] Another!

AZDAK   I am Azdak. [*He gets up and bows. The* BANDIT *also bows.*] The Court welcomes the foreign hermit. Go on with your story, Granny.

OLD WOMAN   Your Honor, that first night I didn't yet know Saint Banditus could work miracles, it was only the cow. But one night, a few days later, the farmer's servants came to take the cow away again. Then they turned round in front of my door and went off without the cow. And bumps as big as a fist sprouted on their heads. So I knew that Saint Banditus had changed their hearts and turned them into friendly people. [*The* BANDIT *roars with laughter.*]

FIRST FARMER   I know what changed them.

AZDAK   That's fine. You can tell us later. Continue.

OLD WOMAN   Your Honor, the next one to become a good man was the farmer Shutoff—a devil, as everyone knows. But Saint Banditus arranged it so he let me off the rent on the little piece of land.

SECOND FARMER   Because my cows were killed in the field. [*The* BANDIT *laughs.*]

OLD WOMAN   [*answering* AZDAK's *sign to continue*]   Then one morning the ham came flying in at my window. It hit me in the small of the back. I'm still lame, Your Honor, look. [*She limps a few steps. The* BANDIT *laughs.*] Your Honor, was there ever a time when a poor old woman could get a ham *without* a miracle? [*The* BANDIT *starts sobbing.*]

AZDAK   [*rising from his chair*]   Granny, that's a question that strikes straight at the Court's heart. Be so kind as to sit here. [*The* OLD WOMAN, *hesitating, sits in the judge's chair.*]

AZDAK   [*sits on the floor, glass in hand, reciting*]

Granny
We could almost call you Granny Grusinia
The Woebegone
The Bereaved Mother
Whose sons have gone to war.
Receiving the present of a cow
She bursts out crying.
When she is beaten
She remains hopeful.
When she's not beaten
She's surprised.
On us
Who are already damned
May you render a merciful verdict
Granny Grusinia!

[*Bellowing at the* FARMERS]   Admit you don't believe in miracles, you atheists! Each of you is sentenced to pay five hundred piasters! For godlessness! Get out! [*The* FARMERS *slink out.*] And you, Granny, and you [*to *the* BANDIT] pious man, empty a pitcher of wine with the Public Prosecutor and Azdak!

SINGER AND CHORUS
And he broke the rules to save them.
Broken law like bread he gave them,
Brought them to shore upon his crooked back.
At long last the poor and lowly
Had someone who was not too holy
To be bribed by empty hands: Azdak.

For two years it was his pleasure
To give the beasts of prey short measure:
He became a wolf to fight the pack.
From All Hallows to All Hallows
On his chair beside the gallows
Dispensing justice in his fashion sat Azdak.

SINGER
But the era of disorder came to an end.
The Grand Duke returned.
The Governor's wife returned.
A trial was held.
Many died.
The people's quarters burned anew.
And fear seized Azdak.
[AZDAK's *judge's chair stands again in the court of justice.* AZDAK *sits on the floor, shaving and talking to* SHAUWA. *Noises outside. In the rear the* FAT PRINCE's *head is carried by on a lance.*]

AZDAK Shauwa, the days of your slavery are numbered, maybe even the minutes. For a long time now I have held you in the iron curb of reason, and it has torn your mouth till it bleeds. I have lashed you with reasonable arguments, I have manhandled you with logic. You are by nature a weak man, and if one slyly throws an argument in your path, you *have* to snap it up, you can't resist. It is your nature to lick the hand of some superior being. But superior beings can be of very different kinds. And now, with your liberation, you will soon be able to follow your natural inclinations, which are low. You will be able to follow your infallible instinct, which teaches you to plant your fat heel on the faces of men. Gone is the era of confusion and disorder, which I find described in the Song of Chaos. Let us now sing that song together in memory of those terrible days. Sit down and don't do violence to the music. Don't be afraid. It sounds all right. And it has a fine refrain. [*He sings.*]

THE SONG OF CHAOS

Sister, hide your face! Brother, take your knife!
The times are out of joint!
Big men are full of complaint
And small men full of joy.
The city says:
"Let us drive the mighty from our midst!"
Offices are raided. Lists of serfs are destroyed.
They have set Master's nose to the grindstone.
They who lived in the dark have seen the light.

The ebony poor box is broken.
Sesnem[2] wood is sawed up for beds.
Who had no bread have full barns.
Who begged for alms of corn now mete it out.

SHAUWA [*refrain*] Oh, oh, oh, oh.
AZDAK [*refrain*]

Where are you, General, where are you?
Please, please, please, restore order!

The nobleman's son can no longer be recognized;
The lady's child becomes the son of her slave-girl
The councilors meet in a shed.
Once, this man was barely allowed to sleep on the wall;
Now, he stretches his limbs in a bed.
Once, this man rowed a boat; now, he owns ships.
Their owner looks for them, but they're his no longer.
Five men are sent on a journey by their master.
"Go yourself," they say, "we have arrived."

SHAUWA [*refrain*] Oh, oh, oh, oh.
AZDAK [*refrain*]

Where are you, General, where are you?
Please, please, please, restore order!

Yes, so it might have been, had order been neglected much longer. But now the Grand Duke has returned to the capital, and the Persians have lent him an army to restore order with. The people's quarters are already aflame. Go and get me the big book I always sit on. [SHAUWA *brings the big book from the judge's chair.* AZDAK *opens it.*] This is the Statute Book and I've always used it, as you can testify. Now I'd better look in this book and see what they can do to me. I've let the down-and-outs get away with murder, and I'll have to pay for it. I helped poverty onto its skinny legs, so they'll hang me for drunkenness. I peeped into the rich man's pocket, which is bad taste. And I can't hide anywhere—everybody knows me because I've helped everybody.

SHAUWA Someone's coming!
AZDAK [*in panic, he walks trembling to the chair*] It's the end. And now they'd enjoy seeing what a Great Man I am. I'll deprive them of that pleasure. I'll beg on my knees for mercy. Spittle will slobber down my chin. The fear of death is in me.

[*Enter Natella Abashwili, the* GOVERNOR'S WIFE, *followed by the* ADJUTANT *and an* IRONSHIRT.]

GOVERNOR'S WIFE What sort of a creature is that, Shalva?
AZDAK A willing one, Your Highness, a man ready to oblige.
ADJUTANT Natella Abashwili, wife of the late Governor, has just returned. She is looking for her two-year-old son, Michael. She has been informed that the child was carried off to the mountains by a former servant.
AZDAK The child will be brought back, Your Highness, at your service.
ADJUTANT They say that the person in question is passing it off as her own.

---

[2] I do not know what kind of wood this is, so I have left the word exactly as it stands in the German original. The song is based on an Egyptian papyrus which Brecht cites as such in his essay, "Five Difficulties in the Writing of the Truth." I should think he must have come across it in Adolf Erman's *Die Literatur der Aegypter*, 1923, p. 130 ff. Erman too gives the word as Sesnem. The same papyrus is quoted in Karl Jaspers' *Man in the Modern Age* (Anchor edition, pp. 18–19) but without the sentence about the Sesnem wood.—E.B.

AZDAK   She will be beheaded, Your Highness, at your service.

ADJUTANT   That is all.

GOVERNOR'S WIFE   [*leaving*]   I don't like that man.

AZDAK   [*following her to door, bowing*]   At your service, Your Highness, it will all be arranged.

5

THE CHALK CIRCLE

SINGER

Hear now the story of the trial
Concerning Governor Abashwili's child
And the determination of the true mother
By the famous test of the Chalk Circle.
[*Law court in Nuka.* IRONSHIRTS *lead* MICHAEL *across stage and out at the back.* IRONSHIRTS *hold* GRUSHA *back with their lances under the gateway until the child has been led through. Then she is admitted. She is accompanied by the former Governor's* COOK. *Distant noises and a fire-red sky.*]

GRUSHA   [*trying to hide*]   He's brave, he can wash himself now.

COOK   You're lucky. It's not a real judge. It's Azdak, a drunk who doesn't know what he's doing. The biggest thieves have got by through him. Because he gets everything mixed up and the rich never offer him big enough bribes, the like of us sometimes do pretty well.

GRUSHA   I *need* luck right now.

COOK   Touch wood. [*She crosses herself.*] I'd better offer up another prayer that the judge may be drunk. [*She prays with motionless lips, while* GRUSHA *looks around, in vain, for the child.*] Why must you hold on to it at any price if it isn't yours? In days like these?

GRUSHA   He's mine. I brought him up.

COOK   Have you never thought what'd happen when she came back?

GRUSHA   At first I thought I'd give him to her. Then I thought she wouldn't come back.

COOK   And even a borrowed coat keeps a man warm, hm? [GRUSHA *nods.*] I'll swear to anything for you. You're a decent girl. [*She sees the soldier* SIMON SHASHAVA *approaching.*] You've done wrong by Simon, though. I've been talking with him. He just can't understand.

GRUSHA   [*unaware of* SIMON's *presence*]   Right now I can't be bothered whether he understands or not!

COOK   He knows the child isn't yours, but you married and not free "till death you do part"—he can't understand *that.*
[GRUSHA *sees* SIMON *and greets him.*]

SIMON   [*gloomily*]   I wish the lady to know I will swear I am the father of the child.

GRUSHA   [*low*]   Thank you, Simon.

SIMON   At the same time I wish the lady to know my hands are not tied nor are hers.

COOK   You needn't have said that. You know she's married.

SIMON   And it needs no rubbing in.
[*Enter an* IRONSHIRT.]

IRONSHIRT   Where's the judge? Has anyone seen the judge?

ANOTHER IRONSHIRT [*stepping forward*] The judge isn't here yet. Nothing but a bed and a pitcher in the whole house!
[*Exeunt* IRONSHIRTS.]

COOK I hope nothing has happened to him. With any other judge you'd have as much chance as a chicken has teeth.

GRUSHA [*who has turned away and covered her face*] Stand in front of me. I shouldn't have come to Nuka. If I run into the Ironshirt, the one I hit over the head . . .
[*She screams. An* IRONSHIRT *had stopped and, turning his back, had been listening to her. He now wheels around. It is the* CORPORAL, *and he has a huge scar across his face.*]

IRONSHIRT [*in the gateway*] What's the matter, Shotta? Do you know her?

CORPORAL [*after staring for some time*] No.

IRONSHIRT She's the one who stole the Abashwili child, or so they say. If you know anything about it you can make some money, Shotta.
[*Exit the* CORPORAL, *cursing.*]

COOK Was it him? [GRUSHA *nods.*] I think he'll keep his mouth shut, or he'd be admitting he was after the child.

GRUSHA I'd almost forgotten him.
[*Enter the* GOVERNOR'S WIFE, *followed by the* ADJUTANT *and two* LAWYERS.]

GOVERNOR'S WIFE At least there are no common people here, thank God. I can't stand their smell. It always gives me migraine.

FIRST LAWYER Madam, I must ask you to be careful what you say until we have another judge.

GOVERNOR'S WIFE But I didn't say anything, Illo Shuboladze. I love the people with their simple straightforward minds. It's only that their smell brings on my migraine.

SECOND LAWYER There won't be many spectators. The whole population is sitting at home behind locked doors because of the riots in the people's quarters.

GOVERNOR'S WIFE [*looking at* GRUSHA] Is that the creature?

FIRST LAWYER Please, most gracious Natella Abashwili, abstain from invective until it is certain the Grand Duke has appointed a new judge and we're rid of the present one, who's about the lowest fellow ever seen in judge's gown. Things are all set to move, you see.
[*Enter* IRONSHIRTS *from the courtyard.*]

COOK Her Grace would pull your hair out on the spot if she didn't know Azdak is for the poor. He goes by the face.
[IRONSHIRTS *begin fastening a rope to a beam.* AZDAK, *in chains, is led in, followed by* SHAUWA, *also in chains. The three* FARMERS *bring up the rear.*]

AN IRONSHIRT Trying to run away, were you? [*He strikes* AZDAK.]

ONE FARMER Off with his judge's gown before we string him up!
[IRONSHIRTS *and* FARMERS *tear off Azdak's gown. His torn underwear is visible. Then someone kicks him.*]

AN IRONSHIRT [*pushing him into someone else*] Want a load of justice? Here it is!
[*Accompanied by shouts of "You take it!" and "Let me have him, Brother!" they throw* AZDAK *back and forth until he collapses. Then he is lifted up and dragged under the noose.*]

GOVERNOR'S WIFE [*who, during this "ballgame," has clapped her hands hysterically*] I disliked that man from the moment I first saw him.

AZDAK [*covered with blood, panting*] I can't see. Give me a rag.

AN IRONSHIRT What is it you want to see?

AZDAK You, you dogs! [*He wipes the blood out of his eyes with his shirt.*] Good morning, dogs! How goes it, dogs! How's the dog world? Does it smell good? Got another boot for me to lick? Are you back at each other's throats, dogs?

[*Accompanied by a* CORPORAL, *a dust-covered* RIDER *enters. He takes some documents from a leather case, looks at them, then interrupts.*]

RIDER Stop! I bring a dispatch from the Grand Duke, containing the latest appointments.

CORPORAL [*bellowing*] Atten—shun!

RIDER Of the new judge it says: "We appoint a man whom we have to thank for saving a life indispensable to the country's welfare—a certain Azdak of Nuka." Which is he?

SHAUWA [*pointing*] That's him, Your Excellency.

CORPORAL [*bellowing*] What's going on here?

AN IRONSHIRT I beg to report that His Honor Azdak was already His Honor Azdak, but on these farmers' denunciation was pronounced the Grand Duke's enemy.

CORPORAL [*pointing at the* FARMERS] March them off! [*They are marched off. They bow all the time.*] See to it that His Honor Azdak is exposed to no more violence.

[*Exeunt* RIDER *and* CORPORAL.]

COOK [*to* SHAUWA] She clapped her hands! I hope he saw it!

FIRST LAWYER It's a catastrophe.

[AZDAK *has fainted. Coming to, he is dressed again in judge's robes. He walks, swaying, toward the* IRONSHIRTS.]

AN IRONSHIRT What does Your Honor desire?

AZDAK Nothing, fellow dogs, or just an occasional boot to lick. [*To* SHAUWA] I pardon you. [*He is unchained.*] Get me some red wine, the sweet kind. [SHAUWA *stumbles off.*] Get out of here, I've got to judge a case. [*Exeunt* IRONSHIRTS. SHAUWA *returns with a pitcher of wine.* AZDAK *gulps it down.*] Something for my backside. [SHAUWA *brings the Statute Book, puts it on the judge's chair.* AZDAK *sits on it.*] I accept.

[*The Prosecutors, among whom a worried council has been held, smile with relief. They whisper.*]

COOK Oh dear!

SIMON A well can't be filled with dew, they say.

LAWYERS [*approaching* AZDAK, *who stands up, expectantly*] A quite ridiculous case, Your Honor. The accused has abducted a child and refuses to hand it over.

AZDAK [*stretching out his hand, glancing at* GRUSHA] A most attractive person. [*He fingers the money, then sits down, satisfied.*] I declare the proceedings open and demand the whole truth. [*To* GRUSHA] Especially from you.

FIRST LAWYER High Court of Justice! Blood, as the popular saying goes, is thicker than water. This old adage . . .

AZDAK [*interrupting*] The Court wants to know the lawyers' fee.

FIRST LAWYER [*surprised*] I beg your pardon? [AZDAK, *smiling, rubs his thumb and index finger.*] Oh, I see. Five hundred piasters, Your Honor, to answer the Court's somewhat unusual question.

AZDAK Did you hear? The question is unusual. I ask it because I listen in quite a different way when I know you're good.

FIRST LAWYER [*bowing*] Thank you, Your Honor. High Court of Justice, of all ties the ties of blood are strongest. Mother and child—is there a more intimate relationship? Can one tear a child from its mother? High Court of Justice, she has conceived it in the holy ecstasies of love. She has carried it in her womb. She has fed it with her blood. She has borne it with pain.

High Court of Justice, it has been observed that the wild tigress, robbed of her young, roams restless through the mountains, shrunk to a shadow. Nature herself . . .

AZDAK [*interrupting, to* GRUSHA] What's your answer to all this and anything else that lawyer might have to say?

GRUSHA He's mine.

AZDAK Is that all? I hope you can prove it. Why should I assign the child to you in any case?

GRUSHA I brought him up like the priest says "according to my best knowledge and conscience." I always found him something to eat. Most of the time he had a roof over his head. And I went to such trouble for him. I had expenses too. I didn't look out for my own comfort. I brought the child up to be friendly with everyone, and from the beginning taught him to work. As well as he could, that is. He's still very little.

FIRST LAWYER Your Honor, it is significant that the girl herself doesn't claim any tie of blood between her and the child.

AZDAK The Court takes note of that.

FIRST LAWYER Thank you, Your Honor. And now permit a woman bowed in sorrow—who has already lost her husband and now has also to fear the loss of her child—to address a few words to you. The gracious Natella Abashwili is . . .

GOVERNOR'S WIFE [*quietly*] A most cruel fate, sir, forces me to describe to you the tortures of a bereaved mother's soul, the anxiety, the sleepless nights, the . . .

SECOND LAWYER [*bursting out*] It's outrageous the way this woman is being treated! Her husband's palace is closed to her! The revenue of her estates is blocked, and she is cold-bloodedly told that it's tied to the heir. She can't do a thing without that child. She can't even pay her lawyer!! [*To the* FIRST LAWYER, *who, desperate about this outburst, makes frantic gestures to keep him from speaking:*] Dear Illo Shuboladze, surely it can be divulged now that the Abashwili estates are at stake?

FIRST LAWYER Please, Honored Sandro Oboladze! We agreed . . . [*To* AZDAK:] Of course it is correct that the trial will also decide if our noble client can take over the Abashwili estates, which are rather extensive. I say "also" advisedly, for in the foreground stands the human tragedy of a mother, as Natella Abashwili very properly explained in the first words of her moving statement. Even if Michael Abashwili were not heir to the estates, he would still be the dearly beloved child of my client.

AZDAK Stop! The Court is touched by the mention of estates. It's a proof of human feeling.

SECOND LAWYER Thanks, Your Honor. Dear Illo Shuboladze, we can prove in any case that the woman who took the child is not the child's mother. Permit me to lay before the Court the bare facts. High Court of Justice, by an unfortunate chain of circumstances, Michael Abashwili was left behind on that Easter Sunday while his mother was making her escape. Grusha, a palace kitchen maid, was seen with the baby . . .

COOK All her mistress was thinking of was what dresses she'd take along!

SECOND LAWYER [*unmoved*] Nearly a year later Grusha turned up in a mountain village with a baby and there entered into the state of matrimony with . . .

AZDAK How'd you get to that mountain village?

GRUSHA On foot, Your Honor. And he was mine.

SIMON I'm the father, Your Honor.

COOK I used to look after it for them, Your Honor. For five piasters.

SECOND LAWYER   This man is engaged to Grusha, High Court of Justice: his testimony is suspect.

AZDAK   Are you the man she married in the mountain village?

SIMON   No, Your Honor, she married a peasant.

AZDAK   [*to* GRUSHA]   Why? [*Pointing at* SIMON.] Is he no good in bed? Tell the truth.

GRUSHA   We didn't get that far. I married because of the baby. So he'd have a roof over his head. [*Pointing at* SIMON.] He was in the war, Your Honor.

AZDAK   And now he wants you back again, huh?

SIMON   I wish to state in evidence . . .

GRUSHA   [*angrily*]   I am no longer free, Your Honor.

AZDAK   And the child, you claim, comes from whoring? [GRUSHA *doesn't answer.*] I'm going to ask you a question: What kind of child is he? A ragged little bastard? Or from a good family?

GRUSHA   [*angrily*]   He's an ordinary child.

AZDAK   I mean—did he have refined features from the beginning?

GRUSHA   He had a nose on his face.

AZDAK   A very significant comment! It has been said of me that I went out one time and sniffed at a rosebush before rendering a verdict—tricks like that are needed nowadays. Well, I'll make it short, and not listen to any more lies. [*To* GRUSHA:] Especially not yours. [*To all the accused*] I can imagine what you've cooked up to cheat me! I know you people. You're swindlers.

GRUSHA   [*suddenly*]   I can understand your wanting to cut it short, now I've seen what you accepted!

AZDAK   Shut up! Did I accept anything from you?

GRUSHA   [*while the* COOK *tries to restrain her*]   I haven't got anything.

AZDAK   True. Quite true. From starvelings I never get a thing. I might just as well starve, myself. You want justice, but do you want to pay for it, hm? When you go to a butcher you know you have to pay, but you people go to a judge as if you were off to a funeral supper.

SIMON   [*loudly*]   When the horse was shod, the horsefly held out its leg, as the saying is.

AZDAK   [*eagerly accepting the challenge*]   Better a treasure in manure than a stone in a mountain stream.

SIMON   A fine day. Let's go fishing, said the angler to the worm.

AZDAK   I'm my own master, said the servant, and cut off his foot.

SIMON   I love you as a father, said the Czar to the peasants, and had the Czarevitch's head chopped off.

AZDAK   A fool's worst enemy is himself.

SIMON   However, a fart has no nose.

AZDAK   Fined ten piasters for indecent language in court! That'll teach you what justice is.

GRUSHA   [*furiously*]   A fine kind of justice! You play fast and loose with us because we don't talk as refined as that crowd with their lawyers.

AZDAK   That's true. You people are too dumb. It's only right you should get it in the neck.

GRUSHA   You want to hand the child over to her, and she wouldn't even know how to keep it dry, she's so "refined"! You know about as much about justice as I do!

AZDAK   There's something in that. I'm an ignorant man. Haven't even a decent pair of pants on under this gown. Look! With me, everything goes on food and drink—I was educated in a convent. Incidentally, I'll fine you ten piasters for contempt of court. And you're a very silly girl, to turn me against you, instead of making eyes at me and wiggling your backside a little to keep me in a good temper. Twenty piasters!

GRUSHA   Even if it was thirty, I'd tell you what I think of your justice, you drunken onion! [*Incoherently.*] How dare you talk to me like the cracked Isaiah on the church window? As if you were somebody? For you weren't born to this. You weren't born to rap your own mother on the knuckles if she swipes a little bowl of salt someplace. Aren't you ashamed of yourself when you see how I tremble before you? You've made yourself their servant so no one will take their houses from them—houses they had stolen! Since when have houses belonged to the bedbugs? But you're on the watch, or they couldn't drag our men into their wars! You bribetaker!

[AZDAK *half gets up, starts beaming. With his little hammer he halfheartedly knocks on the table as if to get silence. As* GRUSHA's *scolding continues, he only beats time with his hammer.*]

I've no respect for you. No more than for a thief or a bandit with a knife! You can do what you want. You can take the child away from me, a hundred against one, but I tell you one thing: only extortioners should be chosen for a profession like yours, and men who rape children! As punishment! Yes, let *them* sit in judgment on their fellow creatures. It is worse than to hang from the gallows.

AZDAK   [*sitting down*]   Now it'll be thirty! And I won't go on squabbling with you—we're not in a tavern. What'd happen to my dignity as a judge? Anyway, I've lost interest in your case. Where's the couple who wanted a divorce? [*To* SHAUWA] Bring 'em in. This case is adjourned for fifteen minutes.

FIRST LAWYER   [*to the* GOVERNOR'S WIFE]   Even without using the rest of the evidence, Madam, we have the verdict in the bag.

COOK   [*to* GRUSHA]   You've gone and spoiled your chances with him. You won't get the child now.

GOVERNOR'S WIFE   Shalva, my smelling salts!

[*Enter a very old couple.*]

AZDAK   I accept. [*The old couple don't understand.*] I hear you want to be divorced. How long have you been together?

OLD WOMAN   Forty years, Your Honor.

AZDAK   And why do you want a divorce?

OLD MAN   We don't like each other, Your Honor.

AZDAK   Since when?

OLD WOMAN   Oh, from the very beginning, Your Honor.

AZDAK   I'll think about your request and render my verdict when I'm through with the other case. [SHAUWA *leads them back.*] I need the child. [*He beckons* GRUSHA *to him and bends not unkindly toward her.*] I've noticed you have a soft spot for justice. I don't believe he's your child, but if he *were* yours, woman, wouldn't you want him to be rich? You'd only have to say he wasn't yours, and he'd have a palace and many horses in his stable and many beggars on his doorstep and many soldiers in his service and many petitioners in his courtyard, wouldn't he? What do you say— don't you want him to be rich?

[GRUSHA *is silent.*]

SINGER

Hear now what the angry girl thought but did not say:

Had he golden shoes to wear
He'd be cruel as a bear.

Evil would his life disgrace.
He'd laugh in my face.

Carrying a heart of flint
Is too troublesome a stint.
Being powerful and bad
Is hard on a lad.

Then let hunger be his foe!
Hungry men and women, no.
Let him fear the darksome night
But not daylight!

AZDAK   I think I understand you, woman.

GRUSHA   [*suddenly and loudly*]   I won't give him up. I've raised him, and he knows me.

[*Enter* SHAUWA *with the* CHILD.]

GOVERNOR'S WIFE   He's in rags!

GRUSHA   That's not true. But I wasn't given time to put his good shirt on.

GOVERNOR'S WIFE   He must have been in a pigsty.

GRUSHA   [*furiously*]   I'm not a pig, but there are some who are! Where did you leave your baby?

GOVERNOR'S WIFE   I'll show you, you vulgar creature! [*She is about to throw herself on* GRUSHA, *but is restrained by her lawyers.*] She's a criminal, she must be whipped. Immediately!

SECOND LAWYER   [*holding his hand over her mouth*]   Natella Abashwili, you promised . . . Your Honor, the plaintiff's nerves . . .

AZDAK   Plaintiff and defendant! The Court has listened to your case, and has come to no decision as to who the real mother is; therefore, I, the judge, am obliged to *choose* a mother for the child. I'll make a test. Shauwa, get a piece of chalk and draw a circle on the floor. [SHAUWA *does so.*] Now place the child in the center. [SHAUWA *puts* MICHAEL, *who smiles at* GRUSHA, *in the center of the circle.*] Stand near the circle, both of you. [*The* GOVERNOR'S WIFE *and* GRUSHA *step up to the circle.*] Now each of you take the child by one hand. [*They do so.*] The true mother is she who can pull the child out of the circle.

SECOND LAWYER   [*quickly*]   High Court of Justice, I object! The fate of the great Abashwili estates, which are tied to the child, as the heir, should not be made dependent on such a doubtful duel. In addition, my client does not command the strength of this person, who is accustomed to physical work.

AZDAK   She looks pretty well fed to me. Pull! [*The* GOVERNOR'S WIFE *pulls the* CHILD *out of the circle on her side;* GRUSHA *has let go and stands aghast.*] What's the matter with you? You didn't pull.

GRUSHA   I didn't hold on to him.

FIRST LAWYER   [*congratulating the* GOVERNOR'S WIFE]   What did I say! The ties of blood!

GRUSHA   [*running to* AZDAK]   Your Honor, I take back everything I said against you. I ask your forgiveness. But could I keep him till he can speak all the words? He knows a few.

AZDAK   Don't influence the Court. I bet you only know about twenty words yourself. All right, I'll make the test once more, just to be certain. [*The two women take up their positions again.*] Pull! [*Again* GRUSHA *lets go of the* CHILD.]

GRUSHA   [*in despair*]   I brought him up! Shall I also tear him to bits? I can't!

AZDAK [*rising*] And in this manner the Court has determined the true mother. [*To* GRUSHA:] Take your child and be off. I advise you not to stay in the city with him. [*To the* GOVERNOR'S WIFE:] And you disappear before I fine you for fraud. Your estates fall to the city. They'll be converted into a playground for the children. They need one, and I've decided it'll be called after me: Azdak's Garden.
[*The* GOVERNOR'S WIFE *has fainted and is carried out by the* LAWYERS *and the* ADJUTANT. GRUSHA *stands motionless.* SHAUWA *leads the* CHILD *toward her.*]
Now I'll take off this judge's gown—it's got too hot for me. I'm not cut out for a hero. In token of farewell I invite you all to a little dance in the meadow outside. Oh, I'd almost forgotten something in my excitement . . . to sign the divorce decree.
[*Using the judge's chair as a table, he writes something on a piece of paper, and prepares to leave. Dance music has started.*]

SHAUWA [*having read what is on the paper*] But that's not right. You've not divorced the old people. You've divorced Grusha!

AZDAK Divorced the wrong couple? What a pity! And I never retract! If I did, how could we keep order in the land? [*To the old couple:*] I'll invite you to my party instead. You don't mind dancing with each other, do you? [*To* GRUSHA *and* SIMON:] I've got forty piasters coming from you.

SIMON [*pulling out his purse*] Cheap at the price, Your Honor. And many thanks.

AZDAK [*pocketing the cash*] I'll be needing this.

GRUSHA [*to* MICHAEL] So we'd better leave the city tonight, Michael? [*To* SIMON] You like him?

SIMON With my respects, I like him.

GRUSHA Now I can tell you: I took him because on that Easter Sunday I got engaged to you. So he's a child of love. Michael, let's dance.
[*She dances with* MICHAEL, SIMON *dances with the* COOK, *the old couple with each other.* AZDAK *stands lost in thought. The dancers soon hide him from view. Occasionally he is seen, but less and less as more couples join the dance.*]

SINGER
And after that evening Azdak vanished and was never seen again.
The people of Grusinia did not forget him but long remembered
The period of his judging as a brief golden age,
Almost an age of justice.
[*All the couples dance off.* AZDAK *has disappeared.*]
But you, you who have listened to the Story of the Chalk Circle,
Take note what men of old concluded:
That what there is shall go to those who are good for it,
Children to the motherly, that they prosper,
Carts to good drivers, that they be driven well,
The valley to the waterers, that it yield fruit.

JOHN OSBORNE
[1929–   ]

Regarded as a leader of England's "angry young men," John Osborne established his place as an important dramatist when his play *Look Back in Anger* was produced in 1956. Although many reviewers thought it a "social outrage" in its harsh criticisms of British social institutions, the play was a spectacular success, running for eighteen months in England, and, when it opened in New York, it won the New York Drama Critics Circle Award as the best foreign play of 1957. Osborne is known as a spokesman both for the post-World War II generation in England and for working class people in rebellion against the status quo and England's ruling classes. Osborne himself comes from a working class family; he remembers his "boyhood in the midst of a brawling, laughing, drinking, moaning" environment provided by his father's pub. After finishing his secondary education and then studying at Belmont College (he did not attend a university), he began acting with repertory companies. While traveling in the provinces with these groups, he learned the crafts of the theater, paying special attention to acting, managing, and writing. Even today, after great success as a playwright, Osborne is a fine actor who often appears in movies and on the stage.

Following *Look Back in Anger*, Osborne wrote *The Entertainer* (1957), which starred Sir Lawrence Olivier, *Epitaph for George Dillon* (1958), *The World of Paul Slickey* (1959), *Luther* (1961), *Inadmissible Evidence* (1964), and *A Patriot for Me* (1965). He also wrote the film versions of *Look Back in Anger, The Entertainer,* and *Tom Jones* (for which he won an Academy Award in 1964). *Luther,* based on the life of Martin Luther, himself an angry man, has captivated American audiences in its Broadway run starring Albert Finney and more recently in a television production starring Robert Shaw. Osborne's *Luther,* along with such plays as Bolt's *A Man for All Seasons* and Anouilh's *Becket,* exemplifies a trend in the modern theater to look to the past for subject matter—particularly for heroic subjects.

LUTHER

JOHN OSBORNE

CAST

KNIGHT	CAJETAN
PRIOR	MILTITZ
MARTIN	LEO
HANS	ECK
LUCAS	KATHERINE
WEINAND	HANS, THE YOUNGER
TETZEL	AUGUSTINIANS, DOMINICANS,
STAUPITZ	HERALD, EMPEROR, PEASANTS, ETC.

ACT ONE

SCENE 1: *The convent of the Augustinian Order of Eremites at Erfurt. 1506*

SCENE 2: *The same. A year later*

SCENE 3: *Two hours later*

Copyright 1962 by Criterion Books, Inc. Reprinted by permission of the publisher from *Luther* by John Osborne (New York: 1962)

ACT TWO

SCENE 1: *The market place, Jüterbog. 1517*
SCENE 2: *The Eremite Cloister. Wittenberg. 1517*
SCENE 3: *The steps of the Castle Church. Wittenberg. Eve of All Saints. 1517*
SCENE 4: *The Fugger Palace. Augsburg. October 1518*
SCENE 5: *A hunting lodge. Magliana, Italy. 1519*
SCENE 6: *The Elster Gate. Wittenberg. 1520*

ACT THREE

SCENE 1: *The Diet of Worms. 1521*
SCENE 2: *Wittenberg. 1525*
SCENE 3: *The Eremite Cloister. Wittenberg. 1530*

NOTE: *At the opening of each act, the Knight appears. He grasps a banner and briefly barks the time and place of the scene following at the audience, and then retires.*

ACT ONE

Scene One

> *The Cloister Chapel of the Eremites of St. Augustine. Erfurt, Thuringia, 1506.* MARTIN *is being received into the Order. He is kneeling in front of the* PRIOR *in the presence of the assembled convent.*

PRIOR   Now you must choose one of two ways: either to leave us now, or give up this world, and consecrate and devote yourself entirely to God and our Order. But I must add this: once you have committed yourself, you are not free, for whatever reason, to throw off the yoke of obedience, for you will have accepted it freely, while you were still able to discard it.

> [*The habit and hood of the Order are brought in and blessed by the* PRIOR.]

PRIOR   He whom it was your will to dress in the garb of the Order, oh Lord, invest him also with eternal life.

> [*He undresses* MARTIN.]

PRIOR   The Lord divest you of the former man and of all his works. The Lord invest you with the new man.

> [*The* CHOIR *sings as* MARTIN *is robed in the habit and hood. The long white scapular is thrown over his head and hung down, before and behind; then he kneels again before the* PRIOR, *and, with his hand on the statutes of the Order, swears the oath.*]

MARTIN   I, brother Martin, do make profession and promise obedience to Almighty God, to Mary the Sacred Virgin, and to you, my brother Prior of this cloister, in the name of the Vicar General of the order of Eremites of the holy Bishop of St. Augustine and his successors, to live without property and in chastity according to the Rule of our Venerable Father Augustine until death.

[*The* PRIOR *wishes a prayer over him, and* MARTIN *prostrates himself with arms extended in the form of a cross.*]

PRIOR   Lord Jesus Christ, our leader and our strength, by the fire of humility you have set aside this servant, Martin, from the rest of Mankind. We humbly pray that this fire will also cut him off from carnal intercourse and from the community of those things done on earth by men, through the sanctity shed from heaven upon him, and that you will bestow on him grace to remain yours, and merit eternal life. For it is not he who begins, but he who endures will be saved. Amen.

[*The* CHOIR *sings Veni Creator Spiritus or perhaps Great Father Augustine. A newly lighted taper is put into* MARTIN's *hands, and he is led up the altar steps to be welcomed by the monks with the kiss of peace. Then, in their midst, he marches slowly with them behind the screen and is lost to sight. The procession disappears, and, as the sound of voices dies away, two men are left alone in the congregation. One of them,* HANS, *gets up impatiently and moves down-stage. It is* MARTIN's FATHER, *a stocky man wired throughout with a miner's muscle, lower-middle class, on his way to become a small, primitive capitalist; bewildered, full of pride and resentment. His companion,* LUCAS, *finishes a respectful prayer and joins him.*]

HANS   Well?

LUCAS   Well?

HANS   Don't 'well' me, you feeble old ninny, what do you think?

LUCAS   Think? Of what?

HANS   Yes, think man, think, what do you think, pen and ink, think of all that?

LUCAS   Oh—

HANS   Oh! Of all these monks, of Martin and all the rest of it, what do you think? You've been sitting in this arse-aching congregation all this time, you've been watching, haven't you? What about it?

LUCAS   Yes, well, I must say it's all very impressive.

HANS   Oh, yes?

LUCAS   No getting away from it.

HANS   Impressive?

LUCAS   Deeply. It was moving and oh—

HANS   What?

LUCAS   You must have felt it, surely. You couldn't fail to.

HANS   Impressive! I don't know what impresses me any longer.

LUCAS   Oh, come on—

HANS   Impressive!

LUCAS   Of course it is, and you know it.

HANS   Oh, you—you can afford to be impressed.

LUCAS   It's surely too late for any regrets, or bitterness, Hans. It obviously must be God's will, and there's an end of it.

HANS   That's exactly what it is—an end of it! Very fine for you, my old friend, very fine indeed. You're just losing a son-in-law, and you can take your pick of plenty more of those where he comes from. But what am I losing? I'm losing a son; mark: a son.

LUCAS   How can you say that?

HANS   How can I say it? I do say it, that's how. Two sons to the plague, and now another. God's eyes! Did you see that haircut? Brother Martin!

LUCAS   There isn't a finer order than these people, not the Dominicans or Franciscans—

HANS Like an egg with a beard.

LUCAS You said that yourself.

HANS Oh, I suppose they're Christians under their damned cowls.

LUCAS There are good, distinguished men in this place, and well you know it.

HANS Yes—good, distinguished men—

LUCAS Pious, learned men, men from the University like Martin.

HANS Learned men! Some of them can't read their own names.

LUCAS So?

HANS So! I—I'm a miner. I don't need books. You can't see to read books under the ground. But Martin's a scholar.

LUCAS He most certainly is.

HANS A Master of Arts! What's he master of now? Eh? Tell me.

LUCAS Well, there it is. God's gain is your loss.

HANS Half these monks do nothing but wash dishes and beg in the streets.

LUCAS We should be going, I suppose.

HANS He could have been a man of stature.

LUCAS And he will, with God's help.

HANS Don't tell me. He could have been a lawyer.

LUCAS Well, he won't now.

HANS No, you're damn right he won't. Of stature. To the Archbishop, or the Duke, or—

LUCAS Yes.

HANS Anyone.

LUCAS Come on.

HANS Anyone you can think of.

LUCAS Well, I'm going.

HANS Brother Martin!

LUCAS Hans.

HANS Do you know why? Lucas: Why? What made him do it?

[*He has ceased to play a role by this time and he asks the question simply as if he expected a short, direct answer.*]

HANS What made him do it?

[LUCAS *grasps his forearm.*]

LUCAS Let's go home.

HANS Why? That's what I can't understand. Why? Why?

LUCAS Home. Let's go home.

[*They go off. The convent bell rings. Some monks are standing at a re-fectory table. After their prayers, they sit down, and, as they eat in silence, one of the Brothers reads from a lectern. During this short scene,* MARTIN, *wearing a rough apron over his habit, waits on the others.*]

READER

What are the tools of Good Works?

First, to love Lord God with all one's heart, all one's soul, and all one's strength. Then, one's neighbour as oneself. Then, not to kill.

Not to commit adultery

Not to steal

Not to covet

Not to bear false witness

To honour all men

To deny yourself, in order to follow Christ

To chastise the body

Not to seek soft living

To love fasting

To clothe the naked
To visit the sick
To bury the dead
To help the afflicted
To console the sorrowing
To prefer nothing to the love of Christ

Not to yield to anger
Not to nurse a grudge
Not to hold guile in your heart
Not to make a feigned peace
To fear the Day of Judgment
To dread Hell
To desire eternal life with all your spiritual longing
To keep death daily before your eyes
To keep constant vigilance over the actions of your life
To know for certain that God sees you everywhere
When evil thoughts come into your heart, to dash them at once on the love
of Christ and to manifest them to your spiritual father
To keep your mouth from evil and depraved talk
Not to love much speaking
Not to speak vain words or such as produce laughter
To listen gladly to holy readings
To apply yourself frequently to prayer
Daily in your prayer, with tears and sighs to confess your past sins to God
Not to fulfil the desires of the flesh
To hate your own will
Behold, these are the tools of the spiritual craft. If we employ these un-
ceasingly day and night, and render account of them on the Day of Judg-
ment, then we shall receive from the Lord in return that reward that He
Himself has promised: Eye hath not seen nor ear heard what God hath
prepared for those that love him. Now this is the workshop in which we
shall diligently execute all these tasks. May God grant that you observe all
these rules cheerfully as lovers of spiritual beauty, spreading around you by
the piety of your deportment the sweet odour of Christ.
[*The convent bell rings. The* MONKS *rise, bow their heads in prayer, and
then move upstage to the steps where they kneel.* MARTIN, *assisted by another Brother, stacks the table and clears it. Presently, they all prostrate
themselves, and, beneath flaming candles, a communal confession begins.*
MARTIN *returns and prostrates himself downstage behind the rest. This
scene throughout is urgent, muted, almost whispered, confidential, secret,
like a prayer.*]

BROTHER   I confess to God, to Blessed Mary and our holy Father Augustine, to
all the saints, and to all present that I have sinned exceedingly in thought,
word and deed by my own fault. Wherefore I pray Holy Mary, all the
saints of God and you all assembled here to pray for me. I confess I did
leave my cell for the Night Office without the Scapular and had to return
for it. Which is a deadly infringement of the first degree of humility, that
of obedience without delay. For this failure to Christ I abjectly seek forgiveness and whatever punishment the Prior and community is pleased
to impose on me.

MARTIN   I am a worm and no man, a byword and a laughing stock. Crush out the worminess in me, stamp on me.

BROTHER   I confess I have three times made mistakes in the Oratory, in psalm singing and Antiphon.

MARTIN   I was fighting a bear in a garden without flowers, leading into a desert. His claws kept making my arms bleed as I tried to open a gate which would take me out. But the gate was no gate at all. It was simply an open frame, and I could have walked through it, but I was covered in my own blood, and I saw a naked woman riding on a goat, and the goat began to drink my blood, and I thought I should faint with the pain and I awoke in my cell, all soaking in the devil's bath.

BROTHER   Let Brother Norbert remember also his breakage while working in the kitchen.

BROTHER   I remember it, and confess humbly.

BROTHER   Let him remember also his greater transgression in not coming at once to the Prior and community to do penance for it, and so increasing his offence.

MARTIN   I am alone. I am alone, and against myself.

BROTHER   I confess it. I confess it, and beg your prayers that I may undergo the greater punishment for it.

MARTIN   How can I justify myself?

BROTHER   Take heart, you shall be punished, and severely.

MARTIN   How can I be justified?

BROTHER   I confess I have failed to rise from my bed speedily enough. I arrived at the Night Office after the Gloria of the 94th Psalm, and though I seemed to amend the shame by not standing in my proper place in the choir, and standing in the place appointed by the Prior for such careless sinners so that they may be seen by all, my fault is too great and I seek punishment.

MARTIN   I was among a group of people, men and women, fully clothed. We lay on top of each other in neat rows about seven or eight across. Eventually, the pile was many people deep. Suddenly, I panicked—although I was on top of the pile—and I cried: what about those underneath? Those at the very bottom, and those in between? We all got up in an orderly way, without haste, and when we looked, those at the bottom were not simply flattened by the weight, they were just their clothes, they were just their clothes, neatly pressed and folded on the ground. They were their clothes, neatly pressed and folded on the ground.

BROTHER   I did omit to have a candle ready at the Mass.

BROTHER   Twice in my sloth, I have omitted to shave, and even excused myself, pretending to believe my skin to be fairer than that of my Brothers, and my beard lighter and my burden also. I have been vain and slothful, and I beg forgiveness and ask penance.

MARTIN   If my flesh would leak and dissolve, and I could live as bone, if I were forged bone, plucked bone and brain, warm hair and a bony heart, if I were all bone, I could brandish myself without terror, without any terror at all—I could be indestructible.

BROTHER   I did ask for a bath, pretending to myself that it was necessary for my health, but as I lowered my body into the tub, it came to me that it was inordinate desire and that it was my soul that was soiled.

MARTIN   My bones fail. My bones fail, my bones are shattered and fall away, my bones fail and all that's left of me is a scraped marrow and a dying jelly.

BROTHER   Let Brother Paulinus remember our visit to our near sister house, and lifting his eyes repeatedly at a woman in the town who dropped alms into his bag.

BROTHER   I remember, and I beg forgiveness.

BROTHER   Then let him remember also that though our dear Father Augustine does not forbid us to see women, he blames us if we should desire them or wish to be the object of their desire. For it is not only by touch and by being affectionate that a man excites disorderly affection in a woman. This can be done also even by looks. You cannot maintain that your mind is pure if you have *wanton* eyes. For a wanton eye is a wanton heart. When people with impure hearts manifest their inclination towards each other through the medium of looks, even though no word is spoken, and when they take pleasure in their desire for each other, the purity of their character has gone even though they may be undefiled by any unchaste act. He who fixes his eyes on a woman and takes pleasure in her glance, must not think that he goes unobserved by his brothers.

MARTIN   I confess that I have offended grievously against humility, being sometimes discontented with the meanest and worst of everything, I have not only failed to declare myself to myself lower and lower and of less account than all other men, but I have failed in my most inmost heart to believe it. For many weeks, many weeks it seemed to me, I was put to cleaning the latrines. I did it, and I did it vigorously, not tepidly, with all my poor strength, without whispering or objections to anyone. But although I fulfilled my task, and I did it well, sometimes there were murmurings in my heart. I prayed that it would cease, knowing that God, seeing my murmuring heart, must reject my work, and it was as good as not done. I sought out my master, and he punished me, telling me to fast for two days. I have fasted for three, but, even so, I can't tell if the murmurings are really gone, and I ask for your prayers, and I ask for your prayers that I may be able to go on fulfilling the same task.

BROTHER   Let Brother Martin remember all the degrees of humility; and let him go on cleaning the latrines.

[*The convent bell rings. After lying prostrate for a few moments, all the* BROTHERS, *including* MARTIN, *rise and move to the* CHOIR. *The office begins, versicle, antiphon and psalm, and* MARTIN *is lost to sight in the ranks of his fellow* MONKS. *Presently, there is a quiet, violent moaning, just distinguishable amongst the voices. It becomes louder and wilder, the cries more violent, and there is some confusion in* MARTIN's *section of the* CHOIR. *The singing goes on with only a few heads turned. It seems as though the disturbance has subsided.* MARTIN *appears, and staggers between the stalls. Outstretched hands fail to restrain him, and he is visible to all, muscles rigid, breath suspended, then jerking uncontrollably as he is seized in a raging fit. Two* BROTHERS *go to him, but* MARTIN *writhes with such ferocity, that they can scarcely hold him down. He tries to speak, the effort is frantic, and eventually, he is able to roar out a word at a time.*]

MARTIN   Not! Me! I am *not!*

[*The attack reaches its height, and he recoils as if he had bitten his tongue and his mouth were full of blood and saliva. Two more* MONKS *come to help, and he almost breaks away from them, but the effort collapses, and they are able to drag him away, as he is about to vomit. The Office continues as if nothing had taken place.*]

[*End of Act One—Scene One*]

ACT ONE

Scene Two

> *A knife, like a butcher's, hanging aloft, the size of a garden fence. The cutting edge of the blade points upwards. Across it hangs the torso of a naked man, his head hanging down. Below it, an enormous round cone, like the inside of a vast barrel, surrounded by darkness. From the upstage entrance, seemingly far, far away, a dark figure appears against the blinding light inside, as it grows brighter. The figure approaches slowly along the floor of the vast cone, and stops as it reaches the downstage opening. It is* MARTIN, *haggard and streaming with sweat.*

MARTIN   I lost the body of a child, a child's body, the eyes of a child; and at the first sound of my own childish voice. I lost the body of a child; and I was afraid, and I went back to find it. But I'm still afraid. I'm afraid, and there's an end of it! But *I* mean . . . [*shouts*] . . . Continually! For instance of the noise the Prior's dog makes on a still evening when he rolls over on his side and licks his teeth. I'm afraid of the darkness, and the hole in it; and I see it sometime of every day! And some days more than once even, and there's no bottom to it, no bottom to my breath, and I can't reach it. Why? Why do you think? There's a bare fist clenched to my bowels and they can't move, and I have to sit sweating in my little monk's house to open them. The lost body of a child, hanging on a mother's tit, and close to the warm, big body of a man, and I can't find it.

[*He steps down, out of the blazing light within the cone, and goes to his cell down* L. *Kneeling by his bed, he starts to try and pray but he soon collapses. From down* R *appear a procession of* MONKS, *carrying various priest's vestments, candles and articles for the altar, for* MARTIN *is about to perform his very first Mass. Heading them is* BROTHER WEINAND. *They pass* MARTIN'S *cell, and, after a few words, they go on, leaving* BROTHER WEINAND *with* MARTIN, *and disappear into what is almost like a small house on the upstage left of the stage: a bagpipe of the period, fat, soft, foolish, and obscene looking.*]

BROTHER WEINAND   Brother Martin! Brother Martin!

MARTIN   Yes.

BROTHER WEINAND   Your father's here.

MARTIN   My father?

BROTHER WEINAND   He asked to see you, but I told him it'd be better to wait until afterwards.

MARTIN   Where is he?

BROTHER WEINAND   He's having breakfast with the Prior.

MARTIN   Is he alone?

BROTHER WEINAND   No, he's got a couple of dozen friends at least, I should say.

MARTIN   Is my mother with him?

BROTHER WEINAND   No.

MARTIN   What did he have to come for? I should have told him not to come.

BROTHER WEINAND   It'd be a strange father who didn't want to be present when his son celebrated his first Mass.

MARTIN   I never thought he'd come. Why didn't he tell me?

BROTHER WEINAND   Well, he's here now, anyway. He's also given twenty guilden to the chapter as a present, so he can't be too displeased with you.

MARTIN   Twenty guilden.

BROTHER WEINAND   Well, are you all prepared?

MARTIN   That's three times what it cost him to send me to the University for a year.

BROTHER WEINAND   You don't look it. Why, you're running all over with sweat again. Are you sick? Are you?

MARTIN   No.

BROTHER WEINAND   Here, let me wipe your face. You haven't much time. You're sure you're not sick?

MARTIN   My bowels won't move, that's all. But that's nothing out of the way.

BROTHER WEINAND   Have you shaved?

MARTIN   Yes. Before I went to confession. Why, do you think I should shave again?

BROTHER WEINAND   No. I don't. A few overlooked little bristles couldn't make much difference, any more than a few imaginary sins. There, that's better.

MARTIN   What do you mean?

BROTHER WEINAND   You were sweating like a pig in a butcher's shop. You know what they say, don't you? Wherever you find a melancholy person, there you'll find a bath running for the devil.

MARTIN   No, no, what did you mean about leaving a few imaginary sins?

BROTHER WEINAND   I mean there are plenty of priests with dirty ears administering the sacraments, but this isn't the time to talk about that. Come on, Martin, you've got nothing to be afraid of.

MARTIN   How do you know?

BROTHER WEINAND   You always talk as if lightning were just about to strike behind you.

MARTIN   Tell me what you meant.

BROTHER WEINAND   I only meant the whole convent knows you're always making up sins you've never committed. That's right—well, isn't it? No sensible confessor will have anything to do with you.

MARTIN   What's the use of all this talk of penitence if I can't feel it.

BROTHER WEINAND   Father Nathin told me he had to punish you only the day before yesterday because you were in some ridiculous state of hysteria, all over some verse in Proverbs or something.

MARTIN   "Know thou the state of thy flocks."

BROTHER WEINAND   And all over the interpretation of one word apparently. When will you ever learn? You must know what you're doing. Some of the brothers laugh quite openly at you, you and your over-stimulated conscience. Which is wrong of them, I know, but you must be able to see why.

MARTIN   It's the single words that trouble me.

BROTHER WEINAND   The moment you've confessed and turned to the altar, you're beckoning for a priest again. Why, every time you break wind they say you rush to a confessor.

MARTIN   Do they say that?

BROTHER WEINAND   It's their favourite joke.

MARTIN   They say that, do they?

BROTHER WEINAND   Martin! You're protected from many of the world's evils in here. You're expected to master them, not be obsessed by them. God bids us hope in His everlasting mercy. Try to remember that.

MARTIN   And you tell me this! What have I gained from coming into this sacred Order? Aren't I still the same? I'm still envious, I'm still impatient, I'm still passionate?

BROTHER WEINAND   How can you ask a question like that?

MARTIN   I do ask it. I'm asking you! What have I gained?

BROTHER WEINAND   In any of this, all we can ever learn is how to die.

MARTIN   That's no answer.

BROTHER WEINAND   It's the only one I can think of at this moment. Come on.

MARTIN   All you teach me in this sacred place is how to doubt—

BROTHER WEINAND   Give you a little praise, and you're pleased for a while, but let a little trial of sin and death come into your day and you crumble, don't you?

MARTIN   But that's all you've taught me, that's really all you've taught me, and all the while I'm living in the Devil's worm-bag.

BROTHER WEINAND   It hurts me to watch you like this, sucking up cares like a leech.

MARTIN   You *will* be there beside me, won't you?

BROTHER WEINAND   Of course, and, if anything at all goes wrong, or if you forget anything, we'll see to it. You'll be all right. But nothing will—you won't make any mistakes.

MARTIN   But what if I do, just one mistake. Just a word, one word—one sin.

BROTHER WEINAND   Martin, kneel down.

MARTIN   Forgive me, Brother Weinand, but the truth is this—

BROTHER WEINAND   Kneel.

[MARTIN *kneels.*]

MARTIN   It's this, just this. All I can feel, all I can feel is God's hatred.

BROTHER WEINAND   Repeat the Apostles' Creed.

MARTIN   He's like a glutton, the way he gorges me, he's a glutton. He gorges me, and then spits me out in lumps.

BROTHER WEINAND   After me. "I believe in God the Father Almighty, maker of Heaven and Earth . . .

MARTIN   I'm a trough, I tell you, and he's swilling about in me. All the time.

BROTHER WEINAND   "And in Jesus Christ, His only Son Our Lord . . .

MARTIN   "And in Jesus Christ, His only Son Our Lord . . .

BROTHER WEINAND   "Who was conceived by the Holy Ghost, born of the Virgin Mary, suffered under Pontius Pilate . . .

MARTIN   [*almost unintelligibly*]   "Was crucified, dead and buried; He descended into Hell; the third day He rose from the dead, He ascended into Heaven, and sitteth on the right hand of God the Father Almighty; from thence He shall come to judge the quick and the dead." And every sunrise sings a song for death.

BROTHER WEINAND   "I believe—"

MARTIN   "I believe—"

BROTHER WEINAND   Go on.

MARTIN   "I believe in the Holy Ghost; the holy Catholic Church; the Communion of Saints; the forgiveness of sins;

BROTHER WEINAND   Again!

MARTIN   "The forgiveness of sins.

BROTHER WEINAND   What was that again?

MARTIN   "I believe in the forgiveness of sins."

BROTHER WEINAND   Do you? Then remember this: St. Bernard says that when we say in the Apostles' Creed "I believe in the forgiveness of sins" each one must believe that *his* sins are forgiven. Well?—

MARTIN   I wish my bowels would open. I'm blocked up like an old crypt.

BROTHER WEINAND   Try to remember, Martin?

MARTIN   Yes, I'll try.

BROTHER WEINAND   Good. Now, you must get yourself ready. Come on, we'd better help you.

[*Some* BROTHERS *appear from out of the bagpipe with the vestments, etc. and help* MARTIN *put them on.*]

MARTIN   How much did you say my father gave to the chapter?
BROTHER WEINAND   Twenty guilden.
MARTIN   That's a lot of money to my father. He's a miner, you know.
BROTHER WEINAND   Yes, he told me.
MARTIN   As tough as you can think of. Where's he sitting?
BROTHER WEINAND   Near the front, I should think. Are you nearly ready?
   [*The Convent bell rings. A procession leads out from the bagpipe.*]
MARTIN   Thank you, Brother Weinand.
BROTHER WEINAND   For what? Today would be an ordeal for any kind of man. In a short while, you will be handling, for the first time, the body and blood of Christ. God bless you, my son.
   [*He makes the sign of the cross, and the other* BROTHERS *leave.*]
MARTIN   Somewhere, in the body of a child, Satan foresaw in me what I'm suffering now. That's why he prepares open pits for me, and all kinds of tricks to bring me down, so that I keep wondering if I'm the only man living who's baited, and surrounded by dreams, and afraid to move.
BROTHER WEINAND   [*really angry by now*]   You're a fool. You're really a fool. God isn't angry with you. It's you who are angry with Him.
   [*He goes out. The* BROTHERS *wait for* MARTIN, *who kneels,*]
MARTIN   Oh, Mary, dear Mary, all I see of Christ is a flame and raging on a rainbow. Pray to your Son, and ask Him to still His anger, for I can't raise my eyes to look at Him. Am I the only one to see all this, and suffer?
   [*He rises, joins the procession and disappears off with it.*
   As the Mass is heard to begin offstage, the stage is empty. Then the light within the cone grows increasingly brilliant, and, presently MARTIN *appears again. He enters through the far entrance of the cone, and advances towards the audience. He is carrying a naked child. Presently, he steps down from the cone, comes downstage, and stands still.*]
MARTIN   And so, the praising ended—and the blasphemy began.
   [*He returns, back into the cone, the light fades as the Mass comes to its end.*]

   [*End of Act One—Scene Two*]

ACT ONE

Scene Three

   The Convent refectory. Some monks are sitting at table with HANS *and* LUCAS. LUCAS *is chatting with the* BROTHERS *eagerly, but* HANS *is brooding. He has drunk a lot of wine in a short time, and his brain is beginning to heat.*

HANS   What about some more of this, eh? Don't think you can get away with it, you know, you old cockchafer. I'm getting me twenty guilden's worth before the day's out. After all, it's a proud day for all of us. That's right, isn't it?
LUCAS   It certainly is.
BROTHER WEINAND   Forgive me, I wasn't looking. Here—
   [*He fills* HANS's *glass.*]
HANS   [*trying to be friendly*]   Don't give me that. You monks don't miss much. Got eyes like gimlets and ears like open drains. Tell me—Come on, then, what's your opinion of Brother Martin?

BROTHER WEINAND   He's a good, devout monk.

HANS   Yes. Yes, well, I suppose you can't say much about each other, can you? You're more like a team, in a way. Tell me, Brother—would you say that in this monastery—or, any monastery you like—you were as strong as the weakest member of the team?

BROTHER WEINAND   No, I don't think that's so.

HANS   But wouldn't you say then—I'm not saying this in any criticism, mind, but because I'm just interested, naturally, in the circumstances—but wouldn't you say that one bad monk, say for instance, one really monster sized, roaring great bitch of a monk, if he really got going, really going, couldn't he get his order such a reputation that eventually, it might even have to go into—what do they call it now—liquidation. That's it. Liquidation. Now, you're an educated man, you understand Latin and Greek and Hebrew—

BROTHER WEINAND   Only Latin, I'm afraid, and a very little Greek.

HANS   [*having planted his cue for a quick, innocent boast*]   Oh, really. Martin knows Latin and Greek, and now he's half-way through Hebrew too, they tell me.

BROTHER WEINAND   Martin is a brilliant man. We are not all as gifted as he is.

HANS   No, well, anyway what would be your opinion about this?

BROTHER WEINAND   I think my opinion would be that the Church is bigger than those who are in her.

HANS   Yes, yes, but don't you think it could be discredited by, say, just a few men?

BROTHER WEINAND   Plenty of people have tried, but the Church is still there. Besides, a human voice is small and the world's very large. But the Church reaches out and is heard everywhere.

HANS   Well, what about this chap Erasmus, for instance?

BROTHER WEINAND   [*politely. He knows* HANS *knows nothing about him*]   Yes?

HANS   Erasmus. [*Trying to pass the ball*] Well, what about him, for instance? What do you think about him?

BROTHER WEINAND   Erasmus is apparently a great scholar, and respected throughout Europe.

HANS   [*resenting being lectured*]   Yes, of course, *I* know who he is, I don't need you to tell me that, what I said was: what do you think about him?

BROTHER WEINAND   Think about him?

HANS   Good God, you won't stand still a minute and let yourself be saddled, will you? Doesn't he criticize the Church or something?

BROTHER WEINAND   He's a scholar, and, I should say, his criticisms could only be profitably argued about by other scholars.

LUCAS   Don't let him get you into an argument. He'll argue about anything, especially if he doesn't know what he's talking about.

HANS   I know what I'm talking about, I was merely asking a question—

LUCAS   Well, you shouldn't be asking questions on a day like today. Just think of it, for a minute, Hans—

HANS   What do you think I'm doing? You soppy old woman!

LUCAS   It's a really "once only" occasion, like a wedding, if you like.

HANS   Or a funeral. By the way, what's happened to the corpse? Eh? Where's Brother Martin?

BROTHER WEINAND   I expect he's still in his cell.

HANS   Well, what's he doing in there?

BROTHER WEINAND   He's perfectly all right, he's a little—disturbed.

HANS   [*pouncing delightedly*]   Disturbed! Disturbed! What's he disturbed about?

BROTHER WEINAND   Celebrating one's first Mass can be a great ordeal for a sensitive spirit.

HANS   Oh, the bread and the wine and all that?

BROTHER WEINAND   Of course; there are a great many things to memorize as well.

LUCAS   Heavens, yes. I don't know how they think of it all.

HANS   I didn't think he made it up as he went along! But doesn't he know we're still here? Hasn't anybody told him we're all waiting for him?

BROTHER WEINAND   He won't be much longer—you'll see. Here, have some more of our wine. He simply wanted to be on his own for a little while before he saw anyone.

HANS   I should have thought he had enough of being on his own by now.

LUCAS   The boy's probably a bit—well, you know, anxious about seeing you again too.

HANS   What's he got to be anxious about?

LUCAS   Well, apart from anything else, it's nearly three years since he last saw you.

HANS   I saw *him*. He didn't see me.

[*Enter* MARTIN.]

LUCAS   There you are, my boy. We were wondering what had happened to you. Come and sit down, there's a good lad. Your father and I have been punishing the convent wine cellar, I'm afraid. Bit early in the day for me, too.

HANS   Speak for yourself, you swirly-eyed old gander. We're not *started* yet, are we?

LUCAS   My dear boy, are you all right? You're so pale.

HANS   He's right though. Brother Martin! Brother Lazarus they ought to call you!

[*He laughs and* MARTIN *smiles at the joke with him.* MARTIN *is cautious,* HANS *too, but manœuvring for position.*]

MARTIN   I'm all right, thank you, Lucas.

HANS   Been sick, have you?

MARTIN   I'm much better now, thank you, father.

HANS   [*relentless*]   Upset tummy, is it? That what it is? Too much fasting I expect. [*Concealing concern*]. You look like death warmed up, all right.

LUCAS   Come and have a little wine. You're allowed that, aren't you? It'll make you feel better.

HANS   I know that milky look. I've seen it too many times. Been sick have you?

LUCAS   Oh, he's looking better already. Drop of wine'll put the colour back in there. You're all right, aren't you, lad?

MARTIN   Yes, what about you—

LUCAS   That's right. Of course he is. He's all right.

HANS   Vomit all over your cell, I expect. [*To* BROTHER WEINAND]. But he'll have to clear that up himself, won't he?

LUCAS   [*to* MARTIN]   Oh, you weren't were you? Poor old lad, well, never mind, no wonder you kept us waiting.

HANS   Can't have his mother coming in and getting down on her knees to mop it all up.

MARTIN   I managed to clean it up all right. How are *you*, father?

HANS   [*feeling an attack, but determined not to lose the initiative*]   Me? Oh, I'm all right. I'm all right, aren't I, Lucas? Nothing ever wrong with me. Your old man's strong enough. But then that's because we've got to be, people like Lucas and me. Because if *we* aren't strong, it won't take any time at all before we're knocked flat on our backs, or flat on our knees, or flat on something or other. Flat on our backs and finished, and we can't afford to be finished because if we're finished, that's it, that's the end, so we just have to stand up to it as best we can. But that's life, isn't it?

MARTIN   I'm never sure what people mean when they say that.

LUCAS   Your father's doing very well indeed, Martin. He's got his own investment in the mine now, so he's beginning to work for himself if you see what I mean. That's the way things are going everywhere now.

MARTIN   [*to* HANS]   You must be pleased.

HANS   I'm pleased to make money. I'm not pleased to break my back doing it.

MARTIN   How's mother?

HANS   Nothing wrong there either. Too much work and too many kids for too long, that's all. [*Hiding embarrassment*]. I'm sorry she couldn't come, but it's a rotten journey as you know, and all that, so she sent her love to you. Oh, yes, and there was a pie too. But I was told [*at* BROTHER WEINAND] I couldn't give it to you, but I'd have to give it to the Prior.

MARTIN   That's the rule about gifts, father. You must have forgotten?

HANS   Well, I hope you get a piece of it anyway. She took a lot of care over it. Oh yes, and then there was Lucas's girl, she asked to be remembered to you.

MARTIN   Oh, good. How is she?

HANS   Didn't she, Lucas? She asked specially to be remembered to Martin, didn't she?

LUCAS   Oh she often talks about you, Martin. Even now. She's married you know.

MARTIN   No, I didn't know.

LUCAS   Oh, yes, got two children, one boy and a girl.

HANS   That's it—two on show on the stall, and now another one coming out from under the counter again—right, Lucas?

LUCAS   Yes, oh, she makes a fine mother.

HANS   And what's better than that? There's only one way of going 'up you' to Old Nick when he does come for you and that's when you show him your kids. It's the one thing—that is, if you've been lucky, and the plagues kept away from you—you can spring it out from under the counter at him. *That* to you! Then you've done something for yourself forever—forever and ever. Amen. [*Pause*]. Come along, Brother Martin, don't let your guests go without. Poor old Lucas is sitting there with a glass as empty as a nun's womb, aren't you, you thirsty little goosey?

MARTIN   Oh, please, I'm sorry.

HANS   That's right, and don't forget your old dad. [*Pause*]. Yes, well, as I say, I'm sorry your mother couldn't come, but I don't suppose she'd have enjoyed it much, although I dare say she'd like to have watched her son perform the Holy Office. Isn't a mother supposed to dance with her son after the ceremony? Like Christ danced with *his* mother? Well, I can't see her doing that. I suppose you think *I'm* going to dance with you instead.

MARTIN   You're not obliged to, father.

HANS   It's like giving a bride away, isn't it?

MARTIN   Not unlike.

[*They have been avoiding any direct contact until now, but now they look at each other, and both relax a little.*]

HANS   [*encouraged*]   God's eyes! Come to think of it, you look like a woman, in all that!

MARTIN   [*with affection*]   Not any woman you'd want, father.

HANS   What do *you* know about it, eh? What do you know about it? [*He laughs but not long*]. Well, Brother Martin.

MARTIN   Well? [*Pause*]. Have you had some fish? Or a roast, how about that, that's what you'd like, isn't it?

HANS   Brother Martin, old Brother Martin. Well, Brother Martin, you had a right old time up there by that altar for a bit, didn't you? I wouldn't have been in your shoes, I'll tell you. All those people listening to you, every word you're saying, watching every little tiny movement, watching for one little lousy mistake. I couldn't keep my eyes off it. We all thought you were going to flunk it for one minute there, didn't we, Lucas?

LUCAS   Well, we had a couple of anxious moments—

HANS   Anxious moments! I'll say there were. I thought to myself, "he's going to flunk it, he can't get through it, he's going to flunk it." What was that bit, you know, the worst bit where you stopped and Brother—

MARTIN   Weinand.

HANS   Weinand, yes, and he very kindly helped you up. He was actually holding you up at one point, wasn't he?

MARTIN   Yes.

BROTHER WEINAND   It happens often enough when a young priest celebrates Mass for the first time.

HANS   Looked as though he didn't know if it was Christmas or Wednesday. We thought the whole thing had come to a standstill for a bit, didn't we? Everyone waiting and nothing happening. What was that bit, Martin, what was it?

MARTIN   I don't remember.

HANS   Yes, you know, the bit you really flunked.

MARTIN   [*rattling it off*]   Receive, oh Holy Father, almighty and eternal God, this spotless host, which I, thine unworthy servant, offer unto thee for my own innumerable sins of commission and omission, and for all here present and all faithful Christians, living and dead, so that it may avail for their salvation and everlasting life. When I entered the monastery, I wanted to speak to God directly, you see. Without any embarrassment, I wanted to speak to him myself, but when it came to it, I dried up—as I always have.

LUCAS   No, you didn't, Martin, it was only for a few moments, besides—

MARTIN   Thanks to Brother Weinand. Father, why do you hate me being here?
[HANS *is outraged at a direct question.*]

HANS   Eh? What do you mean? I don't hate you being here.

MARTIN   Try to give me a straight answer if you can, father. I should like you to tell me.

HANS   What are you talking about, Brother Martin, you don't know what you're talking about. You've not had enough wine, that's your trouble.

MARTIN   And don't say I could have been a lawyer.

HANS   Well, so you could have been. You could have been better than that. You could have been a burgomaster, you could have been a magistrate, you could have been a chancellor, you could have been anything! So what! I don't want to talk about it. What's the matter with you! Anyway, I certainly don't want to talk about it in front of complete strangers.

MARTIN   You make me sick.

HANS   Oh, do I? Well, thank you for that, Brother Martin! Thank you for the truth, anyway.

MARTIN   No, it isn't the truth. It isn't the truth at all. You're drinking too much wine—and I'm . . .

HANS   Drinking too much wine! I could drink this convent piss from here till Gabriel's horn—and from all accounts, that'll blow about next Thursday—so what's the difference? [*Pause.* HANS *drinks.*] Is this the wine you use? Is it? Well? I'm asking a straight question myself now. Is this the wine you use? [*To* MARTIN]. Here, have some.
[MARTIN *takes it and drinks.*]
You know what they say?

MARTIN No, what do they say?
HANS I'll tell you:
> Bread thou art and wine thou art
> And always shall remain so.

[*Pause*]
MARTIN My father didn't mean that. He's a very devout man, I know.
[*Some of the* BROTHERS *have got up to leave.*]
MARTIN [*to* LUCAS] Brother Weinand will show you over the convent. If you've finished, that is.
LUCAS Yes, oh yes, I'd like that. Yes, I've had more than enough, thank you. Right, well, let's go, shall we, Brother Weinand? I'll come back for you, shall I. Hans, you'll stay here?
HANS Just as you like.
LUCAS [*to* MARTIN] You're looking a bit better now, lad. Good-bye, my boy, but I'll see you before I go, won't I?
MARTIN Yes, of course.
[*They all go, leaving* MARTIN *and* HANS *alone together. Pause.*]
HANS Martin, I didn't mean to embarrass you.
MARTIN No, it was my fault.
HANS Not in front of everyone.
MARTIN I shouldn't have asked you a question like that. It was a shock to see you suddenly, after such a long time. Most of my day's spent in silence you see, except for the Offices; and I enjoy the singing, as you know, but there's not much speaking, except to one's confessor. I'd almost forgotten what your voice sounded like.
HANS Tell me, son—what made you get all snarled up like that in the Mass?
MARTIN You're disappointed, aren't you?
HANS I want to know, that's all. I'm a simple man, Martin, I'm no scholar, but I can understand all right. But you're a learned man, you speak Latin and Greek and Hebrew. You've been trained to remember ever since you were a tiny boy. Men like you don't just forget their words!
MARTIN I don't understand what happened. I lifted up my head at the host, and, as I was speaking the words, I heard them as if it were the first time, and suddenly—[*pause*] they struck at my life.
HANS I don't know, I really don't. Perhaps your father and mother are wrong, and God's right, after all. Perhaps. Whatever it is you've got to find, you could only find out by becoming a monk; maybe that's the answer.
MARTIN But you don't believe that. Do you?
HANS No; no I don't.
MARTIN Then say what you mean.
HANS All right, if that's what you want, I'll say just what I mean. I think a man murders himself in these places.
MARTIN [*retreating at once*] I am holy. I kill no one but myself.
HANS I don't care. I tell you it gives me the creeps. And that's why I couldn't bring your mother, if you want to know.
MARTIN The Gospels are the only mother I've ever had.
HANS [*triumphantly*] And haven't you ever read in the Gospels, don't you know what's written in there? "Thou shalt honour thy father and thy mother."
MARTIN You're not understanding me, because you don't want to.
HANS That's fine talk, oh yes, fine, holy talk, but it won't wash, Martin. It won't wash because you can't ever, however you try, you can't ever get away from your body because that's what you live in, and it's all you've got to die in, and you can't get away from the body of your father and your mother! We're bodies, Martin, and so are you, and we're bound to-

gether for always. But you're like every man who was ever born into this world, Martin. You'd like to pretend that you made yourself, that it was *you* who made you—and not the body of a woman and another man.

MARTIN Churches, kings, and fathers—why do they ask so much, and why do they all of them get so much more than they deserve?

HANS You think so. Well, I think I deserve a little more than you've given me—

MARTIN I've given you! I don't have to give you! I *am*—that's all I need to give to you. That's your big reward, and that's all you're ever going to get, and it's more than any father's got a right to. You wanted me to learn Latin, to be a Master of Arts, be a lawyer. All you want is me to justify *you!* Well, I can't, and, what's more, I won't. I can't even justify myself. So just stop asking me what have I accomplished, and what have I done for you. I've done all for you I'll ever do, and that's live and wait to die.

HANS Why do you blame *me* for everything?

MARTIN I don't blame you. I'm just not grateful, that's all.

HANS Listen, I'm not a specially good man, I know, but I believe in God and in Jesus Christ, His Son, and the Church will look after me, and I can make some sort of life for myself that has a little joy in it somewhere. But where is your joy? You wrote to me once, when you were at the University, that only Christ could light up the place you live in, but what's the point? What's the point if it turns out the place you're living in is just a hovel? Don't you think it mightn't be better not to see at all?

MARTIN I'd rather be able to see.

HANS You'd rather see!

MARTIN You really are disappointed, aren't you? Go on.

HANS And why? I see a young man, learned and full of life, my son, abusing his youth with fear and humiliation. You think you're facing up to it in here, but you're not; you're running away, you're running away and you can't help it.

MARTIN If it's so easy in here, why do you think the rest of the world isn't knocking the gates down to get in?

HANS Because they haven't given up, that's why.

MARTIN Well, there it is: you think I've given up.

HANS Yes, there it is. That damned monk's piss has given me a headache.

MARTIN I'm sorry.

HANS Yes, we're all sorry, and a lot of good it does any of us.

MARTIN I suppose fathers and sons always disappoint each other.

HANS I worked for you, I went without for you.

MARTIN Well?

HANS Well! [*almost anxiously*] And if I beat you fairly often, and pretty hard sometimes I suppose, it wasn't any more than any other boy, was it?

MARTIN No.

HANS What do you think it is makes you different? Other men are all right, aren't they? You were stubborn, you were always stubborn, you've always had to resist, haven't you?

MARTIN You disappointed me too, and not just a few times, but at some time of every day I ever remember hearing or seeing you, but, as you say, maybe that was also no different from any other boy. But I loved you the best. It was always *you* I wanted. I wanted your love more than anyone's, and if anyone was to hold me, I wanted it to be you. Funnily enough, my mother disappointed me the most, and I loved her less, much less. She made a gap which no one else could have filled, but all she could do was make it bigger, bigger and more unbearable.

HANS I don't know what any of that means; I really don't. I'd better be going, Martin. I think it's best; and I dare say you've got your various duties to perform.

MARTIN She beat me once for stealing a nut, your wife. I remember it so well, she beat me until the blood came, I was so surprised to see it on my finger-tips; yes, stealing a nut, that's right. But that's not the point. I had corns on my backside already. Always before, when I was beaten for something, the pain seemed outside of me in some way, as if it belonged to the rest of the world, and not only me. But, on that day, for the first time, the pain belonged to me and no one else, it went no further than *my* body, bent between *my* knees and *my* chin.

HANS You know what, Martin, I think you've always been scared—ever since you could get up off your knees and walk. You've been scared for the good reason that that's what you most like to be. Yes, I'll tell you. I'll tell you what! Like that day, that day when you were coming home from Erfurt, and the thunderstorm broke, and you were so piss-scared, you lay on the ground and cried out to St. Anne because you saw a bit of lightning and thought you'd seen a vision.

MARTIN I saw it all right.

HANS And you went and asked her to save you—on condition that you became a monk.

MARTIN I saw it.

HANS Did you? So it's still St. Anne is it? I thought you were blaming your mother and me for your damned monkery?

MARTIN Perhaps I should.

HANS And perhaps sometime you should have another little think about that heavenly vision that wangled you away into the cloister.

MARTIN What's that?

HANS I mean: I hope it really was a vision. I hope it wasn't a delusion and some trick of the devil's. I really hope so, because I can't bear to think of it otherwise. [*Pause*] Good-bye, son. I'm sorry we had to quarrel. It shouldn't have turned out like this at all today.
 [*Pause*]

MARTIN Father—why did you give your consent?

HANS What, to your monkery, you mean?

MARTIN Yes. You could have refused, but why didn't you?

HANS Well, when your two brothers died with the plague . . .

MARTIN You gave me up for dead, didn't you?

HANS Good-bye, son. Here—have a glass of holy wine.
 [*He goes out.* MARTIN *stands, with the glass in his hand and looks into it. Then he drinks from it slowly, as if for the first time. He sits down at the table and sets the glass before him.*]

MARTIN But—but what if it isn't true?

CURTAIN

[*End of Act One*]

DECOR NOTE After the intense private interior of Act One, with its outer darkness and rich, personal objects, the physical effect from now on should be more intricate, general, less personal; sweeping, concerned with men in time rather than particular man in the unconscious; caricature not portraiture, like the popular woodcuts of the period, like Dürer. Down by the apron in one corner there is now a heavily carved pulpit.

ACT TWO

Scene One

> *The market place, Jüterbog, 1517. The sound of loud music, bells as a procession approaches the centre of the market place, which is covered in the banners of welcoming trade guilds. At the head of the slow-moving procession, with its lighted tapers and to the accompaniment of singing, prayers and the smoke of incense, is carried the Pontiff's bull of grace on a cushion and cloth of gold. Behind this the arms of the Pope and the Medici. After this, carrying a large red wooden cross, comes the focus of the procession, JOHN TETZEL, Dominican, inquisitor and most famed and successful indulgence vendor of his day. He is splendidly equipped to be an ecclesiastical huckster, with alive, silver hair, the powerfully calculating voice, range and technique of a trained orator, the terrible, riveting charm of a dedicated professional able to winkle coppers out of the pockets of the poor and desperate.*
>
> *The red cross is taken from* TETZEL *and established prominently behind him, and, from it are suspended the arms of the Pope.*

TETZEL   Are you wondering who I am, or what I am? Is there anyone here among you, any small child, any cripple, or any sick idiot who hasn't heard of me, and doesn't know why I am here? No? Well, speak up then if there is? What, no one? Do you all know me then? Do you all know who I am? If it's true, it's very good, and just as it should be. Just as it should be, and no more than that! However, however—just in case—just in case, mind, there is one blind, maimed midget among you today who can't hear, I will open his ears and wash them out with sacred soap for him! And, as for the rest of you. I know I can rely on you all to listen patiently while I instruct him. Is that right? Can I go on? I'm asking you, is that right, can I go on? I say "can I go on"?

[*Pause*]

Thank you. And what is there to tell this blind, maimed midget who's down there somewhere among you? No, don't look round for him, you'll only scare him and then he'll lose his one great chance, and it's not likely to come again, or if it does come, maybe it'll be too late. Well, what's the good news on this bright day? What's the information you want? It's this! Who is this friar with his red cross? Who sent him, and what's he here for? Don't try to work it out for yourself because I'm going to tell you now, this very minute. I am John Tetzel, Dominican, inquisitor, sub-commissioner to the Archbishop of Mainz, and what I bring you is indulgences. Indulgences made possible by the red blood of Jesus Christ, and the red cross you see standing up here behind me is the standard of those who carry them. Look at it! Go on, look at it! What else do you see hanging from the red cross? Well, what do they look like? Why, it's the arms of his holiness, because why? Because it's him who sent me here. Yes, my friend, the Pope himself has sent me with indulgences for you! Fine, you say, but what are indulgences? And what are they to me? What are indulgences? They're only the most precious and noble of God's gifts to men, that's all they are! Before God, I tell you I wouldn't swap my privilege at this moment with that of St. Peter in Heaven because I've already saved more souls with my indulgences than he could ever have done with all his sermons. You think that's bragging, do you? Well, listen a little more carefully, my friend, because this concerns *you!* Just look at it this way. For every mortal sin you commit, the Church says that after confession and contrition, you've got to do penance—either in this life or in purgatory —for seven years. Seven years! Right? Are you with me? Good. Now then, how many mortal sins are committed by you—by you—in a single day? Just think for one moment: in one single day of your life. Do you know the answer? Oh, not so much as one a day. Very well then, how many in a month? How many in six months? How many in a year? And how many in a whole lifetime? Yes, you needn't shuffle your feet—it doesn't bear thinking about, does it? You couldn't even add up all those years without a merchant's clerk to do it for you! Try and add up all the years of torment piling up! What about it? And isn't there anything you can do about this terrible situation you're in? Do you really want to know? Yes! There is something, and that something I have here with me now up here, letters, letters of indulgence. Hold up the letters so that everyone can see them. Is there anyone so small he can't see? Look at them, all properly sealed, an indulgence in every envelope, and one of them can be yours today, now, before it's too late! Come on, come up as close as you like, you won't squash me so easily. Take a good look. There isn't any one sin so big that one of these letters can't remit it. I challenge any one here, any member of this audience, to present me with a sin, anything, any kind of a sin, I don't care what it is, that I can't settle for him with one of these precious little envelopes. Why, if any one had ever offered violence to the blessed Virgin Mary, Mother of God, if he'd only pay up—as long as he paid up all he could—he'd find himself forgiven. You think I'm exaggerating? You do, do you? Well, I'm authorized to go even further than that. Not only am I empowered to give you these letters of pardon for the sins you've already committed, I can give you pardon for those sins you haven't even committed [*pause . . . then slowly*] but, which, however you *intend* to commit! But, you ask—and it's a fair question—but, you ask, why is our Holy Lord prepared to distribute such a rich grace to me? The answer, my friends, is all too simple. It's so that we can restore the ruined church of St. Peter and St. Paul in Rome! So that it won't have its equal anywhere in the world. This great church contains the bodies not only of the holy apostles Peter and Paul, but of a hundred thousand martyrs and no less than forty-six popes! To say nothing of the relics like St. Veronica's handkerchief, the burning bush of Moses and the very rope with which Judas Iscariot hanged himself! But, alas, this fine old building is threatened with destruction, and all these things with it, if a sufficient restoration fund isn't raised, and raised soon. [*With passionate irony*] . . . Will anyone dare to say that the cause is not a good one? [*Pause.*] . . . Very well, and won't you, for as little as one quarter of a florin, my friend, buy yourself one of these letters, so that in the hour of death, the gate through which sinners enter the world of torment shall be closed against you, and the gate leading to the joy of paradise be flung open for you? And, remember this, these letters aren't just for the living but for the dead too. There can't be one amongst you who hasn't at least one dear one who has departed—and to who knows what? Why, these letters are for them too. It isn't even necessary to repent. So don't hold back, come forward, think of your dear ones, think of yourselves! For twelve groats, or whatever it is we think you can afford, you can rescue your father from agony and yourself from certain disaster. And if you only have the coat on your back to call your own, then strip it off, strip it off now so that you too can obtain grace. For remember: As soon as your money rattles in the box and the cash bell rings, the soul flies out of purgatory and sings! So, come on then. Get your money out! What is it then, have your wits flown away with your faith? Listen then, soon, I shall take down the cross, shut the gates of heaven, and put out the brightness of this sun of grace that shines on you here today.

[*He flings a large coin into the open strong box, where it rattles furiously.*] The Lord our God reigns no longer. He has resigned all power to the Pope. In the name of the Father, and of the Son and of the Holy Ghost. Amen.

[*The sound of coins clattering like rain into a great coffer as the light fades.*]

[*End of Act Two—Scene One*]

ACT TWO

Scene Two

> *The Eremite Cloister, Wittenberg. 1517. Seated beneath a single pear tree is* JOHANN VON STAUPITZ, *Vicar General of the Augustinian Order. He is a quiet, gentle-voiced man in late middle age, almost stolidly contemplative. He has profound respect for* MARTIN, *recognizing in him the powerful potential of insight, sensitivity, courage and, also heroics that is quite outside the range of his own endeavour. However, he also understands that a man of his own limitations can offer a great deal to such a young man at this point in his development, and his treatment of* MARTIN *is a successful astringent mixture of sympathy and ridicule. Birds sing as he reads in the shade, and* MARTIN *approaches, prostrating himself.* STAUPITZ *motions him to his feet.*

MARTIN [*looking up*] The birds always seem to fly away the moment I come out here.

STAUPITZ Birds, unfortunately, have no faith.

MARTIN Perhaps it's simply that they don't like me.

STAUPITZ They haven't learned yet that you mean them no harm, that's all.

MARTIN Are you treating me to one of your allegories?

STAUPITZ Well, you recognized it, anyway.

MARTIN I ought to. Ever since I came into the cloister, I've become a craftsman allegory maker myself. Only last week I was lecturing on Galatians Three, verse three, and I allegorized going to the lavatory.

STAUPITZ [*quoting the verse*] "Are ye so foolish, that ye have begun in the spirit, you would now end in the flesh."

MARTIN That's right. But allegories aren't much help in theology—except to decorate a house that's been already built by argument.

STAUPITZ Well, it's a house you've been able to unlock for a great many of us. I never dreamed when I first came here that the University's reputation would ever become what is has, and in such a short time, and it's mostly due to you.

MARTIN [*very deliberately turning the compliment*] If ever a man could get to heaven through monkery, that man would be me.

STAUPITZ I don't mean that. You know quite well what I mean. I'm talking about your scholarship, and what you manage to do with it, not your monkishness as you call it. I've never had any patience with all your mortifications. The only wonder is that you haven't killed yourself with your prayers, and watchings, yes and even your reading too. All these trials and temptations you go through, they're meat and drink to you.

MARTIN [*patient*] Will you ever stop lecturing me about this?

STAUPITZ Of course not, why do you think you come here—to see me in the garden when you could be inside working?

MARTIN Well, if it'll please you, I've so little time, what with my lectures and study, I'm scarcely able to carry out even the basic requirements of the Rule.

STAUPITZ I'm delighted to hear it. Why do you think you've always been obsessed with the Rule? No, I don't want to hear all your troubles again. I'll tell you why: you're obsessed with the Rule because it serves very nicely as a protection for you.

MARTIN What protection?

STAUPITZ You know perfectly well what I mean, Brother Martin, so don't pretend to look innocent. Protection against the demands of your own instincts, that's what. You see, you think you admire authority, and so you do, but unfortunately, you can't submit to it. So, what you do, by your exaggerated attention to the Rule, you make the authority ridiculous. And the reason you do that is because you're determined to substitute that authority with something else—yourself. Oh, come along, Martin, I've been Vicar General too long not to have made that little discovery. Anyway, you shouldn't be too concerned with a failing like that. It also provides the strongest kind of security.

MARTIN Security? I don't feel *that*.

STAUPITZ I dare say, but you've got it all the same, which is more than most of us have.

MARTIN And how have I managed to come by this strange security?

STAUPITZ Quite simply: by demanding an impossible standard of perfection.

MARTIN I don't see what work or merit can come from a heart like mine.

STAUPITZ Oh, my dear, dear friend, I've sworn a thousand times to our holy God to live piously, and have I been able to keep my vows? No, of course I haven't. Now I've given up making solemn promises because I know I'm not able to keep them. If God won't be merciful to me for the love of Christ when I leave this world, then I shan't stand before Him on account of all my vows and good works, I shall perish, that's all.

MARTIN You think I lavish too much attention on my own pain, don't you?

STAUPITZ Well, that's difficult for me to say, Martin. We're very different kinds of men, you and I. Yes, you do lavish attention on yourself, but then a large man is worth the pains he takes. Like St. Paul, some men must say "I die daily."

MARTIN Tell me, Father, have you never felt humiliated to find that you belong to a world that's dying?

STAUPITZ No, I don't think I have.

MARTIN Surely, this must be the last age of time we're living in. There can't be any more left but the black bottom of the bucket.

STAUPITZ Do you mean the Last Judgment?

MARTIN No. I don't mean that. The Last Judgment isn't to come. It's here and now.

STAUPITZ Good. That's a little better, anyway.

MARTIN I'm like a ripe stool in the world's straining anus, and at any moment we're about to let each other go.

STAUPITZ   There's nothing new in the world being damned, dying or without hope. It's always been like that, and it'll stay like it. What's the matter with you? What are you making funny faces for?

MARTIN   It's nothing, Father, just a—a slight discomfort.

STAUPITZ   Slight discomfort? What are you holding your stomach for? Are you in pain?

MARTIN   It's all right. It's gone now.

STAUPITZ   I don't understand you. What's gone now? I've seen you grabbing at yourself like that before. What is it?

MARTIN   I'm—constipated.

STAUPITZ   Constipated? There's always something the matter with you, Brother Martin. If it's not the gripes, insomnia, or faith and works, it's boils or indigestion or some kind of belly-ache you've got. All these severe fasts——

MARTIN   That's what my father says.

STAUPITZ   Your father sounds pretty sensible to me.

MARTIN   He is, and you know, he's a theologian too, I've discovered lately.

STAUPITZ   I thought he was a miner.

MARTIN   So he is, but he made a discovery years and years ago that took me sweat and labour to dig out of the earth for myself.

STAUPITZ   Well, that's no surprise. There's always some chunk of truth buried down away somewhere which lesser men will always reach with less effort.

MARTIN   Anyway, he always knew that works alone don't save any man. Mind you, he never said anything about faith coming first.

STAUPITZ   [*quoting*] "Oh, well, that's life, and nothing you can do's going to change it."

MARTIN   The same speech.

STAUPITZ   You can't change human nature.

MARTIN   Nor can you.

STAUPITZ   That's right, Martin, and you've demonstrated it only too well in your commentaries on the Gospels and St. Paul. But don't overlook the fact that your father's taken a vow of poverty too, even though it's very different from your own. And he took it the day he told himself, and told *you*, that he was a complete man, or at least, a contented man.

MARTIN   A hog waffling in its own crap is contented.

STAUPITZ   Exactly.

MARTIN   My father, faced with an unfamiliar notion is like a cow staring at a new barn door. Like those who look on the cross and see nothing. All they hear is the priest's forgiveness.

STAUPITZ   One thing I promise you, Martin. You'll never be a spectator. You'll always take part.

MARTIN   How is it you always manage somehow to comfort me?

STAUPITZ   I think some of us are not much more than pretty modest sponges, but we're probably best at quenching big thirsts. How's your tummy?

MARTIN   Better.

STAUPITZ   One mustn't be truly penitent because one anticipates God's forgiveness, but because one already possesses it. You have to sink to the bottom of your black bucket because that's where God judges you, and then look to the wounds of Jesus Christ. You told me once that when you entered the cloister, your father said it was like giving away a bride, and again your father was right. You are a bride and you should hold yourself ready like a woman at conception. And when grace comes and your soul is penetrated by the spirit, you shouldn't pray or exert yourself, but remain passive.

MARTIN   [*smiles*] That's a hard role.

STAUPITZ [*smiles too*] Too hard for you, I dare say. Did you know the Duke's been complaining to me about you?

MARTIN Why, what have I done?

STAUPITZ Preaching against indulgences again.

MARTIN Oh, that—I was very mild.

STAUPITZ Yes, well I've heard your mildness in the pulpit. When I think some-times of the terror it used to be for you, you used to fall up the steps with fright. Sheer fright! You were too frightened to become a Doctor of The-ology, and you wouldn't be now if I hadn't forced you. "I'm too weak, I'm not strong enough. I shan't live long enough!" Do you remember what I said to you?

MARTIN "Never mind, the Lord still has work in heaven, and there are always vacancies."

STAUPITZ Yes, and the Duke paid all the expenses of your promotion for you. He was very cross when he spoke to me, I may say. He said you even made some reference to the collection of holy relics in the Castle Church, and most of those were paid for by the sale of indulgences, as you know. Did you say anything about them?

MARTIN Well, yes, but not about those in the Castle Church. I did make some point in passing about someone who claimed to have a feather from the wing of the angel Gabriel.

STAUPITZ Oh yes, I heard about him.

MARTIN And the Archbishop of Mainz, who is supposed to have a flame from Moses' burning bush.

STAUPITZ Oh dear, you shouldn't have mentioned that.

MARTIN And I just finished off by saying how does it happen that Christ had twelve apostles and eighteen of them are buried in Germany?

STAUPITZ Well, the Duke says he's coming to your next sermon to hear for himself, so try to keep off the subject, if you possibly can. It's All Saints' Day soon, remember, and all those relics will be out on show for everyone to gawp at. The Duke's a good chap, and he's very proud of his collection, and it doesn't help to be rude about it.

MARTIN I've tried to keep off the subject because I haven't been by any means sure about it. Then I did make a few mild protests in a couple of sermons, as I say.

STAUPITZ Yes, yes, but what did you actually say?

MARTIN That you can't strike bargains with God. There's a Jewish, Turkish, Pelagian heresy if you like.

STAUPITZ Yes, more mildness. Go on.

MARTIN I said, oh it was an evil sanction because only *you* could live *your* life, and only you can die your death. It can't be taken over for you. Am I right?

STAUPITZ [*doubtfully*] Yes, what's difficult to understand is why your sermons are so popular.

MARTIN Well, there are plenty who sit out there stiff with hatred, I can tell you. I can see their faces, and there's no mistaking them. But I wanted to tell you something—

STAUPITZ Yes?

MARTIN About all this. The other day a man was brought to me, a shoemaker. His wife had just died, and I said to him, "What've you done for her?" so he said, "I've buried her and commended her soul to God." "But haven't you had a Mass said for the repose of her soul?" "No," he said, "what's the point? She entered heaven the moment she died." So I asked him, "How do you know that?" And he said, "Well, I've proof. that's why." And out of his pocket he took a letter of indulgence.

STAUPITZ   Ah.

MARTIN   He threw it at me, and said, "And if you still maintain that a Mass is necessary, then my wife's been swindled by our most holy father the Pope. Or, if not by him, then by the priest who sold it to me."

STAUPITZ   Tetzel.

MARTIN   Who else?

STAUPITZ   That old tout!

MARTIN   There's another story going around about him which is obviously true because I've checked it at several sources. It seems that a certain Saxon nobleman had heard Tetzel in Jüterbog. After Tetzel had finished his usual performance, he asked him if he'd repeat what he'd said at one stage, that he—Tetzel I mean—had the power of pardoning sins that men intended to commit. Tetzel was very high and mighty, you know what he's like, and said, "What's the matter, weren't you listening? Of course I can give pardon not only for sins already committed but for sins that men *intend* to commit." "Well, then, that's fine," says this nobleman, "because I'd like to take revenge on one of my enemies. You know, nothing much, I don't want to kill him or anything like that. Just a little slight revenge. Now, if I give you ten guilden, will you give me a letter of indulgence that will justify me—justify me freely and completely?" Well, it seems Tetzel made a few stock objections, but eventually agreed on thirty guilden, and they made a deal. The man went away with his letter of indulgence, and Tetzel set out for the next job, which was Leipzig. Well, half-way between Leipzig and Treblen, in the middle of a wood, he was set on by a band of thugs, and beaten up. While he's lying there on the grass in a pool of his own blood, he looks up and sees that one of them is the Saxon nobleman and that they're making off with his great trunk full of money. So, the moment he's recovered enough, he rushes back to Jüterbog, and takes the nobleman to court. And what does the nobleman do? Takes out the letter of indulgence and shows it to Duke George himself—case dismissed!

STAUPITZ   [*laughing*]   Well, I leave you to handle it. But try and be careful. Remember, *I* agree with all you say, but the moment someone disagrees or objects to what you're saying, *that* will be the moment when you'll suddenly recognize the strength of your belief!

MARTIN   Father, I'm never sure of the words till I hear them out loud.

STAUPITZ   Well, that's probably the meaning of the Word. The Word is me, and I am the Word. Anyway, try and be a little prudent. Look at Erasmus: he never really gets into any serious trouble, but he still manages to make his point.

MARTIN   People like Erasmus get upset because I talk of pigs and Christ in the same breath. I must go. [*Clutches himself unobtrusively.*]

STAUPITZ   Well, you might be right. Erasmus is a fine scholar, but there are too many scholars who think they're better simply because they insinuate in Latin what you'll say in plain German. What's the matter, are you having that trouble again? Good heavens! Martin—just before you go: a man with a strong sword will draw it at some time, even if it's only to turn it on himself. But whatever happens, he can't just let it dangle from his belt. And, another thing, don't forget—you began this affair in the name of Our Lord Jesus Christ. You must do as God commands you, of course, but remember, St. Jerome once wrote about a philosopher who destroyed his own eyes so that it would give him more freedom to study. Take care of your eyes, my son, and do something about those damned bowels!

MARTIN   I will. Who knows? If I break wind in Wittenberg, they might smell it in Rome.
[*Exit. Church bells.*]

[*End of Act Two—Scene Two*]

ACT TWO

Scene Three

> *The steps of the Castle Church, Wittenberg, October 31st, 1517. From inside the Church comes the sound of Matins being sung. Sitting on the steps is a child, dirty, half-naked and playing intently by himself.* MARTIN *enters with a long roll of paper. It is his ninety-five theses for disputation against indulgences. As he goes up the steps, he stops and watches the child, absorbed in his private fantasy. He is absorbed by the child, who doesn't notice him at first, but, presently, as soon as the boy becomes aware of an intruder, he immediately stops playing and looks away distractedly in an attempt to exclude outside attention.* MARTIN *hesitates briefly, then puts out his hand to the child, who looks at it gravely and deliberately, then slowly, not rudely, but naturally, gets up and skips away sadly out of sight.* MARTIN *watches him, then walks swiftly back down the steps to the pulpit and ascends it.*

MARTIN   My text is from the Epistle of Paul the Apostle to the Romans, chapter one, verse seventeen: "For therein is the righteousness of God revealed from faith to faith."
[*Pause*]
We are living in a dangerous time. You may not think so, but it could be that this is the most dangerous time since the light first broke upon the earth. It may not be true, but it's very probably true—but, what's most important is that it's an assumption we are obliged to make. We Christians seem to be wise outwardly and mad inwardly, and in this Jerusalem we have built there are blasphemies flourishing that make the Jews no worse than giggling children. A man is not a good Christian because he understands Greek and Hebrew. Jerome knew five languages, but he's inferior to Augustine, who knew only one. Of course, Erasmus wouldn't agree with me, but perhaps one day the Lord will open his eyes for him. But listen! A man without Christ becomes his own shell. We are content with shells. Some shells are whole men and some are small trinkets. And, what are the trinkets? Today is the eve of All Saints, and the holy relics will be on show to you all; to the hungry ones whose lives are made satisfied by trinkets, by an imposing procession and the dressings up of all kinds of dismal things. You'll mumble for magic with lighted candles to St. Anthony for your erysipelas, to St. Valentine for your epilepsy, to St. Sebastian for the pestilence; to St. Laurentis to protect you from fire, to St. Apollonia if you've got the toothache, and to St. Louis to stop your beer from going sour. And tomorrow you'll queue for hours outside the Castle Church so that you can get a cheap-rate glimpse of St. Jerome's tooth, or four pieces each of St. Chrysostom and St. Augustine, and six of St. Bernard. The deacons will

have to link hands to hold you back while you struggle to gawp at four hairs from Our Lady's head, at the pieces of her girdle and her veil stained with her Son's blood. You'll sleep outside with the garbage in the streets all night so that you can stuff your eyes like roasting birds on a scrap of swaddling clothes, eleven pieces from the original crib, one wisp of straw from the manger and a gold piece specially minted by three wise men for the occasion. Your emptiness will be frothing over at the sight of a strand of Jesus' beard, at one of the nails driven into His hands, and at the remains of the loaf at the Last Supper. Shells for shells, empty things for empty men. There are some who complain of these things, but they write in Latin for scholars. Who'll speak out in rough German? Someone's got to bell the cat! For you must be made to know that there's no security, there's no security at all, either in indulgences, holy busywork or anywhere in this world. It came to me while I was in my tower, what they call the monk's sweathouse, the jakes, the john or whatever you're pleased to call it. I was struggling with the text I've given you: "For therein is the righteousness of God revealed, from faith to faith; as it is written, the just shall live by faith." And seated there, my head down, on that privy just as when I was a little boy, I couldn't reach down to my breath for the sickness in my bowels, as I seemed to sense beneath me a large rat, a heavy, wet, plague rat, slashing at my privates with its death's teeth. [*He kneads his knuckles into his abdomen, as if he were suppressing pain. His face runs with sweat.*] I thought of the righteousness of God, and wished his gospel had never been put to paper for men to read; who demanded my love and made it impossible to return it. And I sat in my heap of pain until the words emerged and opened out. "The just shall live by faith." My pain vanished, my bowels flushed and I could get up. I could see the life I'd lost. No man is just because he does just works. The works are just if the man is just. If a man doesn't believe in Christ, not only are his sins mortal, but his good works. This I know; reason is the devil's whore, born of one stinking goat called Aristotle, which believes that good works make a good man. But the truth is that the just shall live by faith alone. I need no more than my sweet redeemer and meditator, Jesus Christ, and I shall praise Him as long as I have voice to sing; and if anyone doesn't care to sing with me, then he can howl on his own. If we are going to be deserted, let's follow the deserted Christ.

[*He murmurs a prayer, descends from the pulpit, then walks up the steps to the Church door, and nails his theses to it. The singing from within grows louder as he walks away.*]

[*End of Act Two—Scene Three*]

ACT TWO

Scene Four

> The Fugger Palace, Augsburg. October 1518. As a backcloth a satirical contemporary woodcut, showing, for example, the Pope portrayed as an ass playing the bagpipes, or a cardinal dressed up as a court fool. Or perhaps Holbein's cartoon of Luther with the Pope suspended from his nose. However, there is a large area for the director and designer to choose from.

Seated at a table is THOMAS DE VIO, *known as Cajetan, Cardinal of San Sisto, General of the Dominican Order, as well as its most distinguished theologian, papal legate, Rome's highest representative in Germany. He is about fifty, but youthful, with a shrewd, broad, outlook, quite the opposite of the vulgar bigotry of* TETZEL, *who enters.*

TETZEL He's here.

CAJETAN So I see.

TETZEL What do you mean?

CAJETAN You look so cross. Is Staupitz with him?

TETZEL Yes. At least *he's* polite.

CAJETAN I know Staupitz. He's a straightforward, four-square kind of a man, and probably very unhappy at this moment. From all accounts, he has a deep regard for this monk—which is all to the good from our point of view.

TETZEL He's worried all right, you can see that. These Augustinians, they don't have much fibre.

CAJETAN What about Dr. Luther? What's he got to say for himself?

TETZEL Too much. I said to him if our Lord the Pope were to offer you a good Bishopric and a plenary indulgence for repairing your church, you'd soon start singing a different song.

CAJETAN Dear, oh, dear, and what did he say to that?

TETZEL He asked me—

CAJETAN Well?

TETZEL He asked me how was my mother's syphilis.

CAJETAN It's a fair question in the circumstances. You Germans, you're a crude lot.

TETZEL He's a pig.

CAJETAN I've no doubt. After all, it's what your country's most famous for.

TETZEL That's what I said to him—you're not on your own ground here, you know. These Italians, they're different. They're not just learned, they're subtle, experienced antagonists. You'll get slung in the fire after five minutes.

CAJETAN And?

TETZEL He said, "I've only been to Italy once, and they didn't look very subtle to me. They were lifting their legs on street corners like dogs."

CAJETAN I hope he didn't see any cardinals at it. Knowing some of them as I do, it's not impossible. Well, let's have a look at this foul-mouthed monk of yours.

TETZEL What about Staupitz?

CAJETAN Let him wait in the corridor. It'll help him to worry.

TETZEL Very well, your eminence. I hope he behaves properly. I've spoken to him.

[TETZEL *goes out and returns presently with* MARTIN, *who advances, prostrates himself, his face to the ground before* CAJETAN. CAJETAN *makes a motion and* MARTIN *rises to a kneeling position, where* CAJETAN *studies him.*]

CAJETAN [*courteous*] Please stand up, Dr. Luther. So you're the one they call the excessive doctor. You don't look excessive to me. Do you feel very excessive?

MARTIN [*conscious of being patronized*] It's one of those words which can be used like a harness on a man.

CAJETAN How do you mean?

MARTIN I mean it has very little meaning beyond traducing him.

CAJETAN   Quite. There's never been any doubt in my mind that you've been misinterpreted all round, and, as you say, traduced. Well, what a surprise you are! Here was I expecting to see some doddering old theologian with dust in his ears who could be bullied into a heart attack by Tetzel here in half an hour. And here you are, as gay and sprightly as a young bull. How old are you, my son?

MARTIN   Thirty-four, most worthy father.

CAJETAN   Tetzel, he's a boy—you didn't tell me! And how long have you been wearing your doctor's ring?

MARTIN   Five years—

CAJETAN   So you were only twenty-nine! Well, obviously, everything I've heard about you is true—you must be a very remarkable young man. I wouldn't have believed there was one doctor in the whole of Germany under fifty. Would you, Brother John?

TETZEL   Not as far as I know.

CAJETAN   I'm certain there isn't. What is surprising, frankly, is that they allowed such an honour to be conferred on anyone so young and inexperienced as a man must inevitably be at twenty-nine.
[*He smiles to let his point get home.*]
Your father must be a proud man.

MARTIN   [*irritated*]   Not at all, I should say he was disappointed and constantly apprehensive.

CAJETAN   Really? Well, that's surely one of the legacies of parenthood to offset the incidental pleasures. Now then, to business. I was saying to Tetzel, I don't think this matter need take up very much of our time. But, before we do start, there's just one thing I would like to say, and that is I was sorry you should have decided to ask the Emperor for safe conduct. That was hardly necessary, my son, and it's a little—well, distressing to feel you have such an opinion of us, such a lack of trust in your Mother Church, and in those who have, I can assure you, your dearest interests at heart.

MARTIN   [*out-manœuvred*]   I—

CAJETAN   [*kindly*]   But never mind all that now, that's behind us, and, in the long run, it's unimportant, after all, isn't it? Your Vicar General has come with you, hasn't he?

MARTIN   He's outside.

CAJETAN   I've known Staupitz for years. You have a wonderful friend there.

MARTIN   I know. I—have great love for him.

CAJETAN   And he certainly has for you, I know. Oh my dear, dear son, this is such a ridiculous, unnecessary business for us all to be mixed up in. It's such a tedious, upsetting affair, and what purpose is there in it? Your entire order in Germany has been brought into disgrace. Staupitz is an old man, and he can't honestly be expected to cope. Not now. I have my job to do, and, make no mistake, it isn't all honey for an Italian legate in your country. You know how it is, people are inclined to resent you. Nationalist feeling and all that—which I respect—but it does complicate one's task to the point where this kind of issue thrown in for good measure simply makes the whole operation impossible. You know what I mean? I mean, there's your Duke Frederick, an absolutely fair, honest man, if ever there was one, and one his holiness values and esteems particularly. Well, he instructed me to present him with the Golden Rose of Virtue, so you can see . . . As well as even more indulgences for his Castle Church. But what happens now? Because of all this unpleasantness and the uproar it's caused throughout Germany, the Duke's put in an extremely difficult position about accepting it. Naturally, he wants to do the right thing by everyone. But he's not going to betray you or anything like that, however much he's set his heart on that Golden Rose, even after all these years. And, of course he's perfectly right. I know he has the greatest regard for you and for some of your ideas—even though, as he's told me—he doesn't agree with a lot of them. No, I can only respect him for all that. So, you see, my dear son, what a mess we are in. Now, what are we going to do? Um? The Duke is unhappy. I am unhappy, his holiness is unhappy, and, you, my son, you are unhappy.

MARTIN [*formal, as if it were a prepared speech*] Most worthy father, in obedience to the summons of his papal holiness, and in obedience to the orders of my gracious lord, the Elector of Saxony, I have come before you as a submissive and dutiful son of the holy Christian church, and acknowledge that I have published the proposition and theses ascribed to me. I am ready now to listen most obediently to my indictment, and if I have been wrong, to submit to your instruction in the truth.

CAJETAN [*impatient*] My son, you have upset all Germany with your dispute about indulgences. I know you're a very learned doctor of the Holy Scriptures, and that you've already aroused some supporters. However, if you wish to remain a member of the Church, and to find a gracious father in the Pope, you'd better listen. I have here, in front of me, three propositions which, by the command of our holy father, Pope Leo the Tenth, I shall put to you now. First, you must admit your faults, and retract all your errors and sermons. Secondly, you must promise to abstain from propagating your opinions at any time in the future. And, thirdly, you must behave generally with greater moderation, and avoid anything which might cause offence or grieve and disturb the Church.

MARTIN May I be allowed to see the Pope's instruction?

CAJETAN No, my dear son, you may not. All you are required to do is confess your errors, keep a strict watch on your words, and not go back like a dog to his vomit. Then, once you have done that, I have been authorized by our most holy father to put everything to rights again.

MARTIN I understand all that. But I'm asking you to tell me where I have erred.

CAJETAN If you insist. [*Rattling off, very fast.*] Just to begin with, here are two propositions you have advanced, and which you will have to retract before anything else. First, the treasure of indulgences does not consist of the sufferings and torments of our Lord Jesus Christ. Second, the man who received the holy sacrament must have faith in the grace that is presented to him. Enough?

MARTIN I rest my case entirely on Holy Scriptures.

CAJETAN The Pope alone has power and authority over all those things.

MARTIN Except Scripture.

CAJETAN Including Scripture. What do you mean?

TETZEL Only the Pope has the right of deciding in matters of Christian faith. He alone and no one else has the power to interpret the meaning of Scripture, and to approve or condemn the views of other men, whoever they are—scholars, councils or the ancient fathers. The Pope's judgement cannot err, whether it concerns the Christian faith or anything that has to do with the salvation of the human race.

MARTIN That sounds like your theses.

TETZEL Burned in the market place by your students in Wittenberg—thank you very much—

MARTIN I assure you, I had nothing to do with that.

CAJETAN Of course. Brother John wasn't suggesting you had.

MARTIN   I can't stop the mouth of the whole world.

TETZEL   Why, your heresy isn't even original. It's no different from Wyclif or Hus.

CAJETAN   True enough, but we mustn't try to deprive the learned doctor of his originality. An original heresy may have been thought of by someone else before you. In fact, I shouldn't think such a thing as an original heresy exists. But it is original so long as it originated in *you*, the virgin heretic.

TETZEL   The time'll come when you'll have to defend yourself before the world, and then every man can judge for himself who's the heretic and schismatic. It'll be clear to everyone, even those drowsy snoring Christians who've never smelled a Bible. They'll find out for themselves that those who scribble books and waste so much paper just for their own pleasure, and are contemptuous and shameless, end up by condemning themselves. People like you always go too far, thank heaven. You play into our hands. I give you a month, Brother Martin, to roast yourself.

MARTIN   You've had your thirty pieces of silver. For the sake of Christ, why don't you betray someone?

CAJETAN   [*to* TETZEL]   Perhaps you should join Staupitz.

TETZEL   Very well, your eminence.

[*He bows and goes out.*]

CAJETAN   In point of fact, he gets eighty guilden a month plus expenses.

MARTIN   What about his vow of poverty?

CAJETAN   Like most brilliant men, my son, you have an innocent spirit. I've also just discovered that he has managed to father two children. So there goes another vow. Bang! But it'll do him no good, I promise you. You've made a hole in that drum for him. I may say there's a lot of bad feelings among the Dominicans about you. I should know—because I'm their General. It's only natural, they're accustomed to having everything their own way. The Franciscans are a grubby, sentimental lot, on the whole, and mercifully ignorant as well. But your people seem to be running alive with scholars and would-be politicians.

MARTIN   I'd no idea that my theses would ever get such publicity.

CAJETAN   Really now!

MARTIN   But it seems they've been printed over and over again, and circulated well, to an extent I'd never dreamed of.

CAJETAN   Oh yes, they've been circulated and talked about wherever men kneel to Christ.

MARTIN   Most holy father, I honour the Holy Roman Church, and I shall go on doing so. I have sought after the truth, and everything I have said I still believe to be right and true and Christian. But I am a man, and I may be deceived, so I am willing to receive instruction where I have been mistaken—

CAJETAN   [*angrily*]   Save your arrogance, my son, there'll be a better place to use it. I can have you sent to Rome and let any of your German princes try to stop me! He'll find himself standing outside the gates of heaven like a leper.

MARTIN   [*stung*]   I repeat, I am here to reply to all the charges you may bring against me—

CAJETAN   No, you're not—

MARTIN   I am ready to submit my theses to the universities of Basle, Freibourg, Louvain or Paris—

CAJETAN   I'm afraid you've not grasped the position. I'm not here to enter into a disputation with you, now or at any other time. The Roman Church is the apex of the world, secular and temporal, and it may constrain with its secular arm any who have once received the faith and gone astray.

Surely I don't have to remind you that it is not bound to use reason to fight and destroy rebels. [*He sighs.*] My son, it's getting late. You must retract. Believe me, I simply want to see this business ended as quickly as possible.

MARTIN Some interests are furthered by finding truth, others by destroying it. I don't care—what pleases or displeases the Pope. He is a man.

CAJETAN [*wearily*] Is that all?

MARTIN He seems a good man, as Popes go. But it's not much for a world that sings out for reformation. I'd say that's a hymn for everyone.

CAJETAN My dear friend, think, think carefully, and see if you can't see some way out of all this. I am more than prepared to reconcile you with the Church, and the sovereign bishop. Retract, my son, the holy father prays for it—

MARTIN But won't you discuss—

CAJETAN Discuss! I've not *discussed* with you, and I don't intend to. If you want a disputation, I dare say Eck will take care of you—

MARTIN John Eck? The Chancellor of Ingolstadt?

CAJETAN I suppose you don't think much of him?

MARTIN He knows theology.

CAJETAN He has a universal reputation in debate.

MARTIN It's understandable. He has a pedestrian style and a judicial restraint and that'll always pass off as wisdom to most men.

CAJETAN You mean he's not original, like you—

MARTIN I'm not an original man, why I'm not even a teacher, and I'm scarcely even a priest. I know Jesus Christ doesn't need my labour or my services.

CAJETAN All right, Martin, I *will* argue with you if you want me to, or, at least, I'll put something to you, because there is something more than your safety or your life involved, something bigger than you and I talking together in this room at this time. Oh, it's fine for someone like you to criticize and start tearing down Christendom, but tell me this, just tell me this: what will you build in its place?

MARTIN A withered arm is best amputated, an infected place is best scoured out, and so you pray for healthy tissue and something sturdy and clean that was crumbling and full of filth.

CAJETAN Can't you see? My son, you'll destroy the perfect unity of the world.

MARTIN Someone always prefers what's withered and infected. But it should be cauterized as honestly as one knows how.

CAJETAN And how honest is that? There's something I'd like to know: suppose you *did* destroy the Pope. What do you think would become of you?

MARTIN I don't know.

CAJETAN Exactly, you wouldn't know what to do because you need him, Martin, you need to hunt him more than he needs his silly wild boar. Well? There have always been Popes, and there always will be, even if they're called something else. They'll have them for people like *you*. You're not a good old revolutionary, my son, you're just a common rebel, a very different animal. You don't fight the Pope because he's too big, but because for your needs he's not big enough.

MARTIN My General's been gossiping—

CAJETAN [*contemptuous*] I don't need Staupitz to explain you to me. Why, some deluded creature might even come to you as a leader of their revolution, but you don't want to break rules, you want to make them. You'd be a master breaker and maker and no one would be able to stand up to you, you'd hope, or ever sufficiently repair the damage you did. I've read some of your sermons on faith. Do you know all they say to me?

MARTIN No.

CAJETAN They say: I am a man struggling for certainty, struggling insanely like a man in a fit, an animal trapped to the bone with doubt.

[MARTIN *seems about to have a physical struggle with himself.*]

CAJETAN Don't you see what could happen out of all this? Men could be cast out and left to themselves for ever, helpless and frightened!

MARTIN Your eminence, forgive me. I'm tired after my journey—I think I might faint soon—

CAJETAN That's what would become of them without their Mother Church—with all its imperfections, Peter's rock, without it they'd be helpless and unprotected. Allow them their sins, their petty indulgences, my son, they're unimportant to the comfort we receive—

MARTIN [*somewhat hysterical*] Comfort! It—doesn't concern me!

CAJETAN We live in thick darkness, and it grows thicker. How will men find God if they are left to themselves each man abandoned and only known to himself?

MARTIN They'll have to try.

CAJETAN I beg of you, my son, I beg of you. Retract.

[*Pause*]

MARTIN Most holy father, I cannot.

[*Pause*]

CAJETAN You look ill. You had better go and rest. [*Pause*] Naturally, you will be released from your order.

MARTIN I—

CAJETAN Yes?

MARTIN As you say, your eminence. Will you refer this matter to the Pope for his decision?

CAJETAN Assuredly. Send in Tetzel.

[MARTIN *prostrates himself, and then kneels.* CAJETAN *is distressed but in control.*]

You know, a time will come when a man will no longer be able to say, "I speak Latin and am a Christian" and go his way in peace. There will come frontiers, frontiers of all kinds—between men—and there'll be no end to them.

[MARTIN *rises and goes out.* TETZEL *returns.*]

TETZEL Yes?

CAJETAN No, of course he didn't—that man hates himself. And if he goes to the stake, Tetzel, you can have the pleasure of inscribing it: he could only love others.

[*End of Act Two—Scene Four*]

ACT TWO

Scene Five

A hunting lodge at Magliana in Northern Italy, 1519. Suspended the arms, the brass balls, of the Medici. KARL VON MILTITZ, *a young Chamberlain of the Pope's household is waiting. There are cries off, and sounds of excitement.* POPE LEO THE TENTH *enters with a* HUNTSMAN, *dogs and* DOMINICANS. *He is richly dressed in hunting clothes and long boots. He is indolent, cultured, intelligent, extremely restless, and well able to assimilate the essence of anything before anyone else. While he is listening, he is able to play with a live bird with apparent distraction. Or shoot at a board with a crossbow. Or generally fidget.* MILTITZ *kneels to kiss his toe.*

LEO I should forget it. I've got my boots on. Well? Get on with it. We're missing the good weather.

[*He sits and becomes immediately absorbed in his own play, as it seems.* MILTITZ *has a letter, which he reads.*]

MILTITZ "To the most blessed father Leo the Tenth, sovereign bishop, Martin Luther, Augustine friar, wishes eternal salvation. I am told that there are vicious reports circulating about me, and that my name is in bad odour with your holiness. I am called a heretic, apostate, traitor and many other insulting names. I cannot understand all this hostility, and I am alarmed by it. But the only basis of my tranquillity remains, as always, a pure and peaceful conscience. Deign to listen to me, most holy father, to me who is like a child.

[LEO *snorts abstractedly.*]

"There have always been, as long as I can remember, complaints and grumbling in the taverns about the avarice of the priests and attacks on the power of the keys. And this has been happening throughout Germany. When I listened to these things my zeal was aroused for the glory of Christ, so I warned not one, but several princes of the Church. But, either they laughed in my face or ignored me. The terror of your name was too much for everyone. It was then I published my disputation, nailing it on the door of the Castle Church here in Wittenberg. And now, most holy father, the whole world has gone up in flames. Tell me what I should do? I cannot retract; but this thing has drawn down hatred on me from all sides, and I don't know where to turn to but to you. I am far too insignificant to appear before the world in a matter as great as this.

[LEO *snaps his fingers to glance at this passage in the letter. He does so and returns it to* MILTITZ *who continues reading.*]

"But in order to quieten my enemies and satisfy my friends I am now addressing myself to you most holy father and speak my mind in the greater safety of the shadow of your wings. All this respect I show to the power of the keys. If I had not behaved properly it would have been impossible for the most serene Lord Frederick, Duke and Elector of Saxony, who shines in your apostolic favour, to have endured me in his University of Wittenberg. Not if I am as dangerous as is made out by my enemies. For this reason, most holy father, I fall at the feet of your holiness, and submit myself to you, with all I have and all that I am. Declare me right or wrong. Take my life, or give it back to me, as you please. I shall acknowledge your voice as the voice of Jesus Christ. If I deserve death, I shall not refuse to die. The earth is God's and all within it. May He be praised through all eternity, and may He uphold you for ever. Amen. Written the day of the Holy Trinity in the year 1518, Martin Luther, Augustine Friar."

[*They wait for* LEO *to finish his playing and give them his full attention. Presently, he gets up and takes the letter from* MILTITZ. *He thinks.*]

LEO Double faced German bastard! Why can't he say what he means? What else?

MILTITZ He's said he's willing to be judged by any of the universities of Germany, with the exception of Leipzig, Erfurt and Frankfurt, which he says are not impartial. He says it's impossible for him to appear in Rome in person.

LEO   I'm sure.

MILTITZ   Because his health wouldn't stand up to the rigours of the journey.

LEO   Cunning! Cunning German bastard! What does Staupitz say for him?

MILTITZ   [*reading hastily from another letter*]   "The reverend father, Martin Luther, is the noblest and most distinguished member of our university. For many years, we have watched his talents—"

LEO   Yes, well we know all about that. Write to Cajetan. Take this down. We charge you to summon before you Martin Luther. Invoke for this purpose, the aid of our very dear son in Christ, Maximilian, and all the other princes in Germany, together with all communities, universities, potentates ecclesiastic and secular. And, once you get possession of him, keep him in safe custody, so that he can be brought before us. If, however, he should return to his duty of his own accord and begs forgiveness, we give you the power to receive him into the perfect unity of our Holy Mother the Church. But, should he persist in his obstinacy and you cannot secure him, we authorize you to outlaw him in every part of Germany. To banish and excommunicate him. As well as all prelates, religious orders, universities, counts, and dukes who do not assist in apprehending him. As for the laymen, if they do not immediately obey your orders, declare them infamous, deprived of Christian burial and stripped of anything they may hold either from the apostolic see or from any lord whatsoever. There's a wild pig in our vineyard, and it must be hunted down and shot. Given under the seal of the Fisherman's Ring, etcetera. That's all.

[*He turns quickly and goes out.*]

[*End of Act Two—Scene Five*]

ACT TWO

Scene Six

> The Elster Gate, Wittenberg. 1520. Evening. A single bell. As a backcloth the bull issued against Luther. Above it a fish-head and bones. The bull is slashed with the reflection of the flames rising round the Elster Gate where the books of canon law, the papal decretals, are burning furiously. MONKS come to and fro with more books and documents, and hurl them on the fire. MARTIN enters and ascends the pulpit.

MARTIN   I have been served with a piece of paper. Let me tell you about it. It has come to me from a latrine called Rome, the capital of the devil's own sweet empire. It is called the papal bull and it claims to excommunicate me, Dr. Martin Luther. These lies they rise up from paper like fumes from the bog of Europe; because papal decretals are the devil's excretals. I'll hold it up for you to see properly. You see the signature? Signed beneath the seal of the Fisherman's Ring by one certain midden cock called Leo, an over-indulged jakes' attendant to Satan himself, a glittering worm in excrement, known to you as his holiness the Pope. You may know him as the head of the Church. Which he may still be: like a fish is the head of a cat's dinner; eyes without sight clutched to a stick of sucked bones. God has told me: there can be no dealings between this cat's dinner and me. And, as for this bull, it's going to roast, it's going to roast and so are the balls of the Medici!

[*He descends and casts the bull into the flames. He begins to shake, as if he were unable to breathe; as if he were about to have another fit. Shaking, he kneels.*]

Oh, God! Oh, God! Oh, thou my God, my God, help me against the reason and wisdom of the world. You must—there's only you—to do it. Breathe into me. Breathe into me, like a lion into the mouth of a stillborn cub. This cause is not mine but yours. For myself, I've no business to be dealing with the great lords of this world. I want to be still, in peace, and alone. Breathe into me, Jesus. I rely on no man, only on you. My God, my God do you hear me? Are you dead? Are you dead? No, you can't die, you can only hide yourself, can't you? Lord, I'm afraid. I am a child, the lost body of a child. I am stillborn. Breathe into me, in the name of Thy Son, Jesus Christ, who shall be my protector and defender, yes, my mighty fortress, breathe into me. Give me life, oh Lord. Give me life.

[MARTIN *prays as the deep red light of the flames floods the darkness around him.*]

[End of Act Two]

ACT THREE

Scene One

> *The Diet of Worms, April 18th, 1521. A gold frontcloth, and on it, in the brightest sunshine of colour, a bold, joyful representation of this unique gathering of princes, electors, dukes, ambassadors, bishops, counts, barons, etc. Perhaps Luther's two-wheeled wagon which brought him to Worms. The mediaeval world dressed up for the Renaissance.*
>
> *Devoid of depth, such scenes are stamped on a brilliant ground of gold. Movement is frozen, recession in space ignored and perspective served by the arrangement of figures, or scenes, one above the other. In this way, landscape is dramatically substituted by objects in layers. The alternative is to do the opposite, in the manner of, say, Altdorfer. Well in front of the cloth is a small rostrum with brass rails sufficient to support one man. If possible, it would be preferable to have this part of the apron projected a little into the audience. Anyway, the aim is to achieve the maximum in physical enlargement of the action, in the sense of physical participation in the theatre, as if everyone watching had their chins resting on the sides of a boxing-ring. Also on the apron, well to the front are several chairs. On one side is a table with about twenty books on it. The table and books may also be represented on the gold cloth. The rostrum has a small crescent of chairs round it. From all corners of the auditorium comes a fanfare of massed trumpets, and, approaching preferably from the auditorium up steps to the apron, come a few members of the Diet audience (who may also be represented on the gold cloth). Preceded by a* HERALD, *and seating themselves on the chairs, they should include* THE EMPEROR CHARLES THE FIFTH *(in front of the rostrum),* ALEANDER, THE PAPAL NUNCIO; ULRICH VON HUTTEN, KNIGHT; THE ARCHBISHOP OF TRIER *and* HIS SECRETARY,

JOHAN VON ECK, *who sit at the table with the books. The trumpets cease, and they wait.* MARTIN *appears from the stage, and ascends the rostrum centre.*

ECK [*rising*]   Martin Luther, you have been brought here by His Imperial Majesty so that you may answer two questions. Do you publicly acknowledge being the author of the books you see here? When I asked you this question yesterday, you agreed immediately that the books were indeed your own. Is that right?

[MARTIN *nods in agreement.*]

When I asked you the second question, you asked if you might be allowed time in which to consider it. Although such time should have been quite unnecessary for an experienced debater and distinguished doctor of theology like yourself, His Imperial Majesty was graciously pleased to grant your request. Well, you have had your time now, a whole day and a night, and so I will repeat the question to you. You have admitted being the author of these books. Do you mean to defend all these books, or will you retract any of them?

[ECK *sits.* MARTIN *speaks quietly, conversationally, hardly raising his voice throughout, and with simplicity.*]

MARTIN   Your serene highness, most illustrious princes and gracious lords, I appear before you by God's mercy, and I beg that you will listen patiently. If, through my ignorance, I have not given anyone his proper title or offended in any way against the etiquette of such a place as this, I ask your pardon in advance for a man who finds it hard to know his way outside the few steps from wall to wall of a monk's cell. We have agreed these books are all mine, and they have all been published rightly in my name. I will reply to your second question. I ask your serene majesty and your gracious lordships to take note that not all my books are of the same kind. For instance, in the first group, I have dealt quite simply with the values of faith and morality, and even my enemies have agreed that all this is quite harmless, and can be read without damaging the most fragile Christian. Even the bull against me, harsh and cruel as it is, admits that some of my books are offensive to no one. Perhaps it's the strange nature of such a questionable compliment, that the bull goes on to condemn these with the rest, which it considers offensive. If I'm to begin withdrawing these books, what should I be doing? I should be condemning those very things my friends and enemies are agreed on. There is a second group of books I have written, and these all attack the power of the keys, which has ravaged Christendom. No one can deny this, the evidence is everywhere and everyone complains of it. And no one has suffered more from this tyranny than the Germans. They have been plundered without mercy. If I were to retract those books now, I should be issuing a licence for more tyranny, and it is too much to ask of me.

I have also written a third kind of book against certain, private, distinguished, and, apparently—highly established—individuals. They are all defenders of Rome and enemies of my religion. In these books, it's possible that I have been more violent than may seem necessary, or, shall I say, tasteful in one who is, after all, a monk. But then, I have never set out to be a saint and I've not been defending my own life, but the teaching of Christ. So you see, again I'm not free to retract, for if I did, the present situation would certainly go on just as before. However, because I am a man and not God, the only way for me to defend what I have written is to employ the same method used by my Saviour. When He was being questioned by Annas, the high priest, about His teaching, and He had been struck in the face by one of the servants, He replied: "If I have spoken lies tell me what the lie is." If the Lord Jesus Himself, who could not err, was willing to listen to the arguments of a servant, how can I refuse to do the same? Therefore, what I ask, by the Mercy of God, is let someone expose my errors in the light of the Gospels. The moment you have done this, I shall ask you to let me be the first to pick up my books and hurl them in the fire.

I think this is a clear answer to your question. I think I understand the danger of my position well enough. You have made it very clear to me. But I can still think of nothing better than the Word of God being the cause of all the dissension among us. For Christ said, "I have not come to bring peace, but a sword. I have come to set a man against his father." We also have to be sure that the reign of this noble, young Prince Charles, so full of promise, should not end in the misery of Europe. We must fear God alone. I commend myself to your most serene majesty and to your lordships, and humbly pray that you will not condemn me as your enemy. That is all.

ECK   [*rising*] Martin, you have not answered the question put to you. Even if it were true that some of your books are innocuous—a point which, incidentally, we don't concede—we still ask that you cut out these passages which are blasphemous; that you cut out the heresies or whatever could be construed as heresy, and, in fact, that you delete any passage which might be considered hurtful to the Catholic faith. His sacred and imperial majesty is more than prepared to be lenient, and, if you will do these things, he will use his influence with the supreme pontiff to see that the good things in your work are not thrown out with the bad. If, however, you persist in your attitude, there can be no question that all memory of you will be blotted out, and everything you have written, right or wrong, will be forgotten.

You see, Martin, you return to the same place as all other heretics—to Holy Scripture. You demand to be contradicted from Scripture. We can only believe that you must be ill or mad. Do reasons have to be given to anyone who cares to ask a question? Any question? Why, if anyone who questioned the common understanding of the Church on any matter he liked to raise, and had to be answered irrefutably from the Scriptures, there would be nothing certain or decided in Christendom. What would the Jews and Turks and Saracens say if they heard us *debating* whether what we have always believed is true or not? I beg you, Martin, not to believe that you, and you alone, understand the meaning of the Gospels. Don't rate your own opinion so highly, so far beyond that of many other sincere and eminent men. I ask you: don't throw doubt on the most holy, orthodox faith, the faith founded by the most perfect legislator known to us, and spread by His apostles throughout the world, with their blood and miracles. This faith has been defined by sacred councils, and confirmed by the Church. It is your heritage, and we are forbidden to dispute it by the laws of the emperor and the pontiff. Since no amount of argument can lead to a final conclusion, they can only condemn those who refuse to submit to them. The penalties are provided and will be executed. I must, therefore, ask again, I must demand that you answer sincerely, frankly and unambiguously, yes or no: will you or will you not retract your books and the errors contained in them.

MARTIN   Since your serene majesty and your lordships demand a simple answer, you shall have it, without horns and without teeth. Unless I am shown by the testimony of the Scriptures—for I don't believe in popes or councils— unless I am refuted by Scripture and my conscience is captured by God's own word, I cannot and will not recant, since to act against one's conscience is neither safe nor honest. Here I stand; God help me; I can do no more. Amen.

[*End of Act Three—Scene One*]

ACT THREE

Scene Two

> *Wittenberg. 1525. A marching hymn, the sound of cannon and shouts of mutilated men. Smoke, a shattered banner bearing the cross and wooden shoe of the Bundschuh, emblem of the Peasants' Movement. A small chapel altar at one side of the stage opposite the pulpit. Centre is a small handcart, and beside it lies the bloody bulk of a peasant's corpse. Downstage stands* THE KNIGHT, *fatigued, despondent, stained and dirty.*

KNIGHT   There was excitement that day. In Worms—that day I mean. Oh, I don't mean now, not now. A lot's happened since then. There's no excitement like that any more. Not unless murder's your idea of excitement. I tell you, you can't have ever known the kind of thrill that monk set off amongst that collection of all kinds of men gathered together there—those few years ago. We all felt it, every one of us, just without any exception, you couldn't help it, even if you didn't want to, and, believe me, most of those people didn't want to. His scalp looked blotchy and itchy, and you felt sure, just looking at him, his body must be permanently sour and white all over, even whiter than his face and like a millstone to touch. He'd sweated so much by the time he'd finished, I could smell every inch of him even from where I was. But he fizzed like a hot spark in a trail of gunpowder going off in us, that dowdy monk, he went off in us, and nothing could stop it, and it blew up and there was nothing we could do, any of us, that was it. I just felt quite sure, quite certain in my own mind nothing could ever be the same again, just simply that. Something had taken place, something had changed and become something else, an event had occurred in the flesh, in the flesh and the breath—like, even like when the weight of that body slumped on its wooden crotchpiece and the earth grew dark. That's the kind of thing I mean by happen, and this also happened in very likely the same manner to all those of us who stood there, friends and enemies alike. I don't think, no I don't think even if I could speak and write like him, I could begin to give you an idea of what we thought, or what some of us thought, of what we might come to. Obviously, we couldn't have all felt quite the same way, but I wanted to burst my ears with shouting and draw my sword, no, not draw it, I wanted to pluck it as if it were a flower in my blood and plunge it into whatever he would have told me to.
[THE KNIGHT *is lost in his own thoughts, then his eyes catch the body of the peasant. He takes a swipe at the cart.*]
If one could only understand him. He baffles me, I just can't make him out. Anyway, it never worked out. [*To corpse*] Did it, my friend? Not the way we expected anyway, certainly not the way *you* expected, but who'd have ever thought we might end up on different sides, him on one and us on the other. That when the war came between you and them, he'd be there beating the drum for *them* outside the slaughter house, and beating it louder and better than anyone, hollering for *your* blood, cutting you up in your thousands, and hanging you up to drip away into the fire for good. Oh well, I suppose all those various groups were out for their different things, or the same thing really, all out for what we could get, and more than any of us had the right to expect. They were all the same, all those big princes and archbishops, the cut rate nobility and rich layabouts, honourable this and thats scrabbling like boars round a swill bucket for every penny those poor

peasants never had. All those great abbots with ther dewlaps dropped and hanging on their necks like goose's eggs, and then those left-over knights, like me for instance, I suppose, left-over men, impoverished, who'd seen better days and were scared and'd stick at nothing to try and make sure they couldn't get any worse. Yes. . . . Not one of them could read the words WAY OUT when it was written up for them, marked out clearly and unmistakably in the pain of too many men. Yes. They say, you know, that the profit motive—and I'm sure you know all about that one—they say that the profit motive was born with the invention of double entry book-keeping in the monasteries. Book-keeping! In the monasteries, and ages before any of us had ever got round to burning them down. But, you know, for men with such a motive, there is only really one entry. The profit is theirs, the loss is someone else's, and usually they don't even bother to write it up.
[*He nudges the corpse with his toe.*]
Well, it was your old loss wasn't it, dead loss, in fact, my friend, you could say his life was more or less a write-off right from the day he was born. Wasn't it? Um? And all the others like him, everywhere, now and after him.
[THE KNIGHT *starts rather weakly to load the body on to the cart.* MARTIN *enters, a book in his hands. They look at each other then* MARTIN *at the* PEASANT. THE KNIGHT *takes his book and glances at it, but he doesn't miss* MARTIN *shrink slightly from the peasant.*]
Another of yours?
[*He hands it back.*]
Do you think it'll sell as well as the others? [*Pause*] I dare say it will. Someone's always going to listen to you. No?
[MARTIN *moves to go, but* THE KNIGHT *stops him.*]
Martin. Just a minute.
[*He turns and places his hand carefully, ritually, on the body in the cart. He smears the blood from it over* MARTIN.]
There we are. That's better.
[MARTIN *makes to move again, but again* THE KNIGHT *stops him.*]
You're all ready now. You even look like a butcher—
MARTIN   God is the butcher—
KNIGHT   Don't you?
MARTIN   Why don't you address your abuse to Him?
KNIGHT   Never mind—you're wearing His apron.
[MARTIN *moves to the stairs of the pulpit.*]
It suits you. [*Pause*] Doesn't it? [*Pause*] That day in Worms [*Pause*] you were like a pig under glass weren't you? Do you remember it? I could smell every inch of you even where I was standing. All you've ever managed to do is convert everything into stench and dying and peril, but you could have done it, Martin, and you were the only one who could have ever done it. You could even have brought freedom and order in at one and the same time.
MARTIN   There's no such thing as an orderly revolution. Anyway, Christians are called to suffer, not fight.
KNIGHT   But weren't we all of us, all of us, without any exceptions to please any old interested parties, weren't we all redeemed by Christ's blood? [*Pointing to the peasant*] Wasn't he included when the Scriptures were being dictated? Or was it just you who was made free, you and the princes you've taken up with, and the rich burghers and—
MARTIN   Free? [*Ascends the pulpit steps.*] The princes blame me, you blame me and the peasants blame me—
KNIGHT   [*following up the steps*]   *You* put the water in the wine didn't you?

MARTIN When I see chaos, then I see the devil's organ and then I'm afraid. Now, that's enough—

KNIGHT You're breaking out again—

MARTIN Go away—

KNIGHT Aren't you?

[MARTIN *makes a sudden effort to push him back down the steps, but* THE KNIGHT *hangs on firmly.*]

MARTIN Get back!

KNIGHT Aren't you, you're breaking out again, you canting pig, I can smell you from here!

MARTIN He heard the children of Israel, didn't He?

KNIGHT Up to the ears in revelation, aren't you?

MARTIN And didn't He deliver them out of the Land of Pharaoh?

KNIGHT You canting pig, aren't you?

MARTIN Well? Didn't He?

KNIGHT Cock's wounds! Don't hold your Bible to my head, piggy, there's enough revelation of my own in there for me, in what I see for myself from here! [*Taps his forehead.*] Hold your gospel against that!

[THE KNIGHT *grabs* MARTIN's *hand and clamps it to his head.*]

KNIGHT You're killing the spirit, and you're killing it with the letter. You've been swilling about in the wrong place, Martin, in your own stink and ordure. Go on! You've got your hand on it, that's all the holy spirit there is, and it's all you'll ever get so feel it!

[*They struggle, but* THE KNIGHT *is very weak by now, and* MARTIN *is able to wrench himself away and up into the pulpit.*]

MARTIN The world was conquered by the Word, the Church is maintained by the Word—

KNIGHT Word? What Word? Word? That word, whatever that means, is probably just another old relic or indulgence, and you know what you did to those! Why, none of it might be any more than poetry, have you thought of that, Martin. Poetry! Martin, you're a poet, there's no doubt about that in anybody's mind, you're a poet, but do you know what most men believe in, in their hearts—because they don't see in images like you do—they believe in their hearts that Christ was a man as we are, and that He was a prophet and a teacher, and they also believe in their hearts that His supper is a plain meal like their own—if they're lucky enough to get it—a plain meal of bread and wine! A plain meal with no garnish and no word. And *you* helped them to begin to believe it!

MARTIN [*pause*] Leave me.

KNIGHT Yes. What's there to stay for? I've been close enough to you for too long. I even smell like you.

MARTIN [*roaring with pain*] I smell because of my own argument, I smell because I never stop disputing with Him, and because I expect Him to keep His Word. Now then! If your peasant rebelled against that Word, that was worse than murder because it laid the whole country waste, and who knows now what God will make of us Germans!

KNIGHT Don't blame God for the Germans, Martin! [*Laughs*] Don't do that! You thrashed about more than anyone on the night they were conceived!

MARTIN Christ! Hear me! My words pour from Your Body! They deserved their death, these swarming peasants! They kicked against authority, they plundered and bargained and all in Your name! Christ, believe me! [*To* THE KNIGHT] I demanded it, I prayed for it, and I got it! Take that lump away! Now, drag it away with you!

[THE KNIGHT *prepares to trundle off the cart and corpse.*]

KNIGHT   All right, my friend. Stay with your nun then. Marry and stew with
    your nun. Most of the others have. Stew with her, like a shuddering infant
    in *her* bed. You think you'll manage?

MARTIN   [*lightly*]   At least my father'll praise me for *that*.

KNIGHT   Your father?

    [THE KNIGHT *shrugs, pushes the cart wearily, and goes off.* MARTIN's *head
    hangs over the edge of the pulpit.*]

MARTIN   I [*whispering*] trust you. . . . I trust you. . . . You've overcome the
    world. . . . I trust you. . . . You're all I wish to have . . . ever. . . .

    [*Slumped over the pulpit, he seems to be unconscious. Then he makes an
    effort to recover, as if he had collapsed in the middle of a sermon.*]

    I expect you must . . . I'm sure you must remember—Abraham. Abraham
    was—he was an old man . . . a . . . very old man indeed, in fact, he was
    a hundred years old, when what was surely, what must have been a miracle
    happened, to a man of his years—a son was born to him. A son. Isaac he
    called him. And he loved Isaac. Well, he loved him with such intensity, one
    can only diminish it by description. But to Abraham his little son was a
    miraculous thing, a small, incessant . . . animal . . . astonishment. And
    in the child he sought the father. But, one day, God said to Abraham: Take
    your little son whom you love so much, kill him, and make a sacrifice of
    him. And in that moment everything inside Abraham seemed to shrivel once
    and for all. Because it had seemed to him that God had promised him life
    through his son. So then he took the boy and prepared to kill him, strapping
    him down to the wood of the burnt offering just as he had been told to do.
    And he spoke softly to the boy, and raised the knife over his little naked
    body, the boy struggling not to flinch or blink his eyes. Never, save in Christ,
    was there such obedience as in that moment, and, if God had blinked, the
    boy would have died then, but the Angel intervened, and the boy was re-
    leased, and Abraham took him up in his arms again. In the teeth of life
    we seem to die, but God says no—in the teeth of death we live. If He butch-
    ers us, He makes us live.

    [*Enter* THE KNIGHT, *who stands watching him, the Bundschuh banner in his
    hands.*]

    Heart of my Jesus save me; Heart of my Saviour deliver me; Heart of my
    Shepherd guard me; Heart of my Master teach me; Heart of my King govern
    me; Heart of my Friend stay with me.

    [*Enter* KATHERINE VON BORA, *his bride, accompanied by two* MONKS. MARTIN
    *rises from the pulpit and goes towards her. A simple tune is played on a
    simple instrument. She takes his hand, and they kneel together centre.* THE
    KNIGHT *watches. Then he smashes the banner he has been holding, and tosses
    the remains onto the altar.*]

[*End of Act Three—Scene Two*]

ACT THREE

Scene Three

> *A hymn. The Eremite Cloister. Wittenberg. 1530. The refectory
> table, and on it two places set, and the remains of two meals.*
> MARTIN *is seated alone. The vigour of a man in his late thirties,*

> *and at the height of his powers, has settled into the tired pain of*
> *a middle age struggling to rediscover strength.*
>
> KATHERINE *enters with a jug of wine. She is a big, pleasant-looking*
> *girl, almost thirty.*

MARTIN   How is he?

KATHERINE   He's all right. He's just coming. Wouldn't let me help him. I think he's been sick.

MARTIN   Poor old chap. After living all your life in a monastery, one's stomach doesn't take too easily to your kind of cooking.

KATHERINE   Wasn't it all right?

MARTIN   Oh, it was fine, just too much for an old monk's shrivelled digestion to chew on, that's all.

KATHERINE   Oh, I see. *You're* all right, aren't you?

MARTIN   Yes, I'm all right, thank you, my dear. [*Smile*] I expect I'll suffer later though.

KATHERINE   You like your food, so don't make out you don't.

MARTIN   Well, I prefer it to fasting. Did you never hear the story of the soldier who was fighting in the Holy Crusades? No? Well, he was told by his officer that if he died in battle, he would dine in Paradise with Christ; and the soldier ran away. When he came back after the battle, they asked him why he'd run away. "Didn't you want to dine with Christ?" they said. And he replied, "No, I'm fasting today."

KATHERINE   I've brought you some more wine.

MARTIN   Thank you.

KATHERINE   Should help you to sleep.

[STAUPITZ *enters, supporting himself with a stick.*]

MARTIN   There you are! I thought you'd fallen down the jakes—right into the devil's loving arms.

STAUPITZ   I'm so sorry. I was—I was wandering about a bit.

MARTIN   Well, come and sit down. Katie's brought us some more wine.

STAUPITZ   I can't get over being here again. It's so odd. This place was full of men. And now, now there's only you, you and Katie. It's very, very strange.

KATHERINE   I shouldn't stay up too long, Martin. You didn't sleep well again last night. I could hear you—hardly breathing all night.

MARTIN   [*amused*] You could hear me hardly breathing?

KATHERINE   You know what I mean. When you don't sleep, it keeps me awake too. Good night, Dr. Staupitz.

STAUPITZ   Good night, my dear. Thank you for the dinner. It was excellent. I'm so sorry I wasn't able to do justice to it.

KATHERINE   That's all right. Martin's always having the same kind of trouble.

STAUPITZ   Yes? Well, he's not changed much then.

MARTIN   Not a bit. Even Katie hasn't managed to shift my bowels for me, have you?

KATHERINE   And if it's not that, he can't sleep.

MARTIN   Yes, Katie, you've said that already. I've also got gout, piles and bells in my ears. Dr. Staupitz has had to put up with all my complaints for longer than you have, isn't that right?

KATHERINE   Well, try not to forget what I said. [*She kisses* MARTIN's *cheeks.*]

MARTIN   Good night, Katie.

[*She goes out.*]

STAUPITZ   Well, *you've* never been so well looked after.

MARTIN   It's a shame everyone can't marry a nun. They're fine cooks, thrifty housekeepers, and splendid mothers. Seems to me there are three ways out of despair. One is faith in Christ, the second is to become enraged by the world and make its nose bleed for it, and the third is the love of a woman. Mind you, they don't all necessarily work—at least, only part of the time. Sometimes, I'm lying awake in the devil's own sweat, and I turn to Katie and touch her. And I say: get me out, Katie, please, Katie, please try and get me out. And sometimes, sometimes she actually drags me out. Poor old Katie, fishing about there in bed with her great, hefty arms, trying to haul me out.

STAUPITZ   She's good.

MARTIN   Wine?

STAUPITZ   Not much. I must go to bed myself.

MARTIN   Help you sleep. You're looking tired.

STAUPITZ   Old. Our old pear tree's in blossom, I see. You've looked after it.

MARTIN   I like to get in a bit in the garden, if I can. I like to think it heals my bones somehow. Anyway, I always feel a bit more pleased with myself afterwards.

STAUPITZ   We'd a few talks under that tree.

MARTIN   Yes.

STAUPITZ   Martin, it's so still. I don't think I'd ever realized how eloquent a monk's silence really was. It was a voice. [*Pause*] It's gone. [*He shakes his head, pause.*] How's your father these days?

MARTIN   Getting old too, but he's well enough.

STAUPITZ   Is he—is he pleased with you?

MARTIN   He was never pleased about anything I ever did. Not when I took my master's degree or when I got to be Dr. Luther. Only when Katie and I were married and she got pregnant. Then he was pleased.

STAUPITZ   Do you remember Brother Weinand?

MARTIN   I ought to. He used to hold my head between my knees when I felt faint in the choir.

STAUPITZ   I wonder what happened to him. [*Pause*] He had the most beautiful singing voice.

MARTIN   My old friend, you're unhappy. I'm sorry. [*Pause*] We monks were really no good to anyone, least of all to ourselves, every one of us rolled up like a louse in the Almighty's overcoat.

STAUPITZ   Yes. Well, you always have a way of putting it. I was always having to give you little lectures about the fanatic way you'd observe the Rule all the time.

MARTIN   Yes, and you talked me out of it, remember? [*Pause*] Father, are *you* pleased with me?

STAUPITZ   Pleased with you? My dear son, I'm not anyone or anything to be pleased with you any more. When we used to talk together underneath that tree you were like a child.

MARTIN   A child.

STAUPITZ   Manhood was something you had to be flung into, my son. You dangled your toe in it longer than most of us could ever bear. But you're not a frightened little monk any more who's come to his prior for praise or blame. Every time you belch now, the world stops what it's doing and listens. Do you know, when I first came to take over this convent, there weren't thirty books published every year. And now, last year it was more like six or seven hundred, and most of those published in Wittenberg too.

MARTIN   The best turn God ever did Himself was giving us a printing press. Sometimes I wonder what He'd have done without it.

STAUPITZ   I heard the other day they're saying the world's going to end in 1532.

MARTIN   It sounds as good a date as any other. Yes—1532. That could easily be the end of the world. You could write a book about it, and just call it that—1532.

STAUPITZ   I'm sorry, Martin. I didn't mean to come and see you after all this time and start criticizing. Forgive me, I'm getting old and a bit silly and frightened, that meal was just too much for me. It wasn't that I didn't—

MARTIN   Please—I'm sorry too. Don't upset yourself. I'm used to critics, John. They just help you to keep your muscles from getting slack. All those hollow cavillers, that subtle clown Erasmus, for instance. He ought to know better, but all he wants to do is to be able to walk on eggs without breaking any. As for that mandrill-arsed English baboon Henry, that leprous son of a bitch never had an idea of his own to jangle on a tomb-stone, let alone call himself Defender of the Faith.

[*Pause.* STAUPITZ *hasn't responded to his attempt at lightness.*]

Still, one thing for Erasmus, he didn't fool about with all the usual cant and rubbish about indulgences and the Pope and Purgatory. No, he went right to the core of it. He's still up to his ears with stuff about morality, and men being able to save themselves. No one does good, not anyone. God is true and one. But, and this is what he can't grasp, He's utterly incomprehensible and beyond the reach of minds. A man's will is like a horse standing between two riders. If God jumps on its back, it'll go where God wants it to. But if Satan gets up there, it'll go where he leads it. And not only that, the horse can't choose its rider. That's left up to them, to those two. [*Pause*] Why are you accusing me? What have I done?

STAUPITZ   I'm not accusing you, Martin. You know that. A just man is his own accuser. Because a just man judges as he is.

MARTIN   What's that mean? I'm not just?

STAUPITZ   You try. What else can you do?

MARTIN   You mean those damned peasants, don't you? You think I should have encouraged them!

STAUPITZ   I don't say that.

MARTIN   Well, what do you say?

STAUPITZ   You needn't have encouraged the princes. They were butchered and *you* got them to do it. And they had just cause, Martin. They did, didn't they?

MARTIN   I didn't say they hadn't.

STAUPITZ   Well, then?

MARTIN   Do you remember saying to me, "Remember, brother, you started this in the name of the Lord Jesus Christ"?

STAUPITZ   Well?

MARTIN   Father, the world can't be ruled with a rosary. They were a mob, a mob, and if they hadn't been held down and slaughtered, there'd have been a thousand more tyrants instead of half a dozen. It was a mob, and because it was a mob it was against Christ. No man can die for another, or believe for another or answer for another. The moment they try they become a mob. If we're lucky we can be persuaded in our own mind, and the most we can hope for is to die each one for himself. Do I have to tell you what Paul says? You read! "Let every soul be subject unto the highest powers. For there is no power but of God: the powers that be are or-dained of God. Whosoever therefore resisteth that power, resisteth the ordinance of God": that's Paul, Father, and that's Scripture! "And they that resist shall receive to themselves damnation."

STAUPITZ   Yes, you're probably right.

MARTIN   "Love worketh no ill to his neighbour: therefore love is the fulfilling of the law."

STAUPITZ   Yes, well it seems to be all worked out. I must be tired.

MARTIN   It was worked out for me.

STAUPITZ   I'd better get off to bed.

MARTIN   They're trying to turn me into a fixed star, Father, but I'm a shifting planet. You're leaving me.

STAUPITZ   I'm not leaving you, Martin. I love you. I love you as much as any man has ever loved most women. But we're not two protected monks chattering under a pear tree in a garden any longer. The world's changed. For one thing, you've made a thing called Germany; you've unlaced a language and taught it to the Germans, and the rest of the world will just have to get used to the sound of it. As we once made the body of Christ from bread, you've made the body of Europe, and whatever our pains turn out to be, they'll attack the rest of the world too. You've taken Christ away from the low mumblings and soft voices and jewelled gowns and the tiaras and put Him back where He belongs. In each man's soul. We owe so much to you. All I beg of you is not to be too violent. In spite of everything, of everything you've said and shown us, there *were* men, *some* men who did live holy lives here once. Don't—don't believe you, only you are right.

[STAUPITZ *is close to tears, and* MARTIN *doesn't know what to do.*]

MARTIN   What else can I do? What can I do?

[*He clutches at his abdomen.*]

STAUPITZ   What is it?

MARTIN   Oh, the old trouble, that's all. That's all.

STAUPITZ   Something that's puzzled me, and I've always meant to ask you.

MARTIN   Well?

STAUPITZ   When you were before the Diet in Worms, and they asked you those two questions—why did you ask for that extra day to think over your reply?

MARTIN   Why?

STAUPITZ   You'd known what your answer was going to be for months. Heaven knows, you told me enough times. Why did you wait?

[*Pause*]

MARTIN   I wasn't certain.

STAUPITZ   And were you? Afterwards?

MARTIN   I listened for God's voice, but all I could hear was my own.

STAUPITZ   *Were* you sure?

[*Pause*]

MARTIN   No.

[STAUPITZ *kisses him.*]

STAUPITZ   Thank you, my son. May God bless you. I hope you sleep better. Goodnight.

MARTIN   Goodnight, Father.

[STAUPITZ *goes out, and* MARTIN *is left alone. He drinks his wine.*]

MARTIN   Oh, Lord, I believe. I believe. I do believe. Only help my unbelief.

[*He sits slumped in his chair.* KATHERINE *enters. She is wearing a nightdress, and carries in her arms* HANS, *their young son.*]

KATHERINE   He was crying out in his sleep. Must have been dreaming again. Aren't you coming to bed?

MARTIN   Shan't be long, Katie. Shan't be long.

KATHERINE   All right, but try not to be too long. You look—well, you don't look as well as you should.

[*She turns to go.*]

MARTIN   Give him to me.

KATHERINE   What?

MARTIN   Give him to me.

KATHERINE   What do you mean, what for? He'll get cold down here.

MARTIN   No, he won't. Please, Katie. Let me have him.

KATHERINE   You're a funny man. All right, but only for five minutes. Don't just sit there all night. He's gone back to sleep now. He'll be having another dream if you keep him down here.

MARTIN   Thank you, Katie.

KATHERINE   There! Keep him warm now! He's *your* son.

MARTIN   I will. Don't worry.

KATHERINE   Well, make sure you do. [*Pausing on way out*] Don't be long now, Martin.

MARTIN   Goodnight, Kate.

[*She goes out, leaving* MARTIN *with the sleeping child in his arms.*]

MARTIN   [*softly*]   What was the matter? Was it the devil bothering you? Um? Was he? Old nick? Up you, old nick. Well, don't worry. One day you might even be glad of him. So long as you can show him your little backside. That's right, show him your backside and let him have it. So try not to be afraid. The dark isn't quite as thick as all that. You know, my father had a son, and he'd to learn a hard lesson, which is a human being is a helpless little animal, but he's not created by his father, but by God. It's hard to accept you're anyone's son, and you're not the father of yourself. So, don't have dreams so soon, my son. *They'll* be having *you* soon enough. [*He gets up.*]

You should have seen me at Worms. I was almost like you that day, as if I'd learned to play again, to play, to play out in the world, like a naked child. "I have come to set a man against his father," I said, and they listened to me. Just like a child. Sh! We must go to bed, mustn't we? A little while, and you *shall* see me. Christ said that, my son. I hope that'll be the way of it again. I hope so. Let's just hope so, eh? Eh? Let's just hope so.

[MARTIN *holds the child in his arms, and then walks off slowly*].

The End.

LORRAINE HANSBERRY
[1930–1965]

Lorraine Hansberry, daughter of a prosperous real estate broker, was captivated by the magic of the theater in her high school days in Chicago where, as she says, she began "sort of hanging around little acting groups, and developing the feeling that the theater embraces everything I like all at one time." Her goal was to be a painter, but, after attending the University of Wisconsin, Chicago's Art Institute, and Roosevelt College, she decided she had no talent as an artist, and subsequently moved to New York in 1950. Then a series of menial jobs followed until she married Robert Nemiroff, song writer and music publisher. Miss Hansberry wrote several plays (left unfinished) before completing *A Raisin in the Sun*, the first play written by a Negro woman to be produced on Broadway, and the first play by a Negro to win the New York Drama Critics Circle Award. Although she was committed to the struggle for civil rights, Miss Hansberry tried to write a play about human beings who happened to be Negroes, not a play "about Negroes." Her second and last Broadway play was *The Sign in Sidney Brustein's Window*, produced by her husband in 1964. In this play once again she proved her great commitment to everyday living, or as she put it, to "caring." The history of how this play managed to remain in production despite mixed reviews and poor attendance is one of the exciting stories of the modern theater, and involves such famous people as Steve Allen, Anne Bancroft, James Baldwin, and many others who contributed time and money to keep the play alive. Unfortunately, during the rehearsals and the performances of *The Sign in Sidney Brustein's Window*, Miss Hansberry was in and out of hospitals, until on January 12, 1965, she died of cancer.

A RAISIN
IN THE SUN

LORRAINE HANSBERRY

To Mama: in gratitude for the dream

What happens to a dream deferred?
Does it dry up
Like a raisin in the sun?
Or fester like a sore—
And then run?
Does it stink like rotten meat:
Or crust and sugar over—
Like a syrupy sweet?

Maybe it just sags
Like a heavy load.

Or does it explode?

—Langston Hughes

© Copyright 1958, 1959 by Lorraine Hansberry. Reprinted by permission of Random House, Inc.
Reprinted by permission of Alfred A. Knopf, Inc. from *The Panther and the Lash.* © Copyright 1967 by Langston Hughes.

RUTH YOUNGER   JOSEPH ASAGAI
TRAVIS YOUNGER   GEORGE MURCHISON
WALTER LEE YOUNGER (BROTHER)   KARL LINDNER
BENEATHA YOUNGER   BOBO
LENA YOUNGER (MAMA)   MOVING MEN

The action of the play is set in Chicago's Southside, sometime between World War II and the present.

ACT ONE

SCENE 1: *Friday morning.*
SCENE 2: *The following morning.*

ACT TWO

SCENE 1: *Later, the same day.*
SCENE 2: *Friday night, a few weeks later.*
SCENE 3: *Moving day, one week later.*

ACT THREE

An hour later.

ACT I

Scene One

The YOUNGER *living room would be a comfortable and well-ordered room if it were not for a number of indestructible contradictions to this state of being. Its furnishings are typical and undistinguished and their primary feature now is that they have clearly had to accommodate the living of too many people for too many years and—they are tired. Still, we can see that at some time, a time probably no longer remembered by the family (except perhaps for* MAMA) *the furnishings of this room were actually selected with care and love and even hope—and brought to this apartment and arranged with taste and pride.*

That was a long time ago. Now the once loved pattern of the couch upholstery has to fight to show itself from under acres of crocheted doilies and couch covers which have themselves finally come to be more important than the upholstery. And here a table or a chair has been moved to disguise the worn places in the carpet; but the carpet has fought back by showing its weariness, with depressing uniformity, elsewhere on its surface. Weariness has, in fact, won in this room. Everything has been

*polished, washed, sat on, used, scrubbed too often. All pre-
tenses but living itself have long since vanished from the very
atmosphere of this room.*

*Moreover, a section of this room, for it is not really a room
unto itself, though the landlord's lease would make it seem so,
slopes backward to provide a small kitchen area, where the
family prepares the meals that are eaten in the living room
proper, which must also serve as dining room. The single window
that has been provided for these "two" rooms is located in this
kitchen area. The sole natural light the family may enjoy in the
course of a day is only that which fights its way through this
little window.*

At left, a door leads to a bedroom which is shared by MAMA *and
her daughter,* BENEATHA. *At right, opposite, is a second room
(which in the beginning of the life of this apartment was
probably a breakfast room) which serves as a bedroom for*
WALTER *and his wife,* RUTH.

Time: Sometime between World War II and the present.
Place: Chicago's Southside.

At Rise: It is morning dark in the living room. TRAVIS *is asleep
on the make-down bed at center. An alarm clock sounds from
within the bedroom at right, and presently* RUTH *enters from
that room and closes the door behind her. She crosses sleepily
toward the window. As she passes her sleeping son she reaches
down and shakes him a little. At the window she raises the
shade and a dusky Southside morning light comes in feebly.
She fills a pot with water and puts it on to boil. She calls to
the boy, between yawns, in a slightly muffled voice.*

RUTH *is about thirty. We can see that she was a pretty girl, even
exceptionally so, but now it is apparent that life has been little
that she expected, and disappointment has already begun to
hang in her face. In a few years, before thirty-five even, she will
be known among her people as a "settled woman."*

She crosses to her son and gives him a good, final, rousing shake.

RUTH   Come on now, boy, it's seven thirty! [*Her son sits up at last, in a stupor
of sleepiness*] I say hurry up, Travis! You ain't the only person in the world
got to use a bathroom! [*The child, a sturdy, handsome little boy of ten or
eleven, drags himself out of the bed and almost blindly takes his towels
and "today's clothes" from drawers and a closet and goes out to the bathroom, which is in an outside hall and which is shared by another family or
families on the same floor.* RUTH *crosses to the bedroom door at right and
opens it and calls in to her husband*] Walter Lee! . . . It's after seven
thirty! Lemme see you do some waking up in there now! [*She waits*] You
better get up from there, man! It's after seven thirty I tell you. [*She waits
again*] All right, you just go ahead and lay there and next thing you know
Travis be finished and Mr. Johnson'll be in there and you'll be fussing
and cussing round here like a mad man! And be late too! [*She waits, at
the end of patience*] Walter Lee—it's time for you to get up!
[*She waits another second and then starts to go into the bedroom, but is
apparently satisfied that her husband has begun to get up. She stops, pulls
the door to, and returns to the kitchen area. She wipes her face with a
moist cloth and runs her fingers through her sleep-disheveled hair in a
vain effort and ties an apron around her housecoat. The bedroom door at
right opens and her husband stands in the doorway in his pajamas, which*

*are rumpled and mismated. He is a lean, intense young man in his middle
thirties, inclined to quick nervous movements and erratic speech habits—
and always in his voice there is a quality of indictment*]

WALTER   Is he out yet?

RUTH   What you mean *out?* He ain't hardly got in there good yet.

WALTER   [*Wandering in, still more oriented to sleep than to a new day*]   Well,
what was you doing all that yelling for if I can't even get in there yet?
[*Stopping and thinking*] Check coming today?

RUTH   They *said* Saturday and this is just Friday and I hopes to God you
ain't going to get up here first thing this morning and start talking to me
'bout no money—'cause I 'bout don't want to hear it.

WALTER   Something the matter with you this morning?

RUTH   No—I'm just sleepy as the devil. What kind of eggs you want?

WALTER   Not scrambled. [RUTH *starts to scramble eggs*] Paper come? [RUTH
points impatiently to the rolled up Tribune *on the table, and he gets it
and spreads it out and vaguely reads the front page*] Set off another bomb
yesterday.

RUTH   [*Maximum indifference*]   Did they?

WALTER   [*Looking up*]   What's the matter with you?

RUTH   Ain't nothing the matter with me. And don't keep asking me that this
morning.

WALTER   Ain't nobody bothering you. [*Reading the news of the day absently
again*] Say Colonel McCormick is sick.

RUTH   [*Affecting tea-party interest*]   Is he now? Poor thing.

WALTER   [*Sighing and looking at his watch*]   Oh, me. [*He waits*] Now what is
that boy doing in that bathroom all this time? He just going to have to
start getting up earlier. I can't be being late to work on account of him
fooling around in there.

RUTH   [*Turning on him*]   Oh, no he ain't going to be getting up no earlier
no such thing! It ain't his fault that he can't get to bed no earlier nights
'cause he got a bunch of crazy good-for-nothing clowns sitting up running
their mouths in what is supposed to be his bedroom after ten o'clock at
night . . .

WALTER   That's what you mad about, ain't it? The things I want to talk about
with my friends just couldn't be important in your mind could they?
[*He rises and finds a cigarette in her handbag on the table and crosses to
the little window and looks out, smoking and deeply enjoying this first
one*]

RUTH   [*Almost matter of factly, a complaint too automatic to deserve emphasis*]
Why you always got to smoke before you eat in the morning?

WALTER   [*At the window*]   Just look at 'em down there . . . Running and
racing to work . . . [*He turns and faces his wife and watches her a moment
at the stove, and then, suddenly*] You look young this morning, baby.

RUTH   [*Indifferently*]   Yeah?

WALTER   Just for a second—stirring them eggs. It's gone now—just for a second
it was—you looked real young again. [*Then, drily*] It's gone now—you
look like yourself again.

RUTH   Man, if you don't shut up and leave me alone.

WALTER   [*Looking out to the street again*]   First thing a man ought to learn
in life is not to make love to no colored woman first thing in the morning.
You all some evil people at eight o'clock in the morning.
[TRAVIS *appears in the hall doorway, almost fully dressed and quite wide
awake now, his towels and pajamas across his shoulders. He opens the door
and signals for his father to make the bathroom in a hurry*]

TRAVIS   [*Watching the bathroom*]   Daddy, come on!

[WALTER *gets his bathroom utensils and flies out to the bathroom*]

RUTH   Sit down and have your breakfast, Travis.

TRAVIS   Mama, this is Friday. [*Gleefully*] Check coming tomorrow, huh?

RUTH   You get your mind off money and eat your breakfast.

TRAVIS   [*Eating*]   This is the morning we supposed to bring the fifty cents to school.

RUTH   Well, I ain't got no fifty cents this morning.

TRAVIS   Teacher say we have to.

RUTH   I don't care what teacher say. I ain't got it. Eat your breakfast, Travis.

TRAVIS   I *am* eating.

RUTH   Hush up now and just eat!

[*The boy gives her an exasperated look for her lack of understanding, and eats grudgingly*]

TRAVIS   You think Grandmama would have it?

RUTH   No! And I want you to stop asking your grandmother for money, you hear me?

TRAVIS   [*Outraged*]   Gaaaleee! I don't ask her, she just gimme it sometimes!

RUTH   Travis Willard Younger—I got too much on me this morning to be—

TRAVIS   Maybe Daddy—

RUTH   *Travis!*

[*The boy hushes abruptly. They are both quiet and tense for several seconds*]

TRAVIS   [*Presently*]   Could I maybe go carry some groceries in front of the supermarket for a little while after school then?

RUTH   Just hush, I said. [*Travis jabs his spoon into his cereal bowl viciously, and rests his head in anger upon his fists*] If you through eating, you can get over there and make up your bed.

[*The boy obeys stiffly and crosses the room, almost mechanically, to the bed and more or less carefully folds the covering. He carries the bedding into his mother's room and returns with his books and cap*]

TRAVIS   [*Sulking and standing apart from her unnaturally*]   I'm gone.

RUTH   [*Looking up from the stove to inspect him automatically*]   Come here. [*He crosses to her and she studies his head*] If you don't take this comb and fix this here head, you better! [TRAVIS *puts down his books with a great sigh of oppression, and crosses to the mirror. His mother mutters under her breath about his "slubbornness"*] 'Bout to march out of here with that head looking just like chickens slept in it! I just don't know where you get your slubborn ways . . . And get your jacket, too. Looks chilly out this morning.

TRAVIS   [*With conspicuously brushed hair and jacket*]   I'm gone.

RUTH   Get carfare and milk money—[*Waving one finger*]—and not a single penny for no caps, you hear me?

TRAVIS   [*With sullen politeness*]   Yes'm.

[*He turns in outrage to leave. His mother watches after him as in his frustration he approaches the door almost comically. When she speaks to him, her voice has become a very gentle tease*]

RUTH   [*Mocking; as she thinks he would say it*]   Oh, Mama makes me so mad sometimes, I don't know what to do! [*She waits and continues to his back as he stands stock-still in front of the door*] I wouldn't kiss that woman good-bye for nothing in this world this morning! [*The boy finally turns around and rolls his eyes at her, knowing the mood has changed and he is vindicated; he does not, however, move toward her yet*] Not for nothing in this world! [*She finally laughs aloud at him and holds out her arms to him and we see that it is a way between them, very old and practiced. He crosses to her and allows her to embrace him warmly but keeps his face fixed with masculine rigidity. She holds him back from her presently and looks at him and runs her fingers over the features of his face. With utter gentleness—]* Now—whose little old angry man are you?

TRAVIS [*The masculinity and gruffness start to fade at last*] Aw gaalee— Mama . . .

RUTH [*Mimicking*] Aw—gaaaaalleeeee, Mama! [*She pushes him, with rough playfulness and finality, toward the door*] Get on out of here or you going to be late.

TRAVIS [*In the face of love, new aggresiveness*] Mama, could I *please* go carry groceries?

RUTH Honey, it's starting to get so cold evenings.

WALTER [*Coming in from the bathroom and drawing a make-believe gun from a make-believe holster and shooting at his son*] What is it he wants to do?

RUTH Go carry groceries after school at the supermarket.

WALTER Well, let him go . . .

TRAVIS [*Quickly, to the ally*] I *have* to—she won't gimme the fifty cents . . .

WALTER [*To his wife only*] Why not?

RUTH [*Simply, and with flavor*] 'Cause we don't have it.

WALTER [*To RUTH only*] What you tell the boy things like that for? [*Reaching down into his pants with a rather important gesture*] Here. son— [*He hands the boy the coin, but his eyes are directed to his wife's.* TRAVIS *takes the money happily*]

TRAVIS Thanks, Daddy.
[*He starts out.* RUTH *watches both of them with murder in her eyes.* WALTER *stands and stares back at her with defiance, and suddenly reaches into his pocket again on an afterthrough*]

WALTER [*Without even looking at his son, still staring hard at his wife*] In fact, here's another fifty cents . . . Buy yourself some fruit today—or take a taxicab to school or something!

TRAVIS Whoopee—
[*He leaps up and clasps his father around the middle with his legs, and they face each other in mutual appreciation; slowly* WALTER LEE *peeks around the boy to catch the violent rays from his wife's eyes and draws his head back as if shot*]

WALTER You better get down now—and get to school, man.

TRAVIS [*At the door*] O.K. Good-bye.
[*He exits*]

WALTER [*After him, pointing with pride*] That's *my* boy. [*She looks at him in disgust and turns back to her work*] You know what I was thinking 'bout in the bathroom this morning?

RUTH No.

WALTER How come you always try to be so pleasant!

RUTH What is there to be pleasant 'bout!

WALTER You want to know what I was thinking 'bout in the bathroom or not!

RUTH I know what you thinking 'bout.

WALTER [*Ignoring her*] 'Bout what me and Willy Harris was talking about last night.

RUTH [*Immediately—a refrain*] Willy Harris is a good-for-nothing loud mouth.

WALTER Anybody who talks to me has got to be a good-for-nothing loud mouth, ain't he? And what you know about who is just a good-for-nothing loud mouth? Charlie Atkins was just a "good-for-nothing loud mouth" too, wasn't he! When he wanted me to go in the dry-cleaning business with him. And now—he's grossing a hundred thousand a year. A hundred thousand dollars a year! You still call *him* a loud mouth!

RUTH   [*Bitterly*]   Oh, Walter Lee . . .

[*She folds her head on her arms over the table*]

WALTER   [*Rising and coming to her and standing over her*]   You tired, ain't you? Tired of everything. Me, the boy, the way we live—this beat-up hole —everything. Ain't you? [*She doesn't look up, doesn't answer*] So tired— moaning and groaning all the time, but you wouldn't do nothing to help, would you? You couldn't be on my side that long for nothing, could you?

RUTH   Walter, please leave me alone.

WALTER   A man needs for a woman to back him up . . .

RUTH   Walter—

WALTER   Mama would listen to you. You know she listen to you more than she do me and Bennie. She think more of you. All you have to do is just sit down with her when you drinking your coffee one morning and talking 'bout things like you do and—[*He sits down beside her and demonstrates graphically what he thinks her methods and tone should be*]—you just sip your coffee, see, and say easy like that you been thinking 'bout that deal Walter Lee is so interested in, 'bout the store and all, and sip some more coffee, like what you saying ain't really that important to you—And the next thing you know, she be listening good and asking you questions and when I come home—I can tell her the details. This ain't no fly-by-night proposition, baby. I mean we figured it out, me and Willy and Bobo.

RUTH   [*With a frown*]   Bobo?

WALTER   Yeah. You see, this little liquor store we got in mind cost seventy-five thousand and we figured the initial investment on the place be 'bout thirty thousand, see. That be ten thousand each. Course, there's a couple of hundred you got to pay so's you don't spend your life just waiting for them clowns to let your license get approved—

RUTH   You mean graft?

WALTER   [*Frowning impatiently*]   Don't call it that. See there, that just goes to show you what women understand about the world. Baby, don't *nothing* happen for you in this world 'less you pay *somebody* off!

RUTH   Walter, leave me alone! [*She raises her head and stares at him vigorously —then says, more quietly*] *Eat* your eggs, they gonna be cold.

WALTER   [*Straightening up from her and looking off*]   That's it. There you are. Man say to his woman: I got me a dream. His woman say: Eat your eggs. [*Sadly, but gaining in power*] Man say: I got to take hold of this here world, baby! And a woman will say: Eat your eggs and go to work. [*Passionately now*] Man say: I got to change my life, I'm choking to death, baby! And his woman say—[*In utter anguish as he brings his fists down on his thighs*]—Your eggs is getting cold!

RUTH   [*Softly*]   Walter, that ain't none of our money.

WALTER   [*Not listening at all or even looking at her*]   This morning, I was lookin' in the mirror and thinking about it . . . I'm thirty-five years old; I been married eleven years and I got a boy who sleeps in the living room —[*Very, very quietly*]—and all I got to give him is stories about how rich white people live . . .

RUTH   Eat your eggs, Walter.

WALTER   *Damn my eggs . . . damn all the eggs that ever was!*

RUTH   Then go to work.

WALTER   [*Looking up at her*]   See—I'm trying to talk to you 'bout myself—

[*Shaking his head with the repetition*]—and all you can say is eat them eggs and go to work.

RUTH [*Wearily*] Honey, you never say nothing new. I listen to you every day, every night and every morning, and you never say nothing new. [*Shrugging*] So you would rather *be* Mr. Arnold than be his chauffeur. So— I would *rather* be living in Buckingham Palace.

WALTER That is just what is wrong with the colored woman in this world . . . Don't understand about building their men up and making 'em feel like they somebody. Like they can do something.

RUTH [*Drily, but to hurt*] There *are* colored men who do things.

WALTER No thanks to the colored woman.

RUTH Well, being a colored woman, I guess I can't help myself none.
[*She rises and gets the ironing board and sets it up and attacks a huge pile of rough-dried clothes, sprinkling them in preparation for the ironing and then rolling them into tight fat balls*]

WALTER [*Mumbling*] We one group of men tied to a race of women with small minds.
[*His sister* BENEATHA *enters. She is about twenty, as slim and intense as her brother. She is not as pretty as her sister-in-law, but her lean, almost intellectual face has a handsomeness of its own. She wears a bright-red flannel nightie, and her thick hair stands wildly about her head. Her speech is a mixture of many things; it is different from the rest of the family's insofar as education has permeated her sense of English—and perhaps the Midwest rather than the South has finally—at last—won out in her inflection; but not altogether, because over all of it is a soft slurring and transformed use of vowels which is the decided influence of the South-side. She passes through the room without looking at either* RUTH *or* WALTER *and goes to the outside door and looks, a little blindly, out to the bathroom. She sees that it has been lost to the Johnsons. She closes the door with a sleepy vengeance and crosses to the table and sits down a little defeated*]

BENEATHA I am going to start timing those people.

WALTER You should get up earlier.

BENEATHA [*Her face in her hands. She is still fighting the urge to go back to bed*] Really—would you suggest dawn? Where's the paper?

WALTER [*Pushing the paper across the table to her as he studies her almost clinically, as though he has never seen her before*] You a horrible-looking chick at this hour.

BENEATHA [*Drily*] Good morning, everybody.

WALTER [*Senselessly*] How is school coming?

BENEATHA [*In the same spirit*] Lovely. Lovely. And you know, biology is the greatest. [*Looking up at him*] I dissected something that looked just like you yesterday.

WALTER I just wondered if you've made up your mind and everything.

BENEATHA [*Gaining in sharpness and impatience*] And what did I answer yesterday morning—and the day before that?

RUTH [*From the ironing board, like someone disinterested and old*] Don't be so nasty, Bennie.

BENEATHA [*Still to her brother*] And the day before that and the day before that!

WALTER [*Defensively*] I'm interested in you. Something wrong with that? Ain't many girls who decide—

WALTER *and* BENEATHA [*In unison*] —"to be a doctor."

[*Silence*]

WALTER Have we figured out yet just exactly how much medical school is going to cost?

RUTH Walter Lee, why don't you leave that girl alone and get out of here to work?

BENEATHA [*Exits to the bathroom and bangs on the door*] Come on out of there, please!

[*She comes back into the room*]

WALTER [*Looking at his sister intently*] You know the check is coming tomorrow.

BENEATHA [*Turning on him with a sharpness all her own*] That money belongs to Mama, Walter, and it's for her to decide how she wants to use it. I don't care if she wants to buy a house or a rocket ship or just nail it up somewhere and look at it. It's hers. Not ours—*hers*.

WALTER [*Bitterly*] Now ain't that fine! You just got your mother's interest at heart, ain't you, girl? You such a nice girl—but if Mama got that money she can always take a few thousand and help you through school too—can't she?

BENEATHA I have never asked anyone around here to do anything for me!

WALTER No! And the line between asking and just accepting when the time comes is big and wide—ain't it!

BENEATHA [*With fury*] What do you want from me, Brother—that I quit school or just drop dead, which!

WALTER I don't want nothing but for you to stop acting holy 'round here. Me and Ruth done made some sacrifices for you—why can't you do something for the family?

RUTH Walter, don't be dragging me in it.

WALTER You are in it—Don't you get up and go work in somebody's kitchen for the last three years to help put clothes on her back?

RUTH Oh, Walter—that's not fair . . .

WALTER It ain't that nobody expects you to get on your knees and say thank you, Brother; thank you, Ruth; thank you, Mama—and thank you, Travis, for wearing the same pair of shoes for two semesters—

BENEATHA [*Dropping to her knees*] Well—I *do*—all right?—thank everybody . . . and forgive me for ever wanting to be anything at all . . . forgive me, forgive me!

RUTH Please stop it! Your mama'll hear you.

WALTER Who the hell told you you had to be a doctor? If you so crazy 'bout messing 'round with sick people—then go be a nurse like other women—or just get married and be quiet . . .

BENEATHA Well—you finally got it said . . . It took you three years but you finally got it said. Walter, give up; leave me alone—it's Mama's money.

WALTER *He was my father, too!*

BENEATHA So what? He was mine, too—and Travis' grandfather—but the insurance money belongs to Mama. Picking on me is not going to make her give it to you to invest in any liquor stores—[*Underbreath, dropping into a chair*]—and I for one say, God bless Mama for that!

WALTER [*To* RUTH] See—did you hear? Did you hear!

RUTH Honey, please go to work.

WALTER Nobody in this house is ever going to understand me.

BENEATHA Because you're a nut.

WALTER Who's a nut?

BENEATHA You—you are a nut. Thee is mad, boy.

WALTER   *[Looking at his wife and his sister from the door, very sadly]*   The world's most backward race of people, and that's a fact.

BENEATHA   *[Turning slowly in her chair]*   And then there are all those prophets who would lead us out of the wilderness—[WALTER *slams out of the house*] —into the swamps!

RUTH   Bennie, why you always gotta be pickin' on your brother? Can't you be a little sweeter sometimes? *[Door opens.* WALTER *walks in]*

WALTER   *[To Ruth]*   I need some money for carfare.

RUTH   *[Looks at him, then warms; teasing, but tenderly]*   Fifty cents? *[She goes to her bag and gets money]* Here, take a taxi.

*[*WALTER *exits.* MAMA *enters. She is a woman in her early sixties, full-bodied and strong. She is one of those women of a certain grace and beauty who wear it so unobtrusively that it takes a while to notice. Her dark-brown face is surrounded by the total whiteness of her hair, and, being a woman who has adjusted to many things in life and overcome many more, her face is full of strength. She has, we can see, wit and faith of a kind that keep her eyes lit and full of interest and expectancy. She is, in a word, a beautiful woman. Her bearing is perhaps most like the noble bearing of the women of the Hereros of Southwest Africa—rather as if she imagines that as she walks she still bears a basket or a vessel upon her head. Her speech, on the other hand, is as careless as her carriage is precise—she is inclined to slur everything—but her voice is perhaps not so much quiet as simply soft]*

MAMA   Who that 'round here slamming doors at this hour?

[She crosses through the room, goes to the window, opens it, and brings in a feeble little plant growing doggedly in a small pot on the window sill. She feels the dirt and puts it back out]

RUTH   That was Walter Lee. He and Bennie was at it again.

MAMA   My children and they tempers. Lord, if this little old plant don't get more sun than it's been getting it ain't never going to see spring again. *[She turns from the window]* What's the matter with you this morning, Ruth? You looks right peaked. You aiming to iron all them things? Leave some for me. I'll get to 'em this afternoon. Bennie honey, it's too drafty for you to be sitting 'round half dressed. Where's your robe?

BENEATHA   In the cleaners.

MAMA   Well, go get mine and put it on.

BENEATHA   I'm not cold, Mama, honest.

MAMA   I know—but you so thin . . .

BENEATHA   *[Irritably]*   Mama, I'm not cold.

MAMA   *[Seeing the make-down bed as* TRAVIS *has left it]*   Lord have mercy, look at that poor bed. Bless his heart—he tries, don't he?

[She moves to the bed TRAVIS *has sloppily made up]*

RUTH   No—he don't half try at all 'cause he knows you going to come along behind him and fix everything. That's just how come he don't know how to do nothing right now—you done spoiled that boy so.

MAMA   Well—he's a little boy. Ain't supposed to know 'bout housekeeping. My baby, that's what he is. What you fix for his breakfast this morning?

RUTH   *[Angrily]*   I feed my son, Lena!

MAMA   I ain't meddling—*[Underbreath; busy-bodyish]* I just noticed all last week he had cold cereal, and when it starts getting this chilly in the fall a child ought to have some hot grits or something when he goes out in the cold—

RUTH   *[Furious]*   I gave him hot oats—is that all right!

MAMA   I ain't meddling. [*Pause*] Put a lot of nice butter on it? [RUTH *shoots her an angry look and does not reply*] He likes lots of butter.

RUTH   [*Exasperated*] Lena—

MAMA   [*To* BENEATHA. MAMA *is inclined to wander conversationally sometimes*] What was you and your brother fussing 'bout this morning?

BENEATHA   It's not important, Mama.

[*She gets up and goes to look out at the bathroom, which is apparently free, and she picks up her towels and rushes out*]

MAMA   What was they fighting about?

RUTH   Now you know as well as I do.

MAMA   [*Shaking her head*] Brother still worrying hisself sick about that money?

RUTH   You know he is.

MAMA   You had breakfast?

RUTH   Some coffee.

MAMA   Girl, you better start eating and looking after yourself better. You almost thin as Travis.

RUTH   Lena—

MAMA   Un-hunh?

RUTH   What are you going to do with it?

MAMA   Now don't you start, child. It's too early in the morning to be talking about money. It ain't Christian.

RUTH   It's just that he got his heart set on that store—

MAMA   You mean that liquor store that Willy Harris want him to invest in?

RUTH   Yes—

MAMA   We ain't no business people, Ruth. We just plain working folks.

RUTH   Ain't nobody business people till they go into business. Walter Lee say colored people ain't never going to start getting ahead till they start gambling on some different kinds of things in the world—investments and things.

MAMA   What done got into you, girl? Walter Lee done finally sold you on investing.

RUTH   No. Mama, something is happening between Walter and me. I don't know what it is—but he needs something—something I can't give him any more. He needs this chance, Lena.

MAMA   [*Frowning deeply*] But liquor, honey—

RUTH   Well—like Walter say—I spec people going to always be drinking themselves some liquor.

MAMA   Well—whether they drinks it or not ain't none of my business. But whether I go into business selling it to 'em *is,* and I don't want that on my ledger this late in life. [*Stopping suddenly and studying her daughter-in-law*] Ruth Younger, what's the matter with you today? You look like you could fall over right there.

RUTH   I'm tired.

MAMA   Then you better stay home from work today.

RUTH   I can't stay home. She'd be calling up the agency and screaming at them, "My girl didn't come in today—send me somebody! My girl didn't come in!" Oh, she just have a fit . . .

MAMA   Well, let her have it. I'll just call her up and say you got the flu—

RUTH   [*Laughing*] Why the flu?

MAMA   'Cause it sounds respectable to 'em. Something white people get, too. They know 'bout the flu. Otherwise they think you been cut up or something when you tell 'em you sick.

RUTH   I got to go in. We need the money.

MAMA Somebody would of thought my children done all but starved to death the way they talk about money here late. Child, we got a great big old check coming tomorrow.

RUTH [*Sincerely, but also self-righteously*] Now that's your money. It ain't got nothing to do with me. We all feel like that—Walter and Bennie and me—even Travis.

MAMA [*Thoughtfully, and suddenly very far away*] Ten thousand dollars—

RUTH Sure is wonderful.

MAMA Ten thousand dollars.

RUTH You know what you should do. Miss Lena? You should take yourself a trip somewhere. To Europe or South America or someplace—

MAMA [*Throwing up her hands at the thought*] Oh, child!

RUTH I'm serious. Just pack up and leave! Go on away and enjoy yourself some. Forget about the family and have yourself a ball for once in your life—

MAMA [*Drily*] You sound like I'm just about ready to die. Who'd go with me? What I look like wandering 'round Europe by myself?

RUTH Shoot—these here rich white women do it all the time. They don't think nothing of packing up they suitcases and piling on one of them big steamships and—swoosh!—they gone, child.

MAMA Something always told me I wasn't no rich white woman.

RUTH Well—what are you going to do with it then?

MAMA I ain't rightly decided. [*Thinking. She speaks now with emphasis*] Some of it got to be put away for Beneatha and her schoolin'—and ain't nothing going to touch that part of it. Nothing. [*She waits several seconds, trying to make up her mind about something, and looks at* RUTH *a little tentatively before going on*] Been thinking that we maybe could meet the notes on a little old two-story somewhere, with a yard where Travis could play in the summertime, if we use part of the insurance for a down payment and everybody kind of pitch in. I could maybe take on a little day work again, few days a week—

RUTH [*Studying her mother-in-law furtively and concentrating on her ironing, anxious to encourage without seeming to*] Well, Lord knows, we've put enough rent into this here rat trap to pay for four houses by now . . .

MAMA [*Looking up at the words "rat trap" and then looking around and leaning back and sighing—in a suddenly reflective mood—*] "Rat trap"—yes, that's all it is. [*Smiling*] I remember just as well the day me and Big Walter moved in here. Hadn't been married but two weeks and wasn't planning on living here no more than a year. [*She shakes her head at the dissolved dream*] We was going to set away, little by little, don't you know, and buy a little place out in Morgan Park. We had even picked out the house. [*Chuckling a little*] Looks right dumpy today. But Lord, child, you should know all the dreams I had 'bout buying that house and fixing it up and making me a little garden in the back—[*She waits and stops smiling*] And didn't none of it happen.

[*Dropping her hands in a futile gesture*]

RUTH [*Keeps her head down, ironing*] Yes, life can be a barrel of disappointments, sometimes.

MAMA Honey, Big Walter would come in here some nights back then and slump down on that couch there and just look at the rug, and look at me and look at the rug and then back at me—and I'd know he was down then . . . really down. [*After a second very long and thoughtful pause; she is seeing back to times that only she can see*] And then, Lord, when I lost that baby—little Claude—I almost thought I was going to lose Big

Walter too. Oh, that man grieved hisself! He was one man to love his children.

RUTH   Ain't nothin' can tear at you like losin' your baby.

MAMA   I guess that's how come that man finally worked hisself to death like he done. Like he was fighting his own war with this here world that took his baby from him.

RUTH   He sure was a fine man, all right. I always liked Mr. Younger.

MAMA   Crazy 'bout his children! God knows there was plenty wrong with Walter Younger—hard-headed, mean, kind of wild with women—plenty wrong with him. But he sure loved his children. Always wanted them to have something—be something. That's where Brother gets all these notions, I reckon. Big Walter used to say, he'd get right wet in the eyes sometimes, lean his head back with the water standing in his eyes and say, "Seem like God didn't see fit to give the black man nothing but dreams—but He did give us children to make them dreams seem worth while." [*She smiles*] He could talk like that, don't you know.

RUTH   Yes, he sure could. He was a good man, Mr. Younger.

MAMA   Yes, a fine man—just couldn't never catch up with his dreams, that's all.

[BENEATHA *comes in, brushing her hair and looking up to the ceiling, where the sound of a vacuum cleaner has started up*]

BENEATHA   What could be so dirty on that woman's rugs that she has to vacuum them every single day?

RUTH   I wish certain young women 'round here who I could name would take inspiration about certain rugs in a certain apartment I could also mention.

BENEATHA   [*Shrugging*] How much cleaning can a house need, for Christ's sakes.

MAMA   [*Not liking the Lord's name used thus*] Bennie!

RUTH   Just listen to her—just listen!

BENEATHA   Oh, God!

MAMA   If you use the Lord's name just one more time—

BENEATHA   [*A bit of a whine*] Oh, Mama—

RUTH   Fresh—just fresh as salt, this girl!

BENEATHA   [*Drily*] Well—if the salt loses its savor—

MAMA   Now that will do. I just ain't going to have you 'round here reciting the scriptures in vain—you hear me?

BENEATHA   How did I manage to get on everybody's wrong side by just walking into a room?

RUTH   If you weren't so fresh—

BENEATHA   Ruth, I'm twenty years old.

MAMA   What time you be home from school today?

BENEATHA   Kind of late. [*With enthusiasm*] Madeline is going to start my guitar lessons today.

[MAMA *and* RUTH *look up with the same expression*]

MAMA   Your *what* kind of lessons?

BENEATHA   Guitar.

RUTH   Oh, Father!

MAMA   How come you done taken it in your mind to learn to play the guitar?

BENEATHA   I just want to, that's all.

MAMA   [*Smiling*] Lord, child, don't you know what to do with yourself? How long it going to be before you get tired of this now—like you got tired of that little play-acting group you joined last year? [*Looking at Ruth*] And what was it the year before that?

RUTH The horseback-riding club for which she bought that fifty-five-dollar riding habit that's been hanging in the closet ever since!

MAMA [*To* BENEATHA] Why you got to flit so from one thing to another, baby?

BENEATHA [*Sharply*] I just want to learn to play the guitar. Is there anything wrong with that?

MAMA Ain't nobody trying to stop you. I just wonders sometimes why you has to flit so from one thing to another all the time. You ain't never done nothing with all that camera equipment you brought home—

BENEATHA I don't flit! I—I experiment with different forms of expression—

RUTH Like riding a horse?

BENEATHA —People have to express themselves one way or another.

MAMA What is it you want to express?

BENEATHA [*Angrily*] Me! [MAMA *and* RUTH *look at each other and burst into raucous laughter*] Don't worry—I don't expect you to understand.

MAMA [*To change the subject*] Who you going out with tomorrow night?

BENEATHA [*With displeasure*] George Murchison again.

MAMA [*Pleased*] Oh—you getting a little sweet on him?

RUTH You ask me, this child ain't sweet on nobody but herself—[*Underbreath*] Express herself!

[*They laugh*]

BENEATHA Oh—I like George all right, Mama. I mean I like him enough to go out with him and stuff, but—

RUTH [*For devilment*] What does *and stuff* mean?

BENEATHA Mind your own business.

MAMA Stop picking at her now, Ruth. [*A thoughtful pause, and then a suspicious sudden look at her daughter as she turns in her chair for emphasis*] What *does* it mean?

BENEATHA [*Wearily*] Oh, I just mean I couldn't ever really be serious about George. He's—he's so shallow.

RUTH Shallow—what do you mean he's shallow? He's *Rich!*

MAMA Hush, Ruth.

BENEATHA I know he's rich. He knows he's rich, too.

RUTH Well—what other qualities a man got to have to satisfy you, little girl?

BENEATHA You wouldn't even begin to understand. Anybody who married Walter could not possibly understand.

MAMA [*Outraged*] What kind of way is that to talk about your brother?

BENEATHA Brother is a flip—let's face it.

MAMA [*To* RUTH, *helplessly*] What's a flip?

RUTH [*Glad to add kindling*] She's saying he's crazy.

BENEATHA Not crazy. Brother isn't really crazy yet—he—he's an elaborate neurotic.

MAMA Hush your mouth!

BENEATHA As for George. Well. George looks good—he's got a beautiful car and he takes me to nice places and, as my sister-in-law says, he is probably the richest boy I will ever get to know and I even like him sometimes— but if the Youngers are sitting around waiting to see if their little Bennie is going to tie up the family with the Murchisons, they are wasting their time.

RUTH You mean you wouldn't marry George Murchison if he asked you someday? That pretty, rich thing? Honey, I knew you was odd—

BENEATHA No I would not marry him if all I felt for him was what I feel now. Besides, George's family wouldn't really like it.

MAMA   Why not?

BENEATHA   Oh, Mama—The Murchisons are honest-to-God-real-*live*-rich colored people, and the only people in the world who are more snobbish than rich white people are rich colored people. I thought everybody knew that. I've met Mrs. Murchison. She's a scene!

MAMA   You must not dislike people 'cause they well off, honey.

BENEATHA   Why not? It makes just as much sense as disliking people 'cause they are poor, and lots of people do that.

RUTH   [*A wisdom-of-the-ages manner. To* MAMA]   Well, she'll get over some of this—

BENEATHA   Get over it? What are you talking about, Ruth? Listen, I'm going to be a doctor. I'm not worried about who I'm going to marry yet—if I ever get married.

MAMA *and* RUTH   *If!*

MAMA   Now, Bennie—

BENEATHA   Oh, I probably will . . . but first I'm going to be a doctor, and George, for one, still thinks that's pretty funny. I couldn't be bothered with that. I am going to be a doctor and everybody around here better understand that!

MAMA   [*Kindly*]   'Course you going to be a doctor, honey, God willing.

BENEATHA   [*Drily*]   God hasn't got a thing to do with it.

MAMA   Beneatha—that just wasn't necessary.

BENEATHA   Well—neither is God. I get sick of hearing about God.

MAMA   Beneatha!

BENEATHA   I mean it! I'm just tired of hearing about God all the time. What has He got to do with anything? Does he pay tuition?

MAMA   You 'bout to get your fresh little jaw slapped!

RUTH   That's just what she needs, all right!

BENEATHA   Why? Why can't I say what I want to around here, like everybody else?

MAMA   It don't sound nice for a young girl to say things like that—you wasn't brought up that way. Me and your father went to trouble to get you and Brother to church every Sunday.

BENEATHA   Mama, you don't understand. It's all a matter of ideas, and God is just one idea I don't accept. It's not important. I am not going out and be immoral or commit crimes because I don't believe in God. I don't even think about it. It's just that I get tired of Him getting credit for all the things the human race achieves through its own stubborn effort. There simply is no blasted God—there is only man and it is he who makes miracles!

[MAMA *absorbs this speech, studies her daughter and rises slowly and crosses to* BENEATHA *and slaps her powerfully across the face. After, there is only silence and the daughter drops her eyes from her mother's face, and* MAMA *is very tall before her*]

MAMA   Now—you say after me, in my mother's house there is still God. [*There is a long pause and* BENEATHA *stares at the floor wordlessly.* MAMA *repeats the phrase with precision and cool emotion*] In my mother's house there is still God.

BENEATHA   In my mother's house there is still God.

[*A long pause*]

MAMA   [*Walking away from* BENEATHA, *too disturbed for triumphant posture. Stopping and turning back to her daughter*] There are some ideas we ain't going to have in this house. Not long as I am at the head of this family.

BENEATHA   Yes, ma'am.

[MAMA *walks out of the room*]

RUTH [*Almost gently, with profound understanding*] You think you a woman, Bennie—but you still a little girl. What you did was childish—so you got treated like a child.

BENEATHA I see. [*Quietly*] I also see that everybody thinks it's all right for Mama to be a tyrant. But all the tyranny in the world will never put a God in the heavens!

[*She picks up her books and goes out*]

RUTH [*Goes to* MAMA's *door*] She said she was sorry.

MAMA [*Coming out, going to her plant*] They frightens me, Ruth. My children.

RUTH You got good children, Lena. They just a little off sometimes—but they're good.

MAMA No—there's something come down between me and them that don't let us understand each other and I don't know what it is. One done almost lost his mind thinking 'bout money all the time and the other done commence to talk about things I can't seem to understand in no form or fashion. What is it that's changing, Ruth?

RUTH [*Soothingly, older than her years*] Now . . . you taking it all too seriously. You just got strong-willed children and it takes a strong woman like you to keep 'em in hand.

MAMA [*Looking at her plant and sprinkling a little water on it*] They spirited all right, my children. Got to admit they got spirit—Bennie and Walter. Like this little old plant that ain't never had enough sunshine or nothing —and look at it . . .

[*She has her back to* RUTH, *who has had to stop ironing and lean against something and put the back of her hand to her forehead*]

RUTH [*Trying to keep* MAMA *from noticing*] You . . . sure . . . loves that little old thing, don't you? . . .

MAMA Well, I always wanted me a garden like I used to see sometimes at the back of the houses down home. This plant is close as I ever got to having one. [*She looks out of the window as she replaces the plant*] Lord, ain't nothing as dreary as the view from this window on a dreary day, is there? Why ain't you singing this morning, Ruth? Sing that "No Ways Tired." That song always lifts me up so—[*She turns at last to see that* RUTH *has slipped quietly into a chair, in a state of semiconsciousness*] Ruth! Ruth honey—what's the matter with you . . . Ruth!

CURTAIN

Scene Two

It is the following morning; a Saturday morning, and house cleaning is in progress at the YOUNGERS. *Furniture has been shoved hither and yon and* MAMA *is giving the kitchen-area walls a washing down.* BENEATHA, *in dungarees, with a handkerchief tied around her face, is spraying insecticide into the cracks in the walls. As they work, the radio is on and a Southside disk-jockey program is inappropriately filling the house with a rather exotic saxophone blues.* TRAVIS, *the sole idle one, is leaning on his arms, looking out of the window.*

TRAVIS Grandmama, that stuff Bennie is using smells awful. Can I go downstairs, please?

MAMA   Did you get all them chores done already? I ain't seen you doing much.

TRAVIS   Yes'm—finished early. Where did Mama go this morning?

MAMA   [*Looking at* BENEATHA]   She had to go on a little errand.

TRAVIS   Where?

MAMA   To tend to her business.

TRAVIS   Can I go outside then?

MAMA   Oh, I guess so. You better stay right in front of the house, though . . . and keep a good lookout for the postman.

TRAVIS   Yes'm. [*He starts out and decides to give his* AUNT BENEATHA *a good swat on the legs as he passes her*] Leave them poor little old cockroaches alone, they ain't bothering you none.
[*He runs as she swings the spray gun at him both viciously and playfully.* WALTER *enters from the bedroom and goes to the phone*]

MAMA   Look out there, girl, before you be spilling some of that stuff on that child!

TRAVIS   [*Teasing*]   That's right—look out now!
[*He exits*]

BENEATHA   [*Drily*]   I can't imagine that it would hurt him—it has never hurt the roaches.

MAMA   Well, little boys' hides ain't as tough as Southside roaches.

WALTER   [*Into phone*]   Hello—Let me talk to Willy Harris.

MAMA   You better get over there behind the bureau. I seen one marching out of there like Napoleon yesterday.

WALTER   Hello, Willy? It ain't come yet. It'll be here in a few minutes. Did the lawyer give you the papers?

BENEATHA   There's really only one way to get rid of them, Mama—

MAMA   How?

BENEATHA   Set fire to this building.

WALTER   Good. Good. I'll be right over.

BENEATHA   Where did Ruth go, Walter?

WALTER   I don't know.
[*He exits abruptly*]

BENEATHA   Mama, where did Ruth go?

MAMA   [*Looking at her with meaning*]   To the doctor, I think.

BENEATHA   The doctor? What's the matter? [*They exchange glances*] You don't think—

MAMA   [*With her sense of drama*]   Now I ain't saying what I think. But I ain't never been wrong 'bout a woman neither.
[*The phone rings*]

BENEATHA   [*At the phone*]   Hay-lo . . . [*Pause, and a moment of recognition*] Well—when did you get back! . . . And how was it? . . . Of course I've missed you—in my way . . . This morning? No . . . house cleaning and all that and Mama hates it if I let people come over when the house is like this . . . You *have?* Well, that's different . . . What is it—Oh, what the hell, come on over . . . Right, see you then.
[*She hangs up*]

MAMA   [*Who has listened vigorously, as is her habit*]   Who is that you inviting over here with this house looking like this? You ain't got the pride you was born with!

BENEATHA   Asagai doesn't care how houses look, Mama—he's an intellectual.

MAMA   *Who?*

BENEATHA   Asagai—Joseph Asagai. He's an African boy I met on campus. He's been studying in Canada all summer.

MAMA   What's his name?

BENEATHA Asagai, Joseph. Ah-sah-guy . . . He's from Nigeria.

MAMA Oh, that's the little country that was founded by slaves way back . . .

BENEATHA No, Mama—that's Liberia.

MAMA I don't think I never met no African before.

BENEATHA Well, do me a favor and don't ask him a whole lot of ignorant questions about Africans. I mean, do they wear clothes and all that—

MAMA Well, now, I guess if you think we so ignorant 'round here maybe you shouldn't bring your friends here—

BENEATHA It's just that people ask such crazy things. All anyone seems to know about when it comes to Africa is Tarzan—

MAMA [*Indignantly*] Why should I know anything about Africa?

BENEATHA Why do you give money at church for the missionary work?

MAMA Well, that's to help save people.

BENEATHA You mean save them from *heathenism*—

MAMA [*Innocently*] Yes.

BENEATHA I'm afraid they need more salvation from the British and the French. [RUTH *comes in forlornly and pulls off her coat with dejection. They both turn to look at her*]

RUTH [*Dispiritedly*] Well, I guess from all the happy faces—everybody knows.

BENEATHA You pregnant?

MAMA Lord have mercy, I sure hope it's a little old girl. Travis ought to have a sister. [BENEATHA *and* RUTH *give her a hopeless look for this grandmotherly enthusiasm*]

BENEATHA How far along are you?

RUTH Two months.

BENEATHA Did you mean to? I mean did you plan it or was it an accident?

MAMA What do you know about planning or not planning?

BENEATHA Oh, Mama.

RUTH [*Wearily*] She's twenty years old, Lena.

BENEATHA Did you plan it, Ruth?

RUTH Mind your own business.

BENEATHA It is my business—where is he going to live, on the *roof*? [*There is silence following the remark as the three women react to the sense of it*] Gee—I didn't mean that, Ruth, honest. Gee, I don't feel like that at all. I —I think it is wonderful.

RUTH [*Dully*] Wonderful.

BENEATHA Yes—really.

MAMA [*Looking at* RUTH, *worried*] Doctor say everything going to be all right?

RUTH [*Far away*] Yes—she says everything is going to be fine . . .

MAMA [*Immediately suspicious*] "She"—What doctor you went to? [RUTH *folds over, near hysteria*]

MAMA [*Worriedly hovering over* RUTH] Ruth honey—what's the matter with you—you sick? [RUTH *has her fists clenched on her thighs and is fighting hard to suppress a scream that seems to be rising in her*]

BENEATHA What's the matter with her, Mama?

MAMA [*Working her fingers in* RUTH's *shoulder to relax her*] She be all right. Women gets right depressed sometimes when they get her way. [*Speaking softly, expertly, rapidly*] Now you just relax. That's right . . . just lean back, don't think 'bout nothing at all . . . nothing at all—

RUTH I'm all right . . . [*The glassy-eyed look melts and then she collapses into a fit of heavy sobbing. The bell rings*]

BENEATHA   Oh, my God—that must be Asagai.

MAMA   [*To* RUTH]   Come on now, honey. You need to lie down and rest awhile
. . . then have some nice hot food.
[*They exit,* RUTH's *weight on her mother-in-law.* BENEATHA, *herself profoundly disturbed, opens the door to admit a rather dramatic-looking young
man with a large package*]

ASAGAI   Hello, Alaiyo—

BENEATHA   [*Holding the door open and regarding him with pleasure*]   Hello
. . . [*Long pause*] Well—come in. And please excuse everything. My mother
was very upset about my letting anyone come here with the place like this.

ASAGAI   [*Coming into the room*]   You look disturbed too . . . Is something
wrong?

BENEATHA   [*Still at the door, absently*]   Yes . . . we've all got acute ghetto-itus.
[*She smiles and comes toward him, finding a cigarette and sitting*] So—sit
down! How was Canada?

ASAGAI   [*A sophisticate*]   Canadian.

BENEATHA   [*Looking at him*]   I'm very glad you are back.

ASAGAI   [*Looking back at her in turn*]   Are you really?

BENEATHA   Yes—very.

ASAGAI   Why—you were quite glad when I went away. What happened?

BENEATHA   You went away.

ASAGAI   Ahhhhhhhh.

BENEATHA   Before—you wanted to be so serious before there was time.

ASAGAI   How much time must there be before one knows what one feels?

BENEATHA   [*Stalling this particular conversation. Her hands pressed together, in
a deliberately childish gesture*]   What did you bring me?

ASAGAI   [*Handing her the package*]   Open it and see.

BENEATHA   [*Eagerly opening the package and drawing out some records and
the colorful robes of a Nigerian woman*]   Oh, Asagai! . . . You got them
for me! . . . How beautiful . . . and the records too! [*She lifts out the
robes and runs to the mirror with them and holds the drapery up in front
of herself*]

ASAGAI   [*Coming to her at the mirror*]   I shall have to teach you how to drape
it properly. [*He flings the material about her for the moment and stands
back to look at her*] Ah—Oh-pay-gay-day, oh-gbah-mu-shay. [*A Yoruba ex-
clamation for admiration*] You wear it well . . . very well . . . mutilated
hair and all.

BENEATHA   [*Turning suddenly*]   My hair—what's wrong with my hair?

ASAGAI   [*Shrugging*]   Were you born with it like that?

BENEATHA   [*Reaching up to touch it*]   No . . . of course not.
[*She looks back to the mirror, disturbed*]

ASAGAI   [*Smiling*]   How then?

BENEATHA   You know perfectly well how . . . as crinkly as yours . . . that's how.

ASAGAI   And it is ugly to you that way?

BENEATHA   [*Quickly*]   Oh, no—not ugly . . . [*More slowly, apologetically*] But
it's so hard to manage when it's, well—raw.

ASAGAI   And so to accommodate that—you mutilate it every week?

BENEATHA   It's not mutilation!

ASAGAI   [*Laughing aloud at her seriousness*]   Oh . . . please! I am only teasing
you because you are so very serious about these things. [*He stands back
from her and folds his arms across his chest as he watches her pulling at her
hair and frowning in the mirror*] Do you remember the first time you met
me at school? . . . [*He laughs*] You came up to me and you said—and I
thought you were the most serious little thing I had ever seen—you said:

[*He imitates her*] "Mr. Asagai—I want very much to talk with you. About Africa. You see, Mr. Asagai, I am looking for my *identity!*"

[*He laughs*]

BENEATHA [*Turning to him, not laughing*] Yes—

[*Her face is quizzical, profoundly disturbed*]

ASAGAI [*Still teasing and reaching out and taking her face in his hands and turning her profile to him*] Well . . . it is true that this is not so much a profile of a Hollywood queen as perhaps a queen of the Nile—[*A mock dismissal of the importance of the question*] But what does it matter? Assimilationism is so popular in your country.

BENEATHA [*Wheeling, passionately, sharply*] I am not an assimilationist!

ASAGAI [*The protest hangs in the room for a moment and* ASAGAI *studies her, his laughter fading*] Such a serious one. [*There is a pause*] So—you like the robes? You must take excellent care of them—they are from my sister's personal wardrobe.

BENEATHA [*With incredulity*] You—you sent all the way home—for me?

ASAGAI [*With charm*] For you—I would do much more . . . Well, that is what I came for. I must go.

BENEATHA Will you call me Monday?

ASAGAI Yes . . . We have a great deal to talk about. I mean about identity and time and all that.

BENEATHA Time?

ASAGAI Yes. About how much time one needs to know what one feels.

BENEATHA You never understood that there is more than one kind of feeling which can exist between a man and a woman—or, at least, there should be.

ASAGAI [*Shaking his head negatively but gently*] No. Between a man and a woman there need be only one kind of feeling. I have that for you . . . Now even . . . right this moment . . .

BENEATHA I know—and by itself—it won't do. I can find that anywhere.

ASAGAI For a woman it should be enough.

BENEATHA I know—because that's what it says in all the novels that men write. But it isn't. Go ahead and laugh—but I'm not interested in being someone's little episode in America or—[*With feminine vengeance*]—one of them! [ASAGAI *has burst into laughter again*] That's funny as hell, huh!

ASAGAI It's just that every American girl I have known has said that to me. White—black—in this you are all the same. And the same speech, too!

BENEATHA [*Angrily*] Yuk, yuk, yuk!

ASAGAI It's how you can be sure that the world's most liberated women are not liberated at all. You all talk about it too much!

[MAMA *enters and is immediately all social charm because of the presence of a guest*]

BENEATHA Oh—Mama—this is Mr. Asagai.

MAMA How do you do?

ASAGAI [*Total politeness to an elder*] How do you do, Mrs. Younger. Please forgive me for coming at such an outrageous hour on a Saturday.

MAMA Well, you are quite welcome. I just hope you understand that our house don't always look like this. [*Chatterish*] You must come again. I would love to hear all about—[*Not sure of the name*]—your country. I think it's so sad the way our American Negroes don't know nothing about Africa 'cept Tarzan and all that. And all that money they pour into these churches when they ought to be helping you people over there drive out them French and Englishmen done taken away your land.

[*The mother flashes a slightly superior look at her daughter upon completion of the recitation*]

ASAGAI   [*Taken aback by this sudden and acutely unrelated expression of sympathy*]   Yes . . . yes . . .

MAMA   [*Smiling at him suddenly and relaxing and looking him over*]   How many miles is it from here to where you come from?

ASAGAI   Many thousands.

MAMA   [*Looking at him as she would* WALTER]   I bet you don't half look after yourself, being away from your mama either. I spec you better come 'round here from time to time and get yourself some decent homecooked meals . . .

ASAGAI   [*Moved*]   Thank you. Thank you very much. [*They are all quiet, then—*]   Well . . . I must go. I will call you Monday, Alaiyo.

MAMA   What's that he call you?

ASAGAI   Oh—"Alaiyo." I hope you don't mind. It is what you would call a nickname, I think. It is a Yoruba word. I am a Yoruba.

MAMA   [*Looking at* BENEATHA]   I—I thought he was from—

ASAGAI   [*Understanding*]   Nigeria is my country. Yoruba is my tribal origin—

BENEATHA   You didn't tell us what Alaiyo means . . . for all I know, you might be calling me Little Idiot or something . . .

ASAGAI   Well . . . let me see . . . I do not know how just to explain it . . . The sense of a thing can be so different when it changes languages.

BENEATHA   You're evading.

ASAGAI   No—really it is difficult . . . [*Thinking*]   It means . . . it means One for Whom Bread—Food—Is Not Enough. [*He looks at her*]   Is that all right?

BENEATHA   [*Understanding, softly*]   Thank you.

MAMA   [*Looking from one to the other and not understanding any of it*]   Well . . . that's nice . . . You must come see us again—Mr.—

ASAGAI   Ah-sah-guy . . .

MAMA   Yes . . . Do come again.

ASAGAI   Good-bye.

[*He exits*]

MAMA   [*After him*]   Lord, that's a pretty thing just went out here! [*Insinuatingly, to her daughter*]   Yes, I guess I see why we done commence to get so interested in Africa 'round here. Missionaries my aunt Jenny!

[*She exits*]

BENEATHA   Oh, Mama! . . .

[*She picks up the Nigerian dress and holds it up to her in front of the mirror again. She sets the headdress on haphazardly and then notices her hair again and clutches at it and then replaces the headdress and frowns at herself. Then she starts to wriggle in front of the mirror as she thinks a Nigerian woman might.* TRAVIS *enters and regards her*]

TRAVIS   You cracking up?

BENEATHA   Shut up.

[*She pulls the headdress off and looks at herself in the mirror and clutches at her hair again and squinches her eyes as if trying to imagine something. Then, suddenly, she gets her raincoat and kerchief and hurriedly prepares for going out*]

MAMA   [*Coming back into the room*]   She's resting now. Travis, baby, run next door and ask Miss Johnson to please let me have a little kitchen cleanser. This here can is empty as Jacob's kettle.

TRAVIS   I just came in.

MAMA   Do as you told. [*He exits and she looks at her daughter*]   Where you going?

BENEATHA   [*Halting at the door*]   To become a queen of the Nile!

[*She exits in a breathless blaze of glory.* RUTH *appears in the bedroom doorway*]

MAMA   Who told you to get up?

RUTH   Ain't nothing wrong with me to be lying in no bed for. Where did Bennie go?

MAMA   [*Drumming her fingers*]   Far as I could make out—to Egypt. [RUTH *just looks at her*] What time is it getting to?

RUTH   Ten twenty. And the mailman going to ring that bell this morning just like he done every morning for the last umpteen years.

[TRAVIS *comes in with the cleanser can*]

TRAVIS   She say to tell you that she don't have much.

MAMA   [*Angrily*]   Lord, some people I could name sure is tight-fisted! [*Directing her grandson*] Mark two cans of cleanser down on the list there. If she that hard up for kitchen cleanser, I sure don't want to forget to get her none!

RUTH   Lena—maybe the woman is just short on cleanser—

MAMA   [*Not listening*]—Much baking powder as she done borrowed from me all these years, she could of done gone into the baking business!

[*The bell sounds suddenly and sharply and all three are stunned—serious and silent—mid-speech. In spite of all the other conversations and distractions of the morning, this is what they have been waiting for, even* TRAVIS, *who looks helplessly from his mother to his grandmother.* RUTH *is the first to come to life again*]

RUTH   [*To* TRAVIS]   Get down them steps, boy!

[TRAVIS *snaps to life and flies out to get the mail*]

MAMA   [*Her eyes wide, her hand to her breast*]   You mean it done really come?

RUTH   [*Excited*]   Oh, Miss Lena!

MAMA   [*Collecting herself*]   Well . . . I don't know what we all so excited about 'round here for. We known it was coming for months.

RUTH   That's a whole lot different from having it come and being able to hold it in your hands . . . a piece of paper worth ten thousand dollars . . . [TRAVIS *bursts back into the room. He holds the envelope high above his head, like a little dancer, his face is radiant and he is breathless. He moves to his grandmother with sudden slow ceremony and puts the envelope into her hands. She accepts it, and then merely holds it and looks at it*] Come on! Open it . . . Lord have mercy, I wish Walter Lee was here!

TRAVIS   Open it, Grandmama!

MAMA   [*Staring at it*]   Now you all be quiet. It's just a check.

RUTH   Open it . . .

MAMA   [*Still staring at it*]   Now don't act silly . . . We ain't never been no people to act silly 'bout no money—

RUTH   [*Swiftly*]   We ain't never had none before—*open it!*

[MAMA *finally makes a good strong tear and pulls out the thin blue slice of paper and inspects it closely. The boy and his mother study it raptly over* MAMA's *shoulders*]

MAMA   Travis! [*She is counting off with doubt*] Is that the right number of zeros.

TRAVIS   Yes'm . . . ten thousand dollars. Gaalee, Grandmama, you rich.

MAMA   [*She holds the check away from her, still looking at it. Slowly her face sobers into a mask of unhappiness*] Ten thousand dollars. [*She hands it to* RUTH] Put it away somewhere, Ruth. [*She does not look at* RUTH; *her eyes seem to be seeing something somewhere very far off*] Ten thousand dollars they give you. Ten thousand dollars.

TRAVIS   [*To his mother, sincerely*]   What's the matter with Grandmama—don't she want to be rich?

RUTH   [*Distractedly*]   You go on out and play now, baby. [TRAVIS *exits.* MAMA *starts wiping dishes absently, humming intently to herself.* RUTH *turns to her, with kind exasperation]* You've gone and got yourself upset.

MAMA [*Not looking at her*] I spec if it wasn't for you all . . . I would just put that money away or give it to the church or something.

RUTH Now what kind of talk is that. Mr. Younger would just be plain mad if he could hear you talking foolish like that.

MAMA [*Stopping and staring off*] Yes . . . he sure would. [*Sighing*] We got enough to do with that money, all right. [*She halts then, and turns and looks at her daughter-in-law hard;* RUTH *avoids her eyes and* MAMA *wipes her hands with finality and starts to speak firmly to* RUTH] Where did you go today, girl?

RUTH To the doctor.

MAMA [*Impatiently*] Now, Ruth . . . you know better than that. Old Doctor Jones is strange enough in his way but there ain't nothing 'bout him make somebody slip and call him "she"—like you done this morning.

RUTH Well, that's what happened—my tongue slipped.

MAMA You went to see that woman, didn't you?

RUTH [*Defensively, giving herself away*] What woman you talking about?

MAMA [*Angrily*] That woman who—

[WALTER *enters in great excitement*]

WALTER Did it come?

MAMA [*Quietly*] Can't you give people a Christian greeting before you start asking about money?

WALTER [*To Ruth*] Did it come? [RUTH *unfolds the check and lays it quietly before him, watching him intently with thoughts of her own.* WALTER *sits down and grasps it close and counts off the zeros*] Ten thousand dollars— [*He turns suddenly, frantically to his mother and draws some papers out of his breast pocket*] Mama—look. Old Willy Harris put everything on paper—

MAMA Son—I think you ought to talk to your wife . . . I'll go on out and leave you alone if you want—

WALTER I can talk to her later—Mama, look—

MAMA Son—

WALTER WILL SOMEBODY PLEASE LISTEN TO ME TODAY!

MAMA [*Quietly*] I don't 'low no yellin' in this house, Walter Lee, and you know it—[WALTER *stares at them in frustration and starts to speak several times*] And there ain't going to be no investing in no liquor stores. I don't aim to have to speak on that again.

[*A long pause*]

WALTER Oh—so you don't aim to have to speak on that again? So *you* have decided . . . [*Crumpling his papers*] Well, *you* tell that to my boy tonight when you put him to sleep on the living-room couch . . . [*Turning to* MAMA *and speaking directly to her*] Yeah—and tell it to my wife, Mama, tomorrow when she has to go out of here to look after somebody else's kids. And tell it to *me*, Mama, every time we need a new pair of curtains and I have to watch *you* go out and work in somebody's kitchen. Yeah, you tell me then!

[WALTER *starts out*]

RUTH Where you going?

WALTER I'm going out!

RUTH Where?

WALTER Just out of this house somewhere—

RUTH [*Getting her coat*] I'll come too.

WALTER I don't want you to come!

RUTH   I got something to talk to you about, Walter.

WALTER   That's too bad.

MAMA   [*Still quietly*]   Walter Lee—[*She waits and he finally turns and looks at her*] Sit down.

WALTER   I'm a grown man, Mama.

MAMA   Ain't nobody said you wasn't grown. But you still in my house and my presence. And as long as you are—you'll talk to your wife civil. Now sit down.

RUTH   [*Suddenly*]   Oh, let him go on out and drink himself to death! He makes me sick to my stomach! [*She flings her coat against him*]

WALTER   [*Violently*]   And you turn mine too, baby! [RUTH *goes into their bedroom and slams the door behind her*] That was my greatest mistake—

MAMA   [*Still quietly*]   Walter, what is the matter with you?

WALTER   Matter with me? Ain't nothing the matter with *me!*

MAMA   Yes there is. Something eating you up like a crazy man. Something more than me not giving you this money. The past few years I been watching it happen to you. You get all nervous acting and kind of wild in the eyes—[WALTER *jumps up impatiently at her words*] I said sit there now, I'm talking to you!

WALTER   Mama—I don't need no nagging at me today.

MAMA   Seem like you getting to a place where you always tied up in some kind of knot about something. But if anybody ask you 'bout it you just yell at 'em and bust out the house and go out and drink somewheres. Walter Lee, people can't live with that. Ruth's a good, patient girl in her way—but you getting to be too much. Boy, don't make the mistake of driving that girl away from you.

WALTER   Why—what she do for me?

MAMA   She loves you.

WALTER   Mama—I'm going out. I want to go off somewhere and be by myself for a while.

MAMA   I'm sorry 'bout your liquor store, son. It just wasn't the thing for us to do. That's what I want to tell you about—

WALTER   I got to go out, Mama—

[*He rises*]

MAMA   It's dangerous, son.

WALTER   What's dangerous?

MAMA   When a man goes outside his home to look for peace.

WALTER   [*Beseechingly*]   Then why can't there never be no peace in this house then?

MAMA   You done found it in some other house?

WALTER   No—there ain't no woman! Why do women always think there's a woman somewhere when a man gets restless. [*Coming to her*] Mama— Mama—I want so many things . . .

MAMA   Yes, son—

WALTER   I want so many things that they are driving me kind of crazy . . . Mama—look at me.

MAMA   I'm looking at you. You a good-looking boy. You got a job, a nice wife, a fine boy and—

WALTER   A job. [*Looks at her*] Mama, a job? I open and close car doors all day long. I drive a man around in his limousine and I say, "Yes, sir; no, sir; very good, sir; shall I take the Drive, sir?" Mama, that ain't no kind of job . . . that ain't nothing at all. [*Very quietly*] Mama, I don't know if I can make you understand.

MAMA   Understand what, baby?

WALTER   [*Quietly*]   Sometimes it's like I can see the future stretched out in front of me—just plain as day. The future, Mama. Hanging over there at the edge of my days. Just waiting for me—a big, looming blank space —full of *nothing.* Just waiting for *me.* [*Pause*] Mama—sometimes when I'm downtown and I pass them cool, quiet-looking restaurants where them white boys are sitting back and talking 'bout things . . . sitting there turning deals worth millions of dollars . . . sometimes I see guys don't look much older than me—

MAMA   Son—how come you talk so much 'bout money?

WALTER   [*With immense passion*]   Because it is life, Mama!

MAMA   [*Quietly*]   Oh—[*Very quietly*]   So now it's life. Money is life. Once upon a time freedom used to be life—now it's money. I guess the world really do change . . .

WALTER   No—it was always money, Mama. We just didn't know about it.

MAMA   No . . . something has changed. [*She looks at him*] You something new, boy. In my time we was worried about not being lynched and getting to the North if we could and how to stay alive and still have a pinch of dignity too . . . Now here come you and Beneatha—talking 'bout things we ain't never even thought about hardly, me and your daddy. You ain't satisfied or proud of nothing we done. I mean that you had a home; that we kept you out of trouble till you was grown; that you don't have to ride to work on the back of nobody's streetcar—You my children—but how different we done become.

WALTER   You just don't understand, Mama, you just don't understand.

MAMA   Son—do you know your wife is expecting another baby? [WALTER *stands, stunned, and absorbs what his mother has said*] That's what she wanted to talk to you about. [WALTER *sinks down into a chair*] This ain't for me to be telling—but you ought to know. [*She waits*] I think Ruth is thinking 'bout getting rid of that child.

WALTER   [*Slowly understanding*]   No—no—Ruth wouldn't do that.

MAMA   When the world gets ugly enough—a woman will do anything for her family. *The part that's already living.*

WALTER   You don't know Ruth, Mama, if you think she would do that.

[RUTH *opens the bedroom door and stands there a little limp*]

RUTH   [*Beaten*] ˙ Yes I would too, Walter. [*Pause*] I gave her a five-dollar down payment.

[*There is total silence as the man stares at his wife and the mother stares at her son*]

MAMA   [*Presently*]   Well—[*Tightly*]   Well—son, I'm waiting to hear you say something . . . I'm waiting to hear how you be your father's son. Be the man he was . . . [*Pause*] Your wife say she going to destroy your child. And I'm waiting to hear you talk like him and say we a people who give children life, not who destroys them—[*She rises*] I'm waiting to see you stand up and look like your daddy and say we done give up one baby to poverty and that we ain't going to give up nary another one . . . I'm waiting.

WALTER   Ruth—

MAMA   If you a son of mine, tell her! (WALTER *turns, looks at her and can say nothing. She continues, bitterly*) You . . . you are a disgrace to your father's memory. Somebody get me my hat.

CURTAIN

ACT II

Scene One

> *Time: Later the same day.*
> *At rise:* RUTH *is ironing again. She has the radio going. Presently* BENEATHA'S *bedroom door opens and* RUTH'S *mouth falls and she puts down the iron in fascination.*

RUTH What have we got on tonight!

BENEATHA [*Emerging grandly from the doorway so that we can see her thoroughly robed in the costume Asagai brought*] You are looking at what a well-dressed Nigerian woman wears—[*She parades for* RUTH, *her hair completely hidden by the headdress; she is coquettishly fanning herself with an ornate oriental fan, mistakenly more like Butterfly than any Nigerian that ever was*] Isn't it beautiful? [*She promenades to the radio and, with an arrogant flourish, turns off the good loud blues that is playing*] Enough of this assimilationist junk! [RUTH *follows her with her eyes as she goes to the phonograph and puts on a record and turns and waits ceremoniously for the music to come up. Then, with a shout—*] OCOMOGO-SIAY!

> [RUTH *jumps. The music comes up, a lovely Nigerian melody.* BENEATHA *listens, enraptured, her eyes far away—"back to the past." She begins to dance.* RUTH *is dumfounded*]

RUTH What kind of dance is that?

BENEATHA A folk dance.

RUTH [*Pearl Bailey*] What kind of folks do that, honey?

BENEATHA It's from Nigeria. It's a dance of welcome.

RUTH Who you welcoming?

BENEATHA The men back to the village.

RUTH Where they been?

BENEATHA How should I know—out hunting or something. Anyway, they are coming back now . . .

RUTH Well, that's good.

BENEATHA [*With the record*]

> *Alundi, alundi*
> *Alundi alunya*
> *Jop pu a jeepua*
> *Ang gu sooooooooooo*
>
> *Ai yai yae . . .*
> *Ayehaye—alundi . . .*

> [WALTER *comes in during this performance; he has obviously been drinking. He leans against the door heavily and watches his sister, at first with distaste. Then his eyes look off—"back to the past"—as he lifts both his fists to the roof, screaming*]

WALTER YEAH . . . AND ETHIOPIA STRETCH FORTH HER HANDS AGAIN! . . .

RUTH [*Drily, looking at him*] Yes—and Africa sure is claiming her own to-night. [*She gives them both up and starts ironing again*]

WALTER [*All in a drunken, dramatic shout*] Shut up! . . . I'm digging them drums . . . them drums move me! . . . [*He makes his weaving way to his wife's face and leans in close to her*] In my *heart of hearts*—[*He thumps his chest*]—I am much warrior!

RUTH [*Without even looking up*] In your heart of hearts you are much drunkard.

WALTER [*Coming away from her and starting to wander around the room, shouting*] Me and Jomo . . . [*Intently, in his sister's face. She has stopped dancing to watch him in this unknown mood*] That's my man, Kenyatta. [*Shouting and thumping his chest*] FLAMING SPEAR! HOT DAMN! [*He is suddenly in possession of an imaginary spear and actively spearing enemies all over the room*] OCOMOGOSIAY . . . THE·LION IS WAK-ING . . . OWIMOWEH! [*He pulls his shirt open and leaps up on a table and gestures with his spear. The bell rings.* RUTH *goes to answer*]

BENEATHA [*To encourage* WALTER, *thoroughly caught up with this side of him*] OCOMOGOSIAY, FLAMING SPEAR!

WALTER [*On the table, very far gone, his eyes pure glass sheets. He sees what we cannot, that he is a leader of his people, a great chief, a descendant of Chaka, and that the hour to march has come*] Listen, my black brothers—

BENEATHA OCOMOGOSIAY!

WALTER —Do you hear the waters rushing against the shores of the coastlands—

BENEATHA OCOMOGOSIAY!

WALTER —Do you hear the screeching of the cocks in yonder hills beyond where the chiefs meet in council for the coming of the mighty war—

BENEATHA OCOMOGOSIAY!

WALTER —Do you hear the beating of the wings of the birds flying low over the mountains and the low places of our land—

[RUTH *opens the door.* GEORGE MURCHISON *enters*]

BENEATHA OCOMOGOSIAY!

WALTER —Do you hear the singing of the women, singing the war songs of our fathers to the babies in the great houses . . . singing the sweet war songs? OH, DO YOU HEAR, MY BLACK BROTHERS!

BENEATHA [*Completely gone*] We hear you, Flaming Spear—

WALTER Telling us to prepare for the greatness of the time—[*To* GEORGE] Black Brother!

[*He extends his hand for the fraternal clasp*]

GEORGE Black Brother, hell!

RUTH [*Having had enough, and embarrassed for the family*] Beneatha, you got company—what's the matter with you? Walter Lee Younger, get down off that table and stop acting like a fool . . .

[WALTER *comes down off the table suddenly and makes a quick exit to the bathroom*]

RUTH He's had a little to drink . . . I don't know what her excuse is.

GEORGE [*To* BENEATHA] Look honey, we're going *to* the theatre—we're not going to be *in* it . . . so go change, huh?

RUTH You expect this boy to go out with you looking like that?

BENEATHA [*Looking at* GEORGE] That's up to George. If he's ashamed of his heritage—

GEORGE Oh, don't be so proud of yourself, Bennie—just because you look eccentric.

BENEATHA How can something that's natural be eccentric?

GEORGE That's what being eccentric means—being natural. Get dressed.

BENEATHA I don't like that, George.

RUTH Why must you and your brother make an argument out of everything people say?

BENEATHA Because I hate assimilationist Negroes!

RUTH Will somebody please tell me what assimila-who-ever means!

GEORGE Oh, it's just a college girl's way of calling people Uncle Toms—but that isn't what it means at all.

RUTH Well, what does it mean?

BENEATHA [*Cutting* GEORGE *off and staring at him as she replies to* RUTH] It means someone who is willing to give up his own culture and submerge himself completely in the dominant, and in this case, *oppressive* culture!

GEORGE Oh, dear, dear, dear! Here we go! A lecture on the African past! On our Great West African Heritage! In one second we will hear all about the great Ashanti empires; the great Songhay civilizations; and the great sculpture of Bénin—and then some poetry in the Bantu—and the whole monologue will end with the word *heritage!* [*Nastily*] Let's face it, baby, your heritage is nothing but a bunch of raggedy-assed spirituals and some grass huts!

BENEATHA Grass huts! [RUTH *crosses to her and forcibly pushes her toward the bedroom*] See there . . . you are standing there in your splendid ignorance talking about people who were the first to smelt iron on the face of the earth! [RUTH *is pushing her through the door*] The Ashanti were performing surgical operations when the English—[RUTH *pulls the door to, with* BENEATHA *on the other side, and smiles graciously at* GEORGE. BENEATHA *opens the door and shouts the end of the sentence defiantly at* GEORGE] —were still tattooing themselves with blue dragons . . . [*She goes back inside*]

RUTH Have a seat, George. [*They both sit.* RUTH *folds her hands rather primly on her lap, determined to demonstrate the civilization of the family*] Warm, ain't it? I mean for September. [*Pause*] Just like they always say about Chicago weather: If it's too hot or cold for you, just wait a minute and it'll change. [*She smiles happily at this cliché of clichés*] Everybody say it's got to do with them bombs and things they keep setting off. [*Pause*] Would you like a nice cold beer?

GEORGE No, thank you. I don't care for beer. [*He looks at his watch*] I hope she hurries up.

RUTH What time is the show?

GEORGE It's an eight-thirty curtain. That's just Chicago, though. In New York standard curtain time is eight forty.

[*He is rather proud of this knowledge*]

RUTH [*Properly appreciating it*] You get to New York a lot?

GEORGE [*Offhand*] Few times a year.

RUTH Oh—that's nice. I've never been to New York.

[WALTER *enters. We feel he has relieved himself, but the edge of unreality is still with him*]

WALTER New York ain't got nothing Chicago ain't. Just a bunch of hustling people all squeezed up together—being "Eastern."

[*He turns his face into a screw of displeasure*]

GEORGE Oh—you've been?

WALTER *Plenty* of times.

RUTH [*Shocked at the lie*] Walter Lee Younger!

WALTER [*Staring her down*] Plenty! [*Pause*] What we got to drink in this house? Why don't you offer this man some refreshment. [*To* GEORGE] They don't know how to entertain people in this house, man.

GEORGE   Thank you—I don't really care for anything.

WALTER   [*Feeling his head; sobriety coming*]   Where's Mama?

RUTH   She ain't come back yet.

WALTER   [*Looking* MURCHISON *over from head to toe, scrutinizing his carefully casual tweed sports jacket over cashmere V-neck sweater over soft eyelet shirt and tie, and soft slacks, finished off with white buckskin shoes*]   Why all you college boys wear them fairyish-looking white shoes?

RUTH   Walter Lee!

[GEORGE MURCHISON *ignores the remark*]

WALTER   [*To* RUTH]   Well, they look crazy as hell—white shoes, cold as it is.

RUTH   [*Crushed*]   You have to excuse him—

WALTER   No he don't! Excuse me for what? What you always excusing me for! I'll excuse myself when I needs to be excused! [*A pause*] They look as funny as them black knee socks Beneatha wears out of here all the time.

RUTH   It's the college *style,* Walter.

WALTER   Style, hell. She looks like she got burnt legs or something!

RUTH   Oh, Walter—

WALTER   [*An irritable mimic*]   Oh, Walter! Oh, Walter! [*To* MURCHISON] How's your old man making out? I understand you all going to buy that big hotel on the Drive? [*He finds a beer in the refrigerator, wanders over to* MURCHISON, *sipping and wiping his lips with the back of his hand, and straddling a chair backwards to talk to the other man*] Shrewd move. Your old man is all right, man. [*Tapping his head and half winking for emphasis*] I mean he knows how to operate. I mean he thinks *big,* you know what I mean, I mean for a *home,* you know? But I think he's kind of running out of ideas now. I'd like to talk to him. Listen, man, I got some plans that could turn this city upside down. I mean I think like he does. *Big.* Invest big, gamble big, hell, lose *big* if you have to, you know what I mean. It's hard to find a man on this whole Southside who understands my kind of thinking—you dig? [*He scrutinizes* MURCHISON *again, drinks his beer, squints his eyes and leans in close, confidential, man to man*] Me and you ought to sit down and talk sometimes, man. Man, I got me some ideas . . .

MURCHISON   [*With boredom*]   Yeah—sometimes we'll have to do that, Walter.

WALTER   [*Understanding the indifference, and offended*]   Yeah—well, when you get the time, man. I know you a busy little boy.

RUTH   Walter, please—

WALTER   [*Bitterly, hurt*]   I know ain't nothing in this world as busy as you colored college boys with your fraternity pins and white shoes . . .

RUTH   [*Covering her face with humiliation*]   Oh, Walter Lee—

WALTER   I see you all all the time—with the books tucked under your arms—going to your [*British A—a mimic*] "clahsses." And for what! What the hell you learning over there? Filling up your heads—[*Counting off on his fingers*]—with the sociology and the psychology—but they teaching you how to be a man? How to take over and run the world? They teaching you how to run a rubber plantation or a steel mill? Naw—just to talk proper and read books and wear white shoes . . .

GEORGE   [*Looking at him with distaste, a little above it all*]   You're all wacked up with bitterness, man.

WALTER   [*Intently, almost quietly, between the teeth, glaring at the boy*]   And you—ain't you bitter, man? Ain't you just about had it yet? Don't you see no stars gleaming that you can't reach out and grab? You happy?— You contented son-of-a-bitch—you happy? You got it made? Bitter? Man,

I'm a volcano. Bitter? Here I am a giant—surrounded by ants! Ants who can't even understand what it is the giant is talking about.

RUTH [*Passionately and suddenly*] Oh, Walter—ain't you with nobody!

WALTER [*Violently*] No! 'Cause ain't nobody with me! Not even my own mother!

RUTH Walter, that's a terrible thing to say!

[BENEATHA *enters, dressed for the evening in a cocktail dress and earrings*]

GEORGE Well—hey, you look great.

BENATHA Let's go, George. See you all later.

RUTH Have a nice time.

GEORGE Thanks. Good night. [*To* WALTER, *sarcastically*] Good night, *Prometheus.*

[BENEATHA *and* GEORGE *exit*]

WALTER [*To* RUTH] Who is Prometheus?

RUTH I don't know. Don't worry about it.

WALTER [*In fury, pointing after* GEORGE] See there—they get to a point where they can't insult you man to man—they got to go talk about something ain't nobody never heard of!

RUTH How do you know it was an insult? [*To humor him*] Maybe Prometheus is a nice fellow.

WALTER Prometheus! I bet there ain't even no such thing! I bet that simple-minded clown—

RUTH Walter—

[*She stops what she is doing and looks at him*]

WALTER [*Yelling*] Don't start!

RUTH Start what?

WALTER Your nagging! Where was I? Who was I with? How much money did I spend?

RUTH [*Plaintively*] Walter Lee—why don't we just try to talk about it . . .

WALTER [*Not listening*] I been out talking with people who understand me. People who care about the things I got on my mind.

RUTH [*Wearily*] I guess that means people like Willy Harris.

WALTER Yes, people like Willy Harris.

RUTH [*With a sudden flash of impatience*] Why don't you all just hurry up and go into the banking business and stop talking about it!

WALTER Why? You want to know why? 'Cause we all tied up in a race of people that don't know how to do nothing but moan, pray and have babies!

[*The line is too bitter even for him and he looks at her and sits down*]

RUTH Oh, Walter . . . [*Softly*] Honey, why can't you stop fighting me?

WALTER [*Without thinking*] Who's fighting you? Who even cares about you?

[*This line begins the retardation of his mood*]

RUTH Well—[*She waits a long time, and then with resignation starts to put away her things*] I guess I might as well go on to bed . . . [*More or less to herself*] I don't know where we lost it . . . but we have . . . [*Then, to him*] I—I'm sorry about this new baby, Walter. I guess maybe I better go on and do what I started . . . I guess I just didn't realize how bad things was with us . . . I guess I just didn't really realize—[*She starts out to the bedroom and stops*] You want some hot milk?

WALTER Hot milk?

RUTH Yes—hot milk.

WALTER Why hot milk?

RUTH 'Cause after all that liquor you come home with you ought to have something hot in your stomach.

WALTER   I don't want no milk.

RUTH   You want some coffee then?

WALTER   No, I don't want no coffee. I don't want nothing hot to drink. [*Almost plaintively*] Why you always trying to give me something to eat?

RUTH   [*Standing and looking at him helplessly*] What else can I give you, Walter Lee Younger?
[*She stands and looks at him and presently turns to go out again. He lifts his head and watches her going away from him in a new mood which began to emerge when he asked her "Who cares about you?"*]

WALTER   It's been rough, ain't it, baby? [*She hears and stops but does not turn around and he continues to her back*] I guess between two people there ain't never as much understood as folks generally thinks there is. I mean like between me and you—[*She turns to face him*] How we gets to the place where we scared to talk softness to each other. [*He waits, thinking hard himself*] Why you think it got to be like that? [*He is thoughtful, almost as a child would be*] Ruth, what is it gets into people ought to be close?

RUTH   I don't know, honey. I think about it a lot.

WALTER   On account of you and me, you mean? The way things are with us. The way something done come down between us.

RUTH   There ain't so much between us, Walter . . . Not when you come to me and try to talk to me. Try to be with me . . . a little even.

WALTER   [*Total honesty*] Sometimes . . . sometimes . . . I don't even know how to try.

RUTH   Walter—

WALTER   Yes?

RUTH   [*Coming to him, gently and with misgiving, but coming to him*]   Honey . . . life don't have to be like this. I mean sometimes people can do things so that things are better . . . You remember how we used to talk when Travis was born . . . about the way we were going to live . . . the kind of house . . . [*She is stroking his head*] Well, it's all starting to slip away from us . . .
[*MAMA enters, and WALTER jumps up and shouts at her*]

WALTER   Mama, where have you been?

MAMA   My—them steps is longer than they used to be. Whew! [*She sits down and ignores him*] How you feeling this evening, Ruth?
[*RUTH shrugs, disturbed some at having been prematurely interrupted and watching her husband knowingly*]

WALTER   Mama, where have you been all day?

MAMA   [*Still ignoring him and leaning on the table and changing to more comfortable shoes*]   Where's Travis?

RUTH   I let him go out earlier and he ain't come back yet. Boy, is he going to get it!

WALTER   Mama!

MAMA   [*As if she has heard him for the first time*]   Yes, son?

WALTER   Where did you go this afternoon?

MAMA   I went downtown to tend to some business that I had to tend to.

WALTER   What kind of business?

MAMA   You know better than to question me like a child, Brother.

WALTER   [*Rising and bending over the table*]   Where were you, Mama? [*Bringing his fists down and shouting*] Mama, you didn't go do something with that insurance money, something crazy?
[*The front door opens slowly, interrupting him, and TRAVIS peeks his head in, less than hopefully*]

TRAVIS [*To his mother*] Mama, I—

RUTH "Mama I" nothing! You're going to get it, boy! Get on in that bedroom and get yourself ready!

TRAVIS But I—

MAMA Why don't you all never let the child explain hisself.

RUTH Keep out of it now, Lena.

[MAMA *clamps her lips together, and* RUTH *advances toward her son menacingly*]

RUTH A thousand times I have told you not to go off like that—

MAMA [*Holding out her arms to her grandson*] Well—at least let me tell him something. I want him to be the first one to hear . . . Come here, Travis. [*The boy obeys, gladly*] Travis—[*She takes him by the shoulder and looks into his face*]—you know that money we got in the mail this morning?

TRAVIS Yes'm—

MAMA Well—what you think your grandmama gone and done with that money?

TRAVIS I don't know, Grandmama.

MAMA [*Putting her finger on his nose for emphasis*] She went out and she bought you a house! [*The explosion comes from* WALTER *at the end of the revelation and he jumps up and turns away from all of them in a fury.* MAMA *continues, to* TRAVIS] You glad about the house? It's going to be yours when you get to be a man.

TRAVIS Yeah—I always wanted to live in a house.

MAMA All right, gimme some sugar then—[TRAVIS *puts his arms around her neck as she watches her son over the boy's shoulder. Then, to* TRAVIS, *after the embrace*] Now when you say your prayers tonight, you thank God and your grandfather—'cause it was him who give you the house—in his way.

RUTH [*Taking the boy from* MAMA *and pushing him toward the bedroom*] Now you get out of here and get ready for your beating.

TRAVIS Aw, Mama—

RUTH Get on in there—[*Closing the door behind him and turning radiantly to her mother-in-law*] So you went and did it!

MAMA [*Quietly, looking at her son with pain*] Yes, I did.

RUTH [*Raising both arms classically*] Praise God! [*Looks at* WALTER *a moment, who says nothing. She crosses rapidly to her husband*] Please, honey—let me be glad . . . you be glad too. [*She has laid her hands on his shoulders, but he shakes himself free of her roughly, without turning to face her*] Oh, Walter . . . a home . . . a home. [*She comes back to* MAMA] Well—where is it? How big is it? How much it going to cost?

MAMA Well—

RUTH When we moving?

MAMA [*Smiling at her*] First of the month.

RUTH [*Throwing back her head with jubilance*] Praise God!

MAMA [*Tentatively, still looking at her son's back turned against her and* RUTH] It's—it's a nice house too . . . [*She cannot help speaking directly to him. An imploring quality in her voice, her manner, makes her almost like a girl now*] Three bedrooms—nice big one for you and Ruth. . . . Me and Beneatha still have to share our room, but Travis have one of his own and [*With difficulty*] I figure if the—new baby—is a boy, we could get one of them double-decker outfits . . . And there's a yard with a little patch of dirt where I could maybe get to grow me a few flowers . . . And a nice big basement . . .

RUTH Walter honey, be glad—

MAMA   [*Still to his back, fingering things on the table*]   'Course I don't want to make it sound fancier than it is . . . It's just a plain little old house—but it's made good and solid—and it will be *ours*. Walter Lee—it makes a difference in a man when he can walk on floors that belong to *him* . . .

RUTH   Where is it?

MAMA   [*Frightened at this telling*]   Well—well—it's out there in Clybourne Park—

[RUTH'S *radiance fades abruptly, and* WALTER *finally turns slowly to face his mother with incredulity and hostility*]

RUTH   Where?

MAMA   [*Matter-of-factly*]   Four o six Clybourne Street, Clybourne Park.

RUTH   Clybourne Park? Mama, there ain't no colored people living in Clybourne Park.

MAMA   [*Almost idiotically*]   Well, I guess there's going to be some now.

WALTER   [*Bitterly*]   So that's the peace and comfort you went out and bought for us today!

MAMA   [*Raising her eyes to meet his finally*]   Son—I just tried to find the nicest place for the least amount of money for my family.

RUTH   [*Trying to recover from the shock*]   Well—well—'course I ain't one never been 'fraid of no crackers, mind you—but—well, wasn't there no other houses nowhere?

MAMA   Them houses they put up for colored in them areas way out all seem to cost twice as much as other houses. I did the best I could.

RUTH   [*Struck senseless with the news, in its various degrees of goodness and trouble, she sits a moment, her fists propping her chin in thought, and then she starts to rise, bringing her fists down with vigor, the radiance spreading from cheek to cheek again*]   Well—well!—All I can say is—if this is my time in life—*my time*—to say good-bye—[*And she builds with momentum as she starts to circle the room with an exuberant, almost tearfully happy release*]—to these Goddamned cracking walls!—[*She pounds the walls*]—and these marching roaches!—[*She wipes at an imaginary army of marching roaches*]—and this cramped little closet which ain't now or never was no kitchen! . . . then I say it loud and good, *Hallelujah! and good-bye misery . . . I don't never want to see your ugly face again!* [*She laughs joyously, having practically destroyed the apartment, and flings her arms up and lets them come down happily, slowly, reflectively, over her abdomen, aware for the first time perhaps that the life therein pulses with happiness and not despair*]   Lena?

MAMA   [*Moved, watching her happiness*]   Yes, honey?

RUTH   [*Looking off*]   Is there—is there a whole lot of sunlight?

MAMA   [*Understanding*]   Yes, child, there's a whole lot of sunlight.

[*Long pause*]

RUTH   [*Collecting herself and going to the door of the room* TRAVIS *is in*]   Well —I guess I better see 'bout Travis. [*To* MAMA]   Lord, I sure don't feel like whipping nobody today!

[*She exits*]

MAMA   [*The mother and son are left alone now and the mother waits a long time, considering deeply, before she speaks*]   Son—you—you understand what I done, don't you? [WALTER *is silent and sullen*]   I—I just seen my family falling apart today . . . just falling to pieces in front of my eyes . . . We couldn't of gone on like we was today. We was going backwards 'stead of forwards—talking 'bout killing babies and wishing each other was dead . . . When it gets like that in life—you just got to do something different, push on out and do something bigger . . . [*She waits*]   I wish you say something, son . . . I wish you'd say how deep inside you you think I done the right thing—

WALTER [*Crossing slowly to his bedroom door and finally turning there and speaking measuredly*] What you need me to say you done right for? *You* the head of this family. You run our lives like you want to. It was your money and you did what you wanted with it. So what you need for me to say it was all right for? [*Bitterly, to hurt her as deeply as he knows is possible*] So you butchered up a dream of mine—you—who always talking 'bout your children's dreams . . .

MAMA Walter Lee—

[*He just closes the door behind him.* MAMA *sits alone, thinking heavily*]

CURTAIN

Scene Two

> *Time: Friday night. A few weeks later.*
> *At rise: Packing crates mark the intention of the family to move.* BENEATHA *and* GEORGE *come in, presumably from an evening out again.*

GEORGE O.K. . . . O.K., whatever you say . . . [*They both sit on the couch. He tries to kiss her. She moves away*] Look, we've had a nice evening; let's not spoil it, huh? . . .

[*He again turns her head and tries to nuzzle in and she turns away from him, not with distaste but with momentary lack of interest; in a mood to pursue what they were talking about*]

BENEATHA I'm *trying* to talk to you.

GEORGE We always talk.

BENEATHA Yes—and I love to talk.

GEORGE [*Exasperated; rising*] I know it and I don't mind it sometimes . . . I want you to cut it out, see—The moody stuff, I mean. I don't like it. You're a nice-looking girl . . . all over. That's all you need, honey, forget the atmosphere. Guys aren't going to go for the atmosphere—they're going to go for what they see. Be glad for that. Drop the Garbo routine. It doesn't go with you. As for myself, I want a nice—[*Groping*]—simple [*Thoughtfully*]—sophisticated girl . . . not a poet—O.K.?

[*She rebuffs him again and he starts to leave*]

BENEATHA Why are you angry?

GEORGE Because this is stupid! I don't go out with you to discuss the nature of "quiet desperation" or to hear all about your thoughts—because the world will go on thinking what it thinks regardless—

BENEATHA Then why read books? Why go to school?

GEORGE [*With artificial patience, counting on his fingers*] It's simple. You read books—to learn facts—to get grades—to pass the course—to get a degree. That's all—it has nothing to do with thoughts.

[*A long pause*]

BENEATHA I see. [*A longer pause as she looks at him*] Good night, George.

[GEORGE *looks at her a little oddly, and starts to exit. He meets* MAMA *coming in*]

GEORGE Oh—hello, Mrs. Younger.

MAMA Hello, George, how you feeling?

GEORGE Fine—fine, how are you?

MAMA Oh, a little tired. You know them steps can get you after a day's work. You all have a nice time tonight?

GEORGE   Yes—a fine time. Well, good night.

MAMA   Good night. [*He exits.* MAMA *closes the door behind her*] Hello, honey. What you sitting like that for?

BENEATHA   I'm just sitting.

MAMA   Didn't you have a nice time?

BENEATHA   No.

MAMA   No? What's the matter?

BENEATHA   Mama, George is a fool—honest. [*She rises*]

MAMA   [*Hustling around unloading the packages she has entered with. She stops*] Is he, baby?

BENEATHA   Yes.

[BENEATHA *makes up* TRAVIS' *bed as she talks*]

MAMA   You sure?

BENEATHA   Yes.

MAMA   Well—I guess you better not waste your time with no fools.

[BENEATHA *looks up at her mother, watching her put groceries in the refrigerator. Finally she gathers up her things and starts into the bedroom. At the door she stops and looks back at her mother*]

BENEATHA   Mama—

MAMA   Yes, baby—

BENEATHA   Thank you.

MAMA   For what?

BENEATHA   For understanding me this time.

[*She exits quickly and the mother stands, smiling a little, looking at the place where* BENEATHA *just stood.* RUTH *enters*]

RUTH   Now don't you fool with any of this stuff, Lena—

MAMA   Oh, I just thought I'd sort a few things out.

[*The phone rings.* RUTH *answers*]

RUTH   [*At the phone*] Hello—Just a minute. [*Goes to door*] Walter, it's Mrs. Arnold. [*Waits. Goes back to the phone. Tense*] Hello. Yes, this is his wife speaking . . . He's lying down now. Yes . . . well, he'll be in tomorrow. He's been very sick. Yes—I know we should have called, but we were so sure he'd be able to come in today. Yes—yes, I'm very sorry. Yes . . . Thank you very much. [*She hangs up.* WALTER *is standing in the doorway of the bedroom behind her*] That was Mrs. Arnold.

WALTER   [*Indifferently*] Was it?

RUTH   She said if you don't come in tomorrow that they are getting a new man . . .

WALTER   Ain't that sad—ain't that crying sad.

RUTH   She said Mr. Arnold has had to take a cab for three days . . . Walter, you ain't been to work for three days! [*This is a revelation to her*] Where you been, Walter Lee Younger? [WALTER *looks at her and starts to laugh*] You're going to lose your job.

WALTER   That's right . . .

RUTH   Oh, Walter, and with your mother working like a dog every day—

WALTER   That's sad too—Everything is sad.

MAMA   What you been doing for these three days, son?

WALTER   Mama—you don't know all the things a man what got leisure can find to do in this city . . . What's this—Friday night? Well—Wednesday I borrowed Willy Harris' car and I went for a drive . . . just me and myself and I drove and drove . . . Way out . . . way past South Chicago, and I parked the car and I sat and looked at the steel mills all day long. I just sat in the car and looked at them big black chimneys for hours. Then I drove back and I went to the Green Hat. [*Pause*] And Thursday—Thursday I borrowed the car again and I got in it and I pointed it the other way and I drove the other way—for hours—way, way up to Wisconsin, and I looked at the farms. I just drove and looked at the farms. Then I drove back and I went to the Green Hat. [*Pause*] And today—today I didn't get the car. Today I just walked. All over the Southside. And I looked at the Negroes and they looked at me and finally I just sat down on the curb at Thirty-ninth and South Parkway and I just sat there and watched the Negroes go by. And then I went to the Green Hat. You all sad? You all depressed? And you know where I am going right now—

[RUTH *goes out quietly*]

MAMA   Oh, Big Walter, is this the harvest of our days?

WALTER   You know what I like about the Green Hat? [*He turns the radio on and a steamy, deep blues pours into the room*] I like this little cat they got there who blows a sax . . . He blows. He talks to me. He ain't but 'bout five feet tall and he's got a conked head and his eyes is always closed and he's all music—

MAMA   [*Rising and getting some papers out of her handbag*]   Walter—

WALTER   And there's this other guy who plays the piano . . . and they got a sound. I mean they can work on some music . . . They got the best little combo in the world in the Green Hat . . . You can just sit there and drink and listen to them three men play and you realize that don't nothing matter worth a damn, but just being there—

MAMA   I've helped do it to you, haven't I, son? Walter, I been wrong.

WALTER   Naw—you ain't never been wrong about nothing, Mama.

MAMA   Listen to me, now. I say I been wrong, son. That I been doing to you what the rest of the world been doing to you. [*She stops and he looks up slowly at her and she meets his eyes pleadingly*] Walter—what you ain't never understood is that I ain't got nothing, don't own nothing, ain't never really wanted nothing that wasn't for you. There ain't nothing as precious to me . . . There ain't nothing worth holding on to, money, dreams, nothing else—if it means—if it means it's going to destroy my boy. [*She puts her papers in front of him and he watches her without speaking or moving*] I paid the man thirty-five hundred dollars down on the house. That leaves sixty-five hundred dollars. Monday morning I want you to take this money and take three thousand dollars and put it in a savings account for Beneatha's medical schooling. The rest you put in a checking account —with your name on it. And from now on any penny that come out of it or that go in it is for you to look after. For you to decide. [*She drops her hands a little helplessly*] It ain't much, but it's all I got in the world and I'm putting it in your hands. I'm telling you to be the head of this family from now on like you supposed to be.

WALTER   [*Stares at the money*]   You trust me like that, Mama?

MAMA   I ain't never stop trusting you. Like I ain't never stop loving you.

[*She goes out, and* WALTER *sits looking at the money on the table as the music continues in its idiom, pulsing in the room. Finally, in a decisive gesture, he gets up, and, in mingled joy and desperation, picks up the money. At the same moment,* TRAVIS *enters for bed*]

TRAVIS   What's the matter, Daddy? You drunk?

WALTER   [*Sweetly, more sweetly than we have ever known him*]   No, Daddy ain't drunk. Daddy ain't going to never be drunk again. . . .

TRAVIS   Well, Good night, Daddy.

[*The* FATHER *has come from behind the couch and leans over, embracing his son*]

WALTER   Son, I feel like talking to you tonight.

TRAVIS About what?

WALTER Oh, about a lot of things. About you and what kind of man you going
to be when you grow up. . . . Son—son, what do you want to be when
you grow up?

TRAVIS A bus driver.

WALTER [*Laughing a little*] A what? Man, that ain't nothing to want to be!

TRAVIS Why not?

WALTER 'Cause, man—it ain't big enough—you know what I mean.

TRAVIS I don't know then. I can't make up my mind. Sometimes Mama asks
me that too. And sometimes when I tell you I just want to be like you—
she says she don't want me to be like that and sometimes she says she
does. . . .

WALTER [*Gathering him up in his arms*] You know what, Travis? In seven
years you going to be seventeen years old. And things is going to be very
different with us in seven years, Travis. . . . One day when you are seventeen I'll come home—home from my office downtown somewhere—

TRAVIS You don't work in no office, Daddy.

WALTER No—but after tonight. After what your daddy gonna do tonight,
there's going to be offices—a whole lot of offices. . . .

TRAVIS What you gonna do tonight, Daddy?

WALTER You wouldn't understand yet, son, but your daddy's gonna make a
transaction . . . a business transaction that's going to change our lives. . . .
That's how come one day when you 'bout seventeen years old I'll come
home and I'll be pretty tired, you know what I mean, after a day of con-
ferences and secretaries getting things wrong the way they do . . . 'cause
an executive's life is hell, man—[*The more he talks the farther away he
gets*] And I'll pull the car up on the driveway . . . just a plain black
Chrysler, I think, with white walls—no—black tires. More elegant. Rich
people don't have to be flashy . . . though I'll have to get something a
little sportier for Ruth—maybe a Cadillac convertible to do her shopping
in. . . . And I'll come up the steps to the house and the gardener will be
clipping away at the hedges and he'll say, "Good evening, Mr. Younger."
And I'll say, "Hello, Jefferson, how are you this evening?" And I'll go
inside and Ruth will come downstairs and meet me at the door and we'll
kiss each other and she'll take my arm and we'll go up to your room to
see you sitting on the floor with the catalogues of all the great schools in
America around you. . . . All the great schools in the world! And—and I'll
say, all right son—it's your seventeenth birthday, what is it you've decided?
. . . Just tell me where you want to go to school and you'll *go*. Just tell
me, what it is you want to be—and you'll *be* it. . . . Whatever you want
to be—Yessir! [*He holds his arms open for* TRAVIS] You just name it, son
. . . [TRAVIS *leaps into them*] and I hand you the world!

[WALTER's *voice has risen in pitch and hysterical promise and on the last
line he lifts* TRAVIS *high*]

[*Blackout*]

Scene Three

*Time: Saturday, moving day, one week later.
Before the curtain rises,* RUTH's *voice, a strident, dramatic church
alto, cuts through the silence.
It is, in the darkness, a triumphant surge, a penetrating statement*

of expectation: "Oh, Lord, I don't feel no ways tired! Children, oh, glory hallelujah!"

As the curtain rises we see that RUTH *is alone in the living room, finishing up the family's packing. It is moving day. She is nailing crates and tying cartons.* BENEATHA *enters, carrying a guitar case, and watches her exuberant sister-in-law.*

RUTH Hey!

BENEATHA [*Putting away the case*] Hi.

RUTH [*Pointing at a package*] Honey—look in that package there and see what I found on sale this morning at the South Center. [RUTH *gets up and moves to the package and draws out some curtains*] Lookahere—hand-turned hems!

BENEATHA How do you know the window size out there?

RUTH [*Who hadn't thought of that*] Oh—Well, they bound to fit something in the whole house. Anyhow, they was too good a bargain to pass up. [RUTH *slaps her head, suddenly remembering something*] Oh, Bennie—I meant to put a special note on that carton over there. That's your mama's good china and she wants 'em to be very careful with it.

BENEATHA I'll do it.

[BENEATHA *finds a piece of paper and starts to draw large letters on it*]

RUTH You know what I'm going to do soon as I get in that new house?

BENEATHA What?

RUTH Honey—I'm going to run me a tub of water up to here . . . [*With her fingers practically up to her nostrils*] And I'm going to get in it—and I am going to sit . . . and sit . . . and sit in that hot water and the first person who knocks to tell *me* to hurry up and come out—

BENEATHA Gets shot at sunrise.

RUTH [*Laughing happily*] You said it, sister! [*Noticing how large* BENEATHA *is absent-mindedly making the note*] Honey, they ain't going to read that from no airplane.

BENEATHA [*Laughing herself*] I guess I always think things have more emphasis if they are big, somehow.

RUTH [*Looking up at her and smiling*] You and your brother seem to have that as a philosophy of life. Lord, that man—done changed so 'round here. You know—you know what we did last night? Me and Walter Lee?

BENEATHA What?

RUTH [*Smiling to herself*] We went to the movies. [*Looking at* BENEATHA *to see if she understands*] We went to the movies. You know the last time me and Walter went to the movies together?

BENEATHA No.

RUTH Me neither. That's how long it been. [*Smiling again*] But we went last night. The picture wasn't much good, but that didn't seem to matter. We went—and we held hands.

BENEATHA Oh, Lord!

RUTH We held hands—and you know what?

BENEATHA What?

RUTH When we come out of the show it was late and dark and all the stores and things was closed up . . . and it was kind of chilly and there wasn't many people on the streets . . . and we was still holding hands, me and Walter.

BENEATHA You're killing me.

[WALTER *enters with a large package. His happiness is deep in him; he cannot keep still with his new-found exuberance. He is singing and wiggling and snapping his fingers. He puts his package in a corner and puts a phonograph record, which he has brought in with him, on the record player. As the music comes up he dances over to* RUTH *and tries to get her to dance with him. She gives in at last to his raunchiness and in a fit of giggling allows herself to be drawn into his mood and together they deliberately burlesque an old social dance of their youth]*

BENEATHA *[Regarding them a long time as they dance, then drawing in her breath for a deeply exaggerated comment which she does not particularly mean]* Talk about—olddddddddddd-fashionedddddddd—Negroes!

WALTER *[Stopping momentarily]* What kind of Negroes?
[He says this in fun. He is not angry with her today, nor with anyone. He starts to dance with his wife again]

BENEATHA Old-fashioned.

WALTER *[As he dances with* RUTH*]* You know, when these *New Negroes* have their convention—*[Pointing at his sister]*—that is going to be the chairman of the Committee on Unending Agitation. *[He goes on dancing, then stops]* Race, race, race! . . . Girl, I do believe you are the first person in the history of the entire human race to successfully brainwash yourself. *[*BENEATHA *breaks up and he goes on dancing. He stops again, enjoying his tease]* Damn, even the N double A C P takes a holiday sometimes! *[*BENEATHA *and* RUTH *laugh. He dances with* RUTH *some more and starts to laugh and stops and pantomimes someone over an operating table]* I can just see that chick someday looking down at some poor cat on an operating table before she starts to slice him, saying . . . *[Pulling his sleeves back maliciously]* "By the way, what are your views on civil rights down there? . . ."
[He laughs at her again and starts to dance happily. The bell sounds]

BENEATHA Sticks and stones may break my bones but . . . words will never hurt me!
*[*BENEATHA *goes to the door and opens it as* WALTER *and* RUTH *go on with the clowning.* BENEATHA *is somewhat surprised to see a quiet-looking middle-aged white man in a business suit holding his hat and a briefcase in his hand and consulting a small piece of paper]*

MAN Uh—how do you do, miss. I am looking for a Mrs.—*[He looks at the slip of paper]* Mrs. Lena Younger?

BENEATHA *[Smoothing her hair with slight embarrassment]* Oh—yes, that's my mother. Excuse me *[She closes the door and turns to quiet the other two]* Ruth! Brother! Somebody's here. *[Then she opens the door. The man casts a curious quick glance at all of them]* Uh—come in please.

MAN *[Coming in]* Thank you.

BENEATHA My mother isn't here just now. Is it business?

MAN Yes . . . well, of a sort.

WALTER *[Freely, the Man of the House]* Have a seat. I'm Mrs. Younger's son. I look after most of her business matters.
*[*RUTH *and* BENEATHA *exchange amused glances]*

MAN *[Regarding* WALTER, *and sitting]* Well—My name is Karl Lindner . . .

WALTER *[Stretching out his hand]* Walter Younger. This is my wife—*[*RUTH *nods politely]*—and my sister.

LINDNER How do you do.

WALTER *[Amiably, as he sits himself easily on a chair, leaning with interest forward on his knees and looking expectantly into the newcomer's face]* What can we do for you, Mr. Lindner!

LINDNER *[Some minor shuffling of the hat and briefcase on his knees]* Well—I am a representative of the Clybourne Park Improvement Association—

WALTER   [*Pointing*]   Why don't you sit your things on the floor?

LINDNER   Oh—yes. Thank you. [*He slides the briefcase and hat under the chair*] And as I was saying—I am from the Clybourne Park Improvement Association and we have had it brought to our attention at the last meeting that you people—or at least your mother—has bought a piece of residential property at—[*He digs for the slip of paper again*]—four o six Clybourne Street. . . .

WALTER   That's right. Care for something to drink? Ruth, get Mr. Lindner a beer.

LINDNER   [*Upset for some reason*]   Oh—no, really. I mean thank you very much, but no thank you.

RUTH   [*Innocently*]   Some coffee?

LINDNER   Thank you, nothing at all.

[BENEATHA *is watching the man carefully*]

LINDNER   Well, I don't know how much you folks know about our organization. [*He is a gentle man; thoughtful and somewhat labored in his manner*] It is one of these community organizations set up to look after—oh, you know, things like block upkeep and special projects and we also have what we call our New Neighbors Orientation Committee . . .

BENEATHA   [*Drily*]   Yes—and what do they do?

LINDNER   [*Turning a little to her and then returning the main force to* WALTER] Well—it's what you might call a sort of welcoming committee, I guess. I mean they, we, I'm the chairman of the committee—go around and see the new people who move into the neighborhood and sort of give them the lowdown on the way we do things out in Clybourne Park.

BENEATHA   [*With appreciation of the two meanings, which escape* RUTH *and* WALTER]   Un-huh.

LINDNER   And we also have the category of what the association calls—[*He looks elsewhere*]—uh—special community problems . . .

BENEATHA   Yes—and what are some of those?

WALTER   Girl, let the man talk.

LINDNER   [*With understated relief*]   Thank you. I would sort of like to explain this thing in my own way. I mean I want to explain to you in a certain way.

WALTER   Go ahead.

LINDNER   Yes. Well. I'm going to try to get right to the point. I'm sure we'll all appreciate that in the long run.

BENEATHA   Yes.

WALTER   Be still now!

LINDNER   Well—

RUTH   [*Still innocently*]   Would you like another chair—you don't look comfortable.

LINDNER   [*More frustrated than annoyed*]   No, thank you very much. Please. Well—to get right to the point I—[*A great breath, and he is off at last*] I am sure you people must be aware of some of the incidents which have happened in various parts of the city when colored people have moved into certain areas—[BENEATHA *exhales heavily and starts tossing a piece of fruit up and down in the air*] Well—because we have what I think is going to be a unique type of organization in American community life—not only do we deplore that kind of thing—but we are trying to do something about it. [BENEATHA *stops tossing and turns with a new and quizzical interest to the man*] We feel—[*gaining confidence in his mission because of the interest in the faces of the people he is talking to*]—we feel that most of the trouble in this world, when you come right down to it—[*He hits his knee*

for emphasis]—most of the trouble exists because people just don't sit
down and talk to each other.

RUTH   [*Nodding as she might in church, pleased with the remark*]   You can
say that again, mister.

LINDNER   [*More encouraged by such affirmation*]   That we don't try hard
enough in this world to understand the other fellow's problem. The other
guy's point of view.

RUTH   Now that's right.

[BENEATHA *and* WALTER *merely watch and listen with genuine interest*]

LINDNER   Yes—that's the way we feel out in Clybourne Park. And that's why
I was elected to come here this afternoon and talk to you people. Friendly
like, you know, the way people should talk to each other and see if we
couldn't find some way to work this thing out. As I say, the whole business
is a matter of *caring* about the other fellow. Anybody can see that you are
a nice family of folks, hard working and honest I'm sure. [BENEATHA *frowns
slightly, quizzically, her head tilted regarding him*] Today everybody knows
what is means to be on the outside of *something*. And of course, there is
always somebody who is out to take the advantage of people who don't
always understand.

WALTER   What do you mean?

LINDNER   Well—you see our community is made up of people who've worked
hard as the dickens for years to build up that little community. They're
not rich and fancy people; just hard-working, honest people who don't
really have much but those little homes and a dream of the kind of community they want to raise their children in. Now, I don't say we are perfect
and there is a lot wrong in some of the things they want. But you've got
to admit that a man, right or wrong, has the right to want to have the
neighborhood he lives in a certain kind of way. And at the moment the
overwhelming majority of our people out there feel that people get along
better, take more of a common interest in the life of the community, when
they share a common background. I want you to believe me when I tell you
that race prejudice simply doesn't enter into it. It is a matter of the people
of Clybourne Park believing, rightly or wrongly, as I say, that for the
happiness of all concerned that our Negro families are happier when they
live in their *own* communities.

BENEATHA   [*With a grand and bitter gesture*]   This, friends, is the Welcoming
Committee!

WALTER   [*Dumfounded, looking at* LINDNER]   Is this what you came marching
all the way over here to tell us?

LINDNER   Well, now we've been having a fine conversation. I hope you'll hear
me all the way through.

WALTER   [*Tightly*]   Go ahead, man.

LINDNER   You see—in the face of all things I have said, we are prepared to
make your family a very generous offer . . .

BENEATHA   Thirty pieces and not a coin less!

WALTER   Yeah?

LINDNER   [*Putting on his glasses and drawing a form out of the briefcase*]   Our
association is prepared, through the collective effort of our people, to buy
the house from you at a financial gain to your family.

RUTH   Lord have mercy, ain't this the living gall!

WALTER   All right, you through?

LINDNER   Well, I want to give you the exact terms of the financial arrangement—

WALTER   We don't want to hear no exact terms of no arrangements. I want to know if you got any more to tell us 'bout getting together?

LINDNER   [*Taking off his glasses*]   Well—I don't suppose that you feel . . .

WALTER   Never mind how I feel—you got any more to say 'bout how people ought to sit down and talk to each other? . . . Get out of my house, man. [*He turns his back and walks to the door*]

LINDNER   [*Looking around at the hostile faces and reaching and assembling his hat and briefcase*]   Well—I don't understand why you people are reacting this way. What do you think you are going to gain by moving into a neighborhood where you just aren't wanted and where some elements— well—people can get awful worked up when they feel that their whole way of life and everything they've ever worked for is threatened.

WALTER   Get out.

LINDNER   [*At the door, holding a small card*]   Well—I'm sorry it went like this.

WALTER   Get out.

LINDNER   [*Almost sadly regarding* WALTER]   You just can't force people to change their hearts, son.
    [*He turns and put his card on a table and exits.* WALTER *pushes the door to with stinging hatred, and stands looking at it.* RUTH *just sits and* BE-NEATHA *just stands. They say nothing.* MAMA *and* TRAVIS *enter*]

MAMA   Well—this all the packing got done since I left out of here this morn-ing. I testify before God that my children got all the energy of the dead. What time the moving men due?

BENEATHA   Four o'clock. You had a caller, Mama.
    [*She is smiling, teasingly*]

MAMA   Sure enough—who?

BENEATHA   [*Her arms folded saucily*]   The Welcoming Committee.
    [WALTER *and* RUTH *giggle*]

MAMA   [*Innocently*]   Who?

BENEATHA   The Welcoming Committee. They said they're sure going to be glad to see you when you get there.

WALTER   [*Devilishly*]   Yeah, they said they can't hardly wait to see your face.
    [*Laughter*]

MAMA   [*Sensing their facetiousness*]   What's the matter with you all?

WALTER   Ain't nothing the matter with us. We just telling you 'bout the gentle-man who came to see you this afternoon. From the Clybourne Park Im-provement Association.

MAMA   What he want?

RUTH   [*In the same mood as* BENEATHA *and* WALTER]   To welcome you, honey.

WALTER   He said they can't hardly wait. He said the one thing they don't have, that they just *dying* to have out there is a fine family of colored people! [*To* RUTH *and* BENEATHA] Ain't that right!

RUTH *and* BENEATHA   [*Mockingly*]   Yeah! He left his card in case—
    [*They indicate the card, and* MAMA *picks it up and throws it on the floor —understanding and looking off as she draws her chair up to the table on which she has put her plant and some sticks and some cord*]

MAMA   Father, give us strength. [*Knowingly—and without fun*] Did he threaten us?

BENEATHA   Oh—Mama—they don't do it like that any more. He talked Brother-hood. He said everybody ought to learn how to sit down and hate each other with good Christian fellowship.
    [*She and* WALTER *shake hands to ridicule the remark*]

MAMA   [*Sadly*]   Lord, protect us . . .

RUTH   You should hear the money those folks raised to buy the house from us. All we paid and then some.

BENEATHA   What they think we going to do—eat 'em?

RUTH   No, honey, marry 'em.

MAMA   [*Shaking her head*]   Lord, Lord, Lord . . .

RUTH   Well—that's the way the crackers crumble. Joke.

BENEATHA   [*Laughingly noticing what her mother is doing*]   Mama, what are you doing?

MAMA   Fixing my plant so it won't get hurt none on the way . . .

BENEATHA   Mama, you going to take *that* to the new house?

MAMA   Un-huh—

BENEATHA   That raggedy-looking old thing?

MAMA   [*Stopping and looking at her*]   It expresses *me*.

RUTH   [*With delight, to* BENEATHA]   So there, Miss Thing!

[WALTER *comes to* MAMA *suddenly and bends down behind her and squeezes her in his arms with all his strength. She is overwhelmed by the suddenness of it and, though delighted, her manner is like that of* RUTH *with* TRAVIS]

MAMA   Look out now, boy! You make me mess up my thing here!

WALTER   [*His face lit, he slips down on his knees beside her, his arms still about her*]   Mama . . . you know what it means to climb up in the chariot?

MAMA   [*Gruffly, very happy*]   Get on away from me now . . .

RUTH   [*Near the gift-wrapped package, trying to catch* WALTER's *eye*]   Psst—

WALTER   What the old song say, Mama . . .

RUTH   Walter—Now?

[*She is pointing at the package*]

WALTER   [*Speaking the lines, sweetly, playfully, in his mother's face*]

> I got wings . . . you got wings . . .
> All God's Children got wings . . .

MAMA   Boy—get out of my face and do some work . . .

WALTER

> When I get to heaven gonna put on my wings,
> Gonna fly all over God's heaven . . .

BENEATHA   [*Teasingly, from across the room*]   Everybody talking 'bout heaven ain't going there!

WALTER   [*To* RUTH, *who is carrying the box across to them*]   I don't know, you think we ought to give her that . . . Seems to me she ain't been very appreciative around here.

MAMA   [*Eying the box, which is obviously a gift*]   What is that?

WALTER   [*Taking it from* RUTH *and putting it on the table in front of* MAMA]   Well—what you all think? Should we give it to her?

RUTH   Oh—she was pretty good today.

MAMA   I'll good you—

[*She turns her eyes to the box again*]

BENEATHA   Open it, Mama.

[*She stands up, looks at it, turns and looks at all of them, and then presses her hands together and does not open the package*]

WALTER   [*Sweetly*]   Open it, Mama. It's for you. [MAMA *looks in his eyes. It is the first present in her life without its being Christmas. Slowly she opens her package and lifts out, one by one, a brand-new sparkling set of gardening tools.* WALTER *continues, prodding*]   Ruth made up the note—read it . . .

MAMA [*Picking up the card and adjusting her glasses*] "To our own Mrs. Miniver—Love from Brother, Ruth and Beneatha." Ain't that lovely . . .

TRAVIS [*Tugging at his father's sleeve*] Daddy, can I give her mine now?

WALTER All right, son. [TRAVIS *flies to get his gift*] Travis didn't want to go in with the rest of us, Mama. He got his own. [*Somewhat amused*] We don't know what it is . . .

TRAVIS [*Racing back in the room with a large hatbox and putting it in front of his grandmother*] Here!

MAMA Lord have mercy, baby. You done gone and bought your grandmother a hat?

TRAVIS [*Very proud*] Open it!
[*She does and lifts out an elaborate, but very elaborate, wide gardening hat, and all the adults break up at the sight of it*]

RUTH Travis, honey, what is that?

TRAVIS [*Who thinks it is beautiful and appropriate*] It's a gardening hat! Like the ladies always have on in the magazines when they work in their gardens.

BENEATHA [*Giggling fiercely*] Travis—we were trying to make Mama Mrs. Miniver—not Scarlett O'Hara!

MAMA [*Indignantly*] What's the matter with you all! This here is a beautiful hat! [*Absurdly*] I always wanted me one just like it!
[*She pops it on her head to prove it to her grandson, and the hat is ludicrous and considerably oversized*]

RUTH Hot dog! Go, Mama!

WALTER [*Doubled over with laughter*] I'm sorry, Mama—but you look like you ready to go out and chop you some cotton sure enough!
[*They all laugh except* MAMA, *out of deference to* TRAVIS' *feelings*]

MAMA [*Gathering the boy up to her*] Bless your heart—this is the prettiest hat I ever owned—[WALTER, RUTH *and* BENEATHA *chime in—noisily, festively and insincerely congratulating* TRAVIS *on his gift*] What are we all standing around here for? We ain't finished packin' yet. Bennie, you ain't packed one book.
[*The bell rings*]

BENEATHA That couldn't be the movers . . . it's not hardly two good yet—
[BENEATHA *goes into her room.* MAMA *starts for door*]

WALTER [*Turning, stiffening*] Wait—wait—I'll get it.
[*He stands and looks at the door*]

MAMA You expecting company, son?

WALTER [*Just looking at the door*] Yeah—yeah . . .
[MAMA *looks at* RUTH, *and they exchange innocent and unfrightened glances*]

MAMA [*Not understanding*] Well, let them in, son.

BENEATHA [*From her room*] We need some more string.

MAMA Travis—you run to the hardware and get me some string cord.
[MAMA *goes out and* WALTER *turns and looks at* RUTH. TRAVIS *goes to a dish for money*]

RUTH Why don't you answer the door, man?

WALTER [*Suddenly bounding across the floor to her*] 'Cause sometimes it hard to let the future begin! [*Stooping down in her face*]

> I got wings! You got wings!
> All Gods children got wings!

[*He crosses to the door and throws it open. Standing there is a very slight little man in a not too prosperous business suit and with haunted frightened eyes and a hat pulled down tightly, brim up, around his forehead.* TRAVIS *passes between the men and exits.* WALTER *leans deep in the man's face, still in his jubilance*]

> When I get to heaven gonna put on my wings,
> Gonna fly all over God's heaven . . .

[*The little man just stares at him*]

> *Heaven*—

[*Suddenly he stops and looks past the little man into the empty hallway*] Where's Willy, man?

BOBO   He ain't with me.

WALTER   [*Not disturbed*]   Oh—come on in. You know my wife.

BOBO   [*Dumbly, taking off his hat*]   Yes—h'you, Miss Ruth.

RUTH   [*Quietly, a mood apart from her husband already, seeing* BOBO]   Hello, Bobo.

WALTER   You right on time today . . . Right on time. That's the way! [*He slaps* BOBO *on his back*] Sit down . . . lemme hear.
[RUTH *stands stiffly and quietly in back of them, as though somehow she senses death, her eyes fixed on her husband*]

BOBO   [*His frightened eyes on the floor, his hat in his hands*]   Could I please get a drink of water, before I tell you about it, Walter Lee?
[WALTER *does not take his eyes off the man.* RUTH *goes blindly to the tap and gets a glass of water and brings it to* BOBO]

WALTER   There ain't nothing wrong, is there?

BOBO   Lemme tell you—

WALTER   Man—didn't nothing go wrong?

BOBO   Lemme tell you—Walter Lee. [*Looking at* RUTH *and talking to her more than to* WALTER] You know how it was. I got to tell you how it was. I mean first I got to tell you how it was all the way . . . I mean about the money I put in, Walter Lee . . .

WALTER   [*With taut agitation now*]   What about the money you put in?

BOBO   Well—it wasn't much as we told you—me and Willy—[*He stops*] I'm sorry, Walter. I got a bad feeling about it. I got a real bad feeling about it . . .

WALTER   Man, what you telling me about all this for? . . . Tell me what happened in Springfield . . .

BOBO   Springfield.

RUTH   [*Like a dead woman*]   What was supposed to happen in Springfield?

BOBO   [*To her*]   This deal that me and Walter went into with Willy—Me and Willy was going to go down to Springfield and spread some money 'round so's we wouldn't have to wait so long for the liquor license . . . That's what we were going to do. Everybody said that was the way you had to do, you understand, Miss Ruth?

WALTER   Man—what happened down there?

BOBO   [*A pitiful man, near tears*]   I'm trying to tell you, Walter.

WALTER   [*Screaming at him suddenly*]   THEN TELL ME, GODDAMMIT . . . WHAT'S THE MATTER WITH YOU?

BOBO   Man . . . I didn't go to no Springfield, yesterday.

WALTER   [*Halted, life hanging in the moment*]   Why not?

BOBO   [*The long way, the hard way to tell*]   'Cause I didn't have no reasons to . . .

WALTER   Man, what are you talking about!

BOBO   I'm talking about the fact that when I got to the train station yesterday morning—eight o'clock like we planned . . . Man—*Willy didn't never show up.*

WALTER   Why . . . where was he . . . where is he?

BOBO   That's what I'm trying to tell you . . . I don't know . . . I waited six hours . . . I called his house . . . and I waited . . . six hours . . . I waited in that train station six hours . . . [*Breaking into tears*] That was all the extra money I had in the world . . . [*Looking up at* WALTER *with the tears running down his face*] Man, *Willy is gone.*

WALTER   Gone, what you mean Willy is gone? Gone where? You mean he went by himself. You mean he went off to Springfield by himself—to take care of getting the license—[*Turns and looks anxiously at* RUTH] You mean maybe he didn't want too many people in on the business down there? [*Looks to* RUTH *again, as before*] You know Willy got his own ways. [*Looks back to* BOBO] Maybe you was late yesterday and he just went on down there without you. Maybe—maybe—he's been callin' you at home tryin' to tell you what happened or something. Maybe—maybe—he just got sick. He's somewhere—he's got to be somewhere. We just got to find him—me and you got to find him. [*Grabs* BOBO *senselessly by the collar and starts to shake him*] We got to!

BOBO   [*In sudden angry, frightened agony*] What's the matter with you, Walter! *When a cat take off with your money he don't leave you no maps!*

WALTER   [*Turning madly, as though he is looking for* WILLY *in the very room*] Willy! . . . Willy . . . don't do it . . . Please don't do it . . . Man, not with that money . . . Man, please, not with that money . . . Oh, God . . . Don't let it be true . . . [*He is wandering around, crying out for* WILLY *and looking for him or perhaps for help from God*] Man . . . I trusted you . . . Man, I put my life in your hands . . . [*He starts to crumple down on the floor as* RUTH *just covers her face in horror.* MAMA *opens the door and comes into the room, with* BENEATHA *behind her*] Man . . . [*He starts to pound the floor with his fists, sobbing wildly*] *That money is made out of my father's flesh* . . .

BOBO   [*Standing over him helplessly*] I'm sorry, Walter . . . [*Only* WALTER'S *sobs reply.* BOBO *puts on his hat*] I had my life staked on this deal, too . . . [*He exits*]

MAMA   [*To* WALTER] Son—[*She goes to him, bends down to him, talks to his bent head*] Son . . . Is it gone? Son, I gave you sixty-five hundred dollars. Is it gone? All of it? Beneatha's money too?

WALTER   [*Lifting his head slowly*] Mama . . . I never . . . went to the bank at all . . .

MAMA   [*Not wanting to believe him*] You mean . . . your sister's school money . . . you used that too . . . Walter? . . .

WALTER   Yessss! . . . All of it . . . It's all gone . . .

[*There is total silence.* RUTH *stands with her face covered with her hands;* BENEATHA *leans forlornly against a wall, fingering a piece of red ribbon from the mother's gift.* MAMA *stops and looks at her son without recognition and then, quite without thinking about it, starts to beat him senselessly in the face.* BENEATHA *goes to them and stops it*]

BENEATHA   Mama!

[MAMA *stops and looks at both of her children and rises slowly and wanders vaguely, aimlessly away from them*]

MAMA   I seen . . . him . . . night after night . . . come in . . . and look at that rug . . . and then look at me . . . the red showing in his eyes . . .

the veins moving in his head . . . I seen him grow thin and old before he was forty . . . working and working and working like somebody's old horse . . . killing himself . . . and you—you give it all away in a day . . .

BENEATHA Mama—

MAMA Oh, God . . . [*She looks up to Him*] Look down here—and show me the strength.

BENEATHA Mama—

MAMA [*Folding over*] Strength . . .

BENEATHA [*Plaintively*] Mama . . .

MAMA Strength!

CURTAIN

ACT III

> *An hour later.*
>
> *At curtain, there is a sullen light of gloom in the living room, gray light not unlike that which began the first scene of Act One. At left we can see* WALTER *within his room, alone with himself. He is stretched out on the bed, his shirt out and open, his arms under his head. He does not smoke, he does not cry out, he merely lies there, looking up at the ceiling, much as if he were alone in the world.*
>
> *In the living room* BENEATHA *sits at the table, still surrounded by the now almost ominous packing crates. She sits looking off. We feel that this is a mood struck perhaps an hour before, and it lingers now, full of the empty sound of profound disappointment. We see on a line from her brother's bedroom the sameness of their attitudes. Presently the bell rings and* BENEATHA *rises without ambition or interest in answering. It is* ASAGAI, *smiling broadly, striding into the room with energy and happy expectation and conversation.*

ASAGAI I came over . . . I had some free time. I thought I might help with the packing. Ah, I like the look of packing crates! A household in preparation for a journey! It depresses some people . . . but for me . . . it is another feeling. Something full of the flow of life, do you understand? Movement, progress . . . It makes me think of Africa.

BENEATHA Africa!

ASAGAI What kind of a mood is this? Have I told you how deeply you move me?

BENEATHA He gave away the money, Asagai . . .

ASAGAI Who gave away what money?

BENEATHA The insurance money. My brother gave it away.

ASAGAI Gave it away?

BENEATHA He made an investment! With a man even Travis wouldn't have trusted.

ASAGAI And it's gone?

BENEATHA Gone!

ASAGAI I'm very sorry . . . And you, now?

BENEATHA Me? . . . Me? . . . Me I'm nothing . . . Me. When I was very small . . . we used to take our sleds out in the wintertime and the only hills we had were the ice-covered stone steps of some houses down the street. And we used to fill them in with snow and make them smooth and slide down them all day . . . and it was very dangerous you know . . . far too steep

. . . and sure enough one day a kid named Rufus came down too fast and hit the sidewalk . . . and we saw his face just split open right there in front of us . . . And I remember standing there looking at his bloody open face thinking that was the end of Rufus. But the ambulance came and they took him to the hospital and they fixed the broken bones and they sewed it all up . . . and the next time I saw Rufus he just had a little line down the middle of his face . . . I never got over that . . .

[WALTER *sits up, listening on the bed. Throughout this scene it is important that we feel his reaction at all times, that he visibly respond to the words of his sister and* ASAGAI]

ASAGAI   What?

BENEATHA   That that was what one person could do for another, fix him up—sew up the problem, make him all right again. That was the most marvelous thing in the world . . . I wanted to do that. I always thought it was the one concrete thing in the world that a human being could do. Fix up the sick, you know—and make them whole again. This was truly being God . . .

ASAGAI   You wanted to be God?

BENEATHA   No—I wanted to cure. It used to be so important to me. I wanted to cure. It used to matter. I used to care. I mean about people and how their bodies hurt . . .

ASAGAI   And you've stopped caring?

BENEATHA   Yes—I think so.

ASAGAI   Why?

[WALTER *rises, goes to the door of his room and is about to open it, then stops and stands listening, leaning on the door jamb*]

BENEATHA   Because it doesn't seem deep enough, close enough to what ails mankind—I mean this thing of sewing up bodies or administering drugs. Don't you understand? It was a child's reaction to the world. I thought that doctors had the secret to all the hurts. . . . That's the way a child sees things—or an idealist.

ASAGAI   Children see things very well sometimes—and idealists even better.

BENEATHA   I know that's what you think. Because you are still where I left off—you still care. This is what you see for the world, for Africa. You with the dreams of the future will patch up all Africa—you are going to cure the Great Sore of colonialism with Independence—

ASAGAI   Yes!

BENEATHA   Yes—and you think that one word is the penicillin of the human spirit: "Independence!" But then what?

ASAGAI   That will be the problem for another time. First we must get there.

BENEATHA   And where does it end?

ASAGAI   End? Who even spoke of an end? To life? To living?

BENEATHA   An end to misery!

ASAGAI   [*Smiling*]   You sound like a French intellectual.

BENEATHA   No! I sound like a human being who just had her future taken right out of her hands! While I was sleeping in my bed in there, things were happening in this world that directly concerned me—and nobody asked me, consulted me—they just went out and did things—and changed my life. Don't you see there isn't any real progress, Asagai, there is only one large circle that we march in, around and around, each of us with our own little picture—in front of us—our own little mirage that we think is the future.

ASAGAI   That is the mistake.

BENEATHA   What?

ASAGAI   What you just said—about the circle. It isn't a circle—it is simply a long line—as in geometry, you know, one that reaches into infinity. And because we cannot see the end—we also cannot see how it changes. And it is very odd but those who see the changes are called "idealists"—and those who cannot, or refuse to think, they are the "realists." It is very strange, and amusing too, I think.

BENEATHA   You—you are almost religious.

ASAGAI   Yes . . . I think I have the religion of doing what is necessary in the world—and of worshipping man—because he is so marvelous, you see.

BENEATHA   Man is foul! And the human race deserves its misery!

ASAGAI   You see: *you* have become the religious one in the old sense. Already, and after such a small defeat, you are worshipping despair.

BENEATHA   From now on, I worship the truth—and the truth is that people are puny, small and selfish. . . .

ASAGAI   Truth? Why is it that you despairing ones always think that only you have the truth? I never thought to see *you* like that. You! Your brother made a stupid, childish mistake—and you are grateful to him. So that now you can give up the ailing human race on account of it. You talk about what good is struggle; what good is anything? Where are we all going? And why are we bothering?

BENEATHA   *And you cannot answer it!* All your talk and dreams about Africa and Independence. Independence and then what? What about all the crooks and petty thieves and just plain idiots who will come into power to steal and plunder the same as before—only now they will be black and do it in the name of the new Independence— You cannot answer that.

ASAGAI   [*Shouting over her*] *I live the answer!* [*Pause*] In my village at home it is the exceptional man who can even read a newspaper . . . or who ever *sees* a book at all. I will go home and much of what I will have to say will seem strange to the people of my village . . . But I will teach and work and things will happen, slowly and swiftly. At times it will seem that nothing changes at all . . . and then again . . . the sudden dramatic events which make history leap into the future. And then quiet again. Retrogression even. Guns, murder, revolution. And I even will have moments when I wonder if the quiet was not better than all that death and hatred. But I will look about my village at the illiteracy and disease and ignorance and I will not wonder long. And perhaps . . . perhaps I will be a great man . . . I mean perhaps I will hold on to the substance of truth and find my way always with the right course . . . and perhaps for it I will be butchered in my bed some night by the servants of empire . . .

BENEATHA   *The martyr!*

ASAGAI   . . . or perhaps I shall live to be a very old man, respected and esteemed in my new nation . . . And perhaps I shall hold office and this is what I'm trying to tell you, Alaiyo; perhaps the things I believe now for my country will be wrong and outmoded, and I will not understand and do terrible things to have things my way or merely to keep my power. Don't you see that there will be young men and women, not British soldiers then, but my own black countrymen . . . to step out of the shadows some evening and slit my then useless throat? Don't you see they have always been there . . . that they always will be. And that such a thing as my own death will be an advance? They who might kill me even . . . actually replenish me!

BENEATHA   Oh, Asagai, I know all that.

ASAGAI   Good! Then stop moaning and groaning and tell me what you plan to do.

BENEATHA   Do?

ASAGAI I have a bit of a suggestion.

BENEATHA What?

ASAGAI [*Rather quietly for him*] That when it is all over—that you come home with me—

BENEATHA [*Slapping herself on the forehead with exasperation born of misunderstanding*] Oh—Asagai—at this moment you decide to be romantic!

ASAGAI [*Quickly understanding the misunderstanding*] My dear, young creature of the New World—I do not mean across the city—I mean across the ocean; home—to Africa.

BENEATHA [*Slowly understanding and turning to him with murmured amazement*] To—to Nigeria?

ASAGAI Yes! . . . [*Smiling and lifting his arms playfully*] Three hundred years later the African Prince rose up out of the seas and swept the maiden back across the middle passage over which her ancestors had come—

BENEATHA [*Unable to play*] Nigeria?

ASAGAI Nigeria. Home. [*Coming to her with genuine romantic flippancy*] I will show you our mountains and our stars; and give you cool drinks from gourds and teach you the old songs and the ways of our people—and, in time, we will pretend that—[*Very softly*]—you have only been away for a day—

[*She turns her back to him, thinking. He swings her around and takes her full in his arms in a long embrace which proceeds to passion*]

BENEATHA [*Pulling away*] You're getting me all mixed up—

ASAGAI Why?

BENEATHA Too many things—too many things have happened today. I must sit down and think. I don't know what I feel about anything right this minute.

[*She promptly sits down and props her chin on her fist*]

ASAGAI [*Charmed*] All right, I shall leave you. No—don't get up. [*Touching her, gently, sweetly*] Just sit awhile and think . . . Never be afraid to sit awhile and think. [*He goes to door and looks at her*] How often I have looked at you and said, "Ah—so this is what the New World hath finally wrought . . ."

[*He exits.* BENEATHA *sits on alone. Presently* WALTER *enters from his room and starts to rummage through things, feverishly looking for something. She looks up and turns in her seat*]

BENEATHA [*Hissingly*] Yes—just look at what the New World hath wrought! . . . Just look! [*She gestures with bitter disgust*] There he is! *Monsieur le petit bourgeois noir*—himself! There he is—Symbol of a Rising Class! Entrepreneur! Titan of the system! [*Walter ignores her completely and continues frantically and destructively looking for something and hurling things to floor and tearing things out of their place in his search.* BENEATHA *ignores the eccentricity of his actions and goes on with the monologue of insult*] Did you dream of yachts on Lake Michigan, Brother? Did you see yourself on that Great Day sitting down at the Conference Table, surrounded by all the mighty bald-headed men in America? All halted, waiting, breathless, waiting for your pronouncements on industry? Waiting for you—Chairman of the Board? [WALTER *finds what he is looking for—a small piece of white paper—and pushes it in his pocket and puts on his coat and rushes out without ever having looked at her. She shouts after him*] I look at you and I see the final triumph of stupidity in the world!

[*The door slams and she returns to just sitting again.* RUTH *comes quickly out of* MAMA'S *room*]

RUTH Who was that?

BENEATHA Your husband.

RUTH Where did he go?

BENEATHA Who knows—maybe he has an appointment at U. S. Steel.

RUTH [*Anxiously, with frightened eyes*] You didn't say nothing bad to him, did you?

BENEATHA Bad? Say anything bad to him? No—I told him he was a sweet boy and full of dreams and everything is strictly peachy keen, as the ofay kids say!

MAMA *enters from her bedroom. She is lost, vague, trying to catch hold, to make some sense of her former command of the world, but it still eludes her. A sense of waste overwhelms her gait; a measure of apology rides on her shoulders. She goes to her plant, which has remained on the table, looks at it, picks it up and takes it to the window sill and sits it outside, and she stands and looks at it a long moment. Then she closes the window, straightens her body with effort and turns around to her children*]

MAMA Well—ain't it a mess in here, though? [*A false cheerfulness, a beginning of something*] I guess we all better stop moping around and get some work done. All this unpacking and everything we got to do. [RUTH *raises her head slowly in response to the sense of the line; and* BENEATHA *in similar manner turns very slowly to look at her mother*] One of you all better call the moving people and tell 'em not to come.

RUTH Tell 'em not to come?

MAMA Of course, baby. Ain't no need in 'em coming all the way here and having to go back. They charges for that too. [*She sits down, fingers to her brow, thinking*] Lord, ever since I was a little girl. I always remembers people saying, "Lena—Lena Eggleston, you aims too high all the time. You needs to slow down and see life a little more like it is. Just slow down some." That's what they always used to say down home— "Lord, that Lena Eggleston is a high-minded thing. She'll get her due one day!"

RUTH No, Lena . . .

MAMA Me and Big Walter just didn't never learn right.

RUTH Lena, no! We gotta go. Bennie—tell her . . . [*She rises and crosses to* BENEATHA *with her arms outstretched.* BENEATHA *doesn't respond*] Tell her we can still move . . . the notes ain't but a hundred and twenty-five a month. We got four grown people in this house—we can work . . .

MAMA [*To herself*] Just aimed too high all the time—

RUTH [*Turning and going to* MAMA *fast—the words pouring out with urgency and desperation*] Lena—I'll work . . . I'll work twenty hours a day in all the kitchens in Chicago . . . I'll strap my baby on my back if I have to and scrub all the floors in America and wash all the sheets in America if I have to—but we got to move . . . We got to get out of here . . .

[MAMA *reaches out absently and pats* RUTH's *hand*]

MAMA No—I sees things differently now. Been thinking 'bout some of the things we could do to fix this place up some. I seen a second-hand bureau over on Maxwell Street just the other day that could fit right there. [*She points to where the new furniture might go.* RUTH *wanders away from her*] Would need some new handles on it and then a little varnish and then it look like something brand-new. And—we can put up them new curtains in the kitchen . . . Why this place be looking fine. Cheer us all up so that we forget trouble ever came . . . [*To Ruth*] And you could get some nice screens to put up in your room round the baby's bassinet . . . [*She looks at both of them, pleadingly*] Sometimes you just got to know when to give up some things . . . and hold on to what you got.

[WALTER *enters from the outside, looking spent and leaning against the door, his coat hanging from him*]

MAMA Where you been, son?

WALTER [*Breathing hard*] Made a call.

MAMA To who, son?

WALTER To The Man.

MAMA What man, baby?

WALTER The Man, Mama. Don't you know who The Man is?

RUTH Walter Lee?

WALTER *The Man.* Like the guys in the streets say—The Man. Captain Boss— Mistuh Charley . . . Old Captain Please Mr. Bossman . . .

BENEATHA [*Suddenly*] Lindner!

WALTER That's right! That's good. I told him to come right over.

BENEATHA [*Fiercely, understanding*] For what? What do you want to see him for!

WALTER [*Looking at his sister*] We going to do business with him.

MAMA   What you talking 'bout, son?

WALTER Talking 'bout life, Mama. You all always telling me to see life like it is. Well—I laid in there on my back today . . . and I figured it out. Life just like it is. Who gets and who don't get. [*He sits down with his coat on and laughs*] Mama, you know it's all divided up. Life is. Sure enough. Between the takers and the "tooken." [*He laughs*] I've figured it out finally. [*He looks around at them*] Yeah. Some of us always getting "tooken." [*He laughs*] People like Willy Harris, they don't never get "tooken." And you know why the rest of us do? 'Cause we all mixed up. Mixed up bad. We get to looking 'round for the right and the wrong; and we worry about it and cry about it and stay up nights trying to figure out 'bout the wrong and the right of things all the time . . . And all the time, man, them takers is out there operating, just taking and taking. Willy Harris? Shoot—Willy Harris don't even count. He don't even count in the big scheme of things. But I'll say one thing for old Willy Harris . . . he's taught me something. He's taught me to keep my eye on what counts in this world. Yeah—[*Shouting out a little*] Thanks, Willy!

RUTH What did you call that man for, Walter Lee?

WALTER Called him to tell him to come on over to the show. Gonna put on a show for the man. Just what he wants to see. You see, Mama, the man came here today and he told us that them people out there where you want us to move—well they so upset they willing to pay us not to move out there. [*He laughs again*] And—and oh, Mama—you would of been proud of the way me and Ruth and Bennie acted. We told him to get out . . . Lord have mercy! We told the man to get out. Oh, we was some proud folks this afternoon, yeah. [*He lights a cigarette*] We were still full of that old-time stuff . . .

RUTH [*Coming toward him slowly*] You talking 'bout taking them people's money to keep us from moving in that house?

WALTER I ain't just talking 'bout it, baby—I'm telling you that's what's going to happen.

BENEATHA Oh, God! Where is the bottom! Where is the real honest-to-God bottom so he can't go any farther!

WALTER See that's the old stuff. You and that boy that was here today. You all want everybody to carry a flag and a spear and sing some marching songs, huh? You wanna spend your life looking into things and trying to find the right and the wrong part, huh? Yeah. You know what's going to happen to that boy someday—he'll find himself sitting in a dungeon, locked in forever

—and the takers will have the key! Forget it, baby! There ain't no causes—
there ain't nothing but taking in this world, and he who takes most is
smartest—and it don't make a damn bit of difference *how*.

MAMA   You making something inside me cry, son. Some awful pain inside me.

WALTER   Don't cry, Mama. Understand. That white man is going to walk in that
door able to write checks for more money than we ever had. It's important
to him and I'm going to help him . . . I'm going to put on the show, Mama.

MAMA   Son—I come from five generations of people who was slaves and share-
croppers—but ain't nobody in my family never let nobody pay 'em no
money that was a way of telling us we wasn't fit to walk the earth. We ain't
never been that poor. [*Raising her eyes and looking at him*] We ain't never
been that dead inside.

BENEATHA   Well—we are dead now. All the talk about dreams and sunlight that
goes on in this house. All dead.

WALTER   What's the matter with you all! I didn't make this world! It was give
to me this way! Hell, yes, I want me some yachts someday! Yes, I want to
hang some real pearls 'round my wife's neck. Ain't she supposed to wear no
pearls? Somebody tell me—tell me, who decides which women is suppose
to wear pearls in this world. I tell you I am a *man*—and I think my wife
should wear some pearls in this world!

[*This last line hangs a good while and* WALTER *begins to move about the
room. The word "Man" has penetrated his consciousness; he mumbles it
to himself repeatedly between strange agitated pauses as he moves about*]

MAMA   Baby, how you going to feel on the inside?

WALTER   Fine! . . . Going to feel fine . . . a man . . .

MAMA   You won't have nothing left then, Walter Lee

WALTER   [*Coming to her*] I'm going to feel fine, Mama. I'm going to look that
son-of-a-bitch in the eyes and say—[*He falters*]—and say, "All right, Mr.
Lindner—[*He falters even more*]—that's your neighborhood out there. You
got the right to keep it like you want. You got the right to have it like you
want. Just write the check and—the house is yours." And, and I am going
to say—[*His voice almost breaks*] And you—you people just put the money
in my hand and you won't have to live next to this bunch of stinking
niggers! . . . [*He straightens up and moves away from his mother, walking
around the room*] Maybe—maybe I'll just get down on my black knees . . .
[*He does so;* RUTH *and* BENNIE *and* MAMA *watch him in frozen horror*] Captain, Mistuh, Bossman. [*He starts crying*] A-hee-hee-hee! [*Wringing his
hands in profoundly anguished imitation*] Yasssssuh! Great White Father,
just gi' ussen de money, fo' God's sake, and we's ain't gwine come out deh
and dirty up yo' white folks neighborhood . . .
[*He breaks down completely, then gets up and goes into the bedroom*]

BENEATHA   That is not a man. That is nothing but a toothless rat.

MAMA   Yes—death done come in this here house. [*She is nodding, slowly, reflectively*] Done come walking in my house. On the lips of my children. You
what supposed to be my beginning again. You—what supposed to be my
harvest. [*To* BENEATHA] You—you mourning your brother?

BENEATHA   He's no brother of mine.

MAMA   What you say?

BENEATHA   I said that that individual in that room is no brother of mine.

MAMA   That's what I thought you said. You feeling like you better than he is
today? [BENEATHA *does not answer*] Yes? What you tell him a minute ago?
That he wasn't a man? Yes? You give him up for me? You done wrote his
epitaph too—like the rest of the world? Well, who give you the privilege?

BENEATHA   Be on my side for once! You saw what he just did, Mama! You saw him—down on his knees. Wasn't it you who taught me—to despise any man who would do that. Do what he's going to do.

MAMA Yes—I taught you that. Me and your daddy. But I thought I taught you something else too . . . I thought I taught you to love him.

BENEATHA Love him? There is nothing left to love.

MAMA There is always something left to love. And if you ain't learned that, you ain't learned nothing. [*Looking at her*] Have you cried for that boy today? I don't mean for yourself and for the family 'cause we lost the money. I mean for him; what he been through and what it done to him. Child, when do you think is the time to love somebody the most; when they done good and made things easy for everybody? Well then, you ain't through learning—because that ain't the time at all. It's when he's at his lowest and can't believe in hisself 'cause the world done whipped him so. When you starts measuring somebody, measure him right, child, measure him right. Make sure you done taken into account what hills and valleys he come through before he got to wherever he is.

[TRAVIS *bursts into the room at the end of the speech, leaving the door open*]

TRAVIS Grandmama—the moving men are downstairs! The truck just pulled up.

MAMA [*Turning and looking at him*] Are they, baby? They downstairs?

[*She sighs and sits.* LINDNER *appears in the doorway. He peers in and knocks lightly, to gain attention, and comes in. All turn to look at him*]

LINDNER [*Hat and briefcase in hand*] Uh—hello . . . [RUTH *crosses mechanically to the bedroom door and opens it and lets it swing open freely and slowly as the lights come up on* WALTER *within, still in his coat, sitting at the far corner of the room. He looks up and out through the room to* LINDNER]

RUTH He's here.

[*A long minute passes and* WALTER *slowly gets up*]

LINDNER [*Coming to the table with efficiency, putting his briefcase on the table and starting to unfold papers and unscrew fountain pens*] Well, I certainly was glad to hear from you people. [WALTER *has begun the trek out of the room, slowly and awkwardly, rather like a small boy, passing the back of his sleeve across his mouth from time to time*] Life can really be so much simpler than people let it be most of the time. Well—with whom do I negotiate? You, Mrs. Younger, or your son here? [MAMA *sits with her hands folded on her lap and her eyes closed as* WALTER *advances.* TRAVIS *goes closer to* LINDNER *and looks at the papers curiously*] Just some official papers, sonny.

RUTH Travis, you go downstairs.

MAMA [*Opening her eyes and looking into* WALTER'S] No. Travis, you stay right here. And you make him understand what you doing, Walter Lee. You teach him good. Like Willy Harris taught you. You show where our five generations done come to. Go ahead, son—

WALTER [*Looks down into his boy's eyes.* TRAVIS *grins at him merrily and* WALTER *draws him beside him with his arm lightly around his shoulders*] Well, Mr. Lindner. [BENEATHA *turns away*] We called you—[*There is a profound, simple groping quality in his speech*]—because, well, me and my family [*He looks around and shifts from one foot to the other*] Well—we are very plain people . . .

LINDNER Yes—

WALTER I mean—I have worked as a chauffeur most of my life—and my wife here, she does domestic work in people's kitchens. So does my mother. I mean—we are plain people . . .

LINDNER Yes, Mr. Younger—

WALTER [*Really like a small boy, looking down at his shoes and then up at the man*] And—uh—well, my father, well, he was a laborer most of his life.

LINDNER [*Absolutely confused*] Uh, yes—

WALTER [*Looking down at his toes once again*] My father almost beat a man to death once because this man called him a bad name or something, you know what I mean?

LINDNER No, I'm afraid I don't.

WALTER [*Finally straightening up*] Well, what I mean is that we come from people who had a lot of pride. I mean—we are very proud people. And that's my sister over there and she's going to be a doctor—and we are very proud—

LINDNER Well—I am sure that is very nice, but—

WALTER [*Starting to cry and facing the man eye to eye*] What I am telling you is that we called you over here to tell you that we are very proud and that this is—this is my son, who makes the sixth generation of our family in this country, and that we have all thought about your offer and we have decided to move into our house because my father—my father—he earned it. [MAMA *has her eyes closed and is rocking back and forth as though she were in church, with her head noding the amen yes*] We don't want to make no trouble for nobody or fight no causes—but we will try to be good neighbors. That's all we got to say. [*He looks the man absolutely in the eyes*] We don't want your money.

[*He turns and walks away from the man*]

LINDNER [*Looking around at all of them*] I take it then that you have decided to occupy.

BENEATHA That's what the man said.

LINDNER [*To* MAMA *in her reverie*] Then I would like to appeal to you, Mrs. Younger. You are older and wiser and understand things better I am sure . . .

MAMA [*Rising*] I am afraid you don't understand. My son said we was going to move and there ain't nothing left for me to say. [*Shaking her head with double meaning*] You know how these young folks is nowadays, mister. Can't do a thing with 'em. Good-bye.

LINDNER [*Folding up his materials*] Well—if you are that final about it . . . There is nothing left for me to say. [*He finishes. He is almost ignored by the family, who are concentrating on* WALTER LEE. *At the door* LINDNER *halts and looks around*] I sure hope you people know what you're doing. [*He shakes his head and exits*]

RUTH [*Looking around and coming to life*] Well, for God's sake—if the moving men are here—LET'S GET THE HELL OUT OF HERE!

MAMA [*Into action*] Ain't it the truth. Look at all this here mess. Ruth, put Travis' good jacket on him . . . Walter Lee, fix your tie and tuck your shirt in, you look just like somebody's hoodlum. Lord have mercy, where is my plant? [*She flies to get it amid the general bustling of the family, who are deliberately trying to ignore the nobility of the past moment*] You all start on down . . . Travis child, don't go empty-handed . . . Ruth, where did I put that box with my skillets in it? I want to be in charge of it myself . . . I'm going to make us the biggest dinner we ever ate tonight . . . Beneatha, what's the matter with them stockings? Pull them things up, girl . . .

[*The family starts to file out as two moving men appear and begin to carry out the heavier pieces of furniture, bumping into the family as they move about*]

BENEATHA Mama, Asagai—asked me to marry him today and go to Africa—

MAMA [*In the middle of her getting-ready activity*] He did? You ain't old enough to marry nobody—[*Seeing the moving men lifting one of her chairs precariously*] Darling, that ain't no bale of cotton, please handle it so we can sit in it again. I had that chair twenty-five years . . .
[*The movers sigh with exasperation and go on with their work*]

BENEATHA [*Girlishly and unreasonably trying to pursue the conversation*] To go to Africa, Mama—be a doctor in Africa . . .

MAMA [*Distracted*] Yes, baby—

WALTER Africa! What he want you to go to Africa for?

BENEATHA To practice there . . .

WALTER Girl, if you don't get all them silly ideas out your head! You better marry yourself a man with some loot . . .

BENEATHA [*Angrily, precisely as in the first scene of the play*] What have you got to do with who I marry!

WALTER Plenty. Now I think George Murchison—
[*He and* BENEATHA *go out yelling at each other vigorously;* BENEATHA *is heard saying that she would not marry* GEORGE MURCHISON *if he were Adam and she were Eve, etc. The anger is loud and real till their voices diminish.* RUTH *stands at the door and turns to* MAMA *and smiles knowingly*]

MAMA [*Fixing her hat at last*] Yeah—they something all right, my children . . .

RUTH Yeah—they're something. Let's go, Lena.

MAMA [*Stalling, starting to look around at the house*] Yes—I'm coming. Ruth—

RUTH Yes?

MAMA [*Quietly, woman to woman*] He finally come into his manhood today, didn't he? Kind of like a rainbow after the rain . . .

RUTH [*Biting her lip lest her own pride explode in front of* MAMA] Yes, Lena.
[WALTER'S *voice calls for them raucously*]

MAMA [*Waving* RUTH *out vaguely*] All right, honey—go on down. I be down directly.
[RUTH *hesitates, then exits.* MAMA *stands, at last alone in the living room, her plant on the table before her as the lights start to come down. She looks around at all the walls and ceilings and suddenly, despite herself, while the children call below, a great heaving thing rises in her and she puts her fist to her mouth, takes a final desperate look, pulls her coat about her, pats her hat and goes out. The lights dim down. The door opens and she comes back in, grabs her plant, and goes out for the last time*]

CURTAIN

GLOSSARY

ACTION   In the *Poetics,* Aristotle says that any literary form that tells a story involves the imitation of human action *(praxis)*. The term action may be most useful for pointing to the general movement of the story before the dramatist has superimposed all the refinements of PLOT. Action could be, for example, the movement in a tragedy from "happiness" to "misery." Francis Fergusson, in *The Idea of a Theater* (1948), suggests that the action of a drama might be interpreted as a progression of infinitive phrases; in *Oedipus Rex* the action might be construed first in the phrase "to cure the sickness that infects Thebes," and then in "to discover the murderer of Laius," and finally in "to accept the truth." In this sense, the action is interpreted and expressed in different ways by each of the main characters.

AGON   A Greek word meaning "public performance" or "contest." The term agon can refer to a dramatic scene showing the main characters engaged in verbal combat. In *Oedipus Rex,* for example, agon can refer to each of Oedipus' "debates": his encounters with Teiresias, Creon, the Messenger, and the Shepherd. See THOUGHT. The term agon is especially appropriate for describing the method of development in a modern "drama of ideas"—such as Shaw's *Cæsar and Cleopatra.*

APOLLONIAN-DIONYSIAC   Opposed terms used by Friedrich Nietzsche in *The Birth of Tragedy* (1872) to refer, respectively, to the poetic impulse toward rationality and controlled form in a literary work, and the poetic impulse which is essentially irrational (perhaps unconscious) and best defined by its associations with music, intoxication, and ecstasy. The affinities of the Apollonian impulse are with symmetry and formal beauty; the affinities of the Dionysiac impulse are with asymmetry and pure energy. It may be possible to interpret almost any literary work as embodying both the Apollonian and Dionysiac impulses.

ASIDE   Lines spoken by one character which are supposedly not heard by the other characters on stage; a dramatic convention whereby the audience is informed of a character's real thoughts or intentions.

CHARACTER   The word character obviously refers to a personage in a drama. But it also denotes the beliefs, habits of mind, moral choices, and MOTIVATION which distinguish one dramatic personage from another. It is in this latter sense that Aristotle uses the term character *(ethos)* as one of the six QUALITATIVE PARTS of drama. See also CHORUS CHARACTER and STOCK CHARACTER.

CHORUS CHARACTER (*Raisonneur*) A character who participates in the action of a play, but who also seems to be a spokesman for the dramatist himself. He provides perceptive commentary on the actions of the other characters, and his remarks are usually tinged with irony. In *Luther,* Staupitz is a chorus character.

CLIMAX The point of most intense emotion in a drama, both for the audience and the CHARACTERS.

COMEDY A play designed to amuse the audience by showing the protagonist moving toward a happy ending, often marriage. Although comedy can deal with serious matters—such as pride, greed, or lust, it seldom condemns evil explicitly. Instead, it ridicules lack of self-knowledge; and the conflict evokes laughter or thoughtful smiles.

COMEDY OF MANNERS A type of comedy concerned with man in his social context: man as he responds to the manners, mores, and morals of his society. This kind of comedy can satirize characters by revealing their social ineptitudes. Comedies of manners often sparkle with witty dialogue between clever, sophisticated people.

COMPLICATION Aristotle used the word complication (*desis*) to refer to the progressive "knotting" of the plot—that period of the play from its beginning up to the DENOUEMENT. In Greek drama, the complication may include everything up to the end of the fourth episode (usually the point where DISCOVERY and REVERSAL take place.) In a general sense, for all drama, the complication consists of an intensification of the play's essential conflicts; characters tend to act at cross-purposes, and the protagonist may become more and more stubborn.

CONVENTION A literary device used by dramatists and accepted by audiences, even though it may be "unrealistic" or "artificial"; examples are SOLILOQUY and ASIDE. In the spirit of the "willing suspension of disbelief" the audience accepts a convention as one of the rules of the game.

CRISIS The "turning point" of a dramatic structure; usually a decision by the protagonist which determines the direction of action of the play. In a tragedy the crisis is often a demonstration of the protagonist's HAMARTIA. The term crisis, however, is *not* part of Aristotle's theory of plot, and it may be applied less appropriately to a Greek drama than to an Elizabethan or a modern drama in which the action is often represented as taking place over a long period of time (weeks, months, or years). In this sense, a crisis usually falls in the third act of a five-act structure, and the second act of a three-act structure.

DEFINING EVENT An early point in a dramatic structure when the essential conflict of the play is clarified both for the characters and the audience; then, the COMPLICATION begins. The defining event (or "inciting moment") usually consists of the protagonist being moved to action, or to a statement of commitment, by some force, challenge, or threat. This sometimes occurs when a dramatist, having introduced his main characters separately, assembles them together for the first time.

DENOUEMENT This French word, like Aristotle's term *lysis,* denotes an "untying"; that part of a plot when conflicts, which have been intensified during the COMPLICATION, are finally resolved.

DISCOVERY Aristotle's term for that point in the PLOT when the protagonist passes suddenly "from ignorance to knowledge." While Aristotle seems to have conceived of discovery generally as a literal "recognition" of one character by another, the term can also refer to the protagonist's perception of the truth of his situation, the *self*-knowledge he finally achieves. See REVERSAL.

DICTION   The language of a play. See IMAGERY. Diction (*lexis*) is the fourth of Aristotle's six QUALITATIVE PARTS of drama; it can be considered as a stage in the dramatist's composition of a play, his "making of verses"—which is partly delimited by THOUGHT.

EPILOGUE   A speech or poem delivered after the last scene of a play. It may be in the nature of a thematic summary, or a kind of appeal for applause.

EPISODE   In the structure of a Greek drama, the episodes are the sections of action and dialogue that alternate with the choric odes. In modern drama, the term episode can refer to any brief, unified portion of the play, and can often be used interchangeably with the term "scene."

EXPOSITION   The background information necessary for the audience to understand the developing action. Most exposition is given in the opening scenes of a drama. Unless a dramatist uses a convention such as a "narrator," it is difficult to make exposition seem natural and well motivated, for example, when one character passes on "news" to another, or when the audience is able to infer past action from a conversation taking place in the present.

FOIL   Usually a minor character whom the dramatist contrasts with a major character (most often the protagonist), thus "setting off" qualities of personality, and clarifying the play's theme. In *Antigone,* for example, Ismene is a foil to her sister Antigone, particularly in regard to the moral dilemma that the play raises. Similarly, Luther's father is a foil to his son in *Luther.*

FORESHADOWING   Clues or hints that prepare the audience for some future action or event. In *Antigone,* Teiresias warns Creon (and the audience) of forthcoming catastrophes. Similarly, in *A View From the Bridge,* the narrator is constantly preparing the audience for Eddie's tragic defeat.

HAMARTIA   Given the essential line of action in tragedy—the passage of an essentially good man from happiness to misery—it is necessary for the dramatist to guide the reaction of the audience, so that it does not become one of disgust, revulsion, or pure shock at the sight of innocent suffering. Aristotle used the term "hamartia" to refer to the dramatist's "assigning" some personal responsibility to the protagonist for his eventual catastrophe—generally an "error of judgment"; hamartia literally means "missing the mark" (as with an arrow). Later critics, however, have preferred another metaphor: the "tragic flaw," an essential chink in the protagonist's moral capability. See HUBRIS. The hamartia usually occurs (or is most fully revealed) at the play's CRISIS.

IMAGE   An aspect of dramatic DICTION whereby words and phrases suggest concrete, physical, or descriptive details such as sounds, odors, colors, and tactile sensations. A good example is *Antony and Cleopatra*, II, ii, 191–197:

> The barge she sat in, like a burnish'd throne,
> Burn'd on the water. The poop was beaten gold;
> Purple the sails, and so perfumed that
> The winds were lovesick with them; the oars were silver,
> Which to the tune of flutes kept stroke, and made
> The water which they beat to follow faster,
> As amorous of their strokes.

IMAGERY A pattern of figurative language which supports and expands the theme of a literary work. In drama the imagery is usually in speeches made by characters who are, for the moment at least, filled with emotion, and who thus slip easily into the use of metaphors and similes. Such imagery generally gives a physical equivalent for a *state of mind* (for example, "darkness" suggesting ignorance or hopelessness). Most often, imagery "builds" from a literal situation. In *Hamlet,* for example, all of the major characters use images of "poison" —and these images suggest such things as spiritual corruption, lust, slander, and lying; but these images are also tied to the literal fact that Hamlet's father was murdered with poison.

IMITATION Aristotle's term (*mimesis*) for the "representational" aspect of drama—for example, men on stage, acting out a story by pretending to be other men. Imitation should not be taken as a pejorative term which would deemphasize the dramatist's creativity; it refers directly to the active "making" of a unified work of art with its own internal coherence. The dramatist's act of "imitating" may resolve itself into the successive stages of the six QUALITATIVE PARTS of drama: the "construction" of plot, the "development" of character, and so on.

INCITING MOMENT (See DEFINING EVENT)

MELODRAMA Literally, "middle drama"—between TRAGEDY and COMEDY. Melodramas are often pretentiously serious plays which stress plot but not character. The protagonist may become involved in violent, sensational, and thrilling action, but melodrama tends to eschew genuinely human motivations, and generally ends with a kind of "poetic justice."

MOTIVATION The reasons—moral, psychological, economic, and so on—for a character's behavior; that which causes a character to act.

MUSIC Aristotle used the term music (*melos*) to refer to the fifth of drama's QUALITATIVE PARTS: the "rhythm" of the speeches, and the rhythm and melody of the choric odes, important for developing the play's "mood" and guiding the audience's emotions. Aristotle's point holds for modern drama as well: the cadence of Shakespearean blank verse, the "clipped" quality of diction in modern realistic drama, the incidental use of music in a play (for example, the chants of the monks in *Luther,* the background music in *The Glass Menagerie*) all add to the emotional effect, and perhaps also to the play's meaning.

NATURALISM Like REALISM, a revolt against what its exponents felt to be the artificialities of the WELL-MADE PLAY and of romantic drama. Because of its preoccupation with social, psychological, and economic determinism, in its characterization, naturalistic drama often focuses on determining causes. Zola speaks of the "slice of life" style of naturalism, but actually, naturalists selected and arranged their subject matter with great care—particularly in drama, as in Gorky's *The Lower Depths.*

PATHOS Aristotle's term for "scenes of suffering" (usually the protagonist's) in a tragedy. Such scenes are important in the development of the plot. They may serve as an expiation for evil deeds, and may stir the audience to pity. In an expanded sense, the term pathos can refer to the emotion of pity itself, which often dominates the tone of a tragedy at its conclusion, and can be "expressed" in the speeches of the characters, or by a narrator or chorus.

PERIPETY (See REVERSAL)

PICTURE-FRAME STAGE   Acting area or stage framed by a PROSCENIUM ARCH which divides the players from the audience; the stage does not extend out into the audience, but is recessed into the back wall. Having the audience thus "look into" the scene may add to the illusion of reality.

PLOT   The dramatist's selection and arrangement of incidents in the story he treats. Plot is a principle of unity which governs such questions as where and how to "open" the story; few successful plays try to give the protagonist's life history, from birth to death and, given the nature of the ACTION that the dramatist chooses to develop, there are "appropriate" points by which the story can be limited. Aristotle called plot the "soul" of a drama; it might also be understood as the final form of the action, the progress from initial COM-PLICATION to eventual DENOUEMENT. It can include such stages as DISCOVERY, REVERSAL, and PATHOS, and, especially in tragedy, it emphasizes cause-effect relationships.

PROLOGUE   In Greek drama, the section of dialogue and action which precedes the entrance of the chorus; in modern drama, an introductory speech delivered before the first scene of a play.

PROSCENIUM   Derived from the Greek work *proskienion,* meaning the "space before the scene," the term proscenium refers to the wall separating the stage from the auditorium—as well as the "opening" in that wall, through which the spectator views the play.

PROSCENIUM ARCH   The arch enclosing the opening in the proscenium wall; see PICTURE-FRAME STAGE.

PROTAGONIST   The central character of a drama; literally, its "first contestant." See AGON.

QUALITATIVE PARTS OF DRAMA   According to Aristotle, dramas can be analyzed not only through their *chronological* development, from first scene to last, but also through their *logical* development of six aspects: PLOT, CHARACTER, THOUGHT, DICTION, MUSIC, and SPECTACLE. These might be considered as actual stages of play-writing: in working out the plot, the dramatist is determining the direction of character-development; in developing his characters, he is determining the kind of thought they will express in their speeches; and so on.

RAISONNEUR   (See CHORUS CHARACTER)

REALISM   Realism seeks to represent life and people as they are, or appear to be, through careful attention to details of costume, speech, and setting. As Tennessee Williams notes, realistic drama uses a "genuine frigidaire and authentic ice-cubes" and its characters "speak exactly as its audience speaks." But unlike naturalistic drama, it does not necessarily adhere to a deterministic philosophy.

REVERSAL   (PERIPETY)   Aristotle's term (*peripeteia*) referring to that part of a dramatic structure in which the protagonist's fortunes undergo a sudden and profound change. Insofar as the reversal is also a reversal of the protagonist's expectations, it should be viewed as a principle of *irony.* Aristotle believed that a reversal was best when it coincided with DISCOVERY; such a scheme is admirably carried out in *Oedipus Rex,* at the end of the fourth episode. The reversal in this play is caused by a discovery; by contrast, the modern tragedy, *A View from the Bridge,* presents a final discovery caused by reversal.

SPECTACLE   Aristotle used the word spectacle (*opsis*) to refer to the visual aspect of drama, and the term can be taken to include such elements as sets, props, costumes, and lighting. Aristotle demoted spectacle to last place among the six QUALITATIVE PARTS of drama, and warned the dramatist against excessive reliance on visual effects to carry the play's essential interest.

SOLILOQUY   A dramatic convention whereby a character talks to himself or to no one in particular; in effect, he thinks aloud. Longer and more complex than an ASIDE, a soliloquy reveals a character's inner conflicts, his reactions to an event or situation, or his motivations.

STOCK CHARACTER   A character type readily recognizable because of frequent use in the history of drama (especially in comedies), and because of conformity to type. In *A Raisin in the Sun*, Lindner's extreme officiousness and hypocrisy (which can be played for comic effects) make him a stock character. See CHARACTER.

THOUGHT   Aristotle's term (*dianoia*) for the "intellectual content" of the characters' speeches. In any drama like the Greek, in which violent physical actions take place off stage and are not presented directly, the ACTION necessarily forms itself around verbal encounters between the main characters; see AGON. Our assessments of the characters are therefore guided to a large extent by how well they argue and the kind of rhetoric they employ. In another sense, however, the term "thought" is often used to refer to the meaning or theme of a play.

TRAGIC FLAW   (See HAMARTIA)

TRAGEDY   A serious play, generally depicting a REVERSAL of fortune—from "happiness" to "misery"—of a man of moral worth (and usually of social stature). Partly through his own error (see HAMARTIA), the protagonist suffers defeat and brings adversity to others. But the "punishment" almost always seems in excess of the "crime"—and thus tragedy is the kind of drama most concerned with such philosophical questions as the meaning of life itself.

TURNING POINT   (See CRISIS)

WELL-MADE PLAY   A carefully plotted, neatly resolved, popular form of drama. The motivation of its characters is plausible but superficial. Originally championed by the French playwright Eugene Scribe (1791–1861), the well-made play is today the essential form of many TV dramas.

INDEX